MY BODY GIVEN FOR YOU

HELMUT HOPING

My Body Given for You

History and Theology of the Eucharist

Translated by Michael J. Miller
from the second expanded German edition

IGNATIUS PRESS   SAN FRANCISCO

Original German edition:
Mein Leib für euch gegeben:
Geschichte und Theologie der Eucharistie
2nd expanded edition
© 2015 by Verlag Herder GmbH, Freiburg im Breisgau, Germany

Cover art: robertharding/stock.adobe.com

Cover design by Riz Boncan Marsella

© 2019 by Ignatius Press, San Francisco
All rights reserved
ISBN 978-1-62164-189-6
Library of Congress Catalogue number 2019931430
Printed in the United States of America ∞

For Alexander Gerken

What was visible in our Savior
has passed over into the Mysteries.

— *Pope Leo the Great*

CONTENTS

FOREWORD TO THE SECOND
EXPANDED EDITION

In the past, dogmatic theology has usually treated the meaning of the Eucharist while disregarding the form of its liturgical celebration, whereas for a long time liturgical studies have been content with the latter. Yet the meaning and the liturgical form of the Eucharist cannot be separated any more than liturgy and dogma or pastoral practice and doctrine can. For the Church's liturgy is not about something external to Christian revelation but, rather, about "revelation accepted in faith and prayer" (Joseph Ratzinger). Nowhere is the Church so much in her element as in the liturgy. Even though the life of the Church does not consist exclusively of the liturgy—among its fundamental actualizations are *martyria* [witness] and *diakonia* [service] also—the liturgy of the Church is nevertheless the source and summit of all Christian life.[1]

Since faith and worship belong together inseparably, this book, which first appeared in German in 2011, combines the systematic theological approach to the Eucharist of dogmatic theology with the perspective of liturgical studies. The book elicited various reactions. A very polemical review by Herbert Vorgrimler (1929–2014) appeared in *Stimmung der Zeit* (2013), and an objective, generally positive discussion of the book by Bertram Stubenrauch in *Theologische Revue* (2013). At the end of his major study on the *Offertorium* (2013; 3rd ed., 2014), Arnold Angenendt approved of my understanding of the sacrifice of Christ and the Church. This year [2015] an Italian edition of the first edition of my *Geschichte und Theologie der Eucharistie* was published by Queriniana.

For the second, expanded edition, the book was examined, revised, and enlarged with a comparative analysis of Eucharistic

[1] Vatican Council II, Constitution on the Sacred Liturgy *Sacrosanctum concilium* (December 4, 1963; hereafter cited as *SC*), 10; Vatican Council II, Dogmatic Constitution on the Church *Lumen gentium* (November 21, 1964; hereafter cited as *LG*), 11.

Prayer II and the historical basis for the text, a chapter on the theology of the words of institution, and a subject index. The appendices contain, in addition to the Latin and English text of Eucharistic Prayer I, the text of parts of the Eucharistic Prayer handed down by Ambrose, the Eucharistic Prayer of the *Apostolic Tradition*, and Eucharistic Prayer II.

When historical figures are first mentioned, the year of birth and the year of death, if certain, are indicated, and in other instances only the year of death, with the exception of the popes of the Catholic Church, in which case the time of their pontificate is noted. Primary sources are cited from the usual editions; magisterial documents of the Catholic Church are cited as far as possible from Denzinger-Hünermann, otherwise by noting the year and chapter or paragraph number. Translations may differ in some details from the editions of the text that are cited. Abbreviations follow the list of abbreviations in the third edition of the *Lexikon für Theologie und Kirche* [with the addition of several standard English-language series of patristic works].

For their enterprising assistance in preparing the new edition of my book on the Eucharist, I thank my coworkers Andrea Hauber, Anna Jaschinski, Moritz Findeisen, Andreas Fritzsch, and Peter Paul Morgalla. To Dr. Stephan Weber, a reader at Herder Verlag, I owe a debt of gratitude for the long-standing good collaboration between publisher and author.

Freiburg im Breisgau, on the Feast of Saint Augustine, 2015

Helmut Hoping

INTRODUCTION

SACRIFICIUM CRUCIS

The Eucharist as the Center of Theology

The Eucharist goes back to the Last Supper of Jesus with his disciples. It is based on the prayer of thanksgiving that Jesus pronounced over the bread and wine at that meal. "Eucharist", derived from the Greek εὐχαριστία, means thanksgiving, praise, and blessing. By the celebration of the Eucharist we usually mean the celebration of Holy Mass. In the narrower sense, the Eucharistic celebration is the second part of the Mass after the Liturgy of the Word. The *Roman Missal* foresees the singing of the *antiphona ad introitum* [entrance antiphon] at the opening of the Mass; nowadays as a rule it is replaced by an opening hymn. *Introitus* means entrance, beginning, or prelude. The function of the *Introitus* is to introduce the theme of the Mass.

Introducing the subject of a book is the job of its introduction. The subject of this book is the history and theology of the Eucharist. The Church celebrates the Eucharist as a memorial of the death and Resurrection of Jesus Christ. The memorial of the Eucharist is more than a remembrance of the Last Supper of Jesus with his disciples. In the Eucharist, the sacrifice of our redemption becomes present sacramentally. The constitution *Sacrosanctum concilium* (1963) of the Second Vatican Council (1962–1965) declares about the sacred liturgy: "At the Last Supper, on the night when He was betrayed, our Savior instituted the eucharistic sacrifice [*sacrificium eucharisticum*] of His Body and Blood. He did this in order to perpetuate the sacrifice of the Cross [*sacrificium crucis*] throughout the centuries until He should come again."[1] Anyone who wants to understand the Eucharist

---

[1] *SC* 47.

must therefore reflect at the same time on Christ's sacrifice on the Cross. This, however, is not possible without having recourse to the understanding of sacrifice in the history of religion. According to Karl Rahner (1904–1984), the dogmatic problem with the term "sacrifice" is to develop a concept of sacrifice that does justice to the general history of religion without doing violence to the New Testament understanding of the sacrifice of Christ on the Cross.[2]

The apostle Paul says about Jesus Christ, the Crucified: "God put [him] forward as an expiation by his blood, to be received by faith" (Rom 3:25). The Cross as a sacrifice of expiation or atonement— what does that mean? Friedrich Nietzsche (1844–1900) saw the sacrifice on the Cross as a relapse into paganism. In the *Antichrist*, he writes: To the sacrifice of the Cross "the deranged reason of the little community formulated an answer that was terrifying in its absurdity: God gave his son as a *sacrifice* for the forgiveness of sins. At once there was an end of the gospels! Sacrifice for sin, and in its most obnoxious and barbarous form: sacrifice of the *innocent* for the sins of the guilty! What appalling paganism!"[3]

From the very beginning, men have offered their sacrifices to gods: food and animal sacrifices, sometimes human sacrifices also, but not in the history of Israel's religion. The account of the binding of Isaac (Gen 22) could originally have been a critique of human sacrifices. According to Paul, whom Nietzsche denounces as a "counterfeiter",[4] the "word of the cross" (1 Cor 1:18) is folly to the Gentiles and a stumbling block to the Jews (1 Cor 1:23). Yet the God of Jesus Christ is not a God of violence who demanded a bloody human sacrifice on Golgotha.[5] This is not the God whom Jesus proclaimed and to whom he entrusted his death even as he experienced abandonment by God. Although the German word *Opfer* can mean either sacrifice

---

[2] See Rahner, "Opfer V. Dogmatisch", in *Lexikon für Theologie und Kirche* (hereafter cited as *LThK*), 2nd ed. (Freiburg im Breisgau: Herder, 1962), 7:1174. Joachim Negel has made a major contribution along these lines with his study on the concept of sacrifice. See Negel, *Ambivalentes Opfer: Studien zur Symbolik, Dialektik und Aporetik eines theologischen Fundamentalbegriffs* (Paderborn et al.: Schöningh, 2005).

[3] Friedrich Nietzsche, *The Antichrist*, translated from the German with an introduction by H.L. Mencken (New York: Alfred A. Knopf, 1920), 117.

[4] Ibid., 119.

[5] Cf. Georg Baudler, *Die Befreiung von einem Gott der Gewalt* (Düsseldorf: Patmos, 1999).

or victim, we must understand the sacrifice on the Cross (*Kreuzesopfer*) in terms of the sacrifice of the life that Jesus laid down for us, not in terms of the Crucified as the victim of violence.[6]

The essence of sacrifice (*Opfer*) is not the violence of the *homo necans*,[7] the victim of violence, or the victimization of the "scapegoat",[8] but rather the gift,[9] even unto the sacrifice of one's own life, as in Jesus' sacrifice on the Cross. In the Good News about the Cross, a "revolution of sacrifice"[10] takes place. The Cross stands for the sacrifice that has been turned around radically, the gift that God himself gives and that man receives. Jesus' death on the Cross is God's utmost gift to us. The Crucified laid down his life, he died for us (*crucifixus etiam pro nobis* [from the Nicene Creed]), in him God "reconciled the world to himself" (cf. 2 Cor 5:19). The crucifixion of Jesus is not sacrificial worship but, rather, the brutal execution of an innocent man. The death of Jesus on the Cross ratified the end of all human sacrificial worship.[11] Nevertheless, the salvific significance of Jesus' death is interpreted in the New Testament with the help of cultic language (for example, Rom 3:25).

---

[6] Cf. Helmut Hoping, *Einführung in die Christologie*, 3rd ed. (Darmstadt: Wissenschaftliche Buchgesellschaft, 2014), 58–62, 156–59. In his important but today largely forgotten dissertation on the concept of sacrifice, Max ten Hompel saw "self-giving" as the essence of the sacrifice on the Cross and of its sacramental presence in the Eucharist. See Max ten Hompel, *Das Opfer als Selbsthingabe und seine ideale Verwirklichung im Opfer Christi: Mit besonderer Berücksichtigung neuerer Kontroversen* (Freiburg: Herder, 1920). Negel, *Ambivalentes Opfer*, pointed out the importance of ten Hompel's dissertation.

[7] "Man the killer". Cf. Walter Burkert, *Homo necans: Interpretationen altgriechischer Opferriten und Mythen*, 2nd ed. (Berlin and New York: Walter de Gruyter, 1997).

[8] Cf. René Girard, *Das Heilige und die Gewalt* (Frankfurt am Main: Fischer-Taschenbuch-Verlag, 1992); Girard, *Ich sah den Satan vom Himmel fallen wie einen Blitz* (Munich: Hanser, 2002); Girard, *Das Ende der Gewalt* (Freiburg: Herder, 2009).

[9] Cf. Marcel Mauss, *The Gift: The Form and Reason for Exchange in Archaic Societies*, trans. W.D. Halls (London: Routledge, 1990); Gerardus van der Leeuw, *Phänomenologie der Religion*, 3rd ed. (Tübingen: Mohr Siebeck, 1970); Maurice Godelier, *Das Rätsel der Gabe: Geld, Geschenke, heilige Objekte* (Munich: Beck, 1999); Marcel Hénaff, *Der Preis der Wahrheit: Gabe, Geld und Philosophie* (Frankfurt am Main: Suhrkamp, 2009).

[10] Cf. Arnold Angenendt, *Die Revolution des geistigen Opfers: Blut—Sündenbock—Eucharistie* (Freiburg: Herder, 2011).

[11] Cf. Christof Gestrich, "Opfer in systematisch-theologischer Perspektive: Gesichtspunkte einer evangelischen Lehre vom Opfer", in *Opfer: Theologische und kulturelle Kontexte*, ed. B. Janowski and M. Welker (Frankfurt am Main: Suhrkamp, 2000), 283, 293; Sigrid Brandt, *Opfer als Gedächtnis: Auf dem Weg zu einer befreienden theologischen Rede vom Opfer* (Münster: Lit., 2001).

This is connected with the fact that on the Cross Jesus laid down his life for us. In what sense can we speak about the Eucharist as a sacrifice? The Eucharist is a sacrifice *sui generis*, for the Eucharistic gifts of bread and wine are different from the animal sacrifices that were offered in the Temple in Jerusalem. They are also different, however, from the grain offerings that people used to offer to God. The Church Fathers call the Eucharist a "rational" or "spiritual sacrifice" (λογικὴ θυσία). Greek philosophy prepared the way for the idea of the spiritual sacrifice, for instance in the writings of Seneca (A.D. 1–65) or of the Jewish philosopher of religion Philo of Alexandria (ca. 15–10 B.C.—A.D. 45–50). Philo thinks that it is not fitting to offer God material gifts and sacrifices. God deserves instead to be thanked. Philo describes thanks as a sort of spiritual sacrifice, as the "sacrifice of thanksgiving" (τῆς εὐχαριστίας θυσία).[12] To express thanks is to give back what we have received: εὐχαριτεῖν (giving thanks) means behaving toward God as someone who has received. The "bread of life" and the "chalice of salvation"[13] are offered to God in order to thank him for the gift that he bestows on us in the Cross of his Son and in the sacrament of the Eucharist. The Eucharist is a sacrifice that is offered in thanksgiving.[14] The central contents of this thanksgiving, as the Bible understands it, are the *magnalia Dei*, God's mighty deeds.

---

[12] Cf. Philo of Alexandria, *De specialibus legibus* I, 297 (quoted from Jutta Leonhardt, *Jewish Worship in Philo of Alexandria* [Tübingen: Mohr Siebeck, 2001], 187). On the theology of sacrifice and thanksgiving in Philo of Alexandria, see Jean Laporte, *La doctrine eucharistique chez Philon d'Alexandrie*, Théologie historique 16 (Paris: Beauchesne, 1972); Laporte, *Théologie liturgique de Philon d'Alexandrie et d'Origène*, Liturgie 6 (Paris: Cerf, 1995).

[13] Eucharistic Prayer I (see appendices).

[14] On the sacrificial character of the Eucharist, cf. Thomas Witt, *Repraesentatio sacrificii: Das eucharistische Opfer und seine Darstellung in den Gebeten und Riten des Missale Romanum 1970: Untersuchungen zur darstellenden Funktion der Liturgie*, Paderborner theologische Studien 31 (Paderborn: Schöningh, 2002); Michael McGuckian, *The Holy Sacrifice of the Mass: A Search for an Acceptable Notion of Sacrifice* (Chicago: Hillenbrand Books; Herefordshire: Gracewing, 2005); Helmut Hoping, "Gottes äusserste Gabe: Die theologische Unverzichtbarkeit der Opfersprache", *Herder Korrespondenz* 56 (2002): 247–51; Hoping, "Freiheit, Gabe, Verwandlung: Zur Hermeneutik des christlichen Opfergedankens", in *Freiheit Gottes und der Menschen*, Festschrift Thomas Pröpper, ed. Michael Böhnke et al. (Regensburg: Pustet, 2006), 417–31; Robert J. Daly, *Sacrifice Unveiled: The True Meaning of Christian Sacrifice* (London and New York: T&T Clark, 2009). Concerning the sacrifice of the Church in the writings of Odo Casel, Karl Rahner, and Hans Urs von Balthasar, cf. Michael Hesse, *Die Eucharistie als Opfer der Kirche: Antwortversuche bei Odo Casel—Karl Rahner—Hans Urs von Balthasar*, Bonner Dogmatische Studien 56 (Würzburg: Echter Verlag, 2015).

The Church's prayer is in the first place praise and thanks, but it also includes petition and, occasionally, lamentation, too.

The official designation for the celebration of the Eucharist is the "Mass", derived from the Latin word *missa*. Until the Middle Ages, the general designations *officium divinum* (divine office) or *opus Dei* (work of God) were predominant. In the East, the celebration of the Eucharist has been called the "Divine Liturgy" since the fifth century. In the Catholic Church, the concept of liturgy first became established beginning with humanism. Liturgy in the narrower sense means today the entire public "cult" or worship of the Roman Rite of the Catholic Church.[15] "Cult" comes from the Latin *cultus*, from which the word "culture" is also derived. In the realm of religion, *cultus* means the worship and adoration that belongs to God. Traditionally we speak therefore also about *cultus debitus* (due worship).

"Liturgy" comes from the Greek λειτουργία. In antiquity, the service of the people or the service done for the people was called λειτουργία.[16] In the Septuagint, the word λειτουργία occurs around one hundred times, forty of them in the sense of worship. In Romans 15:16, Paul calls himself "minister (λειτουργός) of Christ Jesus" and compares his ministry of preaching with the priestly ministry (ἱερουργοῦντα τὸ εὐαγγέλιον τοῦ θεοῦ). In Philippians 2:17, the apostle speaks about "the sacrificial offering (θυσία λειτουργία)" of our faith. Hebrews 8:2 calls Jesus Christ the high priest and mediator of the New Covenant, the minister (λειτουργός) of the true sanctuary. Although it seldom occurs in the New Testament, the concept was adopted early on.[17]

In the liturgy, the Church of the priestly people of God is actualized as the *Ecclesia orans* [praying Church]. Nevertheless, the primary subject of the liturgy is Christ, the true High Priest; the Church is the

---

[15] Cf. Friedrich Kalb, "Liturgie", in *Theologische Realenzyklopödie* 21 (1991), 366; Albert Gerhards, "Liturgie", in *Neues Handbuch theologischer Grundbegriffe*, ed. Peter Eicher, vol. 3 (Munich: Kösel-Verlag, 2005), 7.

[16] Cf. Angelus A. Häussling, "Liturgie I-II: Begriff; systematisch-theologisch", in *LThK*, 3rd ed., vol. 6 (1997), 969–70.

[17] Cf. *Didache* 15, 1, in Ante-Nicene Fathers: The Writings of the Fathers down to A.D. 325, ed. Alexander Roberts and James Donaldson (1885; repr., Peabody, Mass.: Hendrickson, 1995; hereafter cited as ANF), 7:381; *1 Clement* 40–44, in ANF 9:241–42.

secondary subject of the liturgy. The subject of the liturgy is the *totus Christus* [whole Christ], that is, Christ and the members of his Church. The conciliar constitution *Sacrosanctum concilium* says that the sacred liturgy is "an action of Christ the priest and of His Body which is the Church".[18] "The liturgy is the summit toward which the activity of the Church is directed; at the same time, it is the font from which all her power flows."[19] In a special way, this is true of the "eucharistic sacrifice" (*sacrificium eucharisticum*), which is the "fount and apex of the whole Christian life".[20] Pius XII (1939–1958) already called the Eucharist "the culmination and center, as it were, of the Christian religion" (*Christianae religionis caput ac veluti centrum*).[21] According to John Paul II (1978–2005), the Church has her origin and her vital center in the Eucharist.[22] Pope Benedict XVI (2005–2013) reaffirms the last council by describing the Eucharist as the "center and goal of all sacramental life".[23]

When the faithful are gathered for the liturgy in the name of Jesus Christ and in the power of the Holy Spirit, they enter into God's presence so as to give him thanks, in remembrance of his historical salvific deeds, for what he has granted them. In the celebration of the Eucharist, the communion of the faithful (*communio fidelium*) experiences as nowhere else the presence of Christ and of the salvation founded upon him. The Eucharist is the central sacrament of the encounter with Christ. In the Eucharist, Christ is present in manifold ways: he is present not only in the assembled congregation but also in their prayer, in the Word of God in Sacred Scripture, and in the person of the priest who presides over the celebration of the Eucharist.

---

[18] *SC* 7.

[19] *SC* 10: "Attamen Liturgia est culmen ad quod actio Ecclesiae tendit et simul fons unde omnis eius virtus emanat."

[20] *LG* 11: "Sacrificium eucharisticum, totius vitae christianae fontem et culmen."

[21] Heinrich Denzinger, *Enchiridion symbolorum definitionum et declarationum de rebus fidei et morum*, Latin-English, ed. Peter Hünermann, 43rd ed., ed. Robert Fastiggi and Anne Englund Nash for the English edition (San Francisco: Ignatius Press, 2012; hereafter cited as DH), no. 3847.

[22] Cf. John Paul II, Encyclical Letter *Ecclesia de Eucharistia*, On the Eucharist in Its Relationship to the Church (April 17, 2003; hereafter cited as *EE*).

[23] Benedict XVI, Post-Synodal Apostolic Exhortation *Sacramentum caritatis* on the Eucharist as the Source and Summit of the Church's Mission (February 22, 2007; hereafter cited as *SacCar*), nos. 17, 21.

Finally, in a unique way he is present with his Body and his Blood in the signs of bread and wine.[24] For in the "bread of life" and in the "chalice of salvation" we receive the life of Christ that was laid down for us and was transformed through his rising from the dead. Tradition therefore also calls the Eucharistic bread the "medicine of immortality" (*pharmacum immortalitatis*).[25]

In the first half of the twentieth century, the mystery theology of the Benedictine monk Odo Casel (1886–1948) was an important source of initial ideas for liturgical and Eucharistic theology.[26] The goal of his theology was to move the celebration of the saving mystery of Jesus Christ back to the center of Christian life and spirituality. To this day, the chief accomplishment of Casel's theology is the rediscovery of the fact that the mystery of faith and communal worship are one. *Mysterium* for Casel means, first, Holy God himself; next, the mystery of the incarnate Son of God, which culminates in the Paschal Mystery; and, finally, the mystery of the Church and the cultic *mysterium*. When Casel speaks about the Christian cultic and sacrificial *mysterium*, this is done in analogy to the ancient mystery cults; Casel asserts no dependence of the one on the others in the history of religion. However, Casel did not recognize clearly enough the difference between the ancient mystery cults and the Christian cultic *mysterium*. Thus he tends to remove the Paschal Mystery of

---

[24] Cf. SC 7.

[25] Thus Ignatius of Antioch, *To the Ephesians* 20 (*Patrologia cursus completus: Series Graeca*, ed. J.-P. Migne [Paris: Garnier, 1857–1866; hereafter cited as PG], 5:755A; *The Faith of the Early Fathers: A Source-Book of Theological and Historical Passages from the Christian Writings of the Pre-Nicene and Nicene Eras*, selected and trans. W. A. Jurgens [Collegeville, Minn.: Liturgical Press, 1970; hereafter cited as FEF], 19).

[26] Among Casel's works we should mention above all his unfinished "trilogy". Cf. Casel, *The Mystery of Christian Worship*, ed. B. Neunheuser, English trans. (Westminster, Md.: Newman Press, 1962); Casel, *Das christliche Festmysterium* (Paderborn: Bonifacius-Druckerei, 1941); Casel, *Das christliche Opfermysterium: Zur Morphologie und Theologie des eucharistischen Hochgebetes*, ed. V. Warnach, O.S.B. (Graz, Vienna, and Cologne: Verlag Styria, 1968). For interpretations of Casel's mystery theology, cf. Arno Schilson, *Theologie als Sakramententheologie: Die Mysterientheologie Odo Casels*, 2nd ed., Tübinger theologische Studien 18 (Mainz: Matthias-Grünewald-Verlag, 1987); Schilson, "Die Gegenwart des Ursprungs: Überlegungen zur bleibenden Bedeutung der Mysterientheologie Odo Casels", *Liturgisches Jahrbuch* 43 (1993): 6–29; Hans Bernhard Meyer, "Odo Casels Idee der Mysteriengegenwart in neuer Sicht", *Archiv für Liturgiewissenschaft* 28 (1986): 388–95; Maria Judith Krahe, *Der Herr ist der Geist: Studien zur Theologie Odo Casels*, 2 vols. (St. Ottilien: EOS Verlag, 1986).

Christ from the specific place and time of its occurrence.[27] This is connected with the fact that to a great extent Casel's writings disregard the full biblical concept of the remembrance of God and of his saving deeds and, consequently, the relation between the historical saving deed and the remembrance of the congregation gathered for the liturgy.[28]

A critical continuation of the mystery-theological approach was made above all by Gottlieb Söhngen (1892–1971), Johannes Betz (1914–1984), Edward J. Kilmartin, S.J. (1923–1994), and Hans Bernhard Meyer, S.J. (1924–2002).[29] The Paschal Mystery of Christ is an event that becomes present in Christian worship by coming, not out of the realm of the past, but rather out of God's future. For Christ, the glorified Lord, is the one who in laying down his life for us makes himself present through the Spirit. In word and in sacrament, Christ leads the community gathered in his name into the presence of God. The presence of the revelation is based on the presence of the glorified Lord, of the *Christus praesens*. Christ himself is the one who performs the "cult" before God his Father; he becomes the worship of his members "as they come together with him and around him".[30] The liturgy of the Church is the liturgy of the "Son" among us human beings; it is addressed to God, the Father in heaven. The

---

[27] Cf. Schilson, *Theologie der Sakramententheologie*, 207–9; Helmut Hoping, "Die Mysterientheologie Odo Casels und die Liturgiereform", in *Erinnerung an die Zukunft: Das Zweite Vatikanische Konzil*, expanded, updated ed., ed. J. H. Tück (Freiburg: Herder, 2013), 167f.

[28] On the biblical understanding of remembrance, cf. Stephan Wahle, *Gottes-Gedenken: Untersuchungen zum anamnetischen Gehalt christlicher und jüdischer Liturgie*, Innsbrucker theologische Studien 73 (Innsbruck and Vienna: Tyrolia-Verlag, 2006).

[29] Cf. Gottlieb Söhngen, *Der Wesensaufbau des Mysteriums*, Grenzfragen zwischen Theologie und Philosophie 6 (Bonn: Hanstein, 1938); Söhngen, *Das sakramentale Wesen des Messopfers* (Essen: Wibbelt, 1946); Söhngen, "Christi Gegenwart in uns durch den Glauben (Eph 3,17): Ein vergessener Gegenstand unserer Verkündigung von der Messe", in *Die Messe in der Glaubensverkündigung*, ed. Franz Xaver Arnold, 2nd ed. (Freiburg: Herder, 1953), 14–28; Johannes Betz, "Eucharistie als zentrales Mysterium", in *Mysterium Salutis: Grundriß heilsgeschichtlicher Dogmatic*, ed. J. Feiner and M. Löhrer, 4/2 (Einsiedeln: Benziger, 1973), 263–311; Edward J. Kilmartin, *The Eucharist in the West: History and Theology*, ed. R. J. Daly (Collegeville, Minn.: Liturgical Press, 1998), 275–77; Meyer, "Odo Casels Idee der Mysteriengegenwart", 388–95; Hans Bernhard Meyer, *Eucharistie, Geschichte, Theologie, Pastoral*, Handbuch der Liturgiewissenschaft 4 (Regensburg: Pustet, 1989).

[30] Joseph Ratzinger, *The Spirit of the Liturgy*, trans. John Saward (San Francisco: Ignatius Press, 2000), [62–63]; reprinted in Joseph Ratzinger, *Collected Works*, 11 (San Francisco: Ignatius Press, 2014; hereafter cited as *JRCW*), 37.

liturgy is the central milieu of revelation, in which the latter becomes sacramentally present for us.

The liturgy of the Church is founded on "the Passion endured by a man who with his 'I' reaches into the mystery of the living God himself".[31] It inserts "earthly time ... into the time of Jesus Christ and into its present".[32] Liturgy is the celebration of the Paschal Mystery of Christ, the ritual actualization of Christ's redemptive work in his Church—according to the maxim of Pope Leo the Great (440–461): "What was visible in our Redeemer passed over into the mysteries."[33] [In the German Missal,] one of the priest's prayers at the Offertory of the gifts says: "Almighty God, accept the gifts that we offer according to your will. Complete in us the work of redemption and sanctification through the mysteries that we celebrate to your glory. We ask this through Christ, our Lord."[34] Through its ritual form that developed historically, the Eucharist shares in the glory of God's revelation, in its *splendor veritatis*.[35] For in the Church's liturgy, "the Logos himself speaks to us" and comes to us "with his Body and Soul, Flesh and Blood, Divinity and Humanity" in order "to unite us with himself, to make of us one 'body' ".[36]

In this sense, the Eucharist can be considered as *theologia prima*, so to speak, as first theology before all scientific reflection on the faith. Since their beginnings, liturgy and faith have been closely correlated. The Christian liturgy not only decisively influenced the development of the canon of New Testament Scriptures, the primary record of the Christian faith, but also the development of the Christian Creed, which has its authentic place in the liturgy of Christian initiation (catechumenate, baptismal liturgy). The liturgy was therefore a decisive source of theology. In the adage from the patristic era *Lex orandi—lex*

---

[31] Ibid., 34 [57].

[32] Ibid., 36 [61].

[33] Leo the Great, *Sermo* 74, 2 (*PL* 54:398A; Corpus Christianorum Series Latina [Turnhout-Paris, 1953ff.; hereafter cited as CCSL], 138A:457): "Quod itaque Redemptoris nostri conspicuum fuit, in sacramenta transivit."

[34] *Die Feier der Heiligen Messe: Messbuch für die Bistümer des deutschen Sprachgebiets: Autentische Ausgabe für den liturgischen Gebrauch*, 2nd ed. (Einsiedeln et al., 1988; hereafter cited as *MB*), 240–41.

[35] Cf. Romano Guardini, *The Spirit of the Liturgy*, trans. Ada Lane (1937; New York: Crossroad, 1998).

[36] Joseph Ratzinger, "Theology of the Liturgy", in *JRCW* 11:556.

credendi, "The law of praying is the law of believing", the correlation of liturgy and faith is expressed formulaically. The adage goes back to Prosper Tiro of Aquitaine (d. after 455). The unabridged version is: *Legem credendi lex statuat supplicandi*, "The rule of prayer determines the rule of belief."[37]

The historical context of the adage *Lex orandi—lex credendi* is the question about the significance of the intercessory prayer of the liturgy of the Mass for the correct understanding of the correlation of freedom and grace. The intercessions of the litany prayer, which Prosper traces back to apostolic tradition, teach us to think correctly about God's grace and man's freedom.[38] Prosper says that the intercessory prayer of the priest, which he pronounces for the faithful before the Eucharistic Sacrifice and in which he prays for the grace of faith for those who have not yet come to know Christ, expresses the Church's conviction that faith, too, is received from God as a gift. The *lex supplicationis* (1 Tim 2:1–4), which states that prayers should be offered for everyone and everything, even for the faith of those who have not yet found their way to Christ, makes it clear that even the beginning of faith should be regarded as a gift from God.[39] For what do we have, Prosper asks with the apostle Paul, that we have not received from God (cf. 1 Cor 4:7)?

Over the course of time, Prosper's adage acquired a fundamental importance for the relation between liturgy and theology. Christians recognized that the liturgy is (or at least should be) the primary presupposition of theological reflection.[40] On the other hand, the celebration of the Eucharist is made accessible in its entire reality as well as in the diachronic and synchronic understanding thereof only when the authentic doctrinal tradition of the Church is considered, which is connected with the development of the liturgy. Liturgy and dogma

---

[37] Cf. chapter 8 (DH 246). This chapter of the "Capitula Coelestini" is connected with Prosper of Aquitaine, *De vocatione omnium gentium*, 1, 12.

[38] Cf. DH 246 (Indiculus de gratia Dei). As Maieul Cappuyns has demonstrated, the author of the so-called *Capitula Coelestini* was not Pope Celestine I but Prosper of Aquitaine. Cf. Cappuyns, "L'origine des Capitula pseudo-célestiniens contre le semipéligianisme", *Revue Bénédictine* 41 (1929): 156–70.

[39] Cf. Karl Federer, *Liturgie und Glaube: "Legem credendi lex statuat supplicandi": Eine theologigeschichtliche Untersuchung*, Paradosis IV (Fribourg: Paulusverlag, 1950), 15f.

[40] On this subject, see Julia Knop, *Ecclesia orans: Liturgie als Herausforderung für die Dogmatik* (Freiburg: Herder, 2012).

belong together inseparably.[41] Prosper Guéranger (1805–1875) saw liturgy as "Tradition in its most powerful and most solemn form".[42] The Dogmatic Constitution *Dei Verbum* (1965) of the Second Vatican Council includes the public worship (*cultus*) of the Church as part of the *sacra traditio*, the sacred tradition of the Church.[43]

As the source and at the same time the summit of ecclesial life, the Eucharist deserves the full attention of theology. This is true not only for the question of the *ars celebrandi* [art of celebrating] the sacramental rite, but also for the *ars intelligendi* [art of understanding it]. A theology of the Eucharist must not merely set out its meaning; it must keep in view also the form of its celebration. Since sacraments by their nature are liturgical rites, the Eucharist cannot be understood without the *textus sacer* [sacred text] and the other elements of the ritual form. The explanation of and theological reflection on the sacraments always have to consider the "context of the celebrated action".[44] To this day, one often finds in academic theology a separation of liturgical studies on the Eucharist and dogmatic hermeneutics of the sacrament.[45] This book is a contribution toward overcoming this separation.

Thus in the presentation of the history and theology of the Eucharist, problems as framed by historical and systematic liturgical studies are taken up.[46] The Roman Rite, in which the author is at home,

---

[41] A clear connection is found in Cipriano Vagaggini, *Theological Dimensions of the Liturgy: A General Treatise on the Theology of the Liturgy*, trans. Leonard J. Doyle (Collegeville, Minn.: Liturgical Press, 1976).

[42] Prosper Guéranger, *Institutions liturgiques*, 2nd ed. (Paris: Société générale de librairie catholique, 1878), 1:3: "La Liturgie est la tradition même à son plus haut degré de puissance et de sollennité."

[43] Cf. Vatican Council II, Dogmatic Constitution on Divine Revelation *Dei Verbum* (November 18, 1965; hereafter cited as *DV*), no. 8.

[44] Andrea Grillo, "'Intellectus fidei' und 'intellectus ritus': Die überraschende Konvergenz von Liturgietheologie, Sakramententheologie und Fundamentaltheologie", *Liturgisches Jahrbuch* 50 (2000): 163.

[45] The relation between dogmatic theology and liturgical studies is still tense. Proof of this is the polemic against dogmatic theology in Rupert Berger, *Die Feier der Heiligen Messe: Eine Einführung* (Freiburg: Herder, 2009), 58–60, and Friedrich Lurz, *Erhebet die Herzen: Das Eucharistische Hochgebet verstehen* (Kevelaer: Butzon & Bercker, 2011), 15f.

[46] On this subject, see Anton Baumstark, *Vom geschichtlichen Werden der Liturgie*, Ecclesia Orans 10 (Freiburg: Herder, 1923); Baumstark, *Liturgie comparée: Principes et méthodes pour l'étude historique des liturgies chrétiennes*, 3rd ed., Collection Irénikon (Chevetogne, Belgium: Éditions de Chevetogne, 1954); Romano Guardini, "Über die systematische Methode in der

forms the foundation for this *History and Theology of the Eucharist*. Other liturgical families are included where this seemed appropriate. The following pages are neither a history of the Roman Mass, as Josef Andreas Jungmann (1889–1975) presented magisterially in his work *Missarum Sollemnia* [*The Mass of the Roman Rite: Its Origins and Development*] (1948; 6th ed., 2003), nor an explication of the rite of the Mass in the tradition of systematizing Mass commentaries, which includes Johannes Brinktrine (1889–1965) with his book *Die heilige Messe*.[47] Rather, they are a history and theology of the Eucharist, whereby the formal perspective of this book is defined by its interest in the question from systematic theology.[48] Thus the book contains, besides surveys of the history of liturgy, systematic theological chapters on central topics of Eucharistic theology.

Among those treated are the Last Supper of Jesus with his disciples, the celebration of the Eucharist in early Christian times, the understanding of the Eucharist in the patristic era, the medieval controversies over the Eucharist, the doctrine of transubstantiation, Martin Luther's (1483–1546) critique of the Sacrifice of the Mass, his understanding of the Lord's Supper, the debate on the Lord's Supper among the Reformers, the response of the Council of Trent to Luther and the Tridentine and Vatican reform of the Missal. At the end, there are three chapters on the theology of the words of institution, on the status of the ecumenical dialogue about the Lord's Supper, and on the theological hermeneutic of the Eucharist as *sacrament of the gift*.

The liturgical reform introduced by the Second Vatican Council is a reform "the likes of which did not exist previously in the almost two-thousand-year history of the Church".[49] This explains the continual controversies about the reform of the Missal that occurred after

---

Liturgie wissenschaft?", *Jahrbuch für Liturgiewissenschaft* 1 (1921): 97–108; Josef Andreas Jungmann, *The Mass of the Roman Rite*, trans. Francis A. Brunner, C.Ss.R., 2 vols. (New York: Benziger Brothers, 1951, 1955); Cesare Giraudo, *Eucaristia par la chiesa: Prospettive teologiche sull'eucaristia a partire dalla "lex orandi"*, Aloisiana 22 (Rome: Pontificia Univ. Gregoriana, 1989); Reinhard Messner, "Was ist systematische Liturgiewissenschaft?", *Archiv für Liturgiewissenschaft* 40 (1998): 257–74.

[47] Cf. Johannes Brinktrine, *Die heilige Messe*, 5th ed. (Augsburg: Bay Dominus Verlag, 2015).

[48] See also Kilmartin, *Eucharist in the West*.

[49] Andreas Heinz, "25 Jahre Liturgiekonstitution", *Liturgisches Jahrbuch* 38 (1988): 197.

the council. The decision by Pope Benedict XVI to allow Mass again generally in the form from 1962 makes it indispensable to examine more closely the *usus antiquior* [older usage] of the Roman Mass and the question about the unity of the Roman Rite. Interest in the classical form of the Roman Rite continues to exist. And a "reform of the reform", which would have to come about on the basis of *Sacrosanctum concilium*, is still an important concern, even though the question of the liturgy may have receded for the time being into the background during the pontificate of Pope Francis.

Chapter I

CENA DOMINI

The Last Supper of Jesus with His Disciples

In the Roman Rite, the celebration of the *Sacrum Triduum Paschale* begins with the Mass *in Cena Domini*. In the Missal for German-speaking countries, the celebration is entitled "Mass of the Last Supper".[1] The Last Supper, which points ahead to Jesus' offering of his life on the Cross and at the same time symbolically anticipates it, took place in the evening or at night. The oldest Christian sources and tradition, however, do not speak about a supper when they refer to the "Lord's meal" (1 Cor 11:20: κυριακὸν δεῖπνον).[2] The ancient Christian celebration of the Lord's meal is called "Eucharist".[3] With his talk about a Christian supper, Martin Luther introduced a new linguistic convention.[4]

Scholars have various theories about the origin of the Eucharist and of its ritual form. Traditionally the Eucharist is traced back to the Last Supper of Jesus with his disciples: "The history of the

---

[1] *MB* 22.

[2] Thus the Lutheran theologian Hermut Löhr, "Entstehung und Bedeutung des Abendmahls im frühen Christentum", in *Abendmahl*, ed. Hermut Löhr, Themen der Theologie 3 (Tübingen: Mohr Siebeck, 2012), 53. Jacob Kremer thinks that κυριακὸν δεῖπνον refers, not to the Lord's meal, but to the "Lord's food". Cf. Kremer, "'Herrenspeise'—nicht 'Herrenmahl': Zur Bedeutung von κυριακὸν δεῖπνον φαγεῖν (1 Kor 11,20)", in *Schrift und Tradition*, Festschrift J. Ernst, ed. K. Backhaus (Paderborn et al.: Schöningh, 1996), 227–42.

[3] Cf. *Didache* 14 (Fontes Christiani [Freiburg: Herder, 1990ff.; hereafter cited as FC] 1:132–36; ANF 7:381); Ignatius of Antioch, *Ad Ephesios* 13 (PG 5:745B; ANF 1:55); Justin Martyr, *Dialogus cum Tryphone Judaeo* 41, 1 and 3 (PG 6:564B; ANF 1:215).

[4] Cf. Josef Andreas Jungmann, "'Abendmahl' als Name der Eucharistie", *Zeitschrift für katholische Theologie* 93 (1971): 93.

Mass, and also that of its liturgical form, begins in the Cenacle."[5] "The first Holy Mass was said on 'the same night in which He was betrayed'."[6] Moreover, since Hans Lietzmann (1875–1942) there have been different variations on the idea that the Eucharist originated in the circle of Hellenistic Jewish Christianity. According to this hypothesis, the Pauline type of "Lord's Supper" had its origin in Antioch.[7] The "Lord's Supper" is distinguished from the breaking of the bread, which was carried out in joyous expectation of Christ's Second Coming (Acts 2:46) and continued the table fellowship of the historical Jesus.[8]

We can trace to Rudolf Bultmann (1884–1976) the hypothesis that the narrative of the Last Supper consists, not of historically reliable reports, but of etiological cultic legends: Jesus, the theory goes, did have a farewell meal with his disciples before his death, but the words of institution were of post-Paschal origin, for the purpose of attributing to Jesus himself the celebration of the Lord's Supper that was due to Hellenistic influences.[9] Very few contemporary exegetes still support Bultmann's hypothesis of the legendary character of the Last Supper accounts. Of course there are prominent exceptions, for instance, Dominic Crossan of the controversial "Jesus Seminar". He takes the Last Supper of Jesus with his disciples in the form handed down to us as a literary fiction.[10] Jürgen Becker writes in his book on Jesus: "No [Last Supper] text reports the historical event. The purpose of each text is, rather, to justify why the church

---

[5] Josef Andreas Jungmann, *Public Worship*, trans. Clifford Howell, S.J. (Collegeville, Minn.: Liturgical Press, 1958), 89.

[6] Josef Andreas Jungmann, *The Mass of the Roman Rite*, trans. Francis A. Brunner, C.Ss.R., 2 vols. (New York: Benziger Brothers, 1951, 1955), 1:7.

[7] Cf. Hans Lietzmann, *Messe und Herrenmahl: Eine Studie zur Geschichte der Liturgie*, 3rd ed., Arbeiten zur Kirchengeschichte 8 (Berlin: Walter de Gruyter, 1955).

[8] Cf. "Präsenz im Herrenmahl: 1 Kor 11,23–26 im Kontext hellenistischer Religionsgeschichte", in *Amt—Sakrament: Neutestamentliche Perspektiven* (Würzburg: Echter Verlag, 1989), 4f.

[9] Cf. Rudolf Bultmann, *Theology of the New Testament*, trans. Kendrick Grobel (1951; New York: Scribner, 1955), 1:151. So, too, Paul F. Bradshaw, *Reconstructing Early Christian Worship* (Collegeville, Minn.: Liturgical Press, 2010).

[10] Cf. Dominic Crossan, *The Historical Jesus: The Life of a Mediterranean Jewish Peasant* (San Francisco: Harper San Francisco, 1991), 360–67. The "Jesus Seminar" is a group of liberal Anglo-American Scripture scholars. On this topic, see John P. Meier, "The Eucharist at the Last Supper: Did It Happen?", *Theology Digest* 42 (1995): 335–51.

celebrates the Lord's Supper as it does."[11] The Lord's meal did not come about in connection with the Last Supper of Jesus with his disciples. The alleged historical origin of the Eucharist is instead Jesus' praxis at meals generally.[12] The explanatory words of Jesus within the framework of the prayers of blessing over the bread and the wine are secondary.[13]

Yet Hans Lietzmann had already observed: "No bridge leads from the celebration of the original community in Jerusalem to the metaphor likening bread and body: this remains an independent factor that cannot be derived. In other words: the tradition about Jesus' Last Supper, and the metaphor about his death that he uttered at it, is to be acknowledged as a given fact of an historically reliable tradition."[14] Willi Marxsen (1919–1993), too, still supposed at first: "The original form comes so close to the Last Supper of Jesus that no room is left (in the Palestinian primitive community, of course) for an invented etiological cultic legend."[15] A little later, Marxsen adopted Bultmann's position that the accounts of the Last Supper are Hellenistic cultic legends.[16]

Today there is broad acceptance among scholarly exegetes that the Last Supper accounts have a historical core. "If Jesus did *not* give his disciples bread and wine as his body and blood, then the

---

[11] Jürgen Becker, *Jesus of Nazareth*, trans. James E. Crouch (New York: Walter de Gruyter, 1998), 340. Cf. also Jens Schröter, *Das Abendmahl: Frühchristliche Deutungen und Impulse für die Gegenwart* (Stuttgart: Katholisches Bibelwerk, 2006), 123–34, 157–67; Schröter, *Nehmt— esst und trinkt: Das Abendmahl verstehen und feiern* (Stuttgart: Katholisches Bibelwerk, 2010), 122–29; Martin Ebner, *Jesus von Nazaret: Was wir von ihm wissen können* (Stuttgart: Stuttgart Katholisches Bibelwerk, 2007), 152–54.

[12] Likewise Peter Fiedler, "Probleme der Abendmahlsforschung" (1982), in Fiedler, *Studien zur biblischen Grundlegung des christlich-jüdischen Verhältnisses*, Stuttgarter biblische Aufsatzbände 35: Neues Testament (Stuttgart: Katholisches Bibelwerk, 2005), 57; Bernd Kollmann, *Ursprung und Gestalten der frühchristlichen Mahlfeier*, Göttinger theologische Arbeiten 43 (Göttingen: Vandenhoeck & Ruprecht, 1990), 251–58; Matthias Klinghardt, *Gemeinschaftsmahl und Mahlgemeinschaft: Soziologie und Liturgie frühchristlicher Mahlfeiern*, Texte und Arbeiten zum neutestamentlichen Zeitalter 13 (Tübingen and Basel: Francke, 1996).

[13] So, too, Paul F. Bradshaw and Maxwell E. Johnson, *The Eucharistic Liturgies: Their Evolution and Interpretation* (Collegeville, Minn.: Liturgical Press, 2012), 19–24.

[14] Hans Lietzmann, *Messe und Herrenmahl: Eine Studie zur Geschichte der Liturgie*, 3rd ed., Arbeiten zur Kirchengeschichte 8 (Berlin: Walter de Gruyter, 1955), 253.

[15] Willi Marxsen, "Der Ursprung des Abendmahls", *Evangelische Theologie* 12 (1952/1953): 303.

[16] Cf. Willi Marxsen, *Anfangsprobleme der Christologie* (Gütersloh: Mohn, 1960), 46.

Church's eucharistic celebration is empty—a pious fiction and not a reality."[17] On questions about the details, on the other hand, exegetes have widely divergent opinions. This is true not only about the question of which Last Supper account is the oldest, but also about the question of whether it is possible to reconstruct Jesus' words of institution and about the question of when the Last Supper of Jesus took place and what character it had.

A. The Biblical Accounts of the Last Supper

Jesus' common meal with tax collectors and sinners (Mk 2:15; Mt 11:19; Lk 14:21, 15:2) is a sign of the Kingdom of God, which is dawning in his person and in his actions. The banquet parables (for example, Lk 14:21) and the multiplications of the loaves or miraculous feedings (Mt 14:13–21, 15:32–39; Mk 6:30–44, 8:1–9; Lk 9:10–17; Jn 6:1–13) are part of Jesus' message about the Kingdom of God that is beginning. Jesus' festive meals anticipate the table fellowship in the fulfillment of the Kingdom of God (Mt 8:11; cf. Lk 14:25–34 and parallel passages; cf. Is 25:6–8), even though in the New Testament they are not explicitly described as festive meals of the Messiah.[18] As Jesus' eschatological outlook in the Synoptic accounts of the Last Supper shows (Mk 14:25 par.), Jesus' Last Supper with his disciples is related also to the table fellowship in the fulfillment of the Kingdom of God. The Last Supper differs from all other festive meals in that Jesus celebrated it with the Twelve exclusively and connected it very closely with his death.

The memory of Jesus' last meal with his disciples is among the oldest material of the Jesus tradition. The New Testament hands down four accounts of the Last Supper: Matthew 26:26–29; Mark 14:22–25; Luke 22:14–20; 1 Corinthians 11:23–26. With respect to the history of the tradition, Mark 14:22–25 and Matthew 26:26–29 belong together, as do 1 Corinthians 11:23–26 and Luke 22:14–20. The account of the Last Supper that the apostle Paul records in his Letter to the

---

[17] Joseph Ratzinger, *Jesus of Nazareth: Holy Week, From the Entrance into Jerusalem to the Resurrection*, trans. Philip J. Whitmore (San Francisco: Ignatius Press, 2011), 104.

[18] On the motif of the Messianic meal, cf. Enoch 62:14.

Corinthians written around A.D. 54 (1 Cor 11:23–26) very probably points to Antioch around A.D. 40.[19] The group of Hellenists surrounding Stephen has scattered to that Syrian city after his martyrdom (Acts 11:19). In Antioch, the disciples of Jesus were called "Christians" (χριστιανοί) for the first time (Acts 11:26). In literary terms, 1 Corinthians 11:23–26 is the oldest account of the Last Supper.[20]

It is disputed whether this is the case also in terms of tradition history.[21] Whereas 1 Corinthians 11:23–26 is primarily interested in the institution of the Lord's meal by Jesus, the Last Supper account in Mark 14:22–25 is one part of the depiction of Jesus' final days before his death. The Last Supper account in Matthew 26:26–29 is an obvious liturgical and literary elaboration of Mark 14:22–25. The tradition history of the Lucan Last Supper account (Lk 22:14–20)[22] is unclear. It could have been handed down independently of 1 Corinthians 11:23–26 yet may go back to the same Antiochene tradition. Another possibility is a Lucan version of Mark, whereby the possibility should not be ruled out that Luke had access to the Antiochene tradition but linked it with aspects of the version of the Last Supper account in Mark.[23] John the evangelist does tell about a last meal of

[19] Cf. Ulrich Wilckens, *Theologie des Neuen Testaments*, vol. 1, pt. 2, *Jesu Tod und Auferstehung und die Entstehung der Kirche aus Juden und Heiden* (Neukirchen-Vluyn: Neukirchener Verlag, 2003), 77.

[20] Exegetes generally agree that the Gospel according to Mark was composed around A.D. 70, while the Gospels of Matthew, Luke, and John are more recent. Dissenting from the exegetical consensus, Klaus Berger, *Im Anfang war Johannes: Datierung und Theologie des vierten Evangeliums* (Stuttgart: Quell, 1997), regards John's Gospel as the oldest Gospel.

[21] Arguing in favor of the priority of the (pre-)Pauline-Lucan Last Supper account in the history of tradition are, among others: Paul Neuenzeit, *Das Herrenmahl: Studien zur paulinischen Eucharistieauffassung* (Munich: Kösel-Verlag, 1960); Helmut Merklein, "Erwägungen zur Überlieferungsgeschichte der neutestamentlichen Abendmahlstradition", in *Studien zu Jesus und Paulus*, Wissenschaftliche Untersuchungen zum Neuen Testament 43 (Tübingen: Mohr, 1987), 88–101; Hans-Josef Klauck, *Herrenmahl und hellenistischer Kult: Eine religionsgeschichtliche Untersuchung zum ersten Korintherbrief*, Neutestamentliche Abhandlungen, Neue Folge 15 (Münster: Aschendorff, 1982), 285–332.

[22] Today it is assumed that the long version of the account is the original one and was shortened later on by omitting the supposed doublet in Luke 22:19–20.

[23] Cf. Klauck, *Herrenmahl*, 299; Schröter, *Nehmt—esst und trinkt*, 49. Heinz Schürmann, *Eine quellenkritische Untersuchung des lukanischen Abendmahlsberichtes Lk 22, 7–38*, 3 vols. (Münster: Aschendorff, 1953–1957), and Johannes Betz, *Die Eucharistie in der Zeit der griechischen Väter*, vol. 2/1, *Die Realpräsenz des Leibes und Blutes Jesu im Abendmahl nach dem Neuen Testament* (Freiburg: Herder, 1961), 26, attempt to date the Lucan Last Supper account prior to the Pauline one, but hardly anyone today still holds that opinion.

Jesus with his disciples (Jn 13:1), in which Jesus washed the feet of his disciples, but it does not inform us about the course of the meal itself.

In the Synoptics, the accounts of the Last Supper are part of the Passion narratives. The Last Supper account that the evangelist Mark records reads: "And as they were eating, he took bread (ἄρτος), and blessed (εὐλογήσας), and broke (ἔκλασεν) it, and gave (ἔδωκεν) it to them, and said, 'Take (λάβετε); this (τοῦτό) is my body (σῶμα).' And he took a chalice (ποτήριον), and when he had given thanks (εὐχαριστήσας) he gave it to them, and they all drank of it. And he said to them, 'This is my blood (αἷμα) of the covenant (τὸ αἷμα τῆς διαθήκης), which is poured out (ἐκχυννόμενον) for many (ὑπὲρ πολλῶν). Truly, I say to you, I shall not drink again of the fruit of the vine until that day when I drink it new in the kingdom of God'" (Mk 14:22–25).

Over the bread, Jesus spoke a praise/meal blessing (εὐλογήσας), and over the chalice a prayer of thanks (εὐχαριστήσας). The εὐλογία over the bread could have corresponded to the bread-bᵉrākāh at the beginning of a Jewish meal.[24] The prayer of thanks (εὐχαριστία) over the chalice (Mk 14:23) seems to be related to the birkat hammāzôn (prayer after a meal) known from Jewish sources. A difference between εὐλογία and εὐχαριστία can scarcely be discerned, since the prayer of thanks is also a prayer of blessing. The expression σῶμα (Aramaic and Hebrew gūpāh) means "body" and refers to the person of Jesus in his act of laying down his life, like the expression σάρξ/flesh (Aramaic and Hebrew bāśār) in Jesus' discourse in Capernaum.

A chalice in the Old Testament usually has negative connotations. As a cup of wrath, it stands for downfall and destruction (Ps 75:8; Is 51:17, 22; Jer 25:15; Ezek 23:33). The chalice of suffering that Jesus has to drink (Mk 14:36 and parallel passages) is to a great extent interpreted as a cup of wrath: Jesus vicariously took upon himself God's judgment on sinners and thus emptied the cup of divine wrath.[25] Knut

---

[24] Cf. Gerard Rouwhorst, "Christlicher Gottesdienst und der Gottesdienst Israels: Forschungsgeschichte, historische Interaktion, Theology", in *Theologie des Gottesdienstes: Gottesdienst im Leben der Christen; Christliche und jüdische Liturgie*, Gottesdienst der Kirche 2/2 (Regensburg: Pustet, 2008), 556.

[25] Cf. Joachim Gnilka, *Das Evangelium nach Markus (Mk 8,27–16,20)*, Evangelisch-Katholischer Kommentar 2/2 (Zurich and Einsiedeln: Benziger; Neukirchen-Vluyn: Neukirchener Verlag, 1979), 260; Knut Backhaus, "'Lösepreis für viele' (Mk 10,45): Zur Heilsbedeutung des Todes Jesu bei Markus", in *Der Evangelist als Theologe: Studien zum Markusevangelium*, ed. T. Söding, Stuttgarter Biblische Studien 163 (Stuttgart: Verlag Katholisches Bibelwerk, 1995), 101f.

Backhaus (b. 1960) calls this a "daring soteriological exegesis".[26] Yet
it is quite possible that the chalice of suffering stands for God's will,
which hands Jesus over to death for our salvation, without any associated idea of God sentencing Christ to suffer punishment vicariously.
Besides the cup of wrath in the Old Testament, there is also the idea of
the "chalice of salvation" (Ps 116:13). A "cup of blessing" is mentioned
in the pseudepigraphical writing *Joseph and Aseneth* (JosAs 19:5).

In the background of the words over the chalice, "This is my
blood, the blood of the covenant", is the account of the establishment
of the covenant (Ex 24:1–18; cf. also Heb 9:20, where the words over
the chalice are quoted). After sprinkling the people with the blood
of the covenant, Moses ascended Mount Sinai with Aaron and the
seventy elders. There they had the privilege of seeing God and had
a meal in his presence, without perishing at the sight of God's glory:
"And Moses took the blood and threw it upon the people, and said,
'Behold the blood of the covenant which the LORD has made with
you in accordance with all these words.' … And [God] did not lay his
hand on the chief men of the people of Israel; they beheld God, and
ate and drank" (Ex 24:8, 11).[27] With the expression "blood of the covenant", the imminent death of Jesus is explained as the institution of
the eschatological covenant. When Jesus speaks about the blood of the
covenant, it becomes clear that Jesus is dying for Israel. The expression
ὑπὲρ πολλῶν (for many) in the words over the chalice emphasizes that
the death of Jesus is a vicarious death of atonement. The reference here
is to the Suffering Servant of God (Is 53:1–12 LXX) who gives his life
"for the many".[28] Yet Israel has its own mission for the nations. And
thus Jesus dies not only for Israel but also for the people of all nations.[29]

The Last Supper account in Matthew differs only insignificantly
from the one in Mark:

Now as they were eating, Jesus took bread (ἄπτος), and blessed
(εὐλογήσας), and broke (ἔκλασεν) it, and gave (δούς) it to the disciples

---

[26] Ibid., 102.

[27] The Targums *Onkelos* and *Yerushalmi I* combine the ritual establishment of the covenant
with the motive of atonement.

[28] Cf. Rudolf Pesch, *Das Markusevangelium*, vol. 2, *Kommentar zu Kap. 8,27–16,20*, Herders
Theologischer Kommentar zum Neuen Testament 2 (Freiburg: Herder, 1977), 359.

[29] On the discussion about the words over the chalice, see below, chap. 10, "Pro vobis et
pro multis".

and said, "Take (λάβετε), eat (φάγετε); this is my body (σῶμα)." And he took a chalice (ποτήριον), and when he had given thanks (εὐχαριστήσας) he gave it to them, saying, "Drink of it, all of you; for this is my blood of the covenant (τὸ αἷμα τῆς διαθήκης), which is poured out (ἐκχυννόμενον) for many (περὶ πολλῶν) for the forgiveness of sins (εἰς ἄφεσιν ἁμαρτιῶν). I tell you I shall not drink again of this fruit of the vine until that day when I drink it new with you in my Father's kingdom." (Mt 26:26–29)

To a great extent, even in the key words, the account is identical with the Last Supper account in Mark. There are only a few differences, which, however, are quite striking. Before the explanatory words about the bread, in Matthew the verb "take" (λάβετε) is followed by the additional command "eat" (φάγετε). In the words over the chalice, the statement "and they all drank of it" becomes the imperative "Drink of it, all of you." The addition of "for the forgiveness of sins" to the words over the chalice is secondary (cf. Heb 9:12, 15). While Matthew omits the phrase "for the forgiveness of sins" in the preaching about baptism by John the Baptist (Mt 3:1; unlike Mk 1:4; Lk 3:3), he connects it with the words over the chalice.

Ulrich Wilckens (b. 1928) suspects that the expression from the baptismal liturgy, in which it had a permanent place early on, grew up as an addition to the words over the chalice: "The Evangelist cites the *verba testamenti* [words of institution] in the form that he knew from the liturgy of a Eucharistic celebration that followed immediately after the act of baptism."[30] Instead of ὑπὲρ πολλῶν, Matthew reads περὶ πολλῶν, which substantially makes no difference. The expression "for many" is connected with the verb ἐκχυννόμενον, as in Mark. Joachim Jeremias (1900–1979) suspected that the verb ἐκχύννειν contains a reference to the Hebrew text of the fourth Suffering Servant Song (Is 53:12: "Yet he bore the sin of many, and made intercession for the transgressors").[31] In Exodus 29:12 (LXX) the outpouring of the blood of slaughtered animals at the foot of the altar of sacrifice is

---

[30] Ulrich Wilckens, *Theologie des Neuen Testaments*, vol. 1, pt. 2, *Jesu Tod und Auferstehung und die Entstehung der Kirche aus Juden und Heiden* (Neukirchen-Vluyn: Neukirchener Verlag, 2003), 71 (italics added by the author).

[31] Cf. Joachim Jeremias, *Die Abendmahlsworte Jesu*, 3rd ed. (Göttingen: Vandenhoeck & Ruprecht, 1960), 170.

designated as ἐκχέειν and is understood as a cultic act of atonement (cf. Lev 4:18, 25; 17:11).

The Last Supper account recorded by the evangelist Luke reads:

And when the hour came, he sat at table, and the apostles with him. And he said to them, "I have earnestly desired to eat this Passover with you before I suffer; for I tell you I shall not eat it until it is fulfilled in the kingdom of God." And he took a chalice [ποτήριον], and when he had given thanks [εὐχαριστήσας] he said, "Take this, and divide it among yourselves; for I tell you that from now on I shall not drink of the fruit of the vine until the kingdom of God comes." And he took bread [ἄρτος], and when he had given thanks [εὐχαριστήσας] he broke it and gave it to them, saying, "This is my body [σῶμα] which is given for you [ὑπὲρ ὑμῶν διδόμενον]. Do this in remembrance of me." And likewise the chalice [ποτήριον] after supper, saying, "This chalice which is poured out for you [ὑπὲρ ὑμῶν ἐκχυννόμενον] is the new covenant in my blood [ἡ καινὴ διαθήκη ἐν τῷ αἵματί μου]." (Lk 22:14–20)

The account exhibits several peculiarities. The words of institution are preceded by a section that moves the meal into the perspective of the Passover in the end times. Unlike the Marcan and Matthean accounts, in the Lucan account, the eschatological outlook with the statement of renunciation stands at the beginning. In the words over the bread, there is an additional phrase in Luke: "which is given for you". The word εὐχαριστήσας occurs in Luke in reference to the actions with both the bread and the wine. Unlike in Mark 14:22–25, the command to "do this in remembrance" is placed between the words over the bread and those over the cup. In Luke, the words over the chalice are not connected with the formula ὑπὲρ πολλῶν (for many), but are parallel with the words over the bread: ὑπὲρ ὑμῶν (for you). Ulrich Wilckens sees in this a clear liturgical cast of the *verba testamenti* [words of institution] in Luke.[32] As in Mark, ἐκχυννόμενον may mean not only the Blood shed on the Cross, but the appropriation of the salvation founded thereon by drinking from the chalice: the chalice of the covenantal Blood is offered to those who are united with Christ. In Luke, the Scripture verse in the

---

[32] Cf. Wilckens, *Theologie des Neuen Testaments*, 1:72.

background of the words over the chalice is not Exodus 24:8 but Jeremiah 31:31 (LXX) (the new covenant: καινὴ διαθήκη).

This is the case also with the Pauline account of the Last Supper. It reads:

> For I received from the Lord what I also delivered to you, that the Lord Jesus on the night when he was betrayed took bread, and when he had given thanks [εὐχαριστήσας], he broke it, and said, "This is my body which is for you. Do this in remembrance of me." In the same way also the chalice, after supper, saying, "This chalice is the *new covenant* in my blood [ἡ καινὴ διαθήκη ἐν τῷ ἐμῷ αἵματι]. Do this, as often as you drink it, in remembrance of me." For as often as you eat this bread and drink the chalice, you proclaim the Lord's death until he comes. (1 Cor 11:23–26; italics added)

With the chalice of the "new covenant in my blood", the eschatological character of the salvific event is highlighted more prominently. As in Luke, the actions with the bread and the wine are connected with a meal of satiation. Yet it remains unclear whether the actions with the bread and the wine framed the meal, as was the rule in a Jewish meal,[33] or whether they occurred at the end of the meal of satiation.[34]

The Last Supper account recorded by Paul contains the command "do this in remembrance" twice: after the words over the bread and after the words over the chalice. The second remembrance command is followed by an eschatological prospect that—unlike in the Synoptics—is spoken by Jesus in the third person and could hardly be traced back to him personally in this form, but rather comes from a liturgical setting; "For as often as you eat this bread and drink the chalice, you proclaim *the Lord's death* until he comes" (1 Cor 11:26; emphasis added). The twofold remembrance command in Paul as opposed to Luke seems to be secondary, since a later omission of the command after the words over the bread is less likely.[35] It is very

---

[33] Cf. Otfried Hofius, "Herrenmahl und Herrenmahlsparadosis: Erwägungen zu 1 Kor 11,23b–25", in *PaulusStudien*, Wissenschaftliche Untersuchungen zum Neuen Testament 51 (Tübingen: Mohr, 1989), 383f.; Bernd Kollmann, *Ursprung und Gestalten der frühchristlichen Mahlfeier*, Göttinger theologische Arbeiten 43 (Göttingen: Vandenhoeck & Ruprecht, 1990), 42.

[34] Cf. Heinz Schürmann, "Die Gestalt der urchristlichen Eucharistiefeier", in *Ursprung und Gestalt: Erörterungen und Besinnungen zum Neuen Testament*, Kommentare und Beiträge zum Alten und Neuen Testament (Düsseldorf: Patmos, 1970), 85–88.

[35] Cf. Klauck, *Herrenmahl*, 317.

probable that the origin of the remembrance command is the liturgy. The establishment of the Lord's meal must not be understood in the juridical sense as a formal institution. The liturgical cast of the Pauline Last Supper account is evident also in the fact that—unlike the accounts in Mark, Matthew, and Luke—it does not speak about the disciples of Jesus.

Many scholars see in the remembrance command a reference to the influence of Hellenistic memorial meals for the dead on the development of the celebration of the Lord's meal. In identifying common elements between memorial meals for the dead and the early Christian Eucharist, however, they get no farther than external similarities (bread, wine, eating, drinking). The mystery cults may have had some influence on sacramental thinking. The decisive thing here, however, was probably the commemoration of God's saving deeds (*zikkārôn*; Ex 12:14; 13:19: *pæsaḥ*) in Jewish worship. "In the motif of remembrance, Semitic and Hellenistic thought meet."[36] The remembrance command explains how the Christian community understood the Lord's meal: as a remembrance of the life of Jesus given over to death.

Since Jeremias, many exegetes see the explanatory words about the bread and wine as being substantially *ipsissima verba Jesu* [Jesus' very own words]. Of course the recommendations as to how to reconstruct them vary, depending on whether one regards the Marcan line of tradition to be historically prior[37] or the (pre-)Pauline-Lucan tradition, as a large majority of exegetes now maintain.[38] There is a broad consensus that Jesus gave his disciples the broken bread and said: "This is my body."[39] Many scholars think that the explanatory

---

[36] Ibid.

[37] Among those who argue that the pre-Marcan Last Supper tradition is the older one are Pesch, *Markusevangelium* 2:364–77; Thomas Söding, "Das Mahl des Herrn: Zur Gestalt und Theologie der ältesten nachösterlichen Tradition", in *Vorgeschmack: Ökumenische Bemühungen um die Eucharistie*, Festschrift T. Schneider, ed. B.J. Hilberath and D. Sattler (Mainz: Matthias-Grünewald-Verlag, 1995), 134–63.

[38] The majority opinion is advocated by, among others, Knut Backhaus, "Hat Jesus vom Gottesbund gesprochen?" *Theologie und Glaube* 86 (1996): 344f.

[39] Cf. Rudolf Pesch, *Das Abendmahl und Jesu Todesverständnis*, Quaestiones disputatae 80 (Freiburg: Herder, 1978); Merklein, "Erwägungen zur Überlieferungsgeschichte", 157; Michael Theobald, "Das Herrenmahl im Neuen Testament", *Theologische Quartalschrift* 138 (2003): 262; Bernd Heininger, "Das letzte Mahl Jesu: Rekonstruktion und Deutung", in *Mehr als Brot und Wein: Theologische Kontexte der Eucharistie*, ed. W. Haunerland (Würzburg: Echter Verlag, 2005), 26–28.

words refer, not to the bread, but to the action performed with the bread, since the neuter demonstrative pronoun τοῦτο (this) would not agree grammatically with ἄρτος.[40] Yet the demonstrative pronoun τοῦτο may have been chosen to agree with the following noun σῶμα, which is also neuter.[41] Some see the giving-phrase addressed to the disciples, "This is my body which is *for you*" (1 Cor 11:24; emphasis added), as Jesus' explanatory phrase concerning the broken bread.[42] Others reconstruct the explanatory phrase: "This is my body which is *given for many*."[43] Granted, Hebrew and Aramaic do not have the copula "is", yet we may assume that Jesus identified the bread with his body, that is, with his act of laying down his own life in death, and that therefore the "giving-phrase" is at the same time an "explanatory phrase".[44] Moreover, it could be that with the breaking of the bread Jesus intended to refer to his violent death, which is further reinforced by his language about the blood of the covenant.

The words over the chalice, too, in their substance, are frequently traced back to Jesus himself. Of course, sometimes the Blood-formula connected with it is considered to be post-Paschal.[45] For "body" (σῶμα), in Hebrew *bāśār*, means a frail human being,[46] so that an additional mention of blood would not be necessary. Moreover, it is difficult, the argument goes, to derive from the words over the chalice the idea of Jesus' sacrificial, atoning death, which can be found frequently in the New Testament independently of the words

---

[40] Cf. Ulrich Lutz, "Das Herrenmahl im Neuen Testament", *Bibel und Liturgie* 57 (2002): 2–8.

[41] Cf. Gerd Theissen and Annette Merz, *Der historische Jesus: Ein Lehrbuch*, 2nd ed. (Göttingen: Vandenhoeck & Ruprecht, 1997), 373.

[42] Cf. Merklein, "Erwägungen zur Überlieferungsgeschichte", 167; cf. Hofius, "Herrenmahl und Herrenmahlsparadosis", 224–26.

[43] Cf. Löhr, "Entstehung und Bedeutung des Abendmahls", 57.

[44] Cf. ibid., 58.

[45] Cf. Pesch, *Das Abendmahl und Jesu Todesverständnis*, 93–101; Josef Blank, "Weisst du, was Versöhnung heisst? Der Kreuzestod Jesu als Sühne und Versöhnung", in *Sühne und Versöhnung*, ed. J. Blank and J. Werbick, Theologie zur Zeit 1 (Düsseldorf: Patmos, 1987), 81f.; Peter Stuhlmacher, *Biblische Theologie des Neuen Testaments*, vol. 1, *Grundlegung von Jesus zu Paulus* (Göttingen: Vandenhoeck & Ruprecht, 1992), 136f.; Joachim Gnilka, *Jesus of Nazareth: Message and History*, trans. Siegfried S. Schatzmann (Peabody, Mass.: Hendrickson, 1997), 286–88.

[46] Cf. Hans Walter Wolff, *Anthropologie des Alten Testaments*, 4th ed. (Munich: Kaiser, 1984), 49–56.

over the chalice.[47] Scholars also deliberate on whether the original words over the chalice are found in Mark 14:25,[48] while in contrast the words over the chalice in Mark 14:24, which have significance for the theology of covenant and atonement, were formed by analogy with the words over the bread. One argument in favor of this hypothesis could be that the image of the "fruit of the vine" is a Semitic idiom that stands for the beverage wine.[49] The phrase ὑπὲρ πολλῶν, supposedly, could have been connected originally with the words over the bread.[50]

Many scholars rely on a version of the (pre-)Pauline-Lucan words over the chalice that goes back to Jesus, especially since the version in Mark and Matthew could be tolerated only with difficulty by Jewish ears.[51] An argument against this hypothesis is that in Jeremiah 31:31 the idea of the New Covenant is not connected with the idea of a sacrifice or blood, which is why Lietzmann had already assumed that the words over the chalice in Paul are secondary.[52] For linguistic reasons and considering tradition history, "poured out for many" (Mk 14:24) is frequently viewed as original, as opposed to the formula "poured out for you" (Lk 22:20), which has a stronger liturgical emphasis.[53] Since Jeremiah 31:31 has no connection with covenant, blood, and meal, whereas this connection is prepared by Exodus 24:8 (cf. Deut 12:7), and since in the Jewish tradition, too, Jeremiah 31:31 is neither connected with the theme of the forgiveness of sins nor

---

[47] Cf. Michael Theobald, "Leib und Blut Christi: Erwägungen zu Herkunft, Funktion und Bedeutung des sogenannten 'Einsetzungsberichts'", in *Herrenmahl und Gruppenidentität*, ed. M. Ebner, Quaestiones disputatae 221 (Freiburg: Herder, 2007), 126; Söding, "Das Mahl des Herrn", 160.

[48] "Truly, I say to you, I shall not drink again of the fruit of the vine until that day when I drink it new in the kingdom of God."

[49] Cf. Helmut Merklein, *Jesu Botschaft von der Gottesherrschaft*, 3rd ed. (Stuttgart: Verlag Kahtolisches Bibelwerk, 1989), 137–44; Christoph Niemand, "Jesu Abschiedsmahl: Versuche zur historischen Rekonstruktion und seiner theologischen Deutung", in *Forschungen zum Neuen Testament und seiner Umwelt*, Festschrift A. Fuchs, ed. Christoph Niemand (Frankfurt am Main and New York: Lang, 2002), 81–122.

[50] Cf. Theobald, "Das Herrenmahl im Neuen Testament", 262.

[51] Cf. Theissen and Merz, *Der historische Jesus*, 372f.; Theobald, "Das Herrenmahl im Neuen Testament", 266.

[52] Cf. Lietzmann, *Messe und Herrenmahl*, 253.

[53] Cf. Martin Hengel and Anna Maria Schwemer, *Jesus und das Judentum*, Geschichte des frühen Christentums I (Tübingen: Mohr Siebeck, 2007), 584.

related to the messianic meal in Isaiah 25:6–8, ultimately everything speaks in favor of the hypothesis that the reference to Exodus 24:8 in the words over the chalice is original. Why should the more difficult version of the words over the chalice be secondary and not the easier version instead?[54] Nor is this about drinking the physical blood of Jesus; Christ's body and blood both signify his person as he lays down his life for us.

If at the Last Supper with his disciples Jesus already had his violent death in mind, and we must assume this (cf. Mk 2:20; 8:31; 9:31; 10:32f.; Lk 12:50), then it is quite possible that Jesus himself explained his death with the help of the image of the "blood of the covenant" (Ex 24:8) against the background of Isaiah 53 as a vicarious atoning death, especially since the theme of covenant is made explicit in two passages of the Suffering Servant songs (Is 42:6; 49:8).[55] In laying down his life for "the many", Jesus identified himself with the Suffering Servant, who by vicariously substituting his life[56] communicates atonement as God's gift (Is 53:10–12). Since neither the song of the suffering and dying Servant of God nor the notion of a martyr's death appears as scriptural evidence in early Jewish Messianic expectation, it seems rather unlikely that after Easter Christians took up Isaiah 53 to give meaning to Jesus' violent death. It may be historically more likely that Jesus himself was the one who explained his destiny and death in light of the fourth Suffering Servant song.[57] An argument in favor of this is Jesus' statement that the Son of man came "to give his life as a ransom for many" (Mk 10:45b; cf. also Mk 9:31). Connected

---

[54] Cf. Söding, "Das Mahl des Herrn", 141.

[55] Cf. Backhaus, "Hat Jesus vom Gottesbund gesprochen?", 347, 355; Helmut Merklein, "Wie hat Jesus seinen Tod verstanden?", in *Studien zu Jesus und Paulus*, Wissenschaftliche Untersuchungen zum Neuen Testament 105 (Tübingen: Mohr, 1998), 2:183–86; Söding, "Das Mahl des Herrn", 140; Wilckens, *Theologie des Neuen Testaments*, 1:15–18, 65–85; Martin Hengel, "Zur Wirkungsgeschichte von Jes 53 in vorchristlicher Zeit", in *Der leidende Gottesknecht Jes 53 und seine Wirkungsgeschichte*, ed. B. Janowski, Forschungen zum Alten Testament 14 (Tübingen: Mohr, 1996), 49–91; Stuhlmacher, *Biblische Theologie des Neuen Testaments*, 1:125–43.

[56] On the concept of "existential substitution", cf. Peter Stuhlmacher, "Existenzstellvertretung für die vielen: Mk 10,45 (Mt 20,28)", in *Werden und Wirken des Alten Testaments*, Festschrift C. Westermann, ed. R. Albertz et al. (Göttingen: Vandenhoeck und Ruprecht; Neukirchen-Vluyn: Neukirchener Verlag, 1980), 412–27.

[57] Cf. Johannes Betz, *Eucharistie in der Schrift und Patristik*, Handbuch der Dogmengeschichte 4/4a (Freiburg: Herder, 1979), 11.

with the ransom (Is 43:3–4) is the notion of "redeeming a life that has been forfeited" along the lines of "existential substitution".[58] In other passages, too, the Book of Isaiah plays a central role for Jesus, for instance in his interpretation of the Scriptures in the synagogue of Capernaum (Lk 4:16–21; cf. Is 61:1–3a, 6a, 9b–9).

Rudolf Bultmann, too, in his famous academic lecture in 1959, championed the thesis "that we cannot know *how Jesus understood his death*", that his execution happened "as a result of a misunderstanding of his activity as being political", and that there is a possibility "that he went to pieces".[59] In the wake of the "Second Quest", the new historical investigation into Jesus introduced by Ernst Käsemann (1906–1998), a student of Bultmann's, a series of prominent exegetes, through their analyses of Jesus' predictions about his sufferings and of the Last Supper accounts, arrived at the conviction that Jesus understood his death as a death of atonement "for the many".[60] The substance of Jesus' explanatory words over the bread and wine might consist of the following statements: *This is my body, which is given for the many. This is the blood of the [New] Covenant in my blood* or *This is my body. This is my blood of the covenant for the many.*[61]

Yet how can the interpretation of Jesus' death, in connection with the words over the chalice, as a vicarious death of atonement[62] be reconciled with the preaching of God's Kingdom as the central theme of Jesus' activity in Galilee? Anton Vögtle (1910–1996) and Peter Fiedler (1940–2009) advocated the thesis that Jesus' message about the dawning Kingdom of God is incompatible with a vicarious atoning death of Jesus, since God's forgiveness, which Jesus

---

[58] Cf. Bernd Janowski, "Auslösung des verwirkten Lebens", *Zeitschrift für Theologie und Kirche* 79 (1983): 25–59.

[59] Rudolf Bultmann, *Das Verhältnis der urchristlichen Christusbotschaft zum historischen Jesus*, Sitzungsberichte der Heidelberger Akademie der Wissenschaften, Philosophisch-Historische Klasse (Heidelberg: Winter, 1960), 11f.

[60] For example, Joachim Jeremias, Leonhard Goppelt (1911–1973), Otto Betz (1917–2005), and Martin Hengel (1926–2009). Cf. Stuhlmacher, *Biblische Theologie des Neuen Testaments*, 1:126f.

[61] Thus Klauck, *Herrenmahl*, 304–14, and Merklein, "Erwägungen zur Überlieferungsgeschichte", 157–67 (focusing on the Pauline-Lucan Last Supper account). In the case of the words over the chalice, without the bracketed addition, this is Klauck's reconstruction; in the other case—Merklein's reconstruction.

[62] Cf. Martin Hengel, "Der stellvertretende Sühnetod Jesu", *Internationale katholische Zeitschrift Communio* 9 (1980): 1–25, 135–47.

granted to mankind, is not connected with any conditions.[63] Why, then, should any vicarious atoning death of Jesus have been "necessary" at the end? The answer given by Rudolf Pesch (1936–2011), Helmut Merklein (1940–1999), Peter Stuhlmacher, Ulrich Wilckens et al. may well still be the most plausible one: since Israel for the most part did not accept the proclamation of God's kingship, God revealed another opportunity to save Israel, in that his Messiah gave up his own life vicariously "for the many".[64] The farewell meal with the Twelve, who in the eschatological gathering of Jesus represent all Israel, stands for Jesus' sacrifice of his life on the Cross, symbolized by the broken bread and the chalice of the covenant. The broken bread and the corresponding explanatory words stand for the life of Jesus given unto death. The words over the chalice, with the image of bloodshed, reinforce Jesus' surrender of his life even unto death. The Body and Blood of Jesus are not related to each other as body and soul but, rather, stand for his sacrifice of his life.

By the nature of the matter, therefore, the *verba testamenti* may well go back to Jesus himself. Why should the early Christians have invented the course of the Last Supper including Jesus' actions involving the bread and chalice? In order to legitimize the early Christian practice of the Eucharist? Given the extremely short interval of time between Jesus' final days and the beginnings of the Christian Eucharist, this practice itself requires an explanation. "Historians cannot

---

[63] Cf. Anton Vögtle, "Grundfragen der Diskussion um das heilsmittlerische Todesverständnis Jesu", in *Offenbarungsgeschehen und Wirkungsgeschichte: Neutestamentliche Beiträge* (Freiburg: Herder, 1985), 141–67; Peter Fiedler, *Jesus und die Sünder*, Beiträge zur biblischen Exegese und Theologie 3 (Frankfurt am Main: P. Lang; Bern: H. Lang, 1976), 277–83. See also Gerd Häfner, "Nach dem Tod Jesu fragen: Brennpunkte der Diskussion aus neutestamentlicher Sicht", in *Wie heute vom Tod Jesu sprechen? Neutestamentliche, systematisch-theologische und liturgiewissenschaftliche Perspektiven*, ed. G. Häfner and H. Schmidt (Freiburg: Katholische Akademie der Erzdiözese Freiburg, 2002), 154.

[64] Cf. Rudolf Pesch, *Wie Jesus sein Abendmahl hielt: Der Grund der Eucharistie*, 2nd ed. (Freiburg: Herder, 1978), 83; Helmut Merklein, *Die Gottesherrschaft als Handlungsprinzip: Untersuchung zur Ethik Jesu*, 2nd ed., Forschung zur Bibel 34 (Würzburg: Echter Verlag, 1981), 139–44; Merklein, "Wie hat Jesus seinen Tod verstanden?", in *Studien zu Jesus und Paulus*, Wissenschaftliche Untersuchungen zum Neuen Testament 105 (Tübingen: Mohr, 1998), 2:174–89; Stuhlmacher, *Biblische Theologie des Neuen Testaments*, 1:130–43. Hermann Patsch, *Abendmahl und historischer Jesus*, Calwer theologische Monographien: Reihe A. Bibelwissenschaft 1 (Stuttgart: Calwer Verlag, 1972), 141–230, tried with remarkable arguments to demonstrate that Jesus in a commanding way harked back to the idea of a universal atonement in Isaiah 53.

explain how the earliest Christian community could simply have invented the heart of the Eucharistic tradition in so short a time after Jesus' departure."[65] The assumption that Jesus at his farewell meal with his disciples performed a prophetic symbolic action and related bread and wine to his imminent suffering and death therefore meets with wide agreement among New Testament scholars.[66] Moreover, it is scarcely imaginable that the early Christian Eucharist could have arisen without an origin in Jesus' final days.

B. The Last Supper—a Passover Meal?

The Jews connect the Feast of Passover with their rescue from the angel of destruction through the blood of the Paschal lamb, the Exodus, the passage through the Red Sea, and the expectation of the Promised Land, in other words, God's historic actions that are constitutive for his people Israel. The Passover Feast is at the same time the "feast of unleavened bread" (Ex 34:18). Originally it was an independent feast of the barley harvest (Feast of Mazzot), which was later connected with the hasty departure of the Israelites in the wake of their liberation from Egypt. Besides the slaughter of the lambs in the Temple on the Day of Preparation (14 Nisan), the Feast of Passover included the Seder supper on the eve of 15 Nisan.[67] The Synoptics relate that Jesus celebrated the Last Supper with the evening Seder of the Passover Feast and was crucified on the day of the feast. Yet the only foods mentioned besides the Passover lamb are bread (ἄρτος) and wine, which are typical for any kind of Jewish festive meal, but not matzos and bitter herbs. Moreover the word for ἄρτος as a rule means leavened, not unleavened bread; in the Septuagint, the latter is called ἄζυμα (unleavened).

The instructions for the liturgy of the evening Seder (Pesach Haggadah) come from the Mishnah around A.D. 200.[68] The texts, which Joachim Jeremias cited in his study *Die Abendmahlsworte Jesu*

---

[65] Cf. Herbert Vorgrimler, *Sacramental Theology*, trans. Linda M. Maloney (Collegeville, Minn.: Liturgical Press, 1992), 136.

[66] Cf. Theobald, "Leib und Blut Christi", 123f.

[67] According to the Jewish manner of reckoning time, a new day begins after dusk.

[68] Cf. Mishnah, Pesachim 10.

(Jesus' words at the Last Supper) as evidence that the Last Supper of Jesus with his disciples was a Passover Feast, are, however, more recent than was assumed until now. Therefore, they cannot simply be projected back into the time of Jesus. Today scholars assume, rather, that after the destruction of the second Temple in the year A.D. 70, there was a further development of the Pesach Haggadah.[69] Probably the development of the Christian celebration of the Eucharist had an influence on that process.[70]

According to the chronology of Jesus' last days in John, Jesus died, not on the day of the Passover Feast, but on the Day of Preparation before the evening Seder of the Passover Feast. On the Day of Preparation, the lambs for the Passover Feast were slaughtered in the Temple (Jn 18:39). Outside of Jerusalem, the Passover Feast had to be celebrated without the Paschal lamb. Thousands of Jews, therefore, made the pilgrimage to Jerusalem for the Passover Feast. It could be that Paul, too, assumes that the Day of Preparation was the day of Jesus' crucifixion when he says that "Christ, our Paschal Lamb, has been sacrificed" (1 Cor 5:7). The Day of Preparation is 14 Nisan, so that the Last Supper of Jesus with his disciples must have happened at the latest on the evening before that day. Even if it was not a Passover meal, it was celebrated in immediate proximity to the Passover Feast (Jn 13:1).

To this day, exegetical scholarship deals with the question of how to explain the different chronologies of the Synoptics and of the

---

[69] Cf. Günter Stemberger, "Pesachhaggada und Abendmahlsbericht des Neuen Testaments", in *Studien zum rabbinischen Judentum*, Stuttgarter biblische Aufsatzbände 10: Altes Testament (Stuttgart: Katholisches Bibelwerk, 1990), 357–74. Markus Barth, too, assumes that the Passover Haggadah at the time of Jesus can be reconstructed from the treatise "Mishnah, Pesachim 10". Cf. Barth. *Das Mahl des Herrn: Gemeinschaft mit Israel, mit Christus und unter den Gästen* (Neukirchen-Vluyn: Neukirchener Verlag, 1987), 22: "From the Mishnah Treatise Pesachim we can see how the celebration developed in the Hellenistic period and what form it probably had under early rabbinical influence at the time of Jesus, too."

[70] Cf. Israel Yuval, *Pessach und Ostern: Dialog und Polemik in Spätantike und Mittelalter*, Kleine Schriften des Arye-Maimon-Instituts 1 (Trier: Arye-Maimon-Inst., 1999), 10–23; Yuval, *Zwei Völker in deinem Leib: Gegenseitige Wahrnehmung von Juden und Christen in Spätantike und Mittelalter*, German trans. from Hebrew by D. Mach, Jüdische Religion, Geschichte und Kultur 4 (Göttingen: Vandenhoeck & Ruprecht, 2007), 69–75, 210–56. The practice of celebrating a Jewish "Passover" according to the Pesach Haggadah on Holy Thursday after the Mass of the Last Supper, so as to make sure of the historical roots of the Christian celebration of the Eucharist, not only collides with the historical development. It is theologically dubious when Christians imitate a central Jewish rite.

Fourth Gospel. The attempt to harmonize them by assuming different calendars, the official Jerusalem lunar calendar and the solar calendar of Qumran, has hardly any adherents today.[71] What chronology of Jesus' last days is therefore more historically probable? Recently Martin Hengel defended once more the thesis that the Last Supper of Jesus with his disciples was a Passover meal. Following Joachim Jeremias, Hengel presents a series of weighty arguments for it: (1) The Last Supper of Jesus took place in crowded Jerusalem at night; meals at night, however, were not customary among the simple people. (2) This was a true festive meal, since the participants reclined at table on cushions. (3) Explanatory words were spoken over the foods. (4) Finally, the participants sang the Hallel psalms, which in all likelihood were already part of the Pesach Haggadah at the time.[72] Ulrich Wilckens, who likewise assumes that the Last Supper was a Passover meal,[73] sees the bowl from which the disciples ate with Jesus, according to Mark 14:20, as a reference to the bowl with the bitter herbs.[74]

Nevertheless, dating the Last Supper to the night of Passover does not seem very plausible historically. If the Last Supper of Jesus with his disciples was a Passover Feast, this would presuppose that Jesus was tried and then handed over during the night before 15 Nisan and was crucified on the day of the Passover Feast after being sentenced to death by the Roman governor Pilate. Given the commotion in Jerusalem during the Passover Feast, this is difficult to imagine, as it is hardly imaginable that the high priests went to the place of the crucifixion on the Feast of Passover in order to mock the Crucified Lord (Mk 15:31). Another argument against a crucifixion on the Feast of Passover is a passage in Mark where it says that the high priests and the scribes had sought an opportunity "to arrest him by stealth, and kill him; for they said, 'Not during the feast, lest there be a tumult of the people'" (Mk 14:1–2). Thus many scholars today tend to follow the Johannine chronology, according to which

---

[71] According to Annie Jaubert, *La date de la Cène: Calendrier biblique et liturgie chrétienne*, Études bibliques (Paris: Gabalda, 1957), the Last Supper of Jesus was an anticipated Passover meal according to the solar calendar of the Qumran community.

[72] Cf. Hengel and Schwemer, *Jesus und das Judentum*, 583.

[73] Cf. Wilckens, *Theologie des Neuen Testaments*, 1:83.

[74] Cf. ibid., 78.

Jesus was crucified on the Day of Preparation before the beginning of the Passover Feast.[75] Even if the Last Supper of Jesus was presumably not a Passover meal, in any case it was a festive meal, since it was not customary to drink wine with a normal meal.[76]

The Jewish meal included various blessings, which were characterized by anamnetic thanks and praise and also by petitions. The elements that are mentioned occur in every ritualized Jewish festive meal: blessings (*berākôt*) over the bread at the beginning of the meal and the prayer over the "chalice of blessing" at the end of the meal (*birkat hammāzôn*), consisting of two anamnetic blessing formulas (1. Creation; 2. Land/Torah) and an intercessory blessing formula (*birkat jerūšalajim*, prayer for Jerusalem).[77] The *birkat hammāzôn* is considered one of the oldest Jewish prayers, which goes back to the time of the second Temple.[78] At the beginning is the symbolic act of breaking bread with the blessing formula over the bread as a gift of creation. In the case of the "cup of blessing", in addition to the motif of gift of creation there is praise of God as giver of the land and of the covenant as well as the prayer for his eschatological intervention for the benefit of the covenant people. In immediate proximity to the Passover Feast, Jesus at a festive meal with his disciples may have connected the prescribed blessings over broken bread and over the "cup of blessing" (1 Cor 10:16) with special explanatory and giving-phrases.

At the beginning of the meal, Jesus pronounced a blessing over the bread and explained the bread that he distributed to the disciples. After the common meal, the *birkat hammāzôn* over the "cup of blessing" followed, and then the explanation of the chalice with the wine that he handed to the disciples. The statement of renunciation in Luke (Lk 22:15–18) suggests that Jesus himself no longer ate of the bread and drank of the wine; this cannot be ruled out, but the

[75] Thus, for example, John P. Meier, *A Marginal Jew: Rethinking the Historical Jesus*, vol. 1, *The Roots of the Problem and the Person* (New York: Doubleday, 1991), 372–433, and Theissen and Merz, *Der historische Jesus*, 152–54, 373–76; Jürgen Roloff, *Jesus* (Munich: Beck, 2000), 110, and also Ratzinger, *Jesus of Nazareth: Holy Week*, 106–15.

[76] On the use of bread and other foods of the Jewish or early Christian meal, see Klaus Berger, *Manna, Mehl und Sauerteig: Korn und Brot im Alltag der frühen Christen* (Stuttgart: Quell, 1993).

[77] Cf. Reinhard Messner, *Einführung in die Liturgiewissenschaft*, 2nd ed. (Paderborn: Schöningh, 2009), 154.

[78] Cf. Joseph Heinemann, *Prayer in the Talmud: Forms and Patterns* (Berlin and New York: Walter de Gruyter, 1977), 113–22.

question must remain open. When Jesus allows his disciples to drink out of one cup (Mk 14:24; Mt 26:27), he may thereby have deviated from the Jewish custom of the time. Hartmut Gese adopted the thesis that the Last Supper of Jesus with his disciples was the celebration of a thank offering (*zæbaḥ tôdāh*).[79] Εὐχαριστεῖν in fact corresponds to the Hebrew *hôdāh* (to thank), while εὐλογεῖν is the equivalent of *bᵉrākāh* (to bless or to praise). Yet *hôdājôt* (prayers of thanks) occur not only during the celebration of a thank offering (*zæbaḥ tôdāh*) but also at other festive meals.

The Last Supper of Jesus with his disciples was not aimed against the Temple, as Bruce Chilton and others assume. Chilton says that Jesus substituted bread and wine, which are the offerings of the Temple (Num 15:1–10; Ex 29:38), for the animal sacrifices.[80] Gerd Theissen and Annette Merz, too, consider this likely.[81] Of course this would require considerable changes to the traditional text of the explanatory words over the bread and wine. For this text speaks about *Jesus' body and blood* and does not say that the offerings of bread and wine are supposed to replace the animal sacrifices of the Temple. The Acts of the Apostles sees no conflict between the "breaking of the bread" and the Temple worship (at least as far as prayer in the Temple is concerned). It says about the first Christians in Jerusalem: "Day by day, attending the temple together and breaking bread in their homes, they partook of food with glad and generous hearts" (Acts 2:46).[82] In Paul's writings, the imagery of cultic and sacrificial language plays an important role in understanding Christ's death, his own ministry as an apostle, and Christian worship.[83]

---

[79] Cf. Hartmut Gese, "Die Herkunft des Abendmahles", in *Zur biblischen Theologie: Alttestamentliche Vorträge* (Munich: Kaiser, 1977), 107–27. See also David Lindsey, "'Todah' and the Eucharist: The Celebration of the Lord's Supper as a 'Thanks Offering' in the Early Church", *Restoration Quarterly* 39 (1997): 83–100.

[80] Cf. Bruce Chilton, *A Feast of Meaning: Eucharistic Theologies from Jesus through Johannine Circles* (Leiden and New York: Brill, 1994), 46–74; Chilton, *The Temple of Jesus: His Sacrificial Program within a Cultural History of Sacrifice* (University Park, Pa.: Pennsylvania State University Press, 1992), 150–54; also Bernhard Lang, *Heiliges Spiel: Eine Geschichte des christlichen Gottesdienstes* (Munich: Beck, 1998), 241–54.

[81] Cf. Theissen and Merz, *Der historische Jesus*, 359–86; similarly Martin Karrer, *Jesus Christus im Neuen Testament*, Grundrisse zum Neuen Testament 11 (Göttingen: Vandenhoeck & Ruprecht, 1998), 283.

[82] Cf. Jonathan Klawans, "Interpreting the Last Supper: Sacrifice, Spiritualization, and Anti-Sacrifice", *Neutestamentliche Abhandlungen* 48 (2002): 9f.

[83] This is pointed out by Klawans, ibid., 10–15.

The following assumption therefore seems probable: Jesus fore-
saw that he would no longer be able to eat the Paschal lamb. So
he gathered the Twelve for a special farewell meal, in which he
gave himself as the true Lamb and thereby instituted his own Pasch.[84]
This could be what Jesus meant with his mysterious announcement that he would renounce the Pessach: "I have earnestly desired
to eat this Passover with you before I suffer; for I tell you I shall
not eat it until it is fulfilled in the kingdom of God" (Lk 22:15–16).
The decisive thing is no longer the Paschal lamb, but rather the new
Pasch of Jesus' suffering and death. The apostle Paul sees it this way,
too: "Cleanse out the old leaven that you may be new dough, as
you really are unleavened. For Christ, our Paschal Lamb, has been
sacrificed" (1 Cor 5:7). The lamb that has been sacrificed is Christ—
ultimately Paul and John agree on this.

C. The Discourse about the Bread of Heaven
and the Washing of the Feet

In the Gospel of John, nothing at first points to the celebration of
the Eucharist. The centerpieces of the Johannine account of Jesus'
last meal with his disciples are the washing of the feet (13:2–11) and
the *mandatum novum* (new commandment, Jn 13:12–18, 34). Jesus'
decision to wash the feet of his disciples was for the disciples a sign of
his love even to the end (Jn 13:1, 36). For John, the interpretation
of the footwashing as a sign of Jesus' laying down his life is not
opposed to the paradigmatic service of love.[85] What argument can
be made, therefore, against the hypothesis that for John or for Jesus
himself the two things already belong together inseparably?

Some have concluded from the absence of a Last Supper account
that no Eucharist was celebrated at first in the Johannine communities. An argument against this is the third part of the bread of life
discourse (Jn 6:52b–58), which contains very realistic language about

---

[84] So, for example, Meier, *A Marginal Jew*, 1:399; Klawans, "Interpreting the Last Supper",
15f.; Ratzinger, too, agrees with this position in *Jesus of Nazareth: Holy Week*, 114.

[85] Cf. Rudolf Schnackenburg, *Das Johannesevangelium*, vol. 4, pt. 2, of *Herders Theologischer
Kommentar zum Neuen Testament* (Freiburg: Herder, 1971), 7, 12.

eating Jesus' flesh and drinking Jesus' blood. A Eucharistic interpretation is therefore much more obvious.[86] The direct language of the bread of life discourse also makes it unlikely that the lack of an institution account has something to do with the arcane discipline (from the Latin *arcanum*, secret). According to the arcane discipline, cultic customs and rituals were made accessible only to a circle of initiates.[87] Some scholars try to see in the concluding part of the bread of life discourse an editorial continuation that conflicts with the non-sacramental intentions of the evangelist himself.[88] Others, in contrast, trace the concluding part also back to the evangelist.[89] Still others think that it comes from the Johannine school.[90]

Jesus gave the bread of life discourse shortly before the Feast of Passover (Jn 6:4)—after multiplying the loaves (Jn 6:1–15) and walking on the water (Jn 6:16–21). The discourse is introduced by a reference back to the multiplication of the loaves: "However, boats from Tiberias came near the place where they ate the bread after the Lord had given thanks [ἔφαγον τὸν ἄρτον εὐχαριστήσαντος τοῦ κυρίου]" (Jn 6:23). In "the Lord's prayer of thanks", many scholars see a reference to the Christian Eucharist. The centerpiece of the discourse on the bread of life is a midrash on Psalm 78:24:[91] "He rained down upon them manna to eat, and gave them the bread of heaven" (cf. Ex 16:4).[92] The statement "He gave them bread from heaven to eat" (Jn 6:31) is probably based on Wisdom 16:20, Psalm 78:24, and Exodus 16:4, 15.[93] Jesus accuses those who were present at the miracle of the multiplication of the loaves and now listen to him in

[86] Cf. Joachim Gnilka, *Johannesevangelium*, 2nd ed., Neue Echter Bibel: Neues Testament (Würzburg: Echter Verlag, 1985), 50; Marius Reiser, "Eucharistische Wissenschaft: Eine exegetische Betrachtung zu Joh 6,26–59", in *Vorgeschmack: Ökumenische Bemühungen um die Eucharistie*, Festschrift T. Schneider, ed. B.J. Hilberath and D. Sattler (Mainz: Matthias-Grünewald-Verlag, 1995), 164–77.

[87] Thus the explanation by Jeremias, *Abendmahlsworte Jesu*, 130.

[88] For example, Günther Bornkamm, "Die eucharistische Rede im Johannes-Evangelium", *Zeitschrift für die Neutestamentliche Wissenschaft* 47 (1956): 161–69.

[89] For instance, Ulrich Wilckens, "Das Abendmahlzeugnis im vierten Evangelium", *Evangelische Theologie* 18 (1958): 354–71.

[90] Cf. Raymond E. Brown, *The Gospel according to John (I–XII): Introduction, Translation, and Notes* (Garden City, N.Y.: Doubleday, 1966), 286f.

[91] A midrash is a scriptural interpretation in rabbinical Judaism.

[92] Cf. Schnackenburg, *Das Johannesevangelium*, 2:13, 53.

[93] Cf. Betz, *Eucharistie in der Schrift*, 22.

the synagogue of believing, not because of the signs, but because they received bread and ate their fill (Jn 6:27–29). "Do not labor for the food which perishes, but for the food which endures to eternal life, which the Son of man will give to you" (Jn 6:27). This could be a parenthesis to John 6:52b–59, the third part of the bread of life discourse.

The people who are listening to Jesus in the synagogue refer to the manna (Ex 16:4, 31) that their forefathers ate in the desert, about which Scripture says: "He gave them bread from heaven to eat" (cf. Ps 78:24). Jesus replies: "Truly, truly I say to you, it was not Moses who gave you the bread [ἄρτος] from heaven; my Father gives you the true bread [ἄρτος ἀληθινός] from heaven. For the bread of God is that which comes down from heaven, and gives life to the world." Then they asked him: "Lord, give us this bread always." Jesus told them: "I am the bread of life; he who comes to me shall not hunger, and he who believes in me shall never thirst" (Jn 6:32–35). The contrast between manna and the true bread from heaven is to be understood typologically. The manna that Moses gave to the Israelites in the desert to eat is not the bread of life. The true and real bread, in which the manna comes to its fulfillment, is the bread that came down from heaven and gives life to the world. Jesus himself is the "bread of life"[94] in person.

The expression "bread of life" is a metaphorical self-description of Jesus. It is connected with John 6:38 (cf. Jn 6:42), where Jesus says that he came down from heaven and was sent by God to do the Father's will, which is that all who see the Son and believe in him might have eternal life (Jn 6:39). In the bread of life discourse, the bread of life is to be interpreted first in a spiritual-personal way. Evidence of this is the fact that at the beginning of the discourse there is no talk about eating (φαγεῖν) the bread and that the twofold image of hungering and thirsting is used: whoever comes to Jesus will hunger no more; whoever believes in him will no longer thirst. The twofold image links the manna in the desert with the water from the rock (cf. Ex 17:1–7). Probably there is also a connection of the image with statements about wisdom: "Come, eat of my bread and drink of the wine I have mixed" (Prov 9:5). The food and drink of wisdom,

---

[94] Cf. Schnackenburg, *Das Johannesevangelium*, 2:58.

however, do not confer eternal life: "Those who eat me will hunger for more, and those who drink me will thirst for more" (Sir 24:21).

When the people murmur, Jesus explains that no one comes to the Father except through him and no one has seen the Father except the one who is from God (Jn 6:44, 46). After that, Jesus underscores his claim to divine authority by using the ἐγώ εἰμι formula: "I am [ἐγώ εἰμι] the bread of life. Your fathers ate the manna in the wilderness, and they died. This is the bread which comes down from heaven, that a man may eat of it and not die. I am the living bread which came down from heaven; if any one eats of this bread, he will live for ever; and the bread which I shall give for the life of the world is my flesh [σάρξ]" (Jn 6:48–51c). This passage, too, is about fellowship with Jesus, whose origin is heavenly, whereupon the people who listen to Jesus and know him as the son of Joseph protest (Jn 6:41). Jesus, however, refers to the fact that he was sent by the Father in heaven, whom no one has seen except the one who comes from God.

The Eucharistic part of the bread of life discourse, according to Heinz Schürmann, does not yet begin with John 6:51c, because this verse is about Jesus' devotion even unto death.[95] With the theme of "eating", the verse is probably a deliberate transition to the Eucharistic part of the bread of life discourse, which is introduced by John 6:52b.[96] The Jews, who argue among themselves about Jesus' discourse (cf. Ex 17:2), ask: "How can this man give us his flesh to eat?" (Jn 6:52b). Jesus answers them:

> Truly, truly, I say to you, unless you eat [φάγετη] the flesh of the Son of man [υἱὸς ἀνθρώπου] and drink his blood, you have no life in you; he who eats [ὁ τρώγων] my flesh and drinks my blood has eternal life, and I will raise him up at the last day. For my flesh is food indeed [ἀληθής ἐστιν βρῶσις], and my blood is drink indeed [ἀληθής ἐστιν πόσις]. He who eats my flesh and drinks my blood abides in me, and I in him. As the living Father sent me, and I live because of the Father, so he who eats me will live because of me. This is the bread which came down from heaven, not such as the fathers ate and died; he who eats this bread will live for ever." (Jn 6:53–58)

[95] Cf. Heinz Schürmann, "Joh 6,51c—ein Schlüssel zur grossen johanneischen Brotrede", *Biblische Zeitschrift* 2 (1958): 249f.

[96] Cf. Schnackenburg, *Das Johannesevangelium*, 2:83.

Most Greek and Latin Fathers of the Church interpret the bread of life discourse sacramentally, while Clement of Alexandria (d. ca. 215) and Origen (d. ca. 254) refer it to the incarnate Logos, who nourishes us spiritually.[97] Along with numerous Catholic and Lutheran exegetes, we assume here that the bread of life discourse advances from a spiritual/personal to a "sacramental" understanding of the true bread from heaven.[98] The development within the text could be regarded in the context of a *relecture* [rereading] and *reécriture* [rewriting] of the text within the Johannine circle.[99] The reference to the Eucharist, which is anticipated in the bread of life discourse in John 5:23, 27, is in any event obvious in John 6:52b–58.[100] Joachim Gnilka advocates the majority opinion of exegetes when he writes: "The eating is now no longer to be understood figuratively but rather sacramentally."[101]

On the other hand, Jens Schröter thinks that verses John 6:52b–58, too, are exclusively about communion with Christ through faith, which is expressed through the image of eating and drinking.[102] Yet it is striking that "eating" (φαγεῖν) is intensified by "chewing" (τωγεῖν). Other terms in the bread of life discourse that point to the Eucharist are ἄρτος, αἷμα, ἐστιν, and ὑπέρ. Flesh and blood are real food and real drink. The use of the title "Son of man" (υἱὸς ἀνθρώπου) prevents the possible misunderstanding of cannibalism: the physical flesh and blood of Jesus are not received in the Eucharist. He is the glorified Lord, who gives himself with his spirit-filled Flesh and Blood in the Eucharistic gifts. The question of whether the image of the grapevine in John 15:1–8 is connected with the early Christian meal celebration, as is the case in *Didache* 9, 2, must remain open.

It is difficult to tell why the Eucharistic part of the bread of life discourse talks about flesh (σάρξ) instead of about body (σῶμα). It could be a variant translation of the underlying words *gūpāh* and *bāśār*. Thus Ignatius of Antioch (d. ca. 110) uses σάρξ as a Eucharistic

---

[97] On the history of the interpretation, see ibid., 96–102.

[98] Cf. the bibliography, ibid., 87.

[99] Cf. Klaus Scholtissek, *Mit ihm sein und bleiben: Die Sprache der Immanenz in den johanneischen Schriften*, Herders biblische Studien 21 (Freiburg: Herder, 2000), 194–210.

[100] For Johannes Betz, in contrast, the whole bread of life discourse is to be read in a Eucharistic sense. See Betz, *Die Realpräsenz*, II/1:175.

[101] Gnilka, *Johannesevangelium*, 53. Gnilka recognizes in John 6:53–58 a midrash on the Last Supper tradition (Mt 26:26–28 and parallel passages).

[102] Cf. Schröter, *Nehmt—esst und trinkt*, 54–59.

term.[103] Perhaps the Johannine Word-made-flesh Christology plays the decisive role in the designation of the Eucharistic bread as flesh (σάρξ) in John 6:52b–58 (cf. σάρξ Jn 1:14). In any case, the sacramental realism in the last part of the bread of life discourse (some have spoken here about the Capernaite understanding of the Last Supper, since Jesus' bread of life discourse was set in Capernaum) corresponds entirely to the anti-Gnostic emphasis of Johannine Christology. Probably John 6:52b–58 is an objection to the Gnostic-Docetist group that disputed the Incarnation of Jesus and his death on the Cross and refused to receive the Eucharist. Flesh does not mean the reality separated from the blood, but rather the whole man. While the first two parts of the bread of life discourse have an intra-Jewish dispute in view, the third part takes aim against an unorthodox Christian group. The fact that the sacramental elements of bread and wine are not mentioned themselves is no counterargument, for the decisive things are Flesh and Blood as the Son of man's food.

In John 6:52b–58 we are not dealing with a magical understanding of the sacramental meal. The Eucharistic food is not an automatic process that brings about union with Christ. Only by receiving the Eucharistic gifts in faith is a lasting union with Christ bestowed. Mere non-sacramental eating is useless. This is how we are to understand John 6:63, also: "It is the Spirit that gives life, the flesh is of no avail." The Gospel speaks about "chewing" the Eucharistic bread, in order to distinguish the "sacramental eating" from the "figurative eating", that is, receiving in faith Jesus, the Bread of Life, in person. As in the Synoptics, the Eucharist in John is the pledge of eschatological fulfillment. The life bestowed by the Eucharist finds its fulfillment in the resurrection of the dead (Jn 6:54). The sacramental meal is a sign of faith in the revelation of Jesus and participation in his Paschal life.[104]

The symbolic action of washing feet, which the Fourth Gospel mentions as part of Jesus' last meal with his disciples, elucidates the

---

[103] Cf. Ignatius of Antioch, *Ad Romanos* 7 (PG 5:693B; ANF 1:77); Ignatius of Antioch, *Ad Philadelphios* 4 (PG 5:700B; ANF 1:81–82); Ignatius of Antioch, *Ad Smyrnos* 7 (PG 5:713A; ANF 1:89).

[104] Cf. Peter Wick, *Die urchristlichen Gottesdienste: Entstehung und Entwicklung im Rahmen der frühjüdischen Tempel-, Synagogen- und Hausfrömmigkeit*, Beiträge zur Wissenschaft vom Alten und Neuen Testament 150 (Stuttgart, Berlin, Cologne: Kohlhammer, 2002), 334.

meaning of Christ's death, but also that of the Eucharist: to receive the gift of the life that was laid down for us from him who in his death made himself the servant of all. In the Eucharistic bread, we obtain a share in eternal life (Jn 6:33, 50). For John, "the Eucharist is a special way of communicating life and sustaining life through the Son of God ..., who after his death on the cross, as the glorified Son of man, offers his flesh and blood sacramentally to the faithful."[105] The idea of the Real Presence of the incarnate and glorified Christ is no longer remote here, whereby the presence of Christ in the celebration of the breaking of the bread is to be understood personally-sacramentally and not substantially-materially.

At the Mass *In cena Domini*, the washing of the feet is to this day an eloquent sign for Jesus' dedication even unto death. In the liturgy of the Mass of the Last Supper, the washing of the feet takes place right after the homily.[106] In its liturgical context, the footwashing is not a general humanitarian gesture of humility, which one could therefore perform for non-Christians, also. It is instead a liturgical action within the Mass of the Last Supper, which symbolizes Jesus' ministry to his disciples and the disciples' ministry to one another.[107] Through the washing of their feet, the disciples obtain communion with Christ (Jn 13:9). The sacramental interpretation of the footwashing was therefore widespread among the Church Fathers and in the Middle Ages and was championed again and again later, too.[108] The *mandatum novum* is for the disciples to wash one another's feet (Jn 13:14).

[105] Schnackenburg, *Das Johannesevangelium*, 2:100.

[106] Cf. *Missale Romanum ex decreto Sacrosancti Oecumenici Concilii Vaticani II instauratum auctoritate Pauli PP. VI promulgatum, Ioannis Paul PP. II cura recognitum*, editio typica tertia (Vatican City: Libreria editrice vaticana, 2002; hereafter cited as *MR* 2002³). The Roman and German Missals foresee that the feet of twelve men will be washed. On the washing of the feet in the Gospel of John, see John Christopher Thomas, *Footwashing in John 13 and the Johannine Community*, Journal for the Study of the New Testament, Supplement series 61 (Sheffield: JSOT Press, 1991); Christoph Niemand, *Die Fusswaschungserzählung des Johannesevangeliums: Untersuchung zu ihrer Entstehung und Überlieferung im Urchristentum*, Studia Anselmiana 114 (Rome: Pontificio Ateneo S. Anselmo, 1993), 383–95, sees the footwashing in connection with the acceptance of John's disciples, who had already received the baptism of repentance.

[107] On the history of interpreting the footwashing, see Wolfram Lohse, *Die Fusswaschung (Joh 13,1–20): Eine Geschichte ihrer Deutung*, 2 vols. (dissertation, University of Erlangen-Nuremberg, 1967); Georg Richter, *Die Fusswaschung im Johannesevangelium: Geschichte ihrer Deutung*, Biblische Untersuchungen 1 (Regensburg: Pustet, 1967).

[108] Cf. G. Richter, *Die Fusswaschung*, 1–124.

In the Johannine communities, footwashing may have had a special significance as a sign of their love for one another. Ambrose mentions footwashing as part of the sacrament of Baptism.[109] The washing of feet gives participation in Christ. Baptism with water frees from sin; baptismal washing of feet is a remedy against selfish desire.

[109] Cf. Ambrose, *De sacramentis*, 3, 4–5, FC 3:120–23; Ambrose, *De mysteriis*, 31 (FC 3:228f.; Nicene and Post-Nicene Fathers, Second Series, ed. Philip Schaff and Henry Wace [1890; reprinted: Peabody, Mass.: Hendrickson, 1995; hereafter cited as NPNF-2], 10:321). On this topic, see Joseph Schmitz, "Einleitung", in Ambrosius, *De Sacramentis, De Mysteriis—Über die Sakramente, Über die Mysterien*, FC 3 (Freiburg: Herder, 1990), 45.

Chapter II

DIES DOMINICA

The Celebration of the Eucharist in Early Christian Times

"In union with the whole Church, we celebrate the first day of the week as the day on which Christ was raised from the dead."[1] This is how the *Communicantes* begins [in German] in Eucharistic Prayer I on Sundays in Ordinary Time. The Constitution on the Liturgy *Sacrosanctum concilium* notes the inner coherence of Easter, Sunday, and the Eucharist: "By a tradition handed down from the apostles [*ex traditione apostolica*] which took its origin from the very day of Christ's resurrection, the Church celebrates the paschal mystery [*mysterium Paschale*] every eighth day; with good reason this, then, bears the name of the Lord's Day, or Sunday [*dies Domini seu dominica*]."[2] According to the testimony of Scripture, Jesus rose from the dead on the first day of the week (Mk 16:2; Jn 20:1, 19), the day after the Sabbath (κατὰ μίαν σαββάτου). On the first day of the week, therefore, the first Christians celebrated liturgy. According to Jewish tradition, the day after the Sabbath, which concludes the seven-day week, is the first day of the week. According to Christian understanding, the first day of the week is the Lord's Day.[3]

Even for Ignatius of Antioch, living by a calendar regulated "by the Lord's Day"[4] is the distinguishing feature of Christians in contrast to those who celebrate the Sabbath. The earliest witness to the

---

[1] *MB* 465.

[2] *SC* 106.

[3] Cf. Kurt Koch, *Eucharistie: Herz des christlichen Glaubens* (Fribourg: Paulusverlag, 2005), 11; Michael Kunzler, *Sein ist die Zeit: Eine Einführung in Liturgie und Frömmigkeit des Kirchenjahres* (Paderborn: Bonifatius, 2012), 73–113.

[4] Ignatius of Antioch, *Letter to the Magnesians* 9 (PG 5:768A–769A; ANF 1:63).

naming of the first day of the week "Sunday" (ἡλίου ἡμέρα) is Justin Martyr (d. 165).[5] Not only is Sunday the first day of the week, but it is also viewed at the same time as the eighth day, namely, as the day of the New Creation in Christ. The roots of the Sunday celebration of the Lord's Supper go back to apostolic times. On the basis of several New Testament texts (1 Cor 16:2; Acts 20:7–12; Rev 1:10) and other early Christian sources (*Didache*, Ignatius of Antioch),[6] it seems probable that the beginning of the Sunday celebration of the Eucharist goes back to the first half of the first century.[7]

Paul characterizes the Eucharistic meal as the "Lord's Supper" (κυριακὸν δεῖπνον: 1 Cor 11:20). Even the *Didache* (Teaching of the Twelve Apostles)[8] and Ignatius of Antioch[9] call the celebration of the Lord's Supper εὐχαριστία (thanksgiving): "On the Lord's Day of the Lord [κυριακὴ (ἡμέρα) κυρίου] gather together, break bread and give thanks [κλάσετε ἄρτον καὶ εὐχαριστήσατε], after confessing your transgressions so that your sacrifice [θυσία] may be pure."[10] The oldest sources for the existence of the Sunday celebration of the Lord's Supper come from the second century.[11] "On the day which is

---

[5] Cf. Justin Martyr, *First Apology* 67 (*PG* 6:432A; ANF 1:185–86).

[6] Cf. *Didache* 14 (FC 1:132–36; ANF 7:381); Ignatius of Antioch, *Letter to the Magnesians* 9 (*PG* 768A–769A; ANF 1:62–63).

[7] Cf. Robert F. Taft, "The Frequency of the Celebration of the Eucharist throughout History", in *Between Memory and Hope: Readings on the Liturgical Year*, ed. M. E. Johnson (Collegeville, Minn.: Liturgical Press, 2000), 77f. Others doubt the early origin of the Sunday celebration of the Eucharist: Klaus Thraede, "Noch einmal: Plinius d.J. und die Christen", *Zeitschrift für die Neutestamentliche Wissenschaft* 95 (2004): 102–28; Clemens Leonhard, *The Jewish Pesach and the Origins of the Christian Easter*, Open Questions in Current Research (Berlin and New York: Walter de Gruyter, 2006), 119–40 at 123f.; Paul F. Bradshaw and Maxwell E. Johnson, *The Origins of Feasts, Fasts, and Seasons in Early Christianity* (London: SPCK; Collegeville, Minn.: Liturgical Press, 2011), 3–5.

[8] Cf. *Didache*, 9.1 (FC 1:120–23; ANF 7:379–80): Περὶ δὲ τῆς εὐχαριστίας.

[9] Cf. Ignatius of Antioch, *Letter to the Ephesians* 13 (*PG* 5:745B); Ignatius of Antioch, *Letter to the Philadelphians* 4 (*PG* 5:700B; ANF 1:81); Ignatius of Antioch, *Letter to the Smyrnaeans* 7 (*PG* 5:713A; ANF 1:89).

[10] *Didache* 14.1 (FC 1:132f.; FEF 4). The dating of chapter 14 to the first century is not undisputed.

[11] Cf. *Letter of Barnabas* 15.8f. (Klaus Berger and Christiane Nord, *Das Neue Testament und frühchristliche Schriften, übersetzt und kommentiert* [Frankfurt am Main: Insel Verlag, 1999], 257; ANF 1:146–47); Justin Martyr, *First Apology* 67 (*PG* 6:429–32; ANF 1:185–86). Stephen G. Wilson, *Related Strangers: Jews and Christians 70–170 CE* (Minneapolis, Minn.: Fortress Press 1995), 231f., and James Carleton Paget, *The Epistle of Barnabas: Outlook and Background* (Tübingen: Mohr, 1994), 9–30, date the *Letter of Barnabas* around 96–98.

dedicated to the sun, all those who live in the cities or who dwell in the countryside gather in a common meeting."[12] It cannot be determined for certain whether the Eucharist was celebrated on Sunday[13] or (as would be more probable for Jewish Christians) on Saturday evening after the Sabbath, that is, at the beginning of the first day of the week.[14] Since Jesus never opposed the Sabbath, we can assume that Jewish Christians originally continued to celebrate the Sabbath (see Acts 17:2; 18:4). Granted, there is no certain record of this in the New Testament, but James, the spokesperson for the Jewish Christians in Jerusalem, was able to allude to this practice in Acts 15:21.

Sunday is the day of the risen Lord. It is identified as the "*dies dominicae resurrectionis*"[15] or also as the ἀναστάσιμος ἡμέρα (Day of the Resurrection).[16] While "Sun-Christology" is still absent in the writings of Justin Martyr, it became widespread in the fourth century.[17] Christ is the "true Sun", or the "Sun of Salvation" (*sol salutis*). Emperor Constantine I (d. 337) introduced Sunday as a work-free day of rest (A.D. 321). Among other works excepted from the law of Sunday rest were agricultural chores and the holding of markets.[18] The work-free Sunday made unhindered participation in Christian worship possible. It is unclear whether Constantine's decision was

---

[12] Justin Martyr, *First Apology* 67 (*PG* 6:430B; *FEF* 55–56).

[13] Thus Willy Rordorf, *Der Sonntag: Geschichte des Ruhe- und Gottesdiensttages im ältesten Christentum*, Abhandlungen zur Theologie des Alten und Neuen Testaments 43 (Zurich: Zwingli Verlag, 1962), and Rordorf, *Sabbat und Sonntag in der Alten Kirche*, Traditio Christiana 2 (Zurich: Theologische Verlag, 1972), which assumes development of Sunday independently of the Sabbath.

[14] Recent research leans toward this opinion: Gerard Rouwhorst, "The Reception of the Jewish Sabbath in Early Christianity", in *Christian Feast and Festival: The Dynamics of Western Liturgy and Culture*, ed. P. Post et al., Liturgia condenda 12 (Leuven: Peeters, 2001), 251f.; Rouwhorst, "Christlicher Gottesdienst und der Gottesdienst Israels: Forschungsgeschichte, historische Interaktion, *Theologie*", in *Theologie des Gottesdienstes: Gottesdienst im Leben der Christen; Christliche und jüdische Liturgie*, Gottesdienst der Kirche 2/2 (Regensburg: Pustet, 2008), 538; Richard Bauckham, "Sabbath and Sunday in the Post-Apostolic Church", in *From Sabbath to Lord's Day*, ed. D.A. Carson (Grand Rapids, Mich.: Zondervan, 1982), 251–98; Paul F. Bradshaw and Maxwell E. Johnson, *The Origins of Feasts, Fasts, and Seasons in Early Christianity* (London: SPCK; Collegeville, Minn.: Liturgical Press, 2011), 10–13.

[15] Tertullian, *De oratione* 23 (CCSL 1:271; ANF 3:689).

[16] Bradshaw and Johnson, *Origins of Feasts and Seasons*, 14–24, follow traces that lead back to the early third century.

[17] Cf. Martin Wallraff, *Christus versus Sol: Sonnenverehrung und Christentum in der Spätantike* (Münster: Aschendorff, 2001), 41–59.

[18] Cf. *Codex Iustinianus* III, 12, 2.

influenced by the Christians or originated in his own initiative.[19] The first witness for the Christian Sunday as a day of rest is found with Eusebius of Caesarea (d. 339/340).[20] Sunday as a day of rest must not have arisen independently of the Sabbath, since Sunday was not originally linked with the motif of the day of rest after creation.[21] A distinct liturgical form for Saturday is not verifiable until the fourth century. Initially, there were probably no liturgical gatherings of Gentile Christians on the Sabbath.

A. The Christian Meal Celebration in the New Testament

The New Testament has different terms for the Christian meal celebration. The oldest is the term "breaking of the bread". This does not mean an ordinary food, but rather the celebration of the Lord's Supper with the Risen One. In the Acts of the Apostles, it is said of the Christians: "They held steadfastly to the apostles' teaching [διδαχή τῶν ἀποστόλων] and fellowship [κοινωνία], to the breaking of the bread [κλάσις τοῦ ἄρτου] and to the prayers [προσεύχαι].... And day by day [καθ' ἐμέραν], attending the temple together and breaking bread in their homes, they partook of food [μετελάμβανον τροφῆς] with glad and generous hearts" (Acts 2:42, 46). The καθ' ἐμέραν (day by day) in Acts 2:46 refers to the daily stop in the Temple for prayer, not to the "breaking of bread" in the circles of the Jewish Christians. There would hardly have been a daily Eucharist initially in early Christian times. With "breaking of bread", the Eucharistic bread is meant, which bestows participation in the Body of Christ. "The bread which we break, is it not a participation in the body of Christ?" (1 Cor 10:16).

The "breaking of the bread" took place amid eschatological rejoicing (ἀγαλλίασις), in joyful expectation of Christ's Second Coming.[22] The designation of the Eucharist as "breaking of bread" occurs above

---

[19] Cf. Bradshaw and Johnson, *Origins of Feasts and Seasons*, 25.

[20] Cf. Bauckham, "Sabbath and Sunday", 283f.

[21] Cf. Rouwhorst, "Christlicher Gottesdienst", 539.

[22] Cf. *Acta Ioannis* 49 and 109, in *Prex Eucharistica: Textus e variis liturgiis antiquioribus selecti*, Spicilegium Friburgense 12, ed. Anton Hänggi and Irmgard Pahl (Fribourg: Universitaires Suisses, 1968), 76f.; *Acta Ioannis* 49, in *Prex Eucharistica*.

all in Jewish Christian communities. The first Christians were convinced that, in the Eucharist, they already received a share in the eschatological meal toward which Jesus looked ahead at the Last Supper: "Truly, I say to you, I shall not drink again of the fruit of the vine until that day when I drink it new in the kingdom of God" (Mk 14:25; cf. Lk 22:16). According to Acts 2:46, the Jews who had come to believe in Jesus Christ did not completely give up their affiliation to the Temple. Until its destruction, it remained a central place of prayer for the Jewish Christians.

It is possible that the Jewish Christians not only prayed in the Temple but also continued to offer up sacrifices (Acts 21:26; Num 6:1–20); however, this would have been the food offering (minḥāh), not an animal sacrifice. The Temple liturgy also influenced the development of the Christian liturgy, not merely the synagogue services. This is shown above all by the Letter to the Hebrews and the Revelation of John. The framework for the Eucharistic meal in Jerusalem was initially the communal assembly. This included discussions, prayers, proclamation of the Word, care for the poor, and a common meal (Acts 20:9; cf. Acts 2:42). In this context, the Eucharistic bread was broken and the chalice of blessing was administered.[23]

Since, in the community in Corinth, the rich members did not wait for the poor members, who could join the community gathering only later due to the long work day, they immediately consumed the food they had brought with them. And so "one is hungry while another is drunk" (1 Cor 11:21). Paul opposes this: the crucial thing at the gathering is not that one's "own meal" (ἴδιον δεῖπνον) is celebrated but, rather, that the Lord's Supper (κυριακὸν δεῖπνον) is celebrated (1 Cor 11:20f.). The apostle therefore recommends that everyone who is hungry eat and drink at home (1 Cor 11:22, 34), but celebrate the Lord's Supper together (1 Cor 11:33). Whoever humiliates the poor at the Lord's Supper "despise[s] the Church of God" (1 Cor 11:22), he eats and drinks "in an unworthy manner" and "will be guilty of profaning the body and blood of the Lord" (1 Cor 11:27). It is unclear whether the bread and chalice activity framed the

---

[23] Cf. Jacob Kremer, " 'Herrenspeise'—nicht 'Herrenmahl': Zur Bedeutung von κυριακὸν δεῖπνον φαγεῖν (1 Kor 11,20)", in Schrift und Tradition, Festschrift J. Ernst, ed. K. Backhaus (Paderborn et al.: Schöningh, 1996), 234–39.

"satiating meal" as in the Jewish meal,[24] or whether it followed at the end of the satiating meal.[25] In any case, the bread and chalice activity was viewed as constitutive for the Eucharist.[26]

Since the study *Herrenmahl und hellenistischer Kult* (Lord's Supper and Hellenistic Cult) (1982) by Hans-Josef Klauck, the significance of the Last Supper for the emergence of the early Christian Eucharist and its ceremonial form was in part strongly challenged in favor of the meal-culture of the Hellenistic cult. But the Christian Eucharist cannot be derived from the cultic meals of the Greek mystery religions. The relationships and analogies are too superficial, and the Jewish idiolect of the Last Supper is too obvious for that. The early Christian Eucharist cannot be explained by the ritual celebration of meals with bread and wine that we know from Qumran, either, since here, too, the similarities are too superficial.

The Lord's Supper is "Christ-Anamnesis": it is celebrated in "remembrance" (1 Cor 11:24f.; cf. Lk 22:19) of the death and Resurrection of Christ. Anamnesis in the full biblical sense means that the salvation that is based on a founding event becomes present in a ritual action, as is the case with the Exodus event in the Passover celebration. The Eucharistic Christ-Anamnesis is accomplished "in the ritual activity of a cultic meal and in the word".[27] At the basis of it are the liturgically informed narratives of the Lord's Supper with the Risen One (Lk 24:28–32; cf. Acts 10:41; Jn 21:12).

As the *Didache* shows, in the early days of the Eucharist there were initially meal celebrations without explicit anamnesis of the Cross

[24] Cf. Otfried Hofius, "Herrenmahl und Herrenmahlsparadosis: Erwägungen zu 1 Kor 11,23b–25", in *PaulusStudien*, Wissenschaftliche Untersuchungen zum Neuen Testament 51 (Tübingen: Mohr, 1988), 383f.; Bernd Kollmann, *Ursprung und Gestalten der frühchristlichen Mahlfeier*, Göttinger theologische Arbeiten 43 (Göttingen: Vandenhoeck & Ruprecht, 1990), 42.

[25] Cf. Heinz Schürmann, "Die Gestalt der urchristlichen Eucharistiefeier", in *Ursprung und Gestalt: Erörterungen und Besinnungen zum Neuen Testament*, Kommentare und Beiträge zum Alten und Neuen Testament (Düsseldorf: Patmos, 1970), 85–88; Hans-Josef Klauck, "Präsenz im Herrenmahl: 1 Kor 11,23–26 im Kontext hellenistischer Religionsgeschichte", in *Amt—Sakrament: Neutestamentliche Perspektiven* (Würzburg: Echter Verlag, 1989), 320–22.

[26] Cf. Reinhard Messner, "Grundlinien der Entwicklung des eucharistischen Gebets in der frühen Kirche", in *Prex Eucharistica*, vol. 3, pt. 1, ed. A. Gerhards, H. Brakmann, and M. Klöckener, Spicilegium Friburgense: Texte zur Geschichte des kirchlichen Lebens 42 (Fribourg: Academic Press Fribourg and Paulusverlag, 2005), 19.

[27] Reinhard Messner, *Einführung in die Liturgiewissenschaft*, 2nd ed. (Paderborn: Schöningh, 2009), 164.

and Resurrection of Jesus.[28] But this type of Christian meal cele-bration could not become widely accepted. For since the glorified Lord, who was expected in his Second Coming, is none other than the risen Crucified One, the Eucharistic meal celebration could not be severed from Jesus' death on the Cross. Even the oldest report of the Last Supper handed down by the apostle Paul understands the Lord's Supper as a remembrance of the death on the Cross of Jesus, who celebrated the Last Supper "on the night when he was betrayed" (1 Cor 11:23). The broken bread and the chalice of wine are signs of his death for the many. In connection with the command to com-memorate, 1 Corinthians 11:26 states: "As often as you eat this bread and drink the chalice, you proclaim the Lord's death." Since the Eucharist was celebrated as the memorial of the Paschal Mystery, it is altogether possible that the Passion account took the place of table conversation at the Corinthian Lord's Supper.

Paul claims that he received (παρέλαβον) what he handed on (παρέδωκα) to the community of Corinth from the Lord himself, who was handed over (παρεδίδετο). Παραδιδόναι is a stronger form of διδόναι (to give) and means the same as to surrender, to hand over to someone. The Son is handed over not only by men, but also by God himself: God "did not spare his own Son but gave him up [παρέδωκεν] for us all" (Rom 8:32). The Son also gives himself up at the same time: he "loved me and gave himself for me [παραδόντος ἑαυτὸν ὑπὲρ ἐμοῦ]" (Gal 2:20). In dying, Jesus ratifies the pro-existence of his life: the self-surrender of the Son is in accord with the will of the Father, who delivers over the Son. Finally, Jesus is delivered over to the violence of the men who kill him.[29]

The Eucharistic meal is not only a commemoration of the death and Resurrection of Jesus Christ but also an eschatological sign of salvation. The Supper of the Lord is celebrated "until he comes" (1 Cor 11:26) in glory. The Aramaic cry *marana'tha* ("Our Lord, come!" 1 Cor 16:22; Rev 22:20) therefore belonged to the early Christian liturgy. Jesus himself said that he would not drink again from the fruit of the vine until the fulfillment of the Kingdom of

---

[28] See below, section B.

[29] On the multiple meaning of παραδιδόναι, see Hansjürgen Verweyen, *Gottes letztes Wort: Grundriss der Fundamentaltheologie*, 4th ed. (Regensburg: Pustet, 2002), 51–57.

God (Mt 26:29; cf. Mk 14:25; Lk 22:15–18, 30). Thus the Eucharist is characterized by the eschatological tension between "already" and "not yet". The risen Lord is always coming and becomes present in the community. At the same time, the community expects him on "that day" (Mt 26:29) on which he will come again in glory.

The Christian celebration of the Lord's Supper has the form of a prayer of praise and thanksgiving; for this reason, the name "Eucharist" (εὐχαριστία) quickly became established as the name of the Christian celebration of the Lord's Supper. The bread of life and the chalice of blessing, which are distributed in the Christian celebration of the Lord's Supper, are signs of Jesus' surrender of his life in death. When Paul speaks of the body of Christ, he can mean the community in addition to the Eucharistic bread, as in 1 Corinthians 12. He combines the two in 1 Corinthians 10:16f. in the idea of the common participation in the body of Christ: "The cup of blessing which we bless, is it not a participation [κοινωνία] in the blood of Christ? The bread which we break, is it not a participation in the body of Christ? Because there is one bread, we who are many are one body, for we all partake of the one bread" (1 Cor 10:16f.). Κοινωνία means communion through participation. Paul speaks also of the "chalice of the Lord" (ποτήριον τοῦ κυρίου: 1 Cor 11:27; 10:21), which denotes communion with the Blood of Christ and precludes participation in the "cup of demons" (1 Cor 10:21), that is, in idolatry. Paul also speaks of the "table of the Lord" (τράπεζα τοῦ κυρίου), which he distinguishes from the "table of demons" (τράπεζα δαιμονίον: 1 Cor 10:21).

Different hypotheses are advanced regarding the question of the order of events in the early Christian celebration of the Eucharist. The English historian of liturgy Gregory Dix (1901–1952) starts from the premise that the order of events was initially guided by that of the Last Supper, so that the early Christian Eucharist originally encompassed seven actions: (1) Jesus took the bread, (2) broke it, (3) said the prayer of thanks, (4) gave it to his disciples with the corresponding words, (5) then [after the meal] he took the chalice, (6) said the prayer of thanks, and (7) gave it to his disciples with the corresponding words.[30] After the composition of the First Letter to

---

[30] Cf. Gregory Dix, *The Shape of the Liturgy* (1945; London and New York: Continuum, 2005), 48–102.

the Corinthians and the Synoptic Gospels, the Eucharist was separated from the satiating meal, and since then it has encompassed four central actions: (1) *Offertory*: Bread and wine are taken and placed on the altar table; (2) *Prayer*: The presider of the Eucharist says the prayer of thanks over the gifts of bread and wine; (3) *Breaking*: The Eucharistic bread is broken; (4) *Communion*: The Eucharistic bread and the chalice of salvation are distributed.[31]

According to Paul F. Bradshaw, there were different forms of the Christian meal celebration even in the beginning. Given the state of the sources, this seems more convincing than the assumption of a single basic form. One form could have corresponded to the practice in Qumran, in which the prayer of thanks was said over bread and wine before the common meal (1QS6; 1QSa), while it was common in the rabbinic tradition to say the prayer of thanks over the bread before the common meal, and the prayer over the chalice afterward.[32]

Besides the celebration of the Lord's Supper on the first day of the week, there may have already been a yearly Christian Paschal feast in early Christian times.[33] The practice of celebrating the Christian Easter on the night of 14 to 15 Nisan, that is, at the same time as the Jewish Passover, may have been the original practice.[34] The Quartodeciman practice, which interpreted the Passover lamb as a τύπος [type] of Christ, the new and true Paschal Lamb, must have emerged before or shortly after the destruction of the Temple, when the relationship between Christians and Jews was still very close. Less plausible is the assumption that the Quartodeciman Easter celebration

---

[31] About Dix's hypothesis, cf. Paul F. Bradshaw, "Did the Early Eucharist Ever Have a Sevenfold Shape?", *Heythrop Journal* 43 (2002); Simon Jones, "Introduction", in Gregory Dix, *The Shape of the Liturgy*, new ed. (London: Bloomsbury, 2005), x–xxviii. Brian Spinks counts the words "This is my body" and "This is my blood" as separate speech acts and thus, in contrast to Dix, arrives at nine central acts. Cf. Spinks, "Mis-Shapen: Gregory Dix and the Four-Action Shape of the Liturgy", *Lutheran Quarterly* 4 (1990): 161.

[32] Cf. Paul F. Bradshaw, *Eucharistic Origin*, Alcuin Club Collections 80 (London: Oxford University Press, 2004), 43f.

[33] Cf. Gottfried Schille, "Das Leiden des Herrn: Die evangelische Passionstradition und ihr 'Sitz im Leben'", *Zeitschrift für Theologie und Kirche* 52 (1955): 161–205; Rupert Feneberg, *Christliche Passafeier und Abendmahl: Eine bibischhermeneutische Untersuchung der neutestamentlichen Einsetzungsberichte*, Studien zum Alten und Neuen Testament 27 (Munich: Kösel-Verlag, 1971).

[34] Cf. Hansjörg Auf der Maur, *Die Osterfeier in der alten Kirche*, ed. R. Messner (Münster: Lit, 2003).

developed only in the second century in deliberate distinction from the Jewish Passover festival.[35] It is possible that the Passion account with the narrative of the Last Supper was commemorated at the Christian Paschal celebration from the beginning. This would explain the embedding of the Last Supper in a Passover meal in the Synoptic Gospels.[36] From the second century on, the Christian Easter celebration was increasingly observed on the Sunday after 14/15 Nisan.[37]

In opposition to Lietzmann's theory of the double source of the Eucharist, Reginald H. Fuller (1915–2007) advocated the view that the original liturgical place of the Last Supper account, together with the traditional command to commemorate, was a yearly Christian Paschal celebration.[38] The Jews who confessed Jesus as Messiah had continued to celebrate the Passover festival in Jerusalem, while of course believing in the sacrificial death of Jesus as the true eschatological deliverance. Instead of eating the Passover lamb at night, therefore, they fasted, and not until dawn did they commemorate the death and Resurrection of the Crucified One with a festive meal.[39] Erik Peterson (1890–1960) had already speculated that the command to commemorate initially referred to the Easter celebration of the anniversary and the commemoration of Jesus' death.[40]

Michael Theobald sees the Christian Paschal feast not only as the initial context for the cultic etiology of the commemoration command. The Blood-formula ἐν τῷ αἵματί μου, which Theobald considers to be a secondary transformation of the saying over the chalice by the idea of the atoning death of Jesus, also had its original *Sitz im Leben* in the Christian Paschal celebration.[41] Besides the Christian Paschal

[35] Thus Leonhard, *Jewish Pesach*, 435.

[36] This thesis was prepared by Feneberg, *Christliche Paschafeier*.

[37] Cf. Rouwhorst, "Christlicher Gottesdienst", 540–43.

[38] Cf. Reginald H. Fuller, "The Double Origin of the Eucharist", *Biblical Research* 8 (1963): 60–72.

[39] On this subject, compare Bernhard Lohse, *Das Passafest der Quartodezimaner*, Beiträge zur Förderung christlicher Theologie, Reihe 2: Sammlung wissenschaftlicher Monographien 54 (Gütersloh: Bertelsmann, 1953), 74–89.

[40] Cf. Erik Peterson, *Der erste Brief an die Korinther und Paulus Studien*, ed. H.-U. Weidemann (Würzburg: Echter Verlag, 2006), 254.

[41] Cf. Michael Theobald, "Leib und Blut Christi: Erwägungen zu Herkunft, Funktion und Bedeutung des sogenannten 'Einsetzungsberichts'", in *Herrenmahl und Gruppenidentität*, ed. M. Ebner, Quaestiones disputatae 221 (Freiburg: Herder, 2007), 126–29.

celebration, there was another type of Lord's Supper wherein Christ's Parousia, and not his suffering, was central. Gerard Rouwhorst's theory of the definitive difference between Paschal and Sabbath meal is along similar lines.[42] Due to the state of the source material, much must remain open in this regard. Yet there may well have been a yearly Christian Paschal celebration and a weekly celebration of the Lord's Supper even in New Testament times in Jerusalem.

In addition to the Acts of the Apostles and Paul, the Revelation of John also presupposes a Christian meal celebration, but its order of events cannot be reconstructed. The Book of Revelation depicts a meal that distinguishes itself as an ascetic counter-model to the cultic meals of the cultural surroundings with their overindulgence in wine, consumption of meat sacrificed to idols (1 Cor 8:1–13), and sexual debaucheries (Rev 2:14–15, 20): the Christian meal is eating of the Tree of Life (Rev 2:7; 22:2, 14, 19), being fed with the hidden heavenly food of manna (Rev 2:17); it is the wedding feast of the Lamb (Rev 19:6–9), in which Christ is both the host and the guest of the meal (Rev 3:20f.).[43] The meal practice determines whether one belongs to God and the Lamb[44] or to the Whore of Babylon (Rome) and perishes on the deadly gifts of meat and wine that she serves.[45] The earthly meal of Christians is connected with the heavenly liturgy (Rev 19:1–10), which is concretized in the images of the Temple (Rev 7:15; 11:1, 19; 14:15) and the altar (Rev 6:9; 11:1), as well as in hymnic songs such as the Alleluia (Rev 19:1, 3–4, 6), the Trisagion

---

[42] Cf. Rouwhorst, "Christlicher Gottesdienst", 536–39.

[43] Cf. Gerhard Delling, "Zum gottesdienstlichen Stil der Johannes-Apokalypse", in Delling, *Studien zum Neuen Testament und zum hellenistischen Judentum: Gesammelte Aufsätze 1950–1968*, ed. F. Hahn et al. (Göttingen: Vandenhoeck & Ruprecht, 1970), 425–50.

[44] Cf. Thomas Söding, "Gott und das Lamm: Theozentrik und Christologie in der Johannesapokalypse", in *Theologie als Vision: Studien zur Johannes-Offenbarung*, ed. K. Backhaus, Stuttgarter BibelStudien 191 (Stuttgart: Verlag Katholisches Bibelwerk, 2001), 77–120.

[45] It cannot be determined with certainty whether the meal celebration presupposed by the Book of Revelation was celebrated, as by the Therapeutae, with bread and water instead of with bread and wine and consequently prepared the meal asceticism of the Ebionites, Encratites, and other groups. Cf. Hans Joachim Stein, *Frühchristliche Mahlfeiern: Ihre Gestalt und Bedeutung nach der neutestamentlichen Briefliteratur und der Johannesoffenbarung* (Tübingen: Mohr Siebeck, 2008), 319; Andrew B. McGowan, *Ascetic Eucharists: Food and Drink in Early Christian Ritual Meals*, Oxford Early Christian Studies (Oxford: Clarendon Press; New York: Oxford University Press, 1999), 143–74.

(Rev 4:8), and the exclamations declaring God (Rev 4:11) and the Lamb (Rev 5:9–10, 12, 13) worthy.[46]

The Lamb (ἀρνίον, not ἀμνός as in Jn 1:29 and 1 Pet 1:19) is the Christological model of the Book of Revelation and is first encountered in the great vision of Christ in Revelation 5:6–14. The Lamb who "was slain" (Rev 5:12; 13:8; cf. 7:14; 12:11) points to Jesus' death on the Cross, just as the blood of Christ in Revelation 1:5 refers to his vicarious atoning death. In the background of the image of the slain lamb is the blood of the slain Passover lamb (Ex 12:5f.). Christ, the slain Lamb, causes a new People of God to come into existence in the midst of a world of evil (Rev 5:9f.) and protects them from their enemies (Rev 14:1–5). The fact that the Lamb is standing (Rev 5:6; cf. 7:17) refers to the Resurrection and exaltation of Christ. The Risen One participates in the power and glory of God the Father, who sits on the throne. The destruction of the enemies is assigned to the Lamb (Rev 6:16), in order that all those for whom Jesus shed his blood (Rev 5:9) and who have made their clothes white in the blood of the Lamb (Rev 7:14) can participate in the "marriage supper of the Lamb" (Rev 19:9). God and the Lamb impart the eschatological salvation. Therefore, not only sovereignty belongs to them, but also praise and honor (Rev 5:12). A host of angels and saints serve God and the Lamb in adoration and glorification. In the "holy city" (Rev 21:2) of the heavenly Jerusalem, however, there is no longer a visible stone temple, "for its temple is the Lord God the Almighty and the Lamb" (Rev 21:22). The Temple is the place of the presence and worship of God.

The community gathered for the meal awaits the Second Coming of Christ (Rev 22:17, 20). "The present coming of the Lord in the table fellowship imparted by him is understood as an assuring prospect of his future coming."[47] This expectancy finds its liturgical

---

[46] Franz Töth, *Der himmlische Kult: Wirklichkeitskonstruktion und Sinnbildung in der Johannesoffenbarung*, Arbeiten zur Bibel und ihrer Geschichte 22 (Leipzig: Evangelische Verlagsanstalt, 2006), 35, considers it possible that the hymns were already used early in the liturgical gatherings of Christians, even though the Trisagion only slowly made its way into the celebration of the Eucharist. This is tangible for the first time in the anaphora of Serapion (4th century).

[47] Jürgen Roloff, *Die Kirche im Neuen Testament*, Grundrisse zum Neuen Testament 10 (Göttingen: Vandenhoeck & Ruprecht, 1993), 172.

expression at the end of the Book of Revelation in a variation on the oldest prayer invocation, *marana'tha* (1 Cor 16:22). In it, the bridal imagery describes the love of the Church for her Bridegroom, Jesus Christ. "The Spirit and the Bride say, 'Come.' And let him who hears say, 'Come.' And let him who is thirsty come, let him who desires take the water of life without price" (Rev 22:17). The Eucharist is the place of encounter with the glorified, present Lord. The promise that "I stand at the door and knock; if any one hears my voice and opens the door, I will come in to him and eat with him, and he with me" (Rev 3:20) applies to everyone who belongs to Christ.[48] The symbolism of the heavenly city of God depicts the saving space of the gathered community. Indeed, the community gathered for liturgy has no visible temple as a sanctuary (Rev 22:2). Yet this does not lead to the abrogation of the idea of the place of worship, since the liturgy serves God and the Lamb and has the character of adoration (λατρεύειν: Rev 22:3). The Christian meal celebration in the Book of Revelation would therefore certainly have been familiar with an altar table.[49]

The Letter to the Hebrews also presumes the existence of an early Christian meal celebration. The central motif of the Letter to the Hebrews is the glorified High Priest Jesus Christ, the officiant of the New Covenant (Heb 8:1, 9:15), who has entered into the heavenly sanctuary with his blood and has obtained eternal salvation (Heb 9:12). Due to the heavenly origin and permanent duration of the priesthood of Melchizedek,[50] the priest of "God Most High" (Gen 14:18; cf. Ps 110:4), of whom neither birth nor death is mentioned, the Letter to the Hebrews sees him as a type of the High Priesthood of the Son of God. It should be noted here that, according to the interpretation of the Letter to the Hebrews, the biblical type of Melchizedek is patterned after the heavenly reality of the Son. Melchizedek serves to illuminate the everlasting priesthood of Christ, but he otherwise

---

[48] Martin Luther translates Revelation 3:20 with the words: "zu dem werde ich hineingehen und das Abendmahl mit ihm halten" [I will go in to him and have supper with him]. Cf. *Das Neue Testament: Griechisch und Deutsch*, ed. K. and B. Aland, 26th ed. (Stuttgart: Deutsche Bibelgesellschaft, 1986), 639.

[49] Stein, *Frühchristliche Mahlfeiern*, 324, thinks otherwise.

[50] The name means approximately "(My) king is (the god) Zedek" or "(My) King (i.e., divinity) is just."

stays completely in the background. The priesthood of Christ fulfills the earthly priesthood of the Old Covenant.[51] The typology of bread and wine does not yet play a role in the interpretation of the figure of Melchizedek for the Letter to the Hebrews, but it is emphasized time and again by the Church Fathers.[52]

The eternal High Priest Jesus Christ is different from the earthly ministers of sacrifice in that he offered himself up on the Cross.[53] A hallmark of the Old Testament priesthood was that the mortal high priest first had to make atonement for himself (Heb 5:3) before he obtained atonement for the people. While the earthly high priest obtained atonement for the people once a year on the Great Day of Atonement (jôm hakippurîm), the eternal High Priest Jesus Christ advocates "day after day" for those who belong to him, because he offered the decisive sin offering once for all on the Cross. In this way, the end of all human cultic sacrifices is ratified.[54] Every high priest is appointed "to offer gifts and sacrifices". For this reason, it is necessary that the eternal High Priest Jesus Christ offer something as well.

The sacrifice of Christ "is the surrender of his own life, the offering up of himself that was consummated on Golgotha, the lowest place on earth, and achieves heavenly reality"[55] (see Heb 7:27; 10:5–10). The visible offering up of the sacrificial gifts of bread and wine participates in this heavenly reality. The sacrifice of bread and wine that Melchizedek brings to Abraham "was already interpreted as a type of the Eucharist in early Christianity and thus found its way into the Roman Canon of the Mass as 'the holy gifts, the pure sacrifice of your high priest Melchizedek', alongside the 'gifts of your servant, Abel the Just' and the 'sacrifice of our father Abraham.'"[56]

Hebrews 9:20 cites the formula about the blood of the covenant (Ex 28:4) in the wording of the prayer over the chalice in Mark 14:24. Unlike in early Judaism, which relativized the "Canon of

---

[51] Cf. Knut Backhaus, Der Hebräerbrief (Regensburg: Pustet, 2009), 256–75.

[52] Cf. Cyprian, Letter 62.4 (PL 4:375B–376A; ANF 5:359); Ambrose, De mysteriis 45f. (FC 3:238–41; NPNF-2 10:322); Augustine, De civitate Dei 16.22 (CCSL 48:524f.; Nicene and Post-Nicene Fathers, First Series, ed. Philip Schaff [1886; reprinted: Peabody, Mass.: Hendrickson, 1995; hereafter cited as NPNF-1], 2:323).

[53] Cf. Backhaus, Hebräerbrief, 282.

[54] See ibid., 284.

[55] Ibid., 290.

[56] Ibid., 258.

blood" (Lev 17:11) considerably, it remains essential to the interpretation of Scripture in the Letter to the Hebrews (Heb 9:22: "without the shedding of blood there is no forgiveness of sins"). The clearest reference to the Eucharist is generally seen in Hebrews 13:9f.: "Do not be led away by diverse and strange teachings; for it is well that the heart be strengthened by grace [χάρις], not by foods, which have not benefited their adherents. We have an altar [θυσιαστήριον] from which those who serve the tent have no right to eat [φαγεῖν]." While it is true that a non-Eucharistic interpretation of χάρις, θυσιαστήριον, and φαγεῖν is also proposed, because of the strong cult typology in the Letter to the Hebrews, this interpretation is not convincing. *Didache* 10:6 shows that χάρις (Heb 10:29; 12:15) can also mean the grace of the Eucharist. The θυσιαστήριον (Heb 13:10) should be understood typologically, therefore, not as a reference to a Christian altar in the first century. An analogy between the Temple altar and the "table of the Lord" (1 Cor 10:21) is more likely.[57]

Christ is the High Priest of the true tent (Heb 8:2). Hebrews 9:11–14 sees Christ as the High Priest of the New Covenant, who won eternal salvation through his blood and entered into God's presence in the heavenly sanctuary. Through the surrender of his life on the Cross, the culmination of his earthly pro-existence, Christ, who is at the same time Priest and Sacrifice, offers the Father a pure sacrifice. Through it, he makes the space of God's holiness accessible and thus closes forever the gulf between God and mankind. Christ's sacrifices enable man to serve the living God, and this service is not only service to God (*Gottesdienst*, liturgy), but also service to the world (*Weltdienst*).[58] The Letter to the Hebrews shows that Christianity was never a religion distant from worship. As long as cultic activity is not an end in itself, it is in no way unbiblical.[59]

In the First Epistle of Clement (90–100), which is of urban Roman origin like the Epistle to the Hebrews, the cult typology is already expanded to include Christian worship.[60] In 1 Clement 44:4, the offering of sacrifices (προσφέρειν τὰ δῶρα) through the episcopal

---

[57] In Hebrews 6:2, we can see hints of Baptism and the imposition of hands.

[58] Cf. Backhaus, *Hebräerbrief*, 315.

[59] Cf. ibid., 276.

[60] Already in the days of the early Church, a stylistic and thematic affinity between the Letter to the Hebrews and the First Letter of Clement was noted.

officials is discussed. The expression προσφέρειν τὰ δῶρα denotes sacrifices that are offered, in the Greek translation of the Old Testament (Lev 2:1, 4, 13; 4:32; 7:38 LXX, and elsewhere), so that the offering of sacrifices in 1 Clement 44:4 is correlated not only to prayer offerings (θυσίαν αἰνέσεως) (as in 1 Clem 52:3f.; cf. Heb 13:15) but also likewise to the offerings of the Eucharist, as in the writings of Ignatius of Antioch.[61]

B. The Eucharistic Prayers of the Didache

The *Didache* is the oldest surviving Church ordinance.[62] It comes from the Syrian area and addresses questions of ethical life, liturgy, and Church constitution. The composition of the text occurred during New Testament times.[63] Although an early dating of the *Didache* around A.D. 50/65 has not yet been able to gain acceptance,[64] the texts of the *Didache* are, for the most part, older than the final version of the Church ordinance (A.D. 80/100). This is probably true of the Eucharistic Prayers of the *Didache* as well, with their strongly Jewish-Christian coloring.[65] Like the Acts of the Apostles, the *Didache* speaks of "breaking bread" on "the Lord's Day":

[61] Cf. Ignatius of Antioch, *Letter to the Smyrnaeans* 7 (PG 5:713A; ANF 1:89); Ignatius of Antioch, *Letter to the Philadelphians* 4 (PG 5:700B; ANF 1:81–82).

[62] On the rediscovery of the text of the *Didache* by Philotheos Byrennios (1873), see Kurt Niederwimmer, *Die Didache*, 2nd ed. Kommentar zu den Apostolischen Vätern 1 (Göttingen: Vandenhoeck & Ruprecht, 1993), 33–36.

[63] The *Didache* is usually dated to the period around A.D. 80.

[64] Cf. Enrico Mazza, *The Origins of the Eucharistic Prayer*, trans. Ronald E. Lane (Collegeville, Minn.: Liturgical Press, 1995), 12–29 (A.D. 50); Berger, in Berger and Nord, *Neue Testament und frühchristliche Schriften*, 302 (A.D. 65).

[65] Cf. *Didache* 9.1–10.6 (FC 1:120–27; ANF 1:379–80). On this passage, see Thomas J. Talley, "Von der Berakha zur Eucharistia: Das eucharistische Hochgebet der alten Kirche in neuerer Forschung: Ergebnisse und Fragen", *Liturgisches Jahrbuch* 26 (1976): 93–115; Gerard Rouwhorst, "Didache 9–10: A Litmus Test for the Research on Early Christian Eucharist", in *Matthew and the Didache: Two Documents from the Same Jewish Christian Milieu?*, ed. H. van de Sandt (Assen: Royal Van Gorcum; Minneapolis: Fortress Press, 2005.), 143–56. Franz Dünzel, "Herrenmahl ohne Herrenworte? Eucharistische Texte aus der Frühzeit des Christentums", in *Mehr als Brot und Wein: Theologische Kontexte der Eucharistie*, ed. W. Haunerland (Würzburg: Echter Verlag, 2005), 51, dates the *Didache* to around A.D. 90–120. The late dating (first half of the second century) is also the opinion of Niederwimmer, *Didache*, 79.

On the Lord's Day of the Lord [κυριακὴ (ἡμέρα) κυρίου] gather together, break bread and give thanks [κλάσετε ἄρτον καὶ εὐχαριστήσατε], after confessing your transgressions so that your sacrifice [θυσία] may be pure. Let no one who has a quarrel with his neighbor join you until he is reconciled, lest your sacrifice be defiled. For this is that which was proclaimed by the Lord: "In every place and time let there be offered to Me a clean sacrifice [καθαρὰ ἡ θυσία]. For I am a Great King," says the Lord, "and My name is wonderful among the gentiles."[66]

It is very likely that the "breaking bread" refers to the regular Sunday Eucharist, as in Acts 2:42; 20:7, 11, and Luke 24:30, 35.[67] The meal celebration is called a sacrifice (θυσία) (Hebr., minḥāh) in reference to Malachi 1:11. Minḥāh meant the food offering during the time of the Temple. After the destruction of the Jerusalem Sanctuary, minḥāh increasingly denoted the afternoon prayers of the Jews. The "clean sacrifice" that the Christians offer consists of thanksgiving and the breaking of the bread.[68] In Matthew 5:23f., the sacrifice may mean the Temple worship: "So if you are offering your gift at the altar [προσφέρῃς τὸ δῶρόν], and there remember that your brother has something against you, leave your gift there before the altar and go; first be reconciled to your brother, and then come and offer your gift."[69]

The early Christian meal prayers are prayers with a complex structure. Like other prayers, for instance 1 Clement 59–61,[70] the prayer of consecration for baptismal water, or the prayers for ordination, the meal prayers also generally have two parts, an anamnetic and an epicletic part. The early Christian authors, to characterize the

---

[66] Didache 14.1–3 (FC 1:132–35; FEF 4). Part of chapter 14 is regarded as a later addition.

[67] Cf. Paul F. Bradshaw, Eucharistic Origins, Alcuin Club Collections 80 (London: Oxford University Press, 2004), 55–59.

[68] Cf. Reinhard Messner, "Grundlinien der Entwicklung des eucharistischen Gebets in der frühen Kirche", in Prex Eucharistica, vol. 3/1:16. Richard P. C. Hanson, Eucharistic Offering in the Early Church (Bramcote: Grove Books, 1979), 5, turns against this widespread interpretation. He sees in the offering Christ's self-sacrifice as an act of prayer.

[69] The Letter of Barnabas leans more strongly toward an interiorization of the sacrifice. Cf. Der Barnabasbrief, translation and commentary by F. R. Prostmeier (Göttingen: Vandenhoeck & Ruprecht, 1999), 165–89. In 1 Clement 44.4, the expression προσφέρειν τὰ δῶρα presumably means the Eucharistic offertory.

[70] Cf. Hermut Löhr, Studien zum frühchristlichen und frühjüdischen Gebet: Untersuchungen zu 1 Clem 59 bis 61 in seinem literarischen, historischen und theologischen Kontext, Wissenschaftliche Untersuchungen zum Neuen Testament 160 (Tübingen: Mohr Siebeck, 2003).

celebration of the Lord's Supper, speak generally of εὐχαριστεῖν and not of εὐλογεῖν, because εὐχαριστεῖν, which corresponds to the Hebrew *hôdāh*, emphasizes more the character of the prayer as thanksgiving, in contrast to *barak* (εὐλογεῖν, *benedicere*), which more strongly emphasizes the character of the prayer as petition. In the case of the Jewish *bᵉrākôt* (petitions for blessing), short and long petitions are differentiated. The short ones begin with the *bārûk*-formula ("Blessed are you, Lord, our God, King of the universe"), and then comes the reason for the request (*bᵉrākāh*). The longer *bᵉrākôt* open with a short prayer of praise, followed by a remembrance of God's saving deeds, and finally the individual petitions. The longer form of the *bᵉrākôt* is concluded with a short *bᵉrākāh* as a seal.

Chapters 9 and 10 of the *Didache* contain prayers of thanksgiving: over the chalice, the bread, and "after satiation".[71] But are these Eucharistic Prayers or prayers of a non-Eucharistic meal celebration?[72] Formerly, the prevalent opinion was that the prayers of thanksgiving in the *Didache* were not Eucharistic Prayers but, rather, prayers for an *agape* feast.[73] Arthur Vööbus (1909–1988) was one of the first to declare himself in favor of a Eucharistic interpretation.[74] Erik Peterson took up an intermediary position: the prayers were originally Eucharistic Prayers but were later used only at *agape* feasts because they contained no commemoration of the death and Resurrection of Christ, which very early was seen as constitutive for the celebration of the Lord's Supper.[75] Even though we know next to nothing

---

[71] Cf. Rouwhorst, "Didache 9–10".

[72] Arguing in favor of a Eucharist in early *Didache* scholarship were, among others, Adolf von Harnack (1851–1930) and Karl Völker (1866–1937); for an *agape* celebration—Friedrich Wilhelm Kattenbusch (1851–1935) and Gregory Dix. On this topic, cf. Niederwimmer, *Didache*, 176f. It is not possible to go here into all the suggested solutions that have been proposed since the beginning of *Didache* scholarship. A good overview of the research is given in Bradshaw, *Eucharistic Origins*, 26–35. See also Jonathan A. Draper, "The Didache in Modern Research: An Overview", in *The Didache in Modern Research*, Arbeiten zur Geschichte des antiken Judentums und des Urchristentums 37 (Leiden and New York: Brill, 1996), 1–42.

[73] Thus Rudolf Bultmann, Martin Dibelius et al. Cf. Niederwimmer, *Didache*, 178.

[74] Cf. Arthur Vööbus, *Liturgical Traditions in the Didache*, Papers of the Estonian Theological Society in Exile: Scholarly Series 16 (Stockholm: ETSE, 1968).

[75] Cf. Erik Peterson, "Über einige Probleme der Didache-Überlieferung", in *Frühkirche, Judentum und Gnosis: Studien und Untersuchungen* (Rome and Freiburg: Herder, 1969), 146–82. Johannes Betz, "Die Eucharistie in der Didache", *Archiv für Liturgiewissenschaft* 11 (1969): 10–39, agreed with this position.

about the exact sequence of events in the first-century Eucharist, the Eucharistic interpretation of the prayers of thanksgiving in the *Didache* seems more convincing.

The prayers of thanksgiving recall Jewish mealtime prayers. Certain parallels exist also to sayings in the Jewish conversion novel *Joseph and Aseneth*, in which the "blessed bread of life" and the "blessed cup of immortality" are mentioned. In the *Didache*, too, the saving goods, which Jesus revealed and which are communicated through bread and wine, are life and immortality.[76] But the *Didache*'s prayers of thanksgiving are more than the Christianized adoption of Jewish patterns. In chapter 9, the *Didache* initially mentions a thanksgiving (εὐχαριστία) over the chalice and the bread, combined with a petition for the unity of the Church:

> [1] In regard to the Eucharist [περὶ δὲ τῆς εὐχαριστίας]—you shall give thanks [εὐχαριστήσατε] thus: [2] First, in regard to the cup:—We give you thanks, our Father, for the holy vine of David your son, which you have made known to us through Jesus your Son. Glory be to you forever. [3] In regard to the broken bread [κλάσμα]:—We give you thanks, our Father, for the life and knowledge which you have made known to us through Jesus your Son [υἱός]. Glory be to you forever. [4] As this broken bread was scattered on the mountains, but brought together was made one, so gather your Church from the ends of the earth into your kingdom. For yours is the glory and the power through Jesus Christ forever. Let no one eat or drink of the Eucharist with you except those who have been baptized in the name of the Lord; for it was in reference to this that the Lord said: "Do not give that which is holy to dogs."[77]

The meal celebration gets its name from the εὐχαριστία over the chalice and the bread.[78] The Eucharist is meant only for those who are baptized in the name of the Lord. The Jewish model of the *hôdājāh* (praise, thanksgiving) is clearly recognizable in the

---

[76] Cf. *Didache* 10.1–7 (FC 1:122–27).

[77] *Didache* 9.1–5 (FC 1:120–23; FEF 3). Parts of *Didache* 9 recur in the *Constitutiones Apostolorum* 8.25–26 (*Didache* 9.3–5), in the *Euchologium Serapionis* 13, 13 (*Didache* 9.4), and in the Liturgy of Dêr-Balyzeh (*Didache* 9.2–4).

[78] This sequence, which agrees with the *Qiddûš* on the Sabbath, is found in 1 Corinthians 10:16–17.

introductory formula "We give you thanks."[79] The *hôdājôt* also occur in the *Didache*'s after-meal prayer.[80] They doubtlessly derive from the Jewish-Christian milieu and possibly go back to the Palestinian area.[81] The Greek word κλάσμα originally meant, not a whole loaf of bread, but rather a piece of bread. The expression "broken bread" could be meant proleptically. A secondary use of κλάσμα in the sense of ἄρτος ([loaf of] bread) is also conceivable.[82] Chapter 9:4 recalls the petitions for the gathering of Israel in the tenth petition of the *Amidah* and the *Musaf*-prayer on *Yom Kippur*.[83] The Christological title παῖς θεοῦ leads one to think of the theology of the Servant of God in Deutero-Isaiah, which would give a reference to the suffering of Christ. The Eucharistic Prayer of the *Didache* contains no explicit remembrance of the suffering, death, and Resurrection of Christ.[84]

If one assumes the unity of the prayers of thanksgiving in chapters 9 and 10 and their Eucharistic interpretation, then the Eucharist was followed by a satiating meal with a concluding *Post-communio*:

[1] After you have eaten your fill [μετὰ δὲ τὸ ἐμπλησθῆναι], give thanks [εὐχαριστήσατε] thus: [2] We thank you, holy Father, for your holy name [ἁγίου ὀνόματος], which you have caused to dwell in our hearts; and for the knowledge and faith and immortality which you have made known to us through Jesus your Son [παῖς]. Glory be to you forever. [3] You, almighty Master, have created all things for your name's sake, and have given food and drink to men for their enjoyment, so that they might return thanks to you. Upon us, however, you have bestowed spiritual food and drink [πνευματικὴ τρωφὴ καὶ πότον], and eternal life through your Servant. [4] Above all we give you thanks, because you are mighty. Glory be to you forever. [5] Remember, O

---

[79] *Didache* 9.2–3 (FC 1:120f.; *FEF* 3).

[80] Cf. ibid., 10.2.4 (FC 1:122–25).

[81] Cf. Dünzel, "Herrenmahl ohne Herrenworte?", 57.

[82] Cf. Vööbus, *Liturgical Traditions in the Didache*, 35–39, 137–57.

[83] Cf. Rouwhorst, "Didache 9–10", 149.

[84] The *Apostolic Constitutions* (a compilation of Church ordinances, around A.D. 380) add such a memorial. The thanksgiving includes also "the precious blood of Jesus Christ" and "His precious body, whereof we celebrate this representation, as He Himself appointed us, 'to show forth His death'" (*Constitutiones Apostolorum* 7.25.4: SChr 336:54). Besides the Eucharistic prayers of the *Didache*, the *Apostolic Constitutions* contain also the "Clementine Liturgy", a detailed Mass formulary with a voluminous Eucharistic Prayer. Cf. *Constitutiones Apostolorum* 8.12.4–51: SChr 336:178–205 (ed. Hänggi-Paul, 82–95).

Lord, your Church. Deliver it from every evil and perfect it in your love. Gather it from the four winds, sanctified for your kingdom, which you have prepared for it. For yours is the power and the glory forever. [6] Let grace come, and let this world pass away. Osanna to the God of David. If anyone is holy, let him come; if anyone is not, let him repent. Marana Tha. Amen.[85]

It is widely accepted that the *Post-communio* is based on the Jewish after-meal prayer (*birkat hammāzôn*). The holy name in chapter 10 designates God's efficacious presence, which is bestowed through the spiritual food and drink of his Servant, Jesus Christ, which confer eternal life. This could indicate that the Didachist, that is, the Christian author who Christianized the Jewish after-meal prayer, was influenced by the Johannine school.[86] As with chapter 9, chapter 10 also recalls the petitions for the gathering of Israel in the tenth petition of the *Amidah* and of the *Musaf*-prayer on *Yom Kippur*.[87] Like the Aramaic cry *maran'atha*, the liturgical acclamation at the end emphasizes the coming of the Lord in the Eucharist and his expected future coming in glory. The spiritual food and drink that is received through Jesus Christ bestows eternal life. This speaks in favor of the Eucharistic interpretation of the thanksgiving prayers in chapters 9 and 10 of the *Didache*.[88] The difficult conclusion in chapter 10, then, cannot refer to Communion.[89] It is quite conceivable that the author has in mind here participation in eschatological salvation in the fulfillment of the Kingdom of God.[90]

The most common objection to a Eucharistic interpretation of the prayers of thanksgiving is that they contain no anamnesis of the death and Resurrection of Jesus and the words of institution are not cited. Josef Andreas Jungmann, therefore, doubted that chapters 9

---

[85] *Didache* 10.1–7 (FC 1:122–27; *FEF* 3).

[86] Cf. Betz, "Eucharistie in der Didache".

[87] Cf. *Didache* 9.4 (FC 1:122f.); ibid., 10.5 (FC 1:124f.).

[88] Cf. ibid., 9.1–10.6 (FC 1:120–27). Willy Rordorf discerns in the expressions "spiritual food" and "spiritual drink" a clear reference to the Eucharistic species. Yet, according to Rordorf, the reception of the Eucharist follows the prayer in *Didache* 10.1–6. Cf. Willy Rordorf, "La Didaché", in *L'eucharistie des premiers chrétiens*, Le point théologique 17 (Paris: Beauchesne, 1976), 18.

[89] Cf. *Didache*, 10.6 (FC 1:124–27). Thus Niederwimmer, *Didache*, 179.

[90] Cf. Messner, "Entwicklung des eucharistischen Gebets", 12.

and 10 of the *Didache* were about the Eucharist; instead, the prayers presupposed an *agape* celebration.[91] Klaus Wengst and Kurt Niederwimmer agreed with this position.[92] But there is no confirmed indication that the Christian communities in the first two centuries were familiar with an independent *agape* celebration besides the Eucharist.[93] Hence, the *Didache* probably hands on a form of the Eucharist that soon fell out of practice.[94]

In contrast to the Corinthian Lord's Supper, the meal celebration handed down by the *Didache* has the structure of a Jewish main meal, with a *Qiddûš*-chalice at the beginning, the breaking of bread, the meal, and the after-meal prayer (*birkat hammāzôn*).[95] Occasionally, scholars have tried to trace the Eucharist as a whole back to a Christianizing of the *birkat hammāzôn* with the basic form of "Praise—Thanksgiving—Petition".[96] No doubt, the *birkat hammāzôn* was a precursor to the later Eucharistic Prayers,[97] but it was not the only model prayer of the Christian anaphora. The synogogal morning

[91] Cf. Josef Andreas Jungmann, *La Liturgie des premiers siècles: jusqu'à l'époque de Grégoire le Grand*, Lex orandi 33 (Paris, L'Éditions du Cerf, 1962), 63–65.

[92] Cf. Klaus Wengst, *Didache (Apostellehre), Barnabasbrief, Zweiter Klemensbrief, Schrift an Diognet*, Schriften des Urchristentums 2 (Darmstadt: Wiss. Buchges., 1984), 43–57; Niederwimmer, *Didache*, 173–209. Recently Rordorf, too, tends toward this view in "Die Mahlgebete der Didache Kap. 9–10: Ein neuer 'status quaestionis'", *Vigiliae Christianae* 51 (1997): 229–46, although originally he argued for a Eucharistic interpretation of the meal prayers of the *Didache*.

[93] Cf. Andrew B. McGowan, "Naming the Feast: 'Agape' and the Diversity of Early Christian Meals", *Studia Patristica* 30 (1997): 314–18.

[94] Cf. Alfons Fürst, *Die Liturgie der Alten Kirche: Geschichte und Theologie* (Münster: Aschendorff, 2008), 33. Matthias Klinghardt, too, in *Gemeinschaftsmahl und Mahlgemeinschaft: Soziologie und Liturgie frühchristlicher Mahlfeiern*, Texte und Arbeiten zum neutestamentlichen Zeitalter 13 (Tübingen and Basel: Francke, 1996), 98–129, 387–405, argues for a Eucharistic interpretation; at least he sees the meal celebration of the *Didache* in the tradition of the Hellenistic symposium, which, however, on account of the Jewish character of the meal prayers is not likely. Cf. Rouwhorst, "Didache 9–10", 145–47.

[95] Cf. Vööbus, *Liturgical Traditions in the Didache*, 61–171; Mazza, *Origins of the Eucharistic Prayer*, 14. Mazza (cf. ibid., 66–97) interprets the meal celebration in *Didache* 9–10 in the sense of the Pauline Lord's Supper.

[96] Cf. Louis Ligier, "The Origins of the Eucharistic Prayer: From the Last Supper to the Eucharist", *Studia Liturgica* 9 (1973): 161–85; Talley, "Von der Berakha zur Eucharistia"; Herman A.J. Wegman, "Genealogie des Eucharistiegebets", *Archiv für Liturgiewissenschaft* 33 (1991): 193–216.

[97] Cf. Martin Stuflesser and Stephan Winter, *Geladen zum Tisch des Herrn: Die Feier der Eucharistie*, Grundkurs Liturgie 3 (Regensburg: Pustet, 2004), 65.

prayers could likewise have had an influence on the genesis of the
Eucharistic Prayers.

The hypothesis of Hans Lietzmann—that there were originally
two independent Christian meal celebrations—is held infrequently
today. Lietzmann assumed that the first source of the Eucharist was
a table fellowship that Jewish-Christian communities celebrated in
eschatological expectation and joy. He sees Acts 2:42 as evidence of
such a celebration: "They held steadfastly to the apostles' teaching
and fellowship, to the breaking of the bread and to the prayers." This
meal celebration was celebrated in connection with the meal celebrations of Jesus as a sign of the dawning Kingdom of God, without
reference to the Last Supper of Jesus with his disciples. In chapters 9
and 10, Lietzmann saw a developed form of this type of early Christian meal.[98] He differentiated it from the Lord's Supper as a remembrance of the death and Resurrection of Christ, as it was celebrated
in the Pauline communities (1 Cor 11:17–34). Reinhard Messner's
own derivation of the Eucharist is closest to Lietzmann's theory: the
early Christian meal celebration was first developed independently of
the Last Supper of Jesus and continued the table fellowship of Jesus
with his disciples as well as with the poor and outcast.[99] Even so, the
Eucharistic Prayers of the *Didache* definitely include references to an
anamnesis of the Passion, which speak in favor of a connection of the
meal celebration with the Lord's Supper: the identification of Jesus as
servant,[100] which recalls his suffering, as well as the thanksgiving for
life,[101] which could be a reference to the Resurrection of Jesus on
which the new life is founded.

C. The Eucharist as Sacrifice and the Verba Testamenti
(Words of Institution)

As early as the second century, εὐχαριστεῖν and εὐχαριστία designated
not only the thanksgiving and blessing prayer over bread and wine,

---

[98] Cf. Lietzmann, *Messe und Herrenmahl*.
[99] Cf. Messner, "Entwicklung des eucharistischen Gebets", 4.
[100] Cf. *Didache* 9.2–3 (FC 1:120f.).
[101] Cf. ibid., 9.3; 10.2f. (FC 1:120f., 122f.).

but also the celebration[102] and the sanctified signs of bread and wine. Thus, according to Justin, the Lord's Supper is food that has become Eucharist.[103] The verb εὐχαριστεῖν can also be used in the sense of "making into the Eucharist".[104] In the Eucharist, Ignatius of Antioch sees the unity of the Church and unity with Christ designated: "Take care, then, to use one Eucharist, ... for there is one Flesh of our Lord Jesus Christ, and one cup in the union of His Blood; one altar, as there is one bishop with the presbytery and my fellow servants, the deacons."[105] In keeping with the Eucharistic bread of life discourse (Jn 6), Ignatius emphasizes "that the Eucharist is the Flesh [σάρξ] of our Savior Jesus Christ, Flesh which suffered for our sins and which the Father, in his goodness, raised up again."[106] With this, Ignatius underlines the identity of the historical and sacramental body of Christ, without simply equating one with the other: "I desire the Bread of God, which is the Flesh of Jesus Christ, who was of the seed of David; and for drink I desire His Blood, which is love incorruptible."[107]

The Eucharist has to do with the sacrifice, the one θυσιαστήριον. It is possible that in Ignatius' writings θυσιαστήριον already means the Christian altar, unlike in Hebrews 13:10. In any case, the Eucharist has for Ignatius the character of a sacrificial celebration (cf. also 1 Cor 10:21). If the celebration of the Eucharist is identified as a sacrifice (θυσία), this happens above all in connection with the promise of the pure sacrifice in Malachi 1:11. In the surrendering of his life, which is given to us in the Eucharist, Christ offered himself as pure sacrifice. The Eucharist is the remembrance of this sacrifice. This thought is already found in the Letter to the Hebrews: "How much more shall the blood of Christ, who through the eternal Spirit offered himself without blemish (προσήνεγκεν ἄμωμον) to God, purify your conscience from dead works to serve the living God" (Heb 9:14).

Justin Martyr calls the bread and wine over which the bishop speaks the prayer of thanksgiving an offering or oblation (προσφορά).[108] In

---

[102] Cf. ibid., 9.1 (FC 1:120f.); Ignatius of Antioch, *Letter to the Ephesians* 13 (PG 5:745B).

[103] Cf. Justin Martyr, *First Apology* 66 (PG 6:428C): εὐχαριστηθεῖσα τροφή.

[104] Cf. ibid., 66 (PG 6:429A).

[105] Ignatius of Antioch, *Letter to the Philadelphians* 4 (PG 5:700B; FEF 22).

[106] Ignatius of Antioch, *Letter to the Smyrnaeans* 7 (PG 5:713A; FEF 25).

[107] Ignatius of Antioch, *Letter to the Romans* 7 (PG 5:693B; FEF 22).

[108] Cf. Justin Martyr, *Dialogue with Trypho* 41 (PG 6:564B; FEF 60).

the offering of the Eucharist, the pure sacrifice is fulfilled.[109] He understands the preparation of the gifts as an *offering* of the gifts, that is, a type of sacrificial act.[110] Thanksgiving and sacrifice are a response to the gratuitous love of God in Christ, which is bestowed on us in the Eucharist. Justin views the sacrifice of wheat flour (Lev 14:10) as a reference to the bread of the Eucharist in commemoration of the suffering of Jesus.[111] Justin writes on the sacrifice of the Eucharist: "Now, that prayers (εὐχαί) and giving of thanks [εὐχαριστίαι], when offered by worthy men, are the only perfect and well-pleasing sacrifices (θυσίαι) to God, I also admit. For such alone Christians have undertaken to offer, and in the remembrance effected by their solid and liquid food, whereby the suffering of the Son of God which He endured is brought to mind."[112]

The earliest testimony to the order of events in the Sunday Eucharist is found in Justin's first *Apology*.[113] In this context, some have spoken about the "Mass schema",[114] the basic structure of which is still retained today:

And on the day which is dedicated to the sun, all those who live in the cities or who dwell in the countryside gather in a common meeting, and for as long as there is time the Memoirs of the Apostles [= the Gospels] or the writings of the prophets are read. Then, when the reader has finished, the president verbally gives a warning and appeal for the imitation of these good examples. Then we all rise together and offer prayers, and, as we said before, when our prayer is ended, bread is brought forward along with wine and water, and the president likewise gives thanks to the best of his ability, and the people call out their assent, saying the *Amen*. Then there is the distribution to each and the participation in the Eucharistic elements, which also are sent with the deacons to those who are absent. Those who are wealthy and who wish to do so, contribute whatever they themselves wish to give; and the collection is placed with the president, who aids the orphans and the widows, and those who through sickness or

---

[109] Cf. ibid. (*PG* 6:563C).
[110] Cf. ibid., 117 (*PG* 6:746B).
[111] Cf. ibid., 41 (*PG* 6:564B).
[112] Ibid., 117 (*PG* 6:746B–748A; ANF 1:257).
[113] Cf. Justin Martyr, *First Apology* 65 and 67 (*PG* 6:428A-C; 429A–432A).
[114] Cf. Messner, *Einführung in die Liturgiewissenschaft*, 168–70.

any other cause are in need, and those who are imprisoned, and the strangers who are sojourning with us—and in short, he takes care of all who are in need.[115]

The origin of Scripture reading during the Christian liturgy is obscure. Various theories about it are put forward. While Anton Baumstark (1872–1948), Hans Lietzmann, and Gregory Dix were still of the opinion that the Liturgy of the Word had its origin in the synagogal liturgy, this theory is no longer so affirmatively asserted today, due to the rather narrow base for it in the sources. Before the destruction of the Temple in A.D. 70, there would have been only a few synagogues with a liturgical function in the strict sense (but cf. Lk 4:16, 33). Synagogues were communal houses for the purpose of Scripture reading and instruction. Of course, it was not impossible that benedictions were also spoken in the synagogues.[116] In contrast, in the Diaspora, the corresponding gathering spaces were likely primarily houses of prayer. Their designation in Greek as προσευχή (prayer, place of prayer) is especially indicative of this.[117]

Justin does not speak of a reading from the Torah but, rather, from the "memoirs of the apostles" and the "writings of the prophets".[118] The practice of reading excerpts from individual books each week is indicative of the dependence of the Scripture reading in the Christian liturgy on the Jewish Scripture reading, which leads to the idea that the Jewish Sabbath liturgy influenced the Liturgy of the Word

---

[115] Justin Martyr, First Apology 67 (PG 6:429B–C; FEF 55–56). On the early Eucharistic Prayers, see the overview of the research in Geoffrey J. Cuming, "The Early Eucharistic Liturgies in Recent Research", in The Sacrifice of Praise: Studies on the Themes of Thanksgiving and Redemption in the Central Prayer of the Eucharist and Baptismal Liturgies in Honour of Arthur Hubert Couratin, Bibliotheca "Ephemerides liturgicae", Subsidia 19, ed. B.D. Spinks (Rome: C.L.V.–Edizioni liturgiche, 1981), 65–69.

[116] This is considered improbable by Peter von der Osten-Sacken, "Von den jüdischen Wurzeln des christlichen Gottesdienstes", in Liturgie als Theologie, ed. W. Homolka (Berlin: Frank & Timme, 2005), 138. See also Johann Maier, Zwischen den Testamenten: Geschichte und Religion in der Zeit des zweiten Tempels (Würzburg: Echter Verlag, 1990), 243.

[117] Cf. Martin Hengel, "Proseuche und Synagoge: Jüdische Gemeinde, Gotteshaus und Gottesdienst in der Diaspora und Palästina", in Tradition und Glaube, das frühe Christentum in seiner Umwelt, Festgabe für Karl Georg Kuhn zum 65. Geburtstag, ed. G. Jeremias et al. (Göttingen: Vandenhoeck & Ruprecht, 1971), 180; Osten-Sacken, "Von den jüdischen Wurzeln", 137 (here further bibliography on the function of the synagogue in the Diaspora).

[118] On this subject, see Hans Bernhard Meyer, Eucharistie, Geschichte, Theologie, Pastoral, Handbuch der Liturgiewissenschaft 4 (Regensburg: Pustet, 1989), 117.

preceding the Eucharist. The prayer after the presider's speech might have been intercessory prayer.[119] As regards the acclamations of the people in connection with the Eucharistic Prayer, Justin mentions only the people's Amen, which is the only acclamation in the first two centuries that can be verified with certainty. The εὐχαριστία of the presider is verified by the Amen of the people. The introductory dialogue of the Eucharistic Prayer (*dignum et iustum*) is not documented before the third century but may well be older. This is true of the *sursum corda—habemus ad Dominum* as well.[120]

At Communion, the faithful receive the Eucharist. The bread of heaven and the chalice of salvation are called Eucharist because bread and wine are "eucharistized" through the prayer spoken over them.[121] Justin is the earliest witness for Communion outside of the Eucharistic liturgy. Those "absent", to whom the deacons bring Communion, are most likely the sick, whereby the connection of their Communion with the preceding liturgy is emphasized. Justin teaches a somatic Real Presence of the Flesh and Blood of Christ. The analogy to the Incarnation—Justin views the Incarnation as a sacrifice Christ took upon himself—is the key to Justin's understanding of the Eucharist. The Incarnation is the explanation for the presence of Christ in bread and wine. Johannes Betz speaks in this context about the "Eucharistic principle of the Incarnation".[122]

In Justin's writings, we also find the earliest record of the *verba testamenti* outside of the New Testament. However, Justin cites them, not in the context of a Eucharistic Prayer, but rather in a reflection on the Eucharist: "Jesus took bread and, having given thanks, said, 'Do this in remembrance of Me; this is My Body.' And in like manner, taking the cup, and having given thanks, He said, 'This is My Blood.' And He imparted this to them [the apostles] only."[123] While the interpretation of this passage causes no great difficulty, the interpretation of

---

[119] The *First Letter of Clement* records a prayer that is presumably a prayer of the faithful (*oratio fidelium*) taken from the Roman liturgy. Cf. 1 Clement 59.2–61.3 (Berger and Nord, *Neue Testament und frühchristliche Schriften*, 719–21).

[120] Thus Messner, "Entwicklung des eucharistischen Gebets", 39, citing the studies by Robert Taft on the anaphora of the Byzantine Liturgy.

[121] Cf. Justin Martyr, *First Apology* 66 (PG 6:429A).

[122] Betz, *Eucharistie in der Schrift und Patristik*, 34.

[123] Justin Martyr, *The First Apology* 66 (PG 6:429A; FEF 55).

the preceding passage is controversial: "Not as common bread nor common drink do we receive these; but since Jesus Christ our Savior was made incarnate by the word of God and had both flesh and blood for our salvation, so too, as we have been taught, the food which has been made into the Eucharist by the Eucharistic prayer set down by Him [τὴν δι' εὐχῆς λόγου τοῦ παρ' αὐτοῦ εὐχαριστηθεῖσαν τροφήν], and by the change of which our blood and flesh is nourished, is both the flesh and the blood of that incarnated Jesus."[124]

The older research generally viewed the use of τὴν δι' εὐχῆς λόγου τοῦ παρ' αὐτοῦ as a Logos-epiclesis and hence translated it with "prayer about the Logos".[125] This interpretation is followed by Otfried Hofius and Paul F. Bradshaw.[126] Anthony Gelston[127] and Reinhard Messner[128] are of the opinion that the expression refers to the Eucharistic Prayer as a whole, which Justin had in mind but which did not yet contain the words of institution. Geoffrey Cuming, on the other hand, adopts the hypothesis that, with the expression τὴν δι' εὐχῆς λόγου τοῦ παρ' αὐτοῦ (through the prayer of a word from him), Justin is referring to the Eucharistic Prayer including the explanatory words of Jesus about the action with the bread and the chalice.[129] Since Justin compares the Eucharist with the Mithras cult, in which certain formulas were to be spoken as repeatable ritual celebration, it is quite possible that he did in fact have the *verba testamenti* in mind with the

[124] Ibid. (*PG* 6:428C–429A; *FEF* 55).

[125] Cf. Franz-Josef Dölger, *Die Eucharistie nach Inschriften frühchristlicher Zeit* (Münster: Aschendorffsche Verlagsbuchhandlung 1922), 53–57; Betz, *Eucharistie in der Schrift und Patristik*, 34; Betz, *Die Eucharistie in der Zeit der griechischen Väter*, vol. 1/1, *Die Aktualpräsenz der Person und des Heilswerkes Jesu im Abendmahl nach der vorephesinischen griechischen Patristik* (Freiburg: Herder, 1955), 268–72.

[126] Cf. Bradshaw, *Eucharistic Origins*, 92f.

[127] Cf. Anthony Gelston, "ΔΙ' ΕΥΧΗΣ ΛΟΓΟΥ (Justin, *Apology*, I, 66, 2)", *Journal of Theological Studies* 33 (1982): 172–75. So too earlier Edward C. Ratcliff, "The Eucharistic Institution Narrative of Justin Martyr's 'First Apology'", in *Liturgical Studies [of] E. C. Ratcliff*, ed. A. H. Couratin and D. H. Tripp (London: S.P.C.K., 1976), 46.

[128] Cf. Messner, "Entwicklung des eucharistischen Gebets", 25f. In this sense Messner also interprets the epiclesis, by which the bread becomes the Eucharist, according to Irenaeus: "For as the bread from the earth, receiving the invocation of God, is no longer common bread but the Eucharist" (Irenaeus of Lyon, *Against Heresies* 4.18.5: FC 8/4:147; *FEF* 95).

[129] Cf. Geoffrey J. Cuming, "ΔΙ' ΕΥΧΗΣ ΛΟΓΟΥ (Justin, *Apology*, I, 66, 2)", *Journal of Theological Studies* 31 (1980): 80–82. On the controversy between Gelston and Cuming, cf. Michael Heintz, "Justin, 'Apology' I, 66, 2: Cuming and Gelston Revisited", *Studia Liturgica* 33 (2003): 33–36.

expression τὴν δι' εὐχῆς λόγου τοῦ παρ' αὐτοῦ. The Protestant exegete Gerd Theissen also starts from this premise.[130] A formal epiclesis as part of the Eucharistic Prayer is not verifiable with Justin.

At this point it is necessary to investigate the view, held above all by liturgists, that the institution narrative did not find its way into the Eucharistic Prayer until the fourth century. Since the early Eucharistic Prayers were paradigms, not complete formulas, the reference to the absence of the *verba testamenti*, which is used as an argument in this context, is nothing more than an *argumentum ex negativo*. It cannot be ruled out that the *verba testamenti*, which have their own transmission history in East and West,[131] were not mentioned because they were known in the particular local churches. Whether this can also be assumed about the developed East-Syrian anaphora of the apostles Addai and Mari (third century) is disputed, since the earliest manuscripts that do not contain an institution narrative come from the tenth century.[132] Basil of Caesarea (d. 379) could refer to the practice of not recording the *verba testamenti* in writing in his treatise

---

[130] Cf. Gerd Theissen, "Sakralmahl und sakramentales Geschehen: Abstufungen in der Ritualdynamik des Abendmahls", in *Herrenmahl und Gruppenidentität*, Quaestiones disputatae 221 (Freiburg: Herder, 2007), 176f.

[131] Cf. Fritz Hamm, *Die liturgischen Einsetzungsberichte im Sinne vergleichender Liturgiewissenschaft untersucht*, Liturgiegeschichtliche Quellen und Forschungen 23 (Münster: Aschendorffschen Verlagsbuchhandlung, 1928); Josef Andreas Jungmann, *Missarum Sollemnia. Eine genetische Erklärung der römischen Messe*, vol. 1, *Messe im Wandel der Jahrhunderte. Messe und kirchliche Gemeinschaft. Vormesse*, reprint of the 5th rev. ed. (Freiburg: Herder, 1962), 10.

[132] On this discussion, cf. Bernard Botte, "L'anaphora chaldéenne des Apôtres", *Orientalia Christiana Periodica* 15 (1949): 259–76; Brian D. Spinks, "The Original Form of the Anaphora of the Apostles: Suggestion in Light of Maronite Sharar", *Ephemerides liturgicae* 91 (1977): 146–61; Spinks, *Addai and Mari—The Anaphora of the Apostles: A Text for Students*, Grove Liturgical Study 24 (Bramcote: Grove, 1980); Anthony Gelston, *Eucharistic Prayer of Addai and Mari* (Oxford: Clarendon Press; New York: Oxford University Press, 1992); Edward Yarnold, "Anaphoras without Institution Narratives?" *Studia Patristica* 30 (1997): 395–410; Robert F. Taft, "Mass without the Consecration? The Historic Agreement on the Eucharist between the Catholic Church and the Assyrian Church of the East Promulgated 26 October 2001", *Worship* 77 (2003): 482–509; Uwe Michael Lang, ed., *Die Anaphora von Addai und Mari: Studien zu Eucharistie und Einsetzungsworten* (Bonn: Nova & Vetera, 2007); Ansgar Santogrossi, "Historical and Theological Argumentation in Favour of Anaphoras without Institution Narrative", in *Die Anaphora von Addai und Mari: Studien zu Eucharistie und Einsetzungsworten*, ed. U. M. Lang (Bonn: Nova & Vetera, 2007), 175–210; Nicholas V. Russo, "The Validity of the Anaphora of Addai and Mari: Critique of the Critiques", in *Issues in Eucharistic Praying in East and West: Essays in Liturgical and Theological Analysis*, ed. M. E. Johnson (Collegeville, Minn.: Liturgical Press, 2010), 21–62; Dominik Heringer, *Die Anaphora der Apostel Addai und Mari: Ausdrucksformen einer eucharistischen Ekklesiologie* (Göttingen: V & R Unipress, 2013).

On the Holy Spirit (ca. 370): "Which of the saints left us in writing the words of the epiclesis [τῆς ἐπικλήσεως ῥήματα] at the consecration of the Bread of the Eucharist [ἀνάδειξις τοῦ ἄρτου τῆς εὐχαριστίας] and of the Cup of Benediction [ποτηρίου τῆς εὐλογίας]? For we are not content with those words the Apostle or the gospel has recorded, but we say other things also, both before and after; and we regard these other words, which we have received from unwritten teaching, as being of great importance to the mystery."[133] With "those words the Apostle [Paul] or the Gospel has recorded", Basil could be referring to the words of institution, which for him already belonged to the existing tradition. Presumably, "the epiclesis" in the cited passage means the anaphora as an epicletic prayer. Basil had traveled extensively through the Christian East, so his witness is valid for more than just the practice in Cappadocia.

Cesare Giraudo advocated the hypothesis that the early Christian Eucharistic Prayers were modeled after the Jewish *todah*-prayer with its typical double structure (anamnesis—epiclesis with an embolism in the middle) and that the *verba testamenti* were spoken with it as a "Eucharistic embolism".[134] Some scholars received Giraudo's theory very positively.[135] But the development cannot be envisioned as though the *verba testamenti* found their way into the Eucharistic Prayer everywhere at the same time.[136] For the tradition of the Eucharist was not as homogenous as it may previously have been assumed to be.[137]

---

[133] Basil of Caesarea, *De Spiritu Sancto* 27, 66 (FC 12:275; *The Faith of the Early Fathers*, vol. 2, *A Source-Book of Theological and Historical Passages from the Christian Writings of the Post-Nicene and Constantinopolitan Eras through St. Jerome*, selected and trans. W. A. Jurgens [Collegeville, Minn.: Liturgical Press, 1979; hereafter cited as *FEF2*], 19).

[134] Cf. Cesare Giraudo, *La struttura letteraria della preghiera eucaristica: Saggio sulla genesi letteraria di una forma; toda Veterotestamentaria, B'raka Giudaica, Anafori cristiana*, Analecta biblica 92 (Rome: Biblical Institute Press, 1981), 357–70; Giraudo, "Le récit de l'institution dans la prière eucharistique a-t-il de précédents?" *Nouvelle Revue Théologique* 106 (1984): 513–35.

[135] Cf. Thomas J. Talley, "The Literary Structure of the Eucharistic Prayer", *Worship* 58 (1984): 404–19; Xavier Léon-Dufour, *Abendmahl und Abschiedsrede im Neuen Testament* (Stuttgart: Katholisches Bibelwerk, 1983), 62–66.

[136] Cf. Meyer, *Eucharistie*, 99f.

[137] Cf. Paul F. Bradshaw, " 'Zebah Todah' and the Origins of the Eucharist", *Ecclesia Orans* 8 (1991): 245–60; Albert Gerhards, "Entstehung und Entwicklung des Eucharistischen Hochgebets im Spiegel der neueren Forschung: Der Beitrag der Liturgiewissenschaft zur liturgischen Erneuerung", in *Gratias Agamus: Studien zum Eucharistischen Hochgebet*, Festschrift B. Fischer, ed. A. Heinz and H. Rennings (Freiburg: Herder, 1992), 80. Albert Gerhards judges Giraudo's thesis even more positively in Gerhards, "Die literarische Struktur des eucharistischen Hochgebets", *Liturgisches Jahrbuch* 33 (1983): 90–104.

But there is a fairly broad consensus among New Testament scholars, who refer to the more or less strong liturgical influence of the Last Supper narrative as evidence, against the theory that the *verba testamenti* were not incorporated into the prayer over the gifts of bread and wine until the fourth century.[138] On the other hand, Reinhard Messner, among others, argue that the institution narratives, including the Pauline, initially had no relation to the cultic meal celebration of the community and that they are much more concerned with a catechetical tradition, so that no inferences about a cultic ritual are possible.[139]

This theory met with hardly any agreement among exegetes, as it cannot even explain the commemoration command in the Last Supper accounts by Luke and Paul.[140] A formula like 1 Corinthians 10:16f. might sooner be used in catechesis.[141] Besides the commemoration command, there are other additional elements in the Last Supper accounts that support a liturgical *Sitz im Leben*, for instance, the "for you" in the words over the chalice in Paul. To speak of a liturgical influence on the Last Supper narratives does not necessarily mean passing a negative judgment on their historical worth. It is merely impossible to conclude the *ipsissima verba* ("the very words") of Jesus directly from them.[142] Klauck helpfully distinguishes "between cultic tradition or founding narrative (which only establishes worship, without any direct function in the celebration), cultic anamnesis (narrative accompanying worship, meant for recitation), and liturgical rubric or norm for worship (regulating the external course of the celebration)".[143]

Despite the objections of Enrico Mazza,[144] the strongest argument against the hypothesis that the liturgical use of the *verba testamenti* in

---

[138] Cf., for example, Wilckens, *Theologie des Neuen Testaments* 1:73, who describes the oldest accounts of the Last Supper by Mark and Paul as "liturgical texts".

[139] Cf. Messner, "Entwicklung des eucharistischen Gebets", 20; Andrew B. McGowan, "'Is There a Liturgical Text in This Gospel?': The Institution Narratives and Their Early Interpretive Communities", *Journal of Biblical Literature* 118 (1999): 73–97; Bradshaw, *Eucharistic Origins*, 15.

[140] So, too, Rouwhorst, "Didache, 9–10", 155.

[141] Cf. Hans-Josef Klauck, *Herrenmahl und hellenistischer Kult: Eine religionsgeschichtliche Untersuchung zum ersten Korintherbrief*, Neutestamentliche Abhandlungen, Neue Folge 15 (Münster: Aschendorff, 1982), 298.

[142] Cf. ibid.

[143] Ibid.

[144] Cf. Mazza, *Origins of the Eucharistic Prayer*, 66–97.

the celebration of the Lord's Supper cannot be assumed until the fourth century is the account of the Last Supper handed down by Paul (1 Cor 11:23–26).[145] The liturgical use of the *verba testamenti* would consequently go back to New Testament times.[146] According to the opinion of numerous exegetes, the words of institution were recited during the Lord's Supper as cult-anamnesis. This does not mean that the *verba testamenti* were spoken everywhere in the celebration of the Lord's Supper from the beginning. If there were a yearly Christian Easter feast even in early Christian times, it would also be conceivable that a recitation of the *verba testamenti* initially happened only during this celebration[147] and later was gradually adopted in the celebration of the Sunday Eucharist.[148]

---

[145] Jungmann, too, *Opfermesse sowie im Anhang: Messe im Gottesvolk: ein nachkonziliarer Durchblick durch Missarum Sollemnia*, vol. 2 of *Missarum Sollemnia: Eine genetische Erklärung der römischen Messe* (1970; Bonn: Nova et Vetera, 2003), 21, was convinced that in Corinth at the celebration of the Lord's Supper, Jesus' words interpreting the bread and wine were cited. So, too, Stuflesser and Winter, *Geladen zum Tisch des Herrn*, 20, 68–71; Martin Stuflesser, *Eucharistie: Liturgische Feier und theologische Erschliessung* (Regensburg: Pustet, 2013), 34–36.

[146] Cf. Kollmann, *Ursprung und Gestalten*, 170. Klauck, *Herrenmahl und hellenistischer Kult*, 298, assumes that the *verba testamenti* were used initially as a formula accompanying the distribution of Communion.

[147] Cf. Fuller, "Double Origin"; Theobald, "Leib und Blut Christi", 127f.

[148] Cf. Rouwhorst, "Didache 9–10", 155.

Chapter III

OBLATIO MUNDA

The Eucharist in the Patristic Era

"You are indeed Holy, O Lord, and all you have created rightly gives you praise, for through your Son our Lord Jesus Christ, by the power and working of the Holy Spirit, you give life to all things and make them holy, and you never cease to gather a people to yourself, so that from the rising of the sun to its setting a pure sacrifice may be offered to your name."[1] The *Post-sanctus* prayer of Eucharistic Prayer III cites a verse from the Book of Malachi: "For from the rising of the sun to its setting my name is great among the nations, and in every place incense is offered [*sacrificatur*] to my name, and a pure offering [*oblatio munda*; καταρὰ θυσία; in Hebrew *minḥāh*]; for my name is great among the nations, says the LORD of hosts" (Mal 1:11).[2] The *Didache*,[3] Justin Martyr,[4] Irenaeus of Lyon,[5] and after them many

---

[1] *The Roman Missal: Renewed by the Decree of the Most Holy Second Ecumenical Council of the Vatican, Promulgated by authority of Pope Paul VI, and revised at the direction of Pope John Paul II: English translation according to the third typical edition: For Use in the Dioceses of the United States of America: Approved by the United States Conference of Catholic Bishops and confirmed by the Apostolic See* (2010; Washington, D.C.: United States Conference of Catholic Bishops, 2011; hereafter cited as *RM* 2010), 634. The conclusion of the post-*Sanctus* prayer in the *Missale Romanum* reads: "populum tibi congregare non desinis, ut a solis ortu usque ad occasum oblatio munda offeratur nomini tuo" (*MR* 2002³, 585).

[2] Mal 1:11 (Vulgate): "Ab ortu enim solis usque ad occasum magnum est nomen meum in gentibus et in omni loco sacrificatur et offertur nomini meo oblatio munda quia magnum nomen meum in gentibus dicit Dominus exercituum."

[3] Cf. *Didache* 14.3 (FC 1:132–35).

[4] Cf. Justin Martyr, *Dialogus cum Tryphone Judaeo* 117 (PG 6:745A–749A; ANF 1:257a–258b).

[5] Cf. Irenaeus of Lyon, *Adversus haereses* 4.17.5; 4.18.1 (FC 8/4:134–37; 138–139; ANF 1:484).

other writers already refer the promise of the "pure offering" to the Eucharist of the Church that encompasses the nations.[6] During the age of the Church Fathers, this leads to a deepening of the idea of the Eucharistic offering and also to an intensified reflection on the sacramental and ecclesial Body of Christ. Προσφέρειν (*offerre*) becomes a central concept for the celebration of the Eucharist from the second century on.

In the [apocryphal] *Epistle of the Apostles* (ca. 150), the Eucharist is characterized as a "memorial" of Christ's death and of his "Passover" (πάσχα). Pasch in the second century designates both the Christian sacrificial celebration as a whole and also specifically the Eucharistic offering performed during it.[7] The first sure testimony for the existence of a Christian sacrificial celebration is the Easter homily of Melito of Sardis (d. ca. 180).[8] In Asia Minor, πάσχα was usually derived from πάσχειν (to suffer).[9] Actually this derivation is etymologically wrong, but it did eventually form a tradition. The root meaning of the word πάσχα is passover. In this sense, Origen understands Christ's πάσχα to mean his *transitus* from death to life.[10] Augustine (354–430) combines the two meanings together: "Careful and learned scholars have proved that the word 'pasch' is Hebrew, and means not passion but passover. By his passion the Lord passed over from death to life and opened a way for us who believe in his resurrection, that we too may pass over from death to life."[11]

---

[6] Cf. Karl Suso Frank, "Maleachi 1,10ff. in der frühen Väterdeutung: Ein Beitrag zu Opferterminologie und Opferverständnis in der alten Kirche", *Theologie und Philosophie* 53 (1978): 70–79.

[7] Cf. *Epistula Apostolorum* 8.15–18.

[8] Cf. Meliton von Sardes, *Vom Pascha: Die älteste christliche Osterpredigt*, ed. Josef Blank, Sophia 3 (Freiburg: Lambertus, 1963).

[9] Cf. ibid., 46, p. 112; Irenaeus of Lyon, *Epideixis* 25 (FC 8/1:50).

[10] Cf. Origen, *De Pascha* 1.1, in *Die Schrift des Origenes, "Über das Pascha": Textausgabe und Kommentar*, ed. Bernd Witte, Arbeiten zum spätantiken und koptischen Ägypten 4 (Altenberge: Oros, 1993), 88f. Also Jerome, *In Matthaeum* 4.26.2 (CCSL 77:245), and Ambrose, *De sacramentis* 1.12 (FC 3:86f.).

[11] Augustine, *Enarrationes in Psalmos* CXX, 6 (CCSL 40:1791; *The Works of Saint Augustine: A Translation for the 21st Century*, ed. John E. Rotelle, Boniface Ramsey, Augustine Heritage Institute et al. [Brooklyn, N.Y.: New City Press, 1990–2005; hereafter cited as *WSA*], 3/19:514.

A. The Eucharist in Greek Patristic Writings

Irenaeus of Lyon regards the Eucharist as *oblatio*/προσφορά (offering). The Greek theologian originally came from Smyrna and, according to tradition, was the second bishop of Lyon; only two works by him have been preserved: on the one hand, his masterpiece against the Gnostics, Ἔλεγχος καὶ ἀνατροπὴ τῆς ψευδωνύμου γνώσεως, known in Latin by the abbreviated title *Adversus haereses* [*Against the Heresies*] and the Ἐπίδειξις τοῦ ἀποστολικοῦ κηρύγματος (*Proof of the Apostolic Preaching*). In the Greek language, only individual fragments of *Adversus haereses* exist. The work was handed down in Latin, and books 4 and 5 also in Armenian. In book 4 of *Adversus haereses*, Irenaeus comes to speak about the sacrifices of the Old Covenant and their relation to the Eucharist.

Like the *Didache* and Justin Martyr, Irenaeus, too, associates the Eucharist with Malachi 1:11. The Eucharist, the sacrifice of the New Covenant (*Novum Testamentum*), is the offering of the pure sacrifice (*sacrificium purum*).[12] According to Irenaeus, Jesus commanded his apostles at the Last Supper to offer a sacrifice to God:

> Again, giving directions to His disciples to offer to God the first-fruits of His own created things—not as if He stood in need of them, but that they might be themselves neither unfruitful nor ungrateful—He took that created thing, bread, and gave thanks, and said, "This is My body" [Mt 26:26 and parallel passages]. And the cup likewise, which is part of that creation to which we belong, He confessed to be His blood, and taught the new oblation of the new covenant [cf. Mt 26:28 par]; which the Church receiving from the apostles, offers to God throughout all the world, to Him who gives us as the means of subsistence the first-fruits of His own gifts in the New Testament.[13]

Usually Irenaeus uses the concept of sacrifice anabatically—with reference to the offering of bread and wine. However, he can also speak about Christ's Cross katabatically as a sacrifice, which is typologically prefigured in the binding of Isaac (Gen 22:1–18): "God [was pleased] to offer up ... His own beloved and only-begotten Son, as

---

[12] Cf. Irenaeus of Lyon, *Adversus haereses* 4.17.5 (FC 8/4:134–37); ANF 1:484b.
[13] Ibid. (FC 8/4:134f.; ANF 1:484a).

a sacrifice for our redemption."[14] For Irenaeus, the sacrifice that we offer has to do with thanks for God's redemptive salvific action on the Cross. Against the Gnostics, Irenaeus emphasizes that oblations as such have not been set aside (*non genus oblationum reprobatum est*).[15] The kind of sacrifice in the New Covenant, however, has become a different one. God needs no sacrifices; man needs to thank God through sacrifices.[16] We offer to God the pure sacrifice when we thank him.

> The oblation of the Church (*ecclesiae oblatio*), therefore, which the Lord gave instructions to be offered throughout all the world, is accounted with God a pure sacrifice (*purum sacrificium*), and is acceptable to Him; not that He stands in need of a sacrifice from us, but that he who offers is himself glorified in what he does offer, if his gift be accepted...; so that man, being accounted as grateful, by those things in which he has shown his gratitude, may receive that honour which flows from Him.[17]

Irenaeus calls the offering of the Eucharist the *nova oblatio* (new oblation) of the Church,[18] without associating this with the notion that Christ is sacrificed anew each time in the Eucharist, as many medieval theologians would later assume.

Like the author of the *Didache*, Irenaeus demands—with a reference to Matthew 5:23f.—that the offering be brought to the altar with a pure heart.[19] When we offer the sacrifice "with single-mindedness"

[14] Ibid., 4.5.4 (FC 8/4:42f.; ANF 1:467b). On the typological interpretation of Genesis 22 in patristic writings, compare Ernst Dassmann, "'Bindung' und 'Opferung' in jüdischer und patristischer Auslegung", in *Hairesis*, ed. M. Hutter (Münster: Aschendorff, 2002), 1–18; Thomas Böhm, "Die Bindung Isaaks in ausgewählten Texten der Kirchenväter", in *Die Bindung Isaaks: Stimme, Schrift, Bild*, ed. H. Hoping, J. Knop, and T. Böhm, Studien zu Judentum und Christentum (Paderborn: Schöningh, 2009), 128–42.

[15] Cf. Irenaeus of Lyon, *Adversus haereses* 4.18.2 (FC 8/4:138–41; ANF 1:484b–485a).

[16] Cf. ibid., 4.17.1; 4.18.3; 4.18.6 (FC 8/4:124f., 140f., 146f.; ANF 1:482, 485, 486).

[17] Cf. ibid., 4.18.1 (FC 8/4:138; ANF 1:484): "Igitur ecclesiae oblatio, quam dominus docuit offerri in universo mundo, purum sacrificium reputatum est apud Deum et acceptum est ei, non quod indigeat a nobis sacrificium, sed quoniam is qui offert glorificatur ipse in eo quod offert, si accepetur munum eius ... in quibus gratus exstitit homo, in his gratus ei deputatus, eum qui est ab eo percipiat honorem."

[18] Cf. ibid., 4.17.5 (FC 8/4:134–37; ANF 1:484).

[19] Cf. ibid., 4.18.1 (FC 8/4:138f.; ANF 1:484b).

(*sententia pura*),[20] then God accepts our gifts as though from friends.[21] The Church offers (*ecclesia offert*)[22] with the help of the God-given gifts of bread and wine, "rendering thanks for His gift, and thus sanctifying what has been created".[23] With very precise terminology, Irenaeus says that "the Church alone offers this pure oblation (*oblationem puram offert*) to the Creator, offering to Him, with giving of thanks (*offerens cum gratiarum actione*), [the things taken] from His creation."[24] The sacrifice of the Eucharist, however, is more than the offering of bread and wine. Through the epiclesis, the invocation of God (here the specific transubstantiating epiclesis is not yet meant), the gifts of bread and wine become the Body and Blood of Christ, which—and this is formulated against the Gnostics—promise us bodily resurrection: "For as the bread, which is produced from the earth, when it receives the invocation of God, is no longer common bread, but the Eucharist, consisting of two realities, earthly and heavenly; so also our bodies, when they receive the Eucharist, are no longer corruptible, having the hope of the resurrection to eternity."[25]

Through the epiclesis, bread and wine receive the Logos of God. Thus they become the Eucharist and unite those who receive it with the risen Lord and grant a share in eternal life:

When, therefore, the mingled cup and the manufactured bread receives the Word of God [*verbum Dei*/λόγος τοῦ θεοῦ], and the Eucharist of the blood and the body of Christ is made, from which things the substance of our flesh is increased and supported, how can they affirm that the flesh is incapable of receiving the gift of God, which is life eternal, which [flesh] is nourished from the body and blood of the Lord, and is a member of Him?[26]

Irenaeus speaks very realistically about the Body and Blood of Christ: the Eucharistic bread is Christ's own Body, and the chalice

---

[20] Cf. ibid., 4.18.4 (FC 8/4:144f.; ANF 1:485b).
[21] Cf. ibid., 4.18.3 (FC 8/4:142f.; ANF 1:485b).
[22] Cf. ibid., 4.18.4 (FC 8/4:144f.; ANF 1:485b–486a).
[23] Ibid., 4.18.6 (FC 8/4:146f.; ANF 1:486).
[24] Ibid., 4.18.4 (FC 8/4:144f.; ANF 1:485b). "Gratiarum actione" probably corresponds to εὐχαριστία in the non-extant Greek text.
[25] Ibid., 4.18.5 (FC 8/4:146f.; ANF 1:486a).
[26] Ibid., 5.2.3 (FC 8/5:34f.; ANF 1:528).

of blessing contains Christ's own Blood. By that, naturally, Irenaeus does not mean Christ's physical body and his physical blood but, rather, their sacramental reality. The objective of receiving the Eucharistic meal is the communication of the Logos to our mortal nature. As bread and wine receive the Word of God and are transformed into the Eucharist, the Body and Blood of Christ, so too our mortal nature is transformed. The Logos grants us "resurrection 'to the glory of God' [Phil 2:11]", "freely gives to this mortal immortality".[27] Eucharist signifies communication of the Logos, communication of the Word-made-man.

Clement of Alexandria (d. ca. 215): The Christian Platonist emphasizes, along the lines of Philo of Alexandria, that Christians do not offer to God an ordinary, material sacrifice, which God does not need, either, because he lacks nothing. In his main work, *Stromateis*,[28] Clement writes on the sacrifice of the New Covenant: "For this reason we rightly do not sacrifice to God, who, needing nothing, supplies all men with all things; but we glorify Him who gave Himself in sacrifice for us, and also sacrifice ourselves to ever greater frugality and to ever greater freedom from the passions."[29]

Clement, who wants to demonstrate the compatibility of Greek philosophy and Christian faith and also the superiority of faith, regards Christianity as the true philosophy. In Jesus, the incarnate Logos, he sees the Divine Revealer, the Teacher of Wisdom and the High Priest. Christian gnosis (γνῶσις) is the way to attain salvation. Clement distinguishes himself from the heretical Gnostics in that he holds fast to the faith of the apostles, according to which the Flesh (Body) and Blood of Christ are given to us in the signs of bread and wine.[30]

Clement, too, thinks about Christ's presence under the appearances of bread and wine by analogy with the Incarnation. In the consecrated species of bread and wine, the Christian Platonist recognizes

---

[27] Ibid. (FC 8/5:36f.; ANF 1:528b).

[28] The name "Stromateis" (tapestries, patchwork) refers to the miscellaneous, "unsystematic" character of the work.

[29] Clement of Alexandria, *Stromateis* 7.3.14 (Die griechischen christlichen Schriftsteller der ersten drei Jahrhunderte [Leipzig: Hinrichs; Berlin: Akademie-Verlag, 1897ff.; hereafter cited as GCS], 3.11.9–12; ANF 2:527a emended to conform to the German text).

[30] Cf. Clement of Alexandria, *Paidagogos* [*The Instructor*] 1.6.42.3 (GCS 1.115.20–24; ANF 2:217b).

the "incarnate Pneuma" of God. God's Logos, or his Pneuma, enters into a union with the elements:

> [Christ's] flesh figuratively represents to us the Holy Spirit; for the flesh was created by Him. The blood points out to us the Word, for as rich blood the Word has been infused into life; and the union [κρᾶσις, mixture] of both is the Lord, the food [τρωφή] of the babes—the Lord who is Spirit and Word. The food—that is, the Lord Jesus—that is, the Word of God, the Spirit made flesh [πνεῦμα σαρκούμενον], the heavenly flesh sanctified [ἁγιαζομένη σὰρξ οὐράνιος].... The Word Himself, then, the beloved One, and our nourisher, hath shed His own blood for us, to save humanity.[31]

Christ, who as cosmic reason (*die Weltvernunft*) is the source of all truth, gives himself to us in the signs of bread and wine. Here the presence of Christ's Body and Blood is to be understood personally, not in a reified way. In the short work "Who Is the Rich Man That Shall Be Saved?", an exegesis of Mark 10:17–31 about wealth and following Christ, this conviction is expressed poetically: Christ, the "teacher of supercelestial lessons", stands before the soul of the communicant and speaks: "I am He who feeds thee, giving Myself as bread [ἄρτον], of which he who has tasted experiences death no more, and supplying day by day the drink of immortality [πόμα ἀθανασίας]."[32] Like Irenaeus, Clement sees the Eucharist as an oblation (προσφωρά) that has its prerequisite in Christ's sacrifice on the Cross.[33]

Although Clement thinks Platonically, the idea of the change of the sacramental elements is not absent from his writings. Since for Clement the essence of a thing consists in its force, he thinks of the transformation of the gifts of bread and wine as a change of their force.[34] Clement distinguishes between the sacramental Eucharist and the Eucharist of knowledge. As opposed to sacramental Communion, the more suitable manner of communion is for him spiritual communion, which consists of the vision of knowledge:

---

[31] Ibid., 1.6.43.2–3 (GCS 1.115.30—116.6; ANF 2:220b).

[32] Clement of Alexandria, *Quis dives salvetur* 23.4 (GCS 3.175.11–13; ANF 2:598a).

[33] Cf. Clement of Alexandria, *Stromateis* 5.10.66.5 (GCS 2.370.23–25; ANF 2:460a).

[34] Cf. Clement of Alexandria, *Excerpta ex Theodoto* 82.1–2 (GCS 3.132.10–14): here the elements are bread and oil (δύναμει εἰς δύναμιν μεταβέλληται).

Milk will be understood to be catechetical instruction—the first food, as it were, of the soul. And meat is the mystic contemplation [ἐποπτικὴ θεωρία]; for this is the flesh and the blood of the Word, that is, the comprehension of the divine power and essence. "Taste and see that the Lord is Christ," it is said. For so He imparts of Himself to those who partake of such food in a more spiritual manner [πνευματικότερον]; when now the soul nourishes itself, according to the truth-loving Plato. For the knowledge [γνῶσις] of the divine essence is the meat and drink of the divine Word.[35]

For Clement, however, the sacramental and the spiritual understandings of the Eucharist are not mutually exclusive. For spiritual communion, which consists in contemplation or knowledge, he cites Plato,[36] who for him is the foremost authority in Greek philosophy.[37] The communion of the Eucharistic gifts is the comprehension of the visible appearance of the First Principle, understood in Platonic terms.

Origen (d. 254): The second great Alexandrian theologian also distinguishes between sacramental Eucharist and the Eucharist of knowledge. This reinforces the tendency toward a spiritualization of the Eucharist.[38] For Origin, the Eucharist is above all a verbal event; this becomes particularly clear in his commentary on the Last Supper account in Matthew:

This bread that God the Word professes to be his body (*corpus*) is the word that nourishes souls, the word that proceeds from God the Word.... And the drink that God the Word professes to be his blood (*sanguis*) is the word that slakes and gladdens the hearts of those who drink.... So too the bread is the word of Christ, made from that wheat which falls into the earth and brings forth much fruit. For God the Word did not call that visible bread which he held in his hands

---

[35] Clement of Alexandria, *Stromateis* 5.10.66.2–3 (GCS 2.370.14–21; ANF 2:460a).

[36] Cf. among other passages Plato, *Politeia* 6.509b.

[37] Johannes Brinktrine, *Der Messopferbegriff in den ersten zwei Jahrhunderten: Eine biblisch-patristische Untersuchung* (Freiburg: Herder, 1918), 107–9, refers *Stromateis* 5.10.66.3, not to the spiritual, but rather to the sacramental Eucharist. According to Johannes Betz, *Eucharistie in der Schrift und Patristik*, Handbuch der Dogmengeschichte 4/4a (Freiburg: Herder, 1979), 46f., Clement is speaking in the passage cited about the Eucharist of knowledge.

[38] On Christian Platonism in Origen and the other Fathers of the Church, see Endre von Ivánka, *Plato Christianus: Übernahme und Umgestaltung des Platonismus bei den Vätern* (Einsiedeln: Johannes Verlag, 1964).

his body, but rather the Word in whose sacrament (*in cuius mysterio*) that bread is to be broken. And he did not call that visible drink his blood, but rather the Word in whose sacrament that drink was to be poured out. For what else can the body or blood of God the Word be than the Word that nourishes and the Word that gladdens the heart?[39]

The actual sacrament (*mysterium*) is therefore the Word; bread and wine are visible signs which in themselves are neither beneficial nor harmful.[40] For through the word spoken over the bread and wine, the souls of men are supposed to be "eucharistized".[41] The proclaimed word therefore must not be considered less important than the Eucharistic body. For "the word of God too is bread for us",[42] is Eucharistic food.[43] For the spiritual man, the word, as opposed to the visible sign, is even the more suitable presence of the divine Logos. Although Origen tends to spiritualize the Eucharist, we nevertheless find again and again in his writings statements about the Real Presence. Origen does not dispute a sacramental Eucharist, in which the Body and the Blood of Christ are handed to us. The Eucharist is the Flesh (Body) and Blood of the Logos: "When you go up with him [Jesus] to celebrate the Passover, he gives you the chalice of the New Covenant, he gives you the bread of blessing, he bestows his Body and his Blood."[44] Christians "eat as their Passover the Christ who was sacrificed for us (*pascha immolatum Christum pro nobis*) ... and

---

[39] Origen, *In Matthaeum commentariorum*, series 85 (GCS 38.196.19—197.6): "Panis iste, quem deus verbum *corpus* suum esse fatetur, verbum est nutritorium animarum, verbum de deo verbo procedens ... et potus iste, quem deus verbum *sanguinem* suum fatetur, verbum est potans et inebrians praeclare corda bibentium ... sicut et panis est verbum Christi factum de tritico illo quod 'cadens in terram', 'multum reddidit fructum'. Non enim *panem* illum visibilem quem tenebat in manibus *corpus* suum dicebat deus verbum, sed verbum in cuius mysterio fuerat panis ille frangendus. Nec potum illum visibilem *sanguinem* suum dicebat, sed verbum in cuius mysterio potus ille fuerat effundendus. Nam *corpus* dei verbi aut *sanguis* quid aliud potest esse, nisi verbum quod nutrit, et verbum quod 'laetificat cor'?" The work of the Alexandrian theologian is only partly preserved in Greek and has been handed down mainly in the Latin translation by Rufinus.

[40] Cf. Origen, *In Evangelium secundum Matthaeum* 11.14 (GCS 40.57.11—58, 13; ANF 9:443).

[41] Cf. ibid., 16—18 (GCS 10.186.8—189.33; ANF 9:444b—448b).

[42] Origen, *In Exodum homilia* 7.8 (GCS 29.214.24): "Nobis et panis verbum Dei est."

[43] Cf. Origen, *In Numeros homilia* 7.2 (GCS 30.39.27—40.2).

[44] Origen, *Homilia in Jeremiam* 19.13 (GCS 6.169.30—33).

in drinking his Blood as a true drink, they anoint the lintels of the houses of their souls."[45] This anointing could be an allusion to the custom at Communion of touching one's eyes with the host that was previously dipped into the chalice.[46] Origen demands that the Body of the Lord be treated with the utmost care and reverence, "so that not even the smallest crumb falls to the ground, so that nothing of the consecrated gift is lost."[47]

John Chrysostom (d. 407): The great teacher of the Eucharist in Greek patristic writings is John of Antioch, Archbishop of Constantinople, to whom was given in the sixth century the nickname Χρυσόστομος (golden-mouth) on account of his outstanding rhetorical talent. Because of his importance for the Eucharist, John Chrysostom received the honorary title of *doctor eucharistiae*.[48] For John, the symbolic character of the Eucharist consists in the fact that things perceptible to the senses contain a reality that can be grasped only by thought. The form of the Eucharist is the anamnesis of thanksgiving:

> The best guard for the preserving of a benefit is remembrance of the benefit, and perpetual thanksgiving. For this reason too the awesome mysteries, so filled with our great salvation, which are celebrated at each synaxis [communion assembly], are called Eucharist, because they are the anamnesis [commemoration] of many benefits, and they exhibit the summit of God's providence, and in every respect they prepare us to give thanks.[49]

In the Eucharist, the Christ who was crucified for us, who celebrated the Last Supper with his apostles, is present. He himself causes the gifts of bread and wine to become his Body and Blood: "Christ is present. The One who prepared that [Holy Thursday] table is the very One who now prepares this [altar] table."[50] The Eucharist is

---

[45] Origen, *In Matthaeum commentariorum*, series 10 (GCS 38.21.11–15): "manducant etiam pascha immolatum Christum pro nobis ... et per hoc quod bibunt sanguinem eius, verum potum, unguent superlimina domorum animae suae."

[46] Cf. Betz, *Eucharistie in der Schrift und Patristik*, 47.

[47] Origen, *In Exodum homilia* 13.3 (GCS 29.274.9).

[48] Cf. August Naegle, *Die Eucharistielehre des heiligen Johannes Chrysostomus, des Doctor Eucharistiae*, Strassburger theologische Studien 3, 4/5 (Freiburg: Herder, 1900).

[49] John Chrysostom, *In Matthaeum homiliae* 25(26).4 (PG 57:331; FEF 2:111).

[50] John Chrysostom, *De proditione Iudae homiliae* 1.6 (PG 49:380; FEF 2:104).

the remembrance of Christ's death, in which that death is carried out through worship.[51] In the Eucharist "is declared the dread mystery, that God gave Himself for the world."[52] Due to the identity of Christ, who even now is present and effective, the Eucharist celebrated at various places can be only one. The sacrifice of the Eucharist, too, is one, because wherever it is celebrated it is referred to the unique sacrifice of Christ. Hence in all celebrations of the Eucharist, too, only one oblation is offered.

The densest remarks on the Eucharist by John Chrysostom are contained in his Commentary on the Letter to the Hebrews:

> Do we not offer every day? We offer indeed [daily], but making a remembrance of His death, and this [remembrance] is one and not many. How is it one, and not many? Inasmuch as that [Sacrifice] was once for all offered, [and] carried into the Holy of Holies. This is a figure of that [sacrifice] and this remembrance of that.[53]
>
> For we always offer the same [Christ], not one sheep now and to-morrow another, but always the same thing: so that the sacrifice is one. And yet by this reasoning, since the offering is made in many places, are there many Christs? [By no means! Rather,] Christ is one everywhere, being complete here and complete there also, one Body. As then while offered in many places, He is one body and not many bodies; so also [He is] one sacrifice. He is our High Priest, who offered the sacrifice that cleanses us. That we offer now also, which was then offered, which cannot be exhausted. This is done in remembrance of what was then done. For (saith He) "do this in remembrance of Me" (Lk xxii. 19). It is not another sacrifice, as the High Priest, but we offer always the same, or rather we perform a remembrance of a Sacrifice.[54]

At around the same time as Ambrose of Milan (339–397), John Chrysostom regards the *verba testamenti* [words of institution] as the decisive words of consecration. The priest, however, does not effect

---

[51] Cf. John Chrysostom, *In Acta Apostolorum homiliae* 21.4 (PG 60:170; NPNF-1 11:141a): τοῦ θανάτου ἐπιτελουμένου ἐκείνου τῆς φρικτῆς θυσίας.

[52] Ibid.

[53] The meaning of this statement is not clear. Probably it refers to the relation between the Old Testament sacrifice of atonement, the sacrifice on the Cross, and the Eucharistic memorial sacrifice.

[54] John Chrysostom, *In epistolam ad Hebraeos* 17.3 [6] (PL 63:131; NPNF-1 14:449a).

the consecration by his own power. Christ is the one who consecrates the gifts of bread and wine and makes them his Body and Blood: "It is not a man who makes the sacrificial gifts become the Body and Blood of Christ, but He who was crucified for us, Christ Himself. The priest stands there carrying out the action, but the power and the grace is of God. 'This is my Body,' he says. This statement transforms [μεταρρυθμίζει] the gifts."[55]

In the writings of John Chrysostom, we also find already, as later in John of Damascus (d. ca. 754)[56] and Thomas Aquinas (d. 1274),[57] the idea that the efficacy of Christ's words over bread and wine at the Last Supper extends to all celebrations of the Eucharist in the Church. In other passages, Chrysostom ascribes the confection of the Eucharist to the invocation of the Holy Spirit.[58] The Spirit comes down on the gifts and surrounds them; he brings about the mystical sacrifice. Finally, the two elements belong together inseparably: the words of Christ (verba testamenti) and the action of the Spirit (epiclesis of the Spirit).[59]

Theodore of Mopsuestia (d. 428/429): This fellow student of John Chrysostom deals in two chapters of his *Catechetical Homilies* with the Eucharistic sacrifice and the liturgical act of offering it.[60] In Theodore's writings, too, the relation between remembrance and sacrifice

---

[55] John Chrysostom, *De proditione Iudae homiliae* 1.6 (*PG* 49:380; *FEF* 2:104–5).

[56] Cf. John of Damascus, *De fide orthodoxa* 4.13 (*PG* 94:139B–142A; *NPNF*-2 9b:81b–84b).

[57] Cf. Thomas Aquinas, *Summa Theologiae*, III, q. 78, art. 5.

[58] For example, John Chrysostom, *De coemeterio et de cruce* 3 (*PG* 49:397). Additional passages in Betz, *Eucharistie in der Schrift und Patristik*, 104.

[59] This is true also of the Divine Liturgy of St. John Chrysostom, in which the epiclesis to the Holy Spirit follows the *verba testamenti* and the anamnesis: "Send down Your Holy Spirit upon us and upon the gifts here presented,... and make this bread the precious Body of Your Christ ... and that which is in this Cup, the precious Blood of Your Christ." *The Divine Liturgy of Saint John Chrysostom*, at the website of the Greek Orthodox Archdiocese of America https://www.goarch.org/-/the-divine-liturgy-of-saint-john-chrysostom. Christ is therefore the one who truly acts, through the fact that he enables the one who is "clothed with the grace of the priesthood to stand before Your holy Table [altar] and celebrate the Mystery of your holy and pure Body and Your precious Blood" (*The Divine Liturgy of Saint John Chrysostom*, Great Entrance: The Prayer of the Cherubic Hymn).

[60] Cf. Theodore of Mopsuestia, *Homiliae catecheticae* 15.1–16.44 (*FC* 17/2:387–456). Compare Peter Bruns, *Den Menschen mit dem Himmel verbinden: Eine Studie zu den katechetischen Homilien des Theodor von Mopsuestia*, Corpus Scriptorum Christianorum Orientalium, Subsidia 89 (Leuven: Peeters, 1995), 345–70; Simon Gerber, *Theodor von Mopsuestia und das Nicänum: Studien zu den katechetischen Homilien* (Leiden and Boston: Brill, 2000), 225–30.

plays a central role.[61] The Antiochene theologian calls the Eucharistic Prayer ἀναφορὰ τῆς προσφορᾶς (presentation of the sacrifice).[62] In the Eucharist, Theodore sees a memorial of Christ's death.[63] At the same time, he emphasizes that the earthly priest in presenting the Eucharist portrays the High Priest Christ:

> Therefore (on earth) a certain image [εἰκών] of the High Priest must be presented. For this purpose, then, there are those who are appointed to serve with the symbols [τύποι]. We believe that our Lord Christ in fact fulfilled this [service] and still fulfills it, which those who through God's grace [are appointed] priests of the New Covenant, through the Holy Spirit, who truly descended upon them, in the sacraments [μυστήρια], so we believe, fulfill to strengthen and admonish those who partake of the sacraments.[64]

In the offering of the Eucharist, the relation between the sacrifice on the Cross and the Eucharistic Sacrifice should be noted. In the Eucharistic Sacrifice, Christ's sacrifice on the Cross becomes effective: "But all priests of the New Covenant constantly offer, in all places and at all times, one and the same sacrifice, for that sacrifice that was offered for all of us is also one, namely, (the sacrifice) of Christ, who for us accepted death and in offering this sacrifice won perfection for us, as Saint Paul said: 'For by a single offering he has perfected for all time those who are sanctified' (Heb 10:14)."[65] The Eucharist is a sacrifice in which the sacramental renewal of Christ's sacrifice occurs. The visible sacrificial worship is the likeness (ὁμοίωμα) of the heavenly liturgy: "During it we reflect that Christ is in heaven, who for us died, rose and ascended into heaven, that he is the one who is also sacrificed now symbolically [ἐν τύποις]."[66] With that Theodore does not mean that during the sacrifice of the Eucharist a bloody repetition of the sacrifice on the Cross occurs.

---

[61] Cf. Herman A.J. Wegman, *Liturgie in der Geschichte des Christentums* (Regensburg: Pustet, 1994), 153f.

[62] Cf. Theodore of Mopsuestia, *Homiliae catecheticae* 15.19 (FC 17/2:404).

[63] Cf. ibid., 15.7 (FC 17/2:392).

[64] Ibid., 15.19 (FC 17/2:403).

[65] Ibid. (FC 17/2:404).

[66] Ibid., 15.20 (FC 17/2:404).

The Paschal Mystery of Christ is made present sacramentally in the Eucharist offered by the priest under the signs of bread and wine. Theodore says that this happens through the power of the Holy Spirit.[67] Through the Spirit who comes down upon the gifts of bread and wine, they become the Body and Blood of Christ:

> Therefore when the priest says that they [bread and wine] are the Body and Blood of Christ, then he makes it quite clear that they became such through the coming of the Holy Spirit and became immortal through him, since indeed the Body of our Lord, too, which was anointed and received the Spirit has also become clearly visible in this way. In the same way even now, when the Spirit comes, a kind of anointing occurs with the grace that has arrived, which, as we think, bread and wine received after their preparation. We now consider them the Body and Blood of Christ, immortal and incorruptible, impassible and unchangeable by nature [φύσει], as the Body of our Lord became through the Resurrection.[68]

Theodore assigns individual mysteries of salvation from the life of Jesus to the sequence of events in the liturgical action. The presentation of the offerings symbolizes Jesus being led out to his Passion.[69] The placing of the gifts on the altar stands for the burial of Jesus, the altar—for the tomb, and the altar cloth—for the burial cloths.[70] The silence during the Eucharistic liturgy indicates that the disciples hid themselves out of fear during Jesus' Passion and the angels waited in quiet recollection for the Resurrection of Jesus.[71] The designation of the Eucharistic species as "body" and "blood" of Christ stands for the Passion and death of Jesus (Offertory and institutional narrative).[72] The epiclesis that follows corresponds to the Resurrection.

By analogy to the Resurrection of Jesus from the tomb, in which his mortal body received the Holy Spirit and became immortal,

---

[67] Cf. ibid., 16.11 (FC 17/2:430f.).
[68] Ibid., 16.12 (FC 17/2:431).
[69] Cf. ibid., 15.25 (FC 17/2:408).
[70] Cf. ibid., 15.26 (FC 17/2:409f.).
[71] Cf. ibid., 15.28 (FC 17/2:410f.).
[72] Cf. ibid., 15.9; 16.16 (FC 17/2:393, 433f.).

through the epiclesis pronounced by the priest the gifts of bread and wine become the Body and Blood of Christ and thus immortal.[73] The breaking and distribution of the bread, according to Theodore, recalls the appearances of the risen Lord.[74] Communion points once again to the Resurrection: Christ is risen from the altar as though from a kind of tomb and is given to us.[75] Like hardly any other Church Father, Theodore also sets forth the eschatological dimension of the Eucharist. Through the death, Resurrection, and Ascension of Jesus, an age of eternity is inaugurated within history. The risen Crucified One received immortality, in which we gain a share even now through the celebration of the holy mysteries. Therefore the orientation to the *eschaton* [end of the world] is always part of the cultic anamnesis of Christ's Paschal Mystery, too.[76]

B. The Eucharist in Latin Patristic Writings

The Latin Fathers of the Church, like the Greek Fathers, regard the Eucharist as an *oblatio* (offering) and a *sacrificium* (sacrifice). As a whole, however, the Church Fathers in the West are more interested in the gift of the sacramental Body of Christ and also in the ecclesial character of the Eucharist. Significant contributions to the understanding of the Eucharist were made by Tertullian (d. after 220), Cyprian of Carthage (d. 258), Ambrose of Milan, and Augustine (354–430). The last two had considerable influence on the Western doctrine about the Eucharist. The medieval controversies about the Eucharist cannot be understood apart from their understanding of the Eucharist.

Tertullian: In the writings of the theologian from Carthage, in modern-day Tunisia, *oblatio* is the usual term for the Eucharist, since *oratio* and *prex* seem to him too unspecific. To describe the sacrificial character of the Eucharist, Tertullian prefers the expressions *immolare* and *sacrificium*. For Tertullian, the sacrifice of the Eucharist is not a

---

[73] Cf. ibid., 15.10; 16.11f. (FC 17/2:393f., 430f.).
[74] Cf. ibid., 16.17 (FC 17/2:434).
[75] Cf. ibid., 16:26 (FC 17/2:442).
[76] Cf. ibid., 15.3.6; 16.12 (FC 17/2:388f., 391, 431).

bloody sacrifice; the sacrifice of the Eucharist consists, rather, of a *pura prece* [pure prayer].[77] "We are the true adorers and the true priests, who, praying in spirit, sacrifice, in spirit, prayer—a victim proper and acceptable to God."[78] The offering of the *oratio* means the Eucharistic Prayer, which is addressed to God the Father through Christ.[79] The Eucharistic Sacrifice is offered in the form of a sacrifice of praise (*sacrificium laudis*): "Through him then let us continually offer up a sacrifice of praise to God, that is, the fruit of lips that acknowledge his name" (Heb 13:15). In connection with the Eucharistic Prayer, Tertullian speaks about the *gratiarum actiones* or *actio gratiarum* [thanksgiving].[80] Tertullian calls the Mass as a whole the *sacrificiorum orationes* [prayers of sacrifices], "whereby the term might be derived *pars pro toto* [the part standing for the whole] from the Eucharistic Prayer."[81] No fixed formula for the Eucharistic Prayer existed yet in Tertullian's time. While the Eucharistic Prayer was being pronounced, the congregation stood with hands uplifted, facing East, and looked up to heaven.[82] The offering of the *oratio*, however, is not all there is to Eucharistic sacrifice. For in it, Christ's sacrificial death is made present sacramentally.[83]

Tertullian, like most Church Fathers, refers the petition from the Our Father about daily bread to the Eucharistic bread: "For *Christ* is our Bread; because Christ is Life, and bread is life.... Then *we find*, too, that His body is reckoned [as] bread: 'This is my body.' And so, in petitioning for 'daily bread,' we ask for perpetuity in Christ, and

---

[77] Tertullian, *Ad Scapulum* 2.8 (CCSL 2:1128). On the life and theology of Tertullian, see Henrike Maria Zilling, *Tertullian: Untertan Gottes und des Kaisers* (Paderborn: Schöningh, 2004); David E. Wilhite, *Tertullian the African: An Anthropological Reading of Tertullian's Context and Identities*, Millennium-Studien zu Kultur und Geschichte des ersten Jahrtausends n. Chr. 14 (Berlin and New York: Walter de Gruyter, 2007).

[78] Tertullian, *De oratione* 28.3 (CCSL 1:273; ANF 3:690b). "Nos sumus veri adoratores et veri sacerdotes, qui spiritu orantes spiritu sacrificamus orationem hostiam Dei propriam et acceptabilem."

[79] Cf. ibid., 28:1–4 (CCSL 1:273; ANF 3:690b); Tertullian, *Adversus Marcionem* 4.9.9 (CCSL 1:560; ANF 3:357b).

[80] Cf. *Adversus Marcionem*, 1.23.9 (CCSL 1:466; ANF 3:288–89a).

[81] Martin Klöckener, "Das Eucharistische Hochgebet in der nordafrikanischen Liturgie der christlichen Spätantike", in *Prex Eucharistica*, vol. 3, pt. 1, ed. A. Gerhards, H. Brakmann, and M. Klöckener (Fribourg: Academic Press Fribourg and Paulusverlag, 2005), 51.

[82] Cf. ibid., 56.

[83] Cf. Tertullian, *De pudicitia* 9.11 (CCSL 2:1298: ANF 4:83b).

indivisibility from His body."[84] Christ "called the bread His own body", and "thus did He now consecrate His blood in wine."[85] For Christ,

> having taken the bread and given it to His disciples, ... made it His own body, by saying, "This is my body," that is, the figure of my body [*figura corporis mei*]. A figure, however, there could not have been, unless there were first a veritable body. An empty thing, or phantom, is incapable of a figure. If, however, (as Marcion might say,) He pretended the bread was His body, because He lacked the truth of bodily substance, it follows that He must have given bread for us.[86]

Tertullian seeks to give evidence for the reality of Christ's body by means of the blood also:

> He likewise, when mentioning the cup and making the *new* testament to be sealed "in His blood," affirms the reality of His body [*substantiam corporis confirmavit*]. For no blood can belong to a body which is not *a body* of flesh. If any sort of body were presented to our view, which is not one of flesh, not being fleshly, it would not possess blood. Thus, from the evidence of the flesh, we get a proof of the body, and a proof of the flesh from the evidence of the blood.[87]

---

[84] Tertullian, *De oratione* 6.2 (CCSL 1:261; ANF 3:683:b): "Christus enim *panis noster* est, quia vita Christus et vita panis ... tunc quod et corpus eius in pane censetur: *hoc est corpus meum*. Itaque petendo panem quotidianum perpetuitatem postulamus in Christo et individu-itatem a corpore eius."

[85] Tertullian, *Adversus Marcionem* 4.40.3, 5 (CCSL 1:656f.; ANF 3:418b, 419a). Tertullian mentions that the faithful take the Eucharistic bread home and receive it before any other food (*ante omnem cibum*). Cf. Tertullian, *Ad uxorem* 2.5.2 (CCSL 1:389; ANF 4:46b–47a).

[86] Tertullian, *Adversus Marcionem* 4.40.3 (CCSL 1:656; ANF 3:418a-b): "panem et distribu-tum discipulis corpus suum illum fecit *hoc est corpus meum* dicendo, id est *figura corporis mei*. Figura autem non fuisset nisi veritatis esset corpus. Ceterum vacua res, quod est phantasma, figuram capere non posset. Aut si propterea panem corpus sibi finxit, quia corporis carebat veritate, ergo panem debuit tradere pro nobis." It is suspected that the expression *figura corpus mei* was part of the Eucharistic Prayer in Tertullian's time. Cf. Klöckener, "Eucharistische Hochgebet in der nordafrikanischen Liturgie", 52.

[87] Tertullian, *Adversus Marcionem* 4.40.4 (CCSL 1:656f.; ANF 3:418b): "Sic et in calicis mentione testamentum constituens sanguine suo obsignatum substantiam corporis confirma-vit. Nullius enim corporis sanguis potest esse nisi carnis. Nam et si qua corporis qualitas non carnea opponuntur nobis, certe sanguinem nisi carnea non habebit."

Cyprian of Carthage in a certain way wrote the first treatise on the Eucharist with his famous Letter 63. The letter shows that the *verba testamenti* (words of institution) were already a fixed component of the Eucharistic Prayer in Carthage in Cyprian's time. Since Cyprian cites both the Matthean version and also the Pauline, we cannot tell how the liturgical version of the words of institution read.[88] Cyprian describes the Eucharistic Prayer as a *prex* or, when he has individual prayer elements in mind, as *preces*.[89] When Cyprian speaks about *eucharistia*, he very often means the sacramental gifts.[90] The consecrated gifts of bread and wine, for Cyprian, are not only the Body and Blood of Christ; at the same time, they symbolize the Church: the one bread from many grains and the wine pressed from many grapes represent the people of the New Covenant united in Christ.[91] The unity of the Church is of course not only the fruit of the Eucharist but at the same time its prerequisite. The celebration of the Eucharist is the fulfillment and expression of ecclesial unity.[92] The Eucharist cannot be celebrated effectively among heretics, since they do not have the Holy Spirit; for where the Holy Spirit is lacking, the oblation is not sanctified.

Cyprian's sacramental sacrificial language revolves around the concept of offering (*oblatio, offerre*). Like Tertullian, Cyprian, too, associates the idea of sacrifice with the terms *offerre* and *oblatio*.[93] Christ offered his body and blood to the Father as a sacrifice: "Who is more a priest of the most high God than our Lord Jesus Christ, who offered a sacrifice to God the Father, and offered that very same thing which Melchizedek had offered, that is, bread and wine, to wit, His body and blood?"[94] The sacrifice of the Eucharist is celebrated as a memorial

---

[88] Cf. Klöckener, "Das Eucharistische Hochgebet in der nordafrikanischen Liturgie", 60–62.

[89] Cf. Cyprian of Carthage, *Epistola* 40.4 [41.5] (*PL* 4:361C–362A; ANF 5:352a).

[90] Cf. Cyprian of Carthage, *De bono patientiae* 14 (*PL* 4:651C).

[91] Cf. Cyprian of Carthage, *Epistola* 63[62].13 (*PL* 4:383B–384B; ANF 5:362a).

[92] Cf. Cyprian of Carthage, *De unitate ecclesiae* 8 (*PL* 4:472A–473A).

[93] On this subject, see Rupert Berger, *Die Wendung "offerre pro" in der römischen Liturgie* (Münster: Aschendorff, 1965), 55–63.

[94] Cyprian of Carthage, *Epistola* 63[62].4 (*PL* 4:376A; ANF 5:359b): "Nam quis magis sacerdos Dei summi quam Dominus noster Iesus Christus, qui sacrificium Deo Patri obtulit, et obtulit hoc idem quod Melchisedech obtulerat, id est panem et vinum, suum scilicet corpus et sanguinem."

of Christ's death.[95] In it, the ordained priest acts in the person of Christ.[96] He offers a real but unbloody sacrifice. Christ's sacrifice on the Cross becomes present in the sacrifice of the Church. "We make mention of His passion in all sacrifices (for the Lord's passion is the sacrifice which we offer [quod offerimus])."[97] Finally, Christ himself is the one who as High Priest of the New Covenant offers himself in our sacrifice. The interpretation of the Eucharist as a sacrifice is one of Cyprian's most lasting influences on Western theology.

Ambrose develops his doctrine on the Eucharist in his catecheses *De sacramentis* and *De mysteriis*.[98] In them, the bishop of Milan proves to be influenced by Greek theology, especially by the catecheses of Cyril of Jerusalem (d. 386).[99] Like no other Father of the Church, Ambrose emphasizes the transformation of the gifts of bread and wine into the Body and Blood of Jesus Christ.[100] As opposed to the Old Testament shadows (*umbrae*) and prefigurations (*figurae*) of the sacraments (for example, manna, water from the rock), the Eucharist is described as truth (*veritas*) and light (*lux*).[101] Bread and wine are the Body and Blood of Christ not only in faith, but in the sacramental sign. "It is the true Flesh of Christ which was crucified and buried, this is then truly the Sacrament of His Body."[102]

Whereas Ambrose speaks in his work *De fide ad Gratianum* (378/380) about the belief that the gifts of bread and wine "which

---

[95] Cf. ibid., 14 (*PL* 4:383B; ANF 5:362b).

[96] Cf. ibid., 9[10] (*PL* 4:381A; ANF 5:361a).

[97] Cyprian of Carthage, *Epistola* 63.17 (*PL* 4:387A; ANF 5:363a).

[98] Cf. Wenrich Slenczka, *Heilsgeschichte und Liturgie: Studien zum Verhältnis von Heilsgeschichte und Heilsteilhabe anhand liturgischer und katechetischer Quellen des dritten und vierten Jahrhunderts* (Berlin and New York: Walter de Gruyter, 2000), 144–96.

[99] Cf. Betz, *Eucharistie in der Schrift und Patristik*, 147. On the debate about the *Mystagogical Catecheses*, which probably originated, not with Cyril of Jerusalem, but with John of Jerusalem (d. 356–417), cf. Slenczka, *Heilsgeschichte und Liturgie*, 99–143. Unlike Enrico Mazza, *L'anafora eucaristica: Studi sulle origini*, Bibliotheca "Ephemerides liturgicae", Subsidia 62 (Rome: Editione Liturgiche, 1992), 350f., Slenczka assumes, as does Georg Kretschmar, "Die frühe Geschichte der Jerusalemer Liturgie", *Jahrbuch für Liturgie und Hymnologie* 2 (1956/1957): 28f., that the liturgy in Jerusalem had an institutional narrative at the time of the *Mystagogical Catecheses*.

[100] On Ambrose, see Ernst Dassmann, *Ambrosius von Mailand: Leben und Werk* (Stuttgart: Kohlhammer, 2004).

[101] Cf. Ambrose, *De mysteriis* 48–49 (FC 3:242f.; NPNF-2 10:323b–324a).

[102] Ibid., 53 (FC 3:248f.; NPNF-2 10:324b): "Vera utique caro Christi, quae crucifixa est, quae sepulta est: vero ergo carnis illius sacramentum est."

by the mysterious efficacy of holy prayer [*per sacrae orationis myste-rium*] are transformed into the Flesh and the Blood [of Christ]",[103] in his catecheses (from 390 on) he concentrates on the *verba testamenti*. He represents the doctrine, which formed a tradition for the Latin Church, that the elements become Christ's Body and Blood through the words of Christ that the priest pronounces at the "divine Consecration" (*consecratio divina*). Before the Consecration, the bread is ordinary bread; after the Consecration, it is the Body of Christ.

> But that bread is bread before the words of the sacraments (*verba sacramentorum*); when consecration (*consecratio*) has been added, from bread it becomes the flesh of Christ. Let us therefore prove this. How can that which is bread be the body of Christ? By consecration. But in what words and in whose language is the consecration? Those of the Lord Jesus. For all the other things which are said in the earlier parts of the service are said by the priest—praises are offered to God, prayer is asked for the people, for kings, and the rest (cf. 1 Tim 2:1f.); when it comes to the consecration of the venerable sacrament, the priest no longer uses his own language, but he uses the language of Christ. Therefore the word of Christ consecrates this sacrament.[104]

---

[103] Ambrose, *De fide* 4.10.124[125] (FC 47/2:552; NPNF-2 10:278b).

[104] Ambrose, *De sacramentis* 4.14 (FC 3:142f.; quoted in English from: St. Ambrose, *"On the Mysteries" and the Treatise "On the Sacraments" by an Unknown Author*, trans. T. Thompson [London: Society for Promoting Christian Knowledge; New York: Macmillan, 1919], 109–10): "Sed panis iste panis est ante verba sacramentorum; ubi accesserit consecratio, de pane fit caro Christi. Hoc igitur adstruamus, quomodo potest, quis panis est, corpus esse Christi. Consecratio igitur quibus verbis est et cuius sermonibus? Domini Iesu. Nam reliqua omnia, quae dicuntur in superioribus, a sacerdote dicuntur: laus deo, defertur oratio, petitur pro populo, pro regibus, pro ceteris. Ubi venitur, ut conficiatur venerabile sacramentum, iam non suis sermonibus utitur sacerdos, sed utitur sermonibus Christi. Ergo sermo Christi hoc conficit sacramentum." On this subject, see Joseph Schmitz, *Gottesdienst im altchristlichen Mailand: Eine liturgiewissenschaftliche Untersuchung über Initiation und Messfeier während des Jahres zur Zeit des Bischofs Ambrosius (†397)*, Theophaneia 25 (Cologne: Hanstein, 1975), 407–9. A distortion of the position advocated by Ambrose is found in Markus Tymister, "Epiklese und Opfer: Anmerkungen zum Römischen Messkanon", *Gottesdienst* 47 (2007): 154: "The search for an exact 'moment of transformation', however, was imported into our text only at a later time. For the theology of St. Ambrose (d. 397), in whose works we find the oldest known version of the Roman Canon, this question plays no role. The Eucharistic Prayer is viewed as a unity, and one can speak about a completed transformation of the species only after the concluding and assenting *Amen* of the congregation."

"The paradigm for the reality of the sacrament is the performative nature of Christ's word, which stands in the center of the Eucharistic liturgy", so says the philosopher Giorgio Agamben in his analysis on the concept of *mysterium*.[105] Ambrose emphasizes the performative nature of Christ's words for the reality of the Eucharist in another passage, also:

> For that sacrament which you receive is made what it is by the word of Christ. But if the word of Elijah had such power as to bring down fire from heaven [cf. 1 Kings 18:36–38], shall not the word of Christ have power to change the nature of the elements [*ut species mutet elementorum*]?[106]
>
> The Lord Jesus Himself proclaims: "This is My Body" [1 Cor 11:24; Mt 26:26; Mk 14:22; Lk 22:19]. Before the blessing (*benedictio*) of the heavenly words another nature is spoken of, after the consecration (*consecratio*) the Body is signified. He Himself speaks of His Blood. Before the consecration it has another name, after it is called Blood.[107]

Ambrose connects the transformative force of the *verba testamenti* with the creative force of the Divine Word.

> Thou seest, therefore, how effective is the word of Christ. If, therefore, there is such power in the word of the Lord Jesus, that the things which were not began to be, how much more is it effective, that the things previously existing should, without ceasing to exist, be changed into something else [*in aliud commutentur*]?[108]

---

[105] Giorgio Agamben, *Opus Dei: An Archaeology of Duty*, trans. Adam Kotsko (Stanford, Calif.: Stanford University Press, 2013), 87. Agamben suspects that the description of performative speech acts by modern linguistics has its roots in the Eucharistic signification. Cf. ibid., 88.

[106] Ambrose, *De mysteriis* 52 (FC 3:246f.; NPNF-2 10:324b): "Nam sacramentum istud, quod accipis, Christi sermone conficitur. Quod si tantum valuit sermo Heliae, ut ignem de caelo deposceret, non valebit Christi sermo, ut species mutet elementorum?"

[107] Ibid., 54 (FC 3:248f.; NPNF-2 10:324b–325a): "Ipse clamat dominus Iesus: 'Hoc est corpus meum.' Ante benedictionem verborum caelestium alia species nominatur, post consecrationem corpus significatur. Ipse dicit sanguinem suum. Ante consecrationem aliud dicitur, post consecrationem sanguis nuncupatur."

[108] Ambrose, *De sacramentis* 4.15 (FC 3:142–45; Thompson trans., 110): "Vides ergo, quam operatorius sermo sit Christi. Si ergo tanta vis est in sermone domini Iesu, ut inciperent esse, quae non erant, quanto magis operatorius est, ut sint, quae erant, et in aliud commutentur."

It was not the body of Christ before consecration; but after consecration, I tell thee, it is now the body of Christ. *He spake, and* it was
made; *he commanded, and* it was created.[109]

The food offerings not only acquire in the Eucharist a new meaning
but are transformed into the Body and Blood of Christ, a transformation that of course eludes outward inspection, since the *species* or
appearance of the elements continues to exist.[110] The sacred Consecration brings about a real transformation (*mutatio, conversio*) of bread
and wine into the Body and Blood of Christ.[111]

The Lord's words in the account of the institution are described by
Ambrose as *verba sacramentorum*[112] (words of the sacraments) or *sermo
caelestis*[113] (heavenly word). In his catecheses *De mysteriis*, Ambrose says
that the *benedictio consecravit*,[114] and he emphasizes that at the divine
Consecration (*divina consecratio*), Christ's word is what has the power
to change the elements (*Christi sermo species mutet elementorum*).[115] Even
though for Ambrose the somatic Real Presence of Christ in the gifts of
bread and wine is in the foreground, he does take into consideration
likewise the anamnetic dimension of the Eucharistic action: "Therefore dost thou hear that as often as sacrifice is offered (*offertur sacrificium*), the Lord's death, the Lord's resurrection, the Lord's ascension
and the remission of sins is signified [or 'proclaimed'; *significetur*], and
dost thou not take this bread of life daily?"[116]

[109] Ibid., 4.16 (FC 3:144f.; Thompson trans., 111): "non erat corpus Christi ante consecrationem, sed post consecrationem dico tibi, qua iam corpus est Christi. Ipse dixit et factum
est, ipse mandavit et creatum est." On the performative character of the word of Christ that
judges and reveals, cf. Ambrose, *De fide* 4, 7 (PL 16:631; NPNF-2 10:271b), where he cites
Hebrews 4:12.

[110] Cf. Ambrose, *De sacramentis* 4.20 (FC 3:146–49; Thompson trans., 111f.); *De mysteriis* 52
(FC 3:246f.; NPNF-2 10:324b). To designate the process of transformation, Ambrose uses a
series of different terms, besides *convertere*: *consecrare, transfigurare, mutare*, and *commutari*, among
others.

[111] Cf. Ambrose, *De sacramentis* 4.15–16 (FC 3:142–45: Thompson trans., 110–11).

[112] Ibid., 4.14 (FC 3:142; Thompson trans., 109).

[113] Ibid., 4.19 (FC 3:146; Thompson trans., 112).

[114] Ambrose, *De mysteriis* 50 (FC 3:244; NPNF-2 10:324a). Schmitz, *Gottesdienst im
altchristlichen Mailand*, 383f., understands *benedictio consecravit* to mean the *verba testamenti*.

[115] Cf. Ambrose, *De mysteriis* 52 (FC 3:246; NPNF-2 10:324b).

[116] Ambrose, *De sacramentis* 5.25 (FC 3:174f.; Thompson trans., 126): "Ergo tu audis, quod,
quotienscumque offertur sacrificium, mors domini, resurrectio domini, elevatio domini significetur et remissio peccatorum, et panem istum vitae non cottidianus adsumus?"

Augustine, in contrast to Ambrose, emphasizes more the spiritual dimension of the Eucharist and its ecclesial significance. For Augustine, the real gift of the sacrament is accomplished in the union with Christ and with one another.[117] In the Eucharistic elements, he sees the gift of unity presented symbolically. The Eucharist is a sign of Christ's Body, the Church. The bread is the union of many ears of wheat; the wine—the union of many grapes.[118] The Eucharistic bread represents the unity of the many in the one Body of Christ. Union with Christ is also in the background of the practice that spread from North Africa of celebrating the Eucharist on the anniversary of the martyrdom of the Christians who shed their blood for the faith. Augustine's account of the burial of his mother, Monica, is evidence for the celebration of the Eucharist as part of the burial liturgy in Italy as early as the fourth century.[119] It is suspected that the Eucharist, as part of the burial liturgy, repressed the pagan *refrigerium*, a common celebration of the dead at the grave.[120]

In the Eucharist, we receive the mystery of the Body of Christ. "So if it's you that are the body of Christ and its members, it's the mystery meaning you that has been placed on the Lord's table; what you receive is the mystery that means you."[121] "Be what you can see, and receive what you are."[122] These are the famous citations of Augustine. The Body of Christ together with its Head forms the *totus Christus*, the whole Christ. Henri de Lubac showed that the Eucharistic Body was designated as *corpus mysticum* in patristic writings until the early Middle Ages, while the Church was called *corpus verum* [true body]. In the course of the medieval controversies, a change of terminology came about: now the Eucharist is called *corpus verum* and the Church—*corpus mysticum*.[123]

---

[117] Cf. Augustine, *In Iohannis evangelium tractatus* 26.18 (CCSL 36:268: *WSA* 3/12:464).

[118] Cf. ibid., 26.17 (CCSL 36:268: *WSA* 3/12:463–64).

[119] Cf. Augustine, *Confessiones* 9.12.29–33 (CCSL 27:150–52; *WSA* 1/1:231–33).

[120] Cf. Nathan Mitchell, *Cult and Controversy: The Worship of the Eucharist outside the Mass*, Studies in the Reformed Rites of the Catholic Church 4 (Collegeville, Minn.: Liturgical Press, 1990), 32.

[121] Augustine, *Sermo* 272 (*PL* 38:1247; *WSA* 3/7:300): "Si ergo vos estis corpus Christi et membra, mysterium vestrum in mensa Dominica positum est: mysterium vestrum accipitis."

[122] Ibid. (*PL* 38:1247f.; *WSA* 3/7:301): "Estote quod videtis, et accipite quod estis."

[123] Cf. Henri de Lubac, *Corpus Mysticum: The Eucharist and the Church in the Middle Ages: Historical Survey*, trans. Laurence Paul Hemmings and Susan Frank Parsons (Notre Dame, Ind.: University of Notre Dame Press, 2007).

Sacraments in the broader sense are for Augustine signs that refer to divine things[124]—as distinct from magical signs, for which the influence of human forces working supernaturally is claimed. For Augustine, "people could not be gathered together under the name of any religion, whether true or false, if they were not bound together by some sharing of visible signs or sacraments."[125] In *De doctrina christiana*, Augustine proposes a general definition of sign that was regarded as obligatory well into the High Middle Ages: "Signum ... est res praeter speciem quam ingerit sensibus, aliud aliquid ex se faciens in cogitationem venire" (a sign is a thing that, apart from the impression that it presents to the senses, causes of itself some other thing to enter our thoughts).[126] Every *signum* is a *res*, but not every *res* is a *signum*. Augustine subdivides the realm of *res* into *sensibilia*, which are perceived by the senses, and *intelligibilia*, which are accessible only to a mental understanding.[127] Linguistic signs take precedence over non-verbal signs, since everything that is signified by non-verbal signs can be expressed also through linguistic signs, but not vice versa.[128] Letter are signs for words.[129] Augustine's theory of signs is an ontological theory, since reality as a whole is classified under the categories *res* and *signum*, and every

[124] Cf. Augustine, *Epistola* 138.7 (Corpus Scriptorum Ecclesiasticorum Latinorum, ed. by the Austrian Academy of Sciences [Vienna, 1866ff.; hereafter cited as CSEL], 44:131; *WSA* 2/2:228): "Signa cum ad res divina pertinent sacramenta appelantur."

[125] Augustine, *Contra Faustum* 19.11 (CSEL 25:510; *WSA* 1/20:244–45): "In nullam autem nomen religionis, seu verum, seu falsum, coagulari monies possunt, nisi aliquot signaculorum vel sacramentorum visibilium consortio colligentur." On Augustine's theory of signs, cf. Cornelius P. Mayer, *Die Zeichen in der geistigen Entwicklung und in der Theologie des jungen Augustinus*, 2 vols. (1969; Würzburg: Augustinus Verlag, 1974); Simone Raffaele, "Die Semiotik Augustins", in *Zeichen: Semiotik in Theologie und Gottesdienst*, ed. R. Volp (Munich: Kaiser; Mainz: Grünewald, 1982), 79–113.

[126] Augustine, *De doctrina christiana* 2.1 (CCSL 32:32; The Fathers of the Church, 127 vols. [Washington, D.C.: Catholic University of America Press, 1947–2013; hereafter cited as FOC] 2:61). Peter Lombard cites the definition in his *Sentences*. Cf. Augustine, *Sententia in IV libris distinctae* 4.1.3. It is suspected that the source of Augustine's general definition of signs is Origen. Cf. Origen, *In Rom* 4.2 (*PG* 14:968A; SChr 539:208): "*Signum* namque dicitur, cum per hoc quod videtur aliud aliquid indicatur." On Rufinus' Latin translation of the *Commentary on the Letter to the Romans*, see Hammond Bammel, *Der Römerbrieftext des Rufin und seine Origenes-Übersetzung* (Freiburg: Herder, 1985).

[127] Cf. Augustine, *De magistro* 12.39 (Opera 11:182; FOC 59:52): "Namque omnia percipimus, aut sensu corporis aut mente percipimus. Illa sensibilia, haec intelligibilia."

[128] Cf. Augustine, *De doctrina christiana* 2.3 (CCSL 32:34; FOC 2:63–64).

[129] Cf. ibid., 2.4 (CCSL 32:34; FOC 2:64).

science treats either things or signs: "Omnis doctrina vel rerum est
vel signorum."[130]

In discussing signs, Augustine distinguishes between natural signs
(*signa naturalia*) and conventional signs (*signa data*).[131] Augustine
subdivides *signa data* into *signa propria* and *signa translata*, proper and
transferred signs. One example of a transferred sign is the expression
"bull", insofar as it designates, not the animal, but the symbol of the
third evangelist. One complex subclass of *signa translata* is made up
by the sacraments, which are composed of two signs: on the one
hand, visible material (water in Baptism, bread and wine in the
Eucharist), and, on the other hand, the word through which the visible element becomes a sacrament. "Accedit verbum ad elementum et
fit sacramentum" (the word is added to the element, and it becomes
a sacrament).[132] Through the *verbum sacramenti*, the visible element
becomes a *signum sacrum*, a sacred sign.[133]

Now in *De doctrina christiana*, Augustine calls Jesus' discourse about
the bread from heaven in the synagogue of Capernaum (Jn 6) a *figurata locutio*, a figurative speech.[134] The central statement of the speech
reads: "Unless you eat the flesh of the Son of man and drink his
blood, you have no life in you" (Jn 6:53). If this were understood literally, Augustine says, Jesus would be commanding a crime, namely,
to eat the flesh of a human being and to drink his blood.[135] In the case
of the *verba testamenti* that the priest pronounces at the Consecration
over the gifts of bread and wine, however, Augustine says that they
are more than a *tropica locutio* [manner of speaking]. For we receive
Christ's Body and Blood, not only in a figurative sense, but truly.
Even though the somatic Real Presence of Christ in the consecrated
gifts of bread and wine is not emphasized as strongly in Augustine's
writings as in Ambrose's, we still find clear references to it in his
work.[136] Thus Augustine demands that one cannot receive the Body
and Blood of Christ without first having adored. In his Commentary

---

[130] Ibid., 1.2 (CCSL 32:7: FOC 2:28).

[131] Cf. ibid., 2.2 (CCSL 32:32–33; FOC 2:61).

[132] Augustine, *In Iohannis evangelium tractatus* 80.3.5f. (CCSL 36:529).

[133] Cf. Augustine, *De civitate Dei* 10.5.16 (CCSL 47:277; *WSA* 1/6:310).

[134] Cf. Augustine, *De doctrina christiana* 3.16 (CCSL 23:9f.; FOC 2:136).

[135] Cf. ibid.

[136] Cf. Josef Rupert Geiselmann, *Die Eucharistielehre der Vorscholastik*, Forschungen zur
christlichen Literatur- und Dogmengeschichte 15 (Paderborn: Schöningh, 1926), 37.

on the Psalms, he writes: "He walked here below in that flesh, and even gave us that same flesh to eat for our salvation.... No one eats it without first worshipping it."[137]

Therefore, Augustine does not spiritualize the presence of Christ in the sacrament of the Eucharist, as is often maintained. The spiritualistic interpretation of Augustine's teaching on the Eucharist, as championed above all by Protestant scholars, for example, Adolf von Harnack and Friedrich Loofs (1858–1928), is shared by very few today. Catholic Augustine scholarship in the twentieth century, which took great pains to strike a balance between the spiritualistic and the strictly realistic tradition of interpretation, was able to show that Augustine, even before the medieval controversies, gravitates around a realistic or symbolic interpretation of the Eucharist: "Augustine's teaching about the Eucharist has often been interpreted symbolically, as opposed to being understood realistically. It should be clear that this interpretation misses the point. Augustine is still living in an age beyond the opposition 'image or reality'; for him, the image is a real symbol."[138]

In the Eucharist, Augustine recognizes signs in which the Body and Blood of Christ are given to the faithful. Hence Augustine's general definition of signs is insufficient to define the reality of the Eucharist. The sacraments in the narrower sense are signs *sui generis* [in a class of their own]. In their case, the signs are neither natural, as smoke is the sign of fire,[139] nor a symbol, as the cross is for the Christian faith.[140] The sacraments, Augustine says, are "sacred signs" (*sacra signa*),[141] carriers of a hidden, invisible reality. The sacrament of the Eucharist is not given to us only according to the external sign; rather, we truly receive the Body and Blood of Christ.[142] In

---

[137] Augustine, *Enarrationes in Psalmos* 98.9 (CCSL 39:1385; WSA 3/18:474): "Et quia in ipsa carne hic ambulavit, et ipsam carnem nobis manducandam ad salutem dedit; nemo autem illam carnem manducat, nisi prius adoraverit."

[138] Alexander Gerken, *Theologie der Eucharistie* (Munich: Kösel-Verlag, 1973), 91.

[139] Cf. Augustine, *In Iohannis evangelium tractatus* 26.11.19f. (CSEL 36:265; WSA 3/12:458, 464); 80.3.9–12 (CSEL 36:529).

[140] Cf. Augustine, *De doctrina christiana* 2.62[46] (CCSL 32:7; FOC 2:115).

[141] Augustine, *De civitate Dei* 10.5 (CCSL 47:277; WSA 1/6:309).

[142] Cf. ibid., 21.25 (CCSL 48:798; WSA 1/7:484–85): "sed re vera corpus Christi manducare et eius sanguine bibere; hoc est enim in Christo manere, ut in illo et Christus" [To eat Christ's body and drink his blood ... in reality it ... means to abide in Christ in such a way that Christ also abides in us].

one of his letters, Augustine explains that the sacrament of the Body and Blood of Christ is truly the Body and Blood of Christ: "Sacramentum corporis Christi corpus Christi est, sacramentum sanguinis Christi sanguis Christi est."[143]

Augustine distinguishes between the outward sign (*signum*) and the inward reality or power of the sacrament (*res* or *virtus sacramenti*). The sacramental sign is a material object (*elementum*), for example bread, wine, or water, and an interpretive word that is added to the element. The formula that Augustine coined for this is: "Accedit verbum ad elementum et fit sacramentum."[144] The unity of word and matter is characteristic of the celebration of the sacraments; on this is founded also their cosmic dimension. Yet in order to be effective, the word added to the element must be a word of faith.[145] The space of the sacraments is therefore formed by the Church as the communion that hands down the faith. In order for the sacrament to become effective in human beings, a "conversion of heart" (*conversio cordis*)[146] is necessary.

For Augustine, the Eucharist bestows fellowship or communion with Christ: "This, therefore, is eating that food and drinking that drink: abiding in Christ and having him abide in oneself."[147] Someone who stops short at the outward sign, who is not open to the actual reality (*res*) of the sacrament (*sacramentum*), someone who partakes of it in a fleshly manner, does not partake of Jesus Christ in truth. When Jesus says that the Spirit is the one who gives life, but the flesh is of no avail (Jn 6:63), then according to Augustine he is admonishing us not to misunderstand him:

> Understand what I have told you in a spiritual way. You are not asked to eat this body that you can see; nor to drink the blood that will be shed by those who will crucify me. What I have revealed to you

---

[143] Augustine, *Epistola* 98.9 (CCSL 31:531; *WSA* 2/1:431).

[144] Augustine, *In Iohannis evangelium tractatus* 80.3 (CCSL 36:529): "The word is added to the element and the sacrament is effected."

[145] Cf. ibid. (CCSL 36:529).

[146] Augustine, *De baptismo* 4.25.32 (CSEL 51:260).

[147] Augustine, *In Iohannis evangelium tractatus* 26.18 (CCSL36:268; *WSA* 3/12:464): "Hoc est ergo manducare illam escam, et illum bibere potum, in Christo manere, et illum manentem in se habere."

is something mysterious, something that when understood spiritually will mean life for you. Although it is to be celebrated in a visible manner, you must understand it in a way that transcends bodily sight.[148]

Bread and wine are signs of a pneumatic reality, the glorified Christ, who died for us and in his self-surrender gives himself anew for us again and again in his Body and Blood. In this sense, Augustine distinguishes between *sacramentum tantum*, the mere sign, and the *res sacramenti*, the reality of the sacrament. Unworthy Communion is *manducare tantum in sacramento*. What matters, however, is to partake not only according to the mere sign: "To eat Christ's body and drink his blood ... in reality it ... means to abide in Christ in such a way that Christ also abides in us."[149] For the sign alone (*sacramentum tantum*) is fleeting.

The sign is not yet regarded by Augustine in its own substantiality but, rather, altogether as a sign and image for the invisible reality given therein. The question about the reality of the sacrament was not fiercely debated until the early Middle Ages. One prerequisite for it was that the understanding of the Eucharist since Isidore of Seville (d. 636) increasingly shifted from the εὐχαριστία as a cultic thanksgiving to which the faithful were called to participate through the *gratias agamus* to the presence of Christ in the sacramental signs. *Gratiarum actio* (thanksgiving) became *bona gratia* (good grace = a literal Latin rendering of *eu-charistia*).[150] The relation of the sacramental-mystical Body to the ecclesial Body of the Lord, which in Augustine's writings is still entirely in the foreground, recedes in importance. This was accompanied by a decline in the reception of Communion by the faithful.

[148] Augustine, *Enarrationes in Psalmos* 98.9 (CCSL39:1386): "Spiritualiter intellegite quod locutus sum; non hoc corpus quod videtis, manducaturi estis, et bibituri illum sanguinem, quem fusuri sunt qui me crucifigent. Sacramentum aliquod vobis commendavi; spiritualiter intellectum vivificabit vos. Etsi necesse est illud visibiliter celebrari, oportet invisibiliter intellegi."

[149] Augustine, *De civitate Dei* 21.25 (CCSL 48:796: *WSA* 1/7:484–85): "sed re vera corpus Christi manducare et eius sanguinem bibere; hoc est enim in Christo manere, ut in illo et Christus."

[150] Cf. Josef Rupert Geiselmann, *Die Abendmahlslehre an der Wende der christlichen Spätantike zum Frühmittelalter* (Munich: Hueber, 1933), 169–261; Josef Andreas Jungmann, *The Mass of the Roman Rite*, trans. Francis A. Brunner, C.Ss.R., 2 vols. (New York: Benziger Brothers, 1951, 1955), 1:82.

Besides the unity of the ecclesial Body of Christ through sharing in the Eucharistic Body of Christ, Augustine emphasizes also the sacrificial character of the Eucharist. He regards self-surrender as the real sacrifice of Christians, who offer themselves in and through Christ, their High Priest. In the offerings that are placed upon the altar, the faithful are symbolically placed, too, along with all that they are.[151] In the Eucharist, the Church offers herself to God as a living sacrifice, indeed, she is offered in the Eucharist by Christ, her High Priest:

> It obviously follows that the whole redeemed city, that is, the congregation and fellowship of the saints, is offered to God as a universal sacrifice through the great priest who, in his passion, offered himself for us in the form of a servant, to the end that we might be the body of such a great head.... This is the sacrifice of Christians: *although many, one body in Christ.* And this is the sacrifice that the Church continually celebrates in the sacrament of the altar (which is well known to the faithful), where it is made plain to her that, in the offering she makes, she herself is offered.[152]

Yet the Eucharistic Sacrifice does not consist exclusively of the self-offering of the faithful. Augustine writes as follows about the presence of the sacrifice on the Cross in the Eucharist: "Has not Christ sacrificed once in himself, and yet in the mystery he is sacrificed for the people, not only during all the solemnities of Easter, but every day, and a person does not lie if, when asked, he replies that Christ is being sacrificed?"[153] The Church's sacrifice re-presents the sacrifice of

---

[151] Cf. Augustine, *Sermo* 227 (PL 38:1099f.; *WSA* 3/6:254–55).

[152] Augustine, *De civitate Dei* 10.6 (CCSL 47:279: *WSA* 1/6:254–55): "profecto efficitur, ut tota ipsa redempta civitas, hoc est congregatio societasque sanctorum, universale sacrificium offeratur Deo per sacerdotum magnum, qui etiam se ipsum obtulit in passione pro nobis, ut tanti capitis corpus essemus, secundum formam servi.... Hoc est sacrificium Christianorum: *multi unum corpus in Christo.* Quod etiam sacramento altaris fidelibus noto frequentat ecclesia, ubi ei demonstratur, quod in ea re, quam offert, ipsa offeratur." Cf. ibid., 10.20 (CCSL 47:294: *WSA* 1/6:328): "Per hoc et sacerdos est, ipse offerens, ipse et oblatio. Cuius rei sacramentum cotidianum esse voluit ecclesiae sacrificium, quae cum ipsius capitis erit, se ipsam per ipsum discet offerre." (At the same time, he [Christ] is also the priest, himself making the offering as well as himself being the offering. And he wanted the sacrifice offered by the Church to be a daily sacrament of his sacrifice, in which the Church, since it is the body of which he is the head, learns to offer its very self through him.)

[153] Augustine, *Epistola* 98.9 (CSEL 34/2:530f.; *WSA* 2/1:431): "Nonne semel immolatus est Christus in se ipso et tamen in sacramento non solum per omnes paschae sollemnitates sed omni die populis immolatur nec utique mentitur, qui interrogatus eum reponderit immolari?"

Christ's Body, in which Christ, the Head of the Body, sacrifices himself and is sacrificed bodily, so that the Church might learn to sacrifice herself through Christ.[154] The sacrifice that is offered is Christ himself (*Christus passus* [Christ who suffered and died]) as the oblation.

Thus Ambrose already describes the altar, under which the relics of the martyrs are buried, as "the place where Christ is the victim".[155] The offering of the oblation occurs through the Consecration: "For even if Christ does not seem to sacrifice (*offerre*) now, nevertheless he is sacrificed on earth when the Body of Christ is sacrificed: indeed, he himself is shown to offer sacrifice in us whose word sanctifies the sacrifice that is offered."[156] The prefiguration for the sacrifice of the Eucharist is the sacrifice of Melchizedek.[157] The Eucharist has the power to uproot sin: the Body and Blood of Christ are a remedy (*medicina*) against the power of sin and death.[158] In Communion, along with the Body and Blood of Christ, we receive anew again and again Christ, who shed his blood for our sins.[159]

In the writings of the Latin Church Fathers of the fifth century, *oblatio* and *sacrificium* are more closely connected with each other. Pope Leo I (440–461) speaks about the Eucharist as *sacrificii oblatio* [offering of sacrifice].[160] In a text by Pope Gregory the Great (590–601), which was cited again and again in the Middle Ages, he says: the sacrifice of the Eucharist reveals "to us mystically the death of the only-begotten Son" (*mortem Unigeniti per mysterium*), who although "living in himself immortal and incorruptible, he is again immolated for us in the mystery of the holy Sacrifice" (*pro nobis iterum immolatur*).[161] "For who of the faithful can have any doubt that at the

---

[154] Cf. Augustine, *De civitate Dei* 10.20 (CCSL 47:294; WSA 1/6:328).

[155] Ambrose, *Epistola* 72[22].13 (CSEL 83/3:134; NPNF-2 10:438b): "locus uti Christus est hostia."

[156] Augustine, *Enarrationes in Psalmos* 38.25 (PL 14:1102A-B): "quia etsi nunc Christus non videtur offerre, tamen ipse offertur in terris quando Christi corpus offertur: imo ipse offerre manifestatur in nobis, cuius sermo sanctificat sacrificium quod offertur."

[157] Cf. Augustine, *De sacramentis* 5.1 (FC 3:156f.; Thompson trans., 117).

[158] Cf. ibid., 4.28 (FC 3:152f.; Thompson trans., 116).

[159] Cf. ibid. On the structure of the celebration of Mass in Milan at the time of Ambrose, see Schmitz, *Gottesdienst im altchristlichen Mailand*, 316–431.

[160] Compare the overview about this expression in Leo Eizenhöfer, "Das Opfer der Gläubigen in den Sermones Leos des Grossen", in *Die Messe in der Glaubensverkündigung*, 2nd ed., ed. F. X. Arnold and B. Fischer (Freiburg: Herder, 1953), 79–107.

[161] Gregory I, *Dialogi* 4.58 (PL 77:425; FOC 39:272–73).

moment of the immolation, at the sound of the priest's voice, the heavens stand open and the choirs of angels are present at the mystery of Jesus Christ. There at the altar the lowliest is united with the most sublime, earth is joined to heaven, the visible and invisible somehow merge into one."[162]

In the sacrifice of the altar, Jesus Christ offers himself in a mysterious way to the Father, so that the work of redemption might be accomplished in us. "For as often as we offer to [Christ] the sacrifice of his Passion, we renew his Passion for our forgiveness."[163] Gregory the Great has in mind no "repetition" of Christ's sacrifice on the Cross, as though Christ suffered again in the sacrifice of the Eucharist. The pope emphasizes the sacramental presence of Christ's sacrifice on the Cross in the offering of the Eucharist.[164] The patristic texts just cited show that the Church's sacrifice consists not only in the memorial of Christ's sacrifice on the Cross and in the self-offering of the faithful, but in the offering of Christ as an oblation.[165] The idea that the Church is the subject that offers Christ's sacrifice was not just a later development in the early Middle Ages.

What did the celebration of the Eucharist look like formally in Augustine's time? After the bishop's homily, the deacon's cry resounded: *versus ad dominum*. This meant that the faithful and the bishop turned around *versus orientem* [to face East].[166] Augustine

---

[162] Ibid. (*PL* 77:425f.; FOC 39:273): "Quis enim fidelium habere dubium possit, in ipsa immolationis hora ad sacerdotis vocem coelos aperiri, in illo Iesu Christi mysterio angelorum chorus adesse, sumis ima sociari, terrena coelestibus iungi, unumque ex visibilibus atque invisibilibus fieri?"

[163] Gregory I, *Homiliarum in Evangelia* 2.37.7 (*PL* 76:1279): "Nam quoties ei hostiam suae passionis offerimus, toties nobis ad absolutionem nostram passionem illius reparamus."

[164] Cf. Gregory I, *Dialogi* 4.57 (*PL* 77:425f.; FOC 39:270–71): Pope Gregory the Great was convinced not only that the work of our salvation is accomplished through the offering of the sacrifice of the Eucharist, but also that miracles are worked in the earthly realm, for instance, the loosing of physical bonds.

[165] The judgment of Stephan Winter, *Eucharistische Gegenwart: Liturgische Redehandlung im Spiegel mittelalterlicher und analytischer Sprachtheorie*, Ratio fidei 13 (Regensburg: Pustet, 2002), 25, is inaccurate when he says "all offertory statements in which the ecclesial communion is the subject of the action ... always have as their object the *sacrificium laudis* [sacrifice of praise] or *bread and wine*, but never the Body and Blood of Jesus Christ" (emphasis added).

[166] Cf. Martin Klöckener, "Die Bedeutung der neu entdeckten Augustinus-Predigten (*Sermones Dolbeau*) für die liturgiegeschichtliche Forschung", in *Augustin prédicateur (395–411): Actes du Colloque International de Chantilly (5–7 Septembre 1996)*, ed. G. Madec, Collection des Études Augustiniennes, Série Antiquité 159 (Paris: Institut d'études augustiennes, 1998), 153f. (cf. Augustin d'Hippo, *Vingt-six sermons au peuple d'afrique*, ed. Dolbeau, 1996).

presupposes that at least parts of the Eucharistic Prayer addressed to the Father, including the words of institution, were spoken by the celebrant from memory (*memoriter tenere*).[167] Permanent components of the Eucharistic Prayer were the introductory dialogue, a prayer of praise and thanksgiving at the beginning (Preface), and the words of institution. One remarkable feature is the use of the singular *Sursum cor* (lift up your heart) in the introductory dialogue (instead of *sursum corda*).[168] Augustine gives us no information about the wording of the anamnesis. The *Sanctus* was not yet a component of the Canon in Augustine's time. In Africa, the *Sanctus* is attested for the first time in a *professio fidei* (profession of faith) from the year 484.[169] There is no sure reference to an epiclesis, either.[170] Instead, Augustine mentions an offertory prayer that thematizes the Church's self-offering.[171] The verbs *benedicere* and *sanctificare*[172] indicate the two central elements of the Canon: thanksgiving and the Consecration of the gifts. Through the "sanctifying" word of the presider at the Eucharistic celebration, bread and wine become the Body and Blood of Christ. Here Augustine understands the Eucharistic elements as real symbols of Christ and, indeed, of the whole Christ (*totus Christus*), Head and Body.[173] A homily ascribed to Augustine speaks about the efficacy of the words over the bread and wine.[174]

The ordained priest who pronounces the Eucharistic Prayer does not consecrate by his own power. Christ, the incarnate Logos, is the one who sanctifies the gifts of bread and wine: "That bread which you can see on the altar, sanctified by the word of God, is the Body of Christ. The cup, or rather what the cup contains, sanctified by

---

[167] Cf. Augustine, *Contra litteras Petiliani* 2.30.68 (CSEL 52:58). On the interpretation of the passage, see Martin Klöckener, "Das eucharistische Hochgebet bei Augustinus: Zu Stand und Aufgaben der Forschung", in *Signum pietatis*, Festschrift C. P. Mayer, ed. A. Zumkeller, O.S.A., Cassiciacum 40 (Würzburg: Augustinus-Verlag, 1989), 474–76.

[168] Cf. Klöckener, "Bedeutung der neu entdeckten Augustinus-Predigten", 150–52.

[169] Cf. Klöckener, "Eucharistische Hochgebet bei Augustinus", 485.

[170] Cf. ibid., 489–92.

[171] Cf. ibid., 492.

[172] Cf. Augustine, *Epistula* 149.16 (CSEL 44:362: *WSA* 2/2:368): "orationes, cum benedicitur et sanctificatur".

[173] Cf. Augustine, *Sermo* 227 (*PL* 38:1099f.; *WSA* 3/6:255). On this topic, cf. Athanase Sage, "L'Eucharistie dans la pensée de saint Augustin", *Revue des études augustiniennes* 15 (1969): 222–27.

[174] Cf. *Sermo Denis* 6.3 (Germain Morin, *Miscellanea Agostiniana* 1 [Rome: Typis Polyglottis Vaticanis, 1930], 14–18).

the word of God, is the Blood of Christ."[175] It is generally acknowledged that the Eucharistic Prayer in Augustine's writings had its own
formula of Consecration. The words of institution can be reconstructed approximately by means of various sermons: "Hoc est corpus
meum.... Hoc est sanguis (meus) qui pro multis effusus est in remissionem peccatorum" (This is my Body.... This is my Blood which
is poured out for many for the forgiveness of sins).[176] In Augustine's
time, the words of Consecration existed in a set form in North
Africa; this is not certain, however, with regard to the institutional
narrative.[177] The *verba testamenti* are not featured as prominently by
Augustine as by Ambrose. Augustine emphasizes more strongly the
unity of the Eucharistic Prayer. In his work *De Trinitate*, he writes:
"that which is taken from the fruits of the earth, and consecrated by
mystic prayers, and taken by us for our spiritual salvation in memory
of what the Lord suffered for us."[178]

C. Eucharistic Prayers: Traditio Apostolica, Ambrose

Traditio Apostolica: The first complete Eucharistic Prayer is found
in the Latin and Ethiopian tradition of the *Traditio Apostolica*
(Ἀποστολικὴ παράδοσις). Manuscripts of this work date from the first
half of the third century to the late fourth century.[179] The tradition

---

[175] Augustine, *Sermo* 227 (*PL* 38:1099: *WSA* 3/6:254): "Panis ille quem videtis in altari
sanctificatur per verbum Dei, Corpus est Christi. Calix ille immo quod habet calix, sanctifi-
catum per verbum Dei, sanguis est Christi."

[176] Cf. Klöckener, "Eucharistische Hochgebet bei Augustinus", 485–89; Klöckener,
"Eucharistische Hochgebet in der nordafrikanischen Liturgie", 91–93. Without stating reasons, Volker Henning Drecoll, "Liturgie bei Augustinus", in *Augustin Handbuch*, ed. V. H.
Drecoll (Tübingen: Mohr Siebeck, 2007), 227f., finds it doubtful that the words of institution
had a place in the Eucharistic Canon used by Augustine.

[177] Cf. Klöckener, "Eucharistische Hochgebet bei Augustinus", 487.

[178] Augustine, *De Trinitate* 3.1.10 (CCSL 50:136; *WSA* 1/5:154): "quod ex fructibus terrae
acceptum et prece mystica consecratum rite sumimus ad salutem spiritualem in memoriam
pro nobis dominicae passionis."

[179] Cf. Paul F. Bradshaw, Maxwell E. Johnson, and L. Edward Phillips, *The Apostolic Tradition: A Commentary*, Hermeia Series, ed. H. W. Altridge (Minneapolis: Fortress Press, 2002),
1–6 and 13–15; Christoph Markschies, "Wer schrieb das sogenannte 'Traditio apostolica':
Neue Hypothesen und Beobachtungen zu einer kaum lösbaren Frage aus der altkirchlichen
Literaturgeschichte", in *Tauffragen und Bekenntnis: Studien zur sogenannten "Traditio Apostolica",
zu den "Interrogationes de fide" und dem "Römischen Glaubensbekenntnis"*, ed. W. Kinzig et al.,
Arbeiten zur Kirchengeschichte 74 (Berlin and New York: Walter de Gruyter, 1999), 1–74.

history points toward the East.[180] Enrico Mazza suspects that the
Eucharistic Prayer of the *Traditio Apostolica* is dependent on the Easter homilies of the second to the fourth centuries (Melito of Sardis,
and so on). The original Greek text of the *Traditio Apostolica* can be
reconstructed only with the help of translations and adaptations. The
most complete manuscript is a Latin text from the late fifth century.
The translation, however, is probably older than written copy (late
fourth century).[181] The Eucharistic Prayer of the *Traditio Apostolica* could have originated in the West Syrian region.[182] The dating
of the Eucharistic Prayer handed down by the *Traditio Apostolica* to
the first half of the fourth century is the most probable one, since the
first epicleses invoking the Spirit developed at that time in the Syrian
region.[183] The decision in the course of the Vatican reform of the
Missal to make the Eucharistic Prayer of the *Traditio Apostolica*
the foundation of the new Eucharistic Prayer II was based on the
attribution at the time of the Eucharistic Prayer to the Roman tradition of the liturgy. But the author of the *Traditio Apostolica* is in all
probability not Hippolytus of Rome.[184]

The Eucharistic Prayer of the *Traditio Apostolica*[185] has the following structure: after the deacon has brought the offering (προσφορά) for

[180] Cf. Wilhelm Geerlings, "Einleitung zur Traditio Apostolica", in *Didache: Zwölf-Apostel-
Lehre: Apostolische Überlieferung*, FC 1 (Freiburg: Herder, 1991), 148.

[181] Cf. ibid., 150.

[182] Cf. Matthieu Smyth, "The Anaphora of the So-Called 'Apostolic Tradition' and the
Roman Eucharistic Prayer", in *Issues in Eucharistic Praying in East and West: Essays in Liturgical
and Theological Analysis*, ed. M. E. Johnson (Collegeville, Minn.: Liturgical Press, 2010), 87–94.

[183] Cf. Edward C. Ratcliff, "The Sanctus and the Pattern of the Early Anaphora", *Journal of
Ecclesiastical History* 1 (1950): 29–36, 125–34; Smyth, "Anaphora of the So-Called 'Apostolic
Tradition'", 94.

[184] Cf. John F. Baldovin, "Eucharistic Prayer II: History of the Latin Text and Rite", in *A
Commentary on the Order of Mass of the Roman Missal*, foreword by Roger Cardinal Mahoney,
ed. E. Foley (Collegeville, Minn.: Liturgical Press, 2001), 311: "Therefore, it is erroneous to
make sweeping generalizations about the anaphora such as: this is *the Roman* anaphora of the
early third century. It is fairly clear that the author was not the early third-century Roman pres-
byter Hippolytus. It is not altogether clear that the document is Roman at all." Martin Stuflesser, *Eucharistie: Liturgische Feier und theologische Erschliessung* (Regensburg: Pustet, 2013), 50,
advocates the view that the Eucharistic Prayer comes from Hippolytus and thus is of Roman
origin, without giving more detailed reasons for it. In the Canon of the *Traditio Apostolica*,
Stuflesser sees a theologically more convincing Roman Eucharistic Prayer in comparison with
the "Canon Romanus".

[185] For an extensive analysis, see Jeremy Driscoll, *Theology at the Eucharistic Table: Master
Themes in the Theological Tradition* (Leominster: Gracewing, 2005).

the Eucharist, the bishop begins the prayer of thanksgiving with an opening dialogue: "The Lord be with you." And the people respond: "And with your spirit." "Hearts on high." "We have them to the Lord." "Let us give thanks." "It is fitting and right."[186] This opening corresponds to the introduction of the Jewish prayer after meals, which starts with "Let us bless/praise the Everlasting One, our God", to which those present respond: "Blessed/Praised be the Everlasting One, our God."[187] After the opening follows an initial anamnesis of the coming, Passion, and death of Jesus:

> And then he shall continue thus: We give thanks to you, God, through your beloved child Jesus Christ, whom, in the last times, you sent to us as savior and redeemer and angel of your will (cf. Is 9:5 LXX), who is your inseparable Word through whom you made all things and who was well pleasing to you. You sent him from heaven into the womb of a virgin, and he was conceived and made flesh in the womb and shown to be your Son, born of the Holy Spirit and the virgin. He fulfilled your will and won for you a holy people, opening wide his hands when he suffered that he might set free from suffering those who believed in you.[188]

After that, the anamnesis is continued with the memory of Christ's descent into the underworld and his Resurrection; then the account of the institution follows:[189]

> When he was handed over to voluntary suffering, in order to dissolve death and break the chains of the devil and harrow hell and illuminate the just and fix a boundary and manifest the resurrection, he took bread, and, giving thanks to you, he said [accipiens panem gratias tibi agens dixit]: take, eat, this is my body [corpus meum], which will be broken for you [confringetur]" (cf. Lk 22:19; 1 Cor 11:24). Likewise

---

[186] Traditio Apostolica 4 (FC 1:223); English translation by Alistair C. Stewart (2nd ed., 2015), 77.

[187] Mishna Berakot 7, 3. Cf. Peter von der Osten-Sacken, "Von den jüdischen Wurzeln des christlichen Gottesdienstes", in Liturgie als Theologie, ed. W. Homolka (Berlin: Frank & Timme, 2005), 152f.

[188] Traditio Apostolica 4 (FC 1:223, 225; Stewart trans., 77–78).

[189] The words of institution are found only in the Latin and Ethiopian versions of the Traditio Apostolica.

with the cup saying: this is my blood [*sanguis meus*] which is poured
out for you [*pro vobis effunditur*]. Whenever you do this, you perform
my commemoration (cf. Lk 22:20; 1 Cor 11:25).[190]

The future tense *corpus meum* ... *confringetur* is found also in the
Eucharistic Prayer recorded by Ambrose of Milan.[191] *Sanguis meus* ...
pro vobis effunditur has its parallel in the long version of the institution
account in Luke. The concluding command to remember recalls
the account of the Last Supper in Paul, who records the command
to remember in the case of the bread, also. In contrast to Ambrose's
version, the Eucharistic Prayer of the *Traditio Apostolica* does not say
that Jesus handed bread and wine to his disciples.[192] After the words
of institution follows another anamnesis of Jesus' death and Resurrection, connected with the offering (oblation) of the bread and chalice, the prayer for the sending of the Holy Spirit upon the Eucharistic
gifts (epiclesis), and a concluding doxology, which is affirmed by the
congregation with their "Amen".

As in the Roman Canon, the connection between *memoria* and
oblatio is found also in the special anamnesis of the Eucharistic Prayer
of the *Traditio Apostolica*:

> Remembering therefore his death and resurrection, we offer you bread
> and cup [*Memores igitur mortis et resurrectionis eius offerimus tibi panem et
> calicem*], giving thanks to you because you have held us worthy to stand
> before you and minister to you as priest. And we ask that you should
> send your Holy Spirit on the offering of the Holy Church, gathering
> [her] into one, may you grant to all the saints who receive for the full-
> ness of the Holy Spirit, for the confirmation of their faith in truth, that
> we may praise and glorify you through your child Jesus Christ, through
> whom be glory and honor to you, with the Holy Spirit in your holy
> church, both now and to the ages of the ages. Amen.[193]

---

[190] *Traditio Apostolica* 4 (FC 1:225, 227; Stewart trans., 78).

[191] Cf. Ambrose, *De sacramentis* 4.21 (FC 3:148f.; Thompson trans., 113). "*Take, and eat ye
all of this; for this is my body, which shall be broken for many.*"

[192] Cf. Paul F. Bradshaw, *Eucharistic Origins*, Alcuin Club Collections 80 (London: Oxford
University Press, 2004), 19f. Since Bradshaw advocates a late dating of the *Traditio Apostolica*,
he sees in the Sacramentary of Serapion (mid-fourth century) the earliest testimony for the
institutional narrative in traditional anaphora.

[193] *Traditio Apostolica* 4 (FC 1:227; Stewart, 78, 79n.).

The Eucharistic Prayer of the *Traditio Apostolica* has only one epiclesis. The Spirit invoked upon the bread and wine should fill those who receive the oblation, gather them into unity, and strengthen them in faith. Other Eucharistic Prayers have a preceding epiclesis with the petition that the Spirit might change the gifts of bread and wine into the Body and Blood of Christ.[194] This epiclesis, however, must always be seen together with the following epiclesis. For the transformation of the oblations into the Body and Blood of Christ occurs with a view to Communion.

At first the presider at the celebration of the Eucharist formulated the great prayer of thanksgiving in a relatively free manner using a preexisting basic model.[195] But soon the Synod of Hippo (393) prescribed that new Eucharistic Prayers must be submitted in advance for a joint examination by the bishops.[196] After the end of the fourth century, the wording of the Eucharistic Prayers was fixed more exactly, above all to protect against the heresies with which the Church increasingly had to contend, whereby there were differences from one local Church to the next. The early Sacramentaries show that for the celebration of the Latin Mass, a great variety of Prefaces existed at first. In the later Sacramentaries and Missals, only a small number of them remained. Not until the Vatican reform of the Missal was the corpus of Prefaces extended again.

The Ambrosian Canon: For the Roman liturgical tradition, besides the *Canon Romanus*,[197] the Canon recorded by Ambrose should be taken into account. In *De sacramentis*, the bishop of Milan cites parts of a Canon that correspond thematically to the prayer segments from *Quam oblationem* to *Supplices te rogamus* of the Roman Canon. They likewise bear the stamp of Roman legal language and show a familiarity with the pagan-Roman style of prayer.[198] The Ambrosian

---

[194] Both forms of epiclesis are found in Theodore of Mopsuestia, *Catechetical Homilies* 16.12f. (FC 17/2:431f.). The "epiclesis of transformation" in the anaphora of the Divine Liturgy of St. John Chrysostom is very precise (μεταβαλὼν τῷ πνεύματι σου τῷ ἁγίῳ [changing them by your Holy Spirit]).

[195] Cf. Achim Budde, *Die ägyptische Basilios-Anaphora: Text—Kommentar—Geschichte*, Jerusalemer theologisches Forum 7 (Münster: Aschendorff, 2004), who demonstrates this using the example of the anaphora of St. Basil.

[196] Cf. Synod of Hippo, canon 21.

[197] Cf. below, chap. 4, section 2.

[198] Cf. Schmitz, *Gottesdienst im altchristlichen Mailand*, 388f.

Eucharistic Prayer may have originated in the North African region. It is more probable that it is an early form of the Roman Canon.[199] For the bishop of Milan was thoroughly familiar with the liturgy in Rome.[200] He emphasizes explicitly that he follows the Roman Church *in liturgicis* [in liturgical matters].[201] The author and place of origin of the Ambrosian Canon, however, cannot be determined with complete certainty on the basis of the sources now available.[202] The explanations of the Canon given by Ambrose, as it became clear, are centered on the mystery of the Consecration.[203] "Wilt thou know that it is consecrated by heavenly words? Hear what the words are. The priest speaks. 'Make for us,' he says, 'this oblation [*Fac nobis hanc oblationem*] approved, ratified, reasonable, acceptable, seeing that it is the figure of the body and blood [*quod est figura corporis et sanguinis*] of our Lord Jesus Christ.' "[204]

After the request for blessing, the institutional narrative follows:

"... The day before he suffered *took bread* in his holy hands, and *looked up to heaven* to thee, holy Father, almighty, everlasting God, and *giving thanks, he blessed* (*gratias agens benedixit*), *brake, and* having broken, delivered it to his apostles and *to his disciples, saying, Take, and eat* ye all of this; for *this is my body, which shall be broken for many* [*pro multis confringetur*]. *Likewise* also *after supper*, the day before he suffered, he *took the cup, looked up to heaven* to thee, holy Father, almighty, everlasting God, and *giving thanks*, blessed it [*gratias agens benedixit*] and delivered it to his apostles and to his disciples, *saying, Take, and drink ye all of*

[199] Thus Brian D. Spinks, "The Roman Canon Missae", in *Prex Eucharistica*, vol. 3/1:132. Joseph Schmitz, "Canon Romanus", in *Prex Eucharistica*, vol. 3/1:281, sees in the Ambrosian Canon, not a preliminary form, but rather an additional form of the *Canon Romanus*.

[200] Cf. Ambrose, *De sacramentis* 3.5 (FC 3:120f.; Thompson trans., 98).

[201] Ibid. (FC 3:122f.; Thompson trans., 98–99). It is not very likely that a Greek-Egyptian tradition underlay the Ambrosian Eucharistic Prayer, as Mazza supposes. Cf. Mazza, *L'anafora eucaristica*, 268–71; Mazza, "Alle origini del canone romano", *Cristianesimo nella storia* 13 (1992): 1–46.

[202] Klaus Gamber, *Missa Romensis: Beiträge zur frühen römischen Liturgie und zu den Anfängen des Missale Romanum* (Regensburg: Pustet, 1970), 59, 73, speculates that there are traces of the North African Eucharistic Prayer in the Ambrosian Canon. At the time of Ambrose and Augustine, the Eucharistic Prayer was still spoken or sung aloud.

[203] Cf. Joseph Schmitz, "Einleitung", in Ambrosius, *De Saramentis, De Mysteriis—Über die Sakramente, Über die Mysterien*, Fontes Christiani 3 (Freiburg: Herder, 1990), 57.

[204] Ambrose, *De sacramentis* 4.21 (FC 3:148f.; Thompson trans., 113).

this; for this is my blood." Observe all those expressions. Those words
are the Evangelists' up to *Take,* whether the body or the blood. After
that they are the words of Christ; *Take, and drink ye all of this; for this
is my blood....* Then learn how great is the sacrament. See what he
says: *As often as ye do this, so often will ye make a memorial of me until I
come again.*[205]

The third part of the Eucharistic Canon is made up of the anamnesis and the post-consecratory prayer of offering.

And the priest says: Therefore having in remembrance [*Ergo memores*]
his most glorious passion and resurrection from the dead and ascension
into heaven, we offer [*offerimus*] to thee this spotless offering [*immaculata hostia*], reasonable offering [*rationabilis hostia*], unbloody offering
[*incruenta hostia*], this holy bread and cup of eternal life: and we ask
and pray [*petimus et precamus*] that thou wouldst receive this oblation
[*oblationem*] on thy altar on high by the hands of thy angels, as thou
didst vouchsafe to receive the presents of thy righteous servant Abel,
and the sacrifice of our patriarch Abraham, and that which the high
priest, Melchizedek offered to thee.[206]

The core elements of the Eucharistic Prayer are the petition for the
sanctification of the gifts, the institutional narrative with the words
of Consecration, the anamnesis of the Passion, death, and Resurrection of Christ, the post-consecratory offering, and the petition
for acceptance. In the petition for the transformation *Fac oblationem,*
as compared with the Roman Canon, the adjectives *benedictam* and
ratam are missing in the description of the oblation. Corresponding
to the *oblatio rationabilis* (λογικὴ θυσία) is the *rationabilis hostia* after the
Consecration. The expression *quod est figura corporis et sanguinis* is to be
understood not only typologically but sacramentally.[207] It has in view
the real figure of the sacrament of the Body and Blood of Christ. In
this sense, Tertullian also speaks about *figura corporis* in connection

---

[205] Ibid., 4.21–22, 26 (FC 3:148f.; Thompson trans., 113–14, 115).

[206] Ibid., 4.27 (FC 3:152f.; Thompson trans., 115–16).

[207] Typologically, Ambrose uses the expression *figura,* for example, in reference to the
manna as a prefiguration of the Eucharistic body. Cf. Ambrose, *De sacramentis* 4.24 (FC
3:105f.; Thompson trans., 114); Ambrose, *De mysteriis* 49 (FC 3:242f.; NPNF-2 10:324a).

with the *verba testamenti*: "Hoc est corpus meum, dicendo, id est figura corporis mei."[208]

According to Jungmann, the expression *quod est figura corporis et
sanguinis* should be understood as follows: the demonstrative *quod* is
used in the Old Latin sense of *quae* and therefore refers to the *oblatio
rationabilis*.[209] *Figura* may also be the root of the term *transfigurare* to
describe the change in the Eucharistic elements; although the latter term does not appear in *De sacramentis*, Ambrose does use it in
De fide ad Gratianum (378–380).[210] In the context of the Ambrosian
understanding of consecration, the expression *figura corporis et sanguinis* refers, not to the elements that have not yet been consecrated,
but rather to the oblations that have already been consecrated.[211] In
patristic writings, the term *figura* is used in a real-symbolic sense for
the sacrament of the Eucharist. Only in the early Middle Ages was
this no longer self-evident, as the Carolingian controversy over the
Eucharist shows.[212]

Like the Roman Canon, Ambrose, too, emphasizes the connection between *memores* and *offerimus*. The command to remember
underscores the significance of the sacrament of the Eucharist, in

---

[208] Tertullian, *Adversus Marcionem* 4.40.2 (CCSL 1:656: ANF 3:418a): "Saying, 'This is my
body', that is, the figure of my body."

[209] Cf. Jungmann, *Mass of the Roman Rite*, 2:188–90. His interpretation was originally
advocated by Odo Casel, too (cf. Casel, "Quam oblationem", *Jahrbuch für Liturgiewissenschaft* 2 [1922]: 100). Later he renounced it and viewed the prayer of petition *Fac oblationem*
merely as a request for acceptance (cf. Casel, "Ein orientalisches Kultwort in abendländischer
Umschmelzung", *Jahrbuch für Liturgiewissenschaft* 11 (1931): 12f.; so, too, Tymister, "Epiklese
und Opfer", 155. Hans-Joachim Schulz, "Ökumenische Aspekte der Darbringungsaussagen
in der erneuerten römischen und in der byzantinischen Liturgie", *Archiv für Liturgiewissenschaft*
19 (1977): 7–28, understands the *quod* in the prayer *Fac oblationem*, not in a relative, but in a
consecutive sense.

[210] Cf. Ambrose, *De fide* 4.10.124 (FC 47/2:552). This work is a treatise against Arianism
for Emperor Gratian.

[211] Some authors disagree: Edward Foley, *From Age to Age: How Christians Have Celebrated
the Eucharist*, 2nd ed. (Collegeville, Minn.: Liturgical Press, 2008), 122; Reinhard Messner, *Die
Messreform Martin Luthers und die Eucharistie der Alten Kirche: Ein Beitrag zu einer systematischen
Liturgiewissenschaft* (Innsbruck: Tyrolia, 1989), 88, 90f. Messner's commentary on the Canon
in *De sacramentis* proceeds independently of the understanding of consecration that Ambrose
illustrated by means of the Canon that he cites. Only in this way can Messner interpret
the prayer segment *petimus et precamus*, which corresponds to the *Supplices* of the Ambrosian
Canon, as a "petition for transformation". Schmitz, *Gottesdienst im altchristlichen Mailand*, 402–4,
gives no explanation for the *Fac oblationem* in his commentary on the Ambrosian Canon.

[212] See below, chap. 4, section 1.

which we celebrate the memorial of Christ's Passion, his Resurrection from the dead, and his Ascension. The petition for acceptance is connected with the prayer *Supra quae*, which recalls the sacrifices of Abel, Abraham, and Melchizedek.[213] The prayer segment *petimus et precamus* corresponds to the *Supplices te rogamus* in the Roman Canon. The gifts that we offer are the spotless, spiritual, and unbloody sacrifice, the holy bread and the cup of eternal life.[214] Ambrose understands this to mean the Body and the Blood of Christ, since for him the consecration of bread and wine occurs through the *verba testamenti*. About the other parts of the Canon Ambrose gives the following information in another passage: "Praises (*laus*) are offered to God, prayer (*oratio*) is asked for the people, for kings, and the rest (cf. 1 Tim 2:1f.)."[215]

[213] Cf. Zenon of Verona, *Tractatus* 1.3.5 (CCSL 22:25): "Quid, quod Melchisedech, summus ipse sacerdos deo acceptissimus huius fuit cicatricis ignarus?" In his statement about the high priest Melchizedek, Zenon (d. 371/372) is closer to the Roman Canon than the Ambrosian Canon is. Many see this as an indication that the Canon recorded by Ambrose is not an early version of the Roman Canon. Cf. Gordon P. Jeanes, ed., *The Origins of the Roman Rite*, ed. and trans. G. P. Jeanes, Alcuin Club, and the Group for the Renewal of Worship 20/Grove Liturgical Study 67 (Bramcote, Nottingham: Grove Books, 1991), 29.

[214] Cf. Ambrose, *De sacramentis* 4.27 (FC 3:152f.; Thompson trans., 115–16).

[215] Ibid., 4.14 (FC 3:142f.; Thompson trans., 110): "laus deo, defertur oratio, petitur pro populo, pro regibus, pro ceteris."

Chapter IV

MISSA ROMANA

The Roman Mass until the Turn of the Second Millennium

In the Fourth Gospel, Jesus says that the true holy place is to be found where God is worshipped in spirit and in truth (cf. Jn 4:23). For Christians, the temple of God is not a visible building for worship but, rather, the Body of Christ. "Do you not know that you are God's temple [ναός] and that God's Spirit dwells in you? If any one destroys God's temple, God will destroy him. For God's temple is holy [ἅγιος], and that temple you are" (1 Cor 3:16f.; cf. Eph 2:22). God's temple is therefore incompatible with idols (cf. 2 Cor 6:16). Since the true holy place is not a limited divine sphere but, rather, the entire Christian community, the celebration of the Eucharist is not bound to a particular holy place, and the worship space as such is therefore not called the precincts of a temple (τέμενος), either. Yet from the beginning, the Christian community gathered for the Eucharist in remodeled rooms. At first, larger rooms in the houses of members of the community served this purpose; later, church buildings.

Individual church buildings did exist already before Emperor Constantine the Great (d. 337). Yet the basilica was the first church structure, and gradually it had its own influence on the shape of the liturgy (Jerusalem, Rome, Constantinople, and so on).[1] In the Romance languages, *ecclesia, église*, became the accepted term to designate the church building. In other languages, the name for the church building (κυριακόν, *Kirche*, church) was applied by extension to the gathering of

---

[1] Cf. Andreas Heinz, *Lebendiges Erbe: Beiträge zur abendländischen Liturgie- und Frömmigkeitsgeschichte* (Tübingen and Basel: Francke, 2010), 36.

the faithful. Since the church building is the visible space for the living temple of God, its arrangement reflects the inner organization of the Church. In Orthodox church architecture, the space for the faithful between the *narthex* (vestibule) and the altar area is designated the *naos* (temple).

For the celebration of the Eucharist, which from the second century on is called *oblatio* (offering), but also *sacrificium* (sacrifice), the name *missa* appears for the first time in the fourth century in Africa, initially to designate the Mass of the catechumens.[2] *Oblatio* and *dominicum sacrificium* or *cena dominica* [Lord's supper] remained the most commonly used terms for the celebration of the Eucharist until the sixth century.[3] Originally *missa* meant dismissal (from *dimissio*/ ἀπόλυσις).[4] The literal meaning of the summons *Ite, missa est* is "Go, this is the dismissal."[5] Even before the sixth century, *missa* took on also the meaning of *oblatio*/προσφορά. Soon *missa* was also used in the sense of prayer.[6] In the African region, the Eucharist was simply called *sacrificium* for a long time.

Already in the early Church, besides the Sunday Eucharist, there were also occasional celebrations of the Eucharist, for instance at the grave of the deceased or for smaller groups in private houses.[7] The Eucharistic bread served the faithful at first also as an apotropaic sign (protective sign) against illnesses, vices, and sins. The practice of Communion in the home on work days persisted in some cases into the seventh century. Nevertheless, the concern that the Eucharist, once taken home, might fall into the hands of sectarians led quite

---

[2] Cf. Council of Carthage (397), canon 84.

[3] Cf. Klaus Gamber, *Liturgie übermorgen: Gedanken zur Geschichte und Zukunft des Gottesdienstes* (Freiburg: Herder, 1966), 107.

[4] Cf. Ambrose, *Epistola* 76.4 (CSEL 82/3:100); Ambrose, *Itinerarium Egeriae* 24.2; 25.1 and 10 (FC 20:226f.; 234f., 240f.). The *Itinerarium Egeriae* is a report of the Spanish pilgrim Egeria (or "Etheria") about the liturgy in Jerusalem. The account of the pilgrimage covers the time from December 16, 383, to June 384.

[5] Cf. Franz-Josef Dölger, "Zu den Zeremonien der Messliturgie III. 'Ite missa est' in kultur- und sprachgeschichtlicher Bedeutung", *Antike und Christentum* 6 (1950): 81–132; Josef Andreas Jungmann, "Von der 'Eucharistia' zur 'Messe'", *Zeitschrift für katholische Theologie* 89 (1967): 29–40.

[6] Cf. Klaus Gamber, *Missa Romensis: Beiträge zur frühen römischen Liturgie und zu den Anfängen des Missale Romanum* (Regensburg: Pustet, 1970), 183–86.

[7] See the sources listed in Robert F. Taft, *Beyond East and West: Problems in Liturgical Understanding*, 2nd ed. (Rome: Edizioni Orientalia Christiana, 2001), 78.

early in many places to the prohibition of Communion outside the church, for example at the Synod of Saragossa (379–381).[8]

Blessed bread, as opposed to Eucharistic bread, was called the *eulogia*.[9] In Orthodox Churches to this day, the *eulogia* is distributed at the end of the Divine Liturgy. Even persons who are not in full ecclesial communion can receive it. The first prohibition against *agape* celebrations was at the Synod of Laodicaea (380).[10] The prohibition was confirmed by the Synods of Hippo (393)[11] and Carthage (419).[12] Since the essence of the Eucharist from the beginning was considered to be the consecration of the bread and cup and the sacramental participation in the Body and Blood of Christ and not the meal of satiation, the Eucharist did not lose its specific form as a sacred meal when it was separated from the meal of satiation. The Eucharistic meal itself is not a meal of satiation but, rather, the Supper of the Lord.

Unlike the celebration of Baptism and of Reconciliation, the celebration of the Eucharist in Christian antiquity was not the object of theological controversies. It was, however, a concurrent topic during the Christological disputes of the fourth and fifth centuries.[13] Thus, for instance, the decision against Arianism led to the modification of the doxologies. Traditionally liturgical prayers were addressed to God the Father, *through* the Son *in* or *with* the Holy Spirit. Since such doxologies fell under the suspicion of subordinationism after the Council of Nicaea (325), doxologies such as "Glory be to the Father with the Son together with the Holy Spirit" or "The Father is worshipped with the Son and (with) the Holy Spirit" were used more and more often. Basil of Caesarea (d. 379) advocated, besides the doxology to the Father "through the Son in the Holy Spirit" that had been customary until then, the doxology to the Father "with the Son together with the Holy Spirit".[14] Following the decision of the Council of Nicaea, liturgical

---

[8] Cf. Nathan Mitchell, *Cult and Controversy: The Worship of the Eucharist outside the Mass*, Studies in the Reformed Rites of the Catholic Church 4 (Collegeville, Minn.: Liturgical Press, 1990), 18f.

[9] Cf. *Traditio Apostolica* 26 (FC 1:278f.; Stewart-Sykes trans., 137).

[10] Cf. Synod of Laodicaea, canon 28.

[11] Cf. Synod of Hippo, canon 29.

[12] Cf. Synod of Carthage, canon 42.

[13] On this subject, see Alfons Fürst, *Die Liturgie der Alten Kirche: Geschichte und Theologie* (Münster: Aschendorff, 2008), 93–96.

[14] Cf. Basil of Caesarea, *De Spiritu Sancto* 1.3 (FC 12:78f.).

prayers were increasingly addressed to the Son as well. Nevertheless, there was clear opposition to this as early as the end of the fourth century. Thus the Synod of Hippo (393) decides: "During ministry at the altar the prayer should always be directed to the Father."[15] Unlike those in many Eastern liturgies, the orations in the Roman liturgy until the ninth century were addressed to the Father. From Gaul spread orations addressed to Christ with the concluding formula, "Lord Jesus Christ, who livest and reignest with God the Father". In the Roman liturgy, however, they remained the exception.

A. The Celebration of Mass in Rome until Late Antiquity

Despite various attempts at reconstruction, the beginnings of the celebration of the Mass in Rome remain for the most part obscure. The predominant language of the liturgy was at first Greek. While in North Africa the Latin language became widespread in the liturgy as early as the turn of the third century, Greek persisted as the liturgical language in Rome well into the fourth century.[16] Latin first became accepted in Rome for the celebration of Baptism, while for the Eucharist Greek was still used extensively until the end of the third century.[17] At the latest under Pope Damasus I (366–384), Latin became established here, too, as the liturgical language;[18] as opposed to the language spoken by the people, this was an elevated cultic language, so that we can speak only in a qualified sense about a vernacular liturgy.[19] For pastoral reasons, the practice of celebrating several Masses on a day in a church developed in the fifth century. In a letter

---

[15] Synod of Hippo, canon 21.

[16] The first Latin translations of the Bible come from the late second century.

[17] Thus the Christian Neoplatonist Marius Victorinus (d. after 363) cites an offertory prayer (*oratio oblationis*) in Greek, from which we can conclude that the liturgy was still celebrated in the Greek language. Cf. Marius Victorinus, *Adversus Arium* 2.8 (*PL* 8:1094).

[18] This is demonstrated by the so-called "Ambrosiaster", an unknown Roman writer of the second half of the fourth century. He cites a Latin Eucharistic Prayer that is already very similar to the later Roman Canon. Cf. Gamber, *Missa Romensis*, 19.

[19] Cf. Winfried Haunerland, "Lingua Vernacula: Zur Sprache der Liturgie nach dem II. Vatikanum", *Liturgisches Jahrbuch* 42 (1992): 219–38; Uwe Michael Lang, "Rhetoric of Salvation: The Origins of Latin as the Language of the Roman Liturgy", in *The Genius of the Roman Rite: Historical, Theological and Pastoral Perspectives on Catholic Liturgy*, ed. U.M. Lang (Chicago: Hillenbrand, 2010), 22–24; Lang, *The Voice of the Church at Prayer: Reflections on Liturgy and Language* (San Francisco: Ignatius Press, 2012), 48–72, 172–80.

to Bishop Dioskuros of Alexandria, Pope Leo I recommends celebrating the Eucharist several times on days when many of the faithful
are expected.[20] In contrast, daily Mass was unknown in Rome until
the fourth century.[21] Nor were there yet any fixed forms for the celebration of Mass on Sundays and feast days or on the feasts of saints.

The basic form of the celebration of Mass in Christian antiquity
was the Eucharist celebrated by the bishop together with his congregation and his clergy. Through Emperor Constantine, the bishops
obtained the status of royal officials and dignitaries, who therefore
wore the appropriate ministerial garments with insignia, both during
and outside of the liturgy.[22] This was true of the priests and deacons, too. Unlike them, the bishops had special prerogatives, such as
the right to a throne, to be accompanied by torches and incense,
to the προσκύνησις (profound bow) and the kiss on the hand.[23] This
was not a human personality cult, since these signs of respect were
meant for Christ, whom the bishop represents in the liturgy.

The following paragraphs describe what the liturgy of the Mass
probably looked like at the time of the pontificate of Gregory the
Great.[24] Beginning in the fourth century, the practice of the liturgical stations developed, whereby the pope, in order to emphasize the
unity of the Roman congregations, traveled to the titular churches
in Rome to visit the *statio* and to celebrate the Eucharist there.[25] A
little later, there is evidence for station liturgies in Antioch, Jerusalem, and Tours, also.[26] Around the year 400, there were already
twenty-five titular churches in Rome, which together formed the

---

[20] Cf. Leo I, *Epistola* 9.2 (*PL* 54:626f.).

[21] On daily Mass in North Africa, see Augustine, *De civitate Dei* 10.20 (CCSL 47:294);
Augustine, *In Iohannis Evangelium tractatus* 26.15 (CCSL 36:267f.).

[22] These included the *lorum* worn by the Byzantine emperor (which gave rise to the *pal-
lium*), the *mappula* (a ceremonial cloth), the *campagi imperiales* (closed shoes like those worn
by the emperors, as opposed to open sandals) and the *camelaucum* (a sort of cap that gave rise
to the miter). The papal *camauro* is reminiscent of the *camelaucum*.

[23] Cf. Theodor Klauser, *Kleine abendländische Liturgiegeschichte: Bericht und Besinnung* (Bonn:
Hanstein, 1965), 37.

[24] See the findings in Hans Bernhard Meyer, *Eucharistie, Geschichte, Theologie, Pastoral*,
Handbuch der Liturgiewissenschaft 4 (Regensburg: Pustet, 1989), 173–82.

[25] On the history of the stational liturgy, see John F. Baldovin, *The Urban Character of Christian Worship: The Origins, Development, and Meaning of Stational Liturgy*, Orientalia Christiana
Analecta 288 (Rome: Pont. Institutum Studiorum Orientalium, 1987).

[26] See Josef Andreas Jungmann, *The Mass of the Roman Rite*, trans. Francis A. Brunner,
C.Ss.R., 2 vols. (New York: Benziger Brothers, 1951, 1955), 1:59.

Roman diocese.[27] Besides the bishop of Rome, the priests celebrated the Eucharist, too. Optatus of Mileve (d. before 400) relates in his treatise against the Donatist bishop Parmenianus that there were churches in Rome in which presbyters presided at the celebration of the Eucharist.[28]

In the structure of the Roman Mass we distinguish the unchangeable parts of the Ordinary (*Kyrie, Gloria, Credo, Sanctus/Benedictus, Agnus Dei*) and the varying parts of the Proper (for example, *Introitus, Graduale*). The *Kyrie* found its way into the Roman Mass in the sixth century. It had its origin in the older litanies to Christ in the East. The *Gloria* also comes from the East, where it had its original place in Morning Prayer in the Liturgy of the Hours. In the fourth century, it was incorporated into the Christmas Mass in Rome on December 25. Finally, Pope Symmachus (498–514) extended the use of the hymn to Sundays and the feasts of martyrs. In the early seventh century, the *Gloria* became a permanent component of the Sunday Mass. The prayer of the day (*Oratio prima*) after the *Gloria* was supposed to sum up the prayers of the people. Under the influence of the Old Gallic word *collectio*, this prayer of the day was therefore designated the *collecta*. The orations for particular occasions are a distinctive feature of the Roman liturgy of the Mass. Whereas parts of the *Ordinarium*, with the exception of the *Credo*, has been established in Rome by the seventh century, the *Proprium* developed more fully only with the compilation of the liturgical books of *antiphonarium* and *cantatorium*.[29] Gregorian chant, the beginnings of which to this day have not been explained clearly, is of course older.[30] The founding of a *schola cantorum* by Pope Gregory the Great is a legend. It is uncertain whether during his pontificate psalms and the Introit were already sung as he entered the station church.

---

[27] Cf. Edward Foley, *From Age to Age: How Christians Have Celebrated the Eucharist*, 2nd ed. (Collegeville, Minn.: Liturgical Press, 2008), 99f. The origin of the designation titular church (*titulus ecclesiae*) is not clear. One theory claims that the name "titular church" goes back to the owner's name set in an inscription on a Roman residence. According to another theory, the titular churches were assigned to the presbyters who were appointed to minister in the Church of Rome.

[28] Cf. Optatus of Mileve, *Contra Parmenianum* 2.4 (SChr 413:86–88).

[29] Cf. James W. McKinnon, *The Advent Project: The Later-Seventh-Century Creation of the Roman Mass Proper* (Berkeley: University of California Press, 2000).

[30] Cf. Foley, *From Age to Age*, 100–102.

Jungmann still assumed that the plan of readings for the Roman Mass was originally threefold (Old Testament reading, New Testament reading, Gospel) and that the first reading was dropped only from the sixth century on.[31] Today it is assumed that in the Roman Mass from the beginning, only an Epistle from the New Testament and the Gospel were read. While Justin and Tertullian seem to have presupposed a regular reading from the Old Testament during the readings from Scripture, in Rome an Old Testament reading was foreseen only by way of exception.[32] Final certainty cannot be obtained in this matter. In the plan of readings mentioned by Augustine, New Testament pericopes predominate, yet the Old Testament takes up more space than in the Roman liturgy of the Mass,[33] in which of course the Proper to a great extent uses verses from the old Testament. In Gaul, Milan, and Spain it was customary to read three pericopes, the first of which was taken from the Old Testament.[34] Usually this reading was from the prophets, less often from the Torah.[35] The Syrian liturgies have four or more readings, two of which are taken from the Old Testament.

The Roman plan of readings includes no continuous reading of biblical books (*lectio continua*). Instead, as the cycles of feasts

[31] Cf. Jungmann, *Mass of the Roman Rite*, 1:395.

[32] Cf. Antoine Chavasse, "L'epistolier romain du Codex Wurtzbourg: Son organisation", *Revue Bénédictine* 91 (1981): 280–331; Chavasse, *Les lectionnaires romains de la messe I-II*, Spicilegii Friburgensis subsidia 22 (Fribourg: Éditions Universitaires, 1993).

[33] Cf. Martin Klöckener,"Die Bedeutung der neu entdeckten Augustinus-Predigten (*Sermones Dolbeau*) für die liturgiegeschichtliche Forschung", in *Augustin prédicateur (395–411): Actes du Colloque International de Chantilly (5–7 Septembre 1996)*, ed. G. Madec, Collection des Études Augustiniennes, Série Antiquité 159 (Paris: Institut d'études augustiniennes, 1998), 135–47; Michael Margoni-Kögler, *Die Perikopen im Gottesdienst bei Augustinus: Ein Beitrag zur Erforschung der liturgischen Schriftlesung in der frühen Kirche*, Veröffentlichungen der Kommission zur Herausgabe des Corpus der Lateinischen Kirchenväter 29; Sitzungsberichte/Österreichische Akademie der Wissenschafter, Philosophisch-Historische Klasse 810 (Vienna: Verlag der Österreichischen Akademie der Wissenschaften, 2010), 29.

[34] Cf. Heinzgerd Brakmann, "Der christlichen Bibel erster Teil in den gottesdienstlichen Traditionen des Ostens und Westens: Liturgiehistorische Anmerkungen zum sog. Stellenwert des Alten/Ersten Testaments im Christentum", in *Streit am Tisch des Wortes? Zur Deutung und Bedeutung des Alten Testaments und seiner Verwendung in der Liturgie*, ed. A. Franz (St. Ottilien: EOS Verlag, 1997), 591–93.

[35] Cf. Gerard Rouwhorst, "The Reading of Scripture in Early Christian Liturgy", in *What Athens Has to Do with Jerusalem: Essays in Classical, Jewish and Early Christian Art and Archeology*, Festschrift G. Forester, ed. L. V. Rutgers, Interdisciplinary Studies in Ancient Culture and Religion 1 (Leuven: Peeters, 2002), 327.

developed, appropriate readings were assigned to particular feast days
and seasons. In the time *per annum* ("ordinary" time), more or less
free selections were presented from the books of the Bible. Only at a
very late date was the principle of sequential reading established. The
Epistle was read at first by a lector, later by a subdeacon, and thus by
a higher cleric. The proclamation of the Gospel was the task of the
deacon. The decision about whether there were two responsorial
psalms on Sundays and feast days depends on the acceptance of a
three-part Roman reading plan. In the East, the Psalm originally had
the function of a Scripture reading independent of the first reading.
The Psalm was therefore proclamation and not a sung interlude. It
is suspected that since the mid-sixth century only parts of the Psalm
were sung in connection with a refrain by the people (the later *Graduale*).[36] The Alleluia is an independent song of praise to the Lord
present in the proclamation of the Gospel. In Rome, this song of
praise was restricted to the Easter season until the time of Gregory the
Great. Afterward, the use of the Alleluia was extended to Christmas
and the other feast days and Sundays, except during Lent.[37]

   It is unclear to what extent there was preaching in the Roman
Mass between the fourth and the sixth century. The homilies of Pope
Leo the Great show that at least the bishop of Rome gave a homily
with some regularity. Before the presentation of the gifts, the baptized (*fideles*) prayed the great intercessory prayer called the *oratio fidelium*. This "Prayer of the Faithful" is modeled on the Jewish prayer
of eighteen petitions, the main prayer at the beginning of worship in
the synagogue. The *oratio fidelium* was introduced by the bishop and
concluded with a *collecta*. Between the two, the congregation perse-
vered in silent prayer. On penitential days, the petitions of the *oratio
fidelium* were prayed kneeling, whereas all stood up for the following
prayer. The deacon called for these postures by exclaiming *Flecta-
mus genua* (Let us bend our knees) and *Levate* (Rise). In the Solemn

[36] Cf. Peter Jeffery, "The Introduction of Psalmody into the Roman Mass by Pope Celestine I (422–33): Reinterpreting a Passage in the *Liber Pontificalis*", *Archiv für Liturgiewissenschaft*
26 (1984): 147–65.

[37] Cf. Ewald Jammers, *Das Alleluja in der gregorianischen Messe: Eine Studie über seine Entstehung und Entwicklung*, Liturgiewissenschaftliche Quellen und Forschungen 55 (Münster:
Aschendorff, 1973).

Intercessions on Good Friday, this form of the Roman *oratio fidelium* has been preserved to this day.

In the East, there was a shorter form of the intercessory prayer, which was called a litany. The deacon presented the individual petitions, and the people responded with *Kyrie eleison* [Lord, have mercy]. The litany has no silent prayer of the faithful. In the time of Pope Gelasius I (492–496), the form of the *Kyrie* litany was adopted in Rome. Thus the petitions of the *deprecatio Gelasii* coincide to a great extent with those of the intercessory prayer of the Church.[38] While the Solemn Intercession was still practiced during the pontificate of Felix II (483–492), at the turn of the sixth century it fell into disuse. The *Veronese Sacramentary* testifies that the *oratio fidelium* was no longer a part of the Roman Mass during the pontificate of Gregory I.[39]

The fact that the Roman Canon itself contains a series of intercessions may have played a role in the suppression of the Prayer of the Faithful.[40] There is no sure evidence for a presentation of the gifts by the faithful in the ancient Roman liturgy of the Mass before Gregory the Great. After the *oratio fidelium*, the deacons brought the gifts of bread and wine for the Liturgy of the Eucharist to the altar. Then came the *oratio super oblata* (prayer over the gifts), the origin of which goes back to the oldest strata of the Roman liturgy. In the fifth century, it was established as a permanent component of the Roman Mass.[41]

---

[38] Cf. Ewald de Clerck, *La "prière universelle" dans les liturgies latines anciennes: Témoignages patristiques et textes liturgiques*, Liturgiewissenschaftliche Quellen und Forschungen 62 (Münster: Aschendorff, 1977), 166–87.

[39] Cf. *Sacramentarium Veronense* 819, Rerum ecclesiasticarum documenta, Series maior, fontes I, ed. Leo C. Mohlberg (Rome, 1956), 102. The *Veronense* is not a sacramentary in the proper sense but, rather, a collection of *libelli* with texts for the celebration of Mass by priests in the Roman titular churches. The *Veronense* is named after the city in which the one extant manuscript of the collection is found. It is also called the *Leoninum*, although it has nothing to do with Pope Leo I directly. It is certain that Popes Leo I and Gelasius I had a decisive influence on the shape of the Roman liturgy, even though the sacramentaries named after them are of a later date. The influence of Pope Gregory the Great is classified today as somewhat less important than in older scholarship. Cf. Andreas Heinz, "Papst Gregor der Grosse und die römische Liturgie: Zum Gregorius-Gedenkjahr 1400 Jahre nach seinem Tod (†604)", *Liturgisches Jahrbuch* 54 (2004): 69–84.

[40] Cf. de Clerck, *La "prière universelle"*, 282–307; Meyer, *Eucharistie*, 177.

[41] Cf. Geoffrey G. Willis, *Further Essays in Early Roman Liturgy* (London: S.P.C.K. for the Alcuin Club, 1968), 122–24.

The Eucharistic Canon, the great prayer of thanksgiving to God, began with the Preface dialogue, which to this day has remained to a great extent unchanged. Unlike the Eastern liturgies, the Roman liturgy of the Mass had only one Eucharistic Prayer (*Canon Romanus*) until the Vatican reform of the liturgy. The structure of the prayer, the genesis of which cannot be fully explained to this day, is different from that of the Eucharistic Prayer in the *Traditio Apostolica* and in most Eastern anaphoras. With its intercessions, the Roman Canon shows a distinct affinity to the Alexandrine tradition.[42] Many suspect that the intercessions had their origin in the third benediction of the *birkat hammāzón* (*birkat jᵉrūšālajīm*, prayer for Jerusalem). In the Christian Eucharistic Prayer, it became the petition for the unity of the Church. A petition for Church unity can be identified from the *Didache* to the anaphora of the Divine Liturgy of Saint Basil the Great.[43]

The *Pater noster* with the introduction *Praeceptis salutaribus moniti* was pronounced as a Eucharistic presider's prayer and concluded by the people with the final petition *sed libera nos a malo* [but deliver us from evil].[44] Next followed the embolism, the addition to the Our Father. This form of the liturgical *Pater noster* may well go back to the fourth century. After the fifth century, the *Pater noster* was more often sung by the priest. In the ancient Roman liturgy, it was followed immediately by the breaking of the Eucharistic bread, which initially occurred without the later sung accompaniment of the *Agnus Dei*. This prayer was introduced into the Roman Mass only by Sergius I (687–701). The pope was from a Syrian family and was familiar with Eastern liturgies, in which the Eucharist bread is referred to as the "Lamb".[45] The form of the Eucharistic bread[46] was at first a ring loaf (*rotula*). The *Liber Pontificalis*, in the context of a description of the life

---

[42] For an analysis, see below, section 2.

[43] Cf. Albert Gerhards, "Entstehung und Entwicklung des Eucharistischen Hochgebets im Spiegel der neueren Forschung: Der Beitrag der Liturgiewissenschaft zur liturgischen Erneuerung", in *Gratias Agamus: Studien zum Eucharistischen Hochgebet*, Festschrift B. Fischer, ed. A. Heinz and H. Rennings (Freiburg: Herder, 1992), 85.

[44] Cf. Jungmann, *Mass of the Roman Rite*, 2:288.

[45] Cf. Foley, *From Age to Age*, 97.

[46] On the history of the host, see Oliver Seifert and Ambrosius Backhaus, eds., *Panis Angelorum: Das Brot der Engel: Kulturgeschichte der Hostie* (Ostfildern: Thorbecke, 2004).

of Pope Zephyrinus (ca. A.D. 200), says that the Host in the form of a *corona consecrata* [consecrated crown] is to be distributed by the priest to the people.[47]

Right after the Communion of the clerics at the altar, Communion was given to the faithful. They received from the bishop or the priest the Body of Christ and from the deacon the Blood of Christ. Presumably the formula of administration was simply *Corpus Christi* or *Sanguis Christi*. The singing of psalms at the distribution of the Eucharist probably goes back to the fourth century. The Communion part of the Mass was concluded by an *oratio ad complendum*, which since the end of the fifth century has been a permanent component of the liturgy. In form and style, it corresponds to the *collecta* (prayer of the day) and the *oratio super oblata* (prayer over the gifts). At the conclusion of the Mass came the *oratio super populum*, a prayer of blessing during which the faithful bowed at the deacon's bidding. The *oratio super populum* is one of the oldest parts of the Roman Mass.[48] The blessing over the faithful, like the homily, remained for a long time the prerogative of bishops. At the time of Saint Augustine, the priest's homily was still controversial in North Africa.

By the end of late antiquity, a liturgy had developed that was completely set down in writing and ritually regulated. While in antiquity the mystery-character of the liturgy dominated, in the transition to the early Middle Ages the element of ritual increased in importance. The clergy were increasingly regarded as the ones responsible for the liturgy. While in late antiquity and the early Middle Ages, it was still customary to say that the laity celebrated Mass together with the bishop, priest, and deacon (*celebrare missam*),[49] we no longer find this manner of speaking in the High Middle Ages. The Canon, recited by the bishop or the priest, became the prayer on which everything depended, and therefore it also had to be recited without error.[50]

---

[47] Cf. *Liber Pontificalis* I, Texte, introduction et commentaire par l'Abbé L. Duchesne (Paris, 1955), 339.

[48] Jungmann, *Mass of the Roman Rite*, 2:428, assumes that it originated in the late third or early fourth century.

[49] Cf. Gregory of Tours, *De gloria condessorum* 65 (PL 71:875C).

[50] So it was already in the *Stowe Missal*, an Irish Mass book from the eighth or ninth century that gives us insight into the Celtic liturgy around 650.

Information about the Roman liturgy in the late seventh century is given by the *Ordines Romani* edited by Michel Andrieu.[51] These are *libelli* recording prescriptions for the performance of the individual liturgical actions, thus ceremonial books, which were later designated as *Ordinarium, Caeremoniale, Liber caeremoniarum,* and so on.[52] The *Ordo Romanus* I regulates the papal Mass, which was celebrated in one of the Roman station churches after a solemn procession setting out from the Lateran.[53]

In the case of a papal Mass, as it is depicted in the *Ordo Romanus* I,[54] the pontifex goes first into the sacristy to put on the liturgical vestments. Then he enters the station church. At the altar, a subdeacon stands with two acolytes. They hold out to the pope an uncovered vessel containing the *sancta* (the consecrated pieces of Eucharistic bread) from the last papal Mass. The pope reverences the *sancta* and decides how many he wants to use for the celebration of the Mass. The unused *sancta* are brought back in a *conditorium.* This is a cupboard used to store the Most Blessed Sacrament in the Lateran.[55] The selected *fermentum* serves as a sort of leaven; it is dipped into the Eucharistic cup to symbolize the connection of the papal Masses. The rite of the *fermentum* was practiced in Rome already in the early fifth century. In a letter to Bishop Decentius of Gubbio, Pope Innocent I (401–417) mentions this rite.[56] In order to document the connection of the papal Mass with the other celebrations of Mass, a part

---

[51] On this subject, see Johannes Nebel, *Die Entwicklung des römischen Messritus im ersten Jahrtausend anhand der Ordines Romani: Eine synoptische Darstellung,* Pontificium Athenaeum S. Anselmi de Urbe, Pontificum Liturgicum Thesis ad Lauream 264 (Rome: Pontificium Athenaeum S. Anselmi de Urbe, Pontificium Institutum Liturgicum, 2000).

[52] Cf. Klauser, *Kleine abendländische Liturgiegeschichte,* 63–75; Meyer, *Eucharistie,* 173–82; Cyrille Vogel, *Medieval Liturgy: An Introduction to the Sources* (Washington, D.C.: Pastoral Press, 1986), 155–60.

[53] Besides the solemn papal Mass, the presbyteral Mass also existed in Rome around 700, which of course in comparison with the Mass of the Roman bishop was considered inferior. A Mass celebrated by a bishop, a Pontifical Mass, outside of Rome is supposed to be celebrated like the papal Mass (cf. *Ordo Romanus* 2.10 [Michel Andrieu, *Les Ordines Romani du haut moyen âge,* vol. 2. (Louvain: Spicilegium Sacrum Lovaniense, 1960), 116]). This decision presumably goes back to an editor commissioned by a Frankish court or by a synod. Cf. Klauser, *Kleine abendländische Liturgiegeschichte,* 74.

[54] Cf. Jungmann, *Mass of the Roman Rite,* 1:67–74; Gamber, *Liturgie übermorgen,* 149–57.

[55] Cf. *Ordo Romanus* 1.48 (ed. Andrieu, 2:82f.).

[56] Cf. Innocent I, *Epistola* 25.5–8 (*PL* 40:556–57).

of the bread consecrated by the pope is brought by an acolyte to the other Roman titular churches.

As the pope enters, after he has arrived at the altar, he reverences the altar by a bow. Immediately he kneels down on the apse side of the altar facing East.[57] When the *schola cantorum* has finished the *Introitus* with the *Gloria Patri* at a sign from the pope, he stands up and kisses the Gospel book and the altar.[58] After that, he goes to the *sedilia* in the middle of the apse. During the *Kyrie* litany, the pope stands *versus orientem* (facing east).[59] When the *schola cantorum* has finished the litany, the pope intones the hymn *Gloria in excelsis Deo*. While the hymn is being sung, the pope again stands *versus orientem*. After the *Gloria in excelsis Deo*, the pope invites the people to pray by saying *Oremus* and then recites the first oration (*collecta*), which is a prayer "gathering up" the individual petitions of the faithful.[60]

Right after the *collecta* follows the Epistle, which is recited at the ambo by the subdeacon designated for that purpose.[61] After the Epistle, a cantor intones the *responsum* at the ambo. Next, another cantor sings the Alleluia.[62] Immediately the deacon assigned to sing the Gospel goes to the pope and asks for his blessing, which the pope bestows with the prayer *Dominus sit in corde tuo et in labiis tuis* (May the Lord be in your heart and on your lips). The deacon goes to the altar and kisses the Gospel book. With the Gospel book he walks in a short procession to the ambo. He is accompanied by two subdeacons with the thurible and two acolytes with candles. After the Gospel, one of the subdeacons presents the Gospel book to all the clerics in the sanctuary to kiss.[63]

Whereas at the time of Leo the Great, the pope still preached regularly, a papal homily around 700 may already have been rare. The *Credo*, the Symbol or Profession of Faith, first became part of the Roman Mass in the eleventh century. Since the *oratio fidelium* had been replaced by the shorter form of the litany, which ultimately was

---

[57] Cf. *Ordo Romanus* 1.49 (ed. Andrieu, 2:83).
[58] Cf. ibid., 50–51 (2:83f.).
[59] Cf. ibid., 52 (2:84).
[60] Cf. ibid., 53 (2:84).
[61] Cf. ibid., 56 (2:86).
[62] Cf. ibid., 57 (2:86).
[63] Cf. ibid., 57–64 (2:86–89).

moved forward to the beginning of the Liturgy of the Word, the Liturgy of the Eucharist began immediately after the proclamation of the Gospel when there was no homily. One remnant of the suppressed Prayer of the Faithful was the introductory formula *Oremus*, which now served as the transition to the Liturgy of the Eucharist.[64]

Unlike in the old Roman liturgy, the bishop of Rome and his assistants accept the gifts from the faithful: the pope, the offering of bread by the aristocracy;[65] the archdeacon, the offering of wine.[66] The loaves are placed into large linen cloths (*sindones*), while the flasks (*amulae*) with the wine are emptied into a chalice. When it is full, the wine is poured into a large container (*scyphus*).[67] The archdeacon selects for the Consecration as many loaves as will be needed for Communion and places them on the altar. Into the chalice is put exclusively the wine that is offered by the pope and his deacons. To it a little water is added. Finally, the pope goes to the altar and places his own *oblatio* (offering) on the altar.[68] The song that the *schola cantorum* intoned at the beginning of the *Offertorium* (antiphon, psalm) is ended at a sign from the pope. Afterward, he pronounces the *oratio super oblata*, the prayer over the offerings.

After the *oratio super oblate*, the Eucharistic Canon begins with the Preface and the *Sanctus*.[69] The Canon was still recited audibly until the late seventh century (at least audibly for the clerics standing nearby). While everyone stood upright for the Preface, the clerics bowed at the *Sanctus*.[70] After the *Sanctus*, the pope again stands upright (*surgit pontifex solus*) and begins to pray the Canon (*intrat in canonem*), while the other clerics continue to bow (*permanent inclinati*). Initially there was probably no elevation of the gifts after the *verba testamenti*; at least it is not mentioned. For the concluding formula of the Canon, the archdeacon stands and elevates the chalice, while the pope elevates the Eucharistic bread.[71] With the optative

---

[64] Cf. Jungmann, *Mass of the Roman Rite*, 1:483f.
[65] Cf. *Ordo Romanus* 1:69 (ed. Andrieu, 2:91).
[66] Cf. ibid., 70 (2:91).
[67] Cf. ibid., 73 (2:91).
[68] Cf. ibid., 84 (2:94).
[69] Cf. ibid., 87 (2:95).
[70] Cf. ibid., 87–88 (2:95f.).
[71] Cf. ibid., 89 (2:96).

blessing, *Pax Domini sit semper vobiscum* (May the peace of the Lord be with you always), the pope introduces the exchange of the Sign of Peace. The archdeacon receives it from the pope and passes it on to the other clerics, according to their rank (bishops, priests, deacons, subdeacons).[72]

Communion is preceded by another longer breaking of the bread, for small round hosts of bread were as yet unknown. The archdeacon takes the Eucharistic bread from the altar and places it in the little bags of the acolytes. They bring them to the bishops and priests, who break the Eucharistic bread into little pieces. At the "fraction" or breaking of the bread, the *Agnus Dei* is sung. When the fraction is over, the pope's oblation is brought to him on a paten to his seat. Then the chalice is given to the pope. He breaks off a piece of the consecrated bread and puts it into the chalice while pronouncing the formula *Fiat commixtio et consecratio* (May this mingling and consecration ...). The complete formula reads: "Fiat commixtio et consecratio corporis et sanguinis domini nostri Iesu Christi accipientibus nobis in vitam aeternam. Amen."[73] The practice of the *commixtio* along with the formula might be of Syrian origin and represent the unity of Christ, whose Body and Blood we receive.

After the pope has received the Body of Christ, the archdeacon gives him the chalice for Communion. From the pope's seat, the archdeacon goes back to the altar and pours some of the consecrated wine into the wine offering of the faithful that is in the *scyphi* (containers) and, as was thought at that time, is consecrated through that mixture.[74]

Next follows the Communion of the bishops, priests, and deacons. From the pope's hand, they receive the Eucharistic bread. The chalice is given to the clerics by the archdeacon at the altar.[75] During the Communion of the faithful, the *schola cantorum* sings the antiphon and the psalm. After Communion, the pope washes his hands[76] and pronounces at the altar *versus orientem* the *oratio ad complendum*

[72] Cf. ibid., 96 (2:98).

[73] "May this mingling and consecration of the Body and Blood of our Lord Jesus Christ be unto eternal life for us who receive it. Amen." Cf. ibid., 98–107 (2:99–102).

[74] Cf. ibid., 108 (2:102).

[75] Cf. ibid., 110 (2:103).

[76] Cf. ibid., 118 (2:106).

(*Postcommunio*).[77] This is followed by a dismissal sung by one of the deacons, *Ite missa est*, to which the congregation responds *Deo gratias*. After that, the pope administers his blessing.[78] At the conclusion, he goes in solemn procession with the bishops, priests, deacons, and acolytes into the sacristy.[79]

B. Canon Romanus: *The Roman Eucharistic Prayer*

The central action of the Eucharist is the prayer of thanksgiving (Eucharistic Prayer). In the Eastern tradition, it is called ἀνάφορα (elevation, offering), in the Latin West—*oratio, prex oblationis*, or *canon actionis*.[80] It is called *canon* because as a guideline and standard it must not be changed by the celebrant. In the fourth century, fixed formulas for the Eucharistic Prayer became widely accepted in the local Churches. The Christological controversies and the concern about orthodox belief may have played a decisive role in this development.[81] The origin and early development of the Roman Canon are largely obscure to this day.[82] Some scholars detect early references to texts from the Roman Canon in the writings of Tertullian, Irenaeus of Lyon, and Zeno of Verona (d. 371/372).[83] The Ambrosian Eucharistic Prayer is evidence that the core of the *Canon Romanus* goes back at least to the fourth century. The Irish *Stowe Missal*

---

[77] Cf. ibid., 123 (2:107).

[78] During the Vatican reform of the Missal, the order of the *Ite missa est* and the blessing was changed.

[79] Cf. *Ordo Romanus*, 1.126 (2:108).

[80] Cf. Gamber, *Missa Romensis*, 56.

[81] Cf. Allan Bouley, *From Freedom to Formula: The Evolution of the Eucharistic Prayer from Oral Improvisation to Written Texts*, Studies in Christian Antiquity 21 (Washington, D.C.: Catholic University of America Press, 1981).

[82] On the Roman Canon, see the critical edition by Bernard Botte, *Le canon de la messe romaine: Édition critique, introduction et notes*, Textes et études liturgiques 2 (Louvain: Abbaye du Mont César, 1935), and *Prex Eucharistica*, ed. Anton Hänggi and Irmgard Pahl (Fribourg: Editions Universitaires, 1968), 424–38.

[83] Cf. Gordon P. Jeanes, "Early Latin Parallels to the Roman Canon? Possible References to a Eucharistic Prayer in Zenon of Verona", *Journal of Theological Studies* 37 (1986): 427–31; Brian D. Spinks, "The Roman Canon Missae", in *Prex Eucharistica*, vol. 3/1, ed. A. Gerhards, H. Brakmann, and M. Klöckener (Fribourg: Academic Press Fribourg and Paulusverlag, 2005), 131.

(eighth-ninth century) ascribes the Roman Canon to Pope Gelasius I (492–496). Between the fourth and the seventh century, the Roman Canon acquired the form that we encounter in the *Sacramentarium Gelasianum Vetus* (seventh century).[84] The oldest manuscripts with the text of the Canon are the Irish *Bobbio Missal* (ca. 700) and the *Missale Francorum* (ca. 725). The parts of the *Canon Romanus* from *Quam oblationem* to the *Supplices* might have existed already in the late fourth century.[85] The Roman Canon exhibits similarities with two Eastern anaphoras, the Alexandrine Anaphora of Mark[86]and the anaphora in the Sacramentary of Serapion of Thmuis (d. ca. 370).[87]

The core of the Roman Eucharistic Prayer goes back to the time of Gregory the Great.[88] The language of the Canon is marked by sacral, ancient Roman legal language.[89] Elements of praise dominate in the Preface and the concluding Doxology. The main section includes the intercessions, the account of institution (as the center of

---

[84] Cf. Leo Cunibert Mohlberg, ed., *Liber Sacramentorum Romanae Ecclesiae ordinis anni circuli* (Rome: Herder, 1960), nos. 1242–55 (183–86). The only manuscript that has been preserved is the one in Chelles, Northern France (ca. 750).

[85] Cf. Geoffrey G. Willis, *Essays in Early Roman Liturgy*, Alcuin Club Collections 46 (London: S.P.C.K. for the Alcuin Club, 1964), 113–17.

[86] Cf. Geoffrey J. Cuming, *The Liturgy of St. Mark: Edited from the Manuscripts with a Commentary*, Orientalia christiana analecta 234 (Rome: Pontificium institutum orientalium, 1990).

[87] Cf. Anton Baumstark, "Das 'Problem' des römischen Messkanons: Eine Retractatio auf geistesgeschichtlichem Hintergrund", *Ephemerides liturgicae* 53 (1939): 204–43; Enrico Mazza, *L'anafora eucaristica: Studi sulle origini*, Bibliotheca "Ephemerides liturgicae", Subsidia 62 (Rome: Editione Liturgiche, 1992), 261–304; Walter D. Ray, "Rome and Alexandria: Two Cities, One Anaphoral Tradition", in *Issues in Eucharistic Praying in East and West: Essays in Liturgical and Theological Analysis*, ed. M. E. Johnson (Collegeville, Minn.: Liturgical Press, 2010), 99–127; Matthieu Smyth, "The Anaphora of the So-Called 'Apostolic Tradition' and the Roman Eucharistic Prayer", in *Issues in Eucharistic Praying in East and West: Essays in Liturgical and Theological Analysis*, ed. M. E. Johnson (Collegeville, Minn.: Liturgical Press, 2010), 76; Maxwell E. Johnson, *The Prayers of Serapion of Thmuis: A Literary, Liturgical and Theological Analysis*, Orientalia Christiana Analecta 249 (Rome: Pontificio istituto orientale, 1995); Michael J. Moreton, "Rethinking the Origin of the Roman Canon", *Studia Patristica* 26 (1993): 65f.

[88] Cf. Cipriano Vagaggini, *Le canon de la messe et la réforme liturgique*, French trans. A.-M. Roguet and P. Rouillard, Lex orandi 41 (Paris: Les Éditions du Cerf, 1967), 78; Louis Bouyer, *Eucharist*, trans. Charles Underhill Quinn (Notre Dame, Ind.: University of Notre Dame Press, 1968), 227–43. Bruno Kleinheyer, *Erneuerung des Hochgebetes* (Regensburg: Pustet, 1969), 24–32, and Vagaggini, *Canon de la messe*, 82–102, bring up the usual critique of the Roman Canon: lack of unified structure, doubling of intercessions, lack of epiclesis of the Spirit, obscurity of the *Supplices te rogamus*, etc. Cf. Vagaggini, *Canon de la messe*, 82–102.

[89] Cf. Joseph Schmitz, "Canon Romanus", in *Prex Eucharistica*, vol. 3/1:282.

the Canon), the pleas for acceptance, and, connected with them, an anamnesis of salvation history. The intercessions are divided in two; the first group of intercessions comes before the account of institution, the second group—after it. Characteristic of the Roman Canon, in comparison to the Eastern anaphoras, are the changing Prefaces. The advanced age of the Canon is shown in its binitarian structure (relation of Father and Son, without explicit mention of the Holy Spirit) and also in the sacrificial typology in the *Supra quae* and the Angel-Christology of the *Supplices te rogamus*.[90]

Introductory dialogue: The liturgical greeting *Dominus vobiscum* at the beginning of the Canon, according to Jewish tradition (Ruth 2:4; 2 Thess 3:16), is an optative blessing ("May the Lord be with you"), whereby *Dominus* refers to Christ. In the congregation's response, *Et cum spiritu tuo*, the word *spiritus* is not a synonym for the second person singular pronoun ("and also with you") but, rather, according to the interpretation of the early Church, refers to the ministerial charism of the celebrant.[91] The greeting dialogue takes the place of the anaclesis (prayer salutation). The offertory thanksgiving can be performed only in the power of Christ and of his Spirit. This is confirmed by the *Sursum corda* and the affirmative response *Habemus ad Dominum*. Although the Roman Eucharistic Prayer as a whole is directed to the Father, *Dominus* might mean Christ here, too, since the memory of him as Savior is being celebrated.[92] The invitation *Gratias agamus Domino Deo nostro* (Let us give thanks to the Lord our God) could be influenced by the *bírkat hāmmazôn*.[93] The response of the faithful, *Dignum et iustum est*, is a confirmation of the thanksgiving.

Vere dignum: The Preface and the *canon actionis* still formed a unit in the *Old Gelasian Sacramentary* and the *Sacramentarium Veronense* (sixth-seventh century). Before the introductory dialogue of the Preface, it says in the *Old Gelasian Sacramentary*: "Incipit canon actionis."[94] The insertion of the *Sanctus* sung by the priest and the people led

---

[90] Cf. Smyth, "Anaphora of the So-Called 'Apostolic Tradition'", 77f.

[91] Cf. Emil J. Lengeling, "Et cum spiritu tuo—Und auch mit dir?", *Römische Quartalschrift* 70 (1975): 225–37.

[92] Cf. Balthasar Fischer, "Vom Beten zu Christus", in *Gott feiern: Theologische Anregung und geistliche Vertiefung zur Feier der Messe und des Stundengebets*, Festschrift T. Schnitzler, ed. J. G. Plöger (Freiburg: Herder, 1980), 96f.

[93] Cf. *Mishnah Berakhot* 7.3; cf. Schmitz, "Canon Romanus", 284.

[94] Mohlberg, *Liber sacramentorum Romanae Ecclesiae ordinis anni circuli*, no. 1242 (183).

to a caesura between the Preface and the prayer segment *Te igitur*. From the Middle Ages on, the Preface was no longer considered part of the Canon. With its dialogical opening and anamnesis of salvation, the Preface is, however, an intrinsic part of the Eucharistic Prayer. The *vere dignum et iustum est* has its counterpart in the *Apostolic Constitutions*: ἄξιον ὡς ἀληθινῶς καὶ δίκαιον.[95] While the *Sacramentarium Hadrianum* contains only fourteen Prefaces, the *Gelasianum* offers over fifty, and the *Sacramentarium Veronense*—more than 250. In the oldest Preface texts, the central component is thanks for creation and redemption by Christ. In the more recent texts, the mystery of the feast or the life of the saint is increasingly mentioned. Under Pope Gregory the Great, there was a considerable reduction of the number of Prefaces.

Sanctus: The *Trisagion* (Thrice-Holy) goes back to Isaiah 6:3, and in the East there is proof of it from the third, or at latest from the fourth, century. Scholars debate the origin of the *Sanctus* (Greek-Alexandrine or Syrian).[96] In the West, it became widely accepted in the fifth century, presumably under Pope Sixtus III (432–440), certainly not already under Pope Sixtus I (116–125), as the *Liber pontificalis* (ca. 530) maintains.[97] That God is holy is the most frequent statement about his nature in the Old Testament. God's holiness means that he is superior to all that is created; it is experienced above all in his salvific deeds. The *Sanctus* is a prayer of praise of the one who is enthroned "in the highest" and nevertheless is close to mankind. It is unclear when the *Sanctus* first became part of the Eucharistic Prayer in the West. As Revelation 4:8, the *First Letter of Clement* (morning

---

[95] *Constitutiones Apostolorum* 8.12.6 (Anton Hänggi and Irmgard Pahl ed., 82).

[96] Cf. Robert F. Taft, "The Interpolation of the Sanctus into the Anaphora: When and Where? A Review of the Dossier", *Orientalia Christiana Periodica* 57 (1991): 281–308; 58 (1992): 83–121; Brian D. Spinks, *The Sanctus in the Eucharistic Prayer* (Cambridge and New York: Cambridge University Press, 1991); Maxwell E. Johnson, "The Origins of the Anaphoral Use of the Sanctus and the Epiclesis Revisited: The Contribution of Gabriele Winkler and Its Implications", in *The Crossroad of Cultures: Studies in Liturgy and Patristics in Honor of Gabriele Winkler*, ed. H.-J. Feulner et al., Orientalia Christiana Analecta 260 (Rome: Pontificio istituto orientale, 2000), 405–42; Gabriele Winkler, *Das Sanctus: Über den Ursprung und die Anfänge des Sanctus und sein Fortwirken*, Orientalia christiana analecta 267 (Rome: Pontificio Istituto orientale, 2002); Albert Gerhards, "Crossing Borders: The Kedusha and the Sanctus: A Case Study of the Convergence of Jewish and Christian Liturgy", in *Jewish and Christian Liturgy and Worship: New Insights into Its History and Interaction*, ed. A. Gerhards and C. Leonhard, Jewish and Christian Perspectives 15 (Leiden and Boston: Brill, 2007), 27–40.

[97] Cf. *Liber pontificalis* 1 (Duchesne ed., 128).

liturgy),[98] and Tertullian (*Te Deum*)[99] show, the *Sanctus* was used at first outside the celebration of the Eucharist. Nor does Augustine say a single word about the *Sanctus* in reference to the celebration of the Eucharist. For North Africa, there is evidence in the second half of the fifth century for the *Sanctus* as a part of the Eucharistic Prayer.[100]

Attempts to reconstruct the earliest form of the *Sanctus* have proved to be difficult; a single original form is rather unlikely. There may be a connection between the *Sanctus* and the recitation of the *qedûšā* at Morning Prayer as well as in the Eighteen Benedictions.[101] Yet unlike the *qedûšā*, the *Sanctus* addresses God directly. The form of address *Deus* came into the *Trisagion* via the Old Latin translation of the Bible. As compared with the *qedûšā*, the *Sanctus* in praising God's glory makes a change from proclamation ("his glory") to acclamation ("your glory"). Moreover, "heaven and earth" are celebrated, which are full of God's glory. Erik Peterson has given a plausible explanation for this: through the Incarnation of Christ, God's glory (*kābôd;* δόξα) came into the world, and with the Resurrection it returned to heaven. Through Christ, heaven and earth are inseparably connected with each other.[102] The expression "heaven and earth", however, is not uniquely Christian; it occurs also in the later Jewish tradition.[103]

The *Sanctus* makes it clear that the Church in her praises is united with the never-ending heavenly praise of the angels. In Gaul, the

---

[98] Cf. 1 Clement 34.6 (Berger and Nord, 705).

[99] Cf. Tertullian, *De oratione* 3.3 (CCSL 1:259).

[100] Cf. Gamber, *Missa Romensis*, 63.

[101] Cf. Anton Baumstark, "Trishagion und Quedusha", *Jahrbücher für Liturgiewissenschaft* 3 (1923): 18–32; Spinks, *Sanctus in the Eucharistic Prayer*, 39–44.

[102] Cf. Erik Peterson, *Das Buch von den Engeln: Stellung und Bedeutung der heiligen Engel im Kultus*, 2nd ed. (Munich: Kösel-Verlag, 1955), 33. Thus, in Peterson's study, this is still associated with the traditional substitution theory aimed against Israel, which claimed that the Church of Jesus Christ replaced Israel as the People of God; on the problems caused by this view, cf. Gerhards, "Crossing Borders", 36f.

[103] Eric Werner has pointed out that the expression "heaven and earth" is found likewise in the Targum version of Isaiah 6:3 (cf. Werner, *The Sacred Bridge*, vol. 1 [New York: De Capo Press, 1959], 285; Werner, *The Sacred Bridge*, vol. 2 [New York: KTAV, 1984], 108–14). On the Jewish tradition, see also David Flusser, "Sanktus und Gloria", in Flusser, *Entdeckungen im Neuen Testament*, vol. 1, *Jesusworte und ihre Überlieferung*, 2nd ed., ed. M. Maier (Neukirchen-Vluyn: Neukirchener Verlag, 1992), 227–29; Brian D. Spinks, "The Jewish Sources for the Sanctus", *Heythrop Journal* 21 (1980): 176; Gerhards, "Crossing Borders", 32f.

Sanctus was sung from the sixth century on, and in Rome, from the seventh, together with the *Hosanna-Benedictus*, which goes back to the shouts of the crowd at the entrance of Jesus into Jerusalem (Mt 21:9; Ps 118:25f.).[104] The Old Egyptian liturgies (Deir Balyzeh; Anaphora of Serapion, Anaphora of Saint Mark) have no *Benedictus*.

Te igitur: The *Sanctus* is followed by the petition that God may accept and bless the oblations.[105] With the divine form of address *clementissime Pater*, the celebrant appeals to the mercy of God, that he may let grace prevail over justice with regard to sinful man. The description of the oblations (*dona, munera, sancta sacrificia illibata*) is usually understood pleonastically. It could also be a gradual intensification in the sacrificial statements. For the *sacrificia* are oblations consecrated by God, not merely offerings (cf. the *Supra quae*). The Eucharistic sacrifice is offered for the "Catholic" Church, that is, the Universal Church spread throughout the world (*pro ecclesia tua sancta Catholica offerimus*). Prayers are offered for her peace and unity, for the pope and the bishops, who have the task of leading the Church and therefore are obliged to stand up for the Catholic, apostolic faith. The formula *una cum famulo tuo Papa nostro N. et Antistite nostro N. et omnibus orthodoxis atque catholicae et apostolicae fidei cultoribus* goes back to Benedict of Aniane (before 750–821), who relies on Gallic-Irish documents.[106] The title *papa* was increasingly reserved for the Roman bishop from the sixth century on. The "presiders" (*antistites*) were the other bishops. As older manuscripts show, the addition of *et Antistite* is a later development. It may have originated outside of Rome.[107] The expression *orthodoxi atque catholicae et apostolicae fidei cultores* does not mean the faithful as a whole but, rather, the bishops in union with the pope, who are the guardians of the true faith.[108]

---

[104] Cf. Gerhards, "Crossing Borders", 33f.

[105] Cf. Jungmann, *Mass of the Roman Rite*, 2:147–52; Willis, *Essays in Early Roman Liturgy*, 124.

[106] Cf. Bernard Capelle, "Et omnibus orthodoxis atque apostolicae fidei cultoribus", in *Travaux liturgiques* (Louvain: Centre Liturgique, 1962), 295f.

[107] Cf. Johannes Brinktrine, *Die heilige Messe*, 5th ed. (Augsburg: Bay Dominus Verlag, 2015), 188.

[108] Cf. Jungmann, *Mass of the Roman Rite*, 2:156; Schmitz, "Canon Romanus", 292. For another view, see Brinktrine, *Heilige Messe*, 186. For Capelle, "Et omnibus orthodoxis", 267, the expression is part of the original material of the Roman Canon.

Memento, Domine: The intercession for the living may have been inserted into the Canon only later.[109] The opening words of the prayer, nevertheless, are a traditional invocation introducing the intercession for the faithful who were remembered in particular. The persons commemorated are called loyal servants (*famuli, famulae*). This probably means the faithful who gave alms for the Church and the poor. At first the names of these persons in the Canon were read aloud by a deacon. For this purpose, diptychs (small tablets) were used on which these names were inscribed.[110] This usage is already mentioned by Innocent I in his letter to the bishop of Gubbio (416). In it, when the pope speaks about the faithful *circumstare*, this must not be understood as though all the faithful used to stand around the altar. Because of the division between the presbyterium and the nave of the church, that was not at all possible.[111]

The practice of reading aloud in the Canon the names of donors must have been abandoned very soon, since in the oldest manuscripts containing the prayer *Memento, Domine* no reference to it remains. The formula *fides et devotio* presumably comes from the military world, where it designated the loyalty and readiness of the soldiers. In the Eucharistic Canon, this means the Christian faith and the devotion of the faithful to God.[112] The phrase *vota reddere* originally meant the keeping of oaths, which was often done through a sacrifice. In the *Memento, Domine*, the formula refers to the cultic action of offering sacrifice,[113] which was performed by the faithful.[114] The later formula *pro quibus tibi offerimus*, which is ascribed to Alcuin (735–804) or to Benedict of Aniane, shows the tendency to see the offering of sacrifice above all as the duty of the consecrated priest.[115] Probably this is connected with the development of private Mass.

Communicantes: Following the *Memento, Domine* is a commemoration of selected saints in the *Communicantes*. Intercessory parts can be traced back to the old Roman Canon of the Mass at the turn of the

---

[109] Cf. Schmitz, "Canon Romanus", 292.

[110] Cf. Jungmann, *Mass of the Roman Rite*, 2:159.

[111] Cf. ibid., 2:166.

[112] Cf. Alfred Stuiber, "Die Diptychon-Formel für die *nomina offerentium* im römischen Messkanon", *Ephemerides liturgicae* 68 (1954): 143f., 146.

[113] Cf. ibid., 134.

[114] Cf. Jungmann, *Mass of the Roman Rite*, 2:166.

[115] Cf. ibid., 2:167.

fifth century.[116] Very early there was already a provision on particular days for the interpolation that commemorated the mystery of the day's feast. It is assumed that the *Communicantes* was originally united with the *Nobis quoque*.[117] The definitive list of saints in the *Communicantes* may have been established by Pope Gregory the Great. At the beginning, besides the Virgin Mary, probably only the Princes of the Apostles, Peter and Paul, were named; the later list included also the other apostles (Matthias is not mentioned) and Paul as well as twelve martyrs (five Roman bishops, one African bishop, two clerics who were not bishops, and four male laymen).[118] The list of the saints leads to the request that God might grant us help and protection through their merits and intercessions. The *Communicantes* concludes with the Mediator formula *Per Christum Dominum*.[119]

Hanc igitur: The prayer for acceptance of the oblation is said immediately before the Consecration. The *Hanc igitur*, which again takes up the *Te igitur*, was not a fixed component of the Roman Canon at first.[120] Its purpose was to pray for individual persons and concerns. At first, it was used only in Masses for a particular occasion and also in votive Masses but not on Sundays and feast days. Pope Gregory the Great made the *Hanc igitur* a fixed element of the Roman Eucharistic Prayer. Outside of Rome, however, special forms continued to exist for a rather long time. The *Missale Romanum* of 1570 contains such forms only for Holy Thursday and also for the time from the Easter Vigil or Vigil of Pentecost until the following Sunday. A proper *Hanc igitur* is found in the 1596 *Pontificale Romanum* for the consecration of a bishop. The 1970 *Missale Romanum* provides, besides the aforementioned special forms, six more interpolations for special occasions.[121]

---

[116] Cf. ibid., 1:55; Gamber, *Missa Romensis*, 67.

[117] Cf. Schmitz, "Canon Romanus", 296.

[118] On the discussion about what criteria determined the ranking of the apostles and the selection of the saints, cf. Schmitz, "Canon Romanus", 297; Neil J. Roy, "The Roman Canon: Deësis in Euchological Form", in *Benedict XVI and the Sacred Liturgy: Proceedings of the First Fota International Liturgy Conference 2008*, ed. N.J. Roy and J.E. Rutherford (Dublin: Four Courts Press, 2010), 181–99.

[119] Cf. *AAS* 54 (1962): 873. Pope John XXIII (1958–1963), whose given name was Angelo Giuseppe (Joseph) Roncalli, inserted the name of St. Joseph into the *Communicantes*.

[120] Cf. Jungmann, *Mass of the Roman Rite*, 2:179.

[121] We should mention here celebrations of the scrutinies, of adult Baptism, of the ordination of a bishop, priest, or deacon, of Matrimony, of the consecration of virgins, and of perpetual profession.

Evidence for the gesture of spreading hands over the oblations during the *Hanc igitur* appears first in the late Middle Ages.[122] The offering of the oblations (bread and wine) is performed by the *servitus nostra*, that is, the ministry of the bishop or priest, and also by the *cuncta familia tua*, the communion of God's faithful. Combined with the request for the acceptance of the oblations that are offered is a prayer for freedom and for inclusion in the band of the elect.

Quam oblationem: The first part of this prayer segment contains the request that God might make the oblation a gift that is blessed (*benedictam*), approved (*adscriptam, ratam*), and accepted (*acceptabilem*) as a spiritual oblation (*oblationem rationabilem*). The expression *oblatio rationabilis* alludes to Romans 12:1, where Paul contrasts pagan worship with λογικὴ λατρεία, worship in accordance with the Logos that is performed in the Holy Spirit.[123] Spiritual worship consists of offering oneself to God as a living, holy, and God-pleasing sacrifice. In the Old Latin translation of the Bible, λογικός in Romans 12:1 (also in 1 Pet 2:2) is translated *rationabilis*. The expressions *adscriptus* (registered, valid) and *ratus* (legally binding) are taken from Roman legal language.

The second part of the *Quam oblationem* consists of a request for the transformation of the gifts into the Body and Blood of Christ. The transformation is not an end in itself. The purpose of the transformation is communion (*ut nobis Corpus et Sanguis fiat dilectissimi Filii tui, Domini nostri Iesu Christi*). The *ut*-clause is to be understood as a purpose clause (in the sense of *ut enim*) and is dependent on the request referring to the *oblatio rationabilis* in the first part. The clause formulates the petition that the oblation might become for us the Body and Blood of Christ.[124] This is an epiclesis, derived from ἐπικαλεῖν τὸ ὄνομα κυρίου, that is, to call on the name of the Lord (cf. Rom 10:12f.). Every liturgical prayer is fundamentally epicletic. The basic epicletic structure of liturgical prayer, however, is different from formal epiclesis. The latter is an invocation of the divine name or of the Holy Spirit upon a person, a gift, or a community. Now it is possible

---

[122] Cf. Brinktrine, *Heilige Messe*, 194.

[123] On possible influences from pagan philosophy, cf. Odo Casel, "Oblatio rationabilis", *Theologische Quartalschrift* 99 (1917/1918), 429–39.

[124] Cf. Casel, "Quam oblationem", *Jahrbuch für Liturgiewissenschaft* 2 (1922): 98.

that the *Quam oblationem* originally was only a plea for the acceptance of the sacrifice.[125] In the context of the Roman Canon, however, Josef Andreas Jungmann and Johannes Brinktrine interpret the *Quam oblationem* correctly as an epiclesis of transformation, even though it is not an explicit epiclesis of the Spirit.[126]

There are no indications whatsoever that the Roman Canon at first contained an epiclesis of the Spirit that was later omitted.[127] The idea that the consecration of the gifts of bread and wine comes about through the *verba testamenti* of the account of institution has defined Latin Eucharistic theology since Ambrose of Milan. Therefore we are not reading a medieval understanding of consecration into an ancient Christian text if we understand the *Quam oblationem* of the Roman Canon as an epiclesis of transformation. Of course Florus of Lyon (d. ca. 850), like Ambrose, does not yet see an antithesis between the consecration of the gifts through the *verba testamenti* and the understanding of the Eucharistic Prayer as a whole as the prayer of consecration.[128] The interpretation of Christ's words as "words of

---

[125] Cf. Casel, "Ein orientalisches Kultwort in abendländischer Umschmelzung", *Jahrbuch für Liturgiewissenschaft* 11 (1931): 12f.

[126] Cf. Jungmann, *Mass of the Roman Rite*, 2:190–91; Brinktrine, *Heilige Messe*, 197. See also Herwegen's epilogue to Casel, "Oblatio rationabilis", 438f. The Ambrosian *Fac oblationem*, like the *Quam oblationem* of the Roman Canon, refers to the sacramental reality of the Body and Blood of Christ. This is not the case in the corresponding prayer of the Anaphora of St. Mark. It is not an epiclesis over the gifts but, rather, an epiclesis over the act of offering, which is to be distinguished from the transformation epiclesis according to the *verba testamenti*. Cf. *Anaphora Marci Evangelistae* (Anton Hänggi and Irmgard Pahl ed., 112f.). See also the *Euchologion Serapionis* (Anton Hänggi and Irmgard Pahl ed., 130f.).

[127] The Spirit-epiclesis of the Georgian Anaphora of St. Peter, a translation of the Roman Canon from the tenth century, is a later addition. The reference in a letter by Pope Gelasius I (cf. *Epistula* 7) is not unequivocal, since the reference to epiclesis here could also mean the entire Canon (cf. *Mass of the Roman Rite* 2:150f., 193–94).

[128] Cf. Florus of Lyon, *Opusculum de expositio Missae* 60 (PL 119:52B–C): "*Qui, pridie quam pateretur accepit panem*, etc., usque ad *haec quotiescumque feceritis, in mei memoriam facietis.* Unde universalis Ecclesia, ut iugem memoriam Domini et Redemptoris celebret, ipse Dominus tradidit apostolis, et apostoli generaliter omni Ecclesiae. In his verbis, sine quibus nulla lingua, nulla regio, nulla civitas, id est nulla pars Ecclesiae catholicae conficere potest, id est consecrare sacramentum corporis et sanguinis Domini ... Christi ergo virtute et verbis semper consecratur et consecrabitur" [*Who on the day before he suffered took bread ... as often as you do these things, you will do it in memory of me.* Hence, in order that the universal Church might celebrate the continual memory of our Lord and Redeemer, the Lord himself handed it down to the apostles, and the apostles to the whole Church. In these words, without which no language, no region, no city, that is, no part of the Catholic Church can confect, that is,

transformation" did not first become generally accepted in the Carolingian era.[129] As the Eucharistic controversy between Paschasius Radbertus and Ratramnus shows, it was already generally assumed in the late eighth century.[130]

Qui pridie: The account of the institution, which goes back to the Old Latin versions of Matthew 26 and 1 Corinthians 11,[131] is grammatically connected with the *Quam oblationem* (*Iesus Christus, qui pridie . . .*) and therefore belongs to the anamnesis of the Canon. In the reform of the *Ordo Missae* in 1969, the supplement *quod pro vobis tradetur* [which will be given up for you] was added to the words over the bread.[132] Various views are advocated by scholars about the origin and meaning of the interpolation *mysterium fidei*.[133] It is uncertain

consecrate the sacrament of the Lord's Body and Blood ... it is consecrated and will always be consecrated by the power and the words of Christ]. At the end of his interpretation of the Canon, Florus speaks about the "conclusio totius consecrationis": *Opusculum de Expositione Missae* 72 (*PL* 119:64A). Florus, however, no longer regarded the oblations in the *Post-Pridie* prayers as *consecranda* [to be consecrated], as Hans-Christian Seraphim, *Von der Darbringung des Leibes Christi in der Messe: Studien zur Auslegungsgeschichte des römischen Messkanons* (University dissertation, Munich, 1970), 30–32, thinks. Cf. Florus of Lyon, *Opusculum de expositio Missae* 74 (*PL* 119:64D–65C).

[129] A contrasting view: Reinhard Messner, *Die Messreform Martin Luthers und die Eucharistie der Alten Kirche: Ein Beitrag zu einer systematischen Liturgiewissenschaft* (Innsbruck: Tyrolia, 1989), 93.

[130] Cf. below chapter 5.1. The "Letter to Redemptus" attributed to Isidore of Seville, which sees the substance of the sacrament of the Eucharist in the words of institution and understands the Ambrosian concept of consecration in legal categories, is spurious and comes from the twelfth century. Cf. Isidore of Seville, *Epistola* 7.2; *Ad Redemptus* (*PL* 83:905D): "To the substance of the sacrament belong the words of God that are pronounced by the priest in the sacred ministry, namely: 'This is my Body.'" On the Eucharistic doctrine of the Letter to Redemptus, cf. Josef Rupert Geiselmann, *Die Abendmahlslehre an der Wende der christlichen Spätantike zum Frühmittelalter* (Munich: Hueber, 1933), 18–163.

[131] Cf. Edward C. Ratcliff, "The Institution Narrative of the Roman Canon Missae: Its Beginning and Early Background", *Studia patristica* 2 (1957): 64–83.

[132] According to Ratcliff, ibid., the reason why the addition handed down by Paul and Luke, *quod pro vobis tradetur*, is absent from the traditional form of the *Canon Romanus* is that Matthew 26:26–28 is the basis of the text of the Canon.

[133] Cf. Jungmann, *Mass of the Roman Rite*, 2:200–201; Jungmann, *Opfermesse sowie im Anhang: Messe im Gottesvolk: ein nachkonziliarer Durchblick durch Missarum Sollemnia*, vol. 2 of *Missarum Sollemnia: Eine genetische Erklärung der römischen Messe* (1970; Bonn: Nova et Vetera, 2003), 67; Schmitz, "Canon Romanus", 302; Moreton, "Rethinking the Origin of the Roman Canon", 64; Winfried Haunerland, *Die Eucharistie und ihre Wirkungen im Spiegel der Euchologie des Missale Romanum*, Liturgiewissenschaftliche Quellen und Forschungen 71 (Münster: Aschendorff, 1989), 136f.

whether the interpolation refers to the mystery of the transformation of the gifts. Odo Casel suspects that the *mysterium fidei* concerns the Paschal Mystery of Christ.[134] The Latin tradition of course referred the *mysterium fidei* to the mystery of the transformation of the gifts.[135] The interpolation first occurs in the *Sacramentarium Gelasianum* (seventh-eighth century). It has a parallel in the words over the bread in the *Apostolic Constitutions*: τοῦτο τὸ μυστήριον τῆς καινῆς διαθήκης.[136] Philippians 2:17 (sacrificial service to the faith) and 1 Timothy 3:9 (content of the Gospel) are mentioned as the biblical source for the *mysterium fidei* in the words over the chalice in the Roman Canon.[137]

In the addition *accepit panem in sanctas ac venerabiles manus suas, et elevatis oculis in caelum ad te Deum, Patrem suum omnipotentem*, the prayerful character and the idea of offering are expressed with particular clarity. The *pro vobis* in the words over the chalice from the Pauline-Lucan Last Supper tradition is probably not original. It is still absent from the *Expositio brevis antiquae liturgiae Gallicanae*.[138] In the words over the chalice, the New Covenant is additionally professed to be an everlasting one (*novi et aeterni testamenti*). The expansion *qui pridie quam nostra omniumque salute pateretur* is foreseen for the Mass of the Lord's Supper on Holy Thursday.[139]

Unde memores: This prayer segment, which must be seen together with the next two prayers (*Supra quae; Supplices te rogamus*), begins with the remembrance of Christ's Passion, his Resurrection, and his Ascension. Mentioned as the subject of the remembrance (*memores*) are the bishop or priest and the holy people. The second part

[134] Cf. Odo Casel, "Das Mysteriengedächtnis der Messliturgie im Lichte der Tradition", *Jahrbuch für Liturgiewissenschaft* 6 (1926): 173.

[135] So, too, in the *Roman Catechism* (1566/1567). Cf. *Catechismus ex Decreto Concilii Tridentini*, pars II, caput IV, no. 23. English edition: *Catechism of the Council of Trent for Parish Priests*, trans. John A. McHugh, O.P., and Charles J. Callan, O.P. (New York: Joseph F. Wagner, 1923).

[136] Cf. *Constitutiones Apostolorum* 8.12.36 (Anton Hänggi and Irmgard Pahl ed., 92).

[137] During the course of the Vatican reform of the Missal, the interpolation *mysterium fidei* was removed from the words over the chalice, placed after them, and combined with a congregational acclamation.

[138] Cf. *Patrologia cursus completus: Series Latina*, ed. J.-P. Migne (Paris: Garnier, 1841–1864; hereafter cited as *PL*), 72:89–98; 93. The exposition is attributed to Germanus of Paris (496–576), but it originated only in the late seventh or early eighth century.

[139] Cf. Jungmann, *Mass of the Roman Rite*, 2:198.

includes the offering (*offerimus*) "of the holy bread of eternal life and of the chalice of perpetual salvation" (*Panem sanctum vitae aeternae, et Calicem salutis perpetuae*). The consecrated gifts are designated *hostia pura, hostia sancta*, and *hostia immaculata*. The offering is an offering in the form of an anamnesis (*memores ... offerimus*: remembering we offer). In the anamnesis of the Eucharistic Prayer of the *Traditio Apostolica*, Christ's death and Resurrection are mentioned; in the Ambrosian Canon and in the Roman Canon, the Ascension, also. In most Eastern Eucharistic Prayers, the anamnesis is elaborated more fully (for example, with a mention of Christ's rest in the tomb, his descent to the netherworld, Christ's Second Coming, and the judgment).

The thesis that the offering in *Unde et memores* originally referred to the *consecranda* (the oblations to be consecrated) and not to the *consecrata* (the consecrated oblations)[140] assumes that the *Supplices te rogamus* is to be regarded as the real transformation epiclesis. Thus far, however, no one has been able to adduce in favor of it any text from the Roman liturgical tradition. In the light of the concept of consecration that has been dominant since Ambrose, the second part of the prayer *Unde et memores* should be understood as the post-consecratory offering of the Body and Blood of Christ.[141] Jungmann rightly sees the *Unde et memores* as the central sacrificial prayer of the Roman Canon. It is "the foremost liturgical expression of the fact that the Mass is actually a sacrifice".[142] It should be noted in this connection that the *principalis offerens*, Christ the High Priest, remains entirely in

[140] Cf. Seraphim, *Von der Darbringung des Leibes Christi in der Messe*; Hans-Joachim Schulz, "Christusverkündigung und kirchlicher Opfervollzug nach den Anamnesetexten der eucharistischen Hochgebete", in *Christuszeugnis der Kirche*, ed. P.-W. Scheele and G. Schneider (Essen: Fredebeul und Koenen, 1970), 102–4; Herwig Aldenhoven, "Darbringung und Epiklese im Eucharistiegebet: Eine Studie über die Struktur des Eucharistiegebetes in den altkatholischen Liturgien im Lichte der Liturgiegeschichte", in *Internationale Kirchliche Zeitschrift* 61 (1971): 173–81.

[141] While Winfried Haunerland does not advocate the thesis that the *Supplices te rogamus* was originally the transformation epiclesis of the Roman Canon, he does, like Seraphim and Messner, formulate clear reservations with regard to a post-consecratory offering of the Body and Blood of Christ, as is expressed in the *Post-Pridie* prayers. Cf. Haunerland, *Eucharistie und ihre Wirkungen*, 106–13, 155f.; also Martin Stuflesser, *Memoria passionis: Das Verständnis von lex orandi und lex credendi am Beispiel des Opferbegriffs in den eucharistischen Hochgebeten nach dem II. Vatikanischen Konzil*, Münsteraner theologische Abhandlungen 51 (Altenberge: Oros, 1998).

[142] Jungmann, *Mass of the Roman Rite*, 2:223.

the background in the *Unde et memores*. That is not so in the following prayer segment.[143]

Supra quae: After the *Unde et memores* follows another plea for acceptance: May God accept the spotless sacrifice of the Church's minister
and of the holy people as he once accepted the gifts (*munera*) of Abel,
the sacrifice (*sacrificium*) of Abraham, and the offering of the high priest
Melchizedek. The plea for acceptance in the *Supra quae*, too, refers
to the offering of the Body and Blood of Christ. According to the
Liber Pontificalis, Pope Leo the Great was the one who had the words
sanctum sacrificium, immaculatam hostiam added to the description of the
sacrifice that Melchizedek offered (bread, wine).[144] The expression
hostia immaculata is already found earlier in the prayer segment *Unde et
memores*. Zeno of Verona already used it in his sermons to designate
Abraham's sacrifice. Moreover, the expression appears in the Ambrosian Canon.[145] The addition *hostia immaculata* characterizes Melchizedek's present of bread and wine as the offering of a sacrifice.[146] The
description of Abel as "just" (*iustus*) is of New Testament origin (cf.
Mt 23:35; Heb 11:4). The title "high priest" (*summus sacerdos*) for Melchizedek comes from Jewish tradition. The sacrifices of Abel, Abraham, and Melchizedek are prefigurations (τύποι) of the Eucharistic
sacrifice. The decisive thing is not the comparison of the oblations
(although this plays a major role in Christian iconography: Abel/
Lamb, Abraham-Isaac/sacrifice on the Cross, Melchizedek/bread and
wine), but rather the disposition in which the sacrifice is offered and,
above all, the favor with which the sacrifice is accepted by God.

Supplices te rogamus: Presumably this prayer segment, too, goes back
to Pope Leo the Great. The first part (*iube haec perferri per manus sancti
Angeli tui in sublime altare tuum, in conspectu divinae maiestatis tuae*), in
comparison with the anaphoras of the Eastern Churches, gives the impression of being a consecration epiclesis.[147] In the context of the
Roman Canon, the *Supplices*, however, is a post-consecratory plea

[143] Cf. ibid.

[144] Cf. *Liber Pontificalis* 1 (ed. Duchesne, 239).

[145] Cf. Jeanes, "Early Latin Parallels?", 431.

[146] Cf. Jungmann, *Mass of the Roman Rite*, 2:231. The reason for the addition was probably heretical groups hostile to the body that were scandalized by the use of wine in the Eucharist.

[147] Cf. Schulz, "Christusverkündigung und kirchlicher Opfervollzug", 124–28; Alden-hoven, "Darbringung und Epiklese im Eucharistiegebet", 170–473.

for acceptance.[148] With a "daring illustration" (Josef Andreas Jungmann), it formulates the plea for a definitive acceptance and reception of the oblations. The cultic image of the heavenly altar comes
from Revelation 8:3–5 and occurs often in the Eastern liturgies.
The singular *per manus angeli*, as opposed to the plural *per manus
angelorum tuorum*, may have been influenced by Isaiah 9:5 (LXX)
(μεγάλης βουλῆς ἄγγελος).[149] The identification of the angel with
the Mediator Jesus Christ, which Thomas Aquinas undertakes,[150]
would then by no means be that misguided.[151] The other interpretation, which sees the angel as a special angel of sacrifice, would
also be possible, especially because from the time of Pope Gregory
the Great there was a widespread, vivid idea that during the Eucharistic sacrifice the heavens would open and choirs of angels would
descend.[152] The comparison of the first part of the *Supplices* with the
epiclesis of Eastern liturgies led some to see the angel as an image
for the Holy Spirit.[153] But the Christological interpretation seems
more plausible.[154]

Some cite, among other things, the Eucharistic Prayer of the *Traditio Apostolica* as an argument against a post-consecratory offering
of the Body and Blood of Christ in the Roman Canon after the
verba testamenti. Of course, with its Sequence *verba testamenti*, anamnesis, epiclesis, the Eucharistic Prayer of the *Traditio Apostolica* does
not represent the Roman Liturgy, as was initially assumed on the
basis of the false attribution of the *Traditio Apostolica* to Hippolytus
of Rome. Hence the Eucharistic Prayer of the *Traditio Apostolica*
has little bearing on the interpretation of the Roman Canon. For
the reconstruction of an originally different concept of the Roman

---

[148] Another view is presented by Aldenhoven, Schulz, and, among others, Messner, *Messreform Martin Luthers*, 91: "The *Supplices* is therefore the epiclesis or the equivalent of an
epiclesis in the Roman Canon.... As a whole, therefore, the Roman Canon, in the sequence
thanksgiving—institutional narrative—anamnesis and epiclesis, corresponds to the testimony
of the ancient and Eastern liturgies."

[149] Thus Moreton, "Rethinking the Origin of the Roman Canon", 65.

[150] Thus Thomas Aquinas, *Summa Theologiae* III, q. 83, art. 4 ad 8.

[151] Schmitz disagrees, "Canon Romanus", 305. On the medieval interpretations of the
conveyance of the sacrifice to the heavenly altar, see Jungmann, *Mass of the Roman Rite*, 2:233.

[152] Cf. Gregory I, *Dialogi* 4.58 (*PL* 77, 427A).

[153] Cf. Jungmann, *Mass of the Roman Rite*, 2:233f.

[154] So too Smyth, "Anaphora of the So-called 'Apostolic Tradition'", 84.

Canon, whereby the first part of the *Supplices* had the function of a request for transformation, appropriate textual findings are lacking. We can apply to this question what Louis Bouyer (1913–2004) writes about the genealogy of the Eucharistic Prayers: "There are too many gaps, and the worst thing is that the further back we go, the more numerous and the wider they are, so that we cannot avoid hypotheses or mere guesses."[155] The fact that in the ancient Church there were Eucharistic Prayers in which the transformation epiclesis came before the institutional narrative is shown by the Eastern anaphora of the liturgical papyrus of Beir Balyzeh in Egypt (ca. 500). Admittedly, the anaphora does not go back to the second century, as was initially assumed. It is, however, as old as the core of the Roman Canon.

The second part of the *Supplices* is a communion epiclesis, without any mention of the Holy Spirit as in the Eucharistic Prayer of the *Traditio Apostolica* at the corresponding place. The gifts of the Body and Blood of Christ are received *ex hac altaris participatione*, from a share in the altar, whereby those who communicate are united with the heavenly altar. Hence the priest prays that we "may be filled with every heavenly blessing" (*omni benedictione caelesti et gratia repleamur*) through the reception of the Body and Blood of Christ.[156]

Memento etiam: The commemoration of the dead was first prayed only on weekdays. As with the commemoration of the living, the names were read aloud by a deacon.[157] From the fifth century on, a commemoration of the dead followed within the *Kyrie* litany. Benedict of Aniane closely associated the commemoration of the dead

---

[155] Louis Bouyer, "The Different Forms of the Eucharistic Prayer and Their Genealogy", in *Studia Patristica* 8 (Papers presented to the Fourth International Conference on Patristic Studies held at Christ Church, Oxford, 1963; part 2: Patres apostolici, historica, liturgica, ascetica et monastica), ed. F. Cross (Berlin: Akademie-Verlag, 1966), 158.

[156] Jungmann, *Messe im Gottesvolk*, 59*, thinks that the debate between East and West over the epiclesis in the Eucharistic Canon first became possible because John Damascene understood the word ἀντίτυπος used for the oblations in the anaphora of St. Basil between the *verba testamenti* and the epiclesis as a mere image in the sense of the iconoclastic controversy (cf. *De fide orthodoxa* 4.13; PG 94:1139–50), instead of in the realistic sense as had been conventional until then. For this argument, Jungmann cites Johannes Betz, *Die Eucharistie in der Zeit der griechischen Väter*, vol. 2/1, *Die Realpräsenz des Leibes und Blutes Jesu im Abendmahl nach dem Neuen Testament* (Freiburg: Herder, 1961), 217–39.

[157] Cf. Elias A. Lowe and André Wilmart, eds., *The Bobbio Missal: A Gallican Mass-Book (Ms. Paris. Lat. 13246)*, Henry Bradshaw Society (Suffolk: Boydell Press, 1991), 12f.

with the Canon.[158] In the *Memento etiam*, it says that the deceased went before us *cum signo fidei, et dormiunt in somno pacis*. The "sign of faith" means Baptism as the sacramental seal of faith. The expression "sleep of peace", which is found in numerous inscriptions on Christian tombs, is an image for death that is found already in the writings of Cicero.[159] Following Christ's example (Mt 9:24; Jn 11:11), Christians called the death of a just man a kind of sleep and understood by this the state between the just man's death and the consummation at the end of the ages. The commemoration of the dead comprises not only those mentioned by name in the *Memento etiam*, but all who have fallen asleep in Christ (Rev 14:13: *qui in Domino moriuntur*). The Church prays that God might grant to them a *locus refrigerii, lucis, et pacis*, a place of refreshment, light, and peace. In a certain sense, an expansion of the communion epiclesis takes place with the commemoration of the dead. The Eucharist as food of eternal life establishes the connection here.[160] The deceased no longer share in the sacramental meal, and instead they are remembered in the *oratio oblationis*.[161]

Nobis quoque: The last prayer segment of the Canon before the two concluding doxologies (*Per quem; Per ipsum*) contains the plea for communion with the saints and forms a certain parallel to the *Communicantes*. John the Baptist stands at the beginning of the list of saints in the *Nobis quoque*. Fourteen saints of the Roman Church follow (seven men and seven women). The *Nobis quoque*, like the commemoration of the dead, is a continuation of the communion epiclesis in the *Supplices. Nos peccatores famuli tui*, who pray that God may give them a share in heavenly glory with the apostles and martyrs, probably means the entire liturgical assembly,[162] not only the celebrating priest and the other clerics.[163] It is debated whether the *Nobis quoque* was connected with the *Supplices* from the beginning or whether it was added later, after the *Memento etiam* became a permanent component of the Canon. It is possible that the *Nobis quoque* was

---

[158] Cf. Jungmann, *Mass of the Roman Rite*, 2:242–46.

[159] Cf. Cicero *Tusculanae Disputationes* 1.38. In Greek mythology, Hypnos, the god of sleep, is the brother of Thanatos, the god of death.

[160] Cf. Schmitz, "Canon Romanus", 307.

[161] Cf. Jungmann, *Mass of the Roman Rite*, 2:240.

[162] This is assumed by Schmitz, "Canon Romanus", 308.

[163] This interpretation is still given by Jungmann, *Mass of the Roman Rite*, 2:249f.

originally associated with the *Communicantes*. The list of saints in the *Nobis quoque* might have developed slowly.[164]

Per quem: In the context of the Roman Canon, the summarizing formula *Per quem*, which is to be distinguished from the actual concluding doxology *Per ipsum*, refers to the Eucharistic gifts. Presumably, however, this was not its primary sense. Earlier, at the end of the Canon there was a blessing of produce. Jungmann assumes that the doxology *Per quem* initially was the concluding formula for variable prayers of blessing and that "the gifts" (*haec omnia bona*) that God sanctifies through Christ meant fruits of the earth.[165] Others argue that the concluding formula *Per quem* was a permanent component of the Canon from the beginning and referred exclusively to the Eucharistic gifts.[166]

Per ipsum: The Canon concludes with a solemn prayer of praise. This corresponds to the Jewish tradition of prayer. The Trinitarian structure is the distinguishing feature of the Christian doxology. The Divine Persons are not listed paratactically, as in the Eucharistic Prayer of the *Traditio Apostolica*. The Trinitarian formula corresponds to the divine economy of salvation. Honor and glory are offered to God through Jesus Christ, the Mediator and High Priest, in union with the Holy Spirit. The formula *in unitate Spiritus Sancti* corresponds to the formula *in sancta Ecclesia tua* in the Eucharistic Prayer of the *Traditio Apostolica*. Yet in the Roman Canon, it may mean, besides the unity of Holy Church,[167] God's Trinitarian unity, also.[168] The elevation of the consecrated gifts at the concluding doxology, which is still the usage today, goes back to the seventh century.[169] The simple rite of elevation, however, became encrusted early on

---

[164] Cf. ibid., 252–56.

[165] Cf. ibid., 260–64. According to the Latin tradition, the oil of the sick to this day is consecrated immediately before the conclusion of the Canon. For pastoral reasons, it can be consecrated together with the other oils after the Liturgy of the Word.

[166] Cf. Jordi Pinelli, "La grande conclusion du Canon romain", *La Maison-Dieu* 88 (1966): 96–115. Kleinheyer, *Erneuerung des Hochgebetes*, 27, calls the *Per quem* a "bit of debris whose existence cannot be justified at all".

[167] Thus Jungmann, *Mass of the Roman Rite*, 2:266.

[168] Thus Bernard Botte, "In unitate Spiritus Sancti", in *L'Ordinaire de la Messe*, Études liturgiques 2, ed. B. Botte and C. Mohrmann (Paris: Éditions du Cerf; Louvain: Abbaye du Mont César, 1953), 133–39.

[169] Cf. *Ordo Romanus* 1.89 (Andrieu ed., 2:96); ibid., 4.55 (Andrieu ed., 2:164). In the classical form of the Mass, the priest elevates the chalice and ciborium only at the concluding words *omnis honor et Gloria*; in the "Novus Ordo", during the whole concluding doxology.

with a series of signs of the cross.[170] The praise of the doxology is concluded by an affirming *Amen* of the people. With their *Amen*, the people endorse, so to speak, the Eucharistic Prayer. During the early Middle Ages, when the Canon was already prayed silently,[171] the concluding doxology was still pronounced aloud, but later only the concluding *per omnia saecula saeculorum*.

C. Carolingian Reform and Allegorical Interpretations of the Mass

The Carolingian liturgy reform was of central importance for the medieval development of the Roman liturgy. The Carolingian rulers, who derived their position from God, saw it as their mission to regulate the practice of religion and of public worship, so as to strengthen the unity of the Frankish empire.[172] Even before the eighth century, some Frankish bishops had sought contact with the Roman liturgy. In 716, Pope Gregory II (715–731) sent a letter to the Church in Bavaria, in which he laid down the Roman liturgy as the norm.[173] Under Pippin the Younger (714–768), the *Sacramentarium Gelasianum / Old Gelasian Sacramentary* came to France. Influence from the Gallic liturgy led to the further development of the Sacramentary (*New Gelasian*). The *Missale Gothicum* (seventh century)[174] and the *Missale Gallicanum Vetus* (seventh-eighth century)[175] give a glimpse into the original Gallic liturgy. Like Bishop Chrodegang (d. 766) in Metz, Pippin introduced the Latin chant of the Roman *schola cantorum*.

Charlemagne (747–814) strove to continue the work of his father, Pippin. The liturgical reform that Charlemagne initiated was part of a more comprehensive reform in education. Charlemagne's efforts

---

[170] Concerning this development that concluded in the eleventh/twelfth century, see Jungmann, *Mass of the Roman Rite*, 2:267–71.

[171] On the principle of silence during the Canon, cf. ibid., 104f.

[172] On the pre-Carolingian liturgy of Gaul, see the short overview in Meyer, *Eucharistie*, 154–57.

[173] Cf. *PL* 89:531–34; 532A.

[174] Cf. *Missale gothicum* (Codex Vaticanus Regensis latinus 317), Rerum ecclesiasticarum documenta: Series maior, Fontes 5, ed. by L. C. Mohlberg (Rome, 1961).

[175] Cf. *Missale Gallicanum Vetus* (Codex Vaticanus palatinus 493), Rerum ecclesiasticarum documenta: Series maior, Fontes 3, ed. L. C. Mohlberg (Rome, 1958). In the case of the *Missale Gallicanum Vetus*, we are dealing with a fragment.

on behalf of grammatically correct speech and writing led in the field of liturgy to an intensification of "formal justice". According to the king's conviction, one prays correctly only with corrected liturgical books.[176] In order to guarantee as uniform a celebration of the Mass as possible, Charlemagne asked Pope Hadrian I (772–795) for an "unadulterated" Sacramentary of Gregory the Great. The version of the *Gregorianum* that the king received between 784 and 791 is called the *Sacramentarium Hadrianum*. The Sacramentary, which was copied in Aachen, served as the specimen copy for the Romanization of the Frankish liturgy. Since the *Sacramentarium Hadrianum* that the king received was incomplete (it contained only the texts of the papal stational liturgy for certain days of the year), a supplement was added to it. Alcuin was once considered its author, but today it is assumed that the *Supplement* was composed by Benedict of Aniane (d. 821).[177]

Louis the Pious (778–840), Charlemagne's successor, sent Amalar of Metz (d. ca. 850) to Rome to ask Pope Gregory IV (827–844) for a new Antiphonary, for the purpose of further adapting the Frankish forms of worship and hymns to the Roman Rite. In 787, Pope Hadrian I urged that the *cantus romanus* (Gregorian chant) be introduced without any change. It is certain that the renewal of the liturgy was carried out consistently in centers like Aachen, Metz, Lyon, and Saint-Riquier, in which Gregorian chant also flourished. The Romanization of liturgical singing, however, was not immediately accepted everywhere.[178] Notker of Saint Gall (d. 912) still marvels

---

[176] Cf. Karl der Grosse, *Admonitio generalis* a. 789, can. 72 (Monumenta Germaniae Historica cap. 1, 60).

[177] Cf. Jean Deshusses, "Le 'Supplément' au sacramentaire grégorien: Alcuin ou Bénoît d'Aniane", *Archiv für Liturgiewissenschaft* 9 (1965): 48–71; Deshusses, *Le Sacramentaire Grégorien: Ses principales formes d'après les plus anciens manuscrits*, vol. 1, *Le sacramentaire, le supplément d'Aniane*, 2nd ed., Spicilegium Friburgense 16 (Fribourg, Éditions Universitaires, 1979); Marcel Metzger, *Geschichte der Liturgie*, authorized German trans. A. Knoop (Paderborn et al.: Schöningh, 1998), 121f.; Hans Bernhard Meyer, "Benedikt von Aniane (ca. 750–821): Reform der monastischen Tagzeiten und Ausgestaltung der römisch-fränkischen Messfeier", in *Liturgiereformen: Historische Studien zu einem bleibenden Grundzug des christlichen Gottesdienstes*, Festschrift A. A. Häussling, vol. 1, *Biblische Modelle und Liturgiereform von der Frühzeit bis zur Aufklärung*, ed. M. Klöckener and B. Kranemann, Liturgiewissenschaftliche Quellen und Forschungen 88 (Münster: Aschendorff, 2002), 255–60. Benedict of Aniane was the abbot of the reform monastery founded in Aniane in 780.

[178] Cf. Pierre Riché, *Die Welt der Karolinger*, 3rd ed. (Stuttgart: Reclam, 2009). A German translation of *La vie quotidienne dans l'empire Carolingien* (Paris: Hachette, 1973), 275.

at the "all-too-great difference between our way of singing and the Roman way".[179] Benedict of Aniane placed all monasteries in the Frankish empire under the Benedictine Rule.[180] At the same time, he undertook an adaptation of the Roman liturgy to the circumstances of worship in the Frankish monasteries and parishes. In 814, he was appointed Abbot of Kornelimünster Abbey in the vicinity of the imperial city of Aachen. Through the Carolingian reforms, the monasteries became a "place of highly official liturgy",[181] and public life, for example legal proceedings, became liturgized.[182]

The main contributors to the standardization of the rite of the Mass in the period after Charlemagne and Louis the Pious were the Ottonian dynasty and Benedictine monasticism. Of all the Benedictine monasteries, Cluny deserves special mention as a culmination of medieval Church liturgy. In contrast, Rome in the ninth century went into a liturgical decline that was stopped in the tenth century by monasteries that had been repopulated by the Cluniacs. The Ottonian rulers Emperor Otto I (912–973) and Otto II (955–983), in connection with their Italian campaigns, supported a comprehensive ecclesiastical reform that also included a renewal of the liturgy. For this the reformers had recourse to liturgical books from beyond the Alps. In this way, Gallic-Frankish traditions arrived in Rome, and the "Roman-Frankish hybrid liturgy" came about, which was foundational for its further development. At around the turn of the millennium, Rome had regained its liturgy in modified form.

The blending of Gallic and Roman liturgy led to a significant dramatization of the liturgy. Examples are the incensation of the altar and Gospel book, the *Gloria tibi Domine* at the Gospel, the liturgy of Palm Sunday with the hymn *Gloria, laus et honor*,[183] the reverencing

---

[179] Cf. Notker the Stammerer, *Gesta Karoli Magni Imperatoris* 1.10, Monumenta Germaniae Historica: Scriptores rerum Germanicarum, nova series 12, ed. by H.F. Haefele (Berlin: Weidmannsche Verlagsbuchhandlung, 1959), 12.

[180] On the Carolingian reform of the monasteries, cf. Dieter Geuenich, "Kritische Anmerkungen zur sogenannten 'anianischen Reform'", in *Mönchtum—Kirche—Herrschaft 750–1000*, Festschrift J. Semmler, ed. D.R. Bauer et al. (Sigmaringen: Thorbecke Verlag, 1998), 99–112.

[181] Arnold Angenendt, *Geschichte der Religiosität im Mittelalter*, 2nd ed. (Darmstadt: Primus Verlag, 2000), 354.

[182] Cf. Ernst H. Kantorowicz, *Laudes Regiae: A Study in Liturgical Acclamations and Mediaeval Ruler Worship* (Berkeley and Los Angeles: University of California Press, 1946).

[183] The author of the hymn is Bishop Theodulf of Orleans (d. 821).

of the cross and the *Improperia* in the Good Friday liturgy, the blessing of the fire, the *Lumen Christi* and the blessing of the Easter candle
with the hymn *Exsultet*, and the blessing of the baptismal water in
the liturgy of the Easter Vigil. The Offertory prayers before the *oratio
super oblate*, too, have their origin in France, and also the *Orate fratres*,
a preliminary form of which is already found in the Sacramentary of
Amiens (ninth century).[184] The *Niceno-Constantinopolitan Creed* had
come into the Frankish Mass from Spain (sixth century) and Ire-
land (eighth-ninth century). At the urging of Henry II (973–1024), it
was prayed at his imperial coronation (1014) by Pope Benedict VIII
(1012–1024). Beginning with the eleventh century, the *Nicene Creed*
became established as a permanent component of the celebration of
Sunday Mass.

The *Rheinish Order of Mass* provides a glimpse of the Roman-
Frankish liturgy of the Mass.[185] It spread from Saint Gall via
Reichenau and Mainz and was also received in Italy and Rome.[186]
The *Rheinish Order of Mass* is regarded as "the original form of the
Ordo for the unchangeable parts of the Mass that was valid from then
on until the Vatican II reform".[187] Bernold of Constance (d. 1100)
had a strong influence on the standardization of the rite of Mass with
his *Micrologus* (ca. 1085).[188] The liturgical reform under Pope Gregory VII (1073–1085) was restricted to minor modifications. Contrary
to the original intentions, it did not lead the Church to restore the
"ordinem romanum et antiquum morem". Yet under Gregory VII,
the individual dioceses became increasingly committed to the form
of the Roman liturgy that had taken shape between the eighth and
eleventh century. The Order of Mass compiled by the prior of the

---

[184] Cf. Jungmann, *Mass of the Roman Rite*, 1:78.

[185] On this subject, see Bonifas Luykx, "Der Ursprung der gleichbleibenden Teile der Hei-
ligen Messe", in *Priestertum und Mönchtum*, ed. T. Bogler, Liturgie und Mönchtum: Laacher
Heft 29 (Maria Laach: Verlag Ars Liturgica, 1961), 72–119; Meyer, *Eucharistie*, 204–8; Andreas
Odenthal, "Ein Formular des 'Rheinischen Messordo' aus St. Aposteln in Köln", *Archiv für
Liturgiewissenschaft* 34 (1992): 333–44; Odenthal, "'Ante conspectum divinae maiestatis tuae
reus assisto': Liturgie- und frömmigkeitsgeschichtliche Untersuchungen zum 'Rheinischen
Messordo' und dessen Beziehungen zur Fuldaer Sacramentartradition", *Archiv für Liturgiewis-
senschaft* 49 (2007): 1–35.

[186] Cf. Michael Fiedrowicz, *Die überlieferte Messe: Geschichte, Gestalt, Theologie* (Mühlheim
an der Mosel: Carthusianus Verlag, 2011), 27.

[187] Meyer, *Eucharistie*, 204.

[188] Cf. Bernold of Constance, *Micrologus* (PL 151:977–1022).

Lateran Church (mid-twelfth century) is the oldest testimony for the practice that the priest recites softly the parts sung by the *schola cantorum* (*Introit, Kyrie, Gloria, Credo, Sanctus, Agnus Dei*) as well as the readings presented by the lector.

The Carolingian reform of the liturgy led to numerous treatises on the liturgy. The best-known is the liturgical commentary by Amalar of Metz in the third part of his *Liber Officialis* (820),[189] in which he carries the then-common allegorical method of scriptural interpretation over to the liturgy.[190] Allegory enables us to "say something other" (ἄλλα ἀγορεύειν) than the literal meaning of the text at hand. The object of the allegorical explanation of the Mass, the beginnings of which go back to the seventh century in the West, is not primarily the text but, rather, the ritual form of the liturgy of the Mass. In the East, liturgical allegory had existed since the fifth century. Theodore of Mopsuestia sees the bringing of the oblations to the altar as a symbol for the burial of Jesus and the transformation of the gifts as a symbol for the Resurrection.[191] In the West, the symbolism of the burial was probably taken up first in the Gallican liturgy (sixth-seventh century). It could not gain general acceptance there, however, since the Offertory procession of the faithful was predominant.[192]

The purpose of Amalar's allegory of the Mass is to uncover the hidden meaning of the celebration of Mass from its gestures, actions, appointed times, and paraments through "typological", "rememorative", "moral", or "anagogical" allegory.[193] "Typological" allegory concentrates on the fulfillment of Old Testament types (*figurae*); "rememorative" allegory—on the events in salvation history; "moral" allegory—on moral instructions; and "anagogical" allegory—on the consummation in the end times. Particular importance is assigned to "rememorative" allegory. It relates the actions of the Mass to events

---

[189] Cf. Amalar of Metz, *Liber Officialis* 3.5–44 (Opera liturgica omnia, ed. J.M. Hanssens [1948], 271–386). The work also has the title *De ecclesiasticis officiis*.

[190] Cf. Wolfgang Steck, *Der Liturgiker Amalarius: Eine quellenkritische Untersuchung zu Leben und Werk eines Theologen der Karolingerzeit*, Münchener theologische Studien 1, Historische Abteilung 35 (St. Ottilien: EOS-Verlag, 2000). Amalar stayed in Byzantium in 813/814, where he may have learned the allegorical explanation of the Mass.

[191] Cf. Theodore of Mopsuestia, *Homiliae Catecheticae* 15.29–32 (FC 17/2:411–13).

[192] Cf. *Expositio antiquae liturgiae Gallicanae* (1971).

[193] In his explanation of the Mass, Amalar refers to the Frankish version of the *Ordo Romanus* II, which was in use in the Church of Metz.

in the life of Jesus: the parts from the *Introitus* to the Gospel symbolize Christ and his hidden and public life; the parts from the *Offertorium* to the concluding doxology of the Canon—the Passion from Palm Sunday to the deposition from the Cross; and finally, the parts from the Our Father to the conclusion—the rest in the tomb, the Resurrection, and the Ascension. Each part of the Canon marks a station of the Passion: the *Sanctus*—the jubilant rejoicing at the entrance of Jesus into Jerusalem; the *verba testamenti*—the dying of Jesus; the *Unde et memores* after the Consecration—his death on the Cross; the prayer *Nobis quoque* toward the end of the Canon—the profession of the centurion beneath the Cross. The *Agnus Dei* is interpreted in terms of the story of Emmaus.[194] Perhaps the best-known example of a "rememorative" allegory of the Mass is the interpretation of the mingling of the consecrated wine with the consecrated bread as a symbol for the unification of Christ's soul and body in his Resurrection.

The allegorical explanation of the Mass tended to tear apart the ritual and the textual levels, the signs (*signa*) and the spoken words (*verba*). Especially in its rememorative form, related to God's salvific deeds, the allegory of the Mass nevertheless helped to make the Mass more accessible for the priest and the faithful. Meanwhile, the katabatic dimension of the liturgy as well as its dynamic-eschatological dimension receded into the background, of course, along with the idea of self-offering, which, however, was retained in principle. Thus Amalar writes in explaining the words of the Canon "haec dona, haec munera, haec sacrificia illibata" (these gifts, oblations and spotless sacrifices): "As Augustine says: If someone wishes to offer gifts to God, he should offer himself, and if he wishes to bring spotless sacrifices, then let him offer humility, praise, and love."[195]

At the instigation of Florus of Lyon, the allegorical explanation of the Mass was forbidden at a Synod of Quiercy.[196] Nevertheless, authors repeatedly had recourse to it, for example Ivo of Chartres (d. 1115), in whose writings we find the following allegorical interpretation of the silence during the Canon: as the high priest enters

---

[194] Cf. Amalar of Metz, *Liber Officialis* 3.22–33 (Hanssens ed., 329–65).

[195] Ibid., 3.23 (334): "Iuxta eundem Augustinem, si quis dona vult Deo offerre, se ipsum offerat; si quis sacrificia inlibata, humilitatem laudemque et caritatem offerat."

[196] Florus of Lyon himself in his own explanation of the Mass has recourse primarily to patristic citations. Cf. Florus of Lyon, *Opusculum de expositione missae* (PL 119:15–72).

the Holy of Holies silently on the Great Day of Atonement to sprin-
kle the panel of the Ark of the Covenant there with the blood of the
sacrificial animal, so with the Canon the priest enters into the Holy
of Holies to offer the memorial of Christ's Blood.[197] As early as the
eighth century, the transition to the quiet recitation of the Canon
had been completed in Gallic lands, presumably under Eastern influence. The principle of silence during the Canon is based on the idea
that the Consecration of the Eucharistic gifts, as Jesus instructed his
Church at the Last Supper, is a dreadful, awe-inspiring event, and
therefore the holy action must be performed in silence. Thereby it
increasingly became the concern of the ordained ministers. In Rome,
the principle of silence during the Canon was generally accepted
by the end of the ninth century. By the eleventh century, the silent
prayers of the priest were also established. The ideal form of celebrating Mass in the High Middle Ages was High Mass celebrated by
a priest, a deacon, and a subdeacon.[198] In monastery churches, even
the daily conventual liturgy was often celebrated with deacon and
subdeacon (missa maior and missa matutinalis).

Even though individual allegorical interpretations by Ivo of Chartres are theologically altogether dubious, his interpretation of the
Canon nevertheless helped to deepen the understanding of the Mass
as a sacrifice. This is true also of the Speculum de mysteriis Ecclesiae,[199]
which is erroneously attributed to Hugh of Saint Victor (d. 1141).
Even though several allegories in it seem to be rather contrived, one
cannot deny that the allegories still have a certain explanatory force.
This is true above all for the interpretation of the double consecration
of bread and wine as a representation of Christ's sacrifice, an interpretation that occurred very early in the Eastern liturgical tradition. But
all things considered, allegories of the Mass obliterated the awareness
that the offering of the faithful and the Church's prayer of thanksgiving are central. As Josef Andreas Jungmann puts it, the Eucharistia

---

[197] Cf. Ivo of Chartres, Sermo 5: Sive opusculum de convenientia veteris et novi sacrificii (PL
162:554A–556C).

[198] As late as the thirteenth century, Thomas Aquinas in his commentary on the Roman
Rite of the Mass presupposes High Mass with deacon and subdeacon, in which the faithful
participated by singing, e.g., the Offertory. Cf. Thomas Aquinas, Summa Theologiae III, q. 83,
art. 4 ad 6.

[199] Cf. PL 177:335–80.

increasingly became an *Epiphania*, and the priest stood by the altar at its service. "The faithful, viewing what he is performing, are like spectators looking on at a mystery-filled drama of our Lord's Way of the Cross."[200]

The allegorical explanation of the Mass reached a zenith in the writings of the Benedictine Rupert of Deutz (d. 1129)[201] from Saint Laurent Abbey in Liège, later the Abbot of Deutz. In *De officiis*, Rupert extends the allegorical interpretation to the priestly vestments.[202] With its allegorical interpretation, the treatise *De sacro altaris mysterio* (1195–1197)[203] by Cardinal Deacon Lothar di Segni, the later Innocent III (1198–1216), served as a model for future explanations of the Mass. We should mention here above all the *Rationale divinorum officiorum*[204] by William Durand of Mende (d. 1296). This "summa of medieval Mass allegory"[205] had been printed more than forty times by the time of the Reformation.

In the early Middle Ages, the number of Masses celebrated increased considerably. The so-called "private Mass" (*missa privata*) developed. Since every celebration of the Mass, even silent Mass (*missa lecta*), with or without the participation of the faithful, has an ecclesial character, the expression "private Mass" is not entirely appropriate. Today we speak about *missa sine populo* [Mass without the people]. The "private Mass" originated in the monastic communities in which there were more and more priests.[206] Daily "private Mass" of monastic priests was a widespread custom already in the eighth century. Soon more and more secular priests, too, followed the example of the monks. The development of the "private Mass" was fostered by the cultic veneration of the relics of saints in altars

---

[200] Jungmann, *Mass of the Roman Rite*, 1:117.

[201] Cf. Josef Andreas Jungmann, *Symbolik der katholischen Kirche* (Stuttgart: Hiersemann, 1960), 27–39.

[202] Cf. Jungmann, *Mass of the Roman Rite*, 1:111.

[203] Cf. Innocent III, *De sacro altaris mysterio* (PL 217:774–916). The treatise is known also by the title *De missarum mysteriis*.

[204] Cf. Durandus of Mende, *Rationale divinorum officiorum*, ed. Johannes Belethus (Neapoli: Josephum Dura, 1859).

[205] Meyer, *Eucharistie*, 213.

[206] On the Western monastery liturgy of the Middle Ages, cf. Angelus A. Häussling, *Mönchskonvent und Eucharistiefeier: Eine Studie über die Messe in der abendländischen Klosterliturgie des frühen Mittelalters und zur Geschichte der Messhäufigkeit*, Liturgiewissenschaftliche Quellen und Forschungen 58 (Münster: Aschendorff, 1973).

and the idea that one could ensure one's personal salvation or that of departed persons by multiplying celebrations of the Mass or by offering a stipend to have a Mass celebrated. In large monasteries, such as Saint Gall and Mainz, there were attempts in the ninth and tenth centuries to create *Ordines* specifically for the Mass of a priest without the participation of the faithful.

The "private Mass" did not fail to cause controversy. Thus a member of a Carthusian monastery was only rarely permitted to celebrate daily. Francis of Assisi pleaded for only one celebration of Mass each day for the whole convent. From the High Middle Ages on, however, "private Mass" became widely accepted. The priest's celebration of daily Mass was regarded as a sacred duty. While the priest celebrated public Mass as a *missa cantata* [sung Mass], a "private Mass" was *read*. "Simplex" priests were trained for the many Masses. These were priests who (without having completed a course of studies in philosophy and theology) were ordained exclusively to offer the Sacrifice of the Mass. At least one assisting cleric was supposed to participate in the "private Mass" of a priest; one of the lower orders beneath the subdiaconate sufficed.[207]

Many priests, though, celebrated not only daily but two or three times a day. As a result of the custom of stipends and the piety centered on seeing the elevation, there was a huge numerical preponderance of silent Masses as compared with celebrations of Solemn Mass.[208] Votive Masses and Masses for the dead had a questionable influence on the quantity of Masses.[209] Mass was celebrated for all sorts of intentions.[210] The priest's daily celebration of Mass and the proliferation of Masses due to the demands of Mass stipends required an ever greater number of side altars on walls, at pillars, or in the semicircle of chapels in Gothic churches. These side altars were at

---

[207] Cf. Jungmann, *Mass of the Roman Rite*, 1:227–28.

[208] Cf. Otto Nussbaum, *Kloster, Priestermönch und Privatmesse: Ihr Verhältnis im Westen von den Anfängen bis zum hohen Mittelalter*, Theophaneia 14 (Bonn: Hanstein, 1961); Arnold Angenendt, "Missa specialis: Zugleich ein Beitrag zur Entstehung der Privatmesse", *Frühmittelalterliche Studien* 17 (1983): 153–221.

[209] The *Old Gelasian Sacramentary* already included Masses for numerous occasions in which prayers for the living and the deceased were presented.

[210] Cf. Adolph Franz, *Die Messe im deutschen Mittelalter: Beiträge zur Geschichte der Liturgie und des religiösen Volkslebens* (Darmstadt: Wissenschaftliche Buchgesellschaft, 1963), 115–330.

first quite simple, but later they were furnished like the main altar with images or reredos, cross, and candlesticks. Mass celebrated by a priest at a side altar was disparagingly called "corner Mass".

In the ninth century, the faithful in many places started to kneel on the floor for the Eucharistic Canon. Seats or pews with kneelers appeared only in the late Middle Ages. The focus on the somatic Real Presence of Christ in the bread and wine promoted kneeling at the Consecration. Kneeling is a sign of the reverence and adoration of the faithful. The reception of the consecrated Host demanded profound reverence and a pure heart. The faithful were therefore admonished not to receive Communion without sufficient preparation. From the Middle Ages on, the *missa sollemnis* declined sharply, while in the monasteries the *missa publica* with the participation of the laity disappeared. Contact of monasteries with the world was reduced to a minimum. Already in the Carolingian period, it became common in the celebration of the Eucharist to use thin wafers that no longer needed to be broken in order to be distributed. The German name for one of these wafers, *Oblate*, is derived from the Latin term for the offerings (*oblata*) of bread and wine. The baked wafers were made of unleavened wheat flour and water. The term for the consecrated wafer is "Host", derived from *hostia* (victim). Since the early Middle Ages, Eucharistic piety has concentrated more and more on the consecrated Host, which complied with the intensified reverence for the Most Blessed Sacrament.

Chapter V

HOC EST ENIM CORPUS MEUM

The Reality of the Eucharist and Veneration of It

"Adoro devote, latens veritas, te quae sub his formis vere latitas."[1] With these words begins the Eucharistic hymn *Adoro (te) devote*, which is attributed to Thomas Aquinas. The hymn "expresses the Eucharistic spirituality of Aquinas in what is probably the densest and most beautiful way".[2] In the Middle Ages, the presence of Christ in the sacrament of the Eucharist was the object of spirited controversies. This was connected with a stronger devotion to the sensibly perceptible reality and a changed understanding of reality. The visible reality was now considered the reality, from which the sign character was distinguished. Already since the conclusion of the patristic era there had been greater concentration on the somatic (bodily) Real Presence of Christ in the Eucharistic gifts.[3] Thus in the Middle Ages developed a strong veneration and worship of the Eucharist that some German scholars have termed *Schaufrömmigkeit* (show piety). If we speak about *Schaufrömmigkeit* here, it is not in the pejorative sense in which it is used by the School of Maria Laach, for instance, but rather to designate a very intensive form of Eucharistic spirituality. In art history, the concept of *Schaufrömmigkeit* is now viewed critically, since it presupposes a dubious separation between an elite and a popular piety.[4]

[1] "Humbly I adore Thee, Verity unseen, who Thy glory hidest 'neath these shadows mean." English translation by Gerard Manley Hopkins, S.J.

[2] Jan-Heiner Tück, *Gabe der Gegenwart: Theologie und Dichtung der Eucharistie bei Thomas von Aquin*, 3rd ed. (Freiburg: Herder, 2014), 305.

[3] Cf. Alexander Gerken, *Theologie der Eucharistie* (Munich: Kösel-Verlag, 1973), 102.

[4] Cf. Gia Toussaint, *Kreuz und Knochen: Reliquien zur Zeit der Kreuzzüge* (Berlin: Reimer, 2011).

In the Eucharistic miracles, popular piety saw a confirmation of the Real Presence of the Body and Blood of Christ. The most renowned Eucharistic miracle of the early Middle Ages occurred at the beginning of the eighth century in Lanciano near Chieti. In the former monastery church of Saint Longinus, today a Franciscan church, a monk who was tormented by doubts about the bodily presence of Jesus in the sacrament of the Eucharist was celebrating Mass as usual. During the Consecration, one part of the consecrated Host turned into bleeding flesh; the wine assumed the appearance of fresh blood, which clotted into five clumps of dried blood of unequal size. The miraculous Host is preserved between two plates of glass in a silver monstrance, borne by two angelic figures, between which stands a glass chalice with the clotted Blood of Christ.[5] In 804, when news spread that a relic of the Precious Blood of Christ had been discovered in Mantua, Pope Leo III traveled to Aachen to see Charlemagne. Many churches claimed that they possessed drops of the Blood shed by Christ on the Cross and venerated it accordingly. Without the Eucharistic Miracle of Lanciano and the veneration of the relics of Christ's Blood, the positions championed in the medieval Eucharistic controversies, some of them very realistic, are incomprehensible.

A. The Medieval Eucharistic Controversies

The Benedictine Abbey of Corbie near Amiens in Picardy, which was closely associated with the Carolingian court, was the point of departure for the first Eucharistic controversy. It is better to call it a Carolingian Eucharistic controversy than "the first debate about the Lord's Supper",[6] since the Eucharist was not designated as the "Last Supper" until Martin Luther's translation of the Bible into German.[7]

---

[5] Cf. Bruno Sammaciccia, *Das Eucharistie-Wunder von Lanciano*, 2nd ed. (Hauteville: Parvis, 1992).

[6] "Erster Abendmahlsstreit"; Hans Jorissen, "Abendmahlsstreit", in *Lexikon für Theologie und Kirche*, 3rd ed. (Freiburg: Herder, 1993), 1:36–39.

[7] On the Carolingian Eucharistic controversy, cf. John F. Fahey, *The Eucharistic Teaching of Ratramn of Corbie*, Dissertationes ad lauream 22 (Mundelein, Ill.: Saint Mary of the Lake Seminary, 1951); Jean-Paul Bouhot, *Ratramne de Corbie: Histoire littéraire et controverses doctrinales* (Paris: Études augustiniennes, 1976); Hans Jorissen, "Wandlungen des philosophischen

The controversy took place in a "revolutionary spiritual situation" that was marked by a "paradigm shift" from a "Platonic-Neoplatonic metaphysics of image and participation" in patristic writings to an Aristotelian way of thinking that was gradually becoming widely accepted.[8] Another factor that explains the controversy was the debate started by Amalarius of Metz about the threefold Body of Christ (*triforme Corpus Christi*), which deviated from the traditional distinction between the historical body of Christ, the Body of the Church, and the Eucharistic Body. Amalarius distinguished between the body of Christ that Mary conceived, which walked on earth, and the body that was buried and rose again.[9] Florus of Lyon saw this as an unacceptable division of the one body of Christ (*corpus tripertitum*).[10] The Synod of Quiercy (838) condemned Amalarius' interpretation.[11] The frequency of Masses in the monasteries, which has already been pointed out, may also have played a role in the Carolingian Eucharistic controversy. The priest-monks celebrated daily and regularly offered the Eucharist for the souls of the deceased.[12]

Finally, the controversy cannot be understood without the *Opus Caroli regis contra synodum*. The *Libri Carolini*—the modern title of the

---

Kontextes als Hintergrund der frühmittelalterlichen Eucharistiestreitigkeiten", in *Streit um das Bild: Das Zweite Konzil von Nizäa (787) in ökumenischer Perspektive*, Studium Universale 9, ed. J. Wohlmuth (Bonn: Bouvier, 1989), 97–111; Celia Chazelle, "Figure, Character, and the Glorified Body in the Carolingian Eucharistic Controversy", *Traditio* 47 (1992): 2–36; Chazelle, *The Crucified God in the Carolingian Era: Theology and Art of Christ's Passion* (Cambridge: Cambridge University Press, 2001); Chazelle, "The Eucharist in Early Mediaeval Europe", in *A Companion to the Eucharist in the Middle Ages*, ed. J.C. Levy and K. van Ausdall, Brill's Companions to Christian Tradition 26 (Leiden and Boston: Brill, 2012), 205–49; Patricia McCormick Zirkel, "Why Should It Be Necessary that Christ Be Immolated Daily?: Paschasius Radbertus on Daily Eucharist", *American Benedictine Review* 47 (1996): 240–59; Willemien Otten, "Between Augustinian Sign and Carolingian Reality: The Presence of Ambrose and Augustine in the Eucharistic Debate between Paschasius Radbertus and Ratramnus of Corbie", *Dutch Review of Church History* 80 (2000): 137–56; Steffen Patzold, "Visibilis creatura—invisibilis salus: Zur Deutung der Wahrnehmung in der Karolingerzeit", in *Zwischen Wort und Bild: Wahrnehmungen und Deutungen im Mittelalter*, ed. H. Bleumer et al. (Cologne: Böhlau, 2010), 79–108.

[8] Cf. Jorissen, "Wandlungen des philosophischen Kontextes", 99.

[9] Cf. Amalarius of Metz, *Liber Officialis* 2.35 (Hanssens ed., 367f.).

[10] Cf. Patzold, "Visibilis creatura", 103.

[11] Cf. Rosamond McKitterick, *The Frankish Church and the Carolingian Reforms 789–895* (London: Royal Historical Society, 1977), 151–53.

[12] Cf. David Ganz, "Theology and the Organisation of Thought", in *The New Cambridge Mediaeval History*, vol. 2 (c. 700–c. 900) (Cambridge: Cambridge University Press, 1995), 778.

work—were composed at the behest of Charlemagne in response to the partially misunderstood decisions of the Second Council of Nicaea (787) in the iconoclastic controversy.[13] Because of inexact translations of the conciliar decrees (for example, the lack of a distinction between worship and veneration) the Frankish court had got the impression that divine worship was due to images. The *Libri Carolini* argue against this, without advocating the iconoclastic destruction of images but rather attributing to images an exclusively aesthetic and pedagogical function whereby image, truth, and reality are separate. Thus the category of image is rejected as being unsuited to the mystery of the Eucharist. This becomes clear in the fourth book of the *Libri Carolini* where it says: "For the Mystery of the Lord's Blood and Body is not to be called an image ... but rather something that was prefigured by types."[14] For Christ did not say "This is an image [*imago*] of the body", but rather he said, "This is [*est*] my body."[15] The mystery of the Lord's Body cannot be called an image (*imago*), because it is a reality (*veritas*) and not a type (*figura*).[16] For Augustine, this separation of image and reality had been inconceivable. This is true also for Ambrose, who can speak about the Eucharistic bread as *figura corporis Christi* because he presupposes a concept of image in which the bread is not only an image for the Body of Christ but that the Body is also present in the image.

Between February 831 and the summer of 832, the monk Paschasius Radbertus (d. ca. 859) composed the treatise *De corpore et sanguine Domini*. This was the first "scientific monograph about the Eucharist".[17] Warin (d. 856), the second Abbot of Corvey Abbey [in Saxony] and a student of Radbertus, had asked for a treatise on the Eucharist

[13] Cf. *Opus Caroli regis contra synodum (Libri Carolini)* (Monumenta Germaniae Historica, Concilia, vol. 2, Supplementum 1), ed. Freeman (1998). According to the results of research by Ann Freeman, the *Libri Carolini* were composed by the West Gothic theologian Theodulf of Orleans (d. 821), who since 800 had been Charlemagne's theological advisor.

[14] *Libri Carolini* 4.14 (Freeman ed., 523): "Non enim sanguinis et corporis Dominici mysterium imago iam nun dicendum est ... sed id quod exemplaribus praefigurabatur."

[15] Cf. ibid. (524): "Nec ait: Haec est imago corporis et sanguinis mei, sed: Hoc est corpus meum, quod pro vobis tradetur."

[16] Cf. ibid.: "Cum ... nec artificium opus vera Christi possit imago dici nec corporis et sanguinis eius mysterium, quod in veritate gestum esse constat, non in figura."

[17] Marius Lepin, *L'idée du sacrifice de la messe d'après les théologiens depuis l'origine jusqu'à nos jours*, 2nd ed. (Paris: Gabriel Beauchesne, 1926).

for his monks. It appears that Radbertus' work did not meet with criticism at first. This changed with the second edition (843/844), which Radbertus sent shortly after his election as Abbot of Corbie Abbey to Charles the Bald (823–877), the youngest son of Louis the Pious from his second marriage. The second edition contains, besides a dedication to the Frankish king, several accounts of Eucharistic miracles from the *Vitae Patrum*. Among the critics of Radbertus were Hrabanus Maurus (d. 856) and Gottschalk of Orbais (d. 867/870). Hinkmar of Rheims (d. 882), who took a stand against Gottschalk on the question of predestination, shared Radbertus' view to a great extent.[18] The question of the Eucharist was intensively discussed in many places in France around the middle of the ninth century.[19]

During a visit in Corbie Abbey, Charles the Bald became acquainted with the monk Ratramnus (d. ca. 870) and asked him for an opinion on the question about the reality of the Body and Blood of Christ in the sacrament of the Eucharist. It could be that the external occasion for the request was Amalarius' condemnation and not Radbertus' treatise on the Eucharist.[20] Generally it is assumed, however, that *De corpore et sanguine Domini* (after 843) was directed by Ratramnus against the work with the same title by Radbertus, who of course is not mentioned by name in it. Radbertus' critics accused him of a "Capharnaite" view of the Eucharist. This means a literal understanding of Jesus' discourse about the Eucharistic bread. Thus Gottschalk charges Radbertus with violating Augustine's commandment, *Christum vorari fas dentibus non est* [it is not right to eat Christ greedily with your teeth], which he himself cites.[21] Yet Radbertus' view of the Eucharist is far more differentiated and has nothing to do with theophagy (Greek: eating God).

In their writings on the reality of the Eucharist, Radbertus and Ratramnus presuppose Augustine's theory of signs. Their discussion

[18] Cf. Hinkmar of Rheims, *De cavendis vitiis et virtutibus expercendis* (Monumenta Germaniae Historiae), ed. D. Nachtmann (1998). On Hinkmar's position, see Chazelle, "Eucharist in Early Medieval Europe", 240–43.

[19] Cf. Patzold, "Visibilis creatura", 91.

[20] Cf. Bouhot, *Ratramne de Corbie*, 85–88; Gary Macy, *The Theologies of the Eucharist in the Early Scholastic Period: A Study of the Salvific Function of the Sacrament according to the Theologians c. 1080–c. 1220* (Oxford: Clarendon Press; New York: Oxford University Press, 1984), 22.

[21] Cf. Gottschalk of Orbais, *De corpore et sanguine Christi* (PL 124) (1879), 326.

is centered, not on the general concept of *signum*, but rather on the specific concept of *figura*, which also occurs in the *Libri Carolini* besides *imago*. *Figura*, from *fingere*, to shape or to form, served in Latin patristic writings as a translation of τύπος, type or example, which occurs several times as early as the New Testament. Thus Paul calls Adam τύπος τοῦ μέλλοντος, *figura futuri*, "a type of the one [Christ] who was to come". Tertullian, who adopts this typology, describes Adam and Moses as *figura Christi*, Eve as *figura ecclesiae* (type of the Church). He also calls the Eucharistic elements of bread and wine *figura*, specifically *figura corporis et sanguinis Christi*. He distinguishes this from the *corpus veritatis*, the historical body of Christ that was perceptible by the senses.[22]

Like Tertullian and Ambrose, Radbertus calls the consecrated gifts of bread and wine the type (*figura*) of the Body and Blood of Christ. Yet in the bread and wine, Christ's Body and Blood are at the same time present *in veritate*; *in figura*, since the Body and Blood of Christ are not perceived by the senses, *in veritate* because Christ is the truth: "*Christus est Veritas*, Veritas autem Christus est",[23] and hence his words, which are spoken by the priest at the Consecration, are true, although the truth of the Body and Blood of Christ may be a truth *in mysterio*.[24] Radbertus' position becomes particularly clear in the following quotation: "Hence because the sacrament is mystical, we cannot deny either that it is a type (*figura*); but if it is a type, then we must ask how it can be reality.... The likeness (*figura*) or impression (*caracter*) of the reality is what is perceived externally, the reality (*veritas*), however, is whatever is correctly understood or believed internally about this mystery. For not every type (*figura*) is a shadow or unreality (*falsitas*)."[25]

---

[22] Cf. Tertullian, *Adversus Marcionem* 3.19.4; ibid., 4.40.3.

[23] Radbertus, *De corpore et sanguine Domini. Cum appendice Epistola ad Fredugardum*, ed. Bedae Paulus, Corpus Christianorum: Continuatio Mediaevalis 16 (1968), c. 5, 18.

[24] Cf. Zirkel, "Why Should It Be Necessary?", 247–52.

[25] Paschasius Radbertus, *De corpore et sanguine Domini* 4 (Paulus ed., 29): "Unde quia mysticum est sacramentum, nec figuram illud negare possumus. Sed si figura est, quaerendum quomodo veritas esse possit.... sit figura vel caracter veritatis quod exterius sentitur, veritas vero quidquod de hoc mysterio interius recte intellegitur aut creditur. Non enim omnis figura umbra vel falsitas." Cf. Chazelle, "Figure, Character, and the Glorified Body", 11; David Appleby, "'Beautiful on the Cross, Beautiful in His Torments': The Place of the Body in the Thoughts of Paschasius Radbertus", *Traditio* 60 (2005): 8–20.

Radbertus associates *figura* and *veritas* by citing Hebrews 1:3. In this passage, Christ, the Son of God, is designated χαρακτὴρ τῆς ὑποστάσεως αὐτοῦ, as an imprint, impression, or likeness of the invisible divine essence.[26] Like many Fathers of the Church, Radbertus thus regards the sacramental presence of Christ by analogy with the Incarnation. As Christ is the likeness (*caracter*) of the invisible God, bread and wine are the likeness (*caracter*) of Christ's Body and Blood. Radbertus compares bread and wine also with written signs, insofar as they are a copy (*caracter*) of spoken words.[27] In the case of the sacrament of the Eucharist, it is important to direct one's perception in a spiritual way toward what is interiorly perceptible, so that in the bread and wine the senses "perceive (*sentire*) nothing other than what is divine, nothing but what is divine".[28]

The proposition that Radbertus was blamed in particular for holding had been taken verbatim from Ambrose: "The true flesh of Christ, which was crucified and buried, is truly the sacrament of his flesh."[29] Radbertus opposes those who maintain that in the Eucharist we receive only the *glorified* Body of Christ, which is in heaven, and in one passage he calls them *haeretici*.[30] He describes this position as heretical since any dissociation of the historical and glorified Body of Christ and his historical, glorified, and sacramental Body would lead to a denial of the Real Presence of Christ. Present in the Eucharist is the historical body of Christ, which was born of Mary and was buried: "Clearly no other [flesh] than that which was born from Mary and suffered on the Cross and rose from the tomb. It is the same, I say, and therefore it is Christ's flesh which to this day is sacrificed for the life of the world, and when it is received worthily it renews

---

[26] Cf. Chazelle, "Eucharist in Early Medieval Europe", 237.

[27] Cf. Radbertus, *De corpore et sanguine Domini* 4 (Paulus ed., 29).

[28] Ibid., 2 (22). On Radbertus' theory of twofold perception, cf. Patzold, "Visibilis creatura", 93–96.

[29] Cf. Radbertus, *De corpore et sanguine Domini* 4 (Paulus ed., 30): "Vera utique caro Christi quae crucifixa est et sepulta, vere illius carnis sacramentum."

[30] Ibid., 18 (100): "Ad vero quid ultimum est, si post resurrectionem hoc dedisset, dicturi essent haeretici, quod incorruptibilis iam Christus et in caelo positus non posset in terris eius caro a fidelibus vorari." On the discussion about the relation between the historical and the Eucharistic Body of Christ, see Jaroslav Pelikan, *The Christian Tradition: A History of the Development of Doctrine*, vol. 3, *The Growth of Medieval Theology (600–1300)* (Chicago: University of Chicago Press, 1978), 190–92.

eternal life in us."[31] For Radbertus, the inward reality of the sacrament of the Eucharist can be only the historical and glorified Body of Christ that suffered on the Cross.[32]

Despite this strong emphasis by Radbertus on the identity of the historical, glorified, and sacramental Body of Christ, the impartial reader of his treatise on the Eucharist is astonished at how frequently it emphasizes that the body of the risen Lord is not a physical but rather a spiritual body, since at the Resurrection of Christ, his body was transformed into a pneumatic one, which Radbertus sees as the basis of the identity of Christ's historical and sacramental Body.[33] Radbertus also underscores repeatedly that the daily sacrifice of Christ in the Eucharist is a mystical sacrifice.[34] "But because it is not right that Christ should be eaten greedily with the teeth, he willed that this bread and wine should be truly created his Body and Blood in mystery through the consecration of the Holy Spirit in power.... Clearly he mentions here none other than his real flesh and his real blood, albeit mystically."[35] The question about the relation of Christ's sacrifice on the Cross and the sacrifice of the Eucharist had already been raised by Alcuin in his Commentary on the Letter to the Hebrews and since then had been discussed intensively.[36]

Radbert assumes that the Consecration of the oblations of bread and wine is effected through the words of Christ (*verba testamenti*) spoken by the priest and the Holy Spirit and does not depend on the

---

[31] Radbertus, *De corpore et sanguine Domini* I (Paulus ed., 15): "non alia plane, quam quae nata est de Maria et passa in cruce et resurrexit de sepulchro. Haec, inquam, ipsa est et ideo Christi est *caro* quae *pro mundi vita* adhuc hodie offertur, et cum digne percipitur, vita utique aeterna in nobis reparatur."

[32] Cf. ibid. (18): "Et si Deus Veritas est, quicquid Christus promisit in hoc mysterio, utique verum est. Et ideo vera Christi caro et sanguis quam qui manducat [et bibit] digne, habet vitam aeternam in se manentem."

[33] This is overlooked by Chazelle, *Crucified God in the Carolingian Era*, 216, when she describes the sacramental Body of Christ as a body in the "physical sense".

[34] Cf. Radbertus, *De corpore et sanguine Domini* 2 (Paulus ed., 23): "in mysterio cottidie veraciter immolatus"; ibid., 4 (28): "vero cotidie pro mundi vita mystice immolari"; Radbertus, *Epistola ad Fredugardum* (Paulus ed., 151): "immolatur pro nobis cottidie in mysterio".

[35] Radbertus, *De corpore et sanguine Domini* 4 (Paulus ed., 27–28): "Sed quia Christum vorari fas dentibus non est, voluit in mysterio hunc panem et vinum vere carnem suam et sanguinem consecratione Spiritus sancti potentialiter creari.... Ubi profecto non aliam quam veram carnem dicit et verum sanguinem licet mystice."

[36] Cf. Alcuin, *Ad Hebraeos* 10 (*PL* 100:1077B-D).

merits (*meritum*) of the priest.[37] Without the working of the Holy Spirit, the *verba testamenti* do not have the power to transform the gifts of bread and wine into the Body and Blood of Christ. Like Ambrose, Radbertus says about the sacrament of the Eucharist that it "is consecrated divinely by the priest on the altar in Christ's word through the Holy Spirit. Hence the Lord himself exclaims: *This is my Body.*"[38] When the priest pronounces the *verba testamenti*, Christ's word becomes reality: "vere hoc fit quod dictum est: *Hoc est corpus meum.*"[39] Radbertus regards the sacramental presence of Christ's Body and Blood as a miracle just like the transformation of the mortal into the glorified Body of Christ. When Radbertus explains that the substance (*substantia*) of the bread and wine becomes the Body and Blood of Christ at their consecration,[40] he already comes very close to the later doctrine of transubstantiation.

Even though Radbertus does not mean the identity of Christ's historical and sacramental Body in the sense of a material identity, his strong emphasis on the identity of the historical and Eucharistic Body does lead to the idea of a sort of "repetition" (*reiteratio*) of Christ's sacrifice on the Cross in the Eucharist: in the sacrifice of the Eucharist, Christ is sacrificed mystically, that is, in an unbloody manner, each day anew as the sacrificial Lamb,[41] so that the Eucharist is called the true sacrifice of a holy offering.[42] "This oblation, moreover, is repeated daily, even though Christ suffered once in the flesh on the Cross and through one and the same suffering of death saved the world once and for all, and from this death the same Christ rose to life, and death no longer has power over him.... And, therefore, because every day

[37] Cf. Radbertus, *De corpore et sanguine Domini* 12 (Paulus ed., 76f.).

[38] Ibid., 4 (28): "quod per sacerdotem super altare in verbo Christi per Spiritum Sanctum divinitus consecratur. Unde ipse Dominus clamat: *Hoc est corpus meum.*"

[39] Ibid., 15 (94). Cf. ibid., 2 (22); ibid., 4 (28). Radbertus develops at length the position that Ambrose takes with regard to Eucharistic Consecration, ibid., 15 (92–97).

[40] Cf. ibid., 3 (27): "Unde nec mirum Spiritus Sanctus qui hominem Christum in utero virginis sine semine creavit, etiam si ipse panis ac vini substantia carnem Christi et sanguinem invisibili potentia quotidie per sacramenti sui sanctificationem operatur."

[41] Cf. ibid., 4 (28); ibid., 9 (53).

[42] Cf. ibid., 9 (64); Radbertus, *Epistola ad Fredugardum* (Paulus ed., 151): "interrogati confitemur Christum cottidie in mysterio immolari *ad celebrationem pertinet sacramenti*, quod semel factum est, quando immolatus est pro salute mundi in seipso. Ac per hoc, quia sic credimus spiritualiter fieri, nec istud est sine ipso quod tunc gestum est sacramento, nec illud reiteratur in facto, ut moriatur Christus, sed immolatur pro nobis cottidie in mysterio."

we fall, every day Christ is sacrificed mystically for us and the Passion of Christ is handed on in mystery."[43] Radbertus' puzzling interpretation, that the historical flesh and blood of Jesus is present under the Eucharistic species and Christ's sacrifice is "repeated" in the Eucharist, could scarcely be explained without the strong fixation on the historical Blood of Christ in early medieval piety.[44]

Charles the Bald had asked Ratramnus for a clarification of the following question: In Communion, do the faithful receive the Body and Blood of Christ *in mysterio* or *in veritate*?[45] Connected with this were further questions that Ratramnus formulates right at the beginning of his opinion: Can Christ's Body and Blood be perceived by the eyes of faith alone or by the senses also? Are the Body and Blood of Christ hidden mysteriously in types (*sub mysterii figura; velatione mysterii*), or are they present in their unveiled, manifest reality (*nulla sub figura; nulla sub obvelatione, sed ipsius veritatis nuda manifestatione*)?[46] Is the Body of Christ that we receive the same body that Mary bore, which died, was buried, and rose again?[47] Since Radbertus disputes any sense perception of Christ's Body and Blood in the bread and wine (with the exception of Eucharistic miracles), and this could hardly have remained hidden from Ratramnus, Celia Chazelle suspects that in Corbie and Corvey there were individual monks who thought that Christ's Body and Blood would change at the Consecration into the substance of bread and wine so that they could be perceived by the senses.[48]

Ratramnus assumes that the Eucharist is celebrated "figuratively or as a memorial of the death of our Lord ... in order to call to mind what happened independently of our present memorial"[49] and cannot

---

[43] Radbertus, *De corpore et sanguine Domini* 9 (Paulus ed., 52f.): "Iteratur autem cotidie haec oblatio, licet Christus semel passus in carne per unam eandem mortis passionem semel salvaverit mundum, ex qua morte idem resurgens ad vitam mors ei ultra non dominabitur.... Et ideo quia cotidie labimur, cotidie pro nobis Christus mystice immolatur et passio Christi in mysterio traditur."

[44] Cf. Arnold Angenendt, *Geschichte der Religiosität im Mittelalter*, 2nd ed. (Darmstadt: Primus Verlag, 2000), 366.

[45] Cf. Ratramnus, *De corpore et sanguine Domini* 2 (Bakhuizen ed., 1974, 42).

[46] Cf. ibid.

[47] Cf. ibid., 5 (44).

[48] Cf. Chazelle, "Figure, Character, and the Glorified Body", 8.

[49] Ratramnus, *De corpore et sanguine Domini* C (Bakhuizen ed., 69): "in figuram sive memoriam dominicae mortis ponatur ut quod gestum est in praeterito presenti revocet memoriae."

be called back, since it is an event of the past.[50] In the memorial (*memoria*), the mystery of Christ's Passion and death becomes present. Hence bread and wine are called the Body and Blood of Christ.[51] Like Radbertus, Ratramnus takes it quite for granted that the oblations of bread and wine are consecrated into the Body and Blood of Christ by the *verba testamenti* spoken by the priest within the context of the Eucharistic Prayer. He cites Ambrose to this effect.[52] The idea of a Consecration of bread and wine through the pronunciation of the *verba testamenti* did not become generally accepted only later in connection with the development of the doctrine of transubstantiation.[53] Rather, it is an elementary assumption of the Carolingian Eucharistic controversy. Furthermore, in the early Middle Ages, it was already the predominant idea that the decisive Consecration of bread and wine into Christ's Body and Blood came about through the *verba testamenti*; this is demonstrated by the description of the *verba testamenti* as *oratio periculosa* (a perilous prayer) in the *Stowe Missal* (eighth-ninth century).[54]

While Radbertus associates *figura* and *veritas* in the concept of imprint (*caracter*), Ratramnus sees them as more strongly antithetical. The latter understands *figura* to mean an image, as in Jesus' words: "I am the bread of life [that has] come down from heaven" (Jn 6:35, 38). Ratramnus compares the words of institution with a *figurata locutio*, as in the words of Jesus about the living bread and the grapevine: "I am the vine, you are the branches" (Jn 15:5).[55] "For substantially neither bread nor vine is Christ, nor are branches apostles."[56] Ratramnus understands *veritas* to mean an unveiled reality (*res manifesta*) that "is

---

[50] Cf. ibid., 37 (43): "eum semel in seipso passus sit et resurrexit nec dies illi iam possint revocari, quoniam praeterierunt."

[51] Cf. ibid., 39–40 (44f.).

[52] Cf. ibid., 53–54 (56).

[53] Thus incorrectly Angenendt, *Geschichte der Religiosität*, 503.

[54] Cf. Raymund Kottje, "Oratio periculosa: Eine frühmittelalterliche Bezeichnung des Kanons?", *Archiv für Liturgiewissenschaft* 10 (1967): 165–68, who in contrast to Nussbaum shows that the expression *oratio periculosa* (as opposed to *oratio mystica*) meant, not the whole Canon, but merely the institutional narrative with the *verba testamenti*.

[55] Cf. Ratramnus, *De corpore et sanguine Domini* 7 (Bakhuizen ed., 34): "Figura est obumbratio quaedam quibusdam velaminibus quod intendit ostendens ... omnia aliud dicunt et aliud innuunt."

[56] Ibid., 8 (35): "nam substantialiter nec panis Christus nec vitis Christus nec palmitis apostoli."

communicated through pure, clear, natural signs. Thus, we say, for example, that Christ was born of the Virgin, suffered, was crucified, died, and was buried."[57] "For we cannot call mystery a reality in which nothing is hidden, nothing escapes the bodily senses, nothing is covered with a veil."[58]

Ratramnus conceives of bread and wine as a type (*figura*) of a spiritual, non-corporeal reality, so that "the bread that is called Christ's Body and the cup that is called Christ's Blood is a type, because it is a mystery, and there is a considerable difference between the body that exists in the form of the mystery and the body that suffered and was buried and rose again. For this is the actual body of the Redeemer, and in it there is nothing typological and no reference to something else."[59] The historical body of Christ, which was raised again, exists *in veritate*. The glorified Body of Christ that we will see in heaven will be manifest to us without type and signs, unlike the sacramental Body of Christ.[60] Ratramnus separates the sacramental body from the glorified Body of Christ and the imperfect knowledge gained through the sacrament from the heavenly vision of Christ's Body.[61] Unlike Radbertus, Ratramnus assumes no substantial transformation of bread and wine into the Body and Blood of Christ. He calls the sacramental Body of Christ that we receive a pledge (*pignus*) and appearance (*species*)[62] of the glorified Body of Christ in heaven that we will behold in the presence of God.[63] We receive Christ's Body and Blood under the veil of the sacramental sign of bread in *mysterio*, not *in veritate*: "Beneath the veil (*velamen*) of the bodily bread and the

---

[57] Ibid. (34): "Veritas vero est, rei manifestae demonstratio, nullis umbrarum imaginibus obvelatae, sed puris et apertis, utque planius eloquamur naturalibus significationibus insinuatae ut pote cum dicitur Christus natus de virgine, passus, crucifixus, mortuus et sepultus."

[58] Ibid., 9 (35): "Quoniam mysterium dici non potest in quo nihil est abditum, nihil a corporalibus sensibus remotum, nihil aliquo velamine contectum."

[59] Ibid., 97 (59): "quod panis qui corpus Christi, et calix, qui sanguis Christi appellatur, figura sit, quia mysterium, et quod non parva differentia sit inter corpus, quod per mysterium existit, et corpus, quod passum est, et sepultum, et resurrexit. Quoniam hoc proprium salvatoris corpus existet, nec in eo vel aliqua figura, vel aliqua significatio." Cf. ibid., 69 (51).

[60] Cf. ibid., 97 (59): "nec in eo vel aliqua figura vel aliqua significatio".

[61] Cf. ibid., 19 (38); *De corpore et sanguine Domini* 16 (37); ibid., 71–72 (52). On this topic, see Chazelle, "Figure, Character, and the Glorified Body", 22; Chazelle, "Eucharist in Early Medieval Europe", 248.

[62] Cf. Ratramnus, *De corpore et sanguine Domini* 96 (Bakhuizen ed., 56).

[63] Cf. ibid.

bodily wine, the spiritual Body of Christ and the spiritual Blood are there."[64] Bread and wine are images or likenesses of the truth of the Body and Blood of Christ in heaven. We are dealing with a presence "according to the invisible substance".[65]

Like Radbertus, Ratramnus cites Ambrose, although the latter assumes that the historical and glorified Body of Christ is identical with the sacramental Body.[66] It is unclear whether Ratramnus misunderstood the position of the bishop of Milan or simply ignored it.[67] In any case, Ratramnus is of the opinion that the bread and wine do not change at the Consecration.[68] In the Eucharistic bread on the altar, the body of Christ that Mary bore and that arose from the dead is signified (signatur).[69] The Eucharistic bread proclaims (clamat) the Body of Christ.[70] For Ratramnus, Christ's presence in the Eucharist is not a corporeal but rather a spiritual one.[71] Of course, this must not be understood symbolically, since the sacrament, according to its entire reality, is a real, participating type (figura, imago) of the heavenly Body of the Lord. In this sense, Ratramnus can speak about a commutatio spiritualis, non corporalis, a transformation that is spiritual, not corporeal, which takes place figurate, hidden under the appearances.[72] What the senses perceive outwardly, bread and wine, is one thing; what is manifested inwardly to the mind of the faithful is another.[73] The faithful who receive the sacrament of the Eucharist are spiritually nourished secundum vero quod creduntur (but according to

---

[64] Ibid., 16 (37): "sub velamento corporei panis corporeique vini spiritale corpus Christi spiritalisque sanguis existet".

[65] Ibid., 49 (55): "secundum invisibilem substantiam".

[66] Cf. ibid., 59–60 (49).

[67] Cf. Fahey, Eucharistic Teaching of Ratram of Corbie, 50–52; David Ganz, Corbie in the Carolingian Renaissance (Sigmaringen: Thorbecke, 1990), 89; Chazelle, "Figure, Character, and the Glorified Body", 5.

[68] Cf. Ratramnus, De corpore et sanguine Domini 12 (Bakhuizen ed., 36).

[69] Cf. ibid., 96 (59).

[70] Cf. ibid., 9 (35).

[71] Cf. Chazelle, "Figure, Character, and the Glorified Body", 24.

[72] This was pointed out by Fahey, Eucharistic Teaching of Ratram of Corbie, and Jorissen, "Abendmahlsstreit", 1:36. Josef Rupert Geiselmann was still of the opinion that Ratramnus advocated an anti-metabolistic symbolism. Cf. Josef Rupert Geiselmann, Die Eucharistielehre der Vorscholastik, Forschungen zur christlichen Literatur- und Dogmengeschichte 15 (Paderborn: Schöningh, 1926).

[73] Cf. Ratramnus, De corpore et sanguine Domini 12 (Bakhuizen ed., 35).

what is believed).[74] The Eucharist bestows on someone who receives it in faith the "living strength" (*virtus vitalis*) of the risen Lord,[75] the "power of the Divine Word" (*divini potentia verbi*).[76]

Fredugard, a monk from Saint-Riquier, whom Radbertus had taught for a time, was concerned that Augustine's description of Jesus' discourse about the Eucharistic bread as a *tropica locutio* could undermine his teacher's position. Radbertus responded to Fredugard with a letter with which he enclosed a compendium of patristic citations and the explanation of the Last Supper from his Commentary on the Gospel of Matthew.[77] In his letter, Radbertus assures his former student that Augustine calls Jesus' discourse on the bread of life a *tropica locutio* because it is not a matter of eating Christ's physical flesh and drinking his physical blood.[78] Augustine was teaching, however, that in the bread and wine we truly receive Christ's Body and Blood. As proof, he adduces the following citation: "Receive in the bread what hung on the Cross, and in the chalice what flowed from the wounded side."[79] We know today that this citation did not originate with Augustine but, rather, with Faustus of Riez.[80] Of course there is a very similar statement in Augustine's Commentary on the Psalms: "And because he [Christ] lived on earth in this flesh, he gave us this flesh as the food of salvation. But no one eats now of this flesh without first having worshipped."[81]

Ratramnus does not do Augustine justice when he transfers the description of Jesus' discourse about the Eucharistic bread as a *figurata locutio* to the *verba testamenti* in such a way that he adheres strictly to the concept of sign (*signum*) and image (*figura*) in *De doctrina christiana*.[82] For Augustine's general definition of sign is insufficient

---

[74] Ibid., 19 (38).

[75] Cf. ibid., 18 (38).

[76] Cf. ibid., 63 (50).

[77] The compendium of patristic citations and the section from Radbertus' Commentary on Matthew are added to the third and fourth edition of his treatise on the Eucharist.

[78] Cf. Radbertus, *Epistola ad Fredugardum* (Paulus ed., 146f.).

[79] Ibid. (147, 149).

[80] Cf. *Sermo Denis* 3 (19.7–9).

[81] Augustine, *Enarrationes in Psalmos* 98.9 (CCSL 39:1385): "Et quia in ipsa carne hic ambulavit, et ipsam carnem nobis manducandam ad salutem dedit: nemo autem illam carnem manducat, nisi prius adoravit."

[82] Cf. Chazelle, "Figure, Character, and the Glorified Body", 27.

to determine his view of the reality of the Eucharist. The sacraments in the narrower sense are signs *sui generis* (in a category of their own). In their case, it is neither a natural sign, as smoke is the sign of fire,[83] nor a symbol, like the cross as a sign for the Christian faith.[84] The sacrament of the Eucharist is not offered to us merely according to the outward sign; in it we truly receive the Body and Blood of Christ—thus Augustine in *De civitate Dei* (413–426).[85] In one of his letters, Augustine explains that the sacrament of Christ's Body and Blood is truly the Body and Blood of Christ: "sacramentum corporis Christi corpus Christi est, sacramentum sanguinis Christi sanguis Christi est."[86] On this point, Radbertus has Augustine on his side, so that he can explain to his student Fredugard that not all who read Augustine will understand him, too: "Ex quo datur intelligi, quia non omnes continui qui beatum Augustinum legunt, eum intellegunt."[87]

The second Eucharistic controversy in the Middle Ages was started by Berengar of Tours (d. 1088), rector of the cathedral school in Tours and after 1040 archdeacon at the Cathedral in Angers. Berengar was a brilliant orator and used the dialectical method, that is, a procedure of deductive argumentation to treat theological questions while taking various positions into consideration. It was opposed by the anti-dialecticians, headed by Peter Damian (d. 1072). When Pope Leo IX (1049–1054) called for an investigation of Berengar's doctrine on the Eucharist, one of Berengar's critics in the person of Lanfranc of Bec (d. 1089) was staying at the papal court. After Berengar learned about his critique, he sent him a letter (1049) with the suggestion that they meet to debate the question of the reality of the Eucharist.

The missive did not reach Lanfranc. Yet at the Synod in Rome (1050), it served as incriminating evidence against Berengar, who did not take part in the synod. Berengar was excommunicated *in absentia.*

---

[83] Cf. Augustine, *In Iohannis evangelium tractatus* 26.11.19f. (CSEL 36:265); 80.3.9–12 (CSEL 36:529).

[84] Cf. Augustine, *De doctrina christiana* 2.46 (CCSL 32:7).

[85] Cf. Augustine, *De civitate Dei* 21.25 (CCSL 48:798): "sed re vera corpus Christi manducare et eius sanguine bibere; hoc est enim in Christo manere, ut in illo et Christus."

[86] Augustine, *Epistola* 98.9 (CCSL 31:531).

[87] Radbertus, *Epistola ad Fredugardum* (Paulus ed., 151).

Only after the excommunication did Berengar and Lanfranc meet in Normandy, without any rapprochement. In September 1050, a synod in Vercelli condemned Ratramnus' treatise on the Eucharist (which meanwhile had falsely been attributed to John Scotus Eriugena [ninth century]) as heterodox, because it speaks about the Eucharist as *signum, figura, pignus*, and *similitudo* of the Body of Christ. Berengar, who cited the treatise by Ratramnus as his authority, was condemned once again at this synod.[88] Another condemnation of Berengar by a synod in Paris followed in 1051. In 1052, a synod in Tours compelled Berengar to interpret the words of institution realistically. Yet as the *Purgatoria Epistula* (ca. 1053) shows, Berengar held fast to his position. At the same time, Durandus of Troarn (d. 1088) produced the first voluminous treatise on the Eucharist against Berengar.[89] In it, the abbot of the monastery in Normandy by the same name defends the concept *figura* by distinguishing between the heavenly manna as *figura figurae* (type of a type) and the Eucharist as *figura substantiae* (type of a substance).[90]

In 1054, another synod in Tours condemned Berengar. At the urging of Hildebrand of Saona, the papal legate and later Pope Gregory VII (1073–1085), Berengar finally traveled to Rome. At the 1059 Synod in Rome, at which Pope Nicholas II (1058–1061) presided, Berengar recanted his position, and his writings were burned. Berengar signed a profession of faith composed by Humberto Cardinal de Silva Candida (d. 1061):

> I, Berengar, ... knowing the true and apostolic faith, anathematize all heresy, especially that with which I have hitherto been blamed: which dares to affirm that the bread and wine that are placed on the altar, after the consecration, are only a sacrament and not the true Body and Blood of our Lord Jesus Christ.... I am in accord with the holy Roman Church and with the Apostolic See and with mouth and heart profess concerning the sacrament of the Lord's table that I hold that faith which the venerable lord Pope Nicholas and this holy synod, by evangelical and apostolic authority, have handed down to be held

---

[88] Cf. Macy, *Theologies of the Eucharist in the Early Scholastic Period*, 35f.

[89] Cf. Durandus of Troarn, *Liber de corpore et sanguine Christi* (PL 149:1375–1424).

[90] Cf. Marc-Aeilko Aris, "Figura", *Das Mittelalter: Perspektiven mediävistischer Forschung* 15, no. 2 (Berlin, 2010): 72–74.

and have confirmed to me: namely, that the bread and wine that are placed on the altar, after the consecration, are not only a sacrament, but also the true Body and Blood of our Lord Jesus Christ and that they are sensibly (*sensualiter*), not only in sacrament (*non solum sacramento*) but in truth (*in veritate*), touched (*tractari*) and broken (*frangi*) by the hands of priests and ground (*atteri*) by the teeth of the faithful, swearing by the holy and consubstantial Trinity and by these most holy Gospels of Christ.[91]

A little more than a hundred years later, Roland Bandinelli, the later Pope Alexander III (1159–1181), disengaged from this extreme realism.[92] When asked whether the Body of Christ is broken (*an corpus frangitur*), Roland answered: The Body of Christ is broken sacramentally but not essentially (*frangitur sacramentaliter et non essentialiter*).[93] Peter Lombard too (d. 1160) teaches that the Body of Christ is broken *sacramentaliter*.[94] Guibert of Nogent/Laon (1055–1125) also opposed the formula of the 1059 oath and proposed important differentiations with regard to the relation of the historical, glorified, and sacramental Body of Christ (*tria corpora*). The glorified Body of Christ is identical with the historical body of Christ with regard to its individuality, but not with its manner of appearance. The sacramental Body of Christ, as *figura* filled with reality, mediates between the historical and the glorified Body of Christ. Thus Guibert seeks to overcome the opposition between *figura* and *veritas* that had cropped up in the first and second Eucharistic controversies.[95]

In order to understand the crude realism of the 1059 oath, we must recall the role of Humberto de Silva Candida in the controversy over unleavened bread. While the Latin West made a transition between the ninth and the eleventh century to using unleavened bread (ἄζυμον) for the Eucharist, the Orthodox Churches, with the exception of the

---

[91] DH 690.

[92] Jean de Montclos, *Lanfranc et Bérengar: La controverse eucharistique du XIᵉ siècle*, Spicilegium sacrum Lovaniense, Études et documents 37 (Louvain: Spicilegium sacrum Lovaniense, 1971), 590, speaks about *ultra-réalisme*.

[93] Cf. the *Sentences* of Roland, later Pope Alexander III, first edited by A. M. Gietl (1891/1969), 233.

[94] Cf. Peter Lombard, *Sententiae* 1.4, d. 12 (ed. Collegii S. Bonaventurae ad Claras Aquas [1981], 306f.).

[95] Cf. Aris, "Figura", 64–70.

Armenians, clung to leavened bread for the Divine Liturgy.[96] The
centuries-old estrangement between East and West was sealed by the
failure to reach unity in the controversy over unleavened bread.[97]
In 1054, a mutual excommunication between Rome and Byzantium followed, which was not lifted until December 7, 1965, by
Pope Paul VI (1963–1978) and the Ecumenical Patriarch Athenagoras (1886–1972). The 1054 excommunication was limited to persons
and for a long time had no schismatic effect, especially in the mind of
the Latin Church.[98]

One of the reasons given for the introduction of unleavened bread
in the Catholic Church is the matzo of the Jewish Passover meal.
The earliest witnesses for unleavened bread are Alcuin and Hrabanus
Maurus. Despite the willingness of Pope Leo IX to be reconciled,
Humberto de Silva Candida and the Patriarch Michael Cerularius of
Constantinople (d. 1059) did not succeed in settling the controversy
over unleavened bread. The patriarch insisted that Jesus had used
leavened bread at the Last Supper and that the use of unleavened
bread was a relapse into Judaism. Moreover, the "Greeks" saw leavened bread as a symbol for the Trinity, in which the leavened bread
represents the Spirit, while unleavened bread was regarded as *corpus
imperfectum et inanimatum*.[99] Humberto de Silva Candida reproached
the Byzantine Church for falsifying the true faith. It is not in keeping
with the authentic doctrine of faith to speak about bread as a symbol.
For after the Consecration, we are no longer dealing with ordinary
bread. We cannot rule out the possibility that Humberto formulated
the oath *Ego Berengarius* with a view to the "Greeks" as well.

After the Synod of Rome (1059), Berengar went back to Tours. In
his *Scriptum contra Synodum*, which has been lost, Berengar recanted
the formula of the oath that he had signed. He maintained that he had
signed it under pressure and attacked Cardinal Humberto.[100] Lanfranc

---

[96] In the Armenian Church, records for the use of leavened bread go back to the sixth
century, but the custom may be older.

[97] Cf. Josef Rupert Geiselmann, *Die Abendmahlslehre an der Wende der christlichen Spätantike
zum Frühmittelalter* (Munich: Hueber, 1933), 73–85, 248–52; Gary Macy, *Treasures from the
Storeroom: Medieval Religion and the Eucharist* (Collegeville, Minn.: Liturgical Press, 1999), 22.

[98] Cf. Axel Bayer, *Spaltung der Christenheit: Das sogenannte Morganländische Schisma von 1054*
(Cologne: Böhlau Verlag, 2004).

[99] Cf. Geiselmann, *Abendmahlslehre an der Wende*, 77.

[100] Cf. Margaret T. Gibson, *Lanfranc of Bec* (Oxford: Clarendon Press, 1978), 70.

of Bec, too (d. 1089), was harshly attacked by Berengar. Lanfranc, who meanwhile had become Abbot of Saint Stephen's in Caen, reacted with the *Liber de corpore et sanguine Domini* (1063).[101] In it he quotes extensively from Berengar's letter against the Synod of Rome.[102] Chapter 18 of Lanfranc's written response lays the foundations for the later doctrine of transubstantiation, even though the terminology is still uncertain in some details.[103] Lanfranc distinguishes between the substance (*substantia*) of the Eucharistic gifts and their visible form (*species visibilis*) and also between the essence (*essentia*) and the qualities or properties (*proprietates*) of the Body of Christ: "Therefore it should be testified that they [bread and wine] are according to their visible appearance what they were before [the Consecration], but according to their inner essence have been transformed into the nature of that reality [Body and Blood of Christ] which they were not before."[104]

With Ambrose, Lanfranc assumes that bread and wine become the Body and Blood of Christ through the *verba testamenti* spoken by the priest: "Before it is consecrated, it is bread. But when the words of Christ are added, it is the Body of Christ."[105] "We believe, therefore, that the earthly substances lying on the altar are sanctified by God in the priestly *mysterium* ... and are transformed into the essence of the Lord's Body, while the outward appearances are retained."[106] Lanfranc was acquainted with the Aristotelian distinction between first and second substance.[107] For him, the transformation of the gifts of bread and wine affects, not their accidental purpose or qualities,

---

[101] In the Reformation era, the work went through more than ten editions between 1528 and 1618.

[102] Lanfranc does not do Berengar justice when he maintains, for example, that the Eucharist is for Berengar only a memorial of Christ's death. Cf. Lanfranc, *De corpore et sanguine Domini adversus Berengarium Turonensem* 22 (*PL* 150:440B-C).

[103] Cf. Gibson, *Lanfranc of Bec*, 90.

[104] Cf. Lanfranc of Bec, *De corpore et sanguine Domini adversus Berengarium Turonensem* 9 (*PL* 150:420D): "Esse quidem secundum visibilem speciem testatur qua erant, commutari vero secundum interiorem essentiam in natural illarum rerum quae antea non erant."

[105] Thus Lanfranc quotes from Ambrose, *De mysteriis* 5: "Antequam consecratur, panis est. Ubi autem verba Christi accesserunt, corpus est Christi." Cf. Lanfranc, *De corpore et sanguine Domini adversus Berengarium Turonensem* 18 (*PL* 150:432A-B).

[106] Lanfranc, *De corpore et sanguine Domini adversus Berengarium Turonensem* 18 (*PL* 150:430 B-C): "Credimus igitur terrenas substantias quae in mensa Dominica, per sacerdotale mysterium, divinitus sanctificantur ... converti in essentiam Dominici corporis, reservatis ipsarum rerum speciebus."

[107] Cf. ibid., 16 (*PL* 150:428B).

but rather their essence. The transformation of the Eucharistic gifts does not signify a material change of bread and wine. The transformation of the gifts is rather an "event" that refers to the metaphysical substance. Since the glorified Body of Christ is not of a material kind, Communion is for Lanfranc at the same time a physical and a spiritual event (*corporaliter, spiritualiter*).[108] "For as the material bread nourishes and sustains the human body, so the spiritual and invisible Body of Christ nourishes and sustains the soul."[109]

Berengar responded to Lanfranc with the treatise *Rescriptum contra Lanfrannum*. The only extant manuscript of the work, which traditionally was entitled *De sacra coena*, is in the Herzog-August-Bibliothek in Wolfenbüttel, where it was discovered in 1770 by Gotthold Ephraim Lessing (1729–1781).[110] In his Rescript, Berengar agrees with Lanfranc that the Eucharistic sacrifice is not a repetition of Christ's sacrifice on the Cross. In the question about the somatic Real Presence of Christ in the gifts of bread and wine, on the other hand, Berengar clearly distinguishes his position from Lanfranc's. The presence of the Body of Christ in heaven rules out the possibility that Christ could be present at the same time on the altar. The perception by the senses of the accidental qualities of bread and wine makes a substantial transformation of the gifts impossible, since a separation of substance and accidents is inconceivable. In Lanfranc's distinction between substance and accidents, Berengar sees a misuse of Aristotelian philosophy.[111] Berengar cites Boethius' commentary on the introduction (*isagoge*) composed by the Neoplatonist Porphyry (d. 301/305) to the Aristotelian doctrine on the categories.[112] While Lanfranc insists that the words of consecration *Hoc est enim corpus meum* are to be understood in the sense of an identity between bread and Body of Christ, Berengar clings to the idea that the *hoc* refers to the visible form of the bread, which is why the bread cannot be transformed into the Body of Christ.[113]

---

[108] Cf. ibid., 19 (*PL* 150:435C).

[109] Cf. ibid., 20 (*PL* 150:438D): "Nam sicut quae iste materialis panis discrete sumptus humanam carnem nutrit et sustentat, sic spirituale et invisibile corpus Christi animam."

[110] Cf. Berengar of Tours, *Rescriptum contra Lanfrannum* (Huygens ed., 1988).

[111] Cf. Aristotle, *Categorias* 2b 6.

[112] Cf. Boethius, *In Isagogen Porphyrii Commenta* 1.2 (CSEL 48:6, 5–10).

[113] Cf. Berengar of Tours, *Rescriptum contra Lanfrannum* 1, fol. 20–21, 30, 36–38 (Huygens ed., 64f., 76, 87f.).

After Lanfranc became archbishop of Canterbury (1070), his student Guitmund of Aversa (d. 1090/1095) took up the task of disputing with Berengar and his followers.[114] In his treatise on the Eucharist that he wrote against Berengar, *De corporis et sanguinis Jesu Christi veritate in Eucharistia* (1073–1075),[115] Guitmund, like Durandus of Troarn (d. 1089), sets out to clarify the concept *figura*. Harking back to Augustine, Guitmund emphasizes that the cultic celebration of the Eucharist can be called *figura*, but not the sacramental elements bread and wine.[116] Guitmund does acknowledge that Berengar's teaching that Christ's Body and Blood are hidden under the forms of bread and wine is somewhat close to his own interpretation.[117] He distances himself also from the crude realism of the oath formula presented to Berengar by Humberto de Silva Candida.[118] With good reason, Berengar's followers would dispute the idea that Christ's Body is divisible or destructible.[119] The Body of Christ cannot be ground up with teeth. Yet, like Lanfranc, Guitmund assumes a *conversio substantialis* of bread and wine that escapes our senses.[120] It could be that Guitmund's treatise was known to the Synod of Poitiers (1075), which takes up the idea of *conversio substantialis*.[121]

Since Berengar distanced himself from his profession of faith in 1059 after his return from Rome, Pope Gregory VII, who had canonized Paschasius Radbertus in 1073, summoned him before the Lenten Synod in Rome in 1079. At it, Berengar once again had to make a formal profession of faith in the Eucharistic presence of Christ. This profession is theologically more balanced than the formula of

---

[114] On Berengar's follows, cf. Macy, *Treasures from the Storeroom*, 59–80.

[115] Guitmund of Aversa, *De veritate corporis et sanguinis Domini nostri Iesu Christi* (*PL* 149:1427–94). The first printed edition of the treatise, which has the literary form of a dialogue between Guitmund and a young monk named Roger, was prepared by Erasmus of Rotterdam during his stay at the University of Freiburg (1530).

[116] Cf. Aris, "Figura", 74–76.

[117] Cf. Guitmund of Aversa, *De veritate corporis et sanguinis Domini nostri Iesu Christi* 1 (*PL* 149:1430C): "aliquo modo nobiscum".

[118] Cf. Henry Chadwick, "Ego Berengarius", in Chadwick, *Tradition and Exploration* (Norwick: Canterbury Press, 1994), 46.

[119] Cf. Guitmund of Aversa, *De veritate corporis et sanguinis Domini nostri Iesu Christi* 1 (*PL* 149:1434A, 1435A).

[120] Guitmund speaks in this connection about *transmutari* and *transire*. Cf. ibid. (*PL* 149:1440B-C); 2 (*PL* 149:1452D).

[121] Cf. Gibson, *Lanfranc of Bec*, 96.

the oath in 1059. It avoids crude realism and integrates the idea of transubstantiation:

> I, Berengar, in my heart believe and with my lips confess that through the mystery of the sacred prayer and the words of our Redeemer the bread and wine that are placed on the altar are substantially (*substantialiter*) changed (*converti*) into the true and proper and living flesh and blood of Jesus Christ, our Lord, and that after consecration it is the true body of Christ that was born of the Virgin and that, offered for the salvation of the world, was suspended on the Cross and that sits at the right hand of the Father, and the true blood of Christ, which was poured out from his side not only through the sign and power of the sacrament (*per signum et virtutem sacramenti*), but in its proper nature and in the truth of its substance (*in proprietate naturae et veritate substantiae*).[122]

The boundary line of the 1079 profession of faith lies in the then widespread opposition of sacrament (*sacramentum*) and reality (*veritas*).[123]

Berengar did submit outwardly to the 1079 profession of faith, but he held fast to his interpretation to the end of his life. This can be reconstructed as follows from the writings of Berengar and those of his critics: Berengar assumes a sensualist concept of substance and therefore disputes the idea that "the substance of the bread yields to the sacrament of the Lord's Body."[124] In his critique of the notion of a transformation of bread and wine, Berengar introduces the concepts *materia/forma, subiectum*, and *id quod in subiecto est* (that which is in the subject = *accidens*) into the doctrine of the Eucharist. In his writing, however, the terms do not have their later meaning; *subiectum* and *forma* are instead synonymous with matter. The form of a thing is for Berengar the sum of its sensibly perceptible properties.[125] Hence in Berengar's view, the substance of the bread and the wine cannot be transformed.[126] One can speak about a change through their

---

[122] DH 700.

[123] Cf. Gerken, *Theologie der Eucharistie*, 115.

[124] Berengar of Tours, *Epistola ad Ascelinum* (PL 150:66B).

[125] Cf. Hans Jorissen, *Die Entfaltung der Transsubstantiationslehre bis zum Beginn der Hochscholastik*, Münsterische Beiträge zur Theologie, 28/1 (Münster: Aschendorffsche Verlagsbuchhandlung, 1965), 6f.

[126] Cf. Berengar of Tours, *Rescriptum contra Lanfrannum* 1, fol. 20–21, 30, 36–38 (Huygens ed., 64f., 76, 87f.).

consecration (*mutatio per consecrationem*) only insofar as a new spiritual reality is added to the substances of bread and wine, through which they become the sacrament (*sacramentum*), sign (*figura*) of the Body and Blood of Christ.

Berengar advocates a kind of impanation: the bread-substance after the Consecration is united with the Body of Christ as Christ's human nature is with his divine nature.[127] What our body receives at Holy Communion is for Berengar ordinary bread, while the soul receives with Christ a spiritual nourishment. Bread and wine are visible signs (*sacramenta*) of a spiritual reality (*res sacramenti*). The presence of Christ in the sacrament exists for Berengar *intellectualiter* and not *substantialiter*. Otherwise, the Body of Christ on the altars would have to be broken into different pieces. The sacramental body of Christ is for Berengar a different one from the historical and glorified Body of Christ.[128] The Consecration does not change the nature of the bread and wine but, rather, gives them a new meaning, which makes them signs of Christ's Body and Blood. There is already a natural similarity between [the former and] its sacramental sign, inasmuch as bread, as bodily food, brings to bear Christ, the Bread of Life.

Berengar's opponents accused him of a reductive, symbolist interpretation of Christ's presence in the sacrament of the Eucharist. Representative in this regard is the critique by Adelmann of Liège (d. 1061) in his letter to Berengar (1052): "About the Body and Blood of the Lord, which every day throughout the earth is sacrificed on the holy altar, you seem to judge, contrary to what the Catholic faith holds, ... that this is neither the true Body nor the true Blood of Christ, but rather a certain figure and likeness thereof."[129] Through the Consecration, in Berengar's view, bread and wine become symbols of Christ's Body and Blood. Josef Rupert Geiselmann (1890–1970) also interprets Berengar in this sense: the sacrament of the Eucharist is "not absolutely but rather in a certain respect Christ's

---

[127] Cf. Lanfranc of Bec, *De corpore et sanguine Domini* 10 (*PL* 150:421A–C); confirmed by Berengar of Tours, *Rescriptum contra Lanfrannum* 3 (Huygens ed., 633).

[128] Cf. Pelikan, *Christian Tradition*, 3:192–95.

[129] Adelmann of Lüttich, *De Eucharistiae sacramento ad Berengarium epistola* (*PL* 143:1290A–B): "et de corpore et sanguine Domini, quod quotidie in universa terra super sanctum altare immolatur, aliter quam fides catholica teneat, sentire videaris ... non esse verum corpus Christi neque verum sanguinem, sed figuram quamdam et similitudinem."

Body and Blood, namely, insofar as it is a symbol or is a *virtus* [power] united with it on the basis of the *benedictio* [blessing]."[130]

Henry Chadwick (1920–2008) and Hans Jorissen (1924–2011), on the other hand, advocate an orthodox interpretation of Berengar's teaching on the Eucharist; in their reading, he thinks that a type or image (*Bild*) is something real and participatory.[131] To support this view, they cite Berengar's response to Adelmann of Liège in the *Purgatoria Epistula* (1053–1055). In it, Berengar explains that he never designated the *res sacramenti* as *figura*, but only the *sacramentum*.[132] In the eleventh century, however, it was theologically no longer possible to speak about the presence of Christ's Body in the Eucharist in the way that Berengar did without thereby causing massive misunderstandings or drawing suspicion upon oneself.[133] Nevertheless, Berengar made an important contribution to the development of sacramental doctrine. Thus his definition of a sacrament as a visible form of an invisible grace (*invisibilis gratiae visibilis forma*) became widely accepted in the Middle Ages as the standard definition. Berengar's distinction between *sacramentum* and *res sacramenti* also became paradigmatic.[134]

The doctrine of a substantial transformation of bread and wine was not immediately adopted at the turn of the twelfth century; this is demonstrated by Rupert of Deutz in his *Liber de divinis officiis*, which has already been cited. Without speaking about a transubstantiation of bread and wine, Rupert teaches a transformation of the gifts of bread and wine into the Body and Blood of Christ.[135] Citing as his authority the formula of Berengar's 1059 oath, he defends the Real Presence of Christ's Body and Blood in the gifts of bread and wine.[136] In Rupert's view, in the consecrated gifts of bread and wine, the Lord's "sacrificial body" (*corpus sacrificii*), freed from all sensible life, is

---

[130] Geiselmann, *Eucharistielehre der Vorscholastik*, 296.

[131] Cf. Jorissen, "Wandlungen des philosophischen Kontextes", 110f.; Jorissen, "Abendmahlsstreit", 1:37f.; Chadwick, "Ego Berengarius", 33–60.

[132] Cf. "Lettre de Bérenger à Adelmann de Liège", in Montclos, *Lanfranc et Bérenger* 533:39–50; 536:120–22.

[133] Cf. Pelikan, *Christian Tradition*, 3:201f.

[134] Cf. Macy, *Theologies of the Eucharist in the Early Scholastic Period*, 40.

[135] On Rupert's understanding of the Eucharist and the criticism expressed against it, cf. Rhaban Haacke, "Zur Eucharistielehre des Rupert von Deutz", *Recherches de théologie ancienne et médiévale* 32 (1965), 20–42.

[136] Cf. Rupert of Deutz, *De divinis officiis* 2.8–9 (FC 33/1:270–81).

present and displays its efficacy in the transformed gifts by imparting "spiritual life" to the faithful at Communion.

B. The Ontology of the Doctrine of Transubstantiation

From the twelfth century on, reports of miraculous bleeding hosts and images of Christ multiplied.[137] Most theologians were cautious about such reports. They viewed the real miracle as the sacramental presence of the Flesh and Blood of Christ in the bread and wine.[138] Albert the Great (1200–1280), Thomas Aquinas, and many others took a transubstantiation of the gifts of bread and wine as their point of departure. According to an anonymous student report, Robertus Pullus (d. 1147/1150) coined the term *transsubstantiatio*.[139] It appeared first in literary form around 1155/1156 in the writings of Roland Bandinelli, later Pope Alexander III.[140] At the Fourth Lateran Council (1215) the doctrine of transubstantiation was proposed in magisterial form:

> There is indeed one universal Church of the faithful ... in which the priest himself, Jesus Christ, is also the sacrifice. His Body and Blood are truly contained in the sacrament of the altar under the appearances of bread and wine, the bread being transubstantiated (*transsubstantiatis*) into the body by the divine power and the wine into the blood, to the effect that we receive from what is his what he has received from what is ours.[141]

The Fourth Lateran Council took place during the pontificate of Innocent III. The fourth book of his treatise *De sacro altaris mysterio*

---

[137] Cf. Peter Browe, *Die eucharistischen Wunder des Mittelalters*, Breslauer Studien zur historischen Theologie 4 (Breslau: Verlag Müller & Seiffert, 1938).

[138] Cf. Angenendt, *Geschichte der Religiosität*, 336.

[139] Cf. Matthias Laarmann, "Transsubstantiation: Begriffsgeschichtliche Materialien und bibliographische Notizen", *Archiv für Liturgiewissenschaft* 41 (1999): 122; Gary Macy, "Theology of the Eucharist in the High Middle Ages", in *A Companion to the Eucharist in the Middle Ages*, ed. J.C. Levy, Brill's Companions to the Christian Tradition 26 (Leiden and Boston: Brill, 2012), 374.

[140] The *Expositio canonis missae* attributed to Peter Damian, in which the word *transsubstantiatio* occurs, is a late work.

[141] DH 802.

(1195–1197) contains a commentary on the *Canon Romanus* from the Consecration to the Our Father. It also discusses unresolved questions of sometimes subtle casuistry, like the question of what happens to the Body of the Lord when a mouse nibbles on the Blessed Sacrament.[142] On the other hand, Innocent III warns against a curiosity that is inappropriate for the mystery of the Mass: "It is safer in such cases to stop short of understanding than to go beyond the limits of understanding."[143] Based on the doctrine of concomitance, whereby the whole Christ is contained as a natural accompanying consequence (*per concomitantiam*) both under the species of the Body and under the species of the Blood, so that the Blood of Christ is received, too, with the Body of Christ, it was possible for a position that was still disputed in the twelfth century to become generally accepted, namely, that Christ is already entirely present after the first Consecration of the bread and not only after the Consecration of the wine is pronounced.

Faith in the substantial Real Presence of Christ in the consecrated species of bread and wine is reckoned as part of the *fides divina*. Well into the late Middle Ages, however, besides *transubstantiation* of bread and wine into Christ's Body and Blood, other theories were advocated, too. Not all theologians regarded the transubstantiation of bread and wine as a surely defined doctrine of the faith.[144] According to the theory of consubstantiation, the substance of bread and wine remains, but with the Consecration the presence of the substance of Christ's Body and Blood is added, so that the substances of bread and

---

[142] The question "Quid sumit mus" had occupied theologians since the early Scholastic period. While Caesarius of Heisterbach (d. around 1245), despite his assumption that the *verum corpus Christi natum ex Virgine* exists under the form of bread, argued that the mouse receives only the *species*, the outward form of the sacrament, since it possesses no spiritual capacity whatsoever to receive the Body of Christ, Petrus Comestor (d. 1178) assumed that the mouse, like a man, receives the Body of Christ. Others answered the question "Quid sumit mus" by saying *nescio* (I do not know) or *Deus novit* (God knows). The decisive epistemological and presence-theoretical distinctions that rule out the possibility of mice and other animals receiving the Body of Christ, if they eat a particle of the consecrated Host, were undertaken by Alexander of Hales (d. 1245). Cf. Marc-Aeilko Aris, "Quid sumit mus: Präsenz (in) der Eucharistie", in *Mediale Gegenwärtigkeit*, ed. Christian Kiening, Medienwandel, Medienwechsel, Medienwissen 1 (Zurich: Chronos, 2007), 179–205.

[143] *PL* 217:861C.

[144] Cf. Paul J. J. M. Bakker, *La raison et le miracle: Les doctrines eucharistiques (c. 1250–c. 1400)*, 2 vols. (dissertation, Catholic University of Nijmegen, 1999); Macy, *Treasures from the Storeroom*, 81–120.

Christ's Body exist together, as well as the wine and Christ's Blood. The annihilation theory maintains that the substances of bread and wine are first destroyed before they are replaced by Christ's Body and Blood. While the theory of consubstantiation understands Christ's presence as, so to speak, a "local presence" under the species of bread and wine, the annihilation theory assumes a "temporal succession" of these substances and assumes that the accidents momentarily exist without substance.

In the thirteenth century, the doctrine of transubstantiation became widely accepted by leading theologians. In the case of Albert the Great,[145] the Aristotelian concept of substance is accepted, although it is simultaneously transformed at a decisive place. For according to Aristotle, there can indeed be substantial changes, but no transformation of essence in which the accidents are completely retained.[146] Thomas Aquinas presents in the treatise on the Eucharist in his *Summa theologiae* a lengthy explanation and justification of the doctrine of transubstantiation.[147] The point of departure is the conviction that Christ, as the risen, glorified Lord, sits in heaven with his glorified Body at the right hand of the Father. Since any presence of Christ in the signs of bread and wine in the sense of a local motion and spatial extension is ruled out, because this contradicts his divine nature, the presence for Thomas can be only a sacramental one, in the sense of a presence of the glorified Body and Blood of Christ. "Christ's body is not in this sacrament definitively, because then it would be only on the particular altar where this sacrament is performed: whereas it is in heaven under its own species and on many other altars under the sacramental species."[148]

The sacramental Real Presence of the Body and Blood of Christ comes about through a substantial change of the gifts of bread and wine (*conversio substantiae*), which is effected by God himself.[149] "By divine power ... the whole substance of the bread is changed into the whole substance of Christ's body, and the whole substance of the wine

---

[145] Cf. Hans Jorissen, *Der Beitrag Alberts des Grossen zur theologischen Rezeption des Aristoteles am Beispiel der Transsubstantiationslehre*, Lectio Albertina 5 (Münster: Aschendorff, 2002).

[146] On the importance of the reception of Aristotle in the development of the doctrine of transubstantiation, cf. Jorissen, *Entfaltung der Transsubstantiationslehre*, 65–154.

[147] Cf. Thomas Aquinas, *Summa theologiae* III, q. 75, art. 2–8.

[148] *Summa theologiae* III, q. 76, art. 5 ad 3.

[149] Cf. *Summa theologiae* III, q. 75, art. 2c ad 2.

into the whole substance of Christ's blood. Hence this is not a formal, but a substantial conversion (*conversio substantialis*); nor is it a kind of natural movement: but, with a name of its own, it can be called 'transubstantiation'."[150] The properties of bread and wine are maintained at their transubstantiation. Nothing about the chemistry of the bread and wine is changed by their Consecration. The concept of substance that Thomas presupposes is a metaphysical concept, and not the concept of a substance in the later scientific sense. For "it is evident to sense that all the accidents of the bread and wine remain after the Consecration."[151] Anything else would be contrary to reason, since sense perception is unerring. The transformation of essence does resemble a natural change, since it does, like the latter, presuppose something. However, it manifests a greater similarity with creation out of nothing. For the transformation of essence, which happens *instantaneously*,[152] brings into being something entirely new; indeed, in Aquinas' opinion, it is more difficult to understand than creation from nothing.[153] The concept of substance refers to the creaturely being (*esse*) or the created subsistence (*subsistentia*) of the bread and wine, which after the Consecration are both immediately maintained by the *virtus divina* of the glorified Lord present in the sacramental sign. Transubstantiation is therefore understood as a transformation of subject, whereby not only the appearance and color continue, but also the fact that the consecrated bread can serve as food like ordinary bread and the consecrated wine keeps its alcoholic content.[154]

---

[150] *Summa theologiae* III, q. 75, art. 4c: "divina virtute ... tota substantia panis convertitur in totam substantiam corporis Christi, et tota substantia vini in totam substantiam sanguinis Christi. Unde haec conversio non est formalis, sed substantialis. Nec continetur inter species motus naturalis, sed proprio nomine potest dici *transsubstantiatio*."

[151] *Summa theologiae* III, q. 75, art. 5c: "Quod sensu apparet, facta consecratione, omnia accidentia panis et vini remanere."

[152] Cf. *Summa theologiae* III, q. 75, art. 7c.

[153] Cf. *Summa theologiae* III, q. 75, art. 8c.

[154] Here the medieval concept of *subiectum* is presupposed. Contrary to the opinion of Dirk Ansorge, "Jenseits von Begriff und Vorstellung: Das Wunder der Eucharistie im Mittelalter", in *Phänomenologie der Gabe: Neue Zugänge zum Mysterium der Eucharistie*, ed. F. Bruckmann, Quaestiones disputatae 270 (Freiburg: Herder, 2015), 95, Thomas does not set out to "separate substance and accident". While Thomas with Avicenna does distinguish between the existence and the essence of a being and its accidents, he expressly denies that accidents could exist without a substance. We must distinguish from this the *dimensio extensiva* of the Eucharistic elements, the bearers of which cannot be Christ's Body and Blood, since Christ's presence in the Eucharist is not a local one (cf. *Summa theologiae* III, qq. 76–77).

For Thomas, the Lord's words at the Last Supper establish the fact
that Jesus Christ is truly present under the appearances of the bread
and wine. In keeping with Aristotelian hylomorphism, Aquinas distinguished between matter and form in the sacrament of the Eucharist.
The matter of the sacrament of the Eucharist is bread and wine;[155]
the form of the sacrament are the words of institution pronounced
over the bread and wine.[156] According to Thomas, three arguments
of fittingness speak in favor of the special presence of Christ in the
Eucharist. First, the sacrifices of the Old Covenant were only shadows
of what was to come. The sacrifice of the New Covenant could therefore not be contained in a sign or a type alone (non solum in significati-
one vel figura), but must be contained in it in truth (in rei veritate). Christ
is made present in the Eucharist; as High Priest of the New Covenant,
he offered himself as a victim: the Christus passus. As a man, he was
"not only priest, but also a perfect victim, being at the same time
victim for sin, victim for a peace-offering, and a holocaust."[157] In the
New Covenant, "the true sacrifice of Christ is presented to the faithful
under the form of bread and wine."[158] Even though Christ is entirely
present in both cases in the signs of bread and wine,[159] the sacramental sign of wine "represents Christ's blood more expressively".[160] For
Thomas, therefore, the words of the Consecration of the chalice (Hic
est calix sanguinis mei ...) are part of the form of the sacrament.[161]

Thomas sees the sacrificial character of the Mass in the double
Consecration and thus in the inward sacrament (res et sacramentum).
"It has the nature of a sacrifice inasmuch as in this sacrament Christ's
Passion is represented, whereby Christ 'offered himself a Victim to
God' (Eph 5:2)."[162] Just as according to Augustine every sign receives

---

[155] Cf. Summa theologiae III, q. 74, art. 1c.

[156] Cf. Summa theologiae III, q. 78, art. 1c.

[157] Summa theologiae III, q. 22, art. 2c: "Christus, inquantum homo, non solum fuit sacerdos, sed etiam hostia perfecta, simul existens hostia pro peccato, et hostia pacificorum, et
holocaustum."

[158] Summa theologiae III, q. 22, art. 6 ad 2.

[159] Cf. Summa theologiae III, q. 76, art. 1–3.

[160] Summa theologiae III, q. 78, art. 3 ad 7: "sanguis seorsum consecratus a corpore expressius
repraesentat passionem Christi."

[161] Cf. Summa theologiae III, q. 78, art. 3c.

[162] Summa theologiae III, q. 79, art. 7c: "Inquantum enim in hoc sacramento repraesentatur
passio Christi, qua Christus 'obtulit se hostiam Deo', ut dicitur Eph 5, habet rationem sacrificii."

its name from the thing signified, so too the celebration of the Eucharist is called a sacrifice (*immolatio*) because it is the sacramental representation of the sacrifice of Jesus Christ.[163] The oblation that the human priest offers is, with regard to its sacramental reality, the same one that Christ offered. The human priest, however, is not the same one, but the same only with regard to the representation (*repraesentatione*). The priest who consecrates in the person of Christ pronounces the transforming words as Christ's words.[164] The priest "bears Christ's image, in whose person and by whose power he pronounces the words of consecration."[165] The words of institution are for Thomas the genuine act of offering and conveyance to God.[166] The sacrifice of the Eucharist, however, brings about no new effect as compared with the sacrifice on the Cross, but rather applies the saving power of the sacrifice on the Cross.

In the communication of the sacrifice (*communicatio sacrificii*), the salvation founded upon Christ's death is received. Christ's presence in the Eucharist corresponds to his love for mankind unto the end. Christ bequeathed the sacrament of the Eucharist to his friends as a "sign of the greatest love" (*maximae caritatis signum*). Finally, the Real Presence of Christ in the Eucharist corresponds to the perfection of faith in the divinity and humanity of Christ, that he gives himself to us entirely in the sacrament of the Eucharist, both his divinity and his humanity.[167] With regard to Communion, too, the Eucharist for Thomas is a sacrifice because through it the work of our redemption is accomplished.[168] "Just as by coming into the world, [Christ] visibly

---

[163] Cf. *Summa theologiae* III, q. 83, art. 1c. The interpretation advocated by Ferdinand Pratzner, *Messe und Kreuzesopfer: Die Krise der sakramentalen Idee bei Luther und in der mittelalterlichen Scholastik* (Vienna: Herder, 1970), 70–76, whereby Thomas acknowledges in the sacrament of Christ's sacrifice only a figurative representation of Christ's sacrifice on the Cross, does not do him justice. A different reading is given by Burkhard Neunheuser, *Eucharistie in Mittelalter und Neuzeit*, Handbuch der Dogmengeschichte 4/4c (Freiburg: Herder, 1963), 40, who interprets the *memoria* and *repraesentatio sacrificii* in Thomas in the sense of a sacramental realism.

[164] Cf. Thomas Aquinas, *Scriptum super quattuor libros Sententiarum* IV, disp. 8, q. 2, art. 1, sol. 4 ad 4.

[165] Thomas Aquinas, *Summa theologiae* III, q. 83, art. 1 ad 3: "gerit imaginem Christi, in cuius persona et virtute verba pronuntiat ad consecrandum."

[166] Cf. *Summa theologiae* III, q. 82, art. 10c: "consecratione sacrificium offertur".

[167] Cf. *Summa theologiae* III, q. 75, art. 1c.

[168] Cf. *Summa theologiae* III, q. 83, art. 1c (alio modo).

bestowed the life of grace upon the world, . . . so also, by coming sacramentally into man, he causes the life of grace."[169]

The question about the reception of Communion has occupied theologians since Lanfranc of Bec. Following Augustine, theologians distinguished between worthy and unworthy Communion. Worthy Communion was called spiritual, while unworthy Communion was described as corporeal or only sacramental (communion of the sign).[170] In the case of worthy reception of the Eucharist, Thomas distinguished spiritual reception in faith with yearning for the sacrament (*spiritualiter manducare*) and full spiritual and sacramental reception.[171] Communion is not only about the individual's personal encounter with Christ. The purpose of the Eucharist is the unity of the Mystical Body of Jesus Christ.[172]

Thomas rejects the teaching that the substance of Christ's Body and Blood exists hidden beneath the substance of the bread and wine (*consubstantiatio*).[173] For the words of institution identify bread and wine with Christ's Body and Blood, which would not be possible if the substance of bread and wine were to continue in existence. Moreover, in the case of a consubstantiation, Christ would have to be present in the sense of a change of place. Alexander of Hales rejected the theory of consubstantiation for reasons of *ratio theologica*, among others, with the argument that Christ wants to show in the sacrament of the Eucharist that he is the Lord of nature. As with consubstantiation, Thomas also rejects the theory of the annihilation of the substance of bread and wine.[174] A confirmation of the doctrine of transubstantiation proposed by the Fourth Lateran Council followed in the year of Aquinas' death at the Second Council of Lyon (1274).[175] But not all medieval theologians were convinced by

---

[169] *Summa theologiae* III, q. 79, art. 1c.: "Qui, sicut in mundum visibiliter veniens, contulit mundo vitam gratiae . . . ita, in hominem sacramentaliter veniens, vitam gratiae operatur."

[170] Cf. Macy, "Theology of the Eucharist in the High Middle Ages", 379.

[171] Cf. *Summa theologiae* III, q. 80, art. 11c.

[172] Cf. *Summa theologiae* III, q. 73, art. 3.

[173] Cf. Thomas Aquinas, *Scriptum super quattuor libros Sententiarum* IV, disp. 11, q. 1, art. 1; Thomas Aquinas, *Summa contra Gentiles* IV, c. 62; *Summa theologiae* III, q. 75, art. 2c.

[174] Cf. Thomas Aquinas, *Scriptum super quattuor libros Sententiarum* IV, disp. 11, q. 1, art. 2; *Summa theologiae* III, q. 75, art. 3c.

[175] Cf. DH 860: "Sacramentum Eucharistiae ex azymo conficit eadem Romana Ecclesia, tenens et docens, quod in ipso sacramento panis vere transsubstantiatur in corpus et vinum in sanguinem Domini nostri Iesu Christi."

the ontology of the doctrine of transubstantiation. Roughly speaking, three theories were advocated: the *coexistence* of the substance of bread and wine with that of the Body and Blood of Christ, the *replacement* of the substance of bread and wine by that of Christ's Body and Blood, and the theory of *transubstantiation*.[176]

John Duns Scotus (d. 1308) considers consubstantiation at least not ruled out by the wording of Scripture, even though the doctrine of the Church demands transubstantiation.[177] Scotus, like Thomas, is a realist and not a nominalist, but he assumes a univocal concept of being. Both being and its determinations are understood as positive divine ordinances (*Setzungen*). There is no room here for the idea of ontological participation, as in Thomas' thought. The sacramental sign is arbitrarily fixed by the Church as an occasion for God's immediate action. Thus God obliged himself to grant the grace of justification with the sacramental sign of Baptism in water. In the case of the sacrament of the Eucharist, God in his *potentia Dei absoluta* causes the substance of the Body of Christ to replace the substance of bread (*successio substantiarum*). Scotus does not explain what happens to the substance of bread.

For William Ockham (1288–1347), too, the Eucharistic presence of Christ is a miracle of God's unrestricted omnipotence.[178] Yet, unlike Scotus, Ockham is a nominalist. For him, substance is what quantity, quality, and so on, set forth by themselves. Quantity and quality are not really distinct from each other, which rules out a *transmutatio substantialis*. Ockham assumes that the Body and Blood are present without quantity in the unchanged substance of bread and wine in a non-*circumscriptive* way.[179] Ockham speaks about a *successio substantiae ad substantiam* in the sense of an addition (*adductio*) of the Body of Christ.[180] Ockham wavers here between the idea of an annihilation

---

[176] Cf. Macy, "Theology of the Eucharist in the High Middle Ages", 375.

[177] Cf. John Duns Scotus, *In IV Sententiarum*, disp. 11, q. 3, nn. 14–20. On Scotus' doctrine of the Eucharist, see David Burr, "Scotus and Transubstantiation", *Mediaeval Studies* 43 (1972): 336–60.

[178] On Ockham's doctrine of the Eucharist, see Gabriel Buescher, *The Eucharistic Teaching of William Ockham* (St. Bonaventure, N.Y.: Franciscan Institute, 1950; 2nd ed., 1974).

[179] Cf. Ockham, *Quaestiones in librum quartum sententiarum* 4 (Reportation), q. 8 = *Opuscula theologica* 7 (ed. Wood-Gedeon), 140.

[180] Cf. Ockham, *Quaestiones in librum quartum sententiarum* 4 (Reportation), q. 8 = *Opuscula theologica* 7 (Wood-Gedeon ed.), 100; Ockham, *Tractatus de corpore Christi* c. 6 = *Opera theologica* 10 (Wood-Gedeon ed.), 100.

of the substance of bread and the idea of the consubstantiality of the substance of Christ's Body and Blood. He regards both as ways of interpreting the doctrine of transubstantiation. As for the question of the sacrament's efficacy, Ockham, like Scotus, denies that bread and wine are instrumental causes for the grace that the sacrament of the Eucharist bestows. The sacramental signs are only indispensable conditions, *conditio sine qua*. God in his omnipotence has decreed that we should receive the Body and Blood of Christ with bread and wine.[181]

Pierre Cardinal d'Ailly (d. 1420), an exponent of nominalism who played an important role at the Council of Constance (1414–1418), handed Ockham's intellectual heritage on to Gabriel Biel (d. 1494). This philosopher and theologian, who taught in Heidelberg and later in Tübingen, was called the last "Scholastic" by his contemporaries; he adopted Scotist and Ockhamist thought in moderate form for pastoral purposes and had a great influence on Martin Luther. Biel's *Expositio canonis missae* (1488) was widely read.[182] In the forms of bread and wine, the Body and Blood of Christ are truly and really contained. Biel rejects a transformation of the substance of bread into the Body of Christ (*transmutatio substantialis*) on the basis of his concept of substance, which he adopted from Ockham. Through divine omnipotence, the substance of Christ's Body replaces the substance of the bread.[183] The *verba consecrationis* for Biel do not have the power to transform (*convertere, mutare*) bread and wine but are only the prerequisite for it. The change is brought about by God alone.[184]

---

[181] Cf. Stephen E. Lahey, "Late Medieval Eucharistic Theology", in *A Companion to the Eucharist in the Middle Ages*, ed. J. C. Levy and K. van Ausdall, Brill's Companions to Christian Tradition 26 (Leiden and Boston: Brill, 2012), 501–3. On the understanding of the sacraments as effective signs in the late Middle Ages, see Ueli Zahnd, *Wirksame Zeichen? Sakramentenlehre und Semiotik in der Scholastik des ausgehenden Mittelalters*, Spätmittelalter, Humanismus, Reformation 80 (Tübingen: Mohr Siebeck, 2014).

[182] Besides the *Expositio canonis missae*, we should consult Biel's *Commentarium in IV libros sententiarum* (1500/1501) for his teaching on the Eucharist. On Biel's Eucharistic doctrine, see Heiko A. Oberman, *The Harvest of Medieval Theology: Gabriel Biel and Late Medieval Nominalism*, the Robert Troup Prize-Treatise for the Year 1962 (Cambridge: Harvard University Press, 1963), 271–80; Rudolf Damerau, *Die Abendmahlslehre des Nominalismus insbesondere die des Gabriel Biel*, Studien zu den Grundlagen der Reformation 1 (Giessen: Schmitz, 1963), 151–222.

[183] Cf. Biel, *Expositio canonis missae*, Lectio 40, D; Biel, *In IV Sententiarum*, disp. 11, q. 1, art. 1, n. 1.

[184] Cf. Biel, *Expositio canonis missae*, Lectio 47, R.

The Body of Christ present under the sign of bread is the same one that Mary bore, that was crucified and rose from the dead. From this it does not follow, in Biel's view, that the Eucharist is a repetition (*reiteratio*) of the sacrifice on the Cross. The Eucharist is a sacrifice because it is a *repraesentatio* and *memoriale* of the sacrifice on the Cross.[185] With regard to the sacrificial character of the celebration of the Mass, Biel emphasizes the unity of the Offertory, the Consecration, and Communion. Biel does not answer the question of how the Mass, as a representation and memorial of the sacrifice on the Cross, is itself a true sacrifice.[186]

In the fifteenth century, the papal Magisterium confirmed once again the doctrine of the transubstantiation of the gifts of bread and wine into the Body and Blood of Christ as taught by the Fourth Lateran Council and the Council of Lyon. The Decree for the Armenians (1439) declares concerning the form and effect of the sacrament of the Eucharist:

> The form of this sacrament is the words of the Savior with which he effected this sacrament; for the priest effects the sacrament by speaking in the person of Christ. It is by the power of these words that the substance of bread is changed into the body of Christ, and the substance of wine into his blood; in such a way, however, that the whole Christ is contained under the species of bread and the whole Christ under the species of wine. Further, the whole Christ is present under any part of the consecrated host or the consecrated wine when separated from the rest.[187]

The gifts of bread and wine, therefore, are consecrated by the *verba testamenti* into the Body and Blood of Christ.

---

[185] Cf. ibid., 53, U: "unum est sacrificium quod obtulit Christus, et quod nos offerimus, quamvis non eodem modo offeratur. Ab ipso quidem oblatum est in mortem, a nobis non in mortem ..., sed in mortis recordationem offertur a nobis. Unde nostra oblatio non est reiteratio suae oblationis, sed repraesentatio." This definition would be adopted by the Council of Trent in its Decree on the Sacrifice of the Mass (1562). Cf. DH 1740–43.

[186] Cf. Hans Bernhard Meyer, *Luther und die Messe: Eine liturgiewissenschaftliche Untersuchung über das Verhältnis Luthers zum Messwesen des späten Mittelalters* (Paderborn: Verlag Bonifacius-Druckerei, 1965), 151–56.

[187] DH 1321.

C. Eucharistic Devotion in the Middle Ages

From the ninth century on, the theology of the Eucharist increasingly revolved around the question of the somatic Real Presence. This does not mean that there was no longer any interest in the celebration of the Eucharist and its rite. Besides the explanation of the rite that Thomas Aquinas gives in his treatise on the Eucharist,[188] we should point out in particular the treatise *De mysterio missae*[189] by his teacher Albert the Great. Applying the *descensus-ascensus* theory of Pseudo-Dionysius the Areopagite, Albert interprets the liturgy as an action leading the faithful to *beatitudo* (blessedness, eternal happiness). He regards the Sacrifice of the Mass as the most effective means of uniting the soul with God. In order to achieve this, a yearning for the highest good is needed. In the first part of the Mass (called the *introitus*), in Albert's view, this yearning for Christ's coming finds expression. In the second part (*instructio*), the worshipper prepares to accept Christ's teachings. The third part (*oblatio*) represents the perfection of the spiritual life in God. During the *oblatio*, the worshipper offers himself to the Lord as a sacrifice; in Communion, which is the pledge of eternal life, he is sanctified through union with Christ.

As early as the fifth century, sacramental Communion had declined sharply in favor of spiritual communion. A synod held in Southern France by Caesarius of Arles (d. 542) declared: "Laymen who do not communicate on Christmas, Easter, and Pentecost are no longer deemed Catholics and should no longer be regarded as such."[190] Yet even the precept of receiving Communion three times a year was often not obeyed. The Fourth Lateran Council (1215) therefore obliged all the faithful "reverently [to] receive the sacrament of the Eucharist at least at Easter".[191] The "parish bann", that is, the obligation to participate in the celebration of Sunday

---

[188] Cf. Thomas Aquinas, *Summa theologiae* III, q. 83: "De ritu huius sacramenti". In his explanation of the rite, Thomas refers, not to silent Mass (*missa solitaria*), but rather to Solemn High Mass.

[189] Cf. Albertus Magnus, *Opera Omnia*, vol. 38: *De mysterio missae*, 1–189 (Borgnet ed., 1899).

[190] Concilium Agathense 18 (CCSL 148:202): "Saeculares vero qui Natale Domini, Pascha, Pentecosten non communicaverint, catholici non credantur, nec inter catholices habeantur."

[191] DH 812.

Mass within one's own parish, had existed since the ninth century. The appearance of the mendicant orders loosened the parish bann, until Pope Leo X (1513–1521) finally abolished it.[192] Since the High Middle Ages, only the Body of Christ was received by lay people when they went to Communion. The fear of dishonoring the Blood of Christ by spilling it played an important role in that development. Theological justification for Communion under the form of bread alone was provided by the Scholastic doctrine of concomitance, whereby the whole Christ with his divinity and humanity is present in both the bread and the wine.

The practice of elevating the consecrated Host spread, perhaps under the influence of Cluny and as a reaction to Berengar of Tours, starting from France.[193] The elevation of the Host was seen as the lifting up of Jesus on the Cross. A distinction should be made between pre- and post-consecratory elevation. In the case of the pre-consecratory elevation, taking hold of the gifts (*accepit*) while speaking the *verba testamenti* developed into an offertory gesture. More and more often, the priest not only took the host in his hands but also raised it high while pronouncing the words of consecration. The Parisian Bishop Odo of Sully (d. 1208) objected to this. Before the Consecration, the host should be lifted only to chest height and held high only after the Consecration was finished, so that it could be seen by everyone.[194] This regulation spread quickly throughout the Church. The elevation of the chalice became a common practice somewhat later, but was first prescribed generally by the 1570 *Missale Romanum* of Pius V (1566–1572).

The elevation of the consecrated Host and the consecrated chalice and the ringing of the bells underscore the moment of transformation through Christ's words (*verba testamenti*). There are records as early as the year 1201 for the tolling of the bells in Cologne at the elevation of the Host. Adoration is inseparably united with the elevation. A second rite of adoration is the priest's genuflection and the kneeling of the faithful, which has been common practice since the thirteenth

---

[192] Cf. Hans Bernhard Meyer, *Eucharistie, Geschichte, Theologie, Pastoral*, Handbuch der Liturgiewissenschaft 4 (Regensburg: Pustet, 1989), 243.

[193] So Meyer suspects; cf. ibid., 233.

[194] Cf. Peter Browe, *Eucharistie im Mittelalter: Liturgiehistorische Forschungen in kulturwissenschaftlicher Absicht*, ed. H. Lutterbach and T. Flammer (Münster: Lit., 2003), 31.

century. Until then a bow was customary. The theological basis for adoration is the understanding that bread and wine become Christ's Body and Blood through the utterance of the *verba testamenti*. More and more often at the elevation, Latin hymns were sung. One example is the hymn "Ave verum corpus natum", which is attributed to Pope Innocent IV (1243–1254) and has been set to music many times, by Wolfgang Amadeus Mozart (1756–1791), among others. In its liturgical version, the hymn reads: "Ave verum corpus natum / ex Maria virgine, / vere passum immolatum / in cruce pro homine, / cuius latus perforatum / vero fluxit sanguine, / esto nobis praegustatum / mortis in examine." (Hail, O true Body, born / of the Virgin Mary, / which truly suffered and was sacrificed / on the Cross for mankind, / whose pierced side / poured out true blood; / be for us a foretaste / in the trial of death.)[195] In the late fourteenth century, most prayers at the elevation were translated [into German]. Besides these, several vernacular prayers developed. Latin and vernacular prayers at the elevation were not regarded as antithetical, and in some cases they were prayed at Communion, also.[196]

The medieval yearning to see the Blessed Sacrament was no doubt the expression of a deep Eucharistic devotion. The sacrament of the Eucharist, however, was perceived by the faithful less and less as heavenly food. Thus some thought that piously beholding the consecrated Host had the same spiritual value as participation in Mass. "For the High and Later Middle Ages, the consecrated Host was the Divine Presence purely and simply and thus the most effective matter for salvation."[197] The whole cultic interest was concentrated on the yearningly awaited "theophany" or manifestation of God that was brought about with the words of transformation. The decisive things were the Consecration and the elevation of the Host. For the faithful, they were the reason for coming to church.[198]

---

[195] *Praegustatum*, "foretaste", implies that sacramental Communion is an anticipation of the everlasting banquet in heaven. In another version, verse 6 reads "fluxit aqua et sanguine" (poured forth water and blood) (cf. Jn 19:34). — TRANS.

[196] Cf. Miri Rubin, *Corpus Christi: The Eucharist in Late Medieval Culture* (Cambridge and New York: Cambridge Univesity Press, 1991), 155–63.

[197] Angenendt, *Geschichte der Religiosität*, 505.

[198] Cf. Josef Andreas Jungmann, *The Mass of the Roman Rite*, trans. Francis A. Brunner, C.Ss.R., 2 vols. (New York: Benziger Brothers, 1951, 1955), 1:119–20.

The miraculous Hosts in the High Middle Ages were seen as a confirmation of the doctrine of transubstantiation. The most renowned Eucharistic miracle in the thirteenth century was the miracle of Bolsena (1263). A Bohemian priest, tormented by doubts about the reality of the Body and Blood of Christ in the Eucharist, which were not even dispelled by a pilgrimage to Rome, asked God for a sign that would dispel all doubt. Upon his return from Rome, the pious cleric celebrated Holy Mass in the Church of Saint Christina in Bolsena. During it the Host in the priest's hand turned red, as though it were living flesh. Twenty drops of blood dripped onto the corporal. The priest saw "the Host as true, blood-spattered flesh, and the drops of blood arranged themselves on the corporal in such a way that they formed the face of the Redeemer streaming with blood."[199]

The presence of Christ's Blood in the celebration of Mass is also illustrated by the Gregorian Mass, one of the most important pictorial themes in Christian iconography.[200] According to the story, during a Mass in the Church of the Holy Cross in Jerusalem, Pope Gregory the Great is said to have had doubts as to whether Christ is truly present in the bread and wine. In order to scatter the doubts, Christ appeared in the flesh as the Man of Sorrows with the instruments of his martyrdom during the celebration of Holy Mass, and his Blood flowed into the chalice and onto the poor souls. The earliest depiction of the *visio Gregorii* is a mosaic icon from the thirteenth or fourteenth century that is found today in the treasury of Holy Cross in Jerusalem. In the Eucharistic miracle of the Gregorian Mass, the intense mysticism of the thirteenth and fourteenth century focused on the Passion and Cross is apparent.

In the second half of the fifteenth century, the pictorial theme of the Gregorian Mass spread in a truly explosive way, especially north of the Alps. Numerous late medieval altarpieces recorded the scene. One reason for this is surely that prayer before altar images that depicted this theme was increasingly associated with an indulgence

---

[199] Peter Browe, *Die Verehrung der Eucharistie im Mittelalter* (Rome: Herder, 1967), 75f.

[200] On the Gregorian Mass, cf. Uwe Westfehling, *Die Messe Gregors des Grossen: Vision, Kunst, Realität* (Cologne: Schnütgen-Museum-Köln, 1982); Esther Maier, *Die Gregorsmesse: Funktionen eines spätmittelalterlichen Bildtypus* (Cologne: Böhlau, 2006); Andreas Gormans and Thomas Lentes, *Das Bild der Erscheinung: Die Gregorsmesse im Mittelalter*, Kult-Bild 3 (Berlin: Reimer, 2007).

for those who prayed. This by no means tells against the importance of the underlying account in strengthening faith in the somatic Real Presence of Christ. Bloody Hosts raised for theologians the problem of the bilocation of Christ's Body: namely, existing in one respect in glorified form in heaven at the right hand of the Father and in another respect in the bloody Host. Thomas Aquinas tried to solve the problem by explaining that the bloody Hosts are sensible demonstrations of Christ's Real Presence in the sacrament of the Eucharist, which in itself is invisible.[201] Articulate criticism of the exaggerated Eucharistic piety associated with the bloody Hosts came from Nikolaus of Kues, Prince Bishop of Brixen/Bressanone (1401–1464). In a pastoral letter written in 1451, three years after he was elevated to the rank of cardinal, he forbade the public display and adoration of bloody Hosts (*hostiae transformatae, pallae rubricatae*), since they were not infrequently counterfeit. The Catholic faith teaches that the risen Body is in the presence of God in glory, and hence his Body, including the Blood, is completely invisible.[202]

Since there was a need to see the Blessed Sacrament outside of the celebration of Mass, too, the monstrance (from *monstrare*, to show) developed in the thirteenth century. This is a precious liturgical display case with a glass compartment in which a consecrated Host is exposed for veneration and adoration. Tabernacles, or "little houses" for the Blessed Sacrament, which were placed on the Gospel side of the altar, served as the place in which to store the monstrance. In processions, the monstrance was carried together with the Most Blessed Sacrament. These processions are called *theophore* [God-bearing] processions. The most important of these processions is the Corpus Christi procession. "Corpus Christi" is the Latin expression for "Body of Christ". The Feast of Corpus Christi goes back to the visions of the mystic Juliana of Mont Cornillon in Liège (d. 1258).[203] The symbolist interpretation of Christ's presence in the Eucharist among the Cathari and the Albigensians led not only to an intense

---

[201] Cf. Thomas Aquinas, *Summa theologiae* III, q. 73.

[202] Cf. Browe, *Eucharistie im Mittelalter*, 281.

[203] On the origin and significance of the feast, see Rubin, *Corpus Christi*, 164–99; Alex Stock, *Poetische Dogmatik: Christologie*, vol. 3, *Leib und Leben* (Paderborn, Munich, Vienna, and Zurich: Schöningh 1998), 305–9. On the spread of the feast, see Browe, *Eucharistie im Mittelalter*, 509–36.

veneration of the sacrament of the altar. The Eucharist became, especially among the Beguines, a privileged place of mystical experiences.
The Beguines were lay women's groups that lived in convent-like
communities. Juliana, an Augustinian choir nun, had had since 1209
various visions concerning the sacrament of the altar. Several times
she saw in her visions a full moon that displayed a broken spot at
the edge.

In the *Vita Julianae* we read:

> When Juliana dedicated herself to prayer in her youth, a great and
> marvelous sign appeared to her. She saw the moon in its splendor, but
> there was a small break in its globe (*apparuit ei luna in suo splendore, cum
> aliquantula tamen sui sphaerici corporis fractione*). She gazed at it for a long
> time and had no idea what it meant. And so she urgently besought the
> Lord to reveal its meaning to her. He revealed to her that the moon
> represented the Church, but the dark spot on the globe signified that
> one feast day was still lacking that he wanted all the faithful to cele-
> brate. It was his will that in order to increase the faith that was now
> diminishing so much at the end of the world, and for the advance of
> the elect in grace, the institution of his saving Sacrament should be
> celebrated on a special day, more than just on Holy Thursday, when
> indeed the Church is occupied with the washing of the feet and the
> memory of his Passion. On this special day, the faithful should make
> up for what is left undone on ordinary days because of their lack of
> devotion and negligence. When Christ had revealed this to the virgin,
> he commissioned her to begin with this celebration herself and to
> announce his command to the world.[204]

From 1240 on, the new feast was celebrated among the Beguines
in Liège. Juliana received support in her cause from Jacques Pan-
taléon, Archdeacon of Liège, the later Pope Urban IV (1261–1264).
During Juliana's lifetime, the bishop of Liège, Robert de Torote
(d. 1246), decreed that in Liège the Feast of Corpus Christi should
be celebrated on the Thursday after the Octave of Trinity Sunday
(1246) to refute Eucharistic heresies (*ad confutandam haereticorum insa-
niam*). During the reign of Bishop Robert's successor, Juliana lost the
backing of her community. In 1247 she left Liège and from 1248 on

---

[204] Translated from German, quoted from Browe, *Verehrung der Eucharistie*, 71f.

lived as a recluse. The Dominican friar Hugh of Saint-Cher (d. 1263), who had become acquainted with the new feast in Liège in 1251, lobbied as Cardinal Legate for its introduction worldwide, which occurred in 1264 thanks to Urban IV.

In the papal bull *Transiturus de hoc mundo* instituting the feast day, the pope associates the *Festum Sanctissimi Corporis Christi* with the victorious triumph over heretical deniers of transubstantiation. Written sources connecting the feast day with the miraculous Host of Bolsena appear only from 1340 on,[205] but we cannot rule out the possibility that Urban's bull was occasioned also by the Eucharistic miracle of Bolsena. A few weeks after the promulgation of the Corpus Christi bull, Urban IV died. His successors had little interest in the new feast. It first became widespread in the Catholic Church during the pontificate of John XXII (1316–1334).[206] Until then, it was spread primarily by the Cistercians and by individual theologians and bishops. The renowned canonist and liturgist William Durandus, Bishop of Mende (d. 1293), promoted the feast through his influential *Rationale divinorum officiorum* (1286).[207]

The first Corpus Christi processions in Germany took place in Cologne, Münster, and Osnabrück. The development of these devotions into a universal feast of the Catholic Church was furthered by the inclusion of the bull *Transiturus* in the *Clementinae Constitutiones* named after Pope Clement V (1304–1314).[208] The Clementine

---

[205] Cf. Dirk Ansorge, "Jenseits von Begriff und Vorstellung: Das Wunder der Eucharistie im Mittelalter", in *Phänomenologie der Gabe: Neue Zugänge zum Mysterium der Eucharistie*, ed. F. Bruckmann, Quaestiones disputatae 270 (Freiburg: Herder, 2015), 76. On the transmission history of the miracle of Bolsena, see Kristen van Ausdall, "Art and Eucharist in the Late Middle Ages", in *A Companion to the Eucharist in the Middle Ages*, ed. I. C. Levy et al., Brill's Companions to the Christian Tradition 26 (Leiden: Brill, 2012), 582–87.

[206] Cf. Angelus A. Häussling, "Literaturbericht zu Fronleichnam", *Jahrbuch für Volkskunde und Kulturgeschichte*, 1986: 228–40.

[207] Cf. Durandus of Mende, *Rationale divinorum officiorum*, ed. Johannes Belethus (Neapoli: Josephum Dura, 1859), 6:115, no. 6 (De Dominica I post Pentecosten): "Et est sciendum quod Urbanus Papa IV statuit fieri festum de Corpore Christi quinta feria post hanc dominicam, et concedens magnam indulgentiam tam clericis officiantibus, quam populis convenientibus ad divina, prout in officio super hoc ordinato habetur" [It should be known that Pope Urban IV decided that the Feast of Corpus Christi should be observed on the Thursday after that Sunday, while granting a rich indulgence both to the clerics who officiate and to the people who gather for the ceremonies, as it says in the Divine Office appointed for that feast].

[208] Cf. Rubin, *Corpus Christi*, 176–85.

decretals are the last medieval compilation of canon law, which was promulgated by Pope John XXII in the year 1317. One year later, the General Chapter of the Dominicans in Lyon decided to introduce the Feast of Corpus Christi. In the early fourteenth century, it became the custom to leave the monstrance with the Most Blessed Sacrament on the altar after the procession and to celebrate Mass in the presence of the Blessed Sacrament exposed. This practice became widely accepted during that same century.[209]

Between 1261 and 1265, Thomas Aquinas was staying in the immediate neighborhood of the papal Curia in Orvieto. There he was probably a *lector* (lecturer) at the Dominican friary. In Orvieto, Thomas was on friendly terms with Pope Urban IV and composed for him the *Catena aurea* ("Golden chain"). This was one of the most renowned catena commentaries on Sacred Scripture, in which a running commentary of a connected scriptural passage is provided by means of citations from the Church Fathers. For the Feast of Corpus Christi, Thomas wrote at the pope's behest the Sequence *Lauda Sion* and the hymns *Pange lingua, Sacris solemniis,* and *Verbum supernum* for Vespers, Matins, and Lauds.[210] Since the studies by the Dominican theologian Pierre-Marie Gy[211] and Ronald Zawilla,[212] Thomas' authorship of the Sequence and the hymns is again considered probable.[213] The Sequence and the hymns reinforce the Eucharistic realism of the doctrine of transubstantiation and give exquisite poetical

[209] It was first forbidden in the aftermath of the Second Vatican Council's reform of the Missal.

[210] Cf. Thomas Aquinas, *Officium de festo Corporis Christi ad mandatum Urbani Papae IV dictum Festum instituentis,* in *Opusculum theologiae* 2 (Spiazzi ed., 1954), 275–81.

[211] Cf. Pierre-Marie Gy, "L'office du Corpus Christi et Thomas d'Aquin: État d'une recherche", *Revue des sciences philosophiques et théologiques* 64 (1980): 491–504; Gy, "L'office du Corpus Christi et la théologie des accidents eucharistiques", *Revue des sciences philosophiques et théologiques* 66 (1982): 81–86; Gy, *La liturgie dans l'histoire* (Paris: Éditions Saint-Paul, Éditions du Cerf, 1990), 223–45.

[212] Cf. Ronald Zawilla, *The Biblical Sources of the Historiae Corporis Christi Attributed to Thomas Aquinas: A Theological Study to Determine Their Authenticity* (Ph.D. dissertation, University of Toronto, 1985).

[213] Cf. Rubin, *Corpus Christi,* 186–96; Jean-Pierre Torrell, *Saint Thomas Aquinas,* trans. Robert Royal, vol. 1, *The Person and His Work* (Washington, D.C.: Catholic University of America Press, 2005), 130–33; Douglas Burnham and Enrico Giaccherini, *The Poetics of Transubstantiation: From Theology to Metaphor* (Aldershot, England, and Burlington, Vt.: Ashgate, 2005); Tück, *Gabe der Gegenwart,* 223–38.

expression to the worship and veneration of the Most Blessed Sacrament. Together with the hymn *Adoro te devote*, the texts of the Divine Office for Corpus Christi helped greatly to enliven medieval veneration of the Eucharist.

To this day, the texts have lost nothing of their beauty and theological power. The Sequence *Lauda Sion* at the Mass on the Feast of Corpus Christi, which Geoffrey Wainwright described as a "doctrinal hymn", is sung after the reading (1 Cor 11:23–29) and before the Gospel (Jn 6:56–59) as a continuation of the Alleluia. The Alleluia verse is intoned after the Gradual and anticipates the opening verse of the Gospel. The Sequence has the character of a solemn hymn of praise. The Corpus Christi Sequence has been set to music by Orlando di Lasso (1532–1594) and Giovanni Pierluigi da Palestrina (d. 1594), among others. The Vespers hymn *Pange lingua* from the Divine Office of Corpus Christi, in which the theme of the Body of Christ is brought up, celebrates the mystery of the Eucharistic transformation. It is "one of the best-known records of medieval Eucharistic spirituality".[214] The last two stanzas have been sung at Benediction since the fifteenth century. In its poetic quality, the hymn is an unsurpassed profession of faith in the transformation of the gifts of bread and wine into the Body and Blood of Christ.[215]

Pange lingua, gloriosi	Sing, my tongue, the Savior's glory,
Corporis mysterium,	of His flesh the mystery sing;
Sanguinisque pretiosi,	of the Blood, all price exceeding,
quem in mundi pretium	shed by our immortal King,
fructus ventris generosi	destined, for the world's
Rex effudit gentium.	redemption,
	from a noble womb to spring.
Nobis datus, nobis natus	Of a pure and spotless Virgin
ex intacta Virgine,	born for us on earth below,
et in mundo conversatus,	He, as Man, with man conversing,
sparso verbi semine,	stayed, the seeds of truth to sow;
sui moras incolatus	then He closed in solemn order
miro clausit ordine.	wondrously His life of woe.

[214] Tück, *Gabe der Gegenwart*, 239.

[215] For an interpretation, see Stock, *Poetische Dogmatik*, 3:309–20; Tück, *Gabe der Gegenwart*, 239–62. English translation by Fr. Edward Caswall (1814–1878).

In supremae nocte cenae
recumbens cum fratribus
observata lege plene
cibis in legalibus,
cibum turbae duodenae
se dat suis manibus.

On the night of that Last Supper,
seated with His chosen band,
He the Pascal victim eating,
first fulfills the Law's command;
then as Food to His Apostles
gives Himself with His own hand.

Verbum caro, panem verum
verbo carnem efficit:
fitque sanguis Christi merum,
et si sensus deficit,
ad firmandum cor sincerum
sola fides sufficit.

Word-made-Flesh, the bread of
    nature
by His word to Flesh He turns;
wine into His Blood He changes—
what though sense no change
    discerns?
Only be the heart in earnest,
faith her lesson quickly learns.

Tantum ergo Sacramentum
veneremur cernui:
et antiquum documentum
novo cedat ritui:
praestet fides supplementum
sensuum defectui.

Down in adoration falling,
Lo! the sacred Host we hail;
Lo! o'er ancient forms departing,
newer rites of grace prevail;
faith for all defects supplying,
where the feeble senses fail.

Genitori, Genitoque
laus et iubilatio,
salus, honor, virtus quoque
sit et benedictio:
procedenti ab utroque
compar sit laudatio.
Amen. Alleluia.

To the everlasting Father,
and the Son who reigns on high,
with the Holy Ghost proceeding
forth from Each eternally,
be salvation, honor, blessing,
might and endless majesty.
Amen. Alleluia.

The hymn *Pange lingua* is modeled on a famous hymn in praise of
the Cross, "Pange lingua gloriosi lauream certaminis", composed in
569 by Venantius Fortunatus (d. 600/610). Since the ninth century,
it had been used in reverencing the cross and in the Liturgy of the
Hours during Passiontide. The hymn of the Divine Office for Corpus Christi starts with praise of the glorified Body of Christ and of
the Precious Blood that the Redeemer, born of the Virgin Mary,
shed for the sins of the world. In poetic form, the hymn differenti-
ates between the historical body of Christ (*natus ex intacta Virgine*),
the glorified Body of Christ (*gloriosi Corporis mysterium*), and the
sacramental Body of Christ (*Verbum caro panem verum, verbo carnem*

efficit).²¹⁶ "The mystery of the flesh" is in the first place the mystery of Christ's body handed over to death.

The Precious Blood that Christ shed as *pretium mundi* is a rephrasing of 1 Peter 1:18–19: "You know that you were ransomed from the futile ways inherited from your fathers, not with perishable things such as silver or gold, but with the precious blood of Christ, like that of a lamb without blemish or spot [*pretiosi sanguine quasi agni immaculati Christi et incontaminati*]" (cf. Ex 12: the spotless lamb/ *agnus paschalis*).²¹⁷ Jesus' sacrifice of his life is the sacrifice of the *rex gentium* (King of nations) who shed his blood for us. This is a universalized form of the inscription over the Cross *Rex Iudaeorum* (Jn 19:19). The statement about the Incarnation of the divine King (*nobis datus, nobis natus ex intacta Virgine*) alludes to Isaiah 9:6 (*parvulus enim natus a nobis et filius datus est nobis*, "for to us a child is born, to us a son is given").²¹⁸

The child born of the Virgin Mary is the incarnate Word of God, which lived on earth and at the end of his life instituted the Mystery of the Eucharist in a "wondrous order" (*miro ordine*). This happened on the night on which the divine King had gathered with his disciples to celebrate the Passover meal in "full observance of the Law" (*observata lege plene*), during which he gave himself to the Twelve with his own hands as food (*cibum turbae duodenae se dat suis manibus*). The gift of the Eucharist is Christ's gift of himself in the signs of bread and wine. The midpoint of the hymn is the transition from God's gift and Christ's self-gift to the mystery of transubstantiation and the adoration associated with it.

The following couplet *verbum caro panem verum/verbo carnem efficit* mentions the efficacious Divine Word, which, according to the Western conviction, as *verbum efficax* in the *verba testamenti* transforms bread

²¹⁶ Cf. Tück, *Gabe der Gegenwart*, 243–47.

²¹⁷ This text is assigned in the *Missale Romanum* as Introit for the Mass on Christmas in the Morning. Cf. Stock, *Poetische Dogmatik*, 3:313.

²¹⁸ Cf. *Missale Romanum ex decreto SS. Concilii Tridentini restitutum Summorum Pontificum cura recognitum*, editio typica 1962, ed. M. Sodi and A. Toniolo (Vatican City: Libreria editrice vaticana, 2007; hereafter cited as MR 1962), 20; MR 2002³, 160; *Die Feier der Heiligen Messe: Messbuch für die Bistümer des deutschen Sprachgebiets: Authentische Ausgabe für den liturgischen Gebrauch; Kleinausgabe: Das Messbuch für alle Tage des Jahres*, herausgegeben im Auftrag der Bischofskonferenzen Deutschlands, Österreichs und der Schweiz sowie der Bischöfe von Luxemburg, Bozen-Brixen und Lüttich, 2nd ed. (Einsiedeln et al., 1988; hereafter cited as MB), 41[42].

and wine into the Body and Blood of Christ.[219] "For Thomas, the words of institution are not declarative but rather performative."[220] Here he stands in the Western tradition founded by Ambrose. Without resorting to the terminology of the theory of transubstantiation, the hymn puts into words the mystery of the Eucharistic transformation, which eludes sensory perception (*sensus deficit*). The "sensory deficit"[221] is remedied by faith alone (*sola fides*), which illumines the heart that knows about the Mystery of the Body and Blood of Christ.

The concluding stanzas articulate veneration of the Blessed Sacrament and thanksgiving for Christ's presence in the sacrament (*tantum ergo sacramentum veneremur cernui*). Faced with the great mystery of the Eucharistic transubstantiation, the worshipper falls on his knees. Given the presence of the *Christus passus* [Christ who has died], this is the appropriate gesture, which as a sign of worship is reserved for God alone. The theme here is not the supersession of Israel and of the Covenant that God made with his people, as the problematic German translation by Maria Luise Thurmair (1912–2005) seems to imply. Thurmair translates *et antiquum documentum novo cedat ritui* with the antithesis "Law of fear" and "meal of love".[222] Thomas' point is that the bloody part of the Passover meal (animal sacrifice) is replaced by Christ's sacrifice of his life.[223] Christ himself, by laying down his life for us, a gift that is given to us in the signs of bread and wine, is the new Paschal Lamb. The new rite is the presence of the *passio Christi* in the sacrament of the Eucharist.[224]

The hymn *Pange lingua* concludes with an artful Trinitarian doxology. Without mentioning the three Divine Persons by name, the mystery of Father, Son, and Spirit is praised. In doing so, Thomas invokes the terminology of the intra-Trinitarian processions (*genitori genitoque*: procession of the Son; *procedenti ab utroque*: procession of the

[219] Cf. Stock, *Poetische Dogmatik*, 3:315; Tück, *Gabe der Gegenwart*, 255.

[220] Tück, *Gabe der Gegenwart*, 256.

[221] Stock, *Poetische Dogmatik*, 3:317.

[222] Cf. Norbert Lohfink, "Das 'Pange Lingua' im 'Gotteslob'", *Bibel und Liturgie* 76 (2003): 276–85.

[223] In the 2013 *Gotteslob* [the new edition of the authorized hymnal in the dioceses of Germany, Austria, and South Tyrol] the verse now reads: "Altes Zeugnis möge weichen, da der neue Brauch begann" ("Let former testimony yield, since the new usage began." This is an exact translation of the original Latin couplet).

[224] Cf. Tück, *Gabe der Gegenwart*, 257.

Spirit). According to the principle of *homotimé* formulated by Basil of Caesarea, equal worship: praise (*laus*), jubilation (*iubilatio*), salvation (*salus*), honor (*honor*), might (*virtus*), and blessing (*benediction*) belongs to each of the Divine Persons in the Trinity. This superabundance of veneration befits the miracle of Christ's Eucharistic gift of himself in the sacrament of the altar.

Chapter VI

SACRIFICIUM MISSAE

The Reformation and the Council of Trent

"Lord, we gladly bring to your altar earthly gifts so as to obtain heavenly ones; we give temporal gifts so as to receive eternal ones."[1] This prayer over the oblations in the *Sacramentarium Veronense* (sixth/seventh century) was understood in the Middle Ages in the sense of a sacramental economy of exchange.[2] The prerequisite for it was the spread of the monetary system and of money offerings to the Church. Mass stipends and Mass intentions led increasingly to the notion of the Eucharistic Sacrifice as a pecuniary-spiritual business. The consequence was that "the medieval theology of the Mass and the associated piety dealt intensively with the value of the Mass and with the question of the fruits of the Mass and their applicability."[3] Reckoning tables that helped to express the "value" of the Mass in monetary terms existed already in the early Middle Ages.[4] Another part of this context was the system of indulgences, which under Pope Leo X was the occasion for Martin Luther's critical disputation theses in 1517; these were generally seen as the beginning of the Reformation. Luther forwarded his theses to Archbishop Albrecht of Mainz (1490–1545),

---

[1] *Sacramentarium Veronense* 91: Month of April (Mohlberg 12): "Altaribus tuis, Domine, munera terrena gratanter offerimus, ut caelestia consequamur; damus temporalia, ut sumamus aeterna."

[2] Cf. Arnold Angenendt, *Geschichte der Religiosität im Mittelalter*, 2nd ed. (Darmstadt: Primus Verlag, 2000), 375.

[3] Hans Bernhard Meyer, "Abendmahlsfeier II (Mittelalter)", in *Theologische Realenzyklopädie* 1 (1977), 285.

[4] Cf. Arnold Angenendt, *Liturgik und Historik: Gab es eine organische Liturgie-Entwicklung?* (Freiburg: Herder 2001), 134.

among others. The nailing of the ninety-five theses to the door of the palace chapel in Wittenberg is a legend.[5]

Luther's critique of the Roman Mass cannot be understood without the theory of the "fruits of the Mass" (*utilitates missae*). The theory says that the celebration of the Mass is connected with the application of particular fruits, which can be understood as quantifiable graces. In the fourteenth and fifteenth centuries, Western Catholics without exception attributed to a Mass:

> a limited value, on account of which it is more beneficial to someone if offered for him alone than if it is offered at the same time for others, too. The authority for this understanding was not so much the theology of the Sacrifice of the Mass ... as the practice of the Church, which allows Mass to be celebrated repeatedly for individuals and forbids the acceptance of several stipends for one Mass.... Furthermore, it necessarily became an urgent wish to have a special Mass celebrated if possible for one's immediate family circle, one's guild, etc., because then one's share in the fruits was greater than in the case of a Mass celebrated for a larger group. This logically led to the multiplication of altars and to the fragmentation of congregations and convents in the late Middle Ages.[6]

We should also mention in this connection the enormous increase in votive Masses for the living and the dead, for good weather, against various illnesses, and against enemy attacks. A not insignificant part of the clergy lived exclusively on income from votive Masses, which were superimposed on the order of the Church's liturgical year. Even on Sundays, votive Masses of all kinds were celebrated.[7] The frequency of Mass became so great that celebrants resorted to continuing a High Mass as a silent Mass after the *Credo* so that the next High Mass could begin then at another

[5] Cf. Thomas Kaufmann, *Geschichte der Reformation* (Frankfurt am Main and Leipzig: Verlag der Weltreligionen, 2009), 155–62. For an extensive discussion of the theses on indulgences and the mythology surrounding them, see Heinz Schilling, *Martin Luther: Rebell in einer Zeit des Umbruchs: Eine Biographie* (Munich: Beck, 2012), 157–79.

[6] Erwin Iserloh, "Der Wert der Messe in der Diskussion der Theologen vom Mittelalter bis zum 16. Jahrhundert", in *Kirche—Ereignis und Institution: Aufsätze und Vorträge*, Reformationsgeschichtliche Studien und Texte, Supplementum 3 (Münster: Aschendorff, 1985), 400f.

[7] Cf. Adolph Franz, *Die Messe im deutschen Mittelalter: Beiträge zur Geschichte der Liturgie und des religiösen Volkslebens* (Darmstadt: Wissenschaftliche Buchgesellschaft, 1963), 115–217.

altar.[8] Luther called the medieval system of Masses "traffic in pur-
gatorial Masses".[9] He described the Catholic Church's mediation of
graces as "commerce".[10] The Reformer's battle against the Roman
Mass was not only related to the theory of the fruits of the Mass,
however, but was aimed against the core of the Catholic doctrine
about the Sacrifice of the Mass.[11]

A. Luther's Battle against the Roman Mass

Luther already formulates his critique of the Sacrifice of the Mass
in his Lecture on the Letter to the Hebrews (1517–1518).[12] "Why
does our offering not stop even now, since we are already completely redeemed and justified by Baptism and repentance? For Christ
is offered every day for us."[13] Luther answers: "We do offer, but as
a memorial of his death, and this is the one sacrifice that was offered
once. I understand this as follows: Christ was offered only once, as it
says in the preceding chapter. But what is offered each day by us is

---

[8] Cf. Erwin Iserloh, *Der Kampf um die Messe in den ersten Jahren der Auseinandersetzung mit Luther* (Münster: Aschendorff, 1952), 12f.

[9] Martin Luther, *Smalcald Articles* (1537), English translation in *Martin Luther's Basic Theological Writings*, ed. Timothy F. Lull (Minneapolis: Fortress Press, 1989), 497–538 at 506; *Der andere Artikel* in *D. Luthers Werke: Kritische Gesamtausgabe* (Weimar: Hermann Böhlau, 1883–2009; hereafter cited as *WA*), 50:206.

[10] Luther, *Vermahnung zum Sakrament des Leibes und Blutes Christi* (1530): *WA* 30; 2:605.

[11] On Luther's critique of the Roman Mass and his understanding of the Lord's Supper, see Hans Bernhard Meyer, *Luther und die Messe: Eine liturgiewissenschaftliche Untersuchung über das Verhältnis Luthers zum Messwesen des späten Mittelalters* (Paderborn: Verlag Bonifacius-Druckerei, 1965); Francis Clark, *Eucharistic Sacrifice and the Reformation*, 2nd ed. (Oxford: Blackwell, 1967); Tom G. A. Hardt, *Venerabilis et adorabilis eucharistia: Eine Studie über die lutherische Abendmahlslehre im 16. Jahrhundert*, Forschungen zur Kirchen- und Dogmengeschichte 42 (Göttingen: Vandenhoeck & Ruprecht, 1988); Reinhard Messner, *Die Messreform Martin Luthers und die Eucharistie der Alten Kirche: Ein Beitrag zu einer systematischen Liturgiewissenschaft* (Innsbruck: Tyrolia, 1989), Wolfgang Simon, *Die Messopfertheologie Martin Luthers: Voraussetzungen, Genese, Gestalt und Rezeption*. Spätmittelalter und Reformation, Neue Reihe 22 (Tübingen: Mohr Siebeck, 2003); Dorothea Wendebourg, "Taufe und Abendmahl", in *Luther Handbuch*, ed. A. Beutel (Tübingen: Mohr Siebeck, 2005), 414–23; Wendebourg, *Essen zum Gedächtnis: Der Gedächtnisbefehl in den Abendmahlstheologien der Reformation*, Beiträge zur historischen Theologie 148 (Tübingen: Mohr Siebeck, 2009).

[12] Cf. Luther, *Die Vorlesung über den Hebräerbrief* (1517–1518): *WA* 57:201–38.

[13] Ibid. (*WA* 57:217.25–27): "Quomodo etiam nunc non cessat oblatio nostra, cum per gratiam baptismi et poenitentiae perfecti et iusti sumus? Quotidie enim Christus offertur pro nobis."

not so much a sacrifice as rather the memorial of that sacrifice, as he said: Do this in memory of me. For he does not suffer whenever his death is commemorated."[14] Here Luther cites John Chrysostom.[15] Yet unlike John, Luther separates Christ's sacrifice and the offering of the Eucharist.[16] Indeed, for Luther, Christ's sacrifice has "ceased altogether" (cessavit omnino).[17]

In the "Sermon on the New Testament" (1520), Luther sharpens his attack on the Roman Mass: it is a sacrifice that the priest offers in order to obtain graces for the Church. Like the system of indulgences, it is a means of "justification through works" to which Luther contrasts the principle of sola fide. Luther sees the fundamental error of the Roman Mass in the fact that it is regarded as a sacrifice to be offered to God and not as a gift to be received from God.[18] "If man is to set about working with God and to receive something from him, then it must happen in such a way that man is not the one who starts and lays the first stone, but rather God alone must go before without any request or desire of man and make him a promise."[19] The Roman Church, Luther's accusation goes, turned the Mass into a work of men: "This has been the fate of the Mass; it has been converted by the teaching of godless men into a good work. They themselves call it an opus operatum, and by it they presume themselves to be all-powerful with God."[20] In Luther's view, the Mass is a gift of God to us, which therefore cannot be offered to him.[21]

---

[14] Ibid. (WA 57:217.27—218.3): "Offerimus quidem sed ad recordationem mortis eius, et haec est una hostia semel oblata. Quod sic intelligo: Christus oblatus est non nisi semel, ut capite praecedente. Quod autem a nobis offertur quotidie, non tam oblatio quam memoria est oblationis illius, sicut dixit: Hoc facite in meam commemorationem. Non enim toties patitur, quoties memorabitur passus."

[15] Cf. John Chrysostom, Homiliae in epistolam ad Hebraeos, cap. 10, hom. 16, 3 (PG 63:131).

[16] Cf. Ferdinand Pratzner, Messe und Kreuzesopfer: Die Krise der sakramentalen Idee bei Luther und in der mittelalterlichen Scholastik (Vienna: Herder, 1970), 27.

[17] Cf. Meyer, Luther und die Messe, 157.

[18] Cf. Luther, Ein Sermo von dem Neuen Testament, das ist, von der heiligen Messe (1520): WA 6:365.23–25; Luther, De captivitate Babylonica ecclesiae (1520): WA 6:512.7–9; 520.13–19; 523.8–10.

[19] Luther, Ein Sermo von dem Neuen Testament, das ist, von der heiligen Messe (1520): WA 6:356.4–6.

[20] Luther, De captivitate Babylonica ecclesiae (1520): WA 6:520.13–15: "Ita de missa contigit, quae impiorum hominum doctrina mutata est in opus bonum, quod ipsi vocant opus operatum, quod apud deum sese omnia praesumunt posse." English: The Babylonian Captivity of the Church, in Lull, 267–314 at 303.

[21] Cf. Meyer, Luther und die Messe, 158; Iserloh, Kampf um die Messe, 9.

Luther regards the Sacrifice of the Mass in the Roman Church as the worst form of idolatry.[22] In order to understand this invective, we must consider that since the early Middle Ages there had been more emphatic language about a "repetition" of the sacrifice on the Cross through the Sacrifice of the Mass, even though it was understood to be the "unbloody" oblation of the Body and Blood of Christ, an offering in which the salvation founded on the sacrifice on the Cross continues to work in history. Luther allows the concept of sacrifice to apply only to the Church's sacrifice of thanks and praise offered to God: "Therefore when one calls the Mass a sacrifice and understands it in that way, it would probably be right to say, not that we offer the sacrament as a sacrifice, but rather that through our praise, prayer, and sacrifice we incite him and give him reason to sacrifice himself for us in heaven and us with him."[23]

In his 1521 work demanding the abolition of private Mass, Luther declares: "Tell us, you parsons of Baal: Where is it written that the Mass is a sacrifice, or where did Christ teach that we should sacrifice blessed bread and wine? Do you not hear? Christ sacrificed himself once; from now on he does not want to be sacrificed by anyone else. He wants us to remember his sacrifice. How can you be so bold as to make a sacrifice out of this commemoration?"[24] In favor of his rejection of the sacrificial character of the Mass, Luther cites a statement from the Letter to the Hebrews to the effect that Christ offered one sacrifice for sins once and for all, so that all cultic sacrifices are abolished (cf. Heb 10:1–18). If the Mass were a sacrifice, it would be a new sacrifice as opposed to the one sacrifice of Christ on the Cross and, therefore, the human work of a sacrifice offered to God. But that means that the one sacrifice of Christ is not enough.[25] Indeed, the sacrifice of the Eucharist cannot be a new sacrifice alongside the sacrifice on the Cross, unless one wants to relativize the salvific importance of Christ's sacrifice. Yet Luther not only opposes the notion of repeating the sacrifice. He also rejects the notion of offering the Eucharist, which can be found already in patristic writings. The sacrament of Christ's sacrifice is for

[22] Cf. Luther, *Ein Sermo von dem Neuen Testament, das ist von der heiligen Messe* (1520): *WA* 6:363.20–24.

[23] Ibid. (*WA* 6:369.11–15).

[24] Luther, *Vom Missbrauch der Messe* (1521): *WA* 8:493.19–24.

[25] Cf. Alexander Gerken, *Theologie der Eucharistie* (Munich: Kösel-Verlag, 1973), 135.

Luther not a visible offering but, rather, a remembrance of Christ's sacrifice on the Cross.[26]

No agreement was reached about the question of the Sacrifice of the Mass. The Catholic Church tried to dissuade Luther from his teachings. Six months after Luther had burned the papal bull *Exsurge Domine* (June 15, 1520), a list of his errors,[27] he was excommunicated by Pope Leo X with the bull *Decet Romanum Pontificem* (January 3, 1521). From 1525 on, since Luther was busy defending the Real Presence of Christ in the sacrament of the Eucharist against Huldrych Zwingli (1484–1531) and the enthusiasts, his critique of the Roman Mass receded at first into the background, but it flared up again after 1530 and increased in its severity. In the *Smalcald Articles* (1537), Luther calls the Roman Mass "the greatest and most horrible abomination" of all "the papal idolatries".[28]

Luther was convinced that the Roman Church would not give up her teaching about the Sacrifice of the Mass. Therefore he declared with resignation in the *Smalcald Articles*: "Accordingly we are and remain eternally divided and opposed the one to the other."[29] John Calvin (1509–1564), too, saw an irreconcilable opposition between the Reformed Lord's Supper and the Roman Mass.[30] He regarded the Roman Mass as a "sacrifice of expiation" intended "to appease God's wrath",[31] which it plainly is not. Like Luther, Calvin, too, allowed that the Lord's Supper was only a sacrifice of thanks and praise. It could be called a sacrifice only in the improper sense, inasmuch as it is "a memorial, an image, and a testimony" of Christ's unique sacrifice on the Cross.[32] The Lord's Supper, however, is not an oblation but, rather, "a *gift* of God, which ought to have been received with thanksgiving".[33] "There is as much

---

[26] Cf. Pratzner, *Messe und Kreuzesopfer*, 55.

[27] Cf. DH 1451–92.

[28] Luther, *Smalcald Articles* (1537/1538), art. 2: *WA* 50:200.9f., 13f.; Lull, 503.

[29] Ibid. (*WA* 50:204.19–21; Lull, 505).

[30] Cf. Calvin, *Institutes of the Christian Religion*, trans. Ford Lewis Battles, ed. John T. McNeill, 2 vols., Library of Christian Classics 20 and 21 (Philadelphia: Westminster Press, 1960), bk. 4, chap. 18, 1–20 (pp. 2:1429–48).

[31] Ibid., 18, 13 (1441).

[32] Cf. ibid., 18, 10 (1439).

[33] Ibid., 18, 7 (1435), emphasis added.

difference between this sacrifice [of the Mass] and the sacrament of the [Last] Supper as there is between *giving* and *receiving*."[34] Christ has "given us a *Table* at which to *feast, not* an *altar* upon which to offer a *victim*."[35]

Luther rejected not only the Mass as a sacrifice of expiation for the living and the deceased but also Eucharistic adoration. The veneration of the consecrated Host within divine worship seemed legitimate to Luther, but he condemned any adoration of the *Corpus Christi* outside of the Mass. He regarded Eucharistic processions as a form of idolatry. Since Luther acknowledges a somatic Real Presence of Christ only in the order of "take, eat, and drink" instituted by Christ, he maintains that in Eucharistic processions ordinary bread is worshipped. Therefore, he advised the faithful to beware of the beloved Feast of Corpus Christi and of venerating the tabernacle, since purely "external worship" lacks the interior qualification by faith.[36] Like Luther, Calvin, too, criticized the Corpus Christi procession: by carrying the consecrated Host about with pomp and holding it up "to be seen, worshipped, and called upon" "in a solemn spectacle", one yields Christ no veneration. Devotion must be "directed to Christ seated in heaven". In Calvin's estimation, to adore the sacrament of the altar is to stop at the "outward sign" and "to worship the gifts in place of the Giver himself", indeed, a form of "idolatry".[37]

Luther regarded the Lord's Supper as God's promise (*promissio*) to forgive sins in the words of the Gospel, joined with the visible signs (*signa, sacramenta*).[38] The promise in the Lord's Supper is made in the words with which Jesus distributed this sacrament to the disciples at its institution.[39] In the *verba testamenti*, therefore, lies "the entire Mass with all its essence, work, usefulness and fruit".[40] According to Luther's understanding, the *verba testamenti* are words of institution,

---

[34] Ibid., 18, 7 (1435), emphasis added.

[35] Ibid., 18, 12 (1440), emphasis in original.

[36] Cf. Luther, *Vom Anbeten des Sacraments des heiligen Leichnams Christi* (1523): *WA* 11:447.

[37] Calvin, *Institutes of the Christian Religion* (1535), 4.17.37 and 36 (McNeill, 1412–13).

[38] Cf. Luther, *The Babylonian Captivity of the Church*, Prelude (1520): *WA* 6:26 (Lull, 300).

[39] Cf. ibid. (*WA* 6:515.17–26; Lull, 300).

[40] Luther, *Ein Sermo von dem Neuen Testament, das ist von der heiligen Messe* (1520): *WA* 6:355.26–27.

consecration, and distribution: *words of institution*, because the celebration of the Lord's Supper goes back to Jesus' last meal with his
disciples; *words of consecration*, because the gifts of bread and wine
become the Body and Blood of Christ through the *verba testamenti*;
words of distribution, because bread and wine, which through the *verba
testamenti* become Christ's Body and Blood, are meant to be distributed. Luther recognizes a corporeal presence of Christ, of course,
only in the celebration (*in usu*) of the sacrament.

The goal of the Eucharist is in fact the fellowship or communion
of the faithful with Christ and with one another. Yet restricting the
somatic Real Presence of Christ to the celebration of the Eucharist
contradicts the practice of the early Church of bringing the Eucharistic bread to the sick without consecrating it again. The question of
the Sacrifice of the Mass was another matter, but on the question
about the Real Presence, an agreement probably could have been
reached between Luther and the Catholic Church. For unlike the
Swiss Reformers, Luther reaffirmed that Christ's Body and Blood
are contained "in", "under", and "with" the bread and wine and
that they are distributed to the faithful in the Lord's Supper. "In",
"under", and "with" the bread and wine—this is the Lutheran formula for "consubstantiation": the coexistence of the Body and Blood
of Christ with the substance of bread and wine.[41]

In dismissing the doctrine that the sacrament works *ex opere operato*,
Luther explains that the sacrament of the Lord's Supper is effective
through faith alone. Yet here there is a misunderstanding of *ex opere
operato*. The efficacy of the sacrament *ex opere operato* does not mean
that it is effective without faith but, rather, that it comes about independently of the celebrant's worthiness. There is certainly biblical
basis for saying that without faith a sacrament is not efficacious, is
unhelpful, and brings down judgment.[42] Yet Luther ventured here
to make an even more pointed statement: "Hence one obtains grace,
not because he receives absolution or is baptized or receives communion or is anointed, but rather because he believes that in this way,
through absolution, baptism, communion, or anointing, he obtains
grace. For the well-known, widely approved saying is true: not the

---

[41] Cf. Luther, *Grosser Katechismus* (1528/1529): *WA* 30.1:223.
[42] Cf. Luther, *The Babylonian Captivity of the Church*: *WA* 6:517.32f. (Lull, 301–2).

sacrament, but rather faith in the sacrament justifies."[43] Luther relies entirely on the gift of faith through which man is justified. The Lord's Supper is the testament and the ever-new promise of the forgiveness of sins with which God joined the signs of bread and wine as signs of the Body and Blood of Jesus Christ. Instituted as a divine seal, the Eucharistic signs confirm the word of forgiveness.

Luther objects not only to the doctrine of the Sacrifice of the Mass and to Eucharistic adoration outside of Mass, but also to the pious practice of beholding the Eucharist, which he sees as a questionable substitute for Communion. Erasmus of Rotterdam (d. 1536), too, criticized the pious folk who hurried over to see as soon as the priests elevated the Body of the Lord. In his diocesan statutes (1564), the bishop of Haarlem reprimanded "the uncouth people who are not instructed in the true religion", who during Holy Mass pay attention to nothing "but to the elevation of the Host. From this comes the abuse that in the cities, in which many Masses are read, they run from one altar to another and do not attend any sacrifice in its entirety."[44] Indeed, this sort of show-piety tended to equate spiritual communion with sacramental Communion of the Body and Blood of Christ as far as their effects were concerned. Thus the faithful did participate in the Mass, but they hardly ever received the sacrament of the altar anymore.

In contrast, Luther demanded the actual reception of Communion, indeed under both species. He rejected Communion only of the Body of Christ (sub una specie) as unscriptural. Hence he demanded the administration of the chalice to the lay people, also. In his sermon on "The Blessed Sacrament of the Holy and True Body of Christ, and the Brotherhoods" (1519), Luther still appeared conciliatory: it is fitting to administer the sacrament under both species, not because one species is insufficient, but rather for the sake of the fullness of the Eucharistic sign.[45] Yet the doctrine of concomitance, which says

---

[43] Luther, Commentariolus in epistolam divi Pauli Apostoli ad Hebreos (1517): WA 57:169.23—170.4: "Inde fit, ut nullus consequitur graciam, quia absolvitur aut baptizatur aut communicatur aut inungitur, sed quia credit sic absolvendo, baptizando, communicando, inungendo se consequi graciam. Verum enim est illud vulgatissimum et probatissimum dictum: non sacramentum, sed fides sacramenti iustificat."

[44] Cited from Peter Browe, Eucharistie im Mittelalter: Liturgiehistorische Forschungen in kulturwissenschaftlicher Absicht, ed. H. Lutterbach and T. Flammer (Münster: Lit., 2003), 507.

[45] Cf. Luther, Sermon von dem hochwürdigen Sakrament des Heiligen Wahren Leichnams Christi und von den Bruderschaften (1519): WA 2:742f. (Lull, 242–66).

that the whole Christ with his divinity and his humanity is present in both the bread and the wine, is in Luther's opinion based too much on human logic to be able to justify Communion under only one species. Against Luther's demand for Communion under both species, contemporary theologians objected that Christ did not order that the chalice be given to lay people and that he gave the Sacrament to the disciples in Emmaus only in the form of bread. Since Jesus intended to ordain the apostles priests at the Last Supper, they would have drunk from the chalice, too. The two species of bread and wine are the sacramental sign of the separation of Christ's Body and Blood and, therefore, important for the Mass as a sacrifice, but not for the Communion of the faithful.

With his work *The Babylonian Captivity of the Church* (1520), Luther had raised three questions that the Catholic Church had to answer: (1) the question about the Sacrifice of the Mass; (2) the question about the doctrine of transubstantiation; and (3) the question about lay people receiving from the chalice. As far as the question of the Real Presence and transubstantiation is concerned, Johannes Eck (1494–1554) and other theologians reaffirmed that Christ's presence in the Eucharist is a sacramental presence, not a presence of the historical body of Christ that was capable of suffering. Christ is not present *circumscriptive* or "in quasi-quantitative form", but rather *in Spiritu Sancto*, like the soul in the body.[46] From transubstantiation, which is a miracle of divine omnipotence, follows the lasting presence of Christ in the consecrated bread and thus the practice of reserving the Eucharist for the celebration of Communion of the sick and Viaticum. Even though Christ is not present in the sacrament in order to be adored but rather to be received, it is nevertheless fitting to carry the consecrated Host in processions, in order to keep alive the memory of the salvation wrought in Christ.

The battle over the Mass during the Age of the Reformation was waged uncompromisingly. The Wittenberg riots in the year 1521 led to violent disturbances of Masses that were being celebrated. Priests who celebrated the Roman Mass were threatened. One of the most

---

[46] Cf. Erwin Iserloh, *Die Eucharistie in der Darstellung des Johannes Eck: Ein Beitrag zur vortridentinischen Kontroverstheologie über das Messopfer*, Reformationsgeschichtliche Studien und Texte 73/74 (Münster: Aschendorff, 1950); Iserloh, *Kampf um die Messe.*

militant enemies of the Sacrifice of the Mass, of private Mass, and of monasticism was the Augustinian monk Gabriel Zwilling (d. 1558). At his instigation, the Augustinian monastery in Wittenberg discontinued the celebration of Mass on October 13, 1521. After his proscription by the Edict of Worms (May 1521), Luther no longer stayed in Wittenberg. In November, several Augustinian monks left the monastery. Besides Zwilling, Karlstadt (1486–1541) and Melanchthon (1497–1560) campaigned for the abolition of the Mass. On the first day of Christmas in 1521, Karlstadt celebrated without liturgical vestments in the city church of Wittenberg a Lord's Supper worship service in the German language. The Offertory and the Canon (up to the words of institution pronounced in German) were omitted and replaced by an exhortation to the communicants. Instead of hosts, ordinary bread was distributed, which the faithful took in their hands. Afterward, the chalice was administered.[47] All of this caused a huge sensation, so that the moderate Melanchthon feared that the movement would roll over him. In 1522, Martin Bucer (1491–1551) also switched to celebrating Lord's Supper worship services in German. In doing so, he did still follow to a great extent the sequence of the medieval Mass, but he used the German language and tossed out the *Canon Missae*, which he considered the expression of the false Roman Catholic theology of sacrifice. Communion was offered under both species.

The oldest German-Lutheran Mass is the *Evangelische Messe* by Kaspar Kantz (1483–1554), which appeared in Nördlingen in 1522. Here, too, the Offertory and Canon are omitted. The beginning of the Preface is retained, followed by a sort of petition for transubstantiation, the words of institution, the Our Father, the *Agnus Dei* (in German), a preparatory prayer, and Communion. Thomas Müntzer (1490–1525), pastor in Allstedt (Thüringen), developed with the *Deutsche-Evangelische Messe* (1524) a new evangelical form of divine worship on the basis of a free translation of the Latin proper chants while keeping the Gregorian melody. This procedure met with harsh criticism from Luther. In his polemic against Karlstadt, *Against the Heavenly Prophets, about Images and Sacrament* (1525), he accused Müntzer of aping the Catholic Mass with his German-language

---

[47] Cf. Karl-Heinz Bieritz, *Liturgik* (Berlin and New York: Walter de Gruyter, 2004), 452.

Gregorian chant.[48] We can assume that Luther's decision not to construct his *German Mass* (1526)[49] on Gregorian chants but rather to create his own texts and melodies was a deliberate attempt to distance himself from Müntzer.[50]

In a 1524 opinion about the prayer of the Canon of the Roman Mass, Luther, too, passes a devastating judgment on the *Canon Romanus*. "*Summa summarum* [Latin: all in all] there is nothing but horrible, blasphemous stuff in the Canon."[51] The critique of the canon related above all to the post-Consecration offering (*offerimus*) of the Body and Blood of Christ, which Luther interpreted as the renewal of Christ's sacrifice on the Cross: "Behold, the blasphemer sacrifices Christ the Son of God for us, who nevertheless sacrificed himself for us only once on the Cross.... Therefore, Christ's Blood is trampled on here and altogether denied."[52] Thus the Mass, a blessing of God upon us (*beneficium Dei*), is turned into man's sacrifice (*sacrificium hominis*). The Offertory prayers were discarded by Luther, too. He regards the Church's sacrifice as an expression of justification through works.[53]

Luther's theology of the Lord's Supper after 1520 found liturgical expression in the two Mass formularies *Formula Missae et Communionis* (1523)[54] and *Deutsche Messe und Ordnung des Gottesdienstes* (1526).[55] The *German Mass* is, in the opinion of the Lutheran liturgist Frieder Schulz (1917–2005), the "concise conclusion of Luther's theological

[48] Cf. Luther, *Wider die himmlischen Propheten, von den Bildern und Sakrament* (1525): *WA* 18:123.19–29.

[49] Cf. Luther, *Deutsche Messe und Ordnung des Gottesdienstes* (1526): *WA* 19:72–113.

[50] The printed formularies for a German-language Mass before Luther's *Deutsche Messe* are: *Testament Jesu Christi* by Johannes Oekolampad (1523), *Evangelische Deutsche Messe* (Worms, 1524), *Deutsche Messe* by Martin Bucer (1524), *Deutsche Evangelische Messe* by Thomas Müntzer (1524), *Evangelische Messe* by Andreas Döber and Andreas Osiander (1525).

[51] Cited from Bieritz, *Liturgik*, 453.

[52] Cited from ibid.

[53] On the principles of the Wittenberg liturgical reform, cf. Reinhard Messner, "Reformen des Gottesdienstes in der Wittenberger Reformation", in *Liturgiereformen*, vol. 1, pt. 1, *Biblische Modelle und Liturgiereformen von der Frühzeit bis zur Aufklärung*, ed. M. Klöckener and B. Kranemann (Münster: Aschendorff, 2002), 81–416.

[54] Cf. Luther, *Formula Missae et Communionis pro Ecclesia Vuittembergensi* (1523): *WA* 12:205–20. The Lord's Supper part is found also in Irmgard Pahl, ed., *Coena Domini*, vol. 1, *Die Abendmahlsliturgie der Reformationskirchen im 16./17. Jahrhundert* (Fribourg: Universitätsverlag, 1983), 33–36.

[55] Cf. Luther, *Formula Missae* (*WA* 19:72–113); English: *An Order of Mass and Communion for the Church at Wittenberg* (1523), Lull, 449–70. On this subject, see Bieritz, *Liturgik*, 457–74.

reflection about the Sunday Mass worship service".[56] The order of divine worship *Formula Missae* goes back to the urging of Luther's friend Nikolaus Hausmann (d. 1538), a pastor in Zwickauer. It is a liturgical resource rather than a Mass formulary. All statements about sacrifice are expunged from it.[57] Polemics against Luther's *Formula Missae* were composed by Hieronymus Emser (1478–1527)[58]and the French humanist and theologian Jodocus Clichtoveus (d. 1543).[59] Luther's *Formula Missae* reflects a "Mass with congregational Communion",[60] which was not a matter of course at that time, since Communion by the faithful had become disengaged from the Mass almost completely in a long process starting with the Middle Ages. Luther's justified concern was to join *missa* and *communio* with each other again.

Except for the sermon, Luther's order of the Mass is still entirely defined by the Latin language. After the *Introitus*, *Kyria*, *Gloria*, and Collect prayer followed the Epistle, *Graduale*, Alleluia, and the Gospel. Luther reversed the sequence of sermon and Creed, since he saw the profession of faith as a reaffirmation of the proclamation of the word. Hence the sermon forms the transition to the Lord's Supper part of the liturgy. The preparation of the gifts of bread and wine occurs either while the profession of faith is being recited or after the sermon. A separate *Offertorium* is no longer foreseen in the order of the Mass. Like the *Graduale*, the *Sanctus* and *Agnus Dei* can be replaced by German songs. The Lord's Supper part includes the Preface, a time of silent prayer, the *verba testamenti*, then the *Sanctus* and *Benedictus* (choir) with the elevation of the bread and the chalice.

---

[56] Thus the Lutheran liturgist Frieder Schulz, "Der Gottesdienst bei Luther", in *Leben und Werk Martin Luthers von 1526–1546*, Festschrift zu seinem 500. Geburtstag, ed. H. Junghans (Göttingen: Vandenhoeck & Ruprecht, 1983), 1:298.

[57] Cf. Luther, *Formula Missae* (*WA* 12:211.20–22): "Proinde omnibus illis repudiatis quae oblationem sonant, cum universo Canone, retineamus, quae pura et sancta sunt, ac sic Missam nostram ordinamur" [Let us, therefore, repudiate everything that smacks of sacrifice, together with the entire canon and retain only that which is pure and holy, and so order our mass (Lull, 456)].

[58] Cf. Hieronymus Emser, *Missae christianorum contra Lutherana missandi formula* (1523).

[59] Cf. Jodocus Clichtoveus, *Propugnaculum Ecclesiae* (1526): Book One.

[60] Frieder Schulz, "Luthers liturgische Reformen: Kontinuität und Innovation", in *Synaxis: Beiträge zur Liturgik*, Zum 80. Geburtstag des Autors im Auftrag der Evangelischen Landeskirche Baden, ed. G. Schwinge (Göttingen: Vandenhoeck & Ruprecht, 1997), 46.

Next comes the *Pater noster*, which is introduced with the traditional *Oremus, praeceptis salutaribus moniti*. The Sign of Peace follows, then the *Agnus Dei*, Communion, the Communion hymn ("Gott sei gelobet und gebenedeiet" [May God be praised and blessed]), and finally the dismissal and blessing (traditional or Aaronic blessing). Besides the omission of the *Offertorium* and the Roman Canon, there were also Masses (Worms, Strasbourg), in which both parts were modified along Protestant lines.[61]

When more and more purely vernacular Lord's Supper worship services were celebrated in the Southern German region, Luther gave up his initial resistance to a Mass completely in German and composed his own order for such a Mass. Luther's *German Mass* was first celebrated on October 29, 1525, in Wittenberg. In 1526, Luther's *Deutsche Messe* appeared in print. While the first part corresponds structurally to the Roman Mass, the Lord's Supper part foresees an extensive restructuring of the earlier order. Luther not only makes considerable changes to the traditional Mass but also demands a change of the traditional common orientation, although he conceded a rather long time of transition for the new prayer orientation *versus ad populum* [with the celebrant turned toward the people]. "But in the correct Mass among nothing but Christians, the altar should not remain so and the priest should always turn toward the people, as no doubt Christ did at the Lord's Supper. Now, let that bide its time."[62] In making his demand, Luther perhaps had in mind the depiction of the Last Supper that Leonardo da Vinci (1452–1519) created as a mural for the refectory of the former Dominican friary Santa Maria delle Grazie in Milan.

Instead of the Introit, Luther's Mass in German has a hymn of praise ("Ich will den Herren loben alle Zeit") or a psalm in German (Luther wanted the whole psalm to be recited and not just the conventional Introit). Next comes the *Kyrie*, which was no longer sung nine times as in the Roman Mass. The postconciliar Catholic liturgical reform did the same thing here as Luther had done. The *Gloria*, which Luther had at first kept as an option, is now dropped entirely. Thus the *Kyrie* is followed by the prayer of the day (Collect)

---

[61] Cf. Bieritz, *Liturgik*, 457f.
[62] Luther, *Deutsche Messe und Ordnung des Gottesdienstes* (1526): *WA* 19:80.28–30.

and the Epistle. Instead of a shortened Gradual, as in the *Formula Missae* (Luther intended to abolish the Sequence entirely), a German hymn comes after the Epistle. Next comes the Gospel. Luther's congregational hymn "Wir glauben all an einen Gott" (We all believe in one God) (1524) replaces the Niceno-Constantinopolitan Creed, which, according to the *Formula Missae*, is sung by the clergyman. The sermon makes the transition to the Lord's Supper part of the liturgy. The Eucharistic liturgy with Offertory and Roman Canon is replaced by congregational Communion in the Lord's Supper part. For this, Luther borrows elements from the medieval Communion of the Faithful outside of Mass (Communion admonition, Our Father as preparation for Communion, distribution of Communion).

As in the *Formula Missae*, so too in his Mass in German, Luther considers the possibility of Communion with the Body of Christ after the Consecration of the bread and Communion with the Blood of Christ after the Consecration of the chalice, but in the Wittenberg Church Order (1533), that idea is dropped again. A paraphrase of the Our Father and the admonition replace the Preface in the German Mass. It is debated whether the intention of the former was to revive the *oratio fidelium* [prayer of the faithful] or to create an equivalent of the Roman Canon.[63] Some have pictured Communion integrated with the words of institution in such a way that the celebrant at the altar sings in the Gospel tone the words of Christ over the bread and immediately afterward distributes the blessed bread without a formula of administration. Then the clergyman (again at the altar) chants in the Gospel tone the words of Christ over the chalice and afterward gives it to the faithful. The Gospel tone makes it clear that the *verba testamenti* for Luther are primarily proclamation. The position of the elevation, which Luther interprets as an "anamnetic accompanying rite",[64] is unclear. The Lutheran liturgist Karl-Heinz Bieritz (1936–2011) thinks that the elevation is prescribed immediately after the words over the bread and chalice.[65] After Communion, the concluding prayer and the Aaronic blessing end the celebration of the Lord's Supper.

[63] Cf. Schulz, "Luthers liturgische Reformen", 51, 53.
[64] Ibid., 51.
[65] Cf. Bieritz, *Liturgik*, 466f.

B. The Intra-Reformation Debate over the Lord's Supper

Although Martin Luther rejected the Catholic doctrine about the Sacrifice of the Mass, in contrast to the Spiritualists, Karlstadt, the Swiss Reformed, and the Enthusiasts, he did defend a kind of somatic Real Presence of Christ in the gifts of bread and wine. The debate among the Reformers over the Lord's Supper[66] is of no less semiotic importance than the Carolingian controversy over the Eucharist. It marks the threshold at which presence and representation diverge.[67] The dispute over the Lord's Supper is at the beginning of the modern debates about the relation between signifier and signified, or of presence and reference.

After 1524, Karlstadt advocated a purely spiritualistic interpretation of the words of institution: with the words of institution, Jesus pointed to himself. Therefore, it is a matter of receiving Jesus spiritually. Huldrych Zwingli (1484–1531) was not convinced by this reading. But he, too, did not interpret the *verba testamenti* in terms of Real Presence but, rather, attributed to them, for instance in his "Commentary on True and False Religion" (1525), an exclusively signifying character.[68] The statement of identity in the *verba testamenti* (*hoc est enim corpus meum* ...) is to be understood in the sense of *significat* (not "this is", but rather "this signifies"). This interpretation, which was announced publicly in late November 1524 in Strasbourg by the Dutchman Hinne Rode/Johann Rhodius (d. 1537), had already been advocated by his compatriot, the lawyer Cornelis Hoen (d. 1524), in a letter in which he cited the work *De sacra eucharistia* by the humanist

---

[66] Overviews of the controversy are given by Joachim Staedtke, "Abendmahl III/3. Reformationszeit", *Theologische Realenzyklopödie* 1 (1977): 106–22; Gerhard May, ed., *Das Marburger Religionsgespräch (1529)*, Texte zur Kirchen- und Theologiegeschichte 13, 2nd ed. (Gütersloh: Mohn, 1979); Thomas Kaufmann, "Abendmahl 3. Reformation", in *Die Religion in Geschichte und Gegenwart: Handwörterbuch für Theologie und Religionswissenschaft*, Study edition, 4th ed. (Tübingen: Mohr, 2008), 1:24–28; Kaufmann, *Geschichte der Reformation*, 522–41; Dietrich Korsch, ed., *Die Gegenwart Jesu Christi im Abendmahl* (Leipzig: Evangelische Verlagsanstalt, 2005).

[67] Cf. Hans Belting, *Das echte Bild: Bildfragen als Glaubensfragen* (Munich: Beck, 2005), 89, 168–72; Joachim von Soosten, "Präsenz und Repräsentation: Die Marburger Unterscheidung", in *Die Gegenwart Jesu Christi im Abendmahl*, ed. D. Korsch (Leipzig: Evangelische Verlagsanstalt, 2005), 99–122.

[68] Cf. Zwingli, *Kommentar über die wahre und die falsche Religion* (1525/1995), 283–95.

Johannes Wessel Gansfort (1419–1489).[69] It is suspected that this letter made its way into the hands of Luther and Zwingli.[70]

In his "Reply to Luther's Sermon against the Enthusiasts" (1527)[71] and his Latin polemic on the Lord's Supper, *Amica Exegesis*,[72] Zwingli objects to Luther's realistic understanding of the presence of Christ in the bread and wine. Zwingli hurls a sharp "Not so!" against Luther's sacramentalism.[73] Zwingli insists on an exclusively figurative interpretation of the *verba institutionis*: "We declare: The words 'This is my body which is given for you' cannot be understood unless they are taken as a *tropus*, that is, as a figure of speech."[74] *Tropica* are "words that stand for something else and are used in a metaphorical, figurative sense".[75] In Zwingli's view, with the Lord's Supper, Christ "instituted the memorial of his death and thanksgiving for it".[76] The words "This is my body" mean nothing other than the *significatio corporis Christi*, which is identical with the *commemoratio corporis* of the institution account understood as a citation.[77] The Lord's Supper is exclusively a commemorative meal, a sign of remembrance and thanksgiving for the once-only redemption. "If you go beyond the meaning of the Lord's Supper as memorial and thanksgiving, you are trying to know more than is necessary."[78]

Zwingli denies that the presence of the crucified and risen Lord in God's eternity is compatible with his sacramental presence in bread and wine. "The notion that Christ's body and blood are in the bread and wine is wrong, because the articles of the Creed say: 'He ascended into heaven, sits at the right hand of God, the Father Almighty; from thence he shall come to judge. . . .' We believe

---

[69] Admittedly, transubstantiation was not disputed by Wessel Gansfort.

[70] Cf. Kaufmann, *Geschichte der Reformation*, 526.

[71] Cf. Zwingli, *Antwort auf die Predigt Luthers gegen die Schwärmer* (1527), in Zwingli, *Schrif ten* 4 (1995), 1–31.

[72] Cf. Zwingli, *Amica exegesis, id est: expositio eucharistiae negocii ad Martinum Lutherum* (1957); *Sämtliche Werke* 5 (ed. Egli), Corpus Reformatorum 92 (1982), 548–758.

[73] Zwingli, *Antwort auf die Predigt Luthers gegen die Schwärmer* (1527/1995), 8.

[74] Ibid., 11.

[75] Ibid., 12.

[76] Ibid., 23.

[77] Cf. Zwingli, *Amica exegesis* (1527/1982), 665.

[78] Zwingli, *Antwort auf die Predigt Luthers gegen die Schwärmer*, 23. Cf. Wendebourg, *Essen zum Gedächtnis*, 70–100.

that he ascended into heaven in the flesh. Accordingly, he cannot be here below on earth."[79] Zwingli disparagingly characterizes Luther's language about the bodily presence of Christ in the bread of the Eucharist as "Roman Catholic talk".[80] Although in Zwingli's *Interpretation and Substantiation of the Theses or Articles* (1523)[81] there was still discourse about a "re-presentation" of Christ's sacrifice in the Mass, it is not to be found in his *Answer to Luther's Sermon against the Enthusiasts* (1527).

The Lord's Supper controversy between Luther and Zwingli ultimately deals with the question of whether the sacrament of the Lord's Supper communicates Christ's grace or only testifies to it.[82] Whereas Luther teaches a Real Presence of Christ with his Body and Blood under the forms of bread and wine, Zwingli see this as endangering Christ's work of redemption in its uniqueness and completeness. Therefore, what is administered in the Lord's Supper is not the Body and Blood of Christ but, rather, bread and wine "as a remembrance, as praise and thanksgiving for the fact that he suffered death and shed his blood for us, so as to blot out our sins thereby".[83] Christ is only spiritually present in the Lord's Supper: "To eat the body of Christ spiritually means nothing else but to rely in one's mind and heart on the mercy and goodness of God through Christ, in other words, in unshakable faith to be certain that God will give us the forgiveness of sins and the joy of eternal happiness."[84]

Between 1518 and 1523, Luther had grappled exclusively with the Roman Catholic understanding of the sacraments. In his work *De instituendis ministris ecclesiae* (1523),[85] he distanced himself from the doctrine of transubstantiation set forth by the Fourth Lateran Council. Presumably Hoen's letter prompted Luther to take a position on the question of the bodily Real Presence of Christ in his work *On Adoration of the Sacrament* (1523). The bodily Real Presence, Luther explains, is brought about by the Divine Word, which "as a living,

---

[79] Zwingli, *Antwort auf die Predigt Luthers gegen die Schwärmer*, 25.
[80] Ibid., 30.
[81] Cf. Zwingli, *Auslegung und Begründung der Thesen oder Artikel* (1523/1995), 133–45.
[82] Cf. Staedtke, "Abendmahl III/3", 107.
[83] Zwingli, *Erklärung des christlichen Glaubens* (1531/1995), 318.
[84] Ibid., 350f.
[85] Cf. Luther, *De instituendis ministris ecclesiae* (1523): *WA* 12:182.19—183.16.

eternal, almighty word" brings with it all "that it signifies, namely, Christ with his flesh and blood and everything that he is and has".[86] From 1526 on, Luther grappled with Zwingli's teaching about the Lord's Supper.

Luther seeks to solve the problem of the bodily presence of Christ in the sacrament of the Lord's Supper by means of his "ubiquity doctrine". "We believe that Christ, according to his human nature, is put over all creatures and fills all things.... Not only according to his divine nature, but also according to his human nature, he is a lord of all things, has all things in his hand, and is present everywhere."[87] The doctrine of ubiquity defended by Luther says that the glorified Body of the crucified, risen, and ascended Lord participates in God's omnipresence and hence can be present at different places at the same time. Many see this as an offense against the rules of the communication of idioms, whereby no statements that apply to Christ's divine nature can be made directly about his human nature. Luther's doctrine of ubiquity is of course only an auxiliary argument. For Luther does not mean that the somatic Real Presence of Christ in the bread and wine is only a form of God's general omnipresence.

The words of institution testify in Luther's view that Jesus Christ with his flesh and blood is present invisibly and in hidden form in the bread and wine.[88] Luther refuses to understand the word *est* merely in the sense of *significat*. Even pagans, he thinks, when they read the institution account, would have to admit that the Real Presence of Christ's Body and Blood is expressed in them.[89] Luther assumes that Christ's Body and Blood are present in the bread and wine in much the same way as the secondary meaning is present in the rhetorical figure of speech synecdoche ("to understand with"): thus the expression "grape juice" can mean the natural juice from grapes, but also wine. Luther uses also as an aid to understanding the image of a purse with a hundred guilders: when we point to the purse with

---

[86] Luther, *Von Anbeten des Sakraments* (1523): *WA* 11:417–56; 433:25–27.

[87] Luther, *Sermon von dem Sakrament des Leibes und Blutes Christi, wider die Schwarmgeister* (1526): *WA* 19:491.17–20; English: *The Sacrament of the Body and Blood of Christ—Against the Fanatics* (Lull, 314–40 at 321).

[88] Cf. Luther, *Dass diese Worte Christi "Das ist mein Leib" noch fest stehen, wider die Schwarmgeister* (1527): *WA* 23:64–322; Luther, *Das Abendmahl Christi, Bekenntnis* (1528): *WA* 26:261–509.

[89] Cf. ibid. (*WA* 26:406.9—407.1; 496.34—497.1).

the money, we say, "That is a hundred guilders", even though the money is not visible. This aid to understanding is liable to cause misunderstandings, since the presence of Christ's Body and Blood in the bread and wine is not a local presence.

While Luther holds fast unwaveringly to the presence of Christ's Body "in", "with", and "under" the sign of bread, Zwingli in contrast sees the bread as a sign that points to the absent Body of Christ—to put it in semiotic terms: the bread is for Zwingli a symbolic sign based on convention, because this is neither an iconic sign, a copy of the object to which it relates, nor an indexical sign that refers to something connected with the sign. For Luther, the sacramental sign transcends merely semiotic representation.[90] Christ makes himself present in the sacrament of the Lord's Supper not only in his divine but also in his whole theandric reality, as he "is corporeally conceived and born, laid in the crib, taken in arms, sits at table during the Last Supper, hangs on the Cross, etc."[91] Luther expressly distances himself from Berengar of Tours and even defends his condemnation.[92] "Now what is the sacrament of the altar? Answer: It is the true Body and the Blood of our Lord Christ in and under the bread and wine; through Christ the command was given to us Christians to eat and to drink."[93] Christ's substantial presence occurs by dint of his words, which are the true creative word of God.[94] From this it follows that the sinner, too, receives the sacrament of the Eucharist (*manducatio impiorum*). The objective *manducatio corporalis et oralis* [bodily, oral eating] assures, in Luther's view, the *extra nos* [the component of the sacrament that is "outside us"] of salvation in receiving Communion.

---

[90] Cf. Belting, *Das echte Bild*, 169.

[91] Luther, *Dass diese Worte Christi "Das ist mein Leib" noch fest stehen* (*WA* 23:177.27–29).

[92] Cf. Luther, *Das Abendmahl Christ, Bekenntnis* (*WA* 26:442.39—443.3).

[93] Luther, *Grosser Katechismus* (1528/1529): *WA* 30.1:223. Wenrich Slenczka, *Heilsgeschichte und Liturgie: Studien zum Verhältnis von Heilsgeschichte und Heilsteilhabe anhand liturgischer und katechetischer Quellen des dritten und vierten Jahrhunderts* (Berlin and New York: Walter de Gruyter, 2000), 91, says that Luther's understanding of Christ's presence under bread and wine is only inadequately rendered by this formula—just like its designation as "consubstantiation" or as "doctrine of co-presence". The Eucharistic Real Presence, as Luther understands it, is not a local presence but rather—analogous to Christ's Incarnation—the "execution of a communication of Christ to the bread". According to von Soosten, Luther understands the *verba testamenti* performatively according to the trope of the Incarnation of the Divine Word. Cf. von Soosten, "Präsenz und Reprasentation", 105f.

[94] Cf. Luther, *Dass diese Worte Christi "Das ist mein Leib" noch fest stehen* (*WA* 23:231.30).

In contrast, Zwingli rejects a *manducatio corporalis* and *manducatio impiorum* [eating by the wicked]. With regard to the eating of the bread and the drinking from the chalice, one can speak only about a *manducatio spiritualis* [spiritual eating].

The controversy led in early October 1529 to the famous "Marburg Colloquy" on religion, in which not only Luther and Zwingli but also Bucer, Melanchthon, Johannes Oekolampad (1482–1531) from Basel, and the Nürnberg Reformer Andreas Osiander (1496/98–1552) participated. Everyone agreed in rejecting the doctrine of transubstantiation and in demanding that the laity receive from the chalice, but not about their understanding of Christ's presence in the Eucharist. Here the views were in some cases widely divergent. According to Osiander's report, Luther wrote the Latin words *Hoc est enim corpus meum* with chalk on the table and covered them with a velvet cloth, which he removed at the climax of the dispute so as to confront his opponents with the "word of God".[95] Because those statements of Christ are there, Luther said in opposition to Zwingli, "I must profess and believe that the Body of Christ is there",[96] which is why the *est* must not be understood only in the sense of signifying (*significare*). Admittedly, Zwingli conceded at the end of the Colloquy that the Lord's Supper can be called a "sacrament of the true Body and Blood of Jesus Christ". Yet that admission signified nothing more than a compromise on the formula. For the Marburg "agreement document" does not reflect the actual positions of Luther and Zwingli. Luther teaches a substantial presence of Christ's Body and Blood in and under the forms of bread and wine.[97] No agreement with Zwingli was possible on this basis.

The Genevan Reformer John Calvin sees the sacrament as "a testimony of divine grace toward us, confirmed by an outward sign (symbol), with mutual attestation of our piety toward him".[98] The bread of the Lord's Supper is a "symbol of Christ's body", the wine—a "symbol of [Christ's] blood".[99] To receive Christ's Body and Blood

---

[95] Cf. May, *Marburger Religionsgespräch*, 52; Kaufmann, *Geschichte der Reformation*, 539.

[96] Luther, *Marburger Religionsgespräch* (1529): *WA* 30.3:137.12f.

[97] Cf. Luther, *Grosser Katechismus* (*WA* 30.1:223.22–24); Luther, *Kleiner Katechismus* (1529): *WA* 30.1:260.1–4.

[98] Calvin, *Institutes of the Christian Religion* (1535) 4.14.1 (McNeill ed., 1277).

[99] Ibid., 4.17.3 (1363).

means for Calvin, however, more than to believe in Christ, for body and blood are not only symbols for the profession of faith. Rather, the faithful receive in the bread and wine the life of Christ.[100] Bread and wine for Calvin are an image for fellowship with Christ.[101] Through bread and wine, the faithful are united with Christ, who is in heaven.[102] Christ does not become present in the gifts of bread and wine, but rather with the signs of bread and wine the faithful grow together with Christ through his Spirit into one body. Thus they become one in body, spirit, and soul with him.[103] Calvin mistakenly understands transubstantiation through the *verba testamenti*, which he calls a "magic incantation",[104] as Christ's local presence.[105] Calvin also interprets the consubstantiality of the Body and Blood of Christ with the bread and wine, as Luther argues, in the sense of a local presence. In this respect, he sees no difference with the doctrine of transubstantiation.[106]

Hence Calvin distances himself from those who say that Christ's Body is given with the bread, in the bread, and under the bread.[107] The bread is called "body" because it is a "sign of the body", in a figurative or analogous sense, that is, in a metaphorical way of speaking (*metonymicus sermo*), as we often encounter in the Bible.[108] To believe that Christ is confined in earthly forms and to adore him in the Eucharistic bread is nothing else than a "perverse opinion" and a blasphemous "superstition".[109] Calvin teaches a *manducatio spiritualis* [spiritual eating], by dint of which the faithful are united with Christ in heaven, and a *manducatio oralis* of the bread. Like Zwingli, Calvin rejects a *manducatio impiorum* in Luther's sense. Only believers receive Christ, not unbelievers.[110] Calvin thus argues for a dynamic spiritual

---

[100] Cf. ibid., 4.17.5 (1365).

[101] Cf. Calvin, *Streitschrift gegen die Artikel der Sorbonne* (1544/1999), 39.

[102] Cf. Calvin, *Der Genfer Katechismus* (1545): De sacramentis (1997), 130f.

[103] Cf. Calvin, *Institutes of the Christian Religion* 4.17.12 (McNeill ed., 1373).

[104] Ibid., 4.17.15 (1377–79).

[105] Cf. ibid., 4.17.13–14 (1373–76).

[106] Cf. ibid., 4.17.16 (1379).

[107] Cf. ibid., 4.17.20 (1383).

[108] Cf. ibid., 4.17.21 (1385).

[109] Calvin, *Petit traité de la sainte Cène*, introductions M. Carbonnier-Burkhard et L. Gagnebin; adaptation moderne de H. Chatelain et P. Marcel (Lyon, 2008), 67.

[110] Cf. Calvin, *Institutes of the Christian Religion* 4.17.33 (McNeill ed., 1406–7).

presence of Christ in the Lord's Supper. The decisive thing is that Calvin understands Christ's Ascension to the right hand of the Father in such a way that Christ's glorified Body is enclosed by heaven and therefore cannot be present under the sign of bread. Christ is present merely in his spirit, which he sends as the Paraclete.[111] The Lord's Supper is therefore about fellowship with Christ in the spirit, about the "testament in Christ's body".[112]

After the unsuccessful Colloquy on religion, there were several attempts to arrive nevertheless at a Lord's Supper fellowship among the Reformed communions. Serving as a foundation for this were the *Confessio Augustana Invariata* (1530) and the *Confessio Tetrapolitana* (1530) of the Upper German States. With the Wittenberg Concord (1536),[113] a compromise was reached between Luther and the Southern German Reformation. The document reads:

> With the bread and wine, the Body of Christ and his Blood are truly and substantially present, offered, and received (*cum pane et vino vere et substantialiter adesse, exhiberi et sumi*). And although they deny that any transubstantiation takes place and do not think that he is locally enclosed in the bread and permanently united with it apart from the use of the sacrament, they do admit that through the sacramental unity the bread is the Body of Christ, that is, they are convinced that together with the bread that is administered, the Body of Christ is truly there and administered at the same time. For outside of the use [of the sacrament], when it is stored in a food container or displayed in procession, as the papists do, they do not think that the Body of Christ is present then. Finally, they think that the institution of this sacrament is valid in the Church and independent of the worthiness of the minister and that of the recipient.[114]

The *Confessio Helvetica Prior* (1536) adopted Zwingli's symbolic doctrine of the Lord's Supper. In opposition, Luther, two years before his

---

[111] Cf. ibid., 4.17.26–27 (1393–95).

[112] Ibid., 4.17.20 (1385).

[113] On the Concord, see the study by Hermann Sasse, *Corpus Christi: Ein Beitrag zum Problem der Abendmahlskonkordie* (Erlangen: Verlag der Ev.-Luth Mission, 1979).

[114] *Wittenberger Konkordie* 1–2 (*Bekenntnisschriften der evangelisch-lutherischen Kirche*, herausgegeben im Gedenkjahr der Augsburgischen Konfession 1930, 12th ed. [Gottingen: Vandenhoeck, 1998; hereafter cited as *BSLK*], 65).

death, composed his *Brief Profession of Faith about the Blessed Sacrament* (1544).[115] In it, he once again defends the bodily presence of Christ, which is communicated substantially but hidden under the bread and wine. In the intra-Reformation controversy about the Lord's Supper, Calvin proved to be more willing to dialogue than Zwingli. Thus he was willing to sign the *Confessio Augustana Variata* (1540), according to which Christ's Body and Blood are really administered "with" the bread and wine. With Heinrich Bullinger (1504–1575), Zwingli's successor in Zurich, Calvin negotiated the *Zurich Agreement* (1549)[116] about their common doctrine of the Lord's Supper. With the *Confessio Helvetica Posterior* (1562), the statements in the *Heidelberg Catechism* (1563), and the *Formula of Concord* (1577),[117] the intra-Reformation debate about the Lord's Supper reached a sort of conclusion. A real understanding between Lutherans and Reformed Christians was not reached.

Among Lutheran written testimonies, the *Confessio Augustana* (*Augsburg Confession*) (1530) is of particular importance for the question of the Real Presence of Christ in the gifts of bread and wine. Deliberately adopting the Fourth Lateran Council, it speaks about the presence of Christ's Body and Blood under the forms of bread and wine: "They teach about the Lord's Supper that Christ's true Body and Blood are truly present under the form of bread and wine and are distributed to those who partake of the Lord's Supper; and they disapprove of those who teach otherwise."[118] In the *Apology of the Augsburg Confession* (1531), we read: "Decimus articulus approbatus est, in quo confitemur nos sentire, quod in coena Domini vere et substantialiter adsint corpus et sanguis Christi et vere exhibeantur cum illis rebus, quae videntur, pane et vino, his qui sacramentum accipiunt."[119]

---

[115] Cf. Luther, *Kurzes Bekenntnis vom Heiligen Sakrament* (1544): *WA* 54:119.141–67.

[116] Cf. Emidio Campi and Ruedi Reich, eds., *Consensus Tigurinus (1549): Die Einigung zwischen Heinrich Bullinger und Johannes Calvin über das Abendmahl*, Werden-Wertung-Bedeutung (Zurich: TVZ, 2009).

[117] Cf. *Formula Concordiae* 7: De coena Domini (*BSLK* 970–1016).

[118] *Confessio Augustana* (hereafter cited as *CA*) 10: "De coena Domini docent quod corpus et sanguis Christi vere adsint et distribuantur vescentibus in coena Domini; et improbant secus docentes" (*BSLK* 64).

[119] *Apologia Confessionis Augustanae* 10 (*BSLK* 247f.). "Article Ten is approved, in which we profess that we think that the body and blood of Christ are truly and substantially present in the Lord's Supper and are truly offered with the things, bread and wine, that are seen by those who receive the sacrament."

Following the Roman Canon, the *Apology* even speaks about a *mutatio* of the bread and wine: "Id enim testatur canon missae, apud illos, in quo aperte orat sacerdos, ut mutato pane ipsum corpus Christi fiat."[120] The doctrine of transubstantiation is of course rejected in the Lutheran confessional documents as "subtle sophistry" and papist teaching.[121]

Unlike the Evangelical Lutheran confessional documents, the Evangelical Reformed confessional documents deny any presence of Christ in and under the forms of bread and wine. The *Zurich Agreement* describes the sacraments as signs and seals of faith; since they are signs, the faithful should not cling to them. About the sacrament of the Eucharist it says:

Insofar as he is man, Christ is nowhere else but in heaven and is not to be sought otherwise but through the Spirit and the understanding of the faith. For this reason, it is an error to try to enclose the Lord under the elements of this world.[122] Therefore we do not accept the interpretation of those who insist on the literal sense of the letter in the particular customary words of Christ, "This is my body", "this is my blood." For we consider it certain that they are to be understood in the figurative sense.[123]

---

[120] Ibid. (*BSLK* 248). "For among [the Catholics], this is attested by the Canon of the Mass, in which the priest plainly prays that when the bread has been changed it might become the very body of Christ."

[121] Cf. *Smalcald Articles* 3, 6 (*BSLK* 452): "De transsubstantiatione subtilitatem sophisticam nihil curamus, qua fingunt panem et vinum relinquere, et amittere naturalem suam substantiam et tantum formam et colorem panis et non verum panem remanere. Optime enim cum sacra scriptura congruit, quod panis adsit et maneat, sicut Paulus ipse nominat: 'Panis quam frangimus.' Et: 'Ita edat de pane'" [As for transubstantiation, we have no regard for the subtle sophistry of those who teach that bread and wine surrender or lose their natural substance and retain only the appearance and shape of bread without any longer being real bread, for (the belief) that bread is and remains there agrees better with the Scriptures, as St. Paul himself states, "The bread which we break" (1 Cor 10:16), and again, "Let a man so eat of the bread" (1 Cor 11:28) (Lull, 529)].

Formula Concordiae 7.35 (*BSLK* 983): "Primum enim his phrasibus ad reiiciendam papisticam transsubstantionem utimur. Deinde etiam sacramentalem unionem substantiae panis non mutatae et corporis Christi hac ratione docere volumus. Ad eundem enim modum hoc dictum: *Verbo caro factum est*" [For first we use these phrases to reject Papist transubstantiation. Then we intend to teach also by this argument the sacramental union of the unchanged substance of bread with the body of Christ. For in the same way Scripture says: *The Word was made flesh* (Jn 1:14)].

[122] *Consensus Tigurinus*, art. 21 (Campi–Reich ed., 152).

[123] Ibid., art. 22 (Campi–Reich ed., 152).

This symbolism rules out language about eating the flesh of Jesus Christ or about the presence of Christ under, with, and in the bread.[124] Eucharistic adoration is also rejected.

> However, if it is not allowed to attach Christ to the bread and the wine through our imagination, it is even much less permissible to adore him in the bread. Although, indeed, the bread is symbol and pledge of our communion with Christ and is offered to us, nevertheless it is a sign, not the thing itself, and it does not have the thing enclosed within it or attached to it. For this reason, those who follow this train of thought in order to adore Christ make an idol out of it.[125]

The *Apology of the Augsburg Confession*[126] and the *Smalcald Articles*[127] condemn the Mass as a sacrifice because they understand it as a work of the Church through which people obtain the remission of their sins. In the *Augsburg Confession*, we find in part 2 about abuses and errors the following explanation: "There was also added the opinion that infinitely increased private Masses, namely, that Christ, by his Passion, had made satisfaction for original sin and instituted the Mass wherein an offering should be made for daily sins, venial and mortal."[128] The critique is directed against an interpretation that views Christ's sacrifice on the Cross as being limited in its efficacy and importance and adds the Sacrifice of the Mass to supplement it.[129] Even though the Mass as sacrifice is denied, the *Apology of the Augsburg Confession* acknowledges that besides Christ's sacrifice on the Cross, there is the *sacrificium eucharisticum*, the Church's sacrifice of thanksgiving. This sacrifice, however, does not bring about the forgiveness of sins or reconciliation. Rather, it is "offered by those who have been reconciled ... , so that we may

---

[124] Cf. ibid., art. 23–25 (Campi-Reich ed., 152f.).

[125] Ibid., art. 26 (Campi-Reich ed., 153).

[126] Cf. *Apologia Confessionis Augustanae* 24 (*BSLK* 349–77).

[127] Cf. *Smalcald Articles*, 1, 2 (*BSLK* 416; Lull, 503).

[128] *CA* 24 (*BSLK* 93): "Accessit opinio, quae auxit privatas missas in infinitum, videlicet quod Christus sua passione satisfecerit pro peccato originis et instituerit missam, in qua fieret oblatio pro cotidianis delictis, mortalibus et venialibus."

[129] The Council of Trent does not teach this but, rather, speaks about a sacramental representation of the sacrifice on the Cross.

thus express our thanks for the remission of sins and for other blessings received."[130]

C. The Sacrament of the Eucharist and the Sacrifice of the Mass

Catholic theologians responded to Luther's rejection of the Sacrifice of the Mass by making a distinction between Christ's sacrifice on the Cross and its sacramental re-presentation, which primarily is the work of Christ himself. The Mass is not a new bloody offering but, rather, an *oblatio sacramentalis*, a sacrifice *in mysterio*, a spiritual sacrifice in relation to the *oblatio corporalis et realis* [bodily and real sacrifice] on the Cross. The celebration of the Mass is a sacramental *memoria* or *repraesentatio passionis Christi* [commemoration or re-presentation of Christ's Passion]. Luther likewise viewed the Lord's Supper as a memorial of the sacrifice, but understood the *memoria* more as a human remembrance.[131]

Johannes Eck (1486–1543), the most famous Catholic theological polemicist, in his treatise in defense of the Mass (1526),[132] defines it as *memoria* and *repraesentatio passionis et oblationis Christi*.[133] Eck relates the expression *repraesentatio* to the sacramental efficacy of Christ's sacrifice, while *memoria* or *recordatio* means more the human remembrance.[134]

> Thus Holy Mother Church, instructed by the Holy Spirit who was given to her as Teacher and Paraclete, repeats daily by her constant re-presentation this unique oblation offered on the altar of the Cross for the salvation of the world, as the only sacrifice that is all-sufficient and most pleasing to God; she testifies to this in the Secret prayer of a certain Sunday when she says: "as often as the commemoration

---

[130] *Apologia Confessionis Augustanae* 24 (*BSLK* 354): "sed fit a reconciliatis, ut pro accepta remissione peccatorum et pro aliis beneficiis acceptis gratias agamus."

[131] Cf. Wendebourg, *Essen zum Gedächtnis*, 40–60, 139–202.

[132] Cf. Eck, *De sacrificio missae libri tres* (Iserloh ed.).

[133] A "memory" and "re-presentation of Christ's Passion and sacrifice". Cf. ibid., 1.10 (Iserloh ed., 62–65); 3.6 (Iserloh ed., 163); 3.6 (Iserloh ed., 169).

[134] Cf. Erwin Iserloh, "Abendmahl III/3: Römisch-katholische Kirche", in *Theologische Realenzyklopädie* (Berlin and New York: Walter de Gruyter, 1999), 125.

of this sacrifice is celebrated, the work of our redemption is accomplished (*exercetur*)."[135]

The liturgical prayer in question is the *Oratio super oblata* (prayer over the gifts = Secret) for the Ninth Sunday after Pentecost.[136] The language in Eck's writings about the "repetition" of Christ's sacrifice is misleading, even though he speaks about a repetition in the *repraesentatio* or *memoria*.[137] The Mass, in Eck's view, is not a new bloody sacrifice but, rather, an *oblatio sacramentalis*, a *mystica oblatio*.[138] For Eck, the unity of the sacrifice on the Cross and the Sacrifice of the Mass consists above all in the identity of the victim. The idea that Christ himself is the *principalis offerens* (chief priest who offers) is not yet operative in Eck's writings. Therefore he can attribute only a limited value to the Mass celebrated by the human priest as compared with many Masses.[139]

The Franciscan theologian Kaspar Schatzgeyer (d. 1527) showed in his treatise on the Mass (1525) the lines along which an agreement might have been sought in the question as to the sacrificial character of the Mass: "That sacrifice, therefore, which the Church and her minister offers on the altar is none other than this: not only a [human] remembrance but also a solemn representation of the sacrifice that Christ made on the Cross."[140] The Mass is a sacrifice, but it is none other than the sacrifice of Christ on the Cross. No repetition of the sacrifice on the Cross takes place in the Sacrifice

---

[135] Eck, *De sacrificio missae* 1.10 (Iserloh ed., 64): "Sic sancta mater ecclesia, edocta Spiritu sancto, qui ei doctor est datus et paraclitus, iugi repraesentatione et quottidiano reiterat hanc unicam oblationem in ara crucis pro salute mundi factam, tanquam solam sufficientissimam hostiam et Deo placentissimam, id quod in dominicae cuiusdam oratione secreta testatur, cum inquit: *quotiens huius hostiae commemoratio celebratur, opus nostrae redemptionis exercetur.*"

[136] The Second Vatian Council cites this prayer in its Constitution *Sacrosanctum concilium* on the Sacred Liturgy when it says that through the liturgy, "most of all in the divine sacrifice of the Eucharist", "'the work of our redemption is accomplished'" (*SC* 2). In the 1970 *Missale Romanum*, this prayer is assigned to the Mass of the Last Supper on Holy Thursday.

[137] Cf. Eck, *De sacrificio missae* 3.8 (Iserloh ed., 172).

[138] Cf. ibid.

[139] Cf. Iserloh, *Kampf um die Messe*, 55.

[140] Kaspar Schatzgeyer, *Tractatus de missa* 2: *De missae sacrificio*, in *Schriften zur Verteidigung der Messe*, ed. Erwin Iserloh and Peter Fabisch, Corpus Catholicorum 37 (Münster: Aschendorff, 1984), 223: "Illa igitur oblatio, quam ecclesia et suus minister in altari offert, aliud non est quam oblationis Christi in cruce factae non modo recordatio, sed et solennis repraesentatio."

of the Mass. It is a presence of the sacrifice on the Cross *in mysterio*, its sacramental presence. To say that the Sacrifice of the Mass is not a work and a sacrifice of the Church means that "the minister of the Church does not perform that work as though he were going to give to God something of his own or else obtain thereby special merit for himself or for others."[141] The fact that Christ himself is the one who performs this oblation in the Mass is not just mentioned incidentally by Schatzgeyer but is central in his response to Luther. In the Old Covenant, Christ's sacrifice already existed in prefigurations. It is present in the most substantial way (*praesentissima*) in the Eucharist.[142] When he speaks about the sacramental presence of the sacrifice of the Cross in the sacrament, Schatzgeyer, unlike Paschasius Radbertus, avoids all terms that suggest a bloody sacrifice, such as *immolatio* or *mactatio*, but also the term *imago*, which had become vacuous since nominalism.[143]

The Dominican theologian Thomas Cardinal Cajetan de Vio (1469–1534), to whom Leo X entrusted Luther's case and who attended the Diet of Augsburg in 1517 as the pope's legate, teaches in his short work *On the Sacrifice and Rite of the Mass against Luther* (1531) that when we speak about the sacrificial victim on the Cross and in the Eucharist, we are speaking about only one sacrifice (*unica hostia*), namely, the Body and Blood of Christ, and only the manner of offering is different (bloody, unbloody).[144] For Christ does not become present in order to be sacrificed then by us, but, rather, he is present *immolationis modo*, in the manner of the victim, as the one who offered himself as victim.[145] The one sacrifice of Christ on the Cross

---

[141] Ibid. (Iserloh ed., 225): "quod illud opus non facit minister ecclesiae, tanquam per hoc aliquid Deo daturus ex suis, aut ut meritum proprium sibi aut aliis per hoc acquisiturus."

[142] Cf. ibid. (Iserloh ed., 229).

[143] Cf. Schatzgeyer, *Schriften zur Verteidigung*, 7–10.

[144] Cf. Cajetan de Vio, *De Missae sacrificio et ritu adversus Lutheranos*, cap. 6 (Lyon, 1587/1995): "Verum hostia cruenta et incruenta non sunt hostiae duae, sed hostia una ... in hostia cruenta Christus in cruce et hostia incruenta Christus in altari, sed esse unicam hostiam" [But the bloody victim and the unbloody victim are not two victims, but one victim ... Christ on the Cross in the bloody sacrifice and Christ on the altar in the unbloody sacrifice, but they are one sacrifice].

[145] Cf. Pratzner, *Messe und Kreuzesopfer*, 60f. Pratzner does not do Cajetan justice when he accuses him of teaching only a symbolic representation of the sacrifice of the Cross in the Eucharist.

is therefore not repeated in the Mass; it becomes present sacramentally. The efficacy of Christ's sacrifice on the Cross can therefore not be supplemented by the Mass but only appropriated. The ministers of the Church do not act in their own name but, rather, *in persona Christi*,[146] the true priest of the New Covenant.[147] Thus Cajetan overcomes the dubious theory of quantifiable fruits of the Mass: the Eucharistic Sacrifice has infinite power *ex opere operato* and cannot be limited to a particular measure.[148]

The Council of Trent[149] took up the questions raised by Luther (sacrificial character of the Mass, doctrine of transubstantiation, laymen receiving from the chalice) and issued three doctrinal documents on the subject: (1) *Decree on the Sacrament of the Eucharist* on the Real Presence of Christ (October 11, 1551),[150] (2) *Doctrine and Canons on Communion under Both Species and the Communion of Young Children* (July 16, 1562) on questions about Holy Communion,[151] and (3) *Doctrine and Canons on the Sacrifice of the Mass* (September 17, 1562) on the question of the Sacrifice of the Mass.[152] In addition, the *Decree on Things to be Observed and Avoided in Celebrating Masses* (September 17, 1562)[153] was approved. The council, which intended to reject errors about the Eucharist and not to define the opinions of theological schools, endeavored to substantiate its teaching about

---

[146] Cf. Cajetan de Vio, *De Missae sacrificio et ritu adversus Lutheranos*, cap. 6: "nam ministri quoque non in personis propriis, sed in persona Christi consecrant corpus et sanguinem Christi" [Now the ministers, too, consecrate the Body and Blood of Christ, not in their own persons, but rather in the person of Christ].

[147] Cf. ibid.: "In Novo Testamento unicus est sacerdos Christus" [In the New Testament Christ is the sole priest].

[148] Cf. Iserloh, "Wert der Messe", 405f.

[149] After a difficult preparatory phase, the Council of Trent was inaugurated on December 13, 1545. Its proceedings were held in three sessions: Session 1 from 1545 to 1547 in Trent and from March 1547 to 1549 in Bologna; Session 2 (1551–1552) in Trent; Session 3 (1562–1563) in Trent. Cf. Hubert Jedin, *A History of the Council of Trent*, trans. Ernest Graf, O.S.B., 2 vols. (St. Louis: Herder Book, 1957–1961); Remigius Bäumer, ed., *Concilium Tridentinum* (Darmstadt: Wissenschaftliche Buchgesellschaft, 1979); John W. O'Malley, *Trent: What Happened at the Council* (Cambridge, Mass.: Belknap Press of Harvard University Press, 2013).

[150] *Decretum de sanctissima eucharistia*, cf. DH 1635–61.

[151] *De doctrina de communione sub utraque specie et parvulorum*, cf. DH 1725–34.

[152] *De doctrina de sanctissimo missae sacrificio*, cf. DH 1738–59.

[153] *Decretum de observandis et vitandis in celebratione missarum*, cf. Conciliorum Oecumenicorum Decreta: Dekrete der Ökumenischen Konzilien, 3 vols., ed. J. Wohlmuth (Paderborn, Munich, Vienna, and Zurich: Schöningh, 1998–2002; hereafter cited as *COD*), 3:736–37.

the Eucharist on the basis of Scripture. In interpreting Scripture, it harked back to the consensus of the Church Fathers.

In the *Decree on the Sacrament of the Eucharist*, the council taught that it was instituted by Jesus at the Last Supper.[154] With regard to Christ's presence in the Eucharistic gifts, it distinguished between the natural manner in which the ascended Lord exists at the Father's right hand and his sacramental presence in the Eucharist.[155] After the Consecration of the bread and wine, "our Lord Jesus Christ ... is truly (*vere*), really (*realiter*), and substantially (*substantialiter*) contained under the appearances of those perceptible realities [canon 1]."[156]

> This has always been the belief of the Church of God that immediately after the consecration the true body and blood of our Lord, together with his soul and divinity, exist under the species of bread and wine. The body exists under the species of bread and the blood under the species of wine by virtue of the words. But the body, too, exists under the species of wine, the blood under the species of bread, and the soul under both species in virtue of the natural connection and concomitance by which the parts of Christ the Lord, who has already risen from the dead to die no more [cf. Rom 6:9], are united together. Moreover, the divinity is present because of its admirable hypostatic union with the body and the soul. [Canons 1 and 3][157]

Through the consecration of bread and wine "there takes place a change (*conversio*) of the whole substance of bread into the substance of the body of Christ our Lord and of the whole substance of wine into the substance of his blood. This change (*conversio*) the holy Catholic Church has fittingly and properly (*convenienter et proprie*) named transubstantiation (*transsubstantiatio*)" [canon 2].[158] The Council of Trent declared the doctrine about the change of the gifts of bread and wine into the Body and Blood of Christ a formal dogma (*dogma revelatum*

---

[154] Cf. DH 1637–38.

[155] Cf. DH 1636.

[156] Ibid.

[157] DH 1640.

[158] DH 1642. For an understanding of transubstantiation at the Council of Trent, see Josef Wohlmuth, *Realpräsenz und Transsubstantiation auf dem Konzil von Trient: Eine historisch-kritische Analyse der Canones 1–4 der Sessio XIII*, vol. 1 (Bern: Lang, 1975).

et declaratum). It did not define, however, the nature of the change (*conversio*) of the bread and wine that is called *transubstantiation*.[159]

The sacrament of the Eucharist is a spiritual food that frees the recipients from the power of death and sin and bestows life. It is a pledge of eternal life and unites the whole Body of Christ through faith, hope, and love.[160] The reservation of the Sacrament for Communion of the sick, which the Council of Nicaea (325) already mentions, is defended by the council.[161] The adoration of the Sacrament reflects the conviction of the lasting presence of Christ under the Eucharistic species.[162] Since Jesus Christ is truly present in this Sacrament, divine worship (*cultus latriae*) is due to him in it. As for the "use" (*usus*) of the sacrament of the altar, the council distinguishes three ways: merely sacramental reception by sinners, exclusively spiritual reception, whereby the bread from heaven is received by desire (*in voto*), and the simultaneously sacramental and spiritual reception by those who approach the Sacrament with the proper disposition.[163] A believer who is in a state of serious sin must receive sacramental absolution before receiving the Eucharist.[164]

The *Decree on the Sacrament of the Eucharist* condemns various errors without ascribing them to specific authors.[165] Condemned are those who think that Christ is present in the Eucharist "only as in a sign or figure (*in signo vel figura*) or by his power".[166] The concept "figure" used here is different from the one found in Ambrose or Paschasius Radbertus. In the Decree on the Eucharist, only Old Testament sacrifices are described as *signum* and *figura*, not the Eucharist, inasmuch as it is the true eschatological sacrament of the one sacrifice of Christ. When the council teaches that the transformation of bread and wine is very fittingly (*aptissime*) called transubstantiation

---

[159] Cf. DH 1642. In his Constitution *Auctorem fidei* (1794) against the Synod of Pistoia (1786), Pope Pius VI (1775–1799) reaffirmed the Council of Trent's definition of the substantial transformation (*transsubstantiatio seu conversio substantiae*) of the gifts of bread and wine as an article of faith (*articulum fidei Tridentinum Concilium definivit*). Cf. DH 2629.

[160] Cf. DH 1638.

[161] Cf. DH 1645.

[162] Cf. DH 1643–44.

[163] Cf. DH 1648.

[164] Cf. DH 1647.

[165] Cf. DH 1651–61.

[166] DH 1651.

(*transsubstantiatio*),[167] it defines a true change of bread and wine. This does not make Aristotelian ontology dogmatic along with it.[168] Condemned are those who maintain that Jesus Christ is present only *in usu*, during the meal,[169] and therefore reject the reservation of the Eucharist for Communion of the sick, Eucharistic adoration, and processions with the Blessed Sacrament.[170]

Eleven years after the first decree was promulgated, after an interruption of the conciliar sessions for several years, the council promulgated in 1562 its *Doctrine and Canons on Communion under Both Species and the Communion of Young Children*.[171] The Communion of the faithful under only one species is defended by the council as Church practice. The faithful are not obliged by divine command to receive Communion under both species. The authority to regulate the administration of the Sacrament belongs to the Church.[172] The faithful are deprived of no grace through Communion under the species of bread alone. For the whole Christ is present under the species of bread.[173] For young children, there is no obligation to make a sacramental Communion, since they cannot lose the grace given by God in Baptism until they reach the age of reason [DH 1730].

The *Decree on the Request for the Granting of the Chalice* [to the laity] was promulgated on September 17, 1562.[174] The question of whether individual local Churches might allow the laity to receive Communion from the chalice was deferred; the decision about it was left to the pope.[175] On April 16, 1564, Pope Pius IV (1559–1565) granted the chalice to the laity in some cases, among others for the dioceses of Mainz and Cologne. The majority of the Catholic population, however, rejected lay reception of Communion from the chalice, since it

---

[167] Cf. DH 1652.
[168] Cf. Karl Rahner, "The Presence of Christ in the Sacrament of the Lord's Supper", in *Theological Investigations*, vol. 4, trans. Kevin Smyth (Baltimore: Helicon Press, 1966), 298; Edward Schillebeeckx, *Die eucharistische Gegenwart: Zur Diskussion über die Realpräsenz* (Düsseldorf: Patmos, 1967).
[169] Cf. DH 1654.
[170] Cf. DH 1656–57.
[171] Cf. DH 1725–34.
[172] Cf. DH 1726–28.
[173] Cf. DH 1729.
[174] Cf. DH 1760.
[175] Cf. ibid.

had meanwhile become a distinguishing feature of Protestantism. In 1584 Pope Gregory XIII (1572–1585) suspended the indult concerning reception from the chalice that had been granted by Pius IV.[176]

Since Martin Luther disputed the sacrificial character of the Mass and rejected the offering of a Eucharistic sacrifice as "altogether terrible idolatry",[177] the Council of Trent found itself faced with the task of expounding the unity but at the same time the difference between the sacrifice on the Cross and the Sacrifice of the Mass. The Decree on the Sacrifice of the Mass[178] distinguished between the bloody sacrifice on the Cross and its sacramental re-presentation in the Eucharist.[179] According to the council's teaching, Christ's sacrifice on the Cross and his priesthood are the *consummatio* of all human sacrifice.[180] Christ offered himself as a sacrifice once for all on the altar of the Cross and thereby brought about eternal redemption. Through his death on the Cross, however, his priesthood was not annihilated.

The universality of Christ's sacrifice was for the council the reason why he left to his Church at the Last Supper a visible sacrifice. Through this sacrifice, the "true and unique sacrifice",[181] the sacrifice offered once on the Cross, was to be made present (*repraesentaretur*) and "its memory [was to be] perpetuated until the end of the world, and its salutary power applied for the forgiveness of ... sins",[182] as is consistent with human nature. The sacrifice

---

[176] The Vatican reform of the Missal started the practice of Communion under both species, which today is universally optional. See *SC* 55.

[177] *Apologia Confessionis Augustanae* 26.97 (*BSLK* 376).

[178] Cf. Erwin Iserloh, "Das tridentinische Messopferdekret in seinen Beziehungen zur Kontroverstheologie der Zeit", in *Il Concilio di Trento e la Riforma Tridentina: Atti del convegno storico internazionale: Trento—2–6 Settembre 1963* (Rome: Herder, 1965), 2:401–39; Iserloh, "Messe als Repraesentatio Passionis in der Diskussion des Konzils von Trient während der Sitzungsperiode in Bologna 1547", in *Liturgie: Gestalt und Vollzug*, Festschrift J. Pascher, ed. W. Dürig (Munich: Hueber, 1963), 138–46. For the largely negative Protestant opinion of the Tridentine Decree on the Sacrifice of the Mass, see Kaufmann, *Geschichte der Reformation*, 673. He thinks that in the Decree on the Sacrifice of the Mass the "restorational/Counter-Reformation character" of the council becomes particularly clear.

[179] On the theories of sacrifice advocated at the council, see Pratzner, *Messe und Kreuzesopfer*, 27–52.

[180] Cf. DH 1739.

[181] DH 1738.

[182] DH 1740.

on the Cross is therefore not a particular historical incident that is self-contained. Rather, it is an event of universal significance and scope. In the celebration of the Eucharist, the one sacrifice of Christ becomes sacramentally present, without being repeated.[183] Any separation of Cross and Mass, of sacrifice and Christ's Body and Blood, is rejected. Christ's Body and Blood are Jesus Christ's laying down of his life for us in its sacramental reality.

On the relation between sacrifice on the Cross and Sacrifice of the Mass, the council taught:

> In this divine sacrifice that is celebrated in the Mass, the same Christ who offered himself once in a bloody manner [cf. Heb 9:14, 27f.] on the altar of the Cross is contained and is offered in an unbloody manner.... Therefore ... this sacrifice is truly propitiatory.... For, the victim is one and the same: the same now offers himself through the ministry of priests who then offered himself on the Cross, only the manner of offering is different.[184]

The central statement of the Decree on the Sacrifice of the Mass reaffirmed the sacramental identity of the sacrifice of the Cross and the Sacrifice of the Mass. Unlike the *Roman Catechism* (1566/1567),[185] the council taught only implicitly the identity of the priest who sacrifices. The Sacrifice of the Mass is "truly propitiatory" and therefore more than an "offering of praise and thanksgiving (*sacrificium laudis et gratiarum actionis*) or ... a simple commemoration (*nuda commemoratio*) of the sacrifice accomplished on the Cross".[186] The Sacrifice of the Mass in no way blasphemes or detracts from Christ's sacrifice on the Cross.[187] For what is received in the Mass are the fruits of Christ's single, unique

---

[183] Cf. Ratzinger, "Book Review b" of Wilhelm Averbeck, *Der Opfercharakter des Abendmahls in der neueren evangelischen Theologie*, in *JRCW* 11:246–48.

[184] DH 1743. Hans-Joachim Schulz, *Ökumenische Glaubenseinheit aus eucharistischer Überlieferung*, Konfessionskundliche und kontroverstheologische Studien 39 (Paderborn: Verlag Bonifacius-Druckerei, 1976), who rejects a post-consecratory offering of Christ's Body and Blood, abruptly declares the council's teaching to be "dogmatic secondary tradition" and notes "the Council's departure from the legitimate linguistic usage of the liturgical tradition" (72,78–81).

[185] Cf. *Catechismus ex Decreto Concilii Tridentini*, pt. 2, chap. 4, nos. 76–77.

[186] DH 1753.

[187] Cf. DH 1754.

sacrifice. The prerequisite for the efficacious reception are an "upright heart" and a "true faith". The faithful should therefore approach God "with fear and reverence, with sorrow and repentance".[188]

Masses in honor of saints were defended by the council against attacks with the argument that the Church does celebrate them in honor of the saints, but the sacrifice is offered to God and not to the saints.[189] Likewise, the council defended the Canon of the Mass as consistent with Scripture and apostolic tradition.[190] Masses without people attending or those in which the priest alone communicates must not be condemned as "private and illicit".[191] They should be viewed instead as "truly communal (vere communes)", "because they are celebrated by a public minister of the Church, not for his own good alone, but for all the faithful who belong to the body of Christ."[192] The council expressly wished that the faithful communicate during the celebration of Mass not only spiritually but also sacramentally: "fideles adstantes non solum spirituali affectu, sed sacramentali etiam Eucharistiae perceptione communicarent."[193] With that the council adopted one of the concerns of the Reformation.

The Council of Trent did not only give answers to the questions raised by Luther concerning lay reception from the chalice, the somatic Real Presence, and the sacrificial character of the Mass. It also made statements about the theologically binding character of liturgical orders for the celebration of the sacraments.[194] In its seventh session, on March 3, 1547, the council declared that no one can say that "the traditional and approved rites of the Catholic Church, to which one customarily adheres in administering the sacraments, can without sin be despised or abandoned arbitrarily by the ministers or be changed by any pastor of the Church into new and different ones."[195] In the Doctrine and Canons on Communion dated July 16, 1562, the

---

[188] DH 1743.
[189] Cf. DH 1744, 1755.
[190] Cf. DH 1745, 1756.
[191] DH 1747.
[192] Ibid.
[193] Ibid.
[194] Cf. Winfried Haunerland, "Einheitlichkeit als Weg der Erneuerung: Das Konzil von Trient und die nachtridentinische Reform der Liturgie", in Liturgiereformen: Historische Studien zu einem bleibenden Grundzug des christlichen Gottesdienstes 1, ed. M. Klöckener and B. Kranemann (Münster: Aschendorff, 2002), 437–44.
[195] COD 3:685.

council established that "in the administration of the sacraments—provided their substance is preserved—there has always been in the Church that power to determine or modify what she judged more expedient for the benefit of those receiving the sacraments or for the reverence due to the sacraments themselves—according to the diversity of circumstances, times, and places."[196]

In the *Decree on the Sacrament of the Eucharist* the Corpus Christi procession was defended against Martin Luther's critique.[197] Since he denied any presence of Christ in the sacrament outside of the celebration, he could see nothing but blasphemy in a procession with the Blessed Sacrament. Luther described the Feast of Corpus Christi as the "most harmful feast of the year".[198] In contrast, the council declared "that it was with true religious devotion that the custom was introduced into the Church of God whereby every year, on a special fixed day of festival, this sublime and venerable Sacrament should be hailed with particular veneration and solemnity and carried with reverence and honor in processions through streets and public places."[199]

The same is true for the practice of reserving Communion and bringing it to the sick.[200] The demand made by the Reformers to use the vernacular in the celebration of the Mass was rejected by the council as inappropriate. A general prohibition of the vernacular in the liturgy was not articulated out of consideration for the Eastern Churches.[201] But anyone who maintained that the Mass may be celebrated exclusively (*tantum*) in the vernacular was threatened by the council with anathema.[202] Connected with the rejection of the vernacular was the demand that pastors "explain during the celebration of Masses some of the readings of the Mass and, among other things, give some instruction about the mystery of this most holy sacrifice, especially on Sundays and feast days."[203]

---

[196] DH 1728.

[197] Cf. DH 1656.

[198] Luther, *Table Talk* (May 1532, no. 3147): *WA Tischreden* 3, 192.

[199] DH 1644.

[200] Cf. DH 1645, 1657.

[201] On the discussion at the council about the use of the vernacular in the liturgy, see Theobald Freudenberger, "Die Messliturgie in der Volkssprache im Urteil des Trienter Konzils", in *Reformatio ecclesiae: Beiträge zu kirchlichen Reformbemühungen von der Alten Kirche bis zur Neuzeit,* Festschrift E. Iserloh, ed. R. Bäumer (Paderborn et al.: Schöningh, 1980) 679–98.

[202] Cf. DH 1759.

[203] DH 1749.

Chapter VII

MISSALE ROMANUM

The History of the "Tridentine" Mass

Demands for a reform of the liturgy had already made themselves heard on the eve of the Reformation. Noteworthy in this connection are the Councils of Constance (1414–1418) and Basel (1431–1437), as well as the reform of the Missal in Brixen/Bressanone under Nicholas of Cusa. The two Camaldolese monks Paolo Giustiniani (1476–1528) and Vincenzo Quirini (d. 1514) insisted in their *Libellus ad Leonem X* (1513) not only on an edition of Sacred Scripture in the vernacular, but also on a greater use of the vernacular in the liturgy.[1] For Solemn High Mass (*summum officium*) celebrated with deacon and subdeacon, vernacular chants (*Leisen* and *Rufe*) at the Introit had already developed in the twelfth and thirteenth centuries, along with tropes in the Sequences and a chant before and after the sermon. Of course clerics urged limiting these vernacular chants, which were not always very demanding musically or textually.[2]

As a result of increased catechetical efforts to educate the faithful, a profusion of vernacular treatises on the Mass were written starting in the fourteenth century. One of the earliest treatises is preserved in an Anglo-Norman manuscript of unknown origin that was composed in the early fourteenth century.[3] In it the laity receive guidance about

---

[1] For an analysis of the *Libellus* addressed to the Medici Pope Leo X, see Albert Gerhards and Benedikt Kranemann, *Einführung in die Liturgiewissenschaft*, 2nd ed. (Darmstadt: Wissenschaftliche Buchgesellschaft, 2008), 88f.

[2] Cf. Philipp Harnoncourt, *Gesamtkirchliche und teilkirchliche Liturgie: Studien zum liturgischen Heiligenkalender und zum Gesang im Gottesdienst unter besonderer Berücksichtigung des deutschen Sprachgebiets* (Freiburg: Herder, 1974), 294–305.

[3] Cf. National Library of France (Paris), MS franc. 13442.

"what you should do and think during each part of the Mass". Texts and illustrations comment on the meaning of the individual actions in a well-known allegory of the Mass. Moreover, the postures and gestures of the faithful and their prayers at the individual parts of the Mass are explained. The objective of these vernacular treatises on the Mass was to make it possible for the laity to participate more actively in the celebration of the Latin Mass. The first complete German exposition of the Mass was published around 1480.[4] The author was probably a priest of the diocese of Augsburg.

The Council of Trent was the first ecumenical council to commission a reform of the liturgical books. Above all, because of the Reformers' criticism of the Roman Mass, a reform of the Missal had become necessary.[5] The foundation for the reform of the Missal was the newly revised edition of the *Ordo missae secundum consuetudinem Sanctae Romanae Ecclesiae* (1502), which the Strasbourg theologian Johannes Burckard (d. 1506), Master of Ceremonies for the Roman Curia from 1483 to 1503, had compiled in the year 1498.[6] In order to understand the significance of the *Missale Romanum*, it is necessary to examine first the origin of the medieval Sacramentaries and their development into the complete Missal.

A. On the Way to the Standard Missal

Numerous Sacramentaries were compiled in Europe from the ninth to the thirteenth century. These are liturgical books that contain the fixed and variable prayers for the celebrant.[7] The Sacramentary in book format developed from the *libelli* (loose-leaf collections), which go back to the fifth century. The *Sacramentarium Leonianum* contains

---

[4] Franz Rudolf Reichert, *Die älteste deutsche Gesamtauslegung der Messe* (ca. 1480; Münster: Aschendorff, 1967).

[5] Cf. Josef Andreas Jungmann, *The Mass of the Roman Rite*, trans. Francis A. Brunner, C.Ss.R., 2 vols. (New York: Benziger Brothers, 1951, 1955), 1:132–35.

[6] Cf. Burckard, *Ordo Missae secundum consuetudinem Sanctae Romanae Ecclesiae* (1502/1904), 121–78. Burckard's "Order of the Mass", the second edition of which in 1502 was reprinted many times, became the most important source for the *Roman Missal*.

[7] On research into sacramentaries, cf. Jean Deshusses, "Les sacramentaires: État actuel de la recherche", *Archiv für Liturgiewissenschaft* 24 (1982): 19–46; Marcel Metzger, *Les sacramentaires*, Typologie des sources du moyen âge occidental 70 (Turnhout: Brepols, 1994).

texts that are ascribed to Pope Leo the Great. Today it is preferably referred to as the *Sacramentarium Veronense* after Verona, the place where it has been preserved. In the strict sense, it is of course not a Sacramentary, since many forms of the Mass are missing, for instance, for Christmas and Easter. The *Veronese Sacramentary* was a private rather than an official collection of Mass texts. The forms of the *Sacramentarium Veronense* refer, among other things, to the Sack of Rome (455) and the episcopal consecration of Pope Vigilius (537). The *Sacramentarium*, therefore, presumably reflects the time between 440 and around 540.

Unlike the *Sacramentarium Veronense*, the *Sacramentarium Gelasianum*[8] contains forms for the Christmas season and Eastertide, for feasts of saints, Sundays in Advent, the Sundays after Pentecost, and various votive Masses. Since the ninth century, the Sacramentary has been ascribed to Pope Gelasius I (492–496).[9] He cannot have been the author, though, since the Sacramentary also contains texts by Pope Vigilius I (537–550). In the *Gelasian Sacramentary*, moreover, elements of the early-medieval Gallican liturgy can be found. The Sacramentary has been preserved in only one copy from the mid-eighth century. This version is called the "Frankish Gelasianum" or "Young Gelasian" Sacramentary as opposed to the "Old Gelasian". The Sacramentary in question is for the priestly liturgy that presumably was introduced in the mid-seventh century in the Roman titular churches. While the *Sacramentarium Gelasianum* is intended for the celebration of Mass by a priest, the *Sacramentarium Gregorianum* contains prayers provided for the papal liturgy. The first versions may go back to the time of Pope Gregory the Great.

Besides the Sacramentaries, other liturgical books were used, for example, the *Collectare* with prayers and short readings for the Liturgy of the Hours along with blessings and prayers for sacramental celebrations. Liturgical books were compiled for the Scripture readings (*Capitulare lectionum; Capitulare evangeliorum*) and for chant. The oldest lists of Epistles (*Würzburger Epistelliste*) and the oldest *Capitulare evangeliorum* (book of Gospel readings) go back to the seventh

---

[8] Only one manuscript is extant, namely, the *Codex Reginensis* 316 of the Vatican Library from the eighth century, presumably from St. Denis.

[9] Cf. *Liber Pontificalis*, 1:255D.

century.[10] The ordinary and proper chants appointed for the cele-bration of the Mass were performed by a cantor and a schola. After the reading, the cantor sang the Gradual from the *Cantatorium* or the *Graduale*, and then the Alleluia or the Tract before the Gospel. From the *Antiphonarium* or the *Antiphonale*, the parts of the *Proprium* were sung by the schola: *Introitus* (entrance chant), *Offertorium* (chant at the presentation of the gifts), and *Communio* (chant at Com-munion).[11] Later, the two books were combined under the name of *Graduale*. The designation *Antiphonarium* or *Antiphonale* became widely accepted for the collection of antiphons for the Liturgy of the Hours.

The chants contained in the *Graduale* and *Antiphonarium* are called "Gregorian" (*gregoriana carmina/cantus romanus*) because they are traced back to the influence of Pope Gregory the Great. This refer-ence first appears in writing in the ninth century in the Prologue of the Monza *Cantatorium*. It reads: "Gregorius praesul ... composuit hunc libellum musicae artis scolae cantorum."[12] Of course no mel-odies have been handed down to us from the time of Gregory the Great. The oldest liturgical books for the chants contain only texts of prayers, while the chant was handed down *viva voce* through liturgical practice. The "notation" of neums, which gave only accentuations but not the exact sequence of notes, did not appear until the tenth century. The best-known and oldest systems of neums are those of Sankt Gallen and Metz.[13] The earliest example of a set choral Mass is the *Missa de Angelis* (thirteenth century).

Ever since Innocent III, the Roman-Frankish Mass, as it was cel-ebrated in the Roman Curia, has become the model for the whole Universal Church. A not insignificant factor in that trend was the

---

[10] Cf. Aimé-Georges Martimort, *Les lectures liturgiques et leurs livres*, Typologie des sources du moyen âge occidental 64 (Turnhout: Brepols, 1992).

[11] Cf. Reinhard Messner, *Einführung in die Liturgiewissenschaft*, 2nd ed. (Paderborn: Schöningh, 2009), 43–48.

[12] "Gregory the Prelate ... composed this little book of musical art for the schola of sing-ers." Cited from Kenneth Levy, *Gregorian Chant and the Carolingians* (Princeton, N.J.: Prince-ton University Press, 1998), 141f.

[13] Cf. Godehard Joppich, "Christologie im Gregorianischen Choral", in *Christologie der Liturgie: Der Gottesdienst der Kirche—Christusbekenntnis und Sinaibund*, ed. K. Richter, Quaestiones disputatae 159 (Freiburg: Herder, 1995), 271–81. In the *Graduale Triplex* (1979), published by the Abbey of Solesmes, they are indicated together with the later square notation.

swift-growing Franciscan Order, which adopted the Order of celebrating Mass *secundum usum Romanae Curiae*. In the thirteenth century,
it was accepted by the General Chapter of the Franciscans (*Indutus
planeta*, 1243) together with the "Breviary of the Roman Church",
the *Ordo* for solemn conventual Mass, and the *Ordo* for silent Mass
composed by the Franciscan General Haimo of Faversham/Kent
(d. 1243). Through the Franciscans, the Roman Rite spread throughout the known world at the time.[14] The particular requirements
of the "private Mass", but especially pastoral reasons, such as the
growing number of parishes, led to the "complete Missal" containing all prayers, readings, and chants for the celebration of Mass. A
prominent example of this type of book is the *Missale Beneventano*
(ca. 1100). The foundation of the first printed Missal (*Missale comple-
tum secundum consuetudinem Romanae Curiae*) was the Missal compiled
in 1220 for the liturgy of the private papal chapel. As early as the
thirteenth century, the *Ordo* for silent Mass developed in the Roman
Curia and also among the Augustinians and the Franciscans; the form
composed by Haimo of Faversham was predominant until the fifteenth century. The rubrics for silent Mass since the fifteenth century
have been based on Burckard's Order of Mass.

During the first session of the Council of Trent (1545–1548),
Bishop Tommaso Campeggi (1483–1564) pleaded for the publication of a standard Missal purged of theologically dubious Sequences.
He also spoke in favor of presenting the readings of the Mass in
the vernacular.[15] The ideas about reforming the Missal that existed
during the Council of Trent can be inferred from a document about
abuses in celebrating Mass. The document was drawn up by a commission headed by Archbishop Ludovico Beccadelli of Ragusa
(1501–1572).[16] The commission compiled a text that mentions a
series of abuses (*abusus missae*) connected with the celebration of the
Mass. Prefaces and Sequences with legendary contents should be

---

[14] Cf. Stephen J. P. van Dijk, *Sources of the Modern Roman Liturgy: The Ordinals from Haymo
of Faversham and Related Documents (1243–1307)*, 2 vols. Studia et Documenta Franciscana
(Leiden: Brill, 1963).

[15] Cf. *Concilium Tridentinum: Diariorum, Actorum, Epistularum, Tractatuum Nova Collectio*, ed.
Societas Goerresiana promovendis inter Germanos catholicos Litterarum Studiis (Freiburg:
Herder, 1901–2001; hereafter cited as *CT*), 1:503.

[16] Cf. *CT* 8:916–21.

omitted as well as Arian tropes (interpolations) in the *Gloria*.[17] The examination of individual expressions and ritual elements is encouraged: for example the designation *immaculata hostia* and *calix salutaris* for the Eucharistic gifts already in the Offertory,[18] the Offertory of the Requiem Mass, and individual votive Masses and series of Masses. One of the demands with regard to external order is that the liturgical vestments of the priest and servers be clean and neat. In response to the criticism of the Reformer, the document pleads for a significant reduction in the number of Masses, for a prohibition of Masses in which fewer than two faithful are present, and the prohibition of silent Masses that are celebrated in parallel with a sung Mass. Priests should celebrate only once a day and accept only one stipend for each Mass.

At the request of the legates to the council, the document was revised, abridged, and summarized into a *Compendium*.[19] A wish is expressed at the beginning of the *Compendium* that, while preserving the legitimate traditions of local Churches, a Missal corresponding to the Roman tradition should be made available, with standard ceremonies, rubrics, and texts according to the usage and the ancient custom of the Roman Church. Much of the material from the *Compendium* was incorporated into the *Decretum de observandis et evitandis in celebratione missarum* (September 17, 1562), but most of the demands were disregarded.[20] The decree obliges bishops to take care that the Sacrifice of the Mass be celebrated as piously and devoutly as possible. The bishops are urged "to forbid and remove everything that entails greed and idolatry, irreverence—which can scarcely be distinguished from unbelief—or superstition, the false mimic of true piety".[21] The council also obliges local bishops to take measures against superstitious practices and departures from the liturgical order and to admonish the faithful to participate in Holy Mass at least on "Sundays and major feast days".[22] The council also opposes the liturgical use of

---

[17] Cf. *CT* 8:916–21.

[18] Cf. *CT* 8:917.

[19] Cf. *CT* 8:921–24.

[20] "Decree on things to be observed and avoided in the celebration of Masses". Cf. *CT* 8:962f.

[21] *COD* 3:736.

[22] *COD* 3:737.

music that contains objectionable and impure elements (*lascivum aut impurum*) as well as "empty, profane chatter, running around, noise and shouting, so that the house of God really appears to be a house of prayer and can be called such".[23] Since the council did not consider itself capable of carrying out a reform of the Missal by itself, it decided in its concluding session on December 4, 1563, to entrust the reform to the pope.[24]

One group within the commission that Pope Pius IV formed immediately after the Council of Trent for the reform of the Breviary and the Missal and that was expanded by his successor, Pius V, voted in favor of the standard Missal (1564). Next came a coordination of Missal and Breviary, for which the commission was likewise competent (calendar, prayer of the day, Gospel reading). Then it undertook a reduction of the feasts of saints and votive Masses, so that the importance of the Sundays and feast days of the Church year and of the liturgical seasons might again become prominent. Of the numerous votive Masses, only the ones in honor of the Holy Cross, the Holy Spirit, the Holy Trinity, and the Mother of God were to be retained. Likewise, all newer Prefaces and Sequences were omitted. Of the immense number of Prefaces, eleven widely approved Prefaces were selected.[25] At the same time, the commission pursued a clearer version of the rubrics and provided for the continuous use of the Vulgate for the scriptural texts.[26] The Offertory procession of the faithful that was still called for by Johannes Burckard was not considered, probably out of fear of abuse by profiteering priests. The Church year, which was overrun with the feasts of saints, was to be pruned back to a large extent. Efforts to reform the field of sacred music were rejected as well as attacks on polyphony, so that, starting with Giovanni Pierluigi da Palestrina (d. 1594), the masterpieces of modern Church music could develop.[27]

[23] Cf. *COD* 3:736.

[24] Cf. *COD* 3:797.

[25] The reduction of the Sequences may also have had something to do with the fact that they are not genuinely Roman. Cf. Winfried Haunerland, "Einheitlichkeit als Weg der Erneuerung: Das Konzil von Trient und die nachtridentinische Reform der Liturgie", in *Liturgiereformen: Historische Studien zu einem bleibenden Grundzug des christlichen Gottesdienstes*, ed. M. Klöckener and B. Kranemann (Münster: Aschendorff, 2002), 1:447.

[26] Cf. Hans Bernhard Meyer, *Eucharistie, Geschichte, Theologie, Pastoral*, Handbuch der Liturgiewissenschaft 4 (Regensburg: Pustet, 1989), 261.

[27] Cf. Jungmann, *Mass of the Roman Rite*, 1:137–38.

B. *The* Missale Romanum *(1570)*

The liturgical reform following the Council of Trent was the first liturgical reform initiated by the central authority of the Church.[28] The *Missale Romanum ex decreto ss. Tridentini restitutum, Pii V. Pont. Max. iussu editum* (Roman Missal restored by decree of the Sacred Council of Trent and published at the command of the Supreme Pontiff Pius V) was introduced for obligatory use by the Bull of Promulgation *Quo primum* (July 14, 1570) wherever there was no particular liturgical tradition at least two hundred years old, as was the case, for example, in Milan, Toledo, or in the Dominican Order. According to the bull of promulgation, the goal of the reform was to "restore the Missal according to the venerable norm and the right of the holy Fathers of the Church" (*ad pristinam sanctorum Patrum normam ac ritum restituerunt*).[29] As a matter of fact, the eleventh-century liturgy of the city of Rome under Pope Gregory VII was the leading influence.

The most drastic action was taken with the changeable parts of the Mass. Of the Sequences, only those of Easter, Pentecost, and Corpus Christi were retained, along with the *Dies irae* of the Requiem Mass.[30] In 1727, the *Stabat mater* was added *ad libitum* as the fifth Sequence for the Memorial of Our Lady of Sorrows. The request made by a few individuals for a revision of the *Canon Romanus*[31] was not granted. The suggestion by several bishops for the Canon to be recited aloud was not adopted, nor was the demand for greater use of the vernacular in the celebration of the Mass,[32] which the Viennese Bishop Friedrich Nausea (d. 1552) had suggested in his opinion on reform at the Council of Trent.[33] After the council, the dean of the collegiate church in Bautzen, Johann Leisentritt (1527–1586), who had been influenced by the Reformation, spoke up along with others

[28] Cf. Haunerland, *Einheitlichkeit als Weg der Erneuerung*, 436.

[29] Cf. Martin Klöckener, "Die Bulle 'Quo primum' Papst Pius V. vom 14. Juli 1570: Zur Promulgation des nachtridentinischen Missale Romanum: Liturgische Quellentexte lateinisch-deutsch", *Archiv für Liturgiewissenschaft* 48 (2008): 44f.

[30] Many missals contained a hundred or more Prefaces, in some cases riddled with superstitious notions.

[31] Cf. *CT* 12:420f.

[32] Cf. Leisentritt, *Kurtze Fragstücke von dem hochwirdigen Sacrament des Altars unter Gestalt Brodts und Weins* (1578).

[33] Bishop Nausea spoke up also for a revision of the Roman Canon (*CT* 12:420f.), the administration of the chalice to the laity, and the abolition of celibacy.

for the use of the vernacular in the Mass. Since the Reformation, however, Mass in the vernacular had become a denominational distinguishing feature.

Following the pattern of Burckard's *Ordo Missae*, the *Missale Romanum* was prefaced with the general rubrics and the *ritus servandus* [rite to be observed] that governs the *missa sine cantu et sine ministris* [Mass without singing and without deacon and subdeacon]. Besides the *missa solitaria* of the priest, various supplements are provided in the *Missale Romanum* for the *missa sollemnis* [Solemn Mass]. Burckard's rite of the Mass may have been selected primarily for practical reasons, since it contains everything that a celebrant must know in celebrating the Mass. It is not true, however, that "the decision in favor of 'silent Mass' celebrated by the individual priest as the basic form of the post-Tridentine renewed Roman liturgy of the Mass"[34] was connected with Burckard's rite of the Mass. For the question about the basic ritual form of the Mass in the 1570 *Missale*, not only the *Ritus servandus* but the whole Missal should be considered; for example, it contains notes for the intonation of the *Gloria* and the *Credo*, for the Prefaces, and so on. The basic form of the Mass is, starting from the Missal, not the *missa solitaria*, but rather the *missa cantata*, or Solemn High Mass, which is celebrated with deacon and subdeacon. Finally, the Roman Mass as a hierarchically articulated liturgy must be thought of in terms of the Pontifical Mass that is celebrated by a bishop.[35]

The 1570 Missal also takes for granted the presence of the faithful at the celebration of Mass, for instance in the instruction that the priest shows the Host and the chalice to the people (*ostendit populo*) after the words of institution and at the end of Mass blesses the people (*deinde benedicit populo*).[36] In the case of silent Mass, of course, the people scarcely participated.[37] Yet the *Ritus servandus* foresees the participation of the faithful during the *Prayers at the foot of the altar*, the *Kyrie*, the

---

[34] Haunerland, *Einheitlichkeit als Weg der Erneuerung*, 447.

[35] Cf. Sven Conrad, F.S.S.P., "Renewal of the Liturgy in the Spirit of Tradition: Perspectives with a View towards the Liturgical Development of the West", *Antiphon* 14/1 (2010): 119–21; Michael Fiedrowicz, *Die überlieferte Messe: Geschichte, Gestalt, Theologie* (Mühlheim an der Mosel: Carthusianus Verlag, 2011), 69–74.

[36] Cf. Haunerland, *Einheitlichkeit als Weg der Erneuerung*, 447.

[37] Cf. ibid.

Orate fratres, the kiss of the *Pax*-Board at Communion, and also when the wine for the ablutions is presented.[38] The post-Tridentine reform did not succeed, however, in reviving the participation of the faithful in the liturgy of the Mass. Although the idea that the faithful offer the Eucharistic Sacrifice together with the priest is found already in the school of Pierre Cardinal de Bérulle (1575–1629), it had little influence. The French Oratory founded by Bérulle produced important explanations of the Mass. The Oratory also distributed guides describing how the faithful should unite themselves in prayer with the priest who offers the Eucharistic Sacrifice.[39]

Burckard's *Ordo* still provided regulations for the so-called *missa sicca* and the *missa bifaciata*.[40] The *missa sicca* (dry Mass) is a celebration according to the form of Mass without the Eucharistic part from the Offertory to the concluding doxology of the Canon. Like the Divine Liturgy of the Presanctified Gifts in the Eastern Churches, the *missa sicca* has its origins in an extended Communion service especially for the sick and the dying, which can be traced back to the seventh century. The *missa sicca* was a common practice above all in the period from the twelfth to the sixteenth century. It replaced the house Masses for the sick and the dying, which had meanwhile been forbidden, but was also celebrated as a substitute for several Masses on the same day.[41] The *missa bifaciata* (or *trifaciata, quadrifaciata*) derives from the fact that an increasing number of priests celebrated several times a day, for pastoral reasons—for example, in the case of pilgrimage Masses, occasional Masses, and votive Masses—or out of personal piety or for financial reasons (stipends). Since bination or trination [celebrating Mass twice or three times a day] was restricted and finally forbidden by Pope Innocent III in 1206, priests began instead to repeat the Liturgy of the Word twice or as many as four times, so as then to continue with the offering of the gifts, the Preface and the Canon. After the Liturgy of the Eucharist, the *Postcommunio* was repeated also. Through this dubious practice, a priest

---

[38] Cf. Meyer, *Eucharistie*, 293.

[39] Jungmann, *Mass of the Roman Rite*, 1:142–43.

[40] Cf. Adolph Franz, *Die Messe im deutschen Mittelalter: Beiträge zur Geschichte der Liturgie und des religiösen Volkslebens* (Darmstadt: Wissenschaftliche Buchgesellschaft, 1963), 73–86.

[41] Cf. Burckard, *Ordo Missae secundum consuetudinem Sanctae Romanae Ecclesiae* (1502/1904) (Legg ed., 173).

supposedly could satisfy several intentions and Mass obligations. The *Missale Romanum* (1570) no longer provides for the *missa sicca* and the *missa bifaciata*.

In the bull promulgating the introduction of the *Missale Romanum*, Pope Pius V ordered that "nothing must be added to Our recently published Missal, nothing omitted from it, nor anything whatsoever be changed within it."[42] Other liturgical books contain similar statements, for example, the *Breviarum Romanum* (1568), the *Pontificale Romanum* (1596), the *Caeremoniale episcoporum* (1600) of Clement VIII (1592–1605), and the *Rituale Romanum* (1614) of Paul V (1605–1621). In the course of the Vatican reform of the liturgy, the "principle of unchangeableness" was cited as an objection to the Missal of Paul VI. Again and again since the Council of Trent, however, there have been changes in the liturgical books of the Church, even though these were not as fundamental as those after Vatican Council II.[43]

Without the invention of book printing, the 1570 *Missale Romanum* could not have gained universal acceptance as the standard Missal of the Roman Catholic Church. Book printing also made it possible to provide educated Catholics with prayer books, which also contained explanations of the Mass. The spread of the *Missale Romanum* was geographically limited at first to Italy, Portugal, the Netherlands, Belgium, Austria, Hungary, and Poland, as well as the new Orders (Jesuits, and so on). In Germany, the *Missale Romanum* was in some cases not introduced until the period between the seventeenth and the nineteenth century (Münster, Trier); Cologne kept its own tradition until 1865. Of course, new editions of the Missal were continually conformed to the *Missale Romanum*. Even in Spain, the Roman Missal was introduced, with the exception of the Mozarabic Churches (Salamanca, Toledo, and Braga).

Via Portugal and Spain, the Roman Missal arrived in North and Latin America and also in the Far East. For a short time, a Chinese translation of the Roman Missal was approved by Pope Paul V. In the debate over the Roman Rite, it was forbidden and was never put to use. Despite the fact that the Council of Trent recognized

---

[42] Klöckener, "Die Bulle 'Quo primum' ", 46f.

[43] Cf. Pierre Jounel, "L'évolution du Missel Romain de Pie IX à Jean XXIII (1846–1962)", *Notitiae* 14 (1978): 246–58.

particular liturgical traditions that were more than two hundred years old, the 1570 *Missale Romanum* led to a comprehensive unification of the celebration of the Mass in the Catholic Church. In some cases, the Missal was introduced even in dioceses with a very old liturgical tradition.[44] Contributing to the unification of the liturgy of the Mass, along with the spread of book printing, was the *Congregatio pro Sacris Ritibus ac Caeremoniis*, which Pope Sixtus V (1585–1590) had established with the Constitution *Immensa aeterni Dei* (January 22, 1588).[45] The task of the Congregation for Sacred Rites and Ceremonies was to supervise the observance of liturgical regulations and the acceptance of the Roman liturgical books.[46]

C. New Editions and Beginnings of Reform

The new edition of the Roman Missal during the reign of Pope Clement VIII (1604) led, among other things, to a new regulation of the concluding blessing, the multiplication of feast days, and also corrections and additions to the rubrics.[47] Another new edition was issued in 1634 by Urban VIII (1623–1644). Besides changes in the verbal form of the rubrics, the hymns in particular were revised for the sake of metrical smoothness and a classical Latin style. Unapproved votive Masses were forbidden. Alexander VII (1655–1667) forbade all translations of the Roman Missal under pain of excommunication (1661). Presumably the pope saw in translations a slippery slope leading to the abolition of the Latin language, which surrounds the liturgy with the "veil of mystery".[48,49] The prohibition of Alexander VII stopped the practice, which went back to the fourteenth

---

[44] Cf. Haunerland, *Einheitlichkeit als Weg der Erneuerung*, 459.

[45] Along with it fourteen other congregations were established.

[46] Cf. Frederick R. McManus, *The Congregation of Rites*, Canon Law Studies 352 (Washington, D.C.: Catholic University of America Press, 1954). With the Apostolic Constitution *Sacra Rituum Congregatio* (1969), Pope Paul VI dissolved the Congregation for Rites and divided its duties between two new congregations, namely, the Sacred Congregation for the Causes of the Saints and the Sacred Congregation for Divine Worship. Today, the latter bears the name "Sacred Congregation for Divine Worship and the Discipline of the Sacraments".

[47] Cf. Fiedrowicz, *Überlieferte Messe*, 44.

[48] Jungmann, *Mass of the Roman Rite*, 1:144.

[49] Cf. ibid., 1:143–44.

century, of explaining the *Ordo Missae* or the whole Mass to the faithful through translations. The idea that the priest entered into the sanctuary with the Canon was not extended to the whole celebration of the Mass. Yet as early as the seventeenth and eighteenth century, priests in many places started reciting the *Canon Romanus* aloud in Latin, while the people responded *Amen* to the individual prayers.[50] The Missal of Meaux (1709) is an example of this practice.[51]

By the reign of Benedict XV (1914–1920), the 1634 *Missale Romanum* had been reprinted several times. Under Clement XIII (1758–1769), the Preface of the Holy Trinity was introduced instead of the *Praefatio communis* (1759). In the Baroque period, Gregorian chant diminished in importance. A great number of new works of Church music were created, which in some cases departed from the corpus of texts that make up the Ordinary of the Mass and acquired a sort of autonomy with regard to the liturgy of the Mass. As early as 1643, the Congregation for Rites demanded, therefore, that Church music must not be an end in itself but, rather, must serve the dignity of the Mass being celebrated. In German-speaking lands, the practice of chanting parts of the Mass in German, which goes back to the High Middle Ages, developed further after the model of the Reformation. Vernacular chants were sung at the Creed, the Offertory, the Elevation, the Our Father, and Communion, and after the final blessing. They were included in the diocesan hymnals published by the bishops in order to meet the need of the faithful to sing hymns and not just to pray the Rosary or meditate on Christ's Passion during Mass. One of the most widely circulated hymnals was the *Cantuale* of Mainz (1605). The Paderborn hymnal (1726) contains German chants also for the *Gloria*, *Sanctus*, and *Agnus Dei*, while the Speyer hymnal (1770) offers a sung Mass for all the parts of the Ordinary.[52] Yet even during the reign of Benedict XIV (1740–1758), there were attempts to revive Gregorian chant. For a long time, however, Gregorian chant had very limited opportunities. Only the educated among the faithful could be reached by the prayer books with the explanations of

[50] Cf. Prosper Guéranger, *Institutions liturgiques*, 2nd ed. (Paris: Société générale de librairie catholique, 1878), 180–83.

[51] Cf. Meyer, *Eucharistie*, 271.

[52] Cf. Jungmann, *Mass of the Roman Rite*, 1:155.

the Mass. For the majority of the faithful, the vernacular hymn offered the only opportunity for more active participation.

Between the seventeenth and the nineteenth century, the Roman liturgy in France was increasingly replaced by the neo-Gallican liturgy. The dominion of reason demanded by the Enlightenment in all matters of faith increasingly led in the area of liturgy to the demand for comprehensibility and simplicity. The Diocesan Synod of Pistoia (September 18–28, 1786) was to become a synonym for an illuminist and at the same time anti-Roman reform.[53] The synod was convoked by the Jansenist-leaning Bishop Scipione de' Ricci of Pistoia-Prato (1741–1810), who used the vernacular in the liturgy. The synod was under the protectorate of the Tuscan Grand Duke Leopold, the later Emperor Leopold II (1747–1792), who composed a memorandum for the synod. The Josephinist reforms in Austria provided a model for the Synod of Pistoia. The synod spoke in favor of a national council as an expression of a national Church largely independent of Rome. It argued that since the Church is a purely spiritual entity, it has no authority in the secular realm. The synod demanded the abolition of all Oratories and Orders, except for the Benedictine Order.

The goal of the synod's program of liturgical reform was to give to the people suitable means "of uniting its voice with the whole Church".[54] The Decree on the Eucharist speaks about the liturgy as "an act common to the priest and the people".[55] From this principle, the synod deduces the introduction of the vernacular in the liturgy, but, given the decisions of the Council of Trent, it does not demand it explicitly. It limits itself to the demand for liturgical books that contain the Order of Mass in the vernacular so that the faithful can help to celebrate. The main argument in favor of introducing the vernacular was 1 Corinthians 14:16–17: "If you bless with the spirit, how can any one in the position of an outsider say

---

[53] The Decrees of the Synod, in *Sacrorum conciliorum nova et amplissima collectio*, ed. G. D. Mansi (Florence and Venice, 1759–1827; Paris: Hubert Welter, 1899–1927; hereafter cited as Mansi), 38:1011–86, were published together with a Pastoral Letter by Bishop de' Ricci and endorsed by the Grand Dukes of Tuscany. In 1791, de' Ricci resigned from his episcopacy and settled in Florence as a private individual after Leopold II withdrew his support.

[54] Synod of Pistoia, *Decree on Prayer*, 24 (Mansi, 38:1076).

[55] Synod of Pistoia, *Decree on the Eucharist*, 2 (Mansi, 38:1036).

the 'Amen' to your thanksgiving when he does not know what you are saying? For you may give thanks well enough, but the other man is not edified."

For the Synod of Pistoia, one logical consequence of the participation of the faithful in the liturgy is Holy Communion for the faithful as part of the celebration of Mass. The connection between the Sacrifice of the Mass and Communion should be reinforced by distributing at Communion Hosts that were consecrated at the Mass during which Communion is received.[56] In every church, there should be only one altar, on which no images or relics at all should stand. The synod rejects images as objects of religious veneration; they are recognized only with regard to their pedagogical function for illiterates. The synod demands the demolition of all side and secondary altars as well as a simple furnishing of all churches. At the same time, it opposes an exuberant practice of pilgrimages and processions, Way of the Cross devotions, and the veneration of the Sacred Heart of Jesus.[57] Moreover, it carefully distances itself from the doctrine of transubstantiation, which does belong to Church doctrine but should not be considered in catechesis.[58] In the Constitution *Auctorem fidei* (1794) directed against the Synod of Pistoia, Pope Pius VI reaffirmed the dogma of the substantial presence of Christ under the species of bread and wine.[59]

In the aftermath of the Synod of Pistoia, an assembly of Tuscan bishops was held in Florence from April 23 to June 5, 1787, to prepare a national council. Yet the attempt to make the reform program of the Synod of Pistoia binding for all Tuscany failed. By a large majority, the assembly of bishops opposed the introduction of the vernacular in the celebration of the sacraments and also the demand that parts of the Mass be recited aloud. A translation of the *Rituale Romanum* for the personal use of the faithful, on the other hand, was deemed appropriate.[60] All in all, during the Enlightenment era, singing by the people in church was systematically promoted. In the

---

[56] Cf. ibid., 6 (Mansi, 38:1040).

[57] Cf. Synod of Pistoia, *Decree on Prayer*, 10–11 (Mansi, 38:1071–72).

[58] Cf. Synod of Pistoia, *Decree on the Eucharist*, 2 (Mansi, 38:1036).

[59] Cf. DH 2629.

[60] Cf. Albert Gerhards, "Die Synode von Pistoia 1786 und ihre Reform des Gottesdienstes", in vol. 1 of *Liturgiereformen*, ed. M. Klöckener and B. Kranemann (Münster: Aschendorff, 2002), 504f.

process, the German sung Masses were combined both with silent Mass and with Solemn High Mass. In the opinion of Josef Andreas Jungmann, "in the German *Singmesse* a form of celebrating the Mass had been found that was both popular and dignified."[61]

One of the most influential Enlightenment-era liturgists was the Church historian Vitus Anton Winter (1754–1814). Winter regarded the primary objective of divine worship as religious-moral enlightenment and betterment of the heart.[62] Winter's program of reforming the Catholic liturgy "in an up-to-date way" served this objective.[63] In it, Winter demanded that Mass be celebrated entirely in the German language, with all parts of it being prayed aloud. Winter's "forms for new Masses" did start with the Roman Missal, but they also set out to make incisive changes: the *Gloria* and the *Agnus Dei* with modified texts were declared to be optional parts of the Mass. The Preface to the Canon was dropped, the Offertory prayers (including the *Oratio super oblata*) were replaced by new prayers. For Johann Michael Sailer (1751–1832), that went too far. In his speech in memory of Winter, Sailer said that Winter had paid his tribute to the spirit of the age, which was trying to replace religion with morality.[64]

Sailer understood the liturgy as a holistic, corporeal, and spiritual expression, the "total expression of religion".[65] The "basic mother

[61] Jungmann, *Mass of the Roman Rite*, 1:156. Individual demands of the Synod of Pistoia were taken up by the liturgical movement and were included in the Constitution on the Liturgy of the Second Vatican Council. Thus, the council recommends that "the faithful, after the priest's communion, receive the Lord's body from the same sacrifice" (*SC* 55). Moreover, the council intends that "the rites should be distinguished by a noble simplicity; they should be short, clear, and unencumbered by useless repetitions" (*SC* 34). As we will see later, however, Vatican Council II did not adopt the demand for a liturgy celebrated entirely in the vernacular.

[62] Cf. Vitus Anton Winter, *Versuche zur Verbesserung der Katholischen Liturgie: Erster Versuch: Prüfung des Wertes und Unwertes unserer liturgischen Bücher* (Munich, 1804); Winter, *Liturgie, was sie sein soll, unter Hinblick auf das, was sie im Christenthum ist, oder Theorie der öffentlichen Gottesverehrung* (Munich: Lindauer, 1809). Cf. Josef Steiner, *Liturgiereform in der Aufklärungszeit: Eine Darstellung am Beispiel Vitus Anton Winters*, Freiburger theologische Studien 100 (Freiburg: Herder, 1976).

[63] Cf. Vitus Anton Winter, *Erstes deutsches kritisches Messbuch* (Munich: Lindauer, 1810).

[64] Cf. Johann Michael Sailer, "Rede zum Andenken an Vitus Anton Winter, Professor und Stadtpfarrer bei St. Jodok in Landshut" (1814), in *Sämtliche Werke unter Anleitung des Verfassers*, ed. J. Widmer (Sulzbach: Seidel, 1830–1841), 38:145.

[65] Johann Michael Sailer, *Neue Beyträge zur Bildung des Geistlichen*, vol. 2 (Munich: Lentner, 1811), 251. On Sailer's reform program, cf. Manfred Probst, *Gottesdienst in Geist und Wahrheit: Die liturgischen Ansichten und Bestrebungen Johann Michael Sailers (1751–1832)*, Studien zur Pastoralliturgie 2 (Regensburg: Pustet, 1976).

tongue of all divine worship"[66] was, in Sailer's view, a liturgical ritual consisting of signs, gestures, actions, and words. Therefore Sailer was not inclined to overestimate the value of the vernacular in the liturgy like many of his contemporaries, even though he did not reject it.[67] The decisive thing in the liturgy, though, was not intellectual understanding: "I say: nothing is accomplished yet with regard to the liturgy by making sure that the people can understand the words of the priest."[68] Sailer considered well-educated priests more important: "Therefore, whoever wants to reform public divine worship should start by training enlightened, godly priests."[69] "If you put a German Missal in front of an unspiritual man at the altar instead of a Latin one, and tell him to recite his Mass from it in German, he will now be a scandal to *the people who understand what he says*, whereas before, when he recited the Latin Mass just as lifelessly, he was unable to disturb the people's devotion with the sound that they did not understand."[70]

The Romantic era led to the revival of Gregorian chant and classical polyphonic singing. In this regard, we should mention Prosper Guéranger above all. Guéranger, the first Abbot of the Benedictine Abbey of Solesmes that he refounded (1833), was not the Ultramontane restorationist that he is often made out to be. Guéranger by no means looked down on the importance of the liturgical traditions of the Eastern Churches. Yet he opposed the neo-Gallican liturgies and demanded a return to the Roman liturgy. By the end of the pontificate of Pius IX (1846–1878), the *Missale Romanum* was reintroduced in all French dioceses. In the course of the renewal kicked off by Guéranger, the *Allgemeiner Deutscher Cäcilien-Verein* (General German Saint Cecilia Association) was founded in Germany in 1868. Through the revival of Gregorian chant and classical polyphony,

---

[66] Sailer, *Neue Beyträge zur Bildung des Geistlichen*, 2:251.

[67] Cf. ibid., 254f. As early as 1783, Sailer has submitted a translation of the prayers of the Mass, including the Roman Canon. Cf. Johann Michael Sailer, *Vollständiges Gebet- und Lesebuch für katholische Christen, aus dem grösseren Werk von ihm selbst herausgezogen* (Munich: Lentner, 1785). Cf. Sailer, *Vollständiges Gebetbuch für katholische Christen*, which he himself excerpted from the larger work (Munich: Lentner, 1785).

[68] Sailer, *Neue Beyträge zur Bildung des Geistlichen*, 2:257.

[69] Ibid., 253.

[70] Ibid., 252.

the combination of vernacular singing at Mass and the Latin Solemn High Mass was in some cases rolled back.

Theologians during the Romantic era were not so much concerned about a change of the liturgy but, rather, about the possibility of a deeper understanding and better participation of the faithful in the liturgy. This was true also for large sectors of the liturgical movement, for which Johann Adam Möhler (1796–1838) and his student Franz Anton Staudenmaier (1800–1856) laid important ecclesiological foundations in German-speaking lands.[71] The Benedictines were particularly important for liturgical education in the nineteenth century. As late as 1857, the prohibition against translating the Roman Missal was renewed by Pius IX. After that, however, it was no longer emphasized or enforced. The *Missel des Fidèles* compiled by Abbot Gérard van Caloen (1853–1932) of Maredsous Abbey was published from 1882 on. This was a Latin-French edition of the Missal to help the lay faithful take part in the liturgy with greater understanding. Anselm Schott (1843–1896), who stayed for a while in Maredsous, was encouraged in the daughter foundation of Beuron to create a comparable work in the German language. In 1844, he published for Beuron Abbey the Latin-German *Missal of the Holy Church*.[72]

In German-speaking countries, the "Schott" became synonymous with the people's missal. One year after Schott's death, vernacular missals were removed from the Index of Forbidden Books by Leo XIII (1878–1903). This led to a boom in people's missals. In 1927, Urbanus Bomm (1901–1982) published the *Laacher-Volksmessbuch*.[73] After that, more and more of the lay faithful read the prayers of the Mass silently along with the priest. The "Schott" and the "Bomm" went through numerous printings. By the beginning of World War II, 1,650,000 copies of "Schott" alone had been sold in forty-five editions. In all, fifteen million copies of the American people's missal

[71] Cf. Waldemar Trapp, *Vorgeschichte und Ursprung der liturgischen Bewegung vorwiegend in Hinsicht auf das deutsche Sprachgebiet* (Regensburg: Pustet, 1940; Münster: Antiquariat Stenderhoff, 1979), 264–67.

[72] Cf. Anselm Schott, *Das Messbuch der Heiligen Kirche* (Freiburg, 1884).

[73] Cf. Urbanus Bomm, *Lateinisch-Deutsches Volksmessbuch—das vollständige römische Messbuch für alle Tage des Jahres, mit Erklärungen und einem Choralanhang* [Latin-German People's Missal—the complete Roman Missal for every day of the year, with explanations and a choral supplement] (1927; Einsiedeln-Cologne: Benziger, 1961; hereafter cited as Bomm).

were printed between 1939 and 1945. We can scarcely overestimate the contribution made by people's missals to a more deliberate participation of the faithful in the celebration of the Mass.

In 1905, Pius X (1903–1914) issued the decree *Sacra Tridentina Synodus*, in which he spoke in favor of frequent and daily Communion.[74] Five years later (1910), the decree *Quam singulari* followed, promoting early First Holy Communion.[75] The two decrees decisively changed the practice of receiving Communion. On July 25, 1920, during the pontificate of Benedict XV, a new edition of the Missal was published; work on it had been conducted already during the reign of Pius X, but its appearance had been delayed by the death of that pope and by World War I (1914–1918). The changes in the 1920 *editio typica* affected primarily the rubrics.[76] Besides that, there was a drastic reduction of the over two hundred *Missae propriae pro aliquibus locis* [Masses proper to some localities]. In addition, new Prefaces were created (St. Joseph, Requiem Mass).[77] Prefaces for the Feasts of Christ the King and the Sacred Heart of Jesus followed in 1925 and 1928. As early as during the reign of Pius IX, there were various deliberations about a reform of the Roman Missal.

[74] Cf. DH 3375–83.
[75] Cf. DH 3530–36.
[76] See the chapter added to the General Rubrics: "*Additiones et variationes in Rubricis Missalis*".
[77] Cf. Fiedrowicz, *Überlieferte Messe*, 45.

Chapter VIII

MYSTERIUM PASCHALE

The Second Vatican Council and the Reform of the Missal

The *oratio fidelium* (prayer of the faithful), the intercessory prayer that is offered after the Creed during celebration of Mass and resembles the great petitions of Good Friday in its joining of petitions and oration of the priest, is one of the important changes to the traditional rite of Mass in the course of the Second Vatican Council's reform of the Missal. The greater consideration for the *participatio actuosa* of the faithful desired by Vatican Council II is expressed in the intercessory prayer of the Mass. The liturgy is not accomplished by one individual but, rather, by the faithful who gather to celebrate the liturgy. In his book *The Spirit of the Liturgy*, Romano Guardini explains:

> Nor does the onus of liturgical action and prayer rest with the individual. It does not even rest with the collective groups, composed of numerous individuals, who periodically achieve a limited and intermittent unity in their capacity as the congregation of a church. The liturgical entity consists rather of the united body of the faithful as such—the Church—a body which infinitely outnumbers the mere congregation. The liturgy is the Church's public and lawful act of worship, and it is performed and conducted by the officials whom the Church herself has designated for the post—her priests.[1]

Or briefly and to the point: "The liturgy is not celebrated by the individual, but by the body of the faithful."[2]

[1] Romano Guardini, *The Spirit of the Liturgy* [1935], trans. Ada Lane (New York: Crossroad, 1998), 19.
[2] Ibid., 36.

Those responsible for the liturgy are the faithful, on the basis of their membership in the Body of Christ through Baptism. Not only the clergy, but the laity, too, are celebrants of the liturgy. The principal celebrant of the liturgy is Jesus Christ, the true High Priest. Nevertheless, the liturgy is executed by the communion of the faithful. Prepared by the liturgical movement, the *missa cum populo* became the basic form of the Mass in the course of the reform of the Missal.[3] The German translation *Feier der Gemeindemesse*, "celebration of Mass with a congregation",[4] is misleading, since, according to Catholic understanding, the Church is a communion of Churches constituted by the local bishops in union with the bishop of Rome. The local congregation is a church of Jesus Christ only in union with the local bishop: "Associated with their bishop in a spirit of trust and generosity, they [the priests] make him present in a certain sense in the individual local congregations"; the priests should "so lead and serve their local community that it may worthily be called by that name, by which the one and entire people of God is signed, namely, the Church of God".[5]

A. Liturgical Movement and Reform of the Liturgy

The liturgical movement had as its goal the deepening and renewal of the liturgical life of the faithful.[6] The movement is closely connected with centers of Benedictine monasticism. The liturgical movement started in the Benedictine congregations of Solesmes and Beuron. The liturgical movement intended to advance the conscious and active participation of the faithful in the celebration of Holy Mass, which was not suitably expressed in the juxtaposition

---

[3] Cf. *Institutio generalis Missalis Romani: General Instruction of the Roman Missal*, 3rd ed. (1970; Washington, D.C.: United States Conference of Catholic Bishops, 2002; hereafter cited as *GIRM*), no. 115. At the beginning of the *Ordo Missae* we read: "Populo congregato, sacerdos cum ministris ad altare accedit, dum cantus ad introitum peragitur" (When the people are gathered, the priest and ministers go to the altar in procession while the Entrance Chant takes place).

[4] *MB* 321.

[5] *LG* 28.

[6] For initial background information, see Theodor Maas-Ewerd, "Liturgische Bewegung", in *LThK* (1997), 992–93.

of the priestly celebration of Mass and private devotions, for example, when the Rosary or Mass devotions from prayer books and hymnals[7] were prayed during the offering of the Eucharist.[8] Catholics who could afford the book used the bilingual people's missals by Schott and Bomm. This led to greater emphasis on the "active participation (*partecipazione attiva*) [of the faithful] in the most holy mysteries and the public, solemn prayer of the Church",[9] which Pope Pius X had called for in his motu proprio *Tra le sollecitudini* (1903).[10] The motu proprio's context was the struggle since the middle of the nineteenth century over the correct form of sacred music. Pius X, who early on had come into contact with the Benedictine movement for the renewal of Gregorian chant, underscored in his motu proprio on sacred music the special dignity of Gregorian chant and wished for more active participation of the faithful in it. For Pius X, the principle of active participation meant above all participation in the sung Mass. For the time being, the theological question of celebrant and of the communal character of the liturgy remained open: Are all the faithful celebrants of the liturgy or only the clergy?

On September 23, 1909, the young Benedictine monk Dom Lambert Beauduin (1873–1960) from Mont César Abbey gave a lecture on "The True Prayer of the Church" at a Catholic congress in Mechelen/Malines. The lecture is considered the inaugural event of the liturgical movement in the twentieth century. Beauduin was primarily concerned, not about new prayer texts, but rather above all about putting the Church's liturgical books, especially the Missal, into the hands of the faithful, so as to ground the piety of the faithful in the sacred liturgy of the Church. The preferred means to this end, in Beauduin's view, were dual-language editions of the Roman liturgical books with a verbatim translation of the Latin

---

[7] Cf. Josef Hacker, *Die Messe in den deutschen Diözesan-Gesang- und Gebetbüchern von der Auflkärungszeit bis zur Gegenwart* (dissertation; Munich: Zink, 1950); Kurt Küppers, *Diözesan-Gesang- und Gebetbücher des deutschen Sprachgebiets im 19. und 20. Jahrhundert* (Münster: Aschendorff, 1987).

[8] Cf. Josef Andreas Jungmann, *The Mass of the Roman Rite*, trans. Francis A. Brunner, C.Ss.R., 2 vols. (New York: Benziger Brothers, 1951, 1955), 1:145–46.

[9] *AAS* 36 (1903/1904): 331.

[10] Cf. ibid., 329–32.

texts.[11] Beauduin called for the broad dissemination of people's missals, the participation of the faithful in the parish Mass, and the abolition of private devotions at Mass. In France and Italy, the liturgical movement was promoted above all by Aimé-Georges Martimort (1911–2000) and Cyprian Vagaggini (1909–1999).

The liturgical movement was especially strong in Germany, sustained by prominent persons including Ildefons Herwegen (1874–1946), Abbot of the Benedictine Abbey at Maria Laach, the Benedictine Odo Casel (1886–1948), Romano Guardini (1885–1968), and the Jesuit Josef Andreas Jungmann. Casel is considered founder of the theology of the mysteries, probably the most significant initiative in liturgical theology in the twentieth century. Jungmann, the great historian of the Roman Mass, advocated moderate changes to the rite of Mass, but pled for the preservation of the common prayer orientation of priest and people. With his milestone book *The Spirit of the Liturgy* (1918), Guardini wrote the theological manifesto of the liturgical movement.[12] Worth mentioning also are Guardini's lectures about the Church. The first lecture, "The Awakening of the Church in the Soul",[13] became famous. Like Beauduin, Guardini linked the notion of the Church as *Corpus Christi mysticum* with the demand for liturgical renewal.

Also important for the liturgical movement in Germany were the journals *Liturgische Zeitschrift* (1928–1933) and *Liturgisches Leben* (1934–1939), both published by the pastor and theologian Johann Pinsk (1891–1957) of Berlin. In Austria, Augustinian Canon Regular Pius Parsch (1884–1954) of Klosterneuburg Abbey founded the popular liturgical movement. Another center of the liturgical movement was the Oratory in Leipzig. The Benedictine movement promoted above

---

[11] Cf. Lambert Beauduin, "La vraie prière de l'Église (1909)", in A. Haquin, *Dom Lambert Beauduin et le renouveau liturgique* (Gembloux: Duculot, 1970), 240: "A more enlightened, more hierarchical piety; less of a need for new devotions; a more natural and thus more beneficial use of the Holy Eucharist; more complete knowledge of the holy Gospels and above all an easier, more accessible and more popular way to go to Christ.... In order to carry out this renewal, it is necessary to popularize the liturgical texts among all the faithful in both languages, with a literal translation.... The people's Missal must become everyone's prayer book."

[12] Cf. also Romano Guardini, *Meditations before Mass*, trans. Elinor Castendyk Briefs (1956; Notre Dame, Ind.: Ave Maria Press, 2014).

[13] Cf. Guardini, *Vom Sinn der Kirche* (Mainz: Matthias-Grünewald, 1922), 1–19.

all the Latin chant Mass—admittedly with only marginal success in German-speaking regions, where congregational singing in the vernacular predominated. Immediately after World War II, prayer books and hymnals for various associations and dioceses were developed. By and by, the faithful began to assume their role in the celebration of Mass, although their activity was still not recognized canonically as liturgical action. The texts of the Mass spoken or sung by the priest were critical. The use of hymns by the congregation was not permitted until the Instruction *Musicam sacram* (1967).[14]

After the Council of Trent, the Low Mass of the priest had increasingly become the dominant form of the Mass. At the beginning of the twentieth century, the *missa lecta* or *missa solitaria* dominated in parishes. In addition, the *missa cantata* and Solemn High Mass were celebrated. With the introduction of the congregational Mass and the *Betsingmesse* ("Pray-and-Sing Mass"), the liturgical movement led to a strengthening of the communal character of the Mass. Through the influence of Romanticism, German hymnody had been confined to the *missa cantata*. Using a popular missal to pray along with the priest no longer satisfied many. In this regard, the liturgical movement led to a change of the previous appearance of the Mass. New forms of participation by the faithful in the liturgical action developed.[15] We should mention first the communal Mass of the *missa dialogata* or *recitata* celebrated in Latin, in which the faithful became actively involved in the parts of the Mass not reserved to the priest.

Proposals for communal Masses were published by Guardini, Parsch, and Maurus Wolter.[16] On the Feast of the Ascension, 1922, in the Church of Saint Gertrud, Parsch celebrated his first "choral Mass" or "Liturgical Mass", in which the *Kyrie, Sanctus,* and *Agnus Dei* were sung in German by the congregation, with the remaining parts of the Ordinary and the Propers of the Mass in German as well.

---

[14] Cf. Second Vatican Council, *Musicam sacram*, Instruction on Music in the Liturgy, no. 32. Cf. *Dokumente zur Erneurung der Liturgie: Dokumente des Apostolischen Stuhls 1963–1973 und des Zweiten Vatikanischen Konzils*, vols. 1–4, ed. H. Rennings with M. Klöckener (Kevelaer and Freiburg, Switzerland, 1983–2008; hereafter cited as *DEL*),

[15] Cf. Philipp Harnoncourt, "Gemeinschaftsmesse", in *LThK*, 3rd ed., vol. 4 (1995), 437–38.

[16] On Guardini, see Theodor Maas-Ewerd, "Auf dem Weg zur 'Gemeinschaftsmesse': Romano Guardinis 'Messandacht' aus dem Jahre 1920", *Erbe und Auftrag* 66 (1990): 450–68.

The readings and prayers were read aloud in German by a lector. To serve the liturgical movement and also the contemporary biblical movement, Parsch founded in 1926 the periodical *Bibel und Liturgie*. Since 1928, the periodical has published standard German texts for the *Ordinarium Missae*. The German High Mass had already developed in isolated cases by the end of the Baroque period. While the faithful sang a German hymn, the priest recited in Latin the corresponding Latin texts from the Missal (see, for example, Franz Schubert's *Deutsche Messe*, which is popular to this day). Besides that, there was the *Betsingmesse*,[17] celebrated in 1933 at the Catholic Conference in Vienna. A prayer leader pronounced the readings and various prayers of the priest in the German language.[18]

The liturgical movement was not primarily about calling into question the organic Roman Mass but, rather, about strengthening the participation of the faithful in celebrating it. Nevertheless, at the beginning of World War II, furious disputes arose over the liturgical movement. That led in 1940 to the founding of the Liturgical Report and, later, of the Liturgical Commission by the bishops' conference in Fulda. In 1942, the same German commission issued "Guidelines for the Liturgical Form of the Divine Services in Parishes". The liturgical movement experienced a revival during the pontificate of Pope Pius XII (1939–1958). In the encyclical *Mystici Corporis* (1943), the Eucharist is presented as the image of the Church's unity: priest and faithful united in prayer offer together the Sacrifice of Christ. With the encyclical *Mediator Dei* (1947),[19] Pius XII acknowledged the efforts of the liturgical movement to renew liturgical life. To be sure, the pope criticized all unauthorized changes to the liturgy of the Church, yet by making a distinction between changeable and unchangeable parts of the liturgy, he opened the way to a liturgical renewal.

Following the encyclical *Mediator Dei*, the Magna Carta of the liturgical movement, Pius XII established on May 28, 1948, a Pontifical Commission for Reform of the Liturgy. Annibale Bugnini, C.M. (1912–1982) became secretary of the commission and later also

---

[17] Cf. Philipp Harnoncourt, "Betsingmesse", in *LThK*, 3rd ed., vol. 2 (1994), 340.

[18] Cf. Theodor Maas-Ewerd, *Die Krise der liturgischen Bewegung in Deutschland und Österreich: Studien zu den Auseinandersetzungen um die "liturgische Frage" in den Jahren 1939 bis 1944*, Studien zur Pastoralliturgie 3 (Regensburg: Pustet, 1981), 637–40.

[19] Cf. DH 3840–55.

the secretary of the conciliar Pre-preparatory Commission for the Liturgy (1959–1962), of the Consilium for Implementing the Constitution on the Reform of the Liturgy of Vatican Council II, and of the Congregation for Divine Worship (1969–1975). On December 30, 1948, the Pontifical Commission published a memorandum in which a reform of the Missal was recommended. One member of the commission and co-signer of the memorandum was Ferdinando Giuseppe Antonelli (1896–1993), later the secretary of the Conciliar Commission for the Liturgy (1962–1963), who immediately after the council was secretary of the Congregation of (Sacred) Rites (1965–1969), and in 1973 was created cardinal.

Initial reforms under Pius XII were the renewal of the Easter Vigil (1951) and of Holy Week (1956). A simplification of the rubrics of the Missal followed with the decree *Cum nostra hac aetate* (1955). Five years later under John XXIII (1958–1963), the *Codex Rubricarum* (1960) appeared, which replaced the general rubrics of the *Missale Romanum* of 1570 and was incorporated into the *Editio typica* of the 1962 Missal. In the motu proprio *Rubricarum instructum* that accompanied the publication of the *Codex* on July 25, 1960,[20] John XXIII explained that the ecumenical council that he had announced on January 25, 1959, would decide about the "higher principles of the general liturgical reform" and thus about further reforms of the Missal.[21] The *Codex Rubricarum* includes several programmatic statements in the general rubrics that later were adopted by Vatican Council II: every celebration of the Mass is a public act of the Church's worship,[22] of her head and her members, which is why the misleading description "private Mass" should be avoided. The Mass "in union with the Divine Office" represents "the summit of all Christian worship".[23] About the active participation of the faithful in the celebration of Mass, it says: "By its nature, the Mass demands that all participants (*omnes adstantes*) take part in it, each in his own way (*secundum modum sibi proprium, eidem participent*)."[24]

---

[20] Cf. Wilhelm Lurz, *Einführung in die neuen Rubriken des Römischen Breviers und Missale* (Munich: Seitz, 1960).

[21] Cf. Hans Bernhard Meyer, *Eucharistie, Geschichte, Theologie, Pastoral*, Handbuch der Liturgiewissenschaft 4 (Regensburg: Pustet, 1989), 272.

[22] Cf. Rubr. gen. no. 269.

[23] Rubr. gen. no. 270.

[24] Rubr. gen. no. 272.

On December 4, 1963, with the solemn promulgation of the Constitution on the Sacred Liturgy *Sacrosanctum concilium* by the Second Vatican Council, something new happened in the history of the Catholic Church. For the first time a general council spoke comprehensively about the liturgy of the Roman Rite and enacted a general renewal of the liturgy with concrete recommendations for reform. The council proposed "points for a kind of reform that there had never been before in the almost two-thousand-year history of the Catholic Church".[25] The concluding document of the Extraordinary Synod of Bishops on the "Mystery of the Church" in 1985 called the liturgical reform the "most visible fruit of the Council".[26] In fact, nowhere was the *aggiornamento* of the Church as concretely tangible, but as controversial, too, as in the question of the liturgy.[27]

The Pre-preparatory Commission for the Liturgy, led by Gaetano Cardinal Cicognani (1881–1962), had concluded its work on the schema (draft) of the Constitution on the Liturgy shortly before the cardinal's death. Because Cardinal Cicognani had reservations about the schema on the liturgy, he hesitated to sign it. At the insistence of his younger brother, Amleto Giovanni Cardinal Cicognani (1883–1973), he finally allowed the schema to pass.[28] In the autumn of 1962, the bishops received the schemas on the liturgy (*Sacrosanctum concilium*) and on revelation (*De fontibus revelationis*). Since there was considerable resistance to the schema on revelation, the Consultor for the Council of Presidents decided to begin with deliberations on the schema for the liturgy. Under the chairmanship of Arcadio María Cardinal Larraona Saralegui (1887–1973), the Conciliar Commission for the Liturgy introduced the schema on the liturgy in the council hall. The secretary of the Conciliar Commission for the Liturgy was Ferdinando Giuseppe Antonelli. In retrospect, many have seen the

[25] Andreas Heinz, "25 Jahre Liturgiekonstitution", *Liturgisches Jahrbuch* 38 (1988): 197.

[26] *DEL* 3, no. 5790. On the genesis of the constitution, the discussion about it at the council, and the history of its influence, cf. Helmut Hoping, " 'Die sichtbarste Frucht des Konzils': Anspruch und Wirklichkeit der erneuerten Liturgie", in *Zweites Vatikanum—vergessene Anstösse, gegenwärtige Fortschreibungen*, ed. G. Wassilowsky, Quaestiones disputatae 207 (Freiburg: Herder, 2004), 90–115; Hoping, "The Constitution *Sacrosanctum Concilium* and the Liturgical Reform", *Annuarium Historiae Conciliorum* 42 (2010): 297–316.

[27] *DEL* 3:5790.

[28] Cf. John W. O'Malley, *What Happened at Vatican II* (Cambridge, Mass.: Belknap Press of Harvard University Press, 2008), 129.

fact that the council began with deliberations on the liturgy as an act of Divine Providence. In that way it became clear to the whole world that the liturgy forms the center of ecclesial life, the renewal of which was the council's concern, after all.[29]

The Council Fathers professed the liturgy to be at the center of the Church.[30] But the fact that the schema on the liturgy

> became the first subject for the Council's discussions really had nothing to do with the majority of the Fathers having an intense interest in the liturgical question. Quite simply, no great disagreements were expected in this area.... It would not have occurred to any of the Fathers to see in this text a "revolution" signifying the "end of the Middle Ages", as some theologians felt they should interpret it subsequently. The work was seen as a continuation of the reforms introduced by Pius X and carried on carefully but resolutely by Pius XII.[31]

The deliberations about the schema on the liturgy did not proceed as harmoniously as some had hoped.[32] Contentious discussions arose above all over the statements on the Eucharist, the use of vernacular languages, concelebration, Communion from the chalice, the reform of the breviary, and the relationship of universal and local Church authority in the implementation of liturgical reforms. The texts in chapter 2, which concerned Holy Mass,[33] were treated between October 30 and November 6, 1962.

---

[29] Cf. Emil J. Lengeling, *Die Konstitution des Zweiten Vatikanischen Konzils über die heilige Liturgie: Lateinisch-deutscher Text mit einem Kommentar von E. J. Lengeling*, Lebendiger Gottesdienst 5/6 (Münster: Verlag Regensburg, 1964), 55.

[30] Cf. Joseph Ratzinger, "The First Session", in *Theological Highlights of Vatican II* (1966; New York/Mahwah, N.J.: Paulist Press, 2009), 19–54, and "Practical Questions...", in ibid., 91–94.

[31] Joseph Ratzinger, *Milestones: Memoirs: 1927–1977*, trans. Erasmo Leiva-Merikakis (San Francisco: Ignatius Press, 1998), 123. Massimo Faggioli of the Bologna School thinks that it was a programmatic decision of the council to begin with the Constitution on the Liturgy and that the document's ecclesiology, in comparison to the one in *Lumen gentium*, is Eucharistic and non-hierarchical, i.e., decentralized. Faggioli regards this as the hermeneutic key for the interpretation of all the conciliar documents. Cf. Faggioli, *True Reform: Liturgy and Ecclesiology in Sacrosanctum Concilium* (Collegeville, Minn.: Liturgical Press, 2012).

[32] Cf. Ralph M. Wiltgen, *The Rhine Flows into the Tiber* (Rockford, Ill.: Tan Books, 1985), 37.

[33] Cf. *SC* 49–58.

On November 14, 1962, after three full weeks of intense deliberations, a vast majority (2162 *placet,* 46 *non placet,* 7 invalid votes) accepted the schema as the basis for continuing deliberations. A first ballot on *Sacrosanctum concilium* was taken on October 14, 1963—after the election of Pope Paul VI. Besides a majority in principle for the schema, there were also numerous *modi* (proposed changes), which in the event, however, did not lead to any major changes. Another ballot on chapter 2 took place on November 20, 1963. Finally, on December 4, 1963, the constitution *Sacrosanctum concilium* was solemnly passed with 2147 yeas, and only 4 votes opposing, then promulgated on the same day—exactly four hundred years after the Council of Trent had entrusted the reform of the Missal to the pope.

The Council Fathers' whole purpose was "to impart an ever-increasing vigor to the Christian life of the faithful".[34] That was to happen by way of *aggiornamento* in the Church. The Constitution on the Sacred Liturgy was to serve the renewal of the liturgy. The Church's liturgy—and the Council Fathers underscore this in the Dogmatic Constitution *Dei Verbum* (1965)—is part of the Church's tradition (*sacra traditio*). This tradition encompasses not only the authentic doctrine of the faith, but also the public worship of the Church.[35] Tradition, however, is not static, but alive; the liturgy of the Church has developed and continues to develop. For there are unchangeable and changeable things in the liturgy.[36] A reform of the liturgy is possible only "in the light of sound tradition",[37] that is, not by a rupture, but by renewal in continuity with the larger tradition of the Church.

The goal of the liturgical reform was a renewal and fostering of the liturgy, which was to be revised "carefully in the light of sound tradition" in order to meet "the circumstances and needs of modern times".[38] *Sacrosanctum concilium* does not speak of a general *reformatio* of the liturgy but, rather, of an *instauratio*, a renewal.[39] The constitution calls for an examination, that is, a revision of the liturgical

[34] *SC* 1.
[35] Cf. *DV* 8.
[36] Cf. *SC* 21.
[37] *SC* 4.
[38] Ibid.
[39] Cf. *SC* 21, 24.

books.[40] The Pre-preparatory Commission for the Liturgy had spoken in addition about revising the liturgical books *ex integro*, that is, as a whole—which amounts to something quite different.[41] The phenomenon of liturgical reform was hardly a novelty. The most significant reforms up to that time were the Carolingian liturgical reform and the post-Tridentine reform. The constitution *Sacrosanctum concilium* was the first document to be issued at the council. It formed the basis of the liturgical reform that started while the council was still in session. As for the reform of the Missal—the core of the liturgical reform—the Council Fathers wished that the rites of the *Ordo* of the Mass "be simplified, due care being taken to preserve their substance", and "be restored to the vigor which they had in the days of the holy Fathers".[42]

The central, guiding liturgical-theological concept of the Second Vatican Council, particularly of *Sacrosanctum concilium*, is the concept of the *mysterium paschale*.[43] Right from the start of the Constitution on the Liturgy, the influence of the sacramental theology of Odo Casel is noticeable, who spoke of the liturgy as the "mystery of Christian worship".[44] "For the liturgy, 'through which the work of our redemption is accomplished' [Secret of the Ninth Sunday after Pentecost], most of all in the divine sacrifice of the Eucharist, is the outstanding means whereby the faithful may express in their lives, and manifest to others, the mystery of Christ and the real

---

[40] Cf. *SC* 25: "Libri liturgici quam primum recognoscantur."

[41] For another opinion, see Josef Andreas Jungmann, "Konstitution über die heilige Liturgie: Einleitung und Kommentar", in *Das Zweite Vatikanische Konzil. Lexikon für Theologie und Kirche*, supplemental vol. 1 (Freiburg, 1966), 34f.

[42] *SC* 50.

[43] The reception occurred above all via French theologians like Louis Bouyer (1913–2004), François-Xavier Durrwell (1912–2005), and Auxiliary Bishop Henri Jenny (1904–1982), later archbishop of Cambrai. Cf. Simon A. Schrott, *Pascha-Mysterium: Zum liturgietheologischen Leitbegriff des Zweiten Vatikanischen Konzils*, Theologie der Liturgie 6 (Regensburg: Pustet, 2014), 37–141.

[44] Cf. Odo Casel, *The Mystery of Christian Worship*, ed. B. Neunheuser, in English trans. (Westminster, Md.: Newman Press, 1962). On the importance of Casel's mystery theology for the liturgical reform, cf. Winfried Haunerland, "Mysterium paschale: Schlüsselbegriff liturgietheologischer Erneuerung", in *Liturgie als Mitte des christlichen Lebens*, ed. George Augustin, Theologie im Dialog 7 (Freiburg: Herder, 2012), 189–209; Helmut Hoping, "Die Mysterientheologie Odo Casels und die Liturgiereform", in *Erinnerung an die Zukunft: Das Zweite Vatikanische Konzil*, expanded, updated ed., ed. J. H. Tück (Freiburg: Herder, 2013).

nature of the true Church."[45] Already by Baptism we are "plunged into the paschal mystery of Christ" and "receive the spirit of adoption as sons 'in which we cry: Abba, Father' (Rom. 8:15), and thus become true adorers whom the Father seeks (cf. John 4:23)."[46] The redemption originating in the Paschal Mystery of Christ is present in the "sacrifice and sacraments, around which the entire liturgical life revolves".[47] The Church of Christ to which we belong through Baptism has never ceased to gather to celebrate the Paschal Mystery of Christ or to give thanks to God, in the power of the Holy Spirit, for the gift of his Son, particularly in the celebration of the Eucharist, the great sacrament of thanksgiving.

The Incarnation of Christ and his Paschal Mystery constitute God's vital saving action, which is made present symbolically in the liturgy of the Church. Christ, the principal subject of all liturgical action, is present to his Church in the Sacrifice of the Mass and in the person of the priest, above all under the Eucharistic species, in the sacraments, in the Word of Scripture, and in the assembled congregation.[48] The council rediscovered the presence of Christ in the proclamation of God's Word, the homily, and the praying Church.[49] Since it was long the custom to speak only of the sacramental, substantial presence of Christ under the Eucharistic species as "Real Presence", it is not surprising that *Sacrosanctum concilium* 7 was one of the most debated articles of the schema on the liturgy.[50]

The liturgy of the Church is defined as the exercise of Christ's priestly office. The basis of the liturgy is the baptismal priesthood of all the faithful. In the liturgy, "sanctification of the man" is signified by signs perceptible by the senses, and is effected "in a way which corresponds with each of these signs; in the liturgy the whole public worship is performed by the Mystical Body of Jesus Christ, that is, by the

---

[45] *SC* 2.

[46] *SC* 6.

[47] Ibid.

[48] Cf. *SC* 7.

[49] Cf. Albert Gerhards, "Gipfelpunkt und Quelle: Intention und Rezeption der Liturgiekonstitution *Sacrosanctum Concilium*", in *Erinnerung an die Zukunft: Das Zweite Vatikanische Konzil*, ed. Jan-Heiner Tück, 2nd ed. (Freiburg: Herder, 2012), 130f.

[50] Cf. Kaczynski, *Theologischer Kommentar zur Konstitution über die heilige Liturgie Sacrosanctum Concilium* (2004), 65f.

Head and His members."[51] Every liturgical celebration of the Church is for that reason "a sacred action surpassing all others (*actio sacra praecellenter*)".[52] In it we take part in the heavenly liturgy celebrated in the holy city, Jerusalem.[53] At the same time, the liturgy is the sanctification of man (*sanctificatio hominis*) and adoration, worship of God (*cultus*), a *sacrum commercium* of divine and human action.[54] Besides the liturgy, the proclamation of the Gospel and works of service are among the basic actions of the Church. Even though the life of the Church is not exhausted in the liturgy,[55] the liturgy is nonetheless "the summit (*culmen*) toward which the activity of the Church is directed; at the same time it is the font (*fons*) from which all her power flows."[56] Besides the liturgy of the Roman Rite, the council also speaks appreciatively about the devotions proper to individual Churches (*sacra excercitia*), regulated by the bishop, and popular devotions (*pia exercitia*).[57]

The liturgy of the Church has a Trinitarian structure. It is the prayer of the Church (*ecclesia orans*) directed to the Father through the Son in the Holy Spirit. The liturgy of the Church is not something that aims to appease God by a sacrifice. God is the one who reconciled us to himself by the death of his Son. In the first place, the liturgy is God's action on behalf of us men. On this is founded the response of the faithful in praise, thanksgiving, petition, and sacrifice. The liturgy of the Church has both a katabatic and an anabatic dimension. Christ, the High Priest at the right hand of the Father, is the "minister of the holies and of the true tabernacle".[58] The liturgy of the Church is the continuation of Christ's priestly work. The liturgical ministry of all the faithful, as distinct from that of the sacred ministers, belongs to them by virtue of their membership, through Baptism, in the Body of Christ. It follows that all the faithful are celebrants of the liturgy.[59] The chief celebrant of the liturgy, however, is Christ, the true High Priest.

[51] *SC* 7.
[52] Ibid.
[53] Cf. *SC* 8.
[54] Cf. *SC* 10.
[55] Cf. *SC* 9, 12.
[56] *SC* 10.
[57] Cf. *SC* 13.
[58] *SC* 8. Cf. Heb 8:2.
[59] Cf. *SC* 14, 26–29.

Latria characterizes and constitutes the Church's liturgy. For although the liturgy of the Church also has a catechetical significance—since in it God speaks to his people and proclaims his glad tidings—it is nevertheless adoration above all; that is, worship of the divine majesty (*cultus divinae maiestatis*).[60] The Council Fathers explain the liturgy's latreutic character with the example of the prayers of the presider (*preces*) that the priest speaks *in persona Christi* and in the name of the Church: they are spoken *ad Deum directae*, that is, addressed to God.[61] In addition, the liturgy has a constitutive eschatological dimension. It is fitting for the Church, whose essence it is to "be both human and divine, visible and yet invisibly equipped",[62] to celebrate in time the earthly liturgy, in union with the heavenly liturgy, which is our future.

> In the earthly liturgy we take part in a foretaste of that heavenly liturgy which is celebrated in the holy city of Jerusalem toward which we journey as pilgrims, where Christ is sitting at the right hand of God, a minister of the holies and of the true tabernacle (cf. Apoc. 21:2; Col. 3:1; Heb. 8:2); we sing a hymn to the Lord's glory with all the warriors of the heavenly army; venerating the memory of the saints, we hope for some part and fellowship with them; we eagerly await the Saviour, Our Lord Jesus Christ, until He, our life, shall appear and we too will appear with Him in glory (cf. Phil. 3:20; Col. 3:4).[63]

The liturgy "shows forth the Church to those who are outside as a sign lifted up among the nations".[64] Christian worship is public; liturgical functions are not private in nature but, rather, form the core of the Church, which is the "sacrament of unity".[65] The liturgy of the Church "is the summit toward which the activity of the Church is directed; at the same time it is the font from which all her power flows."[66] This holds true especially for the Sacrifice of the Eucharist (*sacrificium eucharistiae*), which the Dogmatic Constitution

---

[60] *SC* 33.
[61] Cf. ibid.
[62] *SC* 2.
[63] *SC* 8.
[64] *SC* 2.
[65] *SC* 26.
[66] *SC* 10.

on the Church *Lumen gentium* (1964) calls the "fount and apex of the whole Christian life".[67] In fact, the solemn offering of the Eucharist is the sacramental celebration by which the Church lives, more so than by any other celebration, and through which she gains her identity. Hence, the last encyclical of Pope John Paul II is entitled *Ecclesia de Eucharistia* (2003).[68] Nowhere is the Church of Jesus Christ more herself than in the celebration of the Eucharist, in which she has her source and her center. But just as the spiritual life of the Christian does not consist exclusively of participation in the sacred liturgy, neither can the Church's action consist exclusively of the liturgy. Among the fundamental acts of the Church are preaching and diakonia, which, like the liturgy, find their place in the koinonia (fellowship, communion) of faith.[69]

Starting from the liturgy's essence and significance in the life of the Church, *Sacrosanctum concilium* formulates principles and norms of a general renewal of the Roman Rite of the liturgy,[70] while recognizing all other lawfully approved rites.[71] It is a mixed bag of principles, prominent among which are the two key concepts *participatio plena, conscia et actuosa*,[72] and *mysterium paschale*.[73,74] These are also characterized as formal and material principles of the liturgical reform.[75] The decisive formal principle of the renewal of the liturgy is the principle of active participation (*actuosa participatio*); here, however, it is often overlooked that the Council Fathers "gave priority to mystagogical transparency to the sacred over *actuosa participatio*".[76]

---

[67] *LG* 11.

[68] Cf. *EE*.

[69] Cf. *SC* 9, 11.

[70] Cf. *SC* 3.

[71] Cf. *SC* 4.

[72] Cf. *SC* 11, 14.

[73] Cf. *SC* 5–7, 61.

[74] Cf. Angelus A. Häussling, *Christliche Identität aus der Liturgie: Theologische und historische Studien zum Gottesdienst der Kirche*, Liturgiewissenschaftliche Quellen und Forschungen 79 (Münster: Aschendorff, 1997), 44, 46–57.

[75] Cf. Winfried Haunerland, "Participatio actuosa: Programmwort liturgischer Erneuerung", *Internationale katholische Zeitschrift Communio* 38 (2009): 585–95.

[76] Kurt Koch, "Die Konstitution über die Heilige Liturgie und die nachkonziliare Liturgiereform", in *Papst Benedikt XVI. und sein Schülerkreis*, Kurt Kardinal Koch, *Das Zweite Vatikanische Konzil: Die Hermeneutik der Reform*, ed. S. Ott and S. Wiedenhofer (Augsburg: Sankt Ulrich, 2012), 74.

Mother Church earnestly desires that all the faithful should be led to that fully conscious, and active participation in liturgical celebrations which is demanded by the very nature of the liturgy. Such participation by the Christian people as "a chosen race, a royal priesthood, a holy nation, a redeemed people" (1 Pet. 2:9; cf. 2:4–5), is their right and duty by reason of their baptism. In the restoration and promotion of the sacred liturgy, the full and active participation by all the people is the aim to be considered before all else; for it is the primary and indispensable source from which the faithful are to derive the true Christian spirit.[77]

With the idea of active participation (*participatio actuosa*), the Constitution on the Liturgy seizes on a central concern of the liturgical movement. The conscious and active participation of the faithful in the liturgy presupposes a corresponding liturgical formation, which is demanded emphatically by the Council Fathers.[78] Besides the primary interior participation in the liturgy, there is also an external form of participation.[79] External participation includes gathering together, communal prayer, listening to God's Word, acclamations, liturgical postures and gestures such as standing, kneeling, sitting, and the reception of Communion, but also individual liturgical duties of the laity that the council either revived or recalled—such as the ministry of the acolyte, of the lector, of the cantor, or of the choir. Corresponding to the essence of the Church, the liturgy by its very nature is at once a "hierarchic and communal" action.[80] Therefore, in the liturgy, "each person, minister or layman, who has an office to perform, should do all of, but only, those parts which pertain to his office by the nature of the rite and the principles of liturgy."[81]

For the reform of the liturgy, the Council Fathers list further principles, which are no less important than the principle of active participation. The renewal of the liturgical texts and rites should be drawn up in such a way that they "express more clearly the holy things which they signify; the Christian people, so far as possible,

---

[77] SC 14.
[78] Cf. SC 19.
[79] Cf. ibid.
[80] Cf. the subheading for SC 26–36.
[81] SC 28.

should be enabled to understand them with ease and to take part in them fully, actively, and as befits a community."[82] The principle of simplicity and ease of understanding the liturgy is, together with the principle of active participation, a further principle for the renewal of the liturgy: "The rites should be distinguished by a noble simplicity; they should be short, clear, and unencumbered by useless repetitions; they should be within the people's powers of comprehension, and normally should not require much explanation."[83] Along these lines, the *ordo missae* should be

> revised in such a way that the intrinsic nature and purpose of its several parts, as also the connection between them, may be more clearly manifested, and that devout and active participation by the faithful may be more easily achieved. For this purpose the rites are to be simplified, due care being taken to preserve their substance; elements which, with the passage of time, came to be duplicated, or were added with but little advantage, are now to be discarded; other elements which have suffered injury through accidents of history are now to be restored to the vigor which they had in the days of the holy Fathers, as may seem useful or necessary.[84]

Connected with the principle of simplicity and ease of understanding is the demand for the introduction of the vernacular into the Roman liturgy. The Council Fathers, however, wish that Latin be preserved as the language of the liturgy: "Particular law remaining in force, the use of the Latin language is to be preserved in the Latin rites. But since the use of the mother tongue, whether in the Mass, the administration of the sacraments, or other parts of the liturgy, frequently may be of great advantage to the people, the limits of its employment may be extended. This will apply in the first place to readings and directives, and in some of the prayers and chants."[85] The introduction of vernacular-only missals did indeed follow the council at the request of numerous bishops, despite the predictable result that Latin as the liturgical language would for the most part

[82] *SC* 21.
[83] *SC* 34.
[84] *SC* 50.
[85] *SC* 36.

be lost in local celebrations of Sunday Mass—which was not the council's intention.[86]

The principle that the Council Fathers formulate for a renewal of the liturgy within the greater tradition of the Church is the principle of organic liturgical development, which is found in liturgical historiography already in the work of Anton Baumstark.[87] However one might judge the idea that the Roman liturgy developed organically,[88] under no circumstances did the Council Fathers intend a completely new form of the rite of Mass. According to the will of the Council Fathers, with the liturgical reform in general and the reform of the Missal in particular, "the general laws governing the structure and meaning of the liturgy must be studied."[89] There should "be no innovations unless the good of the Church genuinely and certainly requires them; and care must be taken that any new forms adopted should in some way grow organically from forms already existing."[90] Organic development does not mean that the historic development is determined from the beginning as it is in a seed or that it is accomplished according to inner laws.[91] Rather, the liturgy of the Church resembles an organism that cannot be changed arbitrarily without endangering its life in the long run. In German-speaking liturgical studies, the principle of the organic development of the liturgy has played almost no role in the assessment of the liturgical reform after the council.

[86] For another opinion, see Winfried Haunerland, "Vom 'Gottesdienst' zur 'Gemeindefeier'? Herausforderungen nachkonziliarer Liturgiereform", *Theologisch-praktische Quartalschrift* 153 (2005): 74; Martin Stuflesser, "Actuosa participatio: Zwischen hektischem Aktionismus und neuer Innerlichkeit: Überlegungen zur 'tätigen Teilnahme' am Gottesdienst der Kirche als Recht und Pflicht der Getauften", *Liturgisches Jahrbuch* 59 (2009): 163.

[87] Cf. Anton Baumstark, *Vom geschichtlichen Werden der Liturgie*, Ecclesia Orans 10 (Freiburg: Herder, 1923); Anton Baumstark, *Liturgie comparée: Principes et méthodes pour l'étude historique des liturgies chrétiennes*, 3rd ed., Collection Irénikon (Chevetogne, Belgium: Éditions de Chevetogne, 1954). On the principle of the organic development of the liturgy before Vatican Council II, see Alcuin Reid, *The Organic Development of the Liturgy: The Principles of Liturgical Reform and Their Relation to the Twentieth-Century Liturgical Movement Prior to the Second Vatican Council*, 2nd ed. (San Francisco: Ignatius Press, 2005).

[88] For a critical discussion of this, see Arnold Angenendt, *Liturgik und Historik: Gab es eine organische Liturgie-Entwicklung?* (Freiburg: Herder 2001).

[89] SC 23.

[90] Ibid.

[91] Cf. Baumstark, *Liturgie comparée*, 2f.

The rite of the Mass was to have been restored according to the "norm of the Fathers" (*norma patrum*). For that reason, it could not simply be a matter of returning to an earlier form of the Roman Mass. "Norm of the Fathers" did not mean being guided by a kind of liturgical "archaism".[92] Instead, sound tradition (*sana traditio*) was to be preserved, while at the same time a path for legitimate development (*progressio legitima*) was to be opened, whereby the "general laws governing the structure and meaning of the liturgy"[93] were to be observed, and the experiences with individual preconciliar liturgical reforms were to be taken into consideration.[94]

Active participation is the point of departure for the constitution's statements about the Eucharist, also.[95] For the liturgy is a celebration of the Church,[96] which is why communal celebration takes precedence over its private celebration, in particular in the case of the celebration of Mass. The right of the priest to celebrate *sine populo*, however, should not be curtailed, since every celebration of Mass is a celebration of the Church.[97] By its very essence, however, the liturgy of the Church has the character of a communal celebration. In it, at the same time, the Church is represented as *communio hierarchica*.[98] All exercise a truly liturgical service in the liturgy: not only the sacred ministers, but also the laity. But peculiar to the liturgical celebration is a specific order, within which "each person, minister or layman, who has an office to perform, should do all of, but only, those parts which pertain to his office by the nature of the rite and the principles of liturgy."[99]

---

[92] SC 23. Gerhards, "Gipfelpunkt und Quelle", 141, accuses the reform of the Mass of remaining largely dependent on the Middle Ages, of course without proving this assertion.

[93] SC 23.

[94] Cf. Alcuin Reid, "Sacrosanctum Concilium and the Organic Development of the Liturgy", in *The Genius of the Roman Rite: Historical, Theological, and Pastoral Perspectives on Catholic Liturgy*, ed. U.M. Lang (Chicago: Hillenbrand, 2010), 198–215; Reid, "Eine Präzisierung von 'The Organic Development of the Liturgy'—Das grundlegende Prinzip zur Beurteilung der Reform", in *Römische Messe und Liturgie in der Moderne*, ed. S. Wahle, H. Hoping, and W. Haunerland (Freiburg: Herder, 2013), 73–102.

[95] Cf. *SC* 48.

[96] Cf. *SC* 26.

[97] Cf. *SC* 27.

[98] Cf. Gerhards, "Gipfelpunkt und Quelle", 139.

[99] SC 28.

While preserving the "substantial unity of the Roman rite", the Council Fathers concede that there can be a certain cultural adaptation of the rite. In this sense there is no requirement for "rigid uniformity"[100] in the Roman Rite. It is not stated wherein the substantial unity of the Roman Rite consists. Therefore, it is not surprising that the question about the limits of legitimate liturgical inculturation is debated to this day. The right to regulate the liturgy, in any event, depends "solely on the authority of the Church, that is, on the Apostolic See and, as laws may determine, on the bishop"[101] or belongs to the conference of bishops. Otherwise, no one has the right to regulate the liturgy. It follows that no one, even if he be a priest, "may add, remove, or change anything in the liturgy on his own authority".[102]

The celebration of the Mass is made up of the liturgy of the Word of God (Liturgy of the Word) and the Eucharistic liturgy (Liturgy of the Eucharist), which are inseparably bound together in the celebration of Mass and are a single act of worship.[103] It is emphatically commended that "the faithful, after the priest's communion, receive the Lord's body from the same sacrifice."[104] In certain celebrations of Mass, it may be permitted to offer the faithful Communion under both species.[105] The possibility of concelebration, in which the unity of the priesthood is manifested, should be extended. It is foreseen that a new rite of concelebration will be drawn up for the Pontifical and the Missal.[106] Particularly important is the demand for a more strongly biblical character in the Roman Rite.[107] The Catholic Church is not only "Church of the Sacraments", but also "Church of the Word", and she has to rediscover this. There should be a new cycle of readings for the celebration of Holy Mass, "so that richer fare may be provided for the faithful at the table of God's word. In this way a more representative portion of the holy scriptures will be

---

[100] SC 37.
[101] SC 22.
[102] Ibid.
[103] Cf. SC 56.
[104] SC 55.
[105] Cf. ibid.
[106] SC 57–58.
[107] SC 24, 51.

read to the people in the course of a prescribed number of years."[108] The homily is not only highly recommended, but prescribed for the celebration of Holy Mass on Sundays and holy days of obligation.[109] To be restored is "the common prayer" or "the prayer of the faithful" (*oratio fidelium*), "in which the people are to take part in the petitions".[110] Since the Liturgy of the Word and the Eucharistic liturgy "comprise a single act of worship",[111] the faithful should take part in the entire celebration of Holy Mass. There can be a legitimate local adaptation of the Roman liturgical books "provided the substantial unity of the Roman rite is preserved".[112] All "lawfully acknowledged rites" of the Catholic Church are recognized "to be of equal right and dignity".[113] Thus, the Second Vatican Council reaffirms the recognition of the ancient rites declared by the Council of Trent.

B. Implementation of the Reform of the Missal

The Second Vatican Council had asked for publication of the revised liturgical books as soon as possible (*quam primum*).[114] The constitution *Sacrosanctum concilium*, solemnly adopted on December 4, 1963, was concerned with "a sort of legal framework"[115] for a general liturgical renewal. By February 29, 1964, Pope Paul VI had appointed a panel to implement the reform of the liturgy.[116] The official name of this liturgical panel was *Consilium ad exsequendam Constitutionem de sacra Liturgia*. The *Consilium*, which reported directly to the pope and worked in that configuration until 1969, had to implement the concerns of the Constitution on the Liturgy. First president of

---

[108] *SC* 51.

[109] Cf. *SC* 52.

[110] *SC* 53.

[111] *SC* 56.

[112] *SC* 38: "Servata substantiali unitate ritus romani".

[113] *SC* 4: "omnes ritus legitime agnitos aequo iure atque honore habere."

[114] Cf. *SC* 25.

[115] Ratzinger, "Das Konzil auf dem Weg", in *Joseph Ratzinger, Gesammelte Schriften*, ed. Gerhard Cardinal Müller (Freiburg, Basel, and Vienna: Herder, 2008– ; hereafter cited as *JRGS*), vol. 7/1 (2012), 406.

[116] On the prehistory of the *Consilium*, cf. Piero Marini, *A Challenging Reform: Realizing the Vision of the Liturgical Renewal (1963–1975)* (Collegeville, Minn.: Liturgical Press, 2007), 1–39.

the *Consilium* was Giacomo Cardinal Lercaro (1891–1976), who was succeeded in 1968 by the Swiss Benedictine Benno Cardinal Gut. Paul VI appointed Annibale Bugnini the secretary. At the organizational session of the *Consilium* on January 15, 1964, it was agreed to begin with the reform of the liturgical books. By April 25, 1964, Paul VI adopted the words *Corpus Christi* as the new formula for administering Communion to the faithful.[117] The *Coetus X De Ordine Missae*, a sub-committee of the *Consilium*, met for the first time from May 7–10, 1964, in Trier. In the same year, additional sessions were held in Rome (June 4–7), Fribourg, Switzerland (August 23–28), and again in Rome (September 21–23). At the fourth session, the draft of a modified *Ordo Missae* was produced.

A few days later (September 26, 1964), the instruction *Inter oecumenici* was issued, which took effect on March 7, 1965 (First Sunday of Lent).[118] The instruction for the implementation of the liturgical reform led to the first changes—with more to follow—of the *Ordo Missae*.[119] The instruction regulates, among other things, the extent of vernacular language in the Mass.[120] It also contains guidelines for translating liturgical texts on the basis of article 36 §3 of the Constitution on the Liturgy.[121] In accordance with the constitution, Latin is retained in the Eucharistic Prayer as the language of worship.[122] Nevertheless, several bishops' conferences pressed to allow the vernacular there as well.[123] Even during the council, permission was given for vernacular translations of the Preface (April 27, 1964).[124]

---

[117] Cf. *AAS* 56 (1964): 337f. (*DEL* 1:100).

[118] Cf. *AAS* 56 (1964): 877–900 (*DEL* 1:102–38).

[119] Cf. Sacred Congregation of Rites, Instruction *Inter oecumenici* on Implementing the Constitution on the Sacred Liturgy (September 26, 1964; hereafter cited as *IO*), no. 48 (*DEL* 1:118f.).

[120] Parts that are not allowed in the vernacular are the prayer of the day, the *oratio super oblata*, the Postcommunion, and the Eucharistic Prayer. Cf. *IO* 57 (*DEL* 1:122–24).

[121] Cf. *IO* 40 (*DEL* 1:114–16).

[122] Cf. *SC* 36. "Steps should be taken so that the faithful may also be able to say or to sing together in Latin those parts of the Ordinary of the Mass which pertain to them" (*SC* 54).

[123] For this purpose, they cited *SC* 40, 54.

[124] In German-speaking regions, the Viennese pastor Joseph Ernst Mayer (1905–1998), who had studied the liturgy formally, supported the celebration of Mass entirely in the vernacular. In March 1964, he gave his famous lecture on the reform of the liturgy at the Liturgical Congress in Mainz. Although the Council Fathers had wished for a linguistically mixed celebration of Mass (Latin, vernacular), Mayer described this as "nonsensical". Cf. Mayer, *Zur Liturgie von heute und morgen* (Klosterneuburg: Verlag Österreichisches Katholisches Bibelwerk, 1997), 76.

On January 27, 1965, the new *editio typica* of the *Ordo Missae*[125] with the unaltered *Canon Romanus* was published. The prayers at the foot of the altar (up to the Psalm *Iudica me*, which was omitted) as well as the Offertory prayers were retained. In accordance with the norm of *Inter oecumenici* regarding the vernacular in the liturgy of the Mass, the first dual-language altar missals appeared that same year. Printed in the front of these books was a revision of the *Ritus servandus in celebratione missae*, supplemented by the tract *De defectibus missae celebratione occurrentibus* (mistakes occurring in the celebration of Mass). Approval of the Latin-German altar missal followed on September 25, 1965.[126] The first volume contains the *Ordo Missae* and the proper parts of the Mass from the First Sunday of Advent to the Saturday after Passion Sunday.

On the basis of the Latin-German altar missal, at the beginning of 1966, Beuron Archabbey produced a new edition of the "Schott" pew missal with up-to-date instructions for its use.[127] Reprinted in it is a letter from Amleto Giovanni Cardinal Cicognani (1883–1973) to the archabbot of Beuron, in which the cardinal secretary of state explains that with the appearance of the Latin-German altar missal and the new "Schott", the "connection to the council's Constitution on the Liturgy is accomplished."[128] The altar missal and the people's Mass book, said the cardinal, make it clear that the liturgy is "the summit toward which the activity of the Church is directed; at

---

[125] Cf. *Ordo Missae* (1965); cf. *Notitiae* 1 (1965): 101–2.

[126] About the Latin-German altar missal, cf. Helmut Hoping, "The *Ordo Missae* of 1965: The Latin-German Altar Missal and Liturgical Renewal", in *Benedict XVI and the Roman Missal*, ed. J.E. Rutherford and J. O'Brien, Fota Liturgy Series 4 (Dublin and New York: Four Courts Press, 2013), 292–309; Hans-Jürgen Feulner, "Der *Ordo Missae* von 1965 und das *Missale Romanum* von 1962", in *Römische Messe und Liturgie in der Moderne*, ed. S. Wahle, H. Hoping, and W. Haunerland (Freiburg: Herder, 2013), 103–42. The American (and Australian) "Interim Missal" was introduced as early as November 29, 1964 (First Sunday of Advent), before the effective date of *Inter oecumenici*. On the first vernacular missals in the U.S.A. (1964–1966), see Andreas Bieringer, *A Halfway House to Aggiornamento? Die ersten muttersprachlichen Messbücher in den USA (1964–1966)*, Studien zur Pastoralliturgie 38 (Regensburg: Pustet, 2014).

[127] Cf. Anselm Schott, O.S.B., *Das Messbuch der heiligen Messe: Mit neuen liturgischen Einführungen in Übereinstimmung mit dem Altarmessbuch neugearbeitet von den Benediktinern der Erzabtei Beuron* (Freiburg, Basel, and Vienna, 1966).

[128] A photocopy of the letter from the Cardinal Secretary of State is printed before the 1966 edition of the "Schott" Missal. Klaus Gamber had already pointed this out. Cf. Klaus Gamber, *Alter und neuer Messritus* (Regensburg: Pustet, 1983), 23.

the same time it is the font from which all her power flows."[129] The Congregation for Rites published a negative *responsum* to the question of whether further changes to the *Ordo Missae* or a complete revision of the *Missale Romanum* was anticipated.[130] Both explanations indicate that, on the question about the reform of the liturgy, there were considerable differences of opinion between, on the one side, the *Consilium* operating directly under the pope and, on the other hand, the Congregation for Rites as well as the Secretariat of State.

In accordance with the first instruction concerning proper implementation of the Constitution on the Liturgy, provisions were made for the vernacular in the Mass initially only in the readings, petitions, hymns, greetings, acclamations, and dialogue as well as the Our Father and in the formula for administering Communion.[131] The *Ordo Missae* of 1965 created the possibility of using the vernacular in the liturgy with the exception of the Eucharistic Prayer. The opening prayers and the Liturgy of the Word were removed from the altar and shifted to the *sedilia* and *ambo*. The faithful (*circumstantes*) could take part in the prayers at the foot of the altar in Latin or in the vernacular; these prayers had hardly been changed in the *Ordo Missae* of 1965. Though it was not prescribed, priests now had the option to celebrate the Eucharist *versus populum*.

With the reform of the *Ordo Missae* of 1965, the reform of the Missal was not finished, even though the Congregation of Rites considered it concluded. After publication of the modified *Ordo Missae*, further sessions of the *Coetus X* took place at Le Saulchoir in Paris (June 8–23, 1965) and at Nemi in Metropolitan Rome (September 16–19, 1965). In them, Josef Andreas Jungmann made the case for a reform of the Roman Canon. Cyprian Vagaggini spoke in favor of removing it and replacing it with another. Aimé-Georges Martimort opposed this plan at the plenary session of the *Consilium* in Rome (October 18–22, 1965). Louis Bouyer (1913–2004), a friend of Pope Paul VI who had been appointed to the group working on the *Ordo Missae*, expressed misgivings about the ideas for reform, which in some cases were far-reaching. At the sessions in Le Saulchoir and

---

[129] SC 10.
[130] Cf. *Notitiae* 2 (1966): 32.
[131] Cf. IO 57.

Nemi, a new schema *De Ordine Missae* was discussed. The schema was then to be presented to the synod of bishops through its governing body, which had recently been established by Pope Paul VI with the motu proprio *Apostolica sollicitudo* (September 15, 1965).

On June 20, 1966, Paul VI informed Cardinal Lercaro that the Roman Canon was to remain unchanged. "Two or three others [i.e., new Eucharistic Prayers] are to be composed or found for use at special limited times",[132] although the *ingenium romanum*, that is, the spirit of the Roman liturgy, must be retained.[133] After this signal from the pope, the *Coetus X* once again tackled the work that had been interrupted in the autumn of 1965. The *Ordo Missae* of 1965 did not satisfy the radical reformers of the liturgy around Bugnini. Thus a new Order of the Mass, with numerous changes, was drafted. It went so far as to omit the prayers at the foot of the altar. Of them, only the Introit was retained. However, even this is often not recited in liturgical praxis nowadays. Instead, an entrance hymn is usually sung, which as a rule is unrelated to the verse of the Introit. In place of the prayers at the foot of the altar, a completely new penitential act was inserted. The *Kyrie* and *Gloria* were retained, but the number of invocations was reduced from nine to six. In addition, it went so far as to redesign the order of readings and the *Offertorium* and to insert the *oratio fidelium* (prayers of the faithful). With the approval of the *Consilium*, the *Coetus X* delivered the schema of the so-called *Missa normativa* to Paul VI on July 2, 1966. In April of 1967, the *Consilium* submitted texts for four new Eucharistic Prayers; one of them, a Latin version of the Alexandrian *anaphora* of Saint Basil, would be dropped later.[134]

The second Instruction for Implementing the Constitution on the Liturgy, *Tres abhinc annos*, dated May 4, 1967, represented a turning point.[135] Since the *Ordo Missae* had been changed extensively from

---

[132] Thus Paul VI in an audience with Cardinal Lercaro on June 20, 1966. Cf. Annibale Bugnini, *The Reform of the Liturgy 1948–1975*, trans. Matthew J. O'Connell (Collegeville, Minn.: Liturgical Press, 1990), 346. Cf. Johannes Wagner, *Mein Weg zur Liturgiereform 1936–1986: Erinnerungen* (Freiburg: Herder, 1993), 95.

[133] Cf. Pierre Jounel, "La composition des nouvelles prières eucharistiques", *La Maison-Dieu* 94 (1968): 39.

[134] Cf. ibid., 39–40.

[135] Cf. Sacred Congregation of Rites, Second Instruction on the Orderly Carrying out of the Constitution on the Liturgy *Tres abhinc annos* (May 4, 1967; hereafter cited as *TAA*), 167–94 (*DEL* 1:429–37).

the 1965 version, it was explicitly called a *Novus Ordo Missae*. Permission was given to the competent regional authorities to introduce the vernacular even into the Canon of the Mass.[136] This had been anticipated back on January 31, 1967. In Holland, there had been since 1965 unapproved translations of the Roman Canon and new Prefaces for use in the liturgy. Since February 13, 1967, translations of the Roman Canon had been submitted to the Holy See for confirmation, but they were too free and had been rejected by the Congregation for the Doctrine of the Faith. Permitted *ad interim* were the authorized translations from the people's missals, which originally had not been intended for liturgical use.[137] In the case of new translations of the Roman Canon, the authorities insisted on a faithful and complete translation, as with the other texts of the Mass. In a departure from the 1965 *Ordo Missae*, the instruction *Tres abhinc annos* determined that the priest, together with the faithful, should recite three times the *Domine non sum dignus* at Communion.[138] It was recommended that the priest pray the prayer *Placeat tibi* at the recessional.[139]

On October 12, 1965, the *Consilium* announced that the pope did not consider the reception of Communion in the hand appropriate—a practice that had developed in many lands (above all in Germany, Holland, Belgium, and France).[140] The instruction concerning the celebration and veneration of the Eucharist, *Eucharisticum mysterium* (May 25, 1967),[141] created the option of standing or kneeling when receiving Communion.[142] But reception of Communion on the tongue remained the general norm. A letter from the Secretariat of State dated June 3, 1968, explained that the Holy Father found Communion in the hand to be—in practice—that is, in view of its consequences—"debatable and dangerous".[143] However, in individual cases, bishops' conferences could receive permission to allow Communion in the hand from the Congregation of Rites. In view of protests against Communion in

---

[136] Cf. ibid., 28 (*DEL* 1:436f.).

[137] Cf. *Notitiae* 3 (1967): 326. See also the Decree of the Sacred Congregation of Rites, *De editionibus librorum liturgicorum*, *AAS* 58 (January 27, 1966), no. 5 (*DEL* 1:314).

[138] Cf. *TAA* 13 (*DEL* 1:433).

[139] Cf. ibid., 16 (*DEL* 1:433f.).

[140] Cf. Bugnini, *Reform of the Liturgy*, 640n34.

[141] Cf. *AAS* 59 (1967): 539–73.

[142] Cf. Sacred Congregation of Rites, Instruction on Eucharistic Worship *Eucharisticum mysterium* (May 27, 1967), no. 34.

[143] Bugnini, *Reform of the Liturgy*, 640.

the hand, the permissions that had been granted first to Germany and Belgium were stopped. The *Consilium* circulated a questionnaire to all bishops concerning Communion in the hand. The majority opposed Communion in the hand.[144] But since the spread of Communion in the hand could no longer be stopped in certain countries, the bishops' conferences of those places were allowed by the Congregation for Divine Worship in its instruction *Memoriale Domini* (May 29, 1969)[145] to introduce Communion in the hand as an option—while preserving the freedom of the faithful to choose for themselves the manner of receiving Communion.[146]

Approval of the first German translation of the *Canon Romanus* for liturgical use followed on December 5, 1967, after the text had been confirmed by the Holy See on November 14, 1967.[147] The translation had been composed by a committee headed by Joseph Pascher, a liturgical scholar from Munich, and of course it underwent several changes by the German-speaking bishops.[148] On May 18, 1967, the Congregation of Rites presented an overview of the new modifications to the *Ordo Missae*. On two pages of the document, the relevant texts of the *Novus Ordo Missae* are juxtaposed with those from the *Vetus Ordo Missae*.[149] The consultations about the outline of the *Novus Ordo Missae* were held during the first Roman Synod of Bishops in October 1967. The *schema* met with considerable resistance from the Synod Fathers.[150] In January 1968, trial celebrations of the so-called *missa normativa* took place in the Sistine Chapel and for Pope Paul VI.[151]

---

[144] Cf. ibid., 647. To the question of whether the practice of Communion in the hand should be allowed, out of 2,136 bishops, 567 responded Yes; 1,233—No; 315—*iuxta modum*; and 21 abstained.

[145] Cf. *AAS* 61 (1969): 541–45 (*DEL* 1:811–18).

[146] Cf. *DEL* 1:814f.

[147] Cf. *Gottesdienst* 1 (1967): 28–30. The translation was reviewed by the *Consilium*, the Congregation for the Doctrine of the Faith, and the Sacred Congregation of Rites.

[148] Cf. Theodor Schnitzler, *Der Römische Messkanon: In Betrachtung, Verkündigung und Gebet* (Freiburg: Herder, 1968), 40. Theodor Schnitzler (1910–1982) was a consultor of the *Consilium* and of the Congregation for Divine Worship.

[149] Cf. *Variationes in Ordinem Missae inducendae ad normam Instructionis S.R.C. diei 4 maii 1967* (1967). The complete text is reprinted in *Notitiae* 3 (1967): 195–211.

[150] Cf. Bugnini, *Reform of the Liturgy*, 346–59.

[151] The results of the ballot on the *missa normativa* were 43 votes *non placet* (No); 62 *iuxta modum* (Yes with in some cases considerable reservations); and 4 abstentions out of a total of 187 votes.

The renovated *Offertorium* in particular met with the criticism of
Paul VI. All in all, he wanted as few changes to the Order of Mass
as necessary.[152] On November 6, 1968, he approved the corrections
to the Roman Canon of the Mass.[153] The words of institution of the
Roman Canon were adapted to those of the new Eucharistic Prayers.
The three new Eucharistic Prayers, together with eight new Prefaces,
were published by the Congregation of Rites on May 23, 1968.[154]
On April 6, 1969, the Congregation for Divine Worship (the successor to the Congregation of Rites) published the *Novus Ordo Missae*
together with the *Institutio Generalis*.[155] Three days earlier, Paul VI
had approved the new Roman Missal with his Apostolic Constitution *Missale Romanum* (April 3, 1969).[156] On account of the resistance
to the new reform of the Mass, Paul VI directed the Prefect of the
Congregation for the Doctrine of the Faith to examine the objections
that were raised against the new Mass. So as not to damage the rep-
utation of Paul VI, Franjo Cardinal Šeper (1905–1981), who personally had reservations about the result of the liturgical reform, tried to
dismiss the objections.

A polemic formally entitled *Short Critical Study of the New Order
of Mass* (1969) was circulated under the name *The Ottaviani Intervention*.[157] In it, the reform of the Mass was accused of being incompatible with the statements of the Council of Trent about Holy Mass
and with the 1570 *Missale Romanum*. The polemic was composed by
a group of conservative theologians, bishops, and cardinals from the
extended circle of the "Coetus Internationalis Patrum" (International

[152] Cf. Bugnini, *Reform of the Liturgy*, 364.

[153] Cf. ibid., 383.

[154] Cf. "Preces eucharistica et praefationis", *Notitia* 4 (1968): 156–60 (*DEL* 1:529–34). On
this subject, see the letter and the instructions of the president of the "Consilium", Benno
Cardinal Gut, to the presidents of the bishops' conferences: *Notitiae* 4 (1968): 146–55 (*DEL*
1:535–46).

[155] That is, the *General Instruction on the Roman Missal*. Cf. *Missale Romanum ex decreto
Sacrosancti Oecumenici Concilii Vaticani II instauratum auctoritate Pauli Pp. VI promulgatum, Ordo
Missae* (1970). On the reform of the "*Ordo Missae*", cf. Maurizio Barba, *La riforma conciliare
dell'Ordo Missae: Il percorso storica-redazionale dei riti d'ingresso, di offertorio, e di communion* (Rome:
CLV, 2008).

[156] Cf. *DEL* 1:1373–1736.

[157] Cf. Alfredo Cardinal Ottaviani, *The Ottaviani Intervention: Short Critical Study of the New
Order of Mass* (West Chester, Ohio: Philothea Press, 2010).

Group of [Council] Fathers).[158] Pope Paul VI responded to the criticism of Ottaviani's group in the prologue to the 1970 *Missale Romanum*. In it, he reaffirmed that the reform was consistent with the Roman tradition. On March 26, 1970, the Congregation for Divine Worship published the *editio typica* of the new *Missale Romanum*.[159] Quite striking are the changes that were undertaken in the *General Instruction on the Roman Missal* (GIRM) to the 1969 Order of Mass, above all with regard to the withdrawal of sacrificial language in the rubrics.[160] On the basis of the 1970 *Missale Romanum*, the Missal for the dioceses of the German-speaking regions appeared in 1975.[161] That same year, the *editio typica altera* [second typical edition] of the *Missale Romanum* was promulgated by Pope Paul VI.[162]

The Missal of Paul VI contains the texts and chants assigned to the priest, but it no longer includes the readings. The readings are found in the Lectionary, or Gospel Book, and the chants for the cantor and the schola in the *Graduale Romanum*. The Missal of Paul VI contains more optional variations than the 1570 Missal. The presider's prayers and the Scripture readings, however, cannot be replaced by other texts. In addition to the *Canon Romanus*, the new Missal of 1970 contains three new Eucharistic Prayers. Eucharistic Prayer II is modeled on the *Traditio Apostolica*. Eucharistic Prayer III takes its orientation from the Roman Canon of the Mass and summarizes the sacrificial statements while paying particular attention to the Christocentric ecclesiology of Vatican Council II. It was conceived by the Italian liturgist Cyprian Vagaggini and was modified in crucial passages under the influence of Pope Paul VI. Eucharistic Prayer IV is modeled on an Eastern anaphora of Antiochene origin. The draft of a Eucharistic Prayer with an even stronger resemblance to the Eastern anaphoras,

---

[158] It is prefaced by a letter from Alfredo Cardinal Ottaviani (1890–1979) and Antonio Cardinal Bacci (1885–1971) that summarizes the points of the critique. Cf. Ottaviani, *Ottaviani Intervention*, 33–36.

[159] Cf. *DEL* 1:2060. Official edition: *Missale Romanum ex decreto Sacrosancti Oecumenici Concilii Vaticani II instauratum auctoritate Pauli Pp. VI. promulgatum* (Vatican City, 1970).

[160] Cf. Maurizio Barba, *Institutio generalis Missalis Romani* (Vatican City: Libreria Editrice Vaticana, 2006).

[161] Cf. *MB*.

[162] Cf. *Missale Romanum ex decreto Sacrosancti Oecumenici Concilii Vaticani II instauratum auctoritate Pauli Pp. VI. promulgatum: Editio typica altera* (1975).

especially to the Alexandrian anaphora of Saint Basil, met with the misgivings of the Congregation for the Doctrine of the Faith in 1967 and hence was not pursued further. For only Eucharistic Prayers that correspond to the spirit (*ingenium*) of the Roman liturgical tradition were to be admitted. The expression *mysterium fidei* was removed from the words over the chalice and combined with a new acclamation of the people that refers to the Paschal Mystery of Christ.

The vernacular translations of the *Missale Romanum* were in some cases very loose. This was connected with a change of position in the hermeneutics of translation that had been effected in 1969. The new translations, unlike the unofficial ones of the popular missals, were supposed to become the voice of the praying Church.[163] This signified a particular challenge for the translators. While Vatican Council II was still in session, a congress for translators of liturgical texts took place in Rome. In his address to the participants in the congress on November 10, 1965, Paul VI referred to the difficulties of translation. In doing so, he cited Saint Jerome: "If I translate literally, it sounds nonsensical; if, compelled by necessity, I change something of the syntax and the text, then it gives the appearance that I have performed my task as translator incorrectly."[164] The quotation from Jerome makes it clear that in translating liturgical texts there must be a balance between formal and dynamic equivalence, just as in the translation of biblical texts. The translation of liturgical texts, Paul VI says, should not use colloquial language and should put the depth of the divine mysteries into words adequately. In order to do that, it is necessary to strike a careful balance between Christian Latinity and the vernacular, while taking into account that the new text must be capable of being declaimed or chanted.[165] Translators of liturgical texts should furthermore make sure that the texts are translated completely and that, therefore, no parts are omitted that could be translated without difficulty.[166]

---

[163] Cf. Paul VI, *Allocutio ad interpretes* (November 10, 1965), *Notitiae* 1 (1965): 380 (*DEL* 1:263).

[164] Ibid., 378 (*DEL* 1:262). Cf. Hieronymus, *Praefatio ad Chronicam Eusebii Pamphilii* (*PL* 26:35).

[165] Cf. Paul VI, Address to Translators of Liturgical Texts (November 10, 1965), *Notitiae* 1 (1965): 379 (*DEL* 1:263).

[166] Cf. ibid., 381 (*DEL* 1:265).

On June 21, 1967, Cardinal Lercaro reaffirmed in a letter from the Concilium to the presidents of the bishops' conferences that the Canon must be translated *literale et integrale* and the texts are to be taken "as they are given, without any abridgments or simplifications. The adaptation to the modern language must be straightforward and moderate."[167] In a communiqué dated August 10, 1967, Bugnini referred to the desire of the Holy See "that the various translations of the Roman Canon correspond to one another, so as to preserve a certain agreement at least for this very sacred text of the Eucharistic celebration."[168] In translating the texts, the extremes of excessively antiquated and overly modern language should be avoided.[169] Bugnini recalled, moreover, that it was the pope's wish "that Missals ... in a complete or partial edition always contain the Latin text alongside the vernacular version",[170] as is the case in the bilingual altar missals that have been published since 1965. In the case of the expression *pro multis* in the words over the chalice, the Congregation for the Doctrine of the Faith and the Secretariat of State insisted on a literal translation in all bilingual altar missals. There were also some who spoke in favor of not translating the *verba testamenti*.[171]

The instruction *De interpretatione textuum liturgicorum* (French title: *Comme le prévoit*) of the Consilium for the Liturgy, dated January 15, 1969, marked a turning point.[172] The instruction now required that only the Eucharistic Prayer be translated *integre et fideliter* [in its entirety and faithfully]. It allowed the other prayers to be translated freely and using colloquial language. Moreover, a complete translation was no longer considered necessary, as with the other parts of the Mass. With that, the instruction gave clear priority to the principle of dynamic equivalence over the principle of formal equivalence.[173] On the basis

---

[167] Lercaro, Epistula "Concilii", *Notitiae* 3 (1967): 296 (*DEL* 1:510).

[168] Bugnini, *De interpretatione Canonis Romani*, *Notitiae* 3 (1967): 326 (*DEL* 1:512).

[169] Cf. Consilium, *De interpretatione Canonis Romani* (August 10, 1967), Prooemium and no. 2 (*DEL* 1:512f.).

[170] Bugnini, *De interpretatione Canonis Romani*, *Notitiae* 3 (1967): 327 (*DEL* 1:513).

[171] Cf. Bugnini, *Reform of the Liturgy*, 109n27.

[172] Cf. Consilium, *De interpretatione textuum liturgicorum* (January 25, 1969), *Notitiae* 5 (1969): 3–12 (*DEL* 1:592–605).

[173] Cf. Dennis McManus, "Übersetzungstheorie in *Liturgiam authenticam*", in *Papst Benedikt XVI. und die Liturgie* (Regensburg: Pustet, 2014), 131–49; Uwe Michael Lang, *The Voice of the Church at Prayer: Reflections on Liturgy and Language* (San Francisco: Ignatius Press, 2012), 169–72.

of this decision, the translation of the *Missale Romanum* into the vernacular languages finally took place. This led to very loose translations of the liturgical texts that in some cases strongly favored one interpretation and even outright paraphrases that were increasingly perceived as a problem. And so the Congregation for Divine Worship, by order of John Paul II, introduced a revision of the translations with the fifth instruction on the lawful implementation of the liturgical reform, *Liturgiam authenticam* (March 28, 2001).[174] A first fruit of the revision process is the *Roman Missal* (2011) for English-speaking regions. The new English-language Missal is a completely new translation of the *Missale Romanum* of Paul VI, the third edition of which John Paul II had promulgated in 2002.[175] The instruction formulates "fidelity to the text" and "ease of understanding" as the central principles of translation.[176] Walter Cardinal Kasper calls the decision made by *Liturgiam authenticam* "a perfectly successful rollback" that contradicts "any rational hermeneutic ... because it ignores the fact that every

---

[174] Cf. Congregation for Divine Worship and the Discipline of the Sacraments, Instruction *Liturgiam authenticam* on the Use of the Vernacular Language in the Publication of the Books of the Roman Liturgy (March 28, 2001). Martin Klöckener, "Liturgical Renewal through History", *Studia Liturgica* 44 (2014): 32, claims that *Liturgiam authenticam* is incompatible with the ecclesiology of Vatican Council II but does not prove his thesis.

[175] The most prominent example of the many corrections to the translation is the colloquial response of the faithful "And also with you" to the priest's liturgical greeting "The Lord be with you." Now the response is "And with your spirit", corresponding to the Latin text. The response "Et cum spiritu tuo" refers to the ministerial charism of the priest.

[176] Cf. McManus, "Übersetzungstheorie", 141–44. On *Liturgiam authenticam*, see also Dieter Böhler, "Anmerkungen eines Exegeten zur Instructio Quinta 'Liturgiam Authenticam'", *Liturgisches Jahrbuch* 54 (2004): 205–22; Winfried Haunerland, "Die Leitlinien der Revision: Texttreue und Verständlichkeit", *Gottesdienst* 39 (2005): 153–56. For opinions critical of the instruction, see Peter Jeffery, *Translating Traditions: A Chant Historian Reads Liturgiam authenticam* (Collegeville, Minn.: Liturgical Press, 2005); Klemens Richter, "Die Liturgiekonstitution 'Sacrosanctum Concilium' des Zweiten Vatikanischen Konzils", in *Liturgiereform: Eine bleibende Aufgabe: 40 Jahre Konzilskonstitution über die heilige Liturgie*, ed. K. Richter and T. Sternberg (Münster: Aschendorff, 2004), 39; Reiner Kaczynski, "Angriff auf die Liturgiekonstitution? Anmerkungen zu einer neuen Übersetzer-Instruktion", *Stimmen der Zeit* 219 (2011): 651–66. In their critique of *Liturgiam authenticam*, Richter and Kaczynski are silent about the fact that the Instruction *De interpretatione textuum liturgicorum* had changed the hermeneutic of translation in a one-sided way in favor of dynamic equivalence, which was corrected by *Liturgiam authenticam*. Keith F. Pecklers writes decidedly in favor of dynamic equivalence only, i.e., an approximate correspondence between the contents in the language of origin and in the target language. See Keith F. Pecklers, *Dynamic Equivalence: The Living Language of Christian Worship* (Collegeville, Minn.: Liturgical Press, 2003).

language has its genius, and therefore there can never be a word-for-word translation if the vernacular text is to be truly comprehensible and not disguised Latin."[177] Cardinal Kasper overlooks the fact that *Liturgiam authenticam* demands a literal translation but not a word-for-word translation at all costs. Cardinal Kasper does not discuss the sometimes dubious translations of the Roman Missal that have resulted since 1969, especially in English and German.[178]

The first volume of the 1975 Missal for the dioceses of the German-speaking regions still contained in part 2 the celebration of Mass in Latin for Sundays and feast days.[179] In contrast, the second edition of the Missal in 1988, which to this day is in liturgical use, reprints only the German text, contrary to the will of Paul VI. The altar edition of the 1975 German Missal is made up of two volumes: the first volume contains the "General Introduction to the Missal" and the *Triduum Sacrum*; the second volume, the texts of the Mass without the *Triduum Sacrum*. In addition, there is a one-volume small edition with all the texts, the General Introduction, and the rubrics of the Missal. During the Holy Year 1975, additional Eucharistic Prayers for reconciliation and for special occasions were approved. During that same year, the *Editio typica altera* [second typical edition] of the *Missale Romanum* appeared with a decree dated March 27. The *Editio typica tertia* [third] of the *Missale Romanum*, which was published in 2002 during the pontificate of John Paul II, contains a revised *Institutio Generalis* [General Instruction] and several new prayers. The two Eucharistic Prayers for reconciliation and the Eucharistic Prayers for Masses for special intentions appear as an appendix to the *Ordo*

---

[177] Walter Kasper, "Die liturgische Erneuerung—Die erste und sichtbarste Frucht des Konzils", *Internationale katholische Zeitschrift Communio* 42 (2013): 631. Among the harshest critics of *Liturgiam authenticam* among German-speaking liturgists is Martin Klöckener. Cf. Martin Klöckener, "Die liturgischen Vorstehergebete im Widerstreit: Theologische Begründungen, Anfragen, Konflikte, Perspektiven", in *Gemeinschaft im Danken: Grundfragen der Eucharistiefeier im ökumenischen Gespräch*, ed. Stefan Böntert, Studien zur Pastoralliturgie 40 (Regensburg: Pustet, 2015), 146–68, 171–74.

[178] Concerning the sometimes dubious German translations of the *Missale Romanum* (1970; 1975²), cf. Alex Stock, *Liturgie und Poesie: Zur Sprache des Gottesdienstes* (Kevelaer: Butzon & Bercker, 2010); Stock, *Orationen: Die Tagesgebete im Jahreskreis neu übersetzt und erklärt* (Regensburg: Pustet, 2011); Stock, *Orationen: Die Tagesgebete im Festkreis neu übersetzt und erklärt* (Regensburg: Pustet, 2014). According to Klöckener, "Die liturgischen Vorstehergebete", 166, the Latin texts of the prayers in the German Missal are "as a rule rendered faithfully".

[179] Cf. *MB*, 355–57.

Missae,[180] the Eucharistic Prayers for children as an appendix to the Missal.[181] In the reprinting of the *Editio typica tertia* of the *Missale Romanum* (2008), the children's Eucharistic Prayers were no longer included. The revised German Missal is still not available at the time of this writing [2015]; therefore, the *Grundordnung des Römischen Messbuchs* should be consulted.[182] This is a German translation of the *Institutio Generalis* [GIRM] of the *Editio typica tertia* of the *Missale Romanum* that has been published in advance.

C. The Return of the Traditional Liturgy

"The most striking result of the Council has been the liturgical reform. But this very reform, so eagerly longed for and so joyfully welcomed, has become for many people 'a sign of contradiction'."[183] This was connected with the sometimes substantial changes made to the form of the Roman liturgy that had developed over the centuries. During the reform, liturgists looked to the allegedly golden age of the liturgy in the patristic era. Many liturgists had a very negative view of the medieval liturgy.[184] Thus the historian of liturgy Theodor Klauser (1894–1984) called the Middle Ages "an era of exuberant growth, reinterpretations, and misinterpretation"[185]—a judgment that as a generalization does not do justice to the medieval period. Emil Josef Lengeling (1916–1986) spoke about the "end of the Middle Ages in the liturgy", which was sealed by the liturgical reform of Vatican Council II.[186] The historically questionable picture of the medieval liturgy led during the implementation of the liturgical reform to the dominance of a liturgical archaism. Doubts were voiced as to whether the 1970 Missal was a revised missal in the larger tradition of the Church[187]

---

[180] Cf. *MR* 2002³, 673–706.

[181] Cf. ibid., 1271–88.

[182] Cf. *Missale Romanum, Grundordnung des Römischen Messbuchs* (2007).

[183] Ratzinger, "Catholicism after the Council", *The Furrow* 18/1 (January 1967): 3–23 at 6.

[184] Cf. ibid., 10.

[185] Theodor Klauser, *Kleine abendländische Liturgiegeschichte: Bericht und Besinnung* (Bonn: Hanstein, 1965), 8.

[186] Cf. Richter, "Liturgiekonstitution 'Sacrosanctum Concilium'", 22–23, 25.

[187] Cf. *SC* 23, 25.

or perhaps a new missal canceling out the 1962 Missal, as not only critics but also proponents of the reform of the Missal thought.

Joseph Gelineau (1920–2008), a promoter of the liturgical reform and a member of the Consilium for Implementing the Reform of the Liturgy, explained: "It has to be said bluntly: The Roman Rite as we knew it no longer exists. It has been destroyed. Walls from the original building have toppled, while others have changed their appearance so much that they look today either like a ruin or as a fragmentary foundation of another building."[188] Joseph Ratzinger writes in his autobiography:

> The old building was demolished, and another was built, to be sure largely using materials from the previous one and even using the old building plans. There is no doubt that this new missal in many respects brought with it a real improvement and enrichment; but setting it as a new construction over against what had grown historically, forbidding the results of this historical growth, thereby makes the liturgy appear to be no longer a living development but the product of erudite work and juridical authority; this has caused us enormous harm. For then the impression had to emerge that liturgy is something "made", not something given in advance but something lying within our own power of decision.[189]

In the reform of the liturgy according to the will of the Council Fathers, not only were "the general laws governing the structure and meaning of the liturgy" to be observed; in addition, "there must be no innovations unless the good of the Church genuinely and certainly requires them; and care must be taken that any new forms adopted should in some way grow organically from forms already existing."[190] The changes made to the Roman Missal, some of them very extensive, were justified not only by the principle of *participatio actuosa* but also and primarily by the principle of noble simplicity. The principle comes from the English convert Edmund Bishop (1846–1917).[191] In his famous essay on "The Genius of the

---

[188] Joseph Gelineau, *Die Liturgie von morgen* (Regensburg: Pustet, 1979), 11.

[189] Ratzinger, *Milestones*, 148.

[190] *SC* 23.

[191] Cf. Edmund Bishop, "The Genius of the Roman Rite", in *Liturgica Historica* (Oxford: Clarendon Press, 1918), 1–19.

Roman Rite", Bishop pointed out the noble simplicity and sobriety of the Roman Rite in comparison with the Eastern Rites. In this, Bishop was guided by the ancient form of the liturgy, which he, like many other historians of liturgy in his day, considered the ultimate standard. Anton Baumstark, too, characterized the Roman liturgy in terms of its simplicity, sobriety, and strict form. In Baumstark's opinion, all liturgies developed according to definite laws. One of them is the law of ever greater complexity combined with less and less strictness of form. This judgment does only limited justice to the actual historical developments.

The principle of simplicity formulated by the council must not be understood in the sense of a rationalizing simplification of the liturgy. The Church's liturgy must not be comprehensible for everyone in the sense of a "superficial comprehensibility" (Dieter Böhler). For the Council Fathers, the principle of noble simplicity and easier comprehensibility is not a principle of economy, comparable to Ockham's Razor, but rather a principle of textual coherence and liturgical aesthetics. The Council Fathers were concerned about an objective correspondence between the content and the form of the liturgy. The Roman liturgy may be simple in comparison to the Eastern liturgical families and, indeed, occasionally sober. Nevertheless, we are talking about a complex structure that opens up only to someone who lives with it and through it, which presupposes regular participation in the liturgy and requires a liturgical mystagogy.

The reform of the Mass no doubt produced numerous good fruits, for example, the introduction of the vernacular, the expanded cycle of readings through which both Testaments of Sacred Scripture were opened up to the faithful to a greater extent, the obligatory homily on Sundays and feast days, the *oratio fidelium* (intercessory Prayer of the Faithful), the increase in the number of Prefaces, the three new Eucharistic Prayers (which, however, should not displace the Roman Canon), Communion of the faithful as part of the Mass, the possibility of receiving Communion under both species, and also the renewal of the ministries of lector and cantor. With many of the changes made to the form of the Roman Mass that had grown over the centuries, however, there are doubts as to whether they complied with the principle of organic development of the liturgy. From the long perspective, a balance between preservation and renewal is not always discernible.

We should mention first in this regard the opening part of the Mass, which has been completely reshaped and in its present form is not very convincing: only the *Introitus, Kyrie,* and *Gloria* have been retained, while the prayers at the foot of the altar have been omitted entirely, instead of dividing it up, for example, between the priest and the faithful in a vernacular translation, as the 1965 *Ordo Missae* foresees as a possibility.[192] In the Missal for German-speaking regions, we find in the renovated *Offertorium* a particularly significant example of liturgical archaism: since the summons to prayer *Orate fratres* and the *Suscipiat* of the faithful were regarded as an early medieval aberration, but there was no chance of omitting them without some replacement, they insisted on the option of adding two variants for the German Missal, and at that they succeeded.[193] An example of a massive revision outside of the *Ordo Missae* is the *Missa pro defunctis,* which on the textual level has almost nothing to do with the Requiem that we know from Western music history: the only things left are the first part of the *Introitus* and the *Communio.* The idea of judgment was completely eliminated, and not only the Sequence *Dies irae* but also the second part of the *Introitus,* the *Graduale,* the *Offertorium,* and the *Libera me* were sacrificed.

Given the sometimes radical liturgical reforms, which in many cases clearly went beyond what the Council Fathers had had in mind, it is not surprising that the reforms, particularly the reform of the Missal, called forth critics. Among them were members of the Consilium for Implementing the Reform of the Liturgy, too, such as Louis Bouyer[194] or Giuseppe Ferdinando Cardinal Antonelli, Secretary of the Conciliar Commission for the Liturgy.[195] Antonelli, like Bugnini, was a supporter of the liturgical reform whose main principle and goal he regarded as the demand for active, conscious participation of the faithful in the liturgy. Antonelli advocated a moderate reform of the Roman liturgy. This becomes clear in his

---

[192] Cf. Helmut Hoping, "Der *Introitus* und das Stufengebet als Schwellentexte der römischen Messe", in *Operation am lebenden Objekt: Roms Liturgiereformen von Trient bis zum Vaticanum II,* ed. Stefan Heid (Berlin and Brandenburg: be.bra Wissenschaft Verlag, 2014), 305–15.

[193] Cf. *MB* 346f.

[194] Cf., among other works, Louis Bouyer, *The Decomposition of Catholicism,* trans. Charles Underhill Quinn (Chicago: Franciscan Herald Press, 1969).

[195] Cf. Nicola Giampietro, *The Development of the Liturgical Reform: As Seen by Cardinal Ferdinando Antonelli from 1948 to 1970* (Fort Collins, Col.: Roman Catholic Books, 2010).

ideas for the reform of the *Ordo Missae*, which to a great extent corresponded to those of the Council Fathers.[196] Antonelli was critical of
Bugnini's radical reform program. In his notebook entitled *Note sulla
Riforma Liturgica* (1968–1971), Antonelli writes: "Up to [the time of]
the council, liturgical law was regarded as something sacred (*una cosa
sacra*). For many it no longer exists. Everyone now takes it [for granted]
that they are authorized to do what they like, and many of the young
[priests] do just that."[197] Antonelli blames the "system of experiments"
for this.[198] He complains that the reforms were becoming more and
more radical and chaotic, and many members of the Consilium for the
Liturgy, including bishops, were poorly educated theologically and
had had no liturgical training.[199] In a time of uncertain theology, a
negative, harmful ideology was spreading that called for everything to
be changed.[200] Moreover, the approach to the liturgy was increasingly
"rationalistic". Hence there was reason to fear that while the liturgy
might be reformed, piety would be left behind.[201] Antonelli regards
the changes to the Roman liturgy, some of them radical, as a process

[196] Cf. ibid., 151: "Many will ask what the innovations in the Mass are. A brief reply
may be made. A revision of the *Ordo Missae* is foreseen. It will have to be carried through
with optimum care and attention. The biblical readings will be enriched. The ancient *Oratio fidelium* will be restored. This will take the form of the prayers which are already well
known from Good Friday ceremonies.... A certain use of the vernacular in the Mass is also
envisioned; particularly for the biblical readings, and in certain other parts which will be
determined by the ecclesiastical authority in the various countries, and approved by the Holy
See." Ibid., 149: "Certain parts of the Mass, such as the Canon, remain in Latin, while others,
especially those directed to the people, such as the readings and the restored *Oratio fidelium*,
can take place in the vernacular."

[197] Ibid., 191.

[198] Cf. ibid., 191. "I note that part of the cause for the state of things must be related to the
system of experiments. The Pope granted a faculty permitting experiments to the Consilium,
and this faculty was used extensively by the Consilium."

[199] Cf. ibid., 166: "I am not enthusiastic about this work. I am unhappy at how much the
Commission has changed. It is merely an assembly of people, many of them incompetent, and
others well advanced on the road to novelty. The discussions are extremely hurried. Discussions are based on impressions and the voting is chaotic."

[200] Cf. ibid., 192: "They begin by despising everything that is actually there. This negative
mentality is unjust and pernicious, and unfortunately, Paul VI tends a little bit to this side.
They have all the best intentions, but with this mentality they have only been able to demol-
ish and not to restore."

[201] Cf. ibid., 234: "There is a spirit of criticism and intolerance toward the Holy See which
cannot lead to a good conclusion. Then the whole approach to the liturgy is rationalistic;
there is no concern for true piety. I am afraid that one day we shall have to say of this whole
reform ...: *accepit liturgia recessit devotio*—As the liturgy progressed, devotion [went] backwards."

of desacralizing and secularizing. "The work of desacralization continues on a vast scale. Now they call it secularization."[202]

From the beginning, not only was the reform of the Roman Mass controversial but also the question about the relation of the new rite of Mass to the old rite. Does it replace it, or does it exist side-by-side with it? For a long time that was not clear. Bugnini, who since the refounding of the Congregation for Divine Worship (1969) had been its secretary, therefore sought to reach a decision. Nevertheless, not until October 8, 1974, four years after the publication of the Missal of Paul VI, did the Congregation for Divine Worship publish a notification on the binding character of the New Mass, which says that the Missal of Paul VI took the place of the 1570 *Missale Romanum*.[203] Yet the 1962 Missal continued to be used after 1965. There were not only exceptions for older priests who had difficulties adapting. On November 5, 1971, Paul VI granted for England and Wales an Indult for the celebration of the Tridentine Mass. It had been preceded by a petition to preserve the "Tridentine" Mass. The petition in favor of the classic form of the Latin Mass, as part of a "universal culture", had been signed by numerous prominent Catholics as well as non-Catholics, among them the Catholic convert and British author Graham Greene (1904–1991), the Jewish violinist Yehudi Menuhin (1904–1999), and the famous detective novelist Agatha Christie (1890–1976). The petition was supported by the archbishop of Westminster, John Carmel Cardinal Heenan (1905–1975). Because of the indult granted by Paul VI, the bishops of England and Wales were authorized to allow the celebration of Mass in the *usus antiquior* [older use] for special occasions.[204] English Catholics had a special attachment to the traditional Roman liturgy, since it was the liturgy of numerous martyrs in England. The Indult for England and Wales is called the Agatha Christie Indult, since Paul VI, while reading the signatures to the petition, is said to have exclaimed, "Ah, Agatha Christie!"

---

[202] Ibid., 177.

[203] This is cited by Andrea Grillo, *Beyond Pius V: Conflicting Interpretations of the Liturgical Reform*, trans. B. Hudock (Collegeville, Minn.: Liturgical Press, 2013), 101, in favor of his thesis that the new Missal replaced the old one.

[204] Faggioli, *True Reform*, does not mention at all the fact that even Paul VI through an indult had allowed the celebration of Mass in the *usus antiquior*.

Further appeals to Pope Paul VI to continue allowing the classic rite of Mass were signed by French intellectuals, among them the French author Julien Green (1900–1998) and the philosophers Jacques Maritain (1882–1973) and Gabriel Marcel (1889–1973). However, the development in the 1970s of the priestly Society of Saint Pius X founded by Archbishop Marcel Lefebvre (1905–1991) and committed to the traditional liturgy caused Paul VI to hesitate to grant further indults. For in the case of the SSPX, the "Tridentine" Mass had become a symbol of their rejection of the Second Vatican Council.[205] In 1975, the Society of Saint Pius X lost its canonical status on account of its resistance to the decisions of Vatican Council II, especially about religious liberty and freedom of conscience. The Society proceeded to run its major seminaries and to ordain priests without permission. In 1988, the illicit consecration of bishops caused a schism. The bishops of the Society of Saint Pius X were excommunicated.

Over the course of the unsuccessful efforts to reinstate the Society of Saint Pius X during the reign of John Paul II, the status of the traditional liturgy was clarified. In a letter to the conferences of bishops dated October 3, 1984, the Congregation for Divine Worship gave all bishops of the Catholic Church permission to grant individual churches an indult to celebrate Mass according to the 1962 Missal. In 1986, a commission of cardinals established by John Paul II, which had been set up during the efforts at reconciliation with the Society of Saint Pius X, determined that the classic form of the Roman Mass had never been abolished. In the interest of *pax liturgica* [liturgical peace], the commission recommended allowing all priests of the Latin Rite to celebrate the old Mass at their discretion. While John Paul II did not follow the commission's recommendation, with his Apostolic Letter *Ecclesia Dei* (1988) on the occasion of the illicit episcopal consecrations for the Society of Saint Pius X, the pope did request of all bishops "a wide and generous application of the directives ... for the use of the Roman Missal according to the typical edition of 1962".[206]

Since the SSPX schism, several communities of priests have been founded within the Catholic Church in which the Roman liturgy is celebrated to this day according to the *usus antiquior*, for example,

---

[205] Thus Jean Guitton, *Paul VI Secret* (Paris, 1979), 158f. Cited from Faggioli, *True Reform*, 150.

[206] John Paul II, Apostolic Letter *Ecclesia Dei* (July 2, 1998), 6c.

the Priestly Fraternity of Saint Peter (FSSP). The prerequisite was that they recognize the decisions of Vatican Council II and the 1970 rite of Mass. Individual monasteries, too, above all in the Benedictine tradition, returned to the old liturgy (for example, the Abbey of Sainte-Madeleine du Barroux, the Abbey of Notre-Dame de Fontgombault). In late 2006, a group of French intellectuals headed by the philosopher René Girard published an appeal to allow the old Mass again universally.[207] On the feast of Epiphany 2007, a "Manifesto for the Reauthorization of the Traditional Latin Mass" was published in Germany. It was signed by the author Martin Mosebach, among others.[208] The motu proprio *Summorum Pontificum* by Benedict XVI (July 7, 2007) was followed by general permission to celebrate the traditional Latin liturgy as of September 14, 2007.[209] In his Letter Accompanying the motu proprio, Benedict XVI emphasized that the mid-term goal of the motu proprio was a mutual enrichment of the two forms of the Roman Rite.[210] "There is no contradiction between the two editions of the Roman Missal. In the history of the liturgy there is growth and progress, but no rupture."[211] The motu proprio *Summorum Pontificum* distinguished between the Ordinary Form and the Extraordinary Form of the Roman Rite and emphasized the unity of the Roman in its two forms.[212]

---

[207] Cf. *Le Figaro*, December 16, 2006; *Süddeutsche Zeitung*, December 19, 2006.

[208] Cf. *Die Welt*, January 17, 2007.

[209] Cf. the commentaries by Norbert Lüdecke, "Kanonistische Anmerkungen zum Motu Proprio 'Summorum Pontificum' ", *Liturgisches Jahrbuch* 58 (2008): 3–34; Johannes Nebel, "Die 'ordentliche' und die 'ausserordentliche' Form des römischen Messritus: Versuch einer Orientierungshilfe zum tieferen Verständnis beider Formen", *Forum Katholische Theologie* 25 (2009): 173–213; Wolfgang F. Rothe, *Ein kirchenrechtlicher Kommentar zum Motu proprio "Summorum Pontificum" für Studium und Praxis. Mit einem Vorwort des Vize-Präsidenten der Päpstlichen Kommission "Ecclesia Dei"* (Augsburg: Dominus Verlag, 2009); Gero P. Weishaupt, *Päpstliche Weichenstellungen: Das Motu Proprio Summorum Pontificum Papst Benedikts XVI. und der Begleitbrief an die Bischöfe; ein kirchenrechtlicher Kommentar und Überlegungen zu einer "Reform der Reform"* (Bonn: Verlag für Kultur und Wissenschaft, 2010).

[210] Cf. Benedict XVI, Letter Accompanying the Motu proprio *Summorum Pontificum* (July 7, 2007), 24.

[211] Ibid., 25f.

[212] Cf. Benedict XVI, Apostolic Letter Given Motu Proprio *Summorum Pontificum* on the Use of the Roman Liturgy Prior to the Reform of 1970 (July 7, 2007; hereafter cited as *SP*), art. 1. Benedict XVI does not speak about an "extraordinary rite", as Klemens Richter, "Vom Sinn der Liturgiereform", in *Ein Ritus—zwei Formen: Die Richtlinie Benedikts XVI. zur Liturgie*, ed. A. Gerhards, Theologie kontrovers (Freiburg: Herder, 2008), 67, and Faggioli, *True Reform*, 154, maintain.

With his motu proprio *Summorum Pontificum*, Pope Benedict XVI allowed all priests of the Latin Rite who are not legally impeded in the exercise of their priestly ministry to choose freely, without previous permission by the competent local ecclesiastical authority, between the Missals of 1962 and 1970 when celebrating Mass *sine populo*.[213] In addition, any priest may allow other faithful to attend, insofar as they request it.[214] If a numerically undefined group of the faithful (*coetus fidelium*) requests that Mass be celebrated according to the *usus antiquior*, the local pastors must do everything possible to comply with this wish. On Sundays and feast days, it is permitted to celebrate one of the Masses in the *usus antiquior*.[215] Besides Holy Mass, the sacraments of Baptism, Confirmation, Penance, Extreme Unction, and Matrimony as well as the funeral liturgy can be celebrated according to the older liturgical books.[216] Moreover, priests and deacons are allowed to use the breviary promulgated by John XXIII.[217]

On April 30, 2011, the Pontifical Commission *Ecclesia Dei*, which by then was incorporated into the Congregation for the Doctrine of the Faith, published the Instruction *Universae Ecclesiae* with guidelines for implementing the motu proprio *Summorum Pontificum*.[218] This instruction was the result of the experiences that Catholics had had with the older form of the Roman Rite since the publication of *Summorum Pontificum*. In interpreting and applying the motu proprio, there were unclear points and in some cases altogether different ways of implementing it in the dioceses. The instruction *Universae Ecclesiae* reaffirms that there is no contradiction between the old and the new Mass.[219] The instruction strengthens the older liturgical tradition, which, "on account of its venerable and ancient use ... [is] to be maintained with appropriate honor."[220] The Roman liturgy in the *usus antiquior* should be offered to all the faithful. For it is "a

---

[213] Cf. *SP*, art. 2.

[214] Cf. ibid., art. 4.

[215] Cf. ibid., art. 5, §2.

[216] Cf. ibid., art. 5, §3; art. 9, §1.

[217] Cf. ibid., art. 9, §3.

[218] Cf. Pontifical Commission *Ecclesia Dei*, Instruction *Universae Ecclesiae* on the Application of the Apostolic Letter *Summorum Pontificum* (April 30, 2011).

[219] Cf. ibid., 7.

[220] Ibid., 6.

precious treasure to be preserved".[221] The instruction obliges all bishops to follow the mind (*mens*) of the pope, as it is clearly expressed in the motu proprio.[222] The norms of the law are to be observed and applied exactly.

Next, the instruction makes several clarifications. The first point concerned the faithful who request the celebration of the Roman liturgy in the *usus antiquior*. Like the motu proprio *Summorum Pontificum*, the instruction, too, does not require a minimum size for the group that requests a liturgy in the *usus antiquior* of the rite. In the case of Mass celebrated in the modern form of the Roman Rite, too, there is no minimum requirement for this to take place, and for good reason (for instance, weekday Masses, in which often only very few of the faithful participate). It is not necessary for the faithful who are committed to the traditional form of the Roman Mass to come from one parish. They can also be from various parishes originally, indeed, even from different dioceses.[223] The Roman liturgy in the *usus antiquior* is to be "effectively guarantee[d] and ensur[ed] ... for all who ask for it".[224] The motu proprio *Summorum Pontificum* is therefore to be interpreted for the benefit of the faithful.

If in many places the celebration of Mass in the *usus antiquior* is only granted to the faithful every other week or once a month, even though priests are available for a celebration every Sunday, then this is hardly consistent with the motu proprio and the instruction. For where it is desired, the old Mass should be a normal component of Church life. This is evident, for example, from the fact that the Easter Triduum can be celebrated in a parish church or an oratory in the *usus antiquior*, too.[225] Ideally, the Easter Triduum should be celebrated in the church or oratory designated for liturgies in the *usus antiquior*. If it is not possible to celebrate the Easter Triduum in its entirety in the *usus antiquior*, then even a part of it can be celebrated in the *usus antiquior*. The Triduum, however, is to be celebrated at least once completely in the *forma ordinaria* in a parish or a parish community (pastoral unit, and so on).

---

[221] Ibid., 8a.
[222] Cf. ibid., 13.
[223] Cf. ibid., 15.
[224] Ibid., 8b.
[225] Cf. ibid., 33.

Regardless of the interest of the candidates for priestly ministry and of the rectors, bishops must see to it that future priests master the Latin liturgical language, be acquainted with the *usus antiquior* of the Roman Rite, and, when it is pastorally necessary, also receive practical training in it.[226] This does not have to happen at the major seminary. It can also be done later in special continuing education courses. As for the question about which priests are qualified to celebrate the older form of the Mass, the rule applies that any priest who is not impeded by canon law is regarded as suitable, provided that he has a command of the Latin liturgical language. For example, priests must not be prevented from celebrating Mass in the *usus antiquior* because they are young. Of course they must be familiar with the *usus antiquior* of the Roman Mass. That is to be presumed, inasmuch as they are willing to celebrate Mass in the *usus antiquior*. Otherwise, the opportunity is given to them to learn the older form of the Roman Rite,[227] either from experienced priests of the diocese or from collaborators of the institutes and communities for which the Pontifical Commission *Ecclesia Dei* is competent.[228] The instruction allows the conferral of minor and major orders in the Extraordinary Form of the rite only for institutes of consecrated life and societies of apostolic life that are under the Pontifical Commission *Ecclesia Dei*, and also for other communities that use the liturgical books of the *forma extraordinaria*. Diocesan bishops must use the new pontifical for the ordination of deacons and priests, unless in individual cases they have a special permission to use the old pontifical. That is a wise decision, because it prevents the development of a diocesan clergy split between the older and newer form of the Roman liturgy.

Since conflicts about the correct interpretation and application of the motu proprio *Summorum Pontificum* have arisen again and again, the *Ecclesia Dei* Commission receives the power to settle, with ordinary, vicarious pastoral authority, recourses against the administrative acts of ordinaries whom the complainants assume to be at odds with *Summorum Pontificum*. These decisions bind the ordinaries, unless

---

[226] Cf. ibid., 20.
[227] Cf. ibid., 21.
[228] Cf. ibid., 22.

they are appealed to the Supreme Tribunal of the Apostolic Signatura, which then is authorized to make the final decision.[229] The bishops must not only see to it that the motu proprio is correctly applied, but also make sure that respect is shown for the *usus antiquior* of the Roman Rite in their dioceses.[230] Priests and faithful must not be neglected or marginalized if they celebrate the Mass in the *usus antiquior*. The faithful who request liturgies in the *usus antiquior* and participate in them must not support or belong to groups that dispute the validity and liceity of the celebration of Holy Mass or the sacraments in the Ordinary Form or reject the pope as the Supreme Pastor of the Universal Church.

The apostolic letter *Summorum Pontificum* and the instruction *Universae Ecclesiae* are not intended only for the traditionalists of the Society of Saint Pius X. They are part of the larger context of the crisis of the postconciliar liturgy.[231] There are many reasons why people love the old Mass, rediscover it, or discover it for the first time. One of the reasons surely lies in the perception that in the *usus antiquior* the sacral and cultic character of the Roman Mass is brought to bear more clearly than in the *usus modernus*. Benedict XVI in his motu proprio *Summorum Pontificum* is not concerned about a return to the "Tridentine Mass" across the board but, rather, about a liturgical renewal in the light of tradition. When many critics maintain that the decision by Benedict XVI to reinstate the classic Latin Mass was a betrayal of the Second Vatican Council,[232] then this boils down to the serious charge that Benedict XVI disregarded decisions of an

---

[229] Cf. ibid., 10, §1.

[230] Cf. ibid., 14.

[231] Cf. Robert Spaemann, "Die Präsenz des klassischen römischen Ritus in der katholischen Kirche", in *Der Widerstand gegen die alte Messe*, ed. E. Muschalek (Denkendorf: Van Seth, 2007), 13–54; Georg Muschalek, "Die Rehabilitierung der alten Messe durch Benedikt XVI", in Muschalek, ed., *Der Widerstand gegen die alte Messe* (Denkendorf: Paul van Seth-Verlag, 2007), 55–82.

[232] Cf. Richter, "Liturgiekonstitution 'Sacrosanctum Concilium'", 38. Cf. also Richter, "Zum Verhältnis von Kirchenbild und Liturgie: Die erneuerte Liturgie und der alte Ritus im Widerspruch", in *Objektive Feier und subjektiver Glaube? Beiträge zum Verhältnis von Liturgie und Spiritualität*, Studien zur Pastoralliturgie 32 (Regensburg: Pustet, 2011), 147–69; Richter, "Ein halbes Jahrhundert Sacrosanctum Concilium: Anmerkungen eines Liturgiewissenschaftlers", in *Sacrosanctum Concilium: Eine Relecture der Liturgiekonstitution des 2. Vatikanischen Konzils*, ed. M. Stuflesser, Theologie der Liturgie 1 (Regensburg: Pustet, 2011), 97–115.

ecumenical council.[233] And anyone who disputes the fact that the *usus antiquior* and the *usus modernus* of the Roman Rite are expressions of the same *lex orandi* of the Church and that therefore no antithesis exists in the *lex credendi* is actually calling into question the legitimacy of a more than 1500-year-old liturgical history.[234]

Various terms are used to designate the two forms of the Roman Mass.[235] The motu proprio *Summorum Pontificum* speaks about the *usus ordinarius* and the *usus extraordinarius*, having in view the different diffusion of the two forms. The instruction *Universae Ecclesiae* also designates the old Mass as the *usus antiquior* of the Roman liturgy.[236] The older form of the Roman Mass is also called the "Tridentine" Mass or the "Gregorian Mass", because its core goes back to Pope Gregory the Great. The term "Tridentine" is very commonly used but not quite accurate, since the older Roman Order of the Mass went into the 1570 *Missale Romanum* without major changes. Some speak also about the Traditional Mass. For the new form of the Mass, we likewise encounter the expressions "Mass of Paul VI" or *usus recentior/modernus* [more recent or modern use] of the Roman liturgy.

The *usus antiquior* and the *usus modernus* of the Roman liturgy, according to the legislative will of Benedict XVI, are not two different families of rites. Benedict XVI regards them rather as two forms of the one Roman Rite.[237] *Usus antiquior* and *usus modernus* are expressions of one and the same *lex orandi* [law of prayer] and *lex credendi* [law

---

[233] Faggioli, *True Reform*, 154–55, accuses Benedict of having played into the hands of the "revisionists of the liturgical reform". His motu proprio *Summorum Pontificum* demonstrated "the 'disposability' [optional character] of the liturgical reform of Vatican II".

[234] Cf. Benedikt Kranemann, "Liturgie im Widerspruch: Anfragen und Beobachtungen zum Motu proprio 'Summorum Pontificum' ", in *Ein Ritus—zwei Formen: Die Richtlinie Benedikts XVI. zur Liturgie*, Theologie kontrovers (Freiburg: Herder, 2008), 55f.; Kranemann, "Die Theologie des Pascha-Mysteriums im Widerspruch: Bemerkungen zur traditionalistischen Kritik katholischer Liturgietheologie", in *Exkommunikation oder Kommunikation? Der Weg der Kirche nach dem II. Vatikanum und die Pius-Brüder*, ed. Peter Hünermann, Quaestiones disputatae 236 (Freiburg: Herder, 2009), 123–51; Faggioli, *True Reform*, 96ff.

[235] About the terminology, see Michael Fiedrowicz, *Die überlieferte Messe: Geschichte, Gestalt, Theologie* (Mühlheim an der Mosel: Carthusianus Verlag, 2011), 47–54.

[236] Cf. Pontifical Commission *Ecclesia Dei*, Instruction *Universae Ecclesiae* on the Application of the Apostolic Letter *Summorum Pontificum* (April 30, 2011), nos. 5, 8, 15.

[237] Joseph Cardinal Ratzinger had addressed the question of the unity of the Roman Rite for the first time at greater length at a liturgical conference in Fontgombault. Cf. Ratzinger, "Assessment and Future Prospects", in *JRCW* 11:558–68.

of belief] of the Roman liturgy.[238] Phenomenologically, however, the classic and the modern form of the Roman Rite seem like two different rites, which makes it clear how thoroughgoing the liturgical reforms after the council were. Benedict XVI wanted to keep the *usus antiquior* and *usus modernus* of the Roman Mass together and to prevent them from drifting farther apart from each other. The unity of the Roman Rite to which Benedict XVI adheres is therefore not just a legal definition but at the same time the definition of an objective.

It is uncertain whether it will be possible to convert the two forms again into one; it is also debated whether that is sensible and necessary. The unity of the Roman Rite, however, must not be disputed in the long run. Hence it seems imperative for the two forms at least to draw closer to each other. We should view in this context the demand for a new liturgical movement or "reform of the reform", as it has been formulated by Joseph Ratzinger and others. The idea is a liturgical renewal on the basis of *Sacrosanctum concilium* in the light of the larger liturgical tradition. Benedict XVI hoped that in the future, through a mutual enrichment, the unity of the *lex orandi* of the Roman Rite, and of the *lex credendi* associated with it, might be expressed more strongly in both forms than has been the case so far.[239]

Contrary to a frequent misunderstanding, Benedict XVI did not intend a "(liturgical-) theological about face"[240] or a general return to the old Mass. With his motu proprio *Summorum Pontificum* (2007) and the Instruction *Universae Ecclesiae* (2011), documents with which he strengthened the position of the *usus antiquior* of the Roman liturgy, the objective of Benedict XVI was instead a liturgical reconciliation and a "return to adoration". To put it pointedly, we could say: away from the "pastorally motivated liturgy" of the postconciliar period toward "latreutic liturgy". For although liturgy may also have a catechetical character, it is nevertheless above all a sacred event, indeed, the sanctification of man,[241] and worship and veneration of God, *cultus divinae majestatis*.

---

[238] Cf. *SP*, art. 1.
[239] Cf. Benedict XVI, Letter Accompanying the Motu proprio *Summorum Pontificum* (July 7, 2007), 24.
[240] This is the opinion of Kranemann, "Theologie des Pascha-Mysteriums", 151.
[241] Cf. *SC* 7.

A "reform of the reform"[242] requires us to proceed carefully. Even though the liturgy is not a static structure, nevertheless, one cannot constantly try to make changes to the liturgy. Surely the liturgical renewal started by the Second Vatican Council is a process that cannot be accomplished in one generation. The Council Fathers, of course, did not have a long-term liturgical reform in mind.[243] They spoke neither about a *liturgia semper reformanda* [liturgy that always needs to be reformed] nor about an *ecclesia semper reformanda*, but rather about an *ecclesia semper purificanda* [Church that constantly needs to be purified].[244] Nor was the liturgical reform carried out exclusively by the revision of the liturgical books; rather, it aimed at the renewal of liturgical praxis along the lines of the council's Constitution on the Liturgy. In the long run, this renewal will make many corrections to the liturgical reform necessary. Even though the liturgical tradition of the Church is a living tradition, so that it develops, one cannot constantly be changing the Church's liturgy, which is probably what many people associate with the program of a *liturgia semper reformanda*. Moreover, it must not give again the fatal impression of a "fabricated" liturgy. At a distance of over fifty years now from the Constitution on the Liturgy *Sacrosanctum concilium*, it is surely high time to speak *sine ira et studio* [without anger and zeal] about the light and the dark sides of the liturgical reform.[245]

---

[242] Cf. Aidan Nichols, *Looking at the Liturgy: The Critical View of Its Contemporary Form* (San Francisco: Ignatius Press, 1996); Christophe Geffroy, *Benoît et la "paix liturgique"* (Paris: Cerf, 2008); Nicola Bux, *La riforma di Benedetto XVI.* (Casale Monferrato [Alessandria]: Piemme, 2008); Mauro Gagliardi, *Liturgia fonte de vita: Prospettive teologiche* (Verona: Fede & Cultura, 2009); Claudio Crescimanno, *La riforma della riforma liturgica* (Verona: Fede & Cultura, 2009). About criticism of the allegedly revisionist demand for a "reform of the reform", cf. John F. Baldovin, *Reforming the Liturgy: A Response to the Critics* (Collegeville, Minn.: Liturgical Press, 2008); Baldovin, "Idols and Icons: Überlegungen zum derzeitigen Stand der Liturgiereform", *Liturgisches Jahrbuch* 61 (2011): 154–70; Faggioli, *True Reform*, 153–59.

[243] In Reiner Kaczynski, "Theologischer Kommentar zur Konstitution", 200, the author disagrees but cannot cite any conciliar text as proof.

[244] Cf. *LG* 8.

[245] Cf. Robert Spaemann, Gedanken eines Laien zur Reform der Reform", *Internationale katholische Zeitschrift Communio* 38 (2009): 82–89; Hoping, "Die sichtbarste Frucht des Konzils"; Hoping, "Bewahren und Erneuern: Eine Relecture der Liturgiereform", *Internationale katholische Zeitschrift Communio* 38 (2009): 570–84.

Chapter IX

ORDO MISSAE

The Celebration of Mass and the Unity of the Roman Rite

"Introibo ad altare Dei. Ad Deum qui laetificat iuventutem meam."
In the classic form of the Roman Mass, after "In nomine Patris, et
Filii, et Spiritus Sancti", the priest begins the prayers at the foot of
the altar with the fourth verse of Psalm 43[42]. The prayers at the
foot of the altar were originally a prayer of the priest and the ministers in preparation for the celebration of Mass. However, they can
also be recited alternately by the priest and the faithful. In the reform
of the Missal, the prayers at the foot of the altar, except for the psalm
Iudica me Deus, were initially retained for the *Ordo Missae* (1965) and
the Latin-German altar missal (1965) based on it. Then in the 1970
Missale Romanum, the prayers at the foot of the altar were completely
dropped. Mass begins with the gathering of the faithful, the entrance
procession of the priest, a profound bow, the Introit, the walk to
the presider's chair, and immediately the Sign of the Cross: "In the
name of the Father and of the Son and of the Holy Spirit". The basic
form of the Mass according to the Missal of Paul VI is the *missa cum
populo*, Mass with the people.[1]

---

[1] Cf. *SC* 57, §2.2. Besides the *missa cum populo*, the Missal also regulates Mass with
only one of the faithful who assists the priest (*GIRM* [2010] 252–72). The Second Vatican
Council reaffirmed the legitimacy of the *missa sine populo*: every priest is free to celebrate
even alone (cf. *SC* 57, §2.2). The popes after the council have recommended that priests
celebrate Mass daily and, if necessary, even without the faithful. Thus, most recently, Benedict XVI, *SacCar* 80.

A. The Ordinary Form of the Mass (1970)

The Mass consists of two main parts, Liturgia Verbi (Liturgy of the Word) and Liturgia eucharistica (Liturgy of the Eucharist), framed by the opening and concluding prayers.[2] Corresponding to the two main parts of the Mass, there are two central places for the actions during the celebration of Mass: the ambo as the table of the Word of God (mensa verbi Dei) and the altar as the table of the Body of the Lord (mensa Corporis Domini).[3] The reform of the Mass led to a new appreciation of the Liturgy of the Word, the so-called Mass of the catechumens, which earlier had often been described inappropriately as the "pre-Mass". In contrast, Vatican Council II declares that the Liturgy of the Word and the Liturgy of the Eucharist are so closely united that they form one single act of worship.[4] According to the Missal of Paul VI, the celebration of Sunday Mass has the following structure:

INTRODUCTORY RITES
Introit (procession with hymn)
Reverence to the altar (kissing the altar); with optional incensation
Sign of the Cross
Greeting
Introduction
Penitential Act (general confession);
   [on Sundays, an optional sprinkling of water as a reminder of Baptism]
Kyrie
Gloria in excelsis
Collect/Prayer of the Day

LITURGY OF THE WORD
First Reading
Responsorial Psalm

---

[2] Cf. Johannes H. Emminghaus, Die Messe: Wesen, Gestalt, Vollzug, 5th ed. (Klosterneuburg: Österr. Kathol. Bibelwerk, 1992), 155–302; Hans Bernhard Meyer, Eucharistie, Geschichte, Theologie, Pastoral, Handbuch der Liturgiewissenschaft 4 (Regensburg: Pustet, 1989), 330–63; Reinhard Messner, Einführung in die Liturgiewissenschaft, 2nd ed. (Paderborn: Schöningh, 2009), 171–222.

[3] Cf. SC 48, 51; "Allgemeine Einführung in das Messbuch", in MB 25*–75* (hereafter cited as AEM), no. 8.

[4] Cf. SC 56.

Second Reading
Acclamation before the Gospel (Alleluia, Sequence when
    applicable)
Gospel (incensation optional)
Homily
Creed / Profession of Faith
Universal Prayer / Prayer of the Faithful

LITURGY OF THE EUCHARIST

Preparation of the Gifts
   Offertory hymn
   Presentation of the gifts
   Preparation of the chalice (wine, water)
   Offertory prayer
   Prayer of self-offering
   Optional: incensation of offerings, altar, clergy, and faithful
   Washing of hands
   Prayer over the offerings
Eucharistic Prayer
   Preface
   Sanctus / Benedictus
   Epiclesis
   Institution narrative and Consecration
   Mysterium fidei
   People's acclamation
   Anamnesis
   Oblation
   Communion epiclesis with a prayer for unity
   Intercessions with a commemoration of the saints
   Concluding doxology
   People's acclamation
Communion Rite
   Our Father with embolism and acclamation
   Prayer for peace and the Sign of Peace
   Agnus Dei/breaking of the bread, a piece of which is put into
      the chalice
   Preparatory prayer
   Reception of Holy Communion
   Purification of the vessels
   Thanksgiving
Postcommunion (Concluding prayer)

CONCLUDING RITES
  Announcements
  Blessing
  Dismissal
  Reverence to the altar
  Recessional

Introductory Rites: The Introductory Rites include the two acts of "recollection" (gathering, Sign of the Cross, liturgical greeting with general confession) and prayer (*Kyrie, Gloria,* prayer of the day).[5] After the gathering of the faithful, there can be a short introduction to the proclamation of the Word of God and the celebration of the Eucharist. The opening or processional hymn (*antiphona ad introitum*) should not be omitted. If an entrance hymn is sung instead of the Introit, the theme of the Introit, if possible, should be mentioned, for instance, during the short introduction, which should not have the character of a short homily. During the opening hymn, the priest goes first to the altar. There he reverences the altar (possibly with the deacon and concelebrants) with a kiss. An incensation of the altar may follow. The incense is not an oblation offered to God but, rather, a sign of prayer (Ps 141[140]:2) and veneration. After kissing and incensing the altar, the priest goes to the chair with the other ministers. From there he performs the other Introductory Rites of the Mass. The location and style of the chair should make it clear that the priest is the presider at the celebration of the Eucharist.

After the gathering of the faithful to celebrate Mass and the Introit, the first ritual is the Sign of the Cross, under which the assembled faithful place themselves. After that, the priest greets the congregation with one of the formulas of greeting and blessing provided in the Missal. The Penitential Act has the form of a general confession of sin, but it can also be combined with the *Kyrie* ("Lord, have mercy" combined with petitions/tropes [= interpolations]). These invocations are directed to Christ the Lord. Optional on Sundays is the sprinkling of water as a reminder of Baptism. The *Gloria* that follows ("Glory to God in the highest") is one of the ancient hymns of the Church. In its first stanza, with the song of the angels, the hymn

---

[5] Cf. Messner, *Einführung in die Liturgiewissenschaft,* 171f.

contains praise of the Father and the Son, in the second stanza—a praise of Christ. During the celebration of Mass, the *Gloria* is sung on Sundays outside of Advent and Lent and also on feast days and at special celebrations. The last element of the Introductory Rites is the prayer of the day (*collecta*), which is one of the "presidial" prayers that are prayed by the presider at the celebration of the Eucharist. The prayer of the day is introduced by the priest with an invitation to prayer and is prayed in the name of the faithful ("we-form" of the Collect). It summarizes the prayers of the faithful, which is why it is appropriate to provide a short moment of silence after the *Oremus* (Let us pray). The prayer of the day expresses the particular character of the celebration of Mass on that day. The faithful reaffirm the prayer of the day with their *Amen* (Yes, so be it).

Liturgy of the Word: Its structure resembles that of the worship service of prayers and readings in the synagogue, but it cannot simply be derived from it. It was the council's objective that in liturgical celebrations there was to be "more reading from holy scripture, and it is to be more varied and suitable."[6] "Richer fare" was to be "provided for the faithful at the table of God's word".[7] This was the purpose of the council's decision that "a more representative portion of the holy scriptures will be read to the people in the course of a prescribed number of years."[8] The new Lectionary for the celebration of Mass went into effect of May 22, 1969. It foresees a three-year cycle (A, B, C) for Sundays and a two-year cycle (I, II) for weekdays. Every Sunday, three biblical readings are pronounced (spoken or sung): as a rule, the First Reading is a passage from the Old Testament; the Second Reading, a passage from the New Testament (Epistle); and, finally, the third biblical reading is the Gospel. On weekdays, two readings are pronounced (Reading, Gospel). The ambo is the place for the proclamation of the Word and must therefore be in plain view. The ambo is likewise the place for the Responsorial Psalm, the Gospel Acclamation, and the homily. The Universal Prayer of the Faithful (intercessions) should be read from a separate place. It is to be introduced by the priest and concluded with an oration. The name

---

[6] SC 35.
[7] SC 51.
[8] Ibid.

of the lectern at which the readings are presented is derived from the Greek verb ἀναβαίνειν (to go up). The ambo should therefore be situated at the level of the sanctuary.

The First Reading is followed by a Responsorial Psalm with a refrain or antiphon, which may be replaced by an intermediate hymn only in exceptional cases, since the Responsorial Psalm is part of the proclamation. After the Second Reading (except in Lent), the Alleluia is sung with the appointed verse. This serves to greet Christ, who speaks to the worshipping assembly in the Word of the Gospel. The Alleluia is sung by the faithful standing. While the two readings can be pronounced by a lector, the proclamation of the Gospel during the celebration of the Mass is reserved to the deacon or the priest. According to liturgical tradition, the presider at the celebration of the Mass does not pronounce the Gospel himself when a deacon assists or when the Mass is concelebrated. The regulation makes it clear that the priest or bishop is a hearer of the Word, too. If a deacon is assisting, the deacon always pronounces the Gospel, since this is one of his proper duties.

From time immemorial, the Gospel has been proclaimed with particular solemnity. The deacon, who stands and makes a deep bow before the presider at the Mass, is commissioned to proclaim the Gospel: "May the Lord be in your heart and on your lips, that you may proclaim his Gospel worthily and well, in the name of the Father, and of the Son, and of the Holy Spirit." The blessing is affirmed by the deacon with the *Amen*. If a priest pronounces the Gospel, he bows before the altar and says: "Cleanse my heart and my lips, almighty God, that I may worthily proclaim your holy Gospel." The Gospel Book is carried to the ambo in a little procession accompanied by candles and possibly incense. The deacon marks the Gospel Book and himself with the Sign of the Cross and, if applicable, incenses it before the proclamation, which is introduced by the deacon with the liturgical greeting, "The Lord be with you", to which the people respond, "And with your spirit." The announcement of the Gospel, "A reading from the Holy Gospel according to ...," is followed by the response, "Glory to you, O Lord." After the Gospel, the deacon reaffirms the Good News with the acclamation, "The Gospel of the Lord", and the faithful respond "Praise to you, Lord Jesus Christ." The deacon kisses the

Gospel Book and says softly: "Through the words of the Gospel may our sins be wiped away." The solemn recitation of the Gospel underscores the fact that the risen Lord himself speaks to the worshipping assembly in the Gospel.

The Liturgy of the Word is concluded with the homily (an exposition of the biblical readings and the liturgical texts), the Creed, and the "Prayer of the Faithful". According to canon law currently in force, the homily during the celebration of Mass is reserved to the bishop, priest, and deacon.[9] The Creed is recited or sung on all major feast days and Sundays, whereby the Niceno-Constantinopolitan Creed is called for, although in individual cases, the Apostles' Creed can also be recited. Using the short *Credo* hymns from the *Gotteslob* hymnal is theologically dubious, since they only incompletely reflect the Church's faith. During the intercessory prayers, the following structure is to be observed: (a) petitions for the Church, (b) petitions for the salvation of the world, (c) petitions for those in need, the sick, the departed, (d) petitions for the local congregation.

Liturgy of the Eucharist: This is the second part of the Mass. It is introduced by the Offertory,[10] which is made up of (a) the placing of the Missal, corporal, and purificator on the altar, (b) the preparation of the chalice (wine, water), (c) the presentation of the offerings of bread and wine/Offertory prayers, (d) the prayer of self-offering, (e) possible incensation, (f) washing of the hands, and (g) the prayer over the offerings (*oratio super oblata*). Bread and wine are brought to the altar. The new Offertory prayers are modeled on Jewish prayers of blessing (*b^erākôt*), as grateful praise to the good God from whom we receive bread and wine. Bread and wine are called the fruit of the earth and of the vine and also of human work, as a symbol for the self-offering of the faithful.

---

[9] Cf. *Code of Canon Law*, trans. the Canon Law Society of America (Washington, D.C.: Canon Law Society of America, 1983), can. 767, §1.

[10] On the old and new offertory prayers, cf. Helmut Hoping, "Offerimus tibi, Domine: Die alten und neuen Offertoriumsgebete des römischen Messritus", in *Römische Messe und Liturgie der Moderne*, ed. S. Wahle, H. Hoping, and W. Haunerland (Freiburg: Herder, 2013), 378–95; Manfred Hauke, "Das *Offertorium* als Herausforderung liturgischer Reformen in der Geschichte", in *Operationen am lebenden Objekt: Roms Liturgiereformen von Trient bis zum Vaticanum II*, ed. Stefan Heid (Berlin and Brandenburg: Wissenschaft Verlag, 2014), 317–49.

Blessed are you, Lord God of all creation,
for through your goodness we have received
the bread (wine) we offer you:
fruit of the earth (vine) and work of human hands,
it will become for us the bread of life (our spiritual drink).[11]

The new prayers at the offering of bread and wine that were submitted to Paul VI to review at first contained no expression of offering. The addition "quem (quod) tibi offerimus", "the bread [that]
we offer you", "the wine [that] we offer you", was added only at the
pope's insistence.[12] The German translation of the Offertory prayers
reads, "Lord God,... you give us the bread, fruit of the earth and
of human work. We bring this bread before you so that it might
become for us the bread of life." The German translators obviously
hesitated to render literally the offertory expressions demanded by
Paul VI, on account of the connotation of sacrifice connected with
them. Annibale Bugnini was glad that in most vernacular translations
offerimus was not translated "we offer".[13] Of course *offerimus* must not
be understood as if the Sacrifice of the Mass consisted of wine and
bread.[14] Yet the language of sacrifice is inseparably connected with
the new Offertory prayers, too. This is true even in the German translation, which tries to avoid such language. The translation is guided
by the traditional prayer at the offering of the chalice *in conspectu divinae maiestatis tuae* (in the *Supplices te rogamus* of the Roman Canon).
In the background of the formula are the showbreads offered to God
in the Temple (Ex 25:30). Most priests, however, would hardly be
aware of that when they recite the Offertory prayers *submissa voce*
[in a low voice], any more than the faithful would when they hear
the prayers recited *elata voce* [in a loud voice] and respond with the
familiar acclamation from the *Didache*, "Blessed be God forever." [In

[11] *RM* 2010, 512. Cf. *MR* 2002³, 514: "Benedictus es, Domine, Deus universi, quia de
tua largitate accepimus panem (vinum), quem tibi offerimus, fructum terrae (vitis) et operis
manuum hominum: ex quo nobis fiet panis vitae (potus spiritualis)."

[12] Cf. Annibale Bugnini, *The Reform of the Liturgy 1948–1975*, trans. Matthew J. O'Connell
(Collegeville, Minn.: Liturgical Press, 1990), 371n37.

[13] Ibid., 379. [N.B. In German the verb "to offer", *opfern*, also means "to sacrifice".]

[14] Cf. Emil J. Lengeling, *Die neue Ordnung der Eucharistiefeier: Allgemeine Einführung in das
römische Messbuch: Endgültiger lateinischer und deutscher Text: Einleitung und Kommentar*, 2nd ed.
Lebendiger Gottesdienst 17/18 (Münster: Verlag Regensburg, 1971), 220.

German-speaking countries,] the option of pronouncing the Offertory prayers aloud with the acclamation of the faithful is chosen much too infrequently; it originated in a suggestion by Bugnini, which of course was challenged, since many thought that there should be only one acclamation at the Offertory: the *Amen* after the *oratio super oblata* [prayer over the offerings].[15]

The silent prayer at the mixing of wine with water (an ancient pagan and also Jewish custom) states the close union of the divine and the human nature in Christ as well as the union with Christ that is granted to us. It reads: "By the mystery of this water and wine may we come to share in the divinity of Christ who humbled himself to share in our humanity."[16] It is incomprehensible why the traditional prayer at the mixing of water and wine,[17] which repeats with slight modifications an ancient Roman Christmas prayer, was narrowed down to the theme of Christ's Incarnation while the motif of human dignity and rebirth was cut out. The reason given by Josef Andreas Jungmann, "indeed, what was begun in the Incarnation should happen in the Sacrament; we should receive a share of the divinity of him who became man for us",[18] is not really convincing, since we receive a share in Christ's divinity precisely as human beings created by God and renewed by Christ.

After the offering of the gifts comes the washing of hands. One can understand the decision to shorten the accompanying prayer *Lavabo*, which in the *Novus Ordo* is replaced by the prayer *Lava me*.[19] The

---

[15] Cf. Bugnini, *Reform of the Liturgy*, 371.

[16] *RM* 2010, 512. Cf. *MR* 2002³, 514: "Per huius aquae et vini mysterium eius efficiamur divinitatis consortes, qui humanitatis nostrae fieri dignatus est particeps."

[17] Cf. *MR* 1962, 221: "Deus, qui humanae substantiae dignitatem mirabiliter condidisti, et mirabilius reformasti: da nobis, per huius aquae et vini mysterium, eius divinitatis esse consortes, qui humanitatis nostrae fieri dignatus est particeps, Iesus Christus, Filius tuus, Dominus noster: Qui tecum vivit et regnat in unitate Spiritus Sancti Deus: per omnia saecula saeculorum. Amen" [O God, who established the nature of man in wondrous dignity, and still more admirably restored it, grant that through the mystery of this water and wine, we may be made partakers of his Divinity, who has condescended to become partaker of our humanity, Jesus Christ, your Son, our Lord: who with you lives and reigns in the unity of the Holy Spirit, God, world without end. Amen].

[18] Josef Andreas Jungmann, *Opfermesse sowie im Anhang: Messe im Gottesvolk: ein nachkonziliarer Durchblick durch Missarum Sollemnia*, vol. 2 of *Missarum Sollemnia: Eine genetische Erklärung der römischen Messe* (1970; Bonn: Nova et Vetera, 2003), 55.

[19] Cf. *MR* 2002³, 515: "Lava me, Domine, ab iniquitate mea, et a peccato meo munda me." *RM* 2010, 513: "Wash me, O Lord, from my iniquity, and cleanse me from my sin."

development of the rite of washing hands was motivated not only by hygienic reasons but also by cultic notions of purity, which of course play a role also in Psalm 26[25]. In the new version, the prayer retains only the theme of being spotted by personal sin. The prayer *Suscipe, sancta Trinitas* has been dropped, because it was viewed as a duplication of the intercessions in the Canon. The prayer of blessing over the offerings, *Veni, sanctificator*, which precedes the washing of hands, was omitted in the new Ordo and not replaced. It was viewed as an anticipation of the epiclesis in the Canon. It does make sense, though, to bless the gifts that are selected for the celebration of the Eucharist. The offerings of the faithful used to be blessed; why not, then, the gifts of bread and wine selected for the Eucharist? Whether the blessing ought to have the form of an epiclesis is another question. Of course one could argue that the blessing of the gifts takes place through the new Offertory prayers modeled on the Jewish *bᵉrākôt*.

The formula *In spiritu humilitatis*[20] was retained "probably because it gives striking expression to the meaning of all outward offering, which lies in the *sacrificium invisibile* of the heart".[21] The prayer at the incensation fell victim to the liturgical reform, which is especially regrettable with regard to the short prayers that frame the citation from Psalm 141[140]: "Incensum istud a te benedictum ascendat ad te, Domine: et descendat super nos misericordia tua" [May this incense blessed by You arise before You, O Lord, and may Your mercy come down upon us] and "Accendat in nobis Dominus ignem sui amoris et flammam aeternae caritatis" [May the Lord enkindle in us the fire of his love and the flame of everlasting charity]. As an invitation to prayer that precedes the prayer over the offerings (*oratio super oblata*), the Missal of Pope Paul VI has in all three editions only the *Orate fratres*, which goes back to the eighth century and in its present wording is documented as early as the twelfth century, to which the

---

[20] *MR* 2002³, 515: "In spiritu humilitatis et in animo contrito sucsipiamur a te, Domine; et sic fiat sacrificium nostrum in conspectu tuo hodie, ut placeat tibi, Domine Deus." Ibid., *RM* 2010, 512: "With humble spirit and contrite heart may we be accepted by you, O Lord, and may our sacrifice in your sight this day be pleasing to you, Lord God." The prayer incorporates verses from the prayer of Azariah in Daniel 3:39–40 [KJV-RC: 3:B16–17], which is preserved only in Greek.

[21] Jungmann, *Messe im Gottesvolk*, 55.

faithful respond with the *Suscipiat*.[22] In Germany, the *Orate fratres* is used very seldom nowadays; as was made clear earlier, this is due to a singular arrangement in the Missal for German-speaking countries in which the *Orate fratres* is only one of three variants of the invitation to prayer, the last one (Form C). The second variant, which is often recited, consists of a simple *Oremus* [Let us pray] without any offertory statement (Form B).[23] The first variant (Form A) reads: "Let us pray to God, the almighty Father, that he may accept the gifts of the Church for his praise and for the salvation of the whole world."[24]

In the classic form of the Roman Rite of the Mass, the idea of offering is palpable everywhere in the Offertory, both textually and ritually. In its modern form, it has indeed been weakened but nevertheless retained thanks to several interventions by Paul VI. In the Missal for German-speaking regions, in contrast, one can note in several places the tendency to avoid offertory language, starting with the fact that during the *Offertorium* the prayers talk, not about the "offering of the gifts", but simply about "preparing the gifts", as though the *Offertorium* were merely the technical process of setting the gifts of bread and wine on the altar in connection with the collects of the faithful. The *Oratio super oblata*, the prayer over the offerings at the end of the Offertory, is merely designated the "prayer over the gifts".[25] The *Offertorium*, however, is not just getting the gifts ready but, rather, an *oblatio*, an offering—notwithstanding what the German translation of *Offertorium* by "Preparation of the Gifts" in the rubrics seems to insinuate. Now the typical Latin edition of the *General Instruction on the Roman Missal* does distinguish in the Liturgy of the Eucharist between *praeparatio donorum, prex eucharistica, fractio panis*, and *communio* [preparation of the gifts, Eucharistic Prayer, breaking of the bread, and Communion].[26] But putting out the gifts

---

[22] Cf. *MR* 2002³, 515: "Orate, fratres: ut meum ac vestrum sacrificium acceptabile fiat apud Deum Patrem omnipotentem. Suscipiat Dominus sacrificium de manibus tuis ad laudem et gloriam nominis sui, ad utilitatem quoque nostram totiusque Ecclesiae suae sanctae." *RM* 2010, 513: "Pray, brothers and sisters, that my sacrifice and yours may be acceptable to God, the almighty Father. May the Lord accept the sacrifice at your hands for the praise and glory of his name, for our good and the good of all his holy Church."
[23] Cf. *MB* 346.
[24] Ibid., 346.
[25] Cf. ibid., 346 and passim.
[26] Cf. *GIRM* 72.

(*afferre, deponere*) and offering the gifts (*offerre*) are clearly distinguished in the GIRM as two stages of the *Offertorium*. The offering of the gifts is emphasized also by their elevation and the *oratio super oblata*.[27] Therefore, we must agree with Alex Stock when he observes that the *Offertorium* is more than a "ritual setting of the table".[28] Through the preparation and offering of the gifts of bread and wine, they are withdrawn from ordinary use.

It is debated whether this is made clear by referring to the *oratio super oblata* as *secreta*. Jungmann says that this prayer is called *secreta* because the priest recites it *secretus*, privately.[29] Pierre Battifol (1861–1929) proposed the hypothesis that *Secreta* comes from *secernere* (to set apart) in the sense of *benedicere* [to bless].[30] In any case, bread and wine are not only placed on the altar (which itself is already a ritual sacrificial element anyway, since the altar is not an ordinary table), but bread and wine are offered (*offerimus*)—which is emphasized by the elevation of the gifts. That, though, is the "most basic act of offering",[31] which reaches back from the Consecration of the offerings into the *Offertorium*. The pale translation of *oratio super oblata* with "prayer over the gifts" therefore seems inappropriate.

Prex eucharistica: After the *oratio super oblata* begins the Eucharistic Prayer. While the Roman liturgy until the liturgical reform was acquainted with only one Eucharistic Prayer, the *Canon Romanus*, but compensated with many Prefaces, the Orthodox Churches, with the exception of the Armenian Church, have several Canons. As has been shown, in the early Middle Ages, out of reverence for the "holy words" of the Eucharistic Prayer, celebrants started praying them silently. Only in 1965 was it again permitted to pronounce the Canon out loud and, since 1967, in the vernacular as well. The 1969 *Ordo Missae* contains besides the *Canon Romanus* three new Eucharistic Prayers. Today the Roman Canon is numbered Eucharistic

---

[27] Cf. *GIRM* 73, 77.

[28] Alex Stock, "Gabenbereitung: Zur Logik des Opfers", *Liturgisches Jahrbuch* 53 (2003): 37.

[29] Cf. Josef Andreas Jungmann, *The Mass of the Roman Rite*, trans. Francis A. Brunner, C.Ss.R., 2 vols. (New York: Benziger Brothers, 1951, 1955), 2:90–91.

[30] So too, recently, Arnold Angenendt, *Geschichte der Religiosität im Mittelalter*, 2nd ed. (Darmstadt: Primus Verlag, 2000), 489, and Alexander Saberschinsky, *Einführung in die Feier der Eucharistie: historisch—systematisch—praktisch* (Freiburg: Herder, 2009), 34f.

[31] Stock, "Gabenbereitung", 38.

Prayer I.[32] The second Eucharistic Prayer in the Missal of Paul VI (1970) is a revised and expanded version of the Eucharistic Prayer of the *Traditio Apostolica*.[33] Eucharistic Prayer III is essentially a new creation, which in its sacrificial statements is guided by the Roman Canon.[34] Eucharistic Prayer IV in some parts is modeled on the Eastern Anaphora of Saint Basil.[35] Since Eucharistic Prayer IV contains an extensive praise of God's saving deeds, it is also called the salvation history Eucharistic Prayer. The venerable *Canon Romanus* and Eucharistic Prayer III are assigned to the celebration of Mass on Sundays and feast days, Eucharistic Prayer II mainly to weekdays and special occasions, and Eucharistic Prayer IV especially to Sundays in ordinary time.[36]

In German-speaking regions, the liturgical practice is to a great extent different. The Roman Canon in this country has disappeared almost entirely from the Sunday liturgy. Even in many cathedral churches one encounters it very seldom now. While Eucharistic Prayer III is quite widespread, Eucharistic Prayer IV is rarely used on account of its length. Most often Eucharistic Prayer II is used, on Sundays, too, as a rule. Theodor Schnitzler had already foreseen this development: "In any case, the second Canon, on account of its brevity, will enjoy great popularity."[37] In this country, the second Canon has become, as it were, the "standard canon" for Sundays.[38] In the new edition of *Gotteslob* (2013), only Eucharistic Prayer II is reprinted—indeed, in a new translation approved by the German Bishops' Conference, which, however, has not been recognized by the Apostolic See.[39]

---

[32] Cf. *MR* 2002³, 572–79; *MB* 462–77.

[33] Cf. *MR* 2002³, 580–84; *RM* 2010, 629–33.

[34] Cf. *MR* 2002³, 585–90; *RM* 2010, 634–39.

[35] Cf. *MR* 2002³, 591–96; *RM* 2010, 640–46.

[36] *Missale Romanum, Editio typica tertia* 2002: "Grundordnung des Römischen Messbuchs", Vorabpublikation zum Deutschen Messbuch, 3rd ed. (Bonn: Sekretariat der Dt. Bischofskonferenz, 2007; hereafter cited as *GORM*), no. 365.

[37] Theodor Schnitzler, *Die drei neuen Hochgebete und die neuen Präfationen* (Freiburg: Herder, 1969), 25.

[38] Cf. Friedrich Lurz, *Erhebet die Herzen: Das Eucharistische Hochgebet verstehen* (Kevelaer: Butzon & Bercker, 2011), 16.

[39] In the old *Gotteslob* hymnal, besides Eucharistic Prayer II, the other three Eucharistic Prayers from the Missal of Paul VI were reprinted, also.

The Eucharistic Prayer is introduced by an alternating chant: Priest: "The Lord be with you." Congregation: "And with your spirit." P.: "Lift up your hearts." C.: "We lift them up to the Lord." P.: "Let us give thanks to the Lord our God." C.: "It is right and just." Next comes the Preface, which if possible should be sung. The Eucharistic Prayer is concluded with the doxology before the Our Father. The Preface is not a "foreword" to the Eucharistic Prayer, because the Latin prefix *prae-* is to be understood spatially: before God and the congregation, "the priest praises the Father and thanks him for the entire work of redemption, or, depending on the day, the feast, or the season, for a particular mystery of the Lord's salvific work", says the *Allgemeine Einführung in das Messbuch*.[40] The Missal contains numerous Prefaces for the liturgical year. The tripartite structure of the Preface includes an introduction, praise of God's saving deeds, and the transition to the *Sanctus*.

The threefold *Sanctus* (Holy, Holy, Holy), which is part of the Eucharistic Prayer and is sung or recited by priest and people, is based on the praise of the angels in the account of the Prophet Isaiah's vision (Is 6:3)[41] and on the people's shouts of praise as Jesus entered Jerusalem (Mt 21:9).[42] In contrast to the *Sanctus* in the 1962 *Missale Romanum*, in the new Eucharistic Prayers, a "post-Sanctus" makes a transition to the "epiclesis". Eucharistic Prayer II: "You are indeed Holy, O Lord, the fount of all holiness"; Eucharistic Prayer III: "You are indeed Holy, O Lord, and all you have created rightly gives you praise, for through your Son our Lord Jesus Christ, by the power and working of the Holy Spirit, you give life to all things and make them holy, and you never cease to gather a people to yourself, so that from the rising of the sun to its setting a pure sacrifice may be offered to your name." Eucharistic Prayer IV contains a "post-Sanctus" with an extensive anamnesis. In the case of the "post-Sanctus" of Eucharistic Prayers II and III, an interpolation can be made on particular days recalling the mystery of the feast.

The epiclesis following the "post-Sanctus" is about calling down the Holy Spirit upon the Eucharistic gifts; it is accompanied by two

[40] AEM, no. 55a.
[41] "Holy, Holy, Holy is the Lord of hosts. The whole earth is full of his glory."
[42] "Hosanna to the Son of David! Blessed is he who comes in the name of the Lord! Hosanna in the highest!" Cf. Ps 118:26.

blessing rites: the extension of hands over the gifts and a blessing with the Sign of the Cross. Eucharistic Prayer II: "Make holy, therefore, these gifts, we pray, by sending down your Spirit upon them like the dewfall, so that they may become for us the Body + and Blood of our Lord, Jesus Christ"; Eucharistic Prayer III: ". . . by the same Spirit graciously make holy these gifts we have brought to you for consecration, that they may become the Body + and Blood of your Son our Lord Jesus Christ, at whose command we celebrate these mysteries"; Eucharistic Prayer IV: "May this same Holy Spirit graciously sanctify these offerings, that they may become the Body + and Blood of our Lord Jesus Christ for the celebration of this great mystery, which he himself left us as an eternal covenant." In the Roman Canon, we can recognize an epiclesis in the prayer *Quam oblationem* (accompanied by the outspreading of hands over the gifts), which is prayed immediately before the institution narrative, in which, however, the Holy Spirit is not mentioned by name: "Be pleased, O God, we pray, to bless, acknowledge, and approve this offering in every respect; make it spiritual and acceptable, so that it may become for us the Body and Blood of your most beloved Son, our Lord Jesus Christ."[43]

In the Eastern rites, the epiclesis as a rule follows the words of institution. Since the early Middle Ages, this sparked a debate over which is decisive for the transubstantiation of the gifts: the words of institution (West) or the epiclesis (East). Today in the Catholic Church, there is once again greater emphasis on the unity of the "Eucharistic Prayer" with its central action from the epiclesis to the *Mysterium fidei*. The words of institution of the Roman Canon are not identical with the biblical accounts of the institution but, rather, go back to an ancient liturgical tradition. The Missal distinguishes between the *narratio institutionis* and the *consecratio*.[44] The English Missal speaks about the institutional narrative and the Consecration.[45] After each

---

[43] *RM* 2010, 622; *MR* 2002³, 574: "Quam oblationem tu, Deus, in omnibus, quaesumus, benedictam, adscriptam, ratam, rationabilem, acceptabilemque facere digneris: ut nobis Corpus et Sanguis fiat dilectissimi Filii tui, Domini nostri Iesu Christi."

[44] Cf. *GIRM* 2002³, 79.

[45] Cf. *MB*, no. 55d. Many liturgists dispute a consecration of the gifts of bread and wine by the *verba testamenti*. Cf. Klemens Richter, "Eucharistisches Hochgebet ohne Einsetzungsworte: Überwindung eines zentralen Aspekts scholastischer Sakramententheologie durch die römische Kongregation für die Glaubenslehre", in *Gemeinschaftlich im Danken: Grundfragen der Eucharistiefeier im ökumenischen Gespräch*, ed. by S. Böntert, Studien zur Pastoralliturgie 40 (Regensburg: Pustet, 2015), 69–83.

Consecration, of bread and of wine, the celebrant elevates the consecrated gifts.[46] The interpolation "The mystery of faith" was detached from the words over the chalice and inserted after the words of institution; with the acclamation of the faithful: "We proclaim your Death, O Lord, and profess your Resurrection until you come again."[47] The acclamation of the congregation is followed by the anamnesis (= remembrance) of the salvation founded on Christ. Eucharistic Prayer I: Passion, Resurrection, and Ascension; Eucharistic Prayer II: death and Resurrection; Eucharistic Prayer III: Passion, Resurrection, Ascension, and coming again; Eucharistic Prayer IV mentions in addition Christ's "descent to the realm of the dead".

Connected with the anamnesis is a prayer of oblation and sacrifice that refers to the one-time sacrifice of Christ in which Christ, unlike Melchizedek, is at the same time victim and priest. Here the self-offering of the faithful, which was mentioned already at the offering of the sacrifice, is mentioned once again, as follows in Eucharistic Prayer IV: "Look, O Lord, upon the Sacrifice which you yourself have provided for your Church, and grant in your loving kindness to all who partake of this one Bread and one Chalice that, gathered into one body by the Holy Spirit, they may truly become a living sacrifice in Christ to the praise of your glory." This petition for the fruitful reception of the Body and Blood of Christ is designated the Communion epiclesis.

The post-consecratory *oblatio*, which we encounter already in the Roman Canon (*Unde et memores*),[48] is intensified in the three new Eucharistic Prayers of 1970. Thus the *Memores igitur* of Eucharistic Prayer II says about the Church's sacrifice: "we offer you, Lord, the Bread of life and the Chalice of salvation" (*tibi, Domine, panem vitae*

---

[46] On the debate about the elevation, which liturgists as a rule regard negatively or with reservations, see the balanced essay by Andreas Heinz, "Zeige- und Darbringungsgestus: Zur Bedeutung der Elevations nach den Einsetzungsworten", in *Gemeinschaft im Danken: Grundfragen der Eucharistiefeier im ökumenischen Gespräch*, ed. Stefan Böntert, Studien zur Pastoralliturgie 40 (Regensburg: Pustet, 2015), 126–46.

[47] RM 2010, 624. According to the *Missale Romanum* (1970[1], 2002[3]), the priest or the bishop sings the *Mysterium fidei*, not the deacon. Only in the Missal for German-speaking regions is the summons *Mysterium fidei* assigned to the deacon.

[48] Cf. MR 2002[3], 576: "offerimus ... hostiam immaculatam, panem sanctum vitae aeternae" [we offer ... this spotless victim, the holy Bread of eternal life].

et calicem salutis offerimus).[49] In Eucharistic Prayer IV, the priest prays: "we offer you his Body and Blood" (*offerimus tibi eius Corpus et Sanguinem*).[50] Thus Christ is presented by the Church to God as her sacrifice, which she has received as a gift in the Consecration. The Mass is therefore more than a memorial celebration of the death and Resurrection of Jesus—it is itself an oblation.

Next, after the prayer of offering and sacrifice with the Communion epiclesis, come the intercessions (petitions): for the Church, her officials, and the assembled faithful, and for people who are still far from God (Eucharistic Prayer III); there is also a commemoration of the dead. In Eucharistic Prayers I–III, it is possible to mention deceased individuals by name. The intercessions in Eucharistic Prayer IV also include "all the dead, whose faith you alone have known". All four Eucharistic Prayers contain a commemoration of the martyrs and saints, above all, a commemoration of the Mother of God and of the apostles. In Eucharistic Prayer III, the names of particular saints can also be added (saints of the day, patrons of the church). The last element of the Eucharistic Prayer is the great doxology (= expression of praise), which is the same in all four Eucharistic Prayers. At the concluding doxology, the priest raises the consecrated gifts slightly and says or sings: "Through him, and with him, and in him, O God, almighty Father, in the unity of the Holy Spirit, all glory and honor is yours, for ever and ever." The faithful reaffirm this expression of praise and the entire Eucharistic Prayer with their *Amen*.

Excursus: The Apostolic Tradition *and Eucharistic Prayer II*[51]

The relation between Eucharistic Prayer II and the Eucharistic Prayer of the *Traditio Apostolica* deserves special attention. During the liturgical reform, it was assumed that Hippolytus of Rome was the author of the *Traditio Apostolica*. The Eucharistic Prayer in this Church ordinance would thus be the oldest Roman Eucharistic Prayer. It was brought into play for the reform of the Missal by Hans Küng, since

---

[49] Cf. *MR* 2002³, 582; *RM* 2010, 632.
[50] Cf. *MR* 2002³, 595; *RM* 2010, 644.
[51] See the Latin and English text of the two Eucharistic Prayers in the appendix.

it seemed to him particularly well suited to cater to the reservations of Protestants about the concept of sacrifice in the Roman Canon.[52] Küng accuses the Roman Canon of being fragmentary; others speak about a "ruin" or about structural and thematic deficiencies.[53] The demand to do away with the Roman Canon, however, could not gain general acceptance any more than the demand for a complete revision, which was discussed in the consultation for implementing the liturgical reform. So, finally, three additional Eucharistic Prayers were placed alongside the traditional Roman Canon, among them Eucharistic Prayer II based on the Eucharistic Prayer in the *Traditio Apostolica* attributed to Hippolytus of Rome.

The differences between Eucharistic Prayer II and the one in the *Traditio Apostolica*[54] first have to do with the insertion of the *Sanctus* and a consecratory epiclesis before the *verba testamenti*. Moreover, significant statements in the Eucharistic Prayer of the *Traditio Apostolica* were not adopted. Already in the Preface, abbreviations were made that can be understood only with difficulty. For example, in the *Traditio Apostolica* it says: "We give thanks to you, God, through your beloved child (*puer*) Jesus Christ, whom, in the last times (*in ultimis temporibus*), you sent to us as savior and redeemer and angel of your will (cf. Is 9:5 LXX), who is your inseparable Word through whom you made all things and who was well pleasing to you. You sent him from heaven into the womb of a virgin."[55] The term *puer* (boy, servant) is replaced by *filius* in Eucharistic Prayer II. Mention of the eschatological end times is missing in Eucharistic Prayer II as well as the designation of Christ as the Word inseparable from God the Father by which the undiminished divinity of Jesus is emphasized. The Preface of Eucharistic Prayer II goes on to say: "Fulfilling your will and gaining for you a holy people, he stretched out his hands as he endured his Passion, so as to break the bonds of death and manifest the resurrection."[56] The text of the *Traditio Apostolica*, in contrast,

---

[52] Cf. Hans Küng, "Das Eucharistiegebet—Konzil und Erneuerung der römischen Liturgie", *Wort und Wahrheit* 18 (1963): 106.

[53] Cf. Bruno Kleinheyer, *Erneuerung des Hochgebetes* (Regensburg: Pustet, 1969), 25–29.

[54] Cf. Heinz-Lothar Barth, *Die Mär vom antiken Kanon des Hippolytos: Untersuchungen zur Liturgiereform* (Stuttgart: Sarto-Verlag, 2008), 21–45, 96–112, 132–37.

[55] FC 1: 222–25; Hippolytus, *On the Apostolic Tradition*, trans. Alistair C. Stewart, 2nd ed., Popular Patristic Series 54 (Yonkers, N.Y.: St. Vladimir's Seminary Press, 2015), 78.

[56] RM 2010, 629.

reads: "He fulfilled your will and won for you a holy people, opening wide his hands when he suffered that he might set free from suffering those who believed in you."[57] In Eucharistic Prayer II, the difference between Christ's redemptive deed on the Cross and the acceptance of him in faith is eliminated.

After the *Sanctus* and the consecratory epiclesis, the priest prays in Eucharistic Prayer II: "At the time he was betrayed and entered willingly into his Passion, he took bread...."[58] In the *Traditio Apostolica*, it says immediately after the Preface without any preceding consecratory epiclesis: "When he was handed over to voluntary suffering, in order to dissolve death and break the chains of the devil and harrow hell and illuminate the just and fix a boundary and manifest the resurrection, he took bread."[59] Eucharistic Prayer II departs here considerably from the text of the *Traditio Apostolica*. It does say in the special Preface for Eucharistic Prayer II: "so as to break the bonds of death and manifest the resurrection."[60] However, the devil and his disempowerment as well as Christ's descent into the underworld, which is nonetheless an article of the Apostles' Creed, probably seemed too archaic to the liturgical reformers.

At the offering of the gifts of bread and wine, several differences are immediately apparent. The text of the *Traditio Apostolica* reads: "Remembering therefore his death and resurrection, we offer you bread and cup, giving thanks to you because you have held us worthy to stand before you and minister to you as priest."[61] Eucharistic Prayer II, in contrast, says: "Therefore, as we celebrate the memorial of his Death and Resurrection, we offer (*offerimus*) you, Lord (*Domine*), the Bread of life (*panem vitae*) and the Chalice of salvation (*calicem salutae*), giving thanks that you have held us worthy to be in your presence and minister to you."[62] The expressions *panis vitae* and *calix salutae* emphasize that the offering of the sacrifice involves the consecrated gifts of bread and wine. In a departure from the Eucharistic Prayer of the *Traditio Apostolica*, however, the *Memores igitur* in Eucharistic Prayer II refers no longer to the priest but, rather, to the

[57] FC 1: 224–25; Stewart, 78.
[58] RM 2010, 630.
[59] FC 1: 224–25; Stewart, 78.
[60] RM 2010, 629.
[61] FC 1: 226–27; Stewart, 78.
[62] RM 2010, 632.

faithful gathered to celebrate the Eucharist.[63] In the *Traditio Apostolica*, it refers unambiguously to the ministry of the ordained ministers, which is why Bernard Botte, following the Ethiopic version of the *Traditio Apostolica*, translates the relevant expression into Latin as *adstare coram te et tibi sacerdotium exhibere*[64] [to stand in your presence and to render priestly ministry to you], while Wilhelm Geerlings translates it "to stand before you and to serve you as a priest".[65]

Since an epiclesis in the sense of calling down the Holy Spirit upon the sacrificial gifts after their Consecration would have posed a certain problem for the Roman Rite, the Spirit-epiclesis of the *Traditio Apostolica* became a Communion epiclesis in Eucharistic Prayer II: "Humbly we pray that, partaking of the Body and Blood of Christ, we may be gathered into one by the Holy Spirit."[66] The text of the *Traditio Apostolica* reads: "And we ask that you should send your Holy Spirit to the offering of the holy church (*oblatio sanctae ecclesiae*): gathering [her] into one, may you grant to all the saints who receive for the fullness of the Holy Spirit, for the confirmation of their faith in truth."[67] While this "strengthening of faith" is clearly expressed in the Eucharistic Prayer of the *Traditio Apostolica* and the Roman Canon emphasizes fidelity to the Church's faith, in Eucharistic Prayer II, the aspect of faith has been omitted and replaced by the idea of unity and love: "bring her [the Church, Latin *ecclesia*] to the fullness of charity [*caritas*]."[68] The liturgists hesitated also to speak about the "sacrifice of holy Church". Obviously with Eucharistic Prayer II, they wanted to create a Eucharistic Prayer that no longer contains the idea, rejected by the Protestants, of a sacrifice of the Church that goes beyond

---

[63] This had already been criticized by Bernard Botte, "Die Wendung 'astare coram te et tibi ministrare' im Eucharistischen Hochgebet II", *Bibel und Liturgie* 49 (1976): 101–4.

[64] Cf. Botte, *La Tradition apostolique de Saint Hippolyte: Essai de reconstitution*, 5th rev. ed., ed. Bernard Botte and Albert Gerhards, Liturgiewissenschaftliche Quellen und Forschungen 39 (Münster: Aschendorff, 1989), 17; Wilhelm Geerlings, "Einleitung zur Traditio Apostolica", in *Didache* =: *Zwölf-Apostel-Lehre: Apostolische Überlieferung*, FC 1:226f.

[65] Cf. John F. Baldovin, "Eucharistic Prayer II: History of the Latin Text and Rite", in *A Commentary on the Order of Mass of the Roman Missal*, foreword by Roger Cardinal Mahony, ed. E. Foley (Collegeville, Minn.: Liturgical Press, 2001), 314, in contrast, thinks that whether the expression *adstare coram te et tibi ministrare* refers to the congregation or to the bishop must remain an open question.

[66] RM 2010, 632.

[67] FC 1: 226–27; Stewart, 79, gives this literal translation in a footnote.

[68] RM 2010, 632.

praise and thanks. And so in Eucharistic Prayer II, there is no mention of the sacrifice that, according to the teaching of the Council of Trent, the Church offers through the ministry of her priests.[69]

Communio, Postcommunio, concluding rites: Communion, the sacred meal, unites us with Christ, as the Bread of Life discourse makes clear: "He who eats my flesh and drinks my blood abides in me, and I in him" (Jn 6:56). In the celebration of the Eucharist in the early Church, Communion followed the Eucharistic Prayer immediately.[70] Very early, though, preparatory prayers and rites developed. We should mention above all the Our Father. In the Roman Mass, it has been prayed since the time of Gregory the Great before the rite of peace and the breaking of the bread. Today the Our Father is again spoken or sung by priest and faithful together, whereas, in the "Tridentine Mass", it was sung or spoken by the priest alone and the faithful joined in at the last petition *sed libera nos a malo* (but deliver us from evil). Following the Our Father is the so-called embolism, an interpolation in which the priest prays for peace, God's saving mercy, and protection from error and sin.

Deliver us, Lord, we pray, from every evil, graciously grant peace in our days, that, by the help of your mercy, we may be always free from sin and safe from all distress, as we await the blessed hope and the coming of our Savior, Jesus Christ.

This interpolation goes back to a doxology from the *Didache*.[71]

Another preparatory rite besides the Our Father and the embolism is the Sign of Peace. It is based, not on Jesus' instruction that one must be reconciled with one's brother before the liturgy (Mt 5:23f.), but rather on the Paschal greeting of the risen Lord. The medieval explanations of the liturgy interpret the Sign of Peace in this way, too.[72] The Sign of Peace is preceded by a prayer for peace and the promise of peace, which is reciprocated by the faithful:

---

[69] Cf. DH 1571–72. Quite a few Catholic dogmatic theologians reject an offering of sacrifice by the priest. Bernd Jochen Hilberath, "Eucharistie", in *LThK*, 2nd ed., vol. 3 (1995), 950, writes: "Talk about the offering of sacrifice through the hands of the priest is altogether misleading."

[70] Cf. Justin Martyr, *Apologia I pro Christianis* 65, 67 (PG 6:427, 430).

[71] Cf. *Didache* 9.4 (FC 1:122f.)

[72] In the Eastern liturgy, the rite of peace takes place before the Eucharistic Prayer.

Priest: Lord Jesus Christ, who said to your Apostles, Peace I leave you, my peace I give you, look not on our sins, but on the faith of your Church, and graciously grant her peace and unity in accordance with your will.... The peace of the Lord be with you always.

People: And with your spirit.[73]

After the prayer of peace and the promise of peace, the deacon may invite the faithful to give one another a sign of peace.

In the *Missale Romanum*, the optional invitation reads: *Offerte vobis pacem.*[74] In the German version, the motive of reconciliation has been added, although the *Pax* is about the peace of the risen Lord: "Give one another a sign of peace and reconciliation."[75] In 2007, Benedict XVI asked all the conferences of bishops to vote on the question of whether the Sign of Peace, which often disturbs preparation for Communion, should be moved ahead, for instance, to a place immediately after the Liturgy of the Word, as is the case in other liturgical families. This had been preceded by an order of the pope to the competent dicasteries to examine the possibility of a change of position.

Taking into account ancient and venerable customs and the wishes expressed by the Synod Fathers, I have asked the competent curial offices to study the possibility of moving the sign of peace to another place, such as before the presentation of the gifts at the altar. To do so would also serve as a significant reminder of the Lord's insistence that we be reconciled with others before offering our gifts to God (cf. Mt 5:23ff.).[76]

Why the Sign of Peace was not moved to another place in the Mass is unclear.[77]

During the subsequent breaking of the bread, the *Agnus Dei* (Lamb of God) is sung or recited. In connection with the breaking of the bread, the priest puts a small piece of the Host into the chalice and says quietly: "May this mingling of the Body and Blood of our Lord Jesus Christ bring eternal life to us who receive it."[78] Since small round hosts

---

[73] *RM* 2010, 650.

[74] Cf. *MR* 2002³, 600.

[75] *MB* 519.

[76] *SacCar* 49, n. 150.

[77] The German bishops had spoken up against changing the position of the Sign of Peace.

[78] *RM* 2010, 651.

first appeared in the twelfth century, until then a fraction or breaking of the Eucharistic bread was necessary in order to distribute it, which Paul already interpreted symbolically: the one Bread, which is Christ, is given to the many, so that they may become the one Body of Christ (cf. 1 Cor 10:16f.). The origin of the practice of adding a piece of the Eucharistic Bread to the chalice is unclear. Some trace the practice back to the custom that on set feast days the bishop of Rome would send to the priests of neighboring Churches a small piece of the consecrated Host, which was called the *fermentum*. During their next Mass, the priests put it into the chalice as a sign of their union with the bishop of Rome and as a sign of the unity of Christ's Sacrifice. Others see the mingling as the adoption of a rite that originated in Syria, which is supposed to symbolize Christ's Resurrection and his presence on the altar, as opposed to the separation of bread and wine and the twofold Consecration, which symbolize the Passion and death of Christ.

The breaking of the Eucharistic Bread is followed by a preparatory prayer of the priest. After a genuflection, he takes a piece of the Host, holds it over the chalice, and says: "Behold the Lamb of God, behold him who takes away the sins of the world."[79] The faithful respond: "Lord, I am not worthy that you should enter under my roof, but only say the word and my soul shall be healed."[80] The priest may then add a Communion verse, for example "Blessed are those called to the supper of the Lamb."[81] Before the priest communicates, he says: "May the Body of Christ keep me safe for eternal life", "May the Blood of Christ keep me safe for eternal life."[82] Only *after* the priest's Communion do the faithful communicate, and they receive, if possible, the Body of Christ from the same sacrifice, that is, not from the tabernacle.[83] With the formula "The Body of Christ", they receive the Eucharist. The faithful respond *Amen*.[84]

Communion is received on the tongue or, if the regulations of the local Church allow, in the hand. For Communion under both

[79] *RM* 2010, 653.
[80] Ibid.
[81] Ibid.
[82] Ibid.
[83] Both rules were established by a decree of the Second Vatican Council. Cf. *SC* 55: "The more perfect form of participation in the Mass whereby the faithful, after the priest's communion, receive the Lord's body from the same sacrifice, is strongly recommended."
[84] *RM* 2010, 653.

species, there are three possibilities for those who are not priests: (a) drinking from the chalice, (b) the use of a straw, and (c) the use of a small spoon, with which a host dipped into the chalice is placed in the recipient's mouth. Other forms, such as dipping the consecrated Host into the chalice, are not allowed for those who are not priests.[85] The distribution of Communion is accompanied by the Communion chant or by organ playing. The hymn of thanksgiving after Communion is followed by the concluding prayer (*Postcommunio*). The prayer is pronounced by the priest from the presider's chair or from the altar. The faithful respond to the prayer with their *Amen*. After the *Postcommunio*, there is an opportunity to make important announcements.

After that the priest gives the concluding blessing. The blessing as a rule is imparted with the usual formula: "May almighty God bless you, the Father, and the Son, and the Holy Spirit." On feast days and special occasions, a "solemn blessing" or a "prayer over the faithful" (*oratio super populo*) or a blessing of the weather can be pronounced, also. The faithful respond with their *Amen*. In keeping with a decision of Pope Benedict XVI that goes back to the consultations of the Synod of Bishops in October 2005, there have been four possible dismissals for the celebration of Mass in the Latin Rite since October 2008: *Ite, missa est* (Go forth, the Mass is ended); *Ite, ad Evangelium Domini annuntiandum* (Go and announce the Gospel of the Lord); *Ite in pace, glorificando vita vestra Dominum* (Go in peace, glorifying the Lord by your life); and *Ite in pace* (Go in peace). The congregation responds *Deo gratias*, "Thanks be to God." During the Easter season, the Alleluia is added by the deacon and the congregation.

The new dismissals will be incorporated into the revised version of the Missal for German-speaking regions. [They are included in the recent revised English translation of the Missal.] The formula in the Latin Missal, *Ite, missa est*, is derived from *dimissio* (dismissal). Because the dismissal was associated with the blessing very early on, the word *missa* was understood to include the blessing that God bestows. *Missa* was likewise thought to be connected with *missio*, and the *Ite, missa est* was understood as a mission: "Go, your mission is beginning." All this is connoted in the Latin *Ite, missa est*. "Go in peace" is a very

---

[85] *GORM* 284–87. The possibilities (b) and (c), practically speaking, play no role in Germany, except in the case of Communion of the sick.

loose interpretation of the dismissal. At the conclusion of the Mass, the priest kisses the altar (if deacons and concelebrants participate, they do, too) and goes back with the other ministers to the sacristy.

B. The Extraordinary Form of the Mass (1962)

If the Roman Mass is celebrated on the legal foundation of the motu proprio *Summorum Pontificum* (2007) and the instruction *Universae Ecclesiae* (2011), then, with the exception of religious orders with their own rite of the Mass, it follows the order of the *Missale Romanum* promulgated by John XXIII.[86] The 1962 *Ordo Missae* has the following structure:

MASS OF THE CATECHUMENS
    Prayers at the foot of the altar
        In nomine Patris
        Introibo ad altare Dei
        Iudica me
        Confiteor
        Misereatur / Indulgentiam
        Deus, tu conversus
        Aufer a nobis and *Oramus te*
        Incensation of altar and priest (High Mass)
    Sacrifice of prayer
        Introit (Entrance chant)
        Kyrie
        Gloria
        Collect (prayer of the day)
    Instruction
        Epistle (reading)
        Gradual
        Tract (during Lent and the weeks before Lent)
        Alleluia
        Two Alleluia chants (during the Easter season)

---

[86] An extensive explanation of the classic rite of the Roman Mass is offered by Adrian Fortescue, *The Ceremonies of the Roman Rite Described*, 15th ed. (Tunbridge Wells: Burns & Oates, 2009); a short explanation is given by Michael Fiedrowicz, *Die überlieferte Messe: Geschichte, Gestalt, Theologie* (Mühlheim an der Mosel: Carthusianus Verlag, 2011), 74–124.

Possible Sequence (on particular feast days)
Incensation of the Gospel book (High Mass)
Gospel
Incensation of the priest (High Mass)
Homily
Credo

MASS OF THE FAITHFUL
Preparatory offering
Offertory chant
Suscipe, sancte Pater (offering of the bread)
Deus, qui humanae substantiae (mixing of the wine with water)
Offerimus tibi, Domine (offering of the wine)
In spiritu humilitatis (prayer of self-offering)
Veni, sanctificator (prayer of blessing)
Incensation of the gifts, altar, priest, and people
Lavabo (washing of hands)
Suscipe, sancta Trinitas (prayer of offering up)
Orate, fratres (invitation to prayer)
Suscipiat
Secret (*oratio super oblata*)
Sacrifice: Canon of the Mass
Preface
Sanctus / Benedictus
Te igitur (commendation of the oblations and commemoration of the
Church)
Memento, Domine (commemoration of the living)
Communicantes (commemoration of the saints)
Hanc igitur (petition for the acceptance of the oblations)
Quam oblationem (petition for the transformation of the oblations)
Qui pridie (Consecration)
Unde et memores (commemoration of Christ's redemptive work)
Supra quae (petition for the acceptance of the sacrifice)
Supplices te rogamus (petition for union with Christ's Sacrifice)
Memento etiam (commemoration of the dead)
Nobis quoque (petition for fellowship with the saints)
Per quem and *Per ipsum* (solemn praise of God)
Amen
Sacrificial banquet
Pater noster
Libera nos (continuation of the Our Father)

Breaking of the bread and mingling (with *Pax Domini*)
Agnus Dei
Domine Jesu Christe, qui dixisti (prayer for peace—in High Mass, with
   Sign of Peace)
Preparatory prayers
Communion of the priest
Confiteor
Misereatur/Indulgentiam
Ecce Agnus Dei
Domine, non sum dignus (3×)
Communion of the faithful
Purification
Communion verse
Postcommunion (concluding prayer)

DISMISSAL
Ite, missa est (dismissal)
Placeat tibi (concluding petition)
Benedicat vos (blessing)
Last Gospel
Recessional
Prayers after Holy Mass

Mass of the catechumens: Before the entrance of the priest and the *min-istri*, various accompanying and preparatory prayers are prescribed for the priest (and the servers) in connection with putting on the liturgical vestments. After the entrance, the "pre-Mass", or, rather, the Mass of the catechumens begins; it consists of prayers at the foot of the altar, the sacrifice of prayer, and the instruction. The prayers at the foot of the altar are prayed by the priest and the servers, who in the past were usually clerics, on the steps leading up to the altar. Next come the silent prayer *Aufer a nobis* and the kissing of the altar with its accompanying prayer. Since the Gospels are integrated into the Missal, the kissing of the Gospel book is omitted. While standing at the middle of the altar (or, in Solemn High Mass, while still on the Epistle side, that is, on the right), the priest leads the ninefold *Kyrie* and the *Gloria* on the Sundays and feast days when it is called for. The prayer of the day (*collecta*), which concludes the Instruction and is pronounced on the Epistle side, is preceded by the greeting *Dominus vobiscum*, for which the priest, standing in the middle, kisses the altar and turns toward the people.

The instruction, which corresponds to the Liturgy of the Word in the modern form of the Roman Mass, begins at the Epistle side. The Gradual and Alleluia verse are read there, too, and on penitential days and at Requiem Masses, the Tract and, on particular feast days, the Sequence. After the reading (in Solemn High Mass, this duty belongs to the subdeacon), the Missal is carried to the Gospel side (on the left). The Gospel is read by the priest after he has pronounced the preparatory prayers *Munda cor* and *Dominus sit in corde meo* at the middle of the altar. In a Solemn High Mass, the duty of reciting the Gospel belongs to the deacon. After he has recited the *Munda cor* kneeling and has received the celebrant's blessing with the *Dominus sit in corde tuo*, he walks with the candle- and incense-bearers, and also with the subdeacon, who holds the Gospel book during the proclamation of the Gospel, in procession to the choir stalls. There he proclaims the Gospel facing north, which symbolizes the place of unbelief. The Sunday sermon is not obligatory but is emphatically recommended by the Council of Trent. On Sundays and feast days, the *Credo* is sung or recited. The "Tridentine" Mass has no intercessions (*oratio fidelium*).

Mass of the faithful: The priest begins the presentation of the gifts while standing at the middle of the altar by kissing the altar and pronouncing the greeting *Dominus vobiscum* and reading the Offertory, which is the antiphon of the chant sung at the Offertory. The psalm that this antiphon originally framed was no longer considered in the 1570 *Missale Romanum*. Likewise at the middle of the altar, the priest offers the bread with the prayer *Suscipe, sancte Pater*. Then he pours wine into the chalice, blesses the water that is mixed in with the wine with the prayer *Deus, qui humanae substantiae*, and offers the wine with the prayer *Offerimus tibi, Domine*. The traditional prayers accompanying the offering of the gifts of bread (*Suscipe, sancte Pater*) and wine (*Offerimus tibi, Domine*) already speak in anticipation about the spotless victim (*immaculata hostia*) and the chalice of salvation (*calix salutaris*). Next come the preparatory prayers *In spiritu humilitatis*, the prayer of blessing *Veni, sanctificator*, the washing of hands with the psalm *Lavabo* (Ps 26[25]:6–12), and the prayer of self-offering *Suscipe, sancta Trinitas*. Afterward, the priest recites the invitation to prayer

Orate, fratres, which is followed by the response *Suscipiat*, which the priest himself should recite in the absence of a server. The prayer over the gifts (*oratio super oblata*), which has been spoken quietly since the early Middle Ages, concludes the offering of the sacrificial gifts.

The Canon, which according to the medieval understanding begins after the Preface with the *Te igitur*, is spoken softly by the priest at the middle of the altar—with the exception of the words *Nobis quoque peccatoribus* and the concluding formula of the doxology *Per omnia saecula saeculorum*. Since the Middle Ages, this practice had become accepted everywhere and was prescribed in a binding way by the 1570 *Missale Romanum*. The prayers of the Roman Canon are accompanied by numerous Signs of the Cross, bows, and genuflections. During the *Sanctus*, an additional candle is lit. After the Consecration, the Host and the chalice are elevated; the priest is supposed to show the Host and the chalice to the people (*ostendit populo*). The prayer from *Quam oblationem* to *Supplices te rogamus*, which are some of the oldest in the *Canon Romanus*, emphasize the sacrificial form of the Eucharist, which does not merely consist of the preparation and distribution of the gifts in connection with the Church's sacrifice of praise. Another part of the Eucharist, according to the Catholic understanding of it, is the offering of it before and after the Consecration. The offering of the gifts aims at the transformation of the gifts, but that in turn aims at the transformation of the faithful.

Communion is introduced by the *Pater noster*, recited aloud by the priest, and the last petition, *sed libera nos a malo*, recited by the faithful as a response. The priest breaks the Host and with a particle of it makes three Signs of the Cross over the chalice while speaking aloud the greeting of peace, *Pax Domini sit semper vobiscum*; then he puts the fragment into the chalice, accompanied by the *Haec commixtio*, recited softly. The threefold *Agnus Dei* afterward is spoken aloud, and the preparatory prayers that follow are again recited softly; the first of them is the prayer for peace, *Domine Jesu Christe, qui dixisti*. If the *Pax* (Sign of Peace) is given at the altar (in Solemn High Mass), the priest kisses the altar first. The *Pax* is given by the priest to the deacon, then by the deacon to the subdeacon, and by him to all the other clerics who are in choir. The response to the greeting of peace *Pax tecum* is *et cum spiritu tuo*.

After the prayer of peace and the *Pax* come the priest's preparatory prayers *Domine Iesu Christe* and *Perceptio corporis*. With the accompanying prayer *Panem caelestem*, the priest takes the paten with the Host in his left hand and recites aloud three times the *Domine, non sum dignus*, striking his breast with his right hand at each recitation. The priest's Communion follows with the appropriate accompanying prayers. Before the Communion of the faithful, the priest turns to the people and shows them the consecrated Host with the words, *Ecce Agnus Dei, ecce qui tollit peccata mundi*, whereupon the faithful also recite the threefold *Domine, non sum dignus*. In the classic form of the Roman Mass, the Eucharist is received exclusively on the tongue while kneeling. The ablution of the faithful who have communicated was omitted from the 1570 *Missale Romanum*, but not the wine poured over the priest's thumbs and index fingers during the ablution. Before the ablution, the priest recites the *Quod ore sumpsimus*, during the ablution—the prayer *Corpus tuum, Domine, quod sumpsi*. After the Missal has been brought back to the Epistle side of the altar, the priest reads the Communion verse, kisses the altar in the middle, and after the greeting *Dominus vobiscum* again goes to the Missal on the Epistle side to read aloud the *Postcommunio* (concluding prayer).

Dismissal: The conclusion of the Mass takes place at the middle of the altar. After the priest has kissed the altar, he pronounces once again the greeting *Dominus vobiscum*. After the response follows the dismissal, *Ite, missa est*. Then he turns toward the altar, prays the *Placeat tibi* silently, kisses the altar again, and gives the blessing (*deinde benedicit populum*). The dismissal *Ite, missa est* occurs in the classical form of the Roman Mass before the blessing, since the blessing was originally not part of the Mass but had its place in a separate rite and only later was added to the *Ite, missa est*. After the blessing, the priest on the Gospel side reads the Last Gospel (Jn 1:1–14), which originally had the function of a gesture of blessing.

C. Prayer Orientation and the Ars Celebrandi

The development of the liturgy after the council was largely dominated by the image of the assembled congregation as a meal fellowship and the subject of the liturgy. Some have spoken in this regard about a "superficial horizontalism"[87] in the liturgy. Moreover, the 1970 Missal, with its extensive changes, confirmed the impression that anyone could make liturgy. This is the starting point for those who call for a "reform of the reform". In this connection, their critique questions, among other things, the almost complete elimination of the common prayer orientation in the Mass as it is celebrated today. Is the sacral and cultic character of the Eucharist as well as its sacrificial character suitably expressed in the continuous *celebratio versus populum*? The Council Fathers had declared that the Latin language of the liturgy should be kept but that more room should be given to the vernacular, especially in the Liturgy of the Word.[88] The Council Fathers said nothing about the question of prayer orientation. Instead, *Sacrosanctum concilium* still takes the traditional prayer orientation for granted.[89] Even the rubrics of the *Editio typica* of the *Missale Romanum* (2002) presuppose the traditional prayer orientation.[90] But let us assume that Holy Mass is celebrated according to the Missal of Paul VI in the Latin liturgical language with the exception of the Liturgy of the Word. The celebrating priest would offer the Eucharist from the *Offertorium* on facing in the same direction as the faithful. A priest who celebrated in that way would almost inevitably be accused of trying to reverse the Second Vatican Council, although he had not violated one single regulation of the council or of the postconciliar liturgical reform.

The first instruction on implementing the reform of the liturgy, *Inter oecumenici* (September 26, 1964), did state, still during the council, that it is better for the main altar to be erected separately from the back wall, so that one can walk around it more easily and celebration facing the people is possible (*celebratio versus populum*).[91]

---

[87] Winfried Haunerland, "Mysterium paschale: Schlüsselbegriff liturgietheologischer Erneuerung", in *Liturgie als Mitte des christlichen Lebens*, ed. George Augustin, Theologie im Dialog 7 (Freiburg: Herder, 2012), 201.

[88] Cf. SC 36.

[89] Cf. SC 33.

[90] The rubrics of the "Novus Ordo" say that for the *Orate, fratres*, the *Pax Domini*, the *Ecce Agnus Dei*, and the concluding rite, the priest turns toward the people. This instruction would be superfluous if the rubrics of the "Novus Ordo" presupposed celebration of Mass *versus populum*. The *Editio typica tertia* of the *Missale Romanum* has retained these rubrics. Cf. MR 2002³, 600 (no. 127); 601 (nos. 132f.); 603 (no. 141).

[91] Cf. IO 91 (DEL 1:133).

Celebration *versus populum* was not prescribed, however. Nor was the recommendation in the instruction an invitation to take down existing altars. The instruction answered the question of whether it is permissible to set up a portable altar in the form of a simple table so as to celebrate facing the people by saying: "It is allowed per se, but it is not advisable. For the faithful do participate quite actively in Mass celebrated according to the norm of the *Novus Ordo* even if the altar is set up so that the celebrant turns his back to the people. For the entire Liturgy of the Word is celebrated at the priest's chair or at the ambo facing the people."[92] A Eucharistic liturgy celebrated *versus orientem* or *ad absidem* [facing East or toward the apse], therefore, is in keeping with the spirit of the renewed liturgy. On June 30, 1965, the Consilium for implementing the liturgical reform declared: "In any case, we would like to emphasize that it is not absolutely necessary for fruitful pastoral activity to celebrate the whole Mass *versus populum*. The entire Liturgy of the Word, in which the active participation of the people is realized in a broader form by means of dialogue and song, is already celebrated facing the congregation and has become much more comprehensible today through the use of the vernacular."[93]

In a 1993 *Responsum* from the Congregation for Divine Worship, we read: "The principle that there should be only one altar is theologically more important than the practice of celebrating facing the people."[94] The so-called *celebratio versus populum*, the *Responsum* goes on to say, was permitted, not for theological, but for pastoral reasons:

> It is necessary to explain that the expression "celebrate turning toward the people" has no theological significance, but is only a topographical description. Every Eucharist is celebrated "to the praise and glory of His Name, for our good and the good of all His holy Church." For in the theological sense, the Mass is always directed toward God and to the people. In designing the celebration, one must be careful not to confuse theology and topography, especially when the priest is at

[92] Ibid., 134.

[93] Consilium, "Brief an die Vorsitzenden der Bischofskonferenzen vom 30. Juni 1965", no. 6: *DEL* 1:217.

[94] Congregation for Divine Worship and the Discipline of the Sacraments, Editorial "Pregare ad orientem versus", *Notitiae* 29 (1993): 249.

the altar. Only during the dialogue at the altar does the priest speak to the people. Everything else is prayer to the Father through Jesus Christ in the Holy Spirit. This theology must be visible.[95]

Only during the dialogue parts, therefore, does the priest speak to the people. In contrast, the presider's prayers recited by the priest, including the Eucharistic Prayer pronounced or sung by him at the altar, are directed to God the Father, before whom Christ, the one primarily responsible for the liturgy, gathers us.

Since the Eucharistic liturgy, in the context of which the words of Consecration are spoken, has the character of an offering of thanksgiving (from the *Offertorium* to the concluding doxology of the Eucharistic Prayer), the continuation of the words over the bread, "which is given for you", is no argument for positioning the priest *versus populum*.[96] In a *Responsum* dated September 25, 2000, the Congregation for Divine Worship reaffirmed once again that *celebratio versus populum* is not an obligation and that there can be good reasons for choosing *celebratio versus orientem*, which can also be a symbolic celebration.[97] The opinions just cited show that to this day the change of prayer orientation has never been prescribed and a traditional prayer orientation while offering the Eucharist does not contradict the spirit of the liturgical reform.

The common prayer orientation is to be seen in the context of the phenomenon of "sacred direction", which we encounter in all three major monotheistic religions. In Judaism at the time of the origins of Christianity, believers usually prayed facing Jerusalem, a practice that Orthodox Judaism has retained to this day. In Islam, the rule is, whether inside or outside the mosque, to pray facing Mecca. Uwe Michael Lang deserves credit for having started an objective discussion in the Catholic Church about the common prayer orientation

---

[95] Ibid.

[96] For a contrasting opinion, see Hansjürgen Verweyen, "Liturgie in den frühen Schriften Joseph Ratzingers", in *Ein hörendes Herz: Hinführung zur Theologie und Spiritualität von Joseph Ratzinger/Papst Benedikt XVI.*, ed. M. C. Hastetter and H. Hoping, Ratzinger-Studien 5 (Regensburg: Pustet, 2012), 85–89.

[97] Congregation for Divine Worship and the Discipline of the Sacraments, *Responsa ad quaestiones de nova Institutione Generali Missalis Romani* (September 25, 2000), Protocol no. 2036/00/L, 171–73.

ad Dominum.[98] The claim that the bishop or the priest originally celebrated *versus populum* is a legend, which Otto Nussbaum (1923–1999) did a great deal to spread.[99] As a rule, Christians prayed facing the same direction, *versus orientem*, and that means that most church buildings were apse-oriented, facing the apse, which was often decorated with a cross or with the image of the glorified Christ.[100]

Some churches, like the first major churches in Rome (Lateran and Saint Peter's), were oriented toward the entrance, mainly for topographical reasons. There the Eucharistic liturgy was very probably celebrated facing the opened doors.[101] Since the common prayer orientation might also have consisted of the *circumstantes* praying with the celebrant toward the East "looking upward, namely towards the eastern sky which was considered the place of paradise and the scene of Christ's Second Coming", it is possible that in churches where the apse was in the west, people looked up and "the mosaics [in the apse and the triumphal arch] might have served to direct the attention of the liturgical assembly, whose eyes were raised up during the Eucharistic Prayer. Even the priest at the altar prayed with outstretched, raised arms (like the female figure known from the Roman catacombs as the *Orans*) and no further ritual gestures."[102] The awareness of celebrating facing the people during the Eucharist (*celebrare versus populum*) was in any case independent of the church architecture and was entirely unheard of as a factor in orienting the church building.[103] The decisive thing was that the

[98] Cf. Uwe Michael Lang, *Turning towards the Lord* (San Francisco: Ignatius Press, 2004); Lang, "The Direction of Liturgical Prayer", in *Ever Directed toward the Lord: The Love of God*, ed. U.M. Lang (New York: T&T Clark, 2007), 90–107.

[99] Cf. Otto Nussbaum, "Die Zelebration versus populum und der Opfercharakter der Messe" (1971), in *Geschichte und Reform des Gottesdienstes: Liturgiewissenschaftliche Untersuchungen*, ed. A. Gerhards and H. Brakmann (Paderborn: Schöningh, 1996), 50–70.

[100] Cf. Marcel Metzger, "La place des liturges à l'autel", *Revue des sciences religieuses* 5 (1971): 113–45.

[101] Cf. Klaus Gamber, *Zum Herrn hin! Fragen um Kirchenbau und Gebet nach Osten* (Regensburg: Pustet, 1987), 41–46; Martin Wallraff, *Christus versus Sol: Sonnenverehrung und Christentum in der Spätantike* (Münster: Aschendorff, 2001), 71–78.

[102] Lang, *Turning towards the Lord*, 84. Cf. Fiedrowicz, *Überlieferte Messe*, 142f.

[103] See also the essay by Stefan Heid, "The Early Christian Altar—Lessons for Today", in *Sacred Liturgy: The Source and Summit of the Life and Mission of the Church: The Proceedings of the International Conference on the Sacred Liturgy Sacra Liturgia 2013*, ed. Alcuin Reed (San Francisco: Ignatius Press, 2013), 87–114.

worshipping assembly prayed together with the celebrant toward God (ad Dominum), while awaiting the Second Coming of Christ.

Josef Andreas Jungmann, consultor of the consilium for implementing the liturgical reform, considered it not in every respect appropriate to position the priest facing the people. He did think that Orient-ation in prayer had lost its symbolic significance to a great extent, yet in a new appendix in the fifth edition of Missarum Sollemnia, which appeared in the year the council began, he still defended the principle "that during prayer everyone, including the celebrant, should look toward God in one direction" and that this would "argue in favor of the same position of the celebrant ... at least if one is willing to accept as foundational the idea that the Church is still on the way and does not yet possess God definitively. The principle corresponds also to the movement contained in the Offertory. If the Mass were only a service of instruction and a celebration of Communion, then turning toward the people would be a given; but not if it is above all homage and sacrifice offered to God."[104] Jungmann cites in this connection the fundamental idea of the "open ring" of the church architect Rudolf Schwarz (1897–1961) with a common prayer orientation of priest and congregation.[105]

The one-sided emphasis on "Eucharist as meal" led after Vatican Council II to the model of the congregation assembled around the meal table. The concept of meal, however, which became increasingly central after the council, does not adequately describe the celebration of the Eucharist. Yes, Jesus did institute the memorial of his death and Resurrection within the context of a Jewish feast day meal, but he commanded his disciples to repeat, not the meal, but rather the thanksgiving and praise pronounced over bread and wine, in which the Body and Blood of Christ are given to us in the celebration of the Eucharist. The Eucharist is not a meal of satiation, even though it was initially connected with it. The Last Supper of Jesus with his disciples was not the first celebration of the Eucharist, either, but rather its "institution". Moreover, the altar is primarily the place for the offering

---

[104] Jungmann, Missarum Sollemnia I, 6th ed. (2003), 333. [Translated from German.]

[105] On the work of Rudolf Schwarz, who was closely connected with Romano Guardini and the "Quickborn" Movement, cf. Schwarz, Vom Bau der Kirche, 2nd ed. (Heidelberg: Verlag Lambert Schneider, 1947); Schwarz, Kirchenbau: Welt vor der Schwelle (Heidelberg: Kerle, 1960).

of the Eucharist, and not the meal table in the horizontal perspective. On this subject, Reinhard Messner writes: "The alleged function of the altar as a meal table is a twentieth-century construct that is not free of ideology. Ever since there has been an altar in the celebration of the Eucharist, it has never been a meal table."[106] The altar is the "threshold to heaven"; it symbolizes the opened heaven that is granted to us through the presence of the Lord. The center of the worshipping assembly therefore transcends the circle of the faithful gathered to celebrate the Eucharist. The center of the worshipping assembly is "ec-centric"—as Messner strikingly describes it.[107]

Today, almost without exception, the priest faces the people during the prayers, including those of the Eucharistic Prayer; this is ambivalent, since it creates the impression that the one being addressed is not God but, rather, the congregation. "What does it mean, then, when the presider, while physically *facing the congregation*, speaks to the congregation the prayer that he is actually addressing to God in the name of the congregation as their spokesman? Does this physical gesture not subliminally introduce a new addressee of the prayer? If we look at it without the hardened ideological positions that beset the whole issue ..., praying *versus populum* does represent an act of communication (merely) within the congregation."[108] Ultimately, the center of the Eucharistic celebration has no position: "The true sacred centre is unplaceable and lies beyond place itself, in God."[109] Hans Urs von Balthasar (1905–1988) strikingly spoke with regard to the Eucharist about "liturgy centred on the Father".[110]

The "sacred direction" of the traditional prayer orientation focused the liturgical assembly on its divine origin and its

---

[106] Reinhard Messner, "Gebetsrichtung, Altar und die exzentrische Mitte der Gemeinde", in *Communio-Räume: Auf der Suche nach der angemessenen Raumgestalt katholischer Liturgie*, ed. A. Gerhards (Regensburg: Schnell and Steiner, 2003), 34.

[107] Cf. ibid., 28.

[108] Ibid., 33.

[109] Catherine Pickstock, *After Writing: On the Liturgical Consummation of Philosophy*, 2nd ed. (Oxford: Blackwell, 2000), 174.

[110] Hans Urs von Balthasar, *The Glory of the Lord*, vol. 1, *Seeing the Form*, trans. Erasmo Leiva-Merikakis, 2nd ed. (San Francisco: Ignatius Press, 2009), 575. On the Trinitarian dimension of the liturgy, see Helmut Hoping, "Das Beten Christi und seiner Kirche: Aspekte einer trinitarischen Theologie der Liturgie", in *Liturgie und Trinität*, ed. B. Groen and B. Kranemann, Quaestiones disputatae 229 (Freiburg: Herder, 2008), 88–107.

eschatological goal. *Celebratio versus populum*, with its constant face-to-face relation, necessarily and increasingly gave the impression of a closed circle. A return to the traditional prayer orientation would make it clearer that after the Scripture readings and the homily, the faithful together with the priest offer the Eucharistic Sacrifice in grateful adoration.[111] Since the traditional prayer orientation is not something that can be reinstated overnight, Joseph Ratzinger made the suggestion of placing a cross (crucifix or triumphal cross) on the altar as the "interior 'east' " of faith,[112] as the common orientation of priest and people to the glorified Lord. The Crucified Lord should "be the common point of focus for both priest and praying community".[113] You might think that this suggestion is half-hearted. Yet it should be taken into account that yet another change in the prayer orientation at the present time would cause a lot of uneasiness among the faithful.

Joseph Ratzinger's concern *in liturgicis* (in liturgical matters) is, in contrast to the ideology of rupture, to regain a "hermeneutic of reform" in continuity with the Church's tradition. With regard to the form of celebrating Mass in the *usus modernus*, he argues that it should more clearly show its character as a sacral and cultic action.[114] Even though so far, besides the revision of vernacular translation, no concrete steps have been taken to initiate a "reform of the reform", it is nevertheless on the agenda for the future. For the time being, there will be in the Catholic Church a twofold form of the Roman Rite,

---

[111] Cf. Lang, *Turning towards the Lord*, 128–29. In the case of the Scripture readings, it should be noted that they are not only a form of instruction but also essentially have an anamnetic function. However, they do not have the character of grateful oblation as is the case with the *Offertorium* and the *Prex Eucharistica*.

[112] Joseph Ratzinger, *The Spirit of the Liturgy*, trans. John Saward (San Francisco: Ignatius Press, 2000), 83 [*JRCW* 11:51]. On Ratzinger's liturgical theology, cf. Helmut Hoping, "Kult und Reflexion: Joseph Ratzinger als Liturgietheologe", in *Der Logos-gemässe Gottesdienst: Theologie der Liturgie bei Joseph Ratzinger*, ed. R. Voderholzer, Benedikt-Studien 1 (Regensburg: Pustet, 2009), 12–25.

[113] Ratzinger, *Spirit of the Liturgy*, 83 [*JRCW* 11:51].

[114] Besides the restoration of the common prayer orientation, Joseph Ratzinger mentioned in his concluding lecture, "Assessment and Future Prospects", at the Liturgical Conference in Fontgombault (2001) two more important points in a "reform of the reform": (1) the correction of a wrongly understood liturgical "creativity" and (2) a correct translation of the liturgical books. Cf. Ratzinger, "Assessment and Future Prospects", in *JRCW* 11:564–68. On the importance of sacral language, cf. Fiedrowicz, *Überlieferte Messe*, 150–86.

the *usus antiquior* and the *usus modernus*.[115] This makes all the more important an *ars celebrandi* (manner of celebrating) that is not regarded as an antithesis to the liturgical order. Only in this way can the awareness of the unity of the Roman liturgy be kept alive.[116] In his Letter Accompanying the Motu Proprio *Summorum Pontificum*, Pope Benedict XVI urged Catholics to respect the celebration of Mass and the unity of the Roman Rite and also the liturgical order. For "the most sure guarantee that the Missal of Paul VI can unite parish communities and be loved by them consists in its being celebrated with great reverence in harmony with the liturgical directives. This will bring out the spiritual richness and the theological depth of this Missal."[117]

However, with its interventions modifying the traditional form of the Roman Mass, some of them substantial, the liturgical reform gave the fatal impression that one can "fabricate" the liturgy, which is why quite a few priests thought and to this day think that they must bring the work of the liturgical reformers to completion through "creative" solutions. And so in our Sunday Masses we often experience a terrible formlessness.[118] Then too, in comparison to the time of the council, liturgical education is in a desolate state, which makes it increasingly difficult for the faithful to participate consciously in the liturgy. Walter Cardinal Kasper's talk about "consumptive faith" and "religious illiteracy"[119] applies *mutatis mutandi* also to the state of liturgical education, which is a fundamental prerequisite if the *participatio actuosa* of the faithful is not to be external.

---

[115] In a letter to Dr. Heinz-Lothar Barth, Bonn, dated June 23, 2003, Joseph Ratzinger expressed the opinion that there could be no lasting coexistence of two forms of the Mass in the Roman Rite but that in the long run the goal must be integration and harmony. Cf. Heinz-Lothar Barth, *Ist die traditionelle lateinische Messe antisemitisch? Antwort auf ein Papier des Zentralkomitees der Katholiken*, Brennpunkte Theologie 7 (Altötting: Sarto-Verlag, 2007), 17f.

[116] Cf. *SacCar* 38.

[117] Benedict XVI, Letter Accompanying the Motu Proprio *Summorum Pontificum* (July 7, 2007), 25.

[118] Cf. Martin Mosebach, *The Heresy of Formlessness* (San Francisco: Ignatius Press, 2006). Even though Mosebach with his fundamental critique of the *Novus Ordo* does not do justice to Paul VI and his role in the liturgical reform, the title of his bestseller, which has been translated into many languages, does hit the nail on the head in describing the problem of the postconciliar liturgical development.

[119] Walter Kasper, "Neue Evangelisierung als theologische, pastorale und geistliche Herausforderung", in *Walter Kasper: Gesammelte Schriften*, ed. G. Augustin and K. Krämer with the Kardinal Walter Kasper Institute (Freiburg: Herder, 2007ff., hereafter cited as *WKGS*), 296.

In the year of the promulgation of *Sacrosanctum concilium*, the German bishops were determined "to do everything possible so that the *Constitutio de sacra liturgia* would not merely remain on paper".[120] The chief goal of the council and of the liturgical reform was "to impart an ever increasing vigor to the Christian life of the faithful".[121] Today, a good forty years later, we must soberly state that the liturgical reform in many places did not lead to an ever-increasing vigor of the Christian life of the faithful. In the liturgy, the faithful can indeed follow what is happening at the altar. But they understand it less and less—despite the vernacular liturgy. Add to this a tragic desacralization of the liturgy.[122]

On the occasion of the fortieth anniversary of *Sacrosanctum concilium* (1963/2003), the then-Prefect of the Congregation for the Doctrine of the Faith, Joseph Cardinal Ratzinger, appraised the lasting theological significance of the Constitution on the Sacred Liturgy.[123] Ratzinger has never left any doubt, however, about his opinion that over the course of the liturgical reform the general understanding of liturgy changed fundamentally. Giving thanks in worship no longer seems to be the primary meaning of the liturgy now but, rather, the celebration of the community, in which the faithful who have gathered in Christ's name assure their fellowship. As a result, Christian worship runs the risk of degenerating into a social ritual.[124] The constitution *Sacrosanctum concilium*, however, had called the liturgy "a sacred action" in which "the whole public worship is performed" by Christ, the risen Lord, and the members of his Mystical Body.[125] As "an exercise of

---

[120] Die Deutschen Bischöfe, *Hirtenschreiben an den Klerus* (December 4, 1963), *Liturgischen Jahrbuch* 14 (1964): 85–90 at 86.

[121] *SC* 1.

[122] This has been analyzed from the perspective of the sociology of religion by Kieran Flanagan, *Sociology and Liturgy: Re-presentations of the Holy* (London: Macmillan; New York: St. Martin's Press, 1991), and David Torevell, *Losing the Sacred: Ritual, Modernity and Liturgical Reform* (Edinburgh: T&T Clark, 2000). Torevell is influenced by the "Radical Orthodoxy" movement, among others. See also John Milbank, *Theology and Social Theory: Beyond Secular Reason* (Oxford: Blackwell, 1990); Milbank, *The Word Made Strange: Theology, Language, Culture* (Cambridge, Mass.: Blackwell, 1997); Pickstock, *After Writing*.

[123] Cf. Ratzinger, "Fortieth Anniversary of the Constitution on the Sacred Liturgy", in *JRCW* 11:574–88.

[124] Ratzinger, "The Resurrection as the Foundation of Christian Liturgy—On the Meaning of Sunday for Christian Prayer and Christian Life", in *JRCW* 11:187–206.

[125] *SC* 7.

the priestly office of Jesus Christ" in which man's sanctification is presented and accomplished "by signs perceptible to the senses",[126] the liturgy is "above all things the worship of the divine Majesty".[127] Christian worship is founded on the mystery that "the body of Christ is sacrificed and precisely as sacrificed is living.... Christ communicates himself to us and thus brings us into a real bond with the living God."[128] Christian worship is above all participation in the *Pasch* of Christ, in his *transitus*, or passing over, from death to life.[129] Benedict XVI put the council's statements about the sacral and cultic dimension of the liturgy at the beginning of his motu proprio *Summorum Pontificum*.[130] The connection between Cross and worship is established as a fundamental fact in the New Testament beginnings of the Church: Christ's Cross is understood in terms of the Temple worship, and Christian worship is understood in terms of Christ's Cross.[131]

Anyone who participates in Holy Mass in grateful adoration can tell that there is no contradiction between the old form and the new form of it, neither in the *lex orandi* nor in the *lex credendi*. It is, however, necessary to bring the two forms of the Roman Mass closer to each other in the ritual form of their celebration. For as much as there is a need for a "reform of the reform", it is nevertheless clear also that the liturgy cannot be frozen in the state in which it existed in 1962.[132] It will be decisive for the future of the liturgy to rediscover the unity of *ars celebrandi* and liturgical order and to see no antithesis between them. Above all, an improved cultivation of the *ars celebrandi* is necessary, including an *ars praesendi* [art of presiding].[133] And if the liturgy, correctly understood, really is the holy play of man

---

[126] SC 7.

[127] SC 33.

[128] Ratzinger, *Spirit of the Liturgy*, 43 [*JRCW* 11:25].

[129] Cf. ibid., 34 [*JRCW* 11:19].

[130] Cf. Benedict XVI, Motu proprio *Summorum Pontificum* (July 7, 2007), foreword: "The Supreme Pontiffs have to this day shown constant concern that the Church of Christ should offer worthy worship to the Divine Majesty, 'for the praise and glory of his name' and 'the good of all his holy Church'."

[131] Cf. Knut Backhaus, "Kult und Kreuz: Zur frühchristlichen Dynamik ihrer theologischen Beziehung", *Theologie und Glaube* 86 (1996): 512–43.

[132] Cf. Ratzinger, "Assessment and Future Prospects", in *JRCW* 11:567–68.

[133] Cf. Winfried Haunerland, "Der bleibende Anspruch liturgischer Erneuerung: Herausforderungen und Perspektiven heute", in *Liturgiereform—eine bleibende Aufgabe: 40 Jahre Konzilskonstitution über die heilige Liturgie*, ed. K. Richter and T. Sternberg (Münster: Aschendorff, 2004), 68.

before God, then any arbitrariness and formlessness is inappropriate. Any game, even and especially holy play, follows definite rules that must be observed.[134] If the historically developed ritual form of the Roman Mass is not respected, the celebration of the Eucharist cannot be a "sign of unity and bond of love" (Augustine), either, but rather will remain an object of strife. Since Vatican Council II forbids everyone, even priests, to change the liturgy arbitrarily,[135] the priests who adhere to the Church's liturgical order are not the ones to be held accountable, but rather those who, contrary to the will of the council, disregard it, for example, by using unapproved prayers, by changing the Eucharistic Prayers of the Missal, by omitting the embolism, and so forth.

Walter Cardinal Kasper writes about the liturgical highhandedness that the faithful have had to face for more than forty years now:

> Therefore you cannot keep reinventing the liturgy and tinkering with it to suit your own taste. When I participate in a liturgy, I would rather not be exposed to the subjective fancies and impressions of the one who happens to be celebrating. I experience that as an unreasonable demand; for indeed, I come to help celebrate the Church's liturgy. In the objectivity that is proper to the liturgy, the universal character of the Catholic liturgy is expressed.[136]

Priests, like everyone else who takes on a particular ministry in the liturgy, are bound to be self-effacing, to step back humbly behind their ministry and the objectivity of the prescribed liturgy. This is true for both forms of the Roman Rite. The "Divine" Liturgy (as the Eastern Churches call the celebration of the Eucharist) has an uncontrollable character that rules out any liturgical highhandedness.[137] Freedom to shape the celebration of the Mass, rightly understood, is characterized by the use of the options that legitimately exist for that purpose. And there are quite a few of them in the Missal of Paul VI.

---

[134] Cf. ibid., 66.

[135] Cf. SC 22: "Regulation of the sacred liturgy depends solely on the authority of the Church, that is, on the Apostolic See and, as laws may determine, on the bishop. . . . Therefore no other person, even if he be a priest, may add, remove, or change anything in the liturgy on his own authority."

[136] Walter Kasper, "Gottesdienst nach katholischem Verständnis", in WKGS 10 (Freiburg: Herder, 2010), 137.

[137] Cf. Ratzinger, Spirit of the Liturgy, 167 [JRCW 11:103].

Chapter X

PRO VOBIS ET PRO MULTIS

The Theology of the Words of Institution

The reform of the Missal led also to changes in the words of institution. *Hoc est enim corpus meum*—these words were traditionally spoken by the priest at the Consecration of the bread.[1] The new, expanded version takes up 1 Corinthians 11:24 (Vulgate) and reads: *Hoc est enim Corpus meum, quod pro vobis tradetur.*[2] "This is my body, which will be given up for you."[3] At the Consecration of the wine, the priest says: *Hoc est enim Calix Sanguinis mei ... qui pro vobis et pro multis effundetur in remissionem peccatorum.*[4] "For this is the chalice of my Blood, ... which will be poured out for you and for all for the forgiveness of sins."[5] In the case of the words over the chalice, the non-biblical parenthesis *mysterium fidei* was detached from them and placed after the *verba testamenti* as a response and combined with an acclamation by the people that is based on 1 Corinthians 11:26.[6] While the words of Consecration over the bread were translated literally in the vernacular missals, the *pro multis* in the words over the chalice was freely rendered "for all" in many (but not all) vernacular languages.

---

[1] Cf. *MR* 1962, 306.

[2] *MR* 2002³, 575.

[3] *RM* 2010, 623, 630, 635, 642.

[4] *MR* 2002³, 575.

[5] Thus the German translation in *MB* 473. Cf. "for many" in *RM* 2010, 639, 647, 651, 659.

[6] Cf. *MR* 1962 (2007), 307; *MR* 2002³, 575–76. In the 1965 Latin-German Altar Missal, the *mysterium fidei* is still part of the words over the chalice. Cf. *Lateinisch-deutsches Altarmessbuch, im Auftrag der Fuldaer und der Schweizer Bischofskonferenz*, besorgt von den Liturgischen Kommissionen Deutschlands und der Schweiz, vol. 1 (Einsiedeln and Cologne, 1965), 110*.

The people's missals (in Germany, Schott, Bomm [in the United States, the popular Saint Joseph Missal]) had translated *pro multis* literally as *für viele/*"for many" until the Second Vatican Council.[7] The translation of the Roman Canon approved in 1967 by the bishops of Germany, Austria, Switzerland, and Luxembourg and ratified that same year by the Holy See translated *pro multis* as *für die vielen* (for the many/multitude).[8] Johannes Wagner (1908–1999), a theologian at the council who for many years headed the Germany Liturgical Institute, saw this as the linguistically more interesting variant.[9] In contrast, the translation of the new Eucharistic Prayers published in advance in 1969 no longer has "for the many" in the words over the chalice, but rather "for all".[10] The German-speaking bishops thereby followed the Italian bishops, who advocated rendering the *pro multis* with *per tutti* (for all). So finally, the words *für alle* entered the German edition of the Missal.[11] Over the course of the process of revising the translations of the Roman Missal, in which a literal translation of the *pro multis* was demanded by the instruction *Liturgiam authenticam* (2001), a lively discussion arose over the meaning and translation of the liturgical words over the chalice.[12]

---

[7] Cf. Anselm Schott, *Das vollständige Römische Messbuch: Lateinisch-Deutsch: Mit allgemeinen und besonderen Einführungen im Anschluss an das Messbuch*, ed. Benedictine monks of Beuron Archabbey (Freiburg: Herder, 1958/1962; hereafter cited as Schott), 465f.; Bomm 771; [St. Joseph Missal, 679].

[8] Gd 3 (1969), 152.

[9] Cf. Johannes Wagner, *Mein Weg zur Liturgiereform 1936–1986: Erinnerungen* (Freiburg: Herder, 1993), 289.

[10] The Congregation for Divine Worship later endorsed the translation of the *pro multis* by "for all". Cf. *AAS* 66 (1974): 661.

[11] Cf. *MB* 473.

[12] On the more recent exegetical and systematic-theological discussion, see Franz Prosinger, *Das Blut des Bundes—vergossen für viele? Zur Übersetzung und Interpretation des hyper pollón in Mk 14,24* (Siegburg: Franz Schmitt, 2007); Norbert Baumert and Maria-Irma Seewann, "Eucharistie 'für alle' oder 'für viele'?", *Gregorianum* 89 (2008): 501–32; Michael Theobald, "'Pro multis'—Ist Jesus nicht 'für alle' gestorben? Anmerkungen zu einem römischen Entscheid", in *Gestorben für wen? Zur Diskussion um das "pro multis"*, ed. M. Striet, Theologie kontrovers (Freiburg: Herder, 2007), 29–54; Thomas Söding, "Für euch—für viele—für alle: Für wen feiert die Kirche Eucharistie?", in *Gestorben für wen? Zur Diskussion um das "pro multis"*, ed. M. Striet, Theologie kontrovers (Freiburg: Herder, 2007), 17–27; Albert Gerhards, "Wie viele sind viele? Zur Diskussion um das 'pro multis'", *Herder Korrespondenz* 61 (2007): 79–83; Helmut Hoping, "'Für die vielen': Der Sinn des Kelchwortes der römischen Messe", in *Gestorben für wen? Zur Diskussion um das "pro multis"*, ed. M. Striet, Theologie

A. Jesus Died for Israel and the Gentiles

The words over the chalice in Mark 14:24 read: "This is my blood of the covenant, which is poured out for many" (τοῦτό ἐστιν τὸ αἷμά μου τῆς διαθήκης τὸ ἐκχυννόμενον ὑπὲρ πολλῶν). In Matthew 26:28, we read: "This is my blood of the covenant, which is poured out for many for the forgiveness of sins" (τοῦτο γάρ ἐστιν τὸ αἷμά μου τῆς διαθήκης τὸ περὶ πολλῶν ἐκχυννόμενον εἰς ἄφεσιν ἁμαρτιῶν). The ecumenical German "Unity Translation" of the Bible renders the Greek expression ὑπὲρ or περὶ πολλῶν literally as *für viele*; the corresponding expression in the Latin text of the Vulgate and of the *Missale Romanum* is *pro multis*. But who are the many for whom the Blood of Jesus was poured out? Did Jesus die "for many" or "for all"? Will "many" or "all" be saved? Jesus knew that in Jerusalem he would run the risk of dying. His goal was to gather God's people Israel. For this purpose, he called the twelve disciples as representatives of Israel. Aware of his impending death, Jesus celebrated with the Twelve in immediate proximity to the Passover Feast a last meal, at which he referred the gifts of bread and wine that he handed to the Twelve to his imminent death and thus gave them a share in his Body and Blood. Jesus was not talking about the question of whether "many" or "all" will be saved.[13]

What were the reasons why *pro multis* was translated, not as "for many" or "for the many", but rather as "for all", for which the Latin equivalent is *pro omnibus*? The decisive factors here were the theses of the Lutheran New Testament scholar Joachim Jeremias. In his work *Die Abendmahlsworte Jesu* (1935), Jeremias advocated the view that the expression ὑπὲρ or περὶ πολλῶν is a Semitism: since Aramaic has no

---

kontrovers (Freiburg: Herder, 2007), 65–79; Magnus Striet, "Nur für viele oder doch für alle? Das Problem der Allerlösung und die Hoffnung der betenden Kirche", in *Gestorben für wen? Zur Diskussion um das "pro multis"*, ed. M. Striet, Theologie kontrovers (Freiburg: Herder, 2007), 81–92; Jan-Heiner Tück, "Memoriale passionis: Die Selbstgabe Jesu Christi für alle als Anstoss für eine eucharistische Erinnerungssolidarität", in *Gestorben für wen? Zur Diskussion um das "pro multis"*, ed. M. Striet, Theologie kontrovers (Freiburg: Herder, 2007), 93–100; Tück, "Für viele und für alle: Marginalien zur 'pro multis'-Entscheidung des Papstes", *Internationale katholische Zeitschrift Communio* 41 (2012): 348–56; Manfred Hauke, *"Für viele vergossen": Studie zur sinngetreuen Wiedergabe des pro multis in den Wandlungsworten*, 2nd ed. (Augsburg: Dominus Verlag, 2012); Thomas Marschler, *Für viele: Eine Studie zu Übersetzung und Interpretation des liturgischen Kelchwortes* (Bonn: Nova et Vetera, 2013).

[13] Cf. Gerhard Lohfink, *Gegen die Verharmlosung Jesu* (Freiburg: Herder, 2013), 131f.

adequate word for "all", "for many" means the same as "for all".[14]
"For many" (*rabim*) in Hebrew has an inclusive character and refers
to "the countless numbers, the great multitude, all",[15] while πολλοί,
taken by itself, stands in opposition to "all". Hebrew and Aramaic,
however, can distinguish very well between "many" (*rabim/sagî*) and
"all" (*kol, kûl*), although these terms may shade off into each other in
particular instances. Moreover, the question remains, why did Matthew and Mark choose "for many" in Greek (περὶ or ὑπὲρ πολλῶν),
when linguistically "for all" (περὶ παντῶν) would have been possible?
Jeremias regarded the Fourth Servant Song (Is 52:13—53:12) as the
background for the περὶ or ὑπὲρ πολλῶν: "The righteous one, my
servant, [shall] make many to be accounted righteous ... because ...
he bore the sin of many, and made intercession for the transgressors"
(53:11–12). Without the reference to the Fourth Servant Song, the
words over the chalice in Matthew and Mark can hardly be understood.[16] It is also quite possible that Jesus himself interpreted his death
in light of the Servant of God who "makes himself an offering for sin"
(Is 53:10). Jeremias, however, referred "for many" (*ha-rabim*; πολλοί)
in Isaiah 53 directly to the Gentile world (*gôjim*).[17] The words over
the chalice, therefore, should be translated: the blood "that is poured
out for the Gentiles".[18] Many exegetes have adopted Jeremias' arguments, among them numerous Catholic exegetes.[19] But meanwhile,
the exegetical consensus has been shattered.

The first misgivings about the thesis that "for many" in Hebrew
means "for all" were voiced by the classicist and biblical scholar Max
Zerwick (1901–1975) of the Pontifical Biblical Institute. He says that
the translation depends on the context. Jesus chose the expression
"for many" to remind his disciples of the Servant of God (Is 53). Zerwick, nevertheless, spoke in favor of translating *pro multis* as "for all";
this was because of possible misunderstandings of the expression "for

---

[14] Cf. Joachim Jeremias, *Die Abendmahlsworte Jesu*, 3rd ed. (Göttingen: Vandenhoeck &
Ruprecht, 1960), 170.

[15] Jeremias, "polloi (= viele)", in *Theologische Wörterbuch zum Neuen Testament*, ed. Gerhard
Kittel, vol. 6 (Stuttgart: Kohlhammer, 1959), 536.

[16] Cf. Söding, "Für euch—für viele—für alle", 23.

[17] Cf. Jeremias, *Abendmahlsworte Jesu*, 171–74.

[18] Ibid., 221.

[19] Cf. the overview in Marschler, *Für viele*, 45–53.

many".[20] Several years later, Rudolf Pesch defended the opinion that Isaiah 53 and along with it Mark 14:24 or Matthew 26:28 referred to all Israel and at most indirectly to the nations; today most exegetes assume this also.[21] There are several arguments against identifying the "many" with the Gentile world: the fact that the Twelve to whom Jesus hands the chalice represent Israel,[22] and the image of the "blood of the covenant" with its reference to the Sinai Covenant (cf. Ex 24:8) in Matthew and Mark, and the "new covenant" (cf. Jer 31:31) in Luke and Paul. For in each case, it is a covenant for Israel that is being considered. Jesus' Last Supper was also different in kind from the meals that he ate with sinners. When Matthew 26:27 says that Jesus handed the chalice of salvation to the Twelve with the words, "drink of it, all of you (πάντες)", then it means the Twelve who stand for all Israel. Contrary to what Jeremias assumed, "the many" means all Israel, but indirectly the Gentiles are being considered too, since Israel's election consists precisely in the vocation to be a sign for the nations (cf. Is 56:7; Mk 11:17), so that we can say that Jesus dies not only for Israel but for the Gentiles.

The witnesses of Christ's Resurrection—and Paul sees himself as one of them (1 Cor 15:8)—are convinced that Jesus died for all. In Romans 8:32, the Apostle to the Gentiles says about God: "He ... did not spare his own Son but gave him up for us all" (Rom 8:32). In 2 Corinthians 5:15 Paul speaks even more clearly: "He died for all, that those who live might live no longer for themselves but for him who for their sake died and was raised." Finally, we read in 1 Timothy 2:6 that Jesus laid down his life "as a ransom for all". It has always been the Church's teaching that Jesus died on the Cross for all mankind. In the fifth century, the opinion of a priest in Southern Gaul, that Christ died only for the elect, was condemned.[23] The Augustinian legacy of soteriological particularism, according to which many, indeed most, human beings are lost because they do not come to faith in Christ, obscured God's universal salvific will. Two Synods

---

[20] Cf. Max Zerwick, "Pro vobis et pro multis effundetur", *Notitiae* 6 (1970): 138–40.

[21] Cf. Rudolf Pesch, *Das Markusevangelium*, vol. 2: *Kommentar zu Kap. 8,27–16,20*, Herders Theologischer Kommentar zum Neuen Testament 2 (Freiburg: Herder, 1977), 360; Pesch, *Das Abendmahl und Jesu Todesverständnis*, Quaestiones disputatae 80 (Freiburg: Herder, 1978), 95f.

[22] Cf. Theobald, "Pro multis", 24.

[23] Cf. DH 332.

of Quiercy (849, 853) condemned the denial of this universal salvific will by the monk Gottschalk of Orbais: "Just as there is not, nor has been, nor will be any man whose nature has not been assumed by Christ Jesus our Lord, so also there is not, nor has been, nor will be any man for whom he has not suffered."[24]

In the seventeenth century, the opinion defended by Jansenism that Jesus did not die for all human beings was condemned.[25] On November 8, 1949, the Holy Office (later the Congregation for the Doctrine of the Faith) condemned the rigidly exclusivist soteriology of the Boston Jesuit Leonard Feeney, who thought that with the exception of Catholics and catechumens all people were excluded from eternal salvation. On February 4, 1953, Feeney was excommunicated.[26] This prepared the way for the statement of Vatican Council II about God's universal salvific will and the possibility of salvation for all. God does not just want "all men to be saved and to come to the knowledge of the truth"; all men can be saved, even those who do not know Christ.[27] With that the council did not intend to dispute the real possibility that men may refuse forever to accept God's love. For the gift of salvation founded on the Cross of Christ and his Resurrection must be accepted by man. This means that the blood shed on the Cross for the world's salvation does not redeem people automatically.

The salvation bestowed by God in his incarnate Son must be accepted freely. In the history of soteriology, therefore, a distinction was always made between objective and subjective redemption. Vatican Council II did not abandon that distinction. The universal salvific character of Jesus' death, as expounded by the council, however, became increasingly connected with the hope that finally all men will be saved. For Hans Urs von Balthasar, this hope springs from love of neighbor and love of enemy, which hopes for everything good for a man.[28] Yet we do not know what the final outcome will be for

---

[24] DH 624.

[25] Cf. DH 2005-6.

[26] Cf. Letter of the Holy Office to the Archbishop of Boston, August 8, 1949 (DH 3866–73, esp. 3870).

[27] Cf. LG 13; 16.

[28] Cf. Hans Urs von Balthasar, *Dare We Hope: "That All Men Be Saved"?* with *A Short Discourse on Hell*, trans. David Kipp and Lothar Krauth (San Francisco: Ignatius Press, 1988).

individuals. Given the abyss of wickedness in the human will, we cannot get by theologically with a kind of optimism about salvation that takes it for granted that ultimately everyone is saved. Instead, we must adhere to the real possibility that those who are hardened in evil may shut themselves off forever from God's forgiveness. Therefore we must leave open the question of whether or not all will drink of the fruit of the vine in the fulfillment of God's kingdom (cf. Mk 14:25). The old *Roman Catechism* was still permeated by an exclusivist soteriology.[29] The *Catechism of the Catholic Church* is different in this respect. It assumes a perspective of universal salvation and teaches "that Christ died for all men without exception."[30] The *Catechism* does, however, insist on the real possibility of eternal shipwreck.[31] Nevertheless, the Church has never declared about an individual human being that he is in hell.

B. Participation in the Eucharist

Usually in discussions about the words over the chalice, their context is overlooked. At the Last Supper, Jesus not only interpreted his death. Joseph Pascher had already referred the past participle ἐκχυννόμενον in the words over the chalice—which can mean both "shed" and also "poured out"—to the cup that Jesus hands to his disciples, who also represent Israel and stand for the future Church.[32] The words over the chalice in Luke 22:20 (ὑπὲρ ὑμῶν ἐκχυννόμενον, shed for you) and in 1 Corinthians 11:25f. are addressed to the Twelve or to those who celebrate the Eucharist to commemorate Christ. The Last Supper was an act that instituted a form of worship from which emerged the celebration of the Eucharist, the center of the life of Christ's Church. Therefore, a distinction should be made also between the interpretation of Jesus' saving death with the formula "for all" and the Eucharist, in which the salvation founded on Jesus' death and Resurrection

---

[29] Cf. Tück, "Für viele und für alle", 352.

[30] *Catechism of the Catholic Church*, 2nd ed. (Vatican City: Libreria Editrice Vaticana; Washington, D.C.: United States Catholic Conference, 2000; hereafter cited as *CCC*), 605.

[31] Cf. ibid.,1035.

[32] Cf. Joseph Pascher, *Eucharistia: Gestalt und Vollzug* (Münster: Aschendorff, 1947), 16; so too Baumert and Seewann, "Eucharistie 'für alle' oder 'für viele'?", 507, 511.

is granted to us. We gain a visible, sacramental participation in Christ's death and Resurrection when, united with Christ by faith and Baptism (1 Cor 10:16–18), we receive his Body and Blood.

In the words that the priest pronounces at the Consecration of bread and wine, the Roman Canon joined together the expressions "for you" and "for many": my Body given for you (*pro vobis tradetur*), my Blood, poured out for you and for many (*pro vobis et pro multis effundetur*). With the words of Consecration that have been adopted in the new Eucharistic Prayers, the priest performs a unique "speech act": together with the epiclesis calling down the Holy Spirit upon the gifts of bread and wine, the words of institution form the core of the Eucharistic Prayer and effect the Consecration of bread and wine into the Body and Blood of Christ. The words of institution are also, however, *giving* words. While the traditional version of the words over the bread (*hoc est enim corpus meum*) expressed the idea of the Real Presence,[33] the extension of them underscores also the character of the Eucharist as gift. Joseph Ratzinger strikingly remarks: The Body of Christ "can become gift, because it is given up. Through the act of self-giving it becomes capable of communicating and is itself changed into a gift."[34]

Here it already becomes clear that the Eucharist, among the sacraments, is *the* great sacrament of the gift.[35] The bread of life and the cup of salvation are given to us, and we receive them, as a divine gift. The Church did not receive the Eucharist as one gift among many but, rather, as simply "the gift", Jesus Christ, who gave his life for us men: Christ's Body given for us, Christ's Blood poured out for us. The Eucharist is the sacrament of the encounter with Christ, for the Church and for every individual in her. The goal of the liturgical renewal was "to lead people to a personal encounter with the Lord, present in the Eucharist, and thus with the living God, so that through this contact with Christ's love, the love of his brothers and sisters for one another might also grow."[36] The sacrament of the Eucharist is the most intensive encounter with God and our Lord Jesus Christ.

[33] Cf. Annibale Bugnini, *The Reform of the Liturgy 1948–1975*, trans. Matthew J. O'Connell (Collegeville, Minn.: Liturgical Press, 1990), 454.

[34] Ratzinger, "Eucharist—Communion—Solidarity", in *JRCW* 11:355–70 at 368.

[35] For a more detailed discussion, see chapter 12.

[36] Benedict XVI, Video Message for the Closing of the 50th International Eucharistic Congress in Dublin (June 17, 2012).

Just as Jesus' words at the Last Supper applied immediately to the Twelve, who stand for all Israel, so, too, the words that the priest pronounces over the gifts of bread and wine apply immediately to those who are assembled for the Eucharist, wherever the Eucharist is celebrated throughout the world, in all cultures and nations. Not all are part of the one Body of Christ, and therefore the bread of life and the cup of salvation are not given to all. Thomas Aquinas calls the Eucharist a sign of friendship with those who have come to believe in Christ. The Eucharist is given to those who are united with Christ in his Church. For this reason, it is also misleading to say that the Church celebrates the Eucharist "for all". The intercessions (petitions) of the Eucharistic Prayer do not refer indiscriminately to all, living and deceased, believers and unbelievers, but rather to all believers and those who "sleep in Christ".[37] The universal Prayer of the Faithful after the Creed, in contrast, also formulates concerns about the world, as do the great intercessions on Good Friday. With regard to the dead, it is true that the Eucharist is offered "for the faithful ... who 'have died in Christ' ".[38]

Yet everyone who approaches the table of the Lord in order to receive his Body does so with the others vicariously for all whom God wills to lead to salvation, by paths that he alone knows. The many who make up the one Body of Christ have a responsibility for all who are not (yet) united with Christ through faith and Baptism. "*The Church draws her life from Christ in the Eucharist*; by him she is fed and by him she is enlightened."[39] From the Eucharist every member of Christ's Body receives immortal nourishment for eternal life. Nevertheless, Jesus is and remains significant for all people. Indeed,

[37] Reiner Kaczynski, "Die Interzessionen im Hochgebet", in *Gemeinde im Herrenmahl: Zur Praxis der Messfeier*, ed. T. Maas-Ewerd and K. Richter (Einsiedeln: Benziger, 1976), 310, thinks instead that the intercessions must not be restricted to the circle of those who are in full communion with the Church. Eucharistic Prayer III in German seems to be an exception with regard to its intercessions, for it reads: "Hear, O merciful Father, the prayers of this assembled community and lead to yourself all your sons and daughters who are still far from you" (*Messbuch*, 498). But that is an utterly misleading translation of the Latin text. A more accurate translation of the concluding petition is now found in the new English *Roman Missal* (2010): "Listen graciously to the prayers of this family,... gather to yourself all your children scattered throughout the world."

[38] Cf. *CCC* 1371.

[39] *EE* 6.

he died for all, for everyone who has a human face. Jesus did not die only for a few elect but, rather, for all (2 Cor 5:14; 1 Tim 2:5–6).

A literal translation of the liturgical words over the chalice is not only scriptural; it is also in keeping with tradition, which never understood the *pro multis* in the words over the chalice in the sense of *pro omnibus* (for all). The Fathers of the Church already distinguish between all for whom Jesus died and those who have come to believe.[40] One decisive factor here was probably the early interpretation of Romans 5:19: "For as by one man's disobedience many were made sinners, so by one man's obedience many will be made righteous." The Vulgate translates πολλοί both times with *multi*, since the *multi* [many] who are justified are not all. The *Catechismus Romanus* (1566–1567) summarizes as follows the unanimous doctrinal tradition of understanding the words over the chalice at Mass:

> The next phrase *for you and for many* is taken partly from St. Matthew, partly from St. Luke (Mt 26:28; Lk 22:20). Guided by the Spirit of God, the Catholic Church has made it a single phrase. It is meant to designate the actual effectiveness of the Passion. If we consider its potential efficacy, we would have to say that the Blood of the Savior was shed for all men. But if we look to what it actually achieves in terms of mankind's acceptance of it, we see that it does not extend to the whole, but only to a large part of the human race.[41]

The *Catechism of the Catholic Church* (1993, 2003), which takes the perspective that salvation is universal, nevertheless refers the words over the chalice to the disciples of Jesus or to the congregation celebrating the Eucharist.[42] The older *Katholische Erwachsenen-Katechismus* [Catholic Adult Catechism], in contrast, advocates the thesis, still

---

[40] Cf. Hauke, *"Für viele vergossen"*, 12–32. On the history of theology as a whole, see Marschler, *Für viele*, 83–163.

[41] Cf. *Catechismus Romanus*, pars II, cap. 4, 24 (Rodríguez ed. [1989], 250): "Sed verba illa quae adduntur: *pro vobis et pro multis*, a Mattaeo et Luca singula a singulis sumpta sunt; quae tamen sancta Ecclesia Spiritu Dei instructa simul coniunxit. Pertinent autem ad passionis fructum atque utilitatem declarandam. Nam si eius virtutem inspiciamus, pro omnium salute sanguinem a Salvatore effusum esse fatendum erit; si vero fructum quem ex eo homines perceperint cogitemus, non ad omnes, sed ad multos tantum eam utilitatem pervenisse facile intelligemus."

[42] Cf. *CCC* 1339.

widely disputed then, that "for many" in the words over the chalice in Matthew and Mark objectively means "for all".[43]

C. The Voice of the Churches

From various quarters arguments were made to translate the *pro multis* as "for all", based on the interpolation in the institutional narrative in the Mass of the Lord's Supper on Holy Thursday.[44] "On the night before he accepted his Passion *for our salvation and the salvation of all mankind*" (*pro nostra omniumque salute*).[45] The interpolation is ancient,[46] but it does not refer to the chalice of the covenant that is handed to the disciples but, rather, directly to Christ's death on the Cross. As an argument for a non-literal translation of the *pro multis*, it is just as unsuitable as the last Holy Thursday letter (2005) by Saint John Paul II. It is true that the letter interprets the "for many" in the sense of "for all":

> "*Hoc est enim corpus meum quod pro vobis tradetur.*" The body and the blood of Christ are given for the salvation of man, of the *whole* man and of *all* men. This salvation is *integral* and at the same time *universal*, because no one, unless he freely chooses, is excluded from the saving power of Christ's blood: "*qui pro vobis et pro multis effundetur*". It is a sacrifice offered for "many", as the Biblical text says (Mk 14:24; Mt 26:28; cf. Is 53:11–12); this typical Semitic expression refers to the multitude who are saved by Christ, the one Redeemer, yet at the same time it implies *the totality of human beings* to whom salvation is offered: the Lord's blood is "*shed for you and for all*", as some translations legitimately make explicit. Christ's flesh is truly given "for the life of the world" (Jn 6:51; cf. 1 Jn 2:2).[47]

In comparison to the unanimous doctrinal tradition of the Catholic Church, the above-cited Holy Thursday letter of John Paul II is

---

[43] Cf. *Katholischer Erwachsenen-Katechismus: Das Glaubenbekenntnis der Kirche* (Kevelaer: German Bishops' Conference, 1985), 186.

[44] Cf., e.g., Gerhards, "Wie viele sind viele?", 82.

[45] Cf. *MB* [30].

[46] Cf. *Sacramentarium Gregorianum Hadrianum* (Deshusses ed., 332).

[47] John Paul II, Letter to Priests for Holy Thursday (March 13, 2005), no. 4.

unambiguous but of secondary importance. In the encyclical *Ecclesia de Eucharistia* (2003), the Eucharistic testament of John Paul II, the interpretation of the *pro multis* in the sense of "for all" is not found.[48] The translation of *pro multis* as "for all" had become possible only after, for the vernacular translations of the Roman Missal, the abandonment of the principle of textual fidelity and completeness (translation *littérale et intégrale*). On the basis of the instruction *Liturgiam authenticam* (2011), Francis Cardinal Arinze, Prefect of the Congregation for Divine Worship, informed all bishops that in all vernacular editions of the Roman Missal, the *pro multis* must be rendered literally in the future and the faithful must be prepared for this by catecheses.[49] Since the German-speaking bishops repeatedly refused to correct the translation of the *pro multis*, Benedict XVI ruled in a letter to the president of the German Bishops' Conference dated April 14, 2012, that the *pro multis* is to be translated literally as "for many".[50] Some interpreted the pope's decision as a concession to the traditionalists of Archbishop Marcel Lefebvre's Society of Saint Pius X. It may have given that impression because, concurrently with the letter of Benedict XVI, negotiations were being conducted with the Society of Saint Pius X about a possible return to the Catholic Church, which were not successful since the Society was unwilling to declare its allegiance to Vatican Council II.

The ruling by Benedict XVI on the question about the translation of *pro multis* has its prehistory of course in the instruction *Liturgiam authenticam* (2001). The letter by Benedict XVI on the translation of *pro multis* also reaffirms the principle of textual fidelity that the instruction *Liturgiam authenticam* had demanded for the revision of the vernacular editions of the liturgical books. In the translation of *pro multis* as "for all", Benedict XVI sees one example out of many of the limit of the principle of a merely dynamic equivalent in translating from the original language of the *Missale Romanum* into the

---

[48] Cf. *AAS* 95 (2003): 434–75.

[49] Cf. Congregatio de culto divino et disciplina sacramentorum, *Litterae circulares* (Rome, October 17, 2006), *Notitiae* (Sept./Oct. 2006), Prot. N. 467/05/L, 441–43 (Italian); 453–55 (German). Among the numerous revisions of the English translation in the *Roman Missal* (2010), the translation of *pro multis* is also corrected ("for many" instead of "for all").

[50] Cf. http://www.dbk.de/presse/details/?presseid=2091&cHash=a73624e1fe19363371ca 03c812dbf396 (25 June 2015).

target language of the vernacular missals. In his letter, Benedict XVI demanded out of "respect for the word of Jesus" a literal translation of the *pro multis*. For Benedict XVI, the fact that Jesus died for all is one of the fundamental certainties of our faith. Yet the interpretation of the words over the chalice, with Isaiah 53 in the background, has for Benedict XVI its place in theological interpretation and catechesis.[51]

In his letter about the translation of the *pro multis*, Benedict XVI does not go into the ecumenical dimension of the question, although the anaphora of the Divine Liturgy of the Eastern Churches, the *Book of Common Prayer* of the Anglicans, the Lord's Supper rituals of the Reformation churches, and the missal of the American Methodists do not have the expression "for you and for all" in the words over the chalice—which according to the judgment of the exegete Michael Theobald is "an ecumenical argument, the importance of which should not be underestimated".[52] Martin Luther adhered to the *pro vobis et pro multis* in his Latin Mass formulary (1523). In the "German Mass" (1526), he refers to the words over the chalice to the disciples of Jesus or to the congregation celebrating the Lord's Supper ("for you"). The current practice in the Lutheran-Evangelical regional churches in Germany varies. While in the Württemberg edition of the *Evangelisches Gesangbuch* [*Lutheran Hymnal*] the words over the chalice read "for you and for many",[53] the *Lutheran Hymnal* for the regional church in Baden[54] and the *Evangelische Gottesdiensthandbuch* of the Evangelical Church of the Union (EKU) and of the United Evangelical-Lutheran Church in Germany (VELKD)[55] have the formula "for you" in the words over the chalice. The Catholic Church in many local Churches has gone her separate way in this

---

[51] Already as Archbishop of Munich and Freising, Joseph Ratzinger had expressed misgivings about the translation of *pro multis* as "for all" (cf. Ratzinger, "The Eucharist—Heart of the Church", in *JRCW* 11:249–98 at 255–59). He reaffirmed it in the second volume of his book on Jesus. Cf. Ratzinger, *Jesus of Nazareth: Holy Week* (Vatican City: LEV; San Francisco: Ignatius Press, 2011), 131–44.

[52] Theobald, "Pro multis", 35.

[53] Cf. *Evangelisches Gesangbuch: Ausgabe für die Evangelische Landeskirche in Württemberg*, 2nd ed. (Stuttgart: Gesangbuchverlag, 2007), 1248.

[54] Cf. *Evangelisches Gesangbuch: Ausgabe für die Evangelische Landeskirche in Baden, für die Kirchen Augsburgischen Bekenntnisses und die Reformierte Kirche in Elsass und Lothringen*, 3rd ed. (Karlsruhe: Evangelischer Presseverband für Baden, 1999), no. 025.

[55] Cf. *Evangelisches Gottesdienstbuch: Agende für die Evangelische Kirche der Union und für die Vereinigte Evangelisch-Lutherische Kirche Deutschlands*, 3rd ed. (1999; Berlin: Evangelische Haupt-Bibelges, 2003; hereafter cited as *Agende*), 170.

issue of the *pro multis*, because only the Old Catholics have adopted the translation of *pro multis* as "for all".[56] Above all, the decision of Benedict XVI about the *pro multis* is of decisive importance for the dialogue with the Orthodox Churches. From the Orthodox perspective, Catholic soteriology and eschatology since the Middle Ages are said to have had a tendency to apocatastasis [Origen's doctrine of universal salvation], which is rejected by the Orthodox.

Correcting the translation of the *pro multis* [in the German-speaking Catholic Church] will be a challenge and must be prepared properly. In the new edition of the *Gotteslob* (2013), therefore, the *pro multis* is already rendered as *für viele* (for many).[57] Given the philological, dogmatic, liturgical-theological, and ecumenical arguments in favor of a literal rendering of the *pro multis*, pastoral scruples have to yield the right of way. Nor is it a convincing argument in favor of keeping the existing [non-literal] translation to say that the faithful and the priests have grown accustomed to it by now and that a change would therefore be difficult. After the Second Vatican Council, the faithful had to adapt to many changes in the liturgy. The great majority of them would also accept a correction of the translation of the *pro multis*. The most resistance comes from the priests,[58] who with a correction of the translation of the *pro multis* would be obliged to respect the liturgical order.[59] The universal salvific meaning of Jesus' death would by no means be called into question by a literal translation of the *pro multis*: Jesus died for all. Yet the words of Consecration that the priest pronounces over bread and wine *in persona Christi capitis* apply immediately to the faithful who participate in the Eucharist. The Eucharistic gifts, the bread of life and the cup of salvation, are not handed to all indiscriminately but, rather, to those who are united with Christ by faith and Baptism. A correction of the *pro multis* translation presents an opportunity to reflect anew about the connection between the Passion and the Eucharist, the Cross and the altar.

---

[56] Cf. *Die Feier der Eucharistie im katholischen Bistum der Alt-Katholiken in Deutschland*, für den gottesdienstliche Gebrauch erarbeitet durch die liturgische Kommission [des Katholischen Bistums der Alt-Katholiken, Bonn] und herausgegeben durch Bischof und Synodalvertretung (Munich: Bremberger Verlagsgesellschaft, 1995), 168–223.

[57] *Gotteslob: Katholisches Gebet- und Gesangbuch, Ausgabe für die Erzdiözese Freiburg; gemeinsamer Eigenteil mit der Diözese Rottenburg-Stuttgart* (Freiburg: Herder, 2013), no. 588.5.

[58] Cf. Marschler, *Für viele*, 203f.

[59] Cf. the norm in *SC* 22.

Chapter XI

COMMUNIO EUCHARISTICA

Eucharistic Ecclesiology and Ecumenism

With the "Niceno-Constantinopolitan" Creed (Nicene Creed), we profess "one, holy, catholic and apostolic Church" (*unam sanctam catholicam et apostolicam Ecclesiam*). In comparison to the "Apostles' Creed", the unity and uniqueness of the Church are acknowledged in addition to her holiness, catholicity, and apostolicity.[1] Yet from the beginning there have been divisions in the Church. The major divisions were the one between the Eastern and the Western Church, the separation of the Church of England, and the division in the era of the Reformation. Set in motion by numerous ecumenical initiatives, after war's end in 1945, the "World Council of Churches" was founded (1948). In the wake of the ecumenical movement and the biblical movement, the Catholic Church became open at the Second Vatican Council to ecumenical dialogue with other Churches and ecclesial communities. The encyclical *Satis cognitum* (1896) had inferred from the profession of one, holy, catholic, and apostolic Church that the Church of Christ is "one and the same forever" and that all who are not in union with her "leav[e] the path of salvation".[2] The decree *Unitatis redintegratio* about Christian ecumenism (1965) reasserts the unity and uniqueness of Christ's Church but refrains from condemning those who are not in full communion with the Catholic Church. Instead, it makes an irrevocable commitment to

---

[1] In the churches of the Reformation, we find the profession of "the holy Christian Church" or "the holy universal Christian Church".

[2] DH 3304.

Christian ecumenism: since Christ "founded one Church and one Church only", the Catholic Church sees "the restoration of unity among all Christians" as one of her chief tasks.[3]

The decree *Unitatis redintegratio* formulates the principles for Christian ecumenism from the Catholic perspective. Jesus Christ, who offered himself for us on the Cross as a spotless victim, "in His Church ... instituted the wonderful sacrament of the Eucharist by which the unity of His Church is both signified and made a reality".[4] Through the Holy Spirit, the faithful are united with Christ, so that he can be considered "the principle of the Church's unity". The unity of the Church consists "in ... confessing the one faith, celebrating divine worship in common, and keeping the fraternal harmony of the family of God".[5] An essential part of the Church of Jesus Christ, which is called to unity, is the ministry (*Amt*) of teaching, ruling, and sanctifying that Christ entrusted to the college of the Twelve, among whom he selected Peter, after his profession of faith, in order to build his Church upon him, whereby Christ himself is the chief cornerstone.[6] The Church, according to the Catholic understanding, is an episcopally constituted Church that is led by the successors of the apostles with Peter as their head under the influence of the Holy Spirit.[7]

The Catholic Church regards all who believe in Christ and have received Baptism as brothers and sisters who are "in communion with the Catholic Church even though this communion is imperfect".[8] For through faith and Baptism, they belong to the Church of Jesus Christ. The communion of Christians, however, is not only

---

[3] Vatican Council II, Decree on Ecumenism, *Unitatis redintegratio* (November 21, 1964; hereafter cited as *UR*), 1. About the Decree on Ecumenism, see Johannes Feiner, "Kommentar zu 'Unitatis Redintegratio'", in *LThK*, 2nd ed. (Freiburg: Herder, 1967), 40–123; Bernd Jochen Hilberath, "Theologischer Kommentar zum Dekret über den Ökumenismus 'Unitatis redintegratio'", in *Herders Theologischer Kommentar zum 2. Vatikanischen Konzil*, vol. 3, ed. P. Hünermann and B.J. Hilberath (Freiburg: Herder, 2005), 69–223. On the history of Christian ecumenism and on ecumenical theology, see Friederike Nüssel and Dorothea Sattler, *Einführung in die ökumenische Theologie* (Darmstadt: Wissenschaftliche Buchgesellschaft, 2008).

[4] *UR* 2.
[5] Ibid.
[6] Cf. ibid.
[7] Cf. ibid.
[8] *UR* 3.

an invisible Church hidden from worldly view.[9] The visible and the invisible Church are not two different things; "they form one complex reality which coalesces from a human and a divine element."[10] There is much that unites the Christians of different Churches and ecclesial communities with each other, such as the written Word of God, Baptism, the profession of faith, prayer and praise of God, liturgical celebrations, to some extent even the sacrament of the Eucharist and other sacraments, as in the Orthodox Churches, with which the Catholic Church is bound together by "a brotherly union of faith and sacramental life".[11]

A. Eucharist: Sacrament of Unity

In the ecumenism of the Christian churches, bi- and multilateral dialogues after the Second Vatican Council led to important instances of *rapprochement* in questions concerning faith and the sacraments.[12] The ecumenical challenge confronting the churches today is to reach an understanding about the Church and her unity, and that means about the goal of ecumenism. Quite different notions about it exist in some cases in the Christian churches.[13] The Catholic Church and the Orthodox Churches share the conviction that the Church by her

---

[9] Cf. Luther, *De servo arbitrio* (1525): *WA* 18:652: "abscondita est Ecclesia, latent sancti."

[10] *LG* 8.

[11] *UR* 14.

[12] Cf. Oliver Schuegraf, *Der einen Kirche Gestalt geben: Ekklesiologie in den Dokumenten der Konsensökumene*, Jerusalemer Theologisches Forum (Münster: Aschendorff, 2001).

[13] Cf. on this subject, Heinrich Fries and Karl Rahner, *Unity of the Churches: An Actual Possibility*, trans. Ruth C. L. Gritsch and Eric W. Gritsch (Philadelphia: Fortress Press; New York: Paulist Press, 1985); Heinrich Fries and Otto Hermann Pesch, *Streiten für die eine Kirche* (Munich: Kösel-Verlag, 1987); Eilert Herms, *Einheit der Christen in der Gemeinschaft der Kirchen: Die ökumenische Bewegung der römischen Kirche im Lichte der reformatorischen Theologie; Antwort auf den Rahner-Plan*, Kirche und Konfession 24 (Göttingen: Vandenhoeck & Ruprecht, 1984); Harding Meyer, *That All May Be One: Perceptions and Models of Ecumenicity*, trans. William G. Rusch (Grand Rapids, Mich.: Eerdmans, 1999); Wolfgang Thönissen, *Gemeinschaft durch Teilhabe an Jesus Christus: Ein katholisches Modell für die Einheit der Kirchen* (Freiburg: Herder, 1996); Georg Hintzen and Wolfgang Thönissen, *Kirchengemeinschaft möglich? Einheitsverständnis und Einheitskonzepte in der Diskussion*, Thema Ökumene 1 (Paderborn: Bonifatius, 2001); Wolfgang Thönissen, *"Unitatis redintegratio": 40 Jahre Ökumenismusdekret—Erbe und Auftrag*, Konfessionskundliche Schriften 23 (Paderborn: Bonifatius; Frankfurt am Main: Lemback, 2005).

nature is a Eucharistic communion and exists through this Eucharistic communion.[14] For the Byzantine theologian Nicholas Kabasilas (d. after 1391), the meaning of the Church is expressed most clearly in the Eucharist; in it, she also finds the supreme fulfillment of her life in Christ.[15] Important contributions to Eucharistic ecclesiology came from the Russian theologian-in-exile Nicholas Afanasyev (1893–1963),[16] the Greek-Orthodox theologian Ioannis Zizioulas,[17] and the Russian-Orthodox theologian Alexander Schmemann (1921–1983).[18]

Beginnings of a Eucharistic ecclesiology are found also in the Dogmatic Constitution on the Church *Lumen gentium* (1965)[19] and in the decree *Unitatis redintegratio* on ecumenism.[20] The Church is communion, fellowship of the Word of Christ and of his Body, which causes the Church to become a people. The Church came about when the Lord gave his Body and Blood under the forms of bread and wine "for the many" and the Church received the commission: "Do this in memory of me." The Church comes from the Eucharist, and at her heart is a Eucharistic assembly. The idea of Church

[14] Cf. Albert Rauch, ed., *Die Eucharistie der Einen Kirche: Eucharistische Ekklesiologie: Perspektiven und Grenzen*, Regensburger Ökumenisches Symposium 1981 (Munich: Verlagsgesellschaft Gerrhard Kaffke, 1983).

[15] Cf. Kabasilas, *De vita in Christo* 4 (*PG* 150:585B).

[16] Cf. Nicolas Afanassieff [Nikolay Afanasyer], *La primauté de Pierre dans l'Église orthodoxe* (Neuchâtel: Delachaux & Niestlé, 1960); Afanassieff, *The Church of the Holy Spirit*, trans. Vitaly Permiakov and ed. with an introduction by Michael Plekon, foreword by Rowan Williams (Notre Dame, Ind.: University of Notre Dame Press, 2012). On Afanasyev's Eucharistic ecclesiology, see Peter Plank, *Die Eucharistieversammlung als Kirche: Zur Entstehung und Entwicklung der eucharistischen Ekklesiologie Nikolaj Afanasjevs (1893–1966)*, Das östliche Christentum, Neue Folge 31 (Würzburg: Augustinus, 1980).

[17] Cf. Jean Zizioulas, *L'eucharistie, l'évêque et l'église durant les trois premiers siècles*, Theophanie (Paris: Deslée de Brouwer, 1994); Zizioulas, *Being as Communion: Studies in Personhood and the Church* (Crestwood, N.Y.: St. Vladimir's Seminary Press, 1985); Zizioulas, *Communion and Otherness: Further Studies in Personhood and the Church*, ed. P. McPartlan (London and New York: T&T Clark, 2006); Zizioulas, "Die Eucharistie in der neuzeitlichen orthodoxen Theologie", in *Die Anrufung des Heiligen Geistes im Abendmahl: Viertes Theologisches Gespräch zwischen dem Ökumenischen Patriarchat und der Evangelischen Kirche in Deutschland*, Beiheft zur Ökumenischen Rundschau 31 (Frankfurt am Main: Otto Lembeck, 1977), 163–79; Paul McPartlan, *The Eucharist Makes the Church: Henri de Lubac and Jean Zizioulas in Dialogue* (Edinburgh: T&T Clark, 1993).

[18] Cf. Alexander Schmemann, *Eucharistie: Sakrament des Gottesreiches*, with an introduction by J.-H. Tück, 2nd ed. (Freiburg: Johannes-Verlag Einsiedeln, 2012).

[19] Cf. *LG* 3.

[20] Cf. *UR* 15.

as *communio* is founded on this fact, also.[21] For *communio* is Church above all as Eucharistic communion/fellowship. The intrinsic connection between Church and Eucharist is made clear by the threefold meaning of the expression *corpus Christi*, too. As was shown, *corpus Christi* designates the historical body of Jesus Christ, the Eucharistic Body, and the ecclesial Body of Christ that consists of many members. Eucharistic ecclesiology underscores the fact that the Eucharist is not an isolated individual sacrament alongside other sacramental signs; instead, Eucharistic Communion and ecclesial communion are most intimately interconnected.[22]

Between those who participate to the full extent in the celebration of the Eucharist and receive Holy Communion, there must be nothing fundamentally divisive; after all, through their participation in the Body and Blood of Christ, they are "one body and one Spirit" [Eph 4:4]. First Corinthians 10:16–17 is a sort of "proof text" for the understanding of the Church as a Eucharistic communion: "The cup of blessing which we bless, is it not a participation in the blood of Christ? The bread which we break, is it not a participation in the body of Christ? Because there is one bread, we who are many are one body, for we all partake of the one bread." *Communion in Christ*

---

[21] By now it is almost impossible to survey the literature on the subject. See Joseph Ratzinger, "Communion—Community—Mission", in *Behold the Pierced One*, trans. Graham Harrison (San Francisco: Ignatius Press, 1986), 71–100; Ratzinger, "The Universal Church and the Particular Church", in *Called to Communion*, trans. Adrian Walker (San Francisco: Ignatius Press, 1996), 75–103; Walter Kasper, *Die Kirche Jesu Christi*, WKGS, 11 (2008), 15–120; Kasper, "Kirche als Communio", in *WKGS* 11 (2008), 405–20; Kasper, "Communio: Die Leitidee der katholischen ökumenischen Theologie", in *WKGS* 14 (2012), 137–67; Gisbert Greshake, "Communio—Schlüsselbegriff der Dogmatik", in *Gemeinsam Kirche sein: Theorie und Praxis der Communio*, Festschrift O. Saier (Freiburg: Herder, 1992), 90–121; Bernd Jochen Hilberath, "Kirche als Communio", *Theologische Quartalschrift* 174 (1994): 45–65; Joachim Drumm and Winfried Aymans, "Communio", in *Lexikon für Theologie und Kirche*, 3rd ed. (Freiburg: Herder, 1994), 2:1280–84; Rolf Schäfer, "Communio 1. Dogmatisch", in *Die Religion in Geschichte und Gegenwart: Handwörterbuch für Theologie und Religionswissenschaft*, 4th ed. (Tübingen: Mohr, 1999), 2:435–37; Winfried Aymans, "Communio IV. Kirchenrechtlich", in *Die Religion in Geschichte und Gegenwart: Handwörterbuch für Theologie und Religionswissenschaft*, 4th ed. (Tübingen: Mohr, 1999), 2:439–40; Reinhild Ahlers, *Communio eucharistica: Eine kirchenrechtliche Untersuchung zur Eucharistie im Codex iuris canonici*, Eichstätter Studien, new series 29 (Regensburg: Pustet, 1990).

[22] Cf. Wolfgang Thönissen, "Einheitsverständnis und Einheitsmodell nach katholischer Lehre", in *Kirchengemeinschaft möglich? Einheitsverständnis und Einheitskonzepte in der Diskussion*, ed. G. Hitzen and W. Thönissen, Thema Ökumene 1 (Paderborn: Bonifatius, 2001), 73–125.

through participation—this is the key to the Catholic understanding of ecclesial unity. Through the sacrament of the Eucharist, "the unity of His Church is both signified and made a reality."[23] Yet how could those who participate in the Body and Blood of Christ be one if there were something divisive in their understanding of the Eucharistic and ecclesial Body of Christ? "Therefore, the reciprocal unity of all those communities who celebrate the Eucharist is not something external added to Eucharistic ecclesiology, but rather its internal condition."[24]

The one and only Church of Jesus Christ, Vatican Council II teaches, is fully realized in the Catholic Church (*subsistit in Ecclesia catholica*), which is led by the college of bishops with the successor of Peter at its head.[25] The Church of Jesus Christ is not simply identical to the Catholic Church (hence *subsistit in* and not *est*), but it does stand in an essential relation to her.[26] The expression *subsistit in* is an ecclesiological "escape clause" (Lothar Ullrich), but does reaffirm that the Church of Jesus Christ exists in the Catholic Church. Much was written about the *subsistit in* during the years after the council.[27] The whole ecumenical problem lies in the distinction made by the

---

[23] *UR* 2.

[24] Joseph Ratzinger, "The Ecclesiology of Vatican II", Conference of Cardinal Ratzinger at the opening of the Pastoral Congress of the Diocese of Aversa (Italy). September 15, 2001, *L'Osservatore Romano*, January 23, 2002: 5.

[25] Cf. *LG* 8.

[26] Ibid.: "Haec Ecclesia, in hoc mundo ut societas constituta et ordinata, subsistit in Ecclesia catholica, a successore Petri et Episcopis in eius communione gubernata, licet extra eius compaginem elementa plura sanctificationis et veritatis inveniantur quae, ut dona Ecclesiae Christi propria, ad unitatem catholicam impellunt" [This Church, constituted and organized in the world as a society, subsists in the Catholic Church, which is governed by the successor of Peter and by the Bishops in communion with him, although many elements of sanctification and of truth are found outside of its visible structure. These elements, as gifts belonging to the Church of Christ, are forces impelling toward catholic unity].

[27] On the debate, which we cannot go into here, see Kasper, "Zur Theologie und Praxis des bischöflichen Amtes", in *WKGS* 12 (2009); Kasper, "Das Verhältnis von Universalkirche und Ortskirche", in *WKGS* 11 (2008); Kasper, *Katholische Kirche: Wesen—Wirklichkeit— Sendung* (Freiburg: Herder, 2011), 234–38; Ratzinger, "The Ecclesiology of the Constitution *Lumen gentium*", in *Pilgrim Fellowship of Faith: The Church as Communion*, trans. Henry Taylor (San Francisco: Ignatius Press, 2005); Ratzinger, "Questions about the Structure and Duties of the Synod of Bishops", in *Church, Ecumenism, and Politics*, trans. Michael J. Miller (San Francisco: Ignatius Press, 2008), 51–66; Ratzinger, "Universal Church and the Particular Church"; Medard Kehl, "Die eine Kirche und die vielen Kirchen", *Stimmen der Zeit* 219 (2001): 3–16; Kehl, "Zum jüngsten Disput um das Verhältnis von Universalkirche und Ortskirchen", in *Kirche in ökumenischer Perspektive*, Festschrift W. Kasper, ed. P. Walter et al. (Freiburg: Herder,

council between *subsistit in* and *est*.[28] The statement is correctly inter-preted only if we avoid both an ecclesiological pluralism that regards all churches and ecclesial communities as equivalent and also an ecclesiological exclusivity that simply equates the Church of Jesus Christ with the Catholic Church.[29] "The Council is trying to tell us that the Church of Jesus Christ may be encountered in this world as a concrete agent in the Catholic Church."[30] We should hold fast to the claim that the Catholic Church is irreplaceably the one true Church. At the same time, we should allow room for acknowledging elements of the true Church outside the Catholic Church.[31] Because of the division that still exists between the churches, the catholicity of the Catholic Church cannot be expressed fully.[32] This does not mean, however, that the Church "is nothing more than a collection (divided, but still possessing a certain unity) of Churches and ecclesial communities".[33] According to the Catholic understanding, there is

---

2003), 81–101; Alexandra von Teuffenbach, *Die Bedeutung des subsistit in (LG 8): Zum Selbstver-ständnis der katholischen Kirche* (Munich: Herbert Utz, 2002); Peter Walter, "Ein Blick zurück und nah vorne aus dem Abstand von fast vierzig Jahren am Beispiel des Verhältnisses von Orts- und Universalkirche", in *Zweites Vatikanum—vergessene Anstösse, gegenwärtige Fortschrei-bungen*, ed. G. Wassilowsky, Quaestiones disputatae 207 (Freiburg: Herder, 2004), 116–36; Karl J. Becker, "Subsistit in", *L'Osservatore Romano*, December 5–6, 2005: 6–7; Francis A. Sullivan, "Quaestio Disputata: A Response to Karl Becker on the Meaning of 'subsistit in'", *Theological Studies* 67 (2006): 395–409; Sullivan, "Further Thoughts on the Meaning of subsistit in", *Theological Studies* 71 (2010): 133–47; Peter Hofmann, "Kirche als universale concre-tum: Der 'Streit der Kardinäle' und seine fundamentaltheologischen Voraussetzungen", in *Primato pontificio ed episcopato: Dal primo millenio al Concilio Ecumenico Vaticano II: Studi in onore dell'Archivescovo Agostino Marchetto*, ed. J. Ehret (Vatican City: Libreria Editrice Vaticana, 2013), 391–426; Walter Kasper, "Der 'Streit der Kardinäle'—neu aufgelegt: Eine Zumutung, die man sich nicht bieten lassen kann", *Stimmen der Zeit* 231 (2013): 119–23. For suggestions from patristic writings and Orthodox theology as to an understanding of universal Church and par-ticular Church, see Lothar Lies, *Eucharistie in ökumenischer Verantwortung* (Graz: Styria, 1996).

[28] Cf. Ratzinger, "The Ecclesiology of the Constitution *Lumen gentium*", 147.

[29] Another view is presented by Bernd Jochen Hilberath, "Eucharistie und Kirchenge-meinschaft", in *Die Kirche—erfahrbar und sichtbar in Amt und Eucharistie: Zur Problematik der Stel-lungn von Amt und Abendmahl im ökumenischen Gespräch*, ed. J. G. Piepke, Veröffentlichungen des Missionspriesterseminars St. Augustin bei Bonn (Nettetal: Steyler, 2006), 44.

[30] Ratzinger, "The Ecclesiology of the Constitution *Lumen gentium*", 147.

[31] This follows from the Relatio of the Council's Doctrinal Commission. Cf. Giuseppe Alberigo, Franca Magistretti, *Constitutionis dogmaticae Lumen gentium synopsis historica* (Bologna: Istituto per le scienze religiose, 1975), 440.

[32] Cf. UR 4.

[33] Congregation for the Doctrine of the Faith, Declaration *Mysterium Ecclesiae* (1973), no. 1 (DH 4530).

one single Church of Christ, which subsists in the Catholic Church and is governed by the successor of Peter and by the bishops in communion with him.[34]

> The Catholic Church is convinced that the fullness of all means of salvation exists in her alone. The Church of Jesus Christ subsists in her alone in a secure [*unverlierbar*] and lasting way. In her also, therefore, the unity essential to the Church already exists. Her unity, however, is wounded as a result of the divisions. These wounds are to be healed through ecumenical dialogue; through it, the incomplete unity should be brought to full unity.[35]

Whether the ecclesial communities (*Communitates ecclesiales*) can be described as churches (*ecclesiae*) as the Catholic Church understands them[36] was a controversial question at the Second Vatican Council[37] and has remained so to this day. The Lutheran and Reformed communities of faith, in any case, are not churches according to the Catholic understanding, nor do they want to be such.[38]

The Declaration of the Congregation for the Doctrine of the Faith *Dominus Iesus* (2000) denies the churches of the Reformation full ecclesial status, because they have no valid episcopate and have not preserved the original, complete essence of the Eucharistic mystery: they are not churches in the proper sense (*sensu proprio Ecclesiae non sunt*).[39] What was meant by this ambiguous formulation was that the churches of the Reformation that regard themselves as Church are not churches according to the Catholic understanding of the term. Cardinal Kasper suggested speaking about a "different type of church".[40]

---

[34] Cf. ibid.

[35] Kasper, *Katholische Kirche*, 235f.

[36] Cf. *UR* 19.

[37] Cf. Feiner, "Kommentar zu 'Unitatis Redintegratio' ", 55f.

[38] The Council of the Evangelical Church in Germany responded to the Vatican Declaration *Dominus Iesus* with the document *Kirchengemeinschaft nach evangelischem Verständnis: Ein Votum zum geordneten Miteinander bekenntnisverschiedener Kirchen* [Ecclesial Communion according to the Lutheran-Evangelical Understanding: A vote in favor of the ordered coexistence of churches with different professions of faith] (2001).

[39] Cf. Congregation for the Doctrine of the Faith, Declaration *Dominus Iesus* on the Unicity and Salvific Universality of Jesus Christ and the Church (August 6, 2000), no. 17 (DH 5088). This judgment was confirmed by the document "Responses to Some Questions regarding Certain Aspects of the Doctrine on the Church" (June 29, 2007) (DH 5108).

[40] Walter Kasper, "Situation und Zukunft der Ökumene", in *WKGS* 14 (2012), 357.

In any case, the churches of the Reformation are churches lacking something crucial for full ecclesial status according to the Catholic understanding, above all episcopal and priestly ministry, as well as the full reality of the celebration of the Eucharist, which is connected with it. Nevertheless, numerous elements of ecclesial status are found in them.[41]

With the statement that "elements and endowments which together go to build up and give life to the Church itself, can exist outside the visible boundaries of the Catholic Church",[42] the council goes beyond the previous view. For the elements are not just any kind of elements but, rather, "institutional ecclesial elements"[43] or "sacramental structural elements",[44] like Christian faith and Baptism, which establish a fundamental unity between the Churches and ecclesial communities. The Catholic Church recognizes the particular churches separated from Rome as true Churches (*ecclesiae*) and even describes them as "sister Churches"[45] that are united with the Catholic Church in the communion of faith and sacramental life.[46] The Eastern Churches not in union with Rome are Churches in the full sense. For these Churches are distinguished by the fact that they possess true sacraments within the apostolic succession, above all priesthood and the Eucharist. A *communicatio in sacris* with the Orthodox Churches, that is, reception of the sacraments reciprocally (Penance, Eucharist, Anointing of the Sick) would therefore be possible.[47] Ultimately, all that is lacking for full unity is union

---

[41] The Dogmatic Constitution *Lumen gentium* on the Church speaks about "many elements of sanctification and of truth" that as "gifts belonging to the Church of Christ ... are forces impelling towards Catholic unity" (*LG* 8). Although this is said about the churches of the Reformation, it is still meant according to their own self-understanding.

[42] *UR* 3.

[43] Johannes Feiner, "Kommentar zu 'Unitatis Redintegratio'", in *LThK*, 2nd ed. (Freiburg: Herder, 1967), 57.

[44] Medard Kehl, *Die Kirche: Eine katholische Ekklesiologie* (Würzburg: Echter Verlag, 1992), 419.

[45] Paul VI, Letter *Anno ineunte* to Patriarch Athenagoras I of Constantinople (July 25, 1967), 852f.; John Paul II, Encyclical *Slavorum Apostoli* (June 2, 1985), 807; John Paul II, Encyclical *Ut unum sint* (May 25, 1995), 954f., 957; Congregation for the Doctrine of the Faith, "Note on the expression 'Sister Churches'" (June 9, 2000).

[46] Vatican Council II uses the expression "sister Churches" to describe the fraternal relations between particular Churches. Cf. *UR* 14.

[47] Cf. *UR* 14–15.

with the bishop of Rome; reaching an understanding about this continues to be difficult.

The Church as a concrete reality is manifested in the individual local congregation, which is centered on the Eucharistic assembly. In the Eucharistic assembly, however, the whole worldwide Church is present.[48] The individual congregation is the Church of Jesus Christ only in union with the communion of the particular or local Church represented by the bishop and led by him, in union with the Universal Church. The priestly ministry is inseparable from the episcopal ministry. In the unity of faith, of sacramental life, and of ministry, the unity of the Church finds its visible expression. Therefore, from the Catholic perspective, this unity must be the goal of the ecumenical movement.[49]

Participation in the Body and Blood of Christ presupposes Baptism as the sacramental event of justification. Baptism "envisages a complete profession of faith, complete incorporation in the system of salvation such as Christ willed it to be, and finally complete ingrafting in eucharistic communion".[50] This implies no devaluation of Baptism, for it is the permanent foundation of Christian life (cf. Rom 6; 1 Cor 12:13). Baptism establishes an irrevocable sacramental bond of unity among all who are reborn through it. Those who believe in Christ and have received Baptism are "in communion with the Catholic Church even though this communion is imperfect".[51] "Yet worship in common (*communicatio in sacris*) is not to be considered as a means to be used indiscriminately for the restoration of Christian unity."[52] This is true particularly for the celebration of the Eucharist, which like no other sacrament is a sign of ecclesial unity. From the Catholic perspective, and all the more according to

---

[48] The *communio* of the Eucharist at the level of the local Churches and in the Universal Church has been rediscovered by individual theologians from the Reformation tradition, too. Cf. Wolfhart Pannenberg, *Kirche und Ökumene*, vol. 3 of *Beiträge zur systematischen Theologie* (Göttingen: Vandenhoeck & Ruprech, 2000), 11–22; Gunther Wenz, "Communio Ecclesiarum: Die theologische Relevanz der ökumenischen Verständigung: Bestimmung und Beleuchtung einer protestantischen Zentralperspektive", *KNA Dokumentation* 7 (July 10, 2001): 1–10.

[49] Cf. Thönissen, "Einheitsverständnis und Einheitsmodell", 93, 95.

[50] *UR* 22.

[51] *UR* 3.

[52] *UR* 8.

the Orthodox view, Eucharistic communion presupposes full ecclesial communion.[53] For the sacramental consolidation of ecclesial
koinonia occurs in the Eucharist. The concept "unity in reconciled
diversity" runs up against its limitations in the different understandings of Church, Eucharist, and ministry. In the foreseeable future,
we cannot count on any consensus about our understanding of
Church and ministry, which would be required for fellowship at the
Lord's Supper. On the other hand, there are no fundamental objections to Eucharistic communion between the Catholic Church and
the Orthodox Churches, since the latter, even without full communion with the bishop of Rome, are episcopally constituted particular Churches in which Holy Orders and the other sacraments are
validly administered.

Demands for Catholic-Lutheran fellowship at the Lord's Supper
often emphasize that Christ is the Lord of his supper and he invites
all. This interprets the Eucharist one-sidedly along the lines of the
meals that Jesus ate with sinners as a sign of God's unconditional
grace, while ignoring the difference between those meals with sinners, Jesus' Last Supper with his disciples, and the Eucharist. Someone who regards the Lord's Supper as being directly connected with
the doctrine on justification must ask himself what still stands in the
way of Lord's Supper fellowship between Catholics and Protestants,
after a successful agreement on the doctrine of justification: God justifies man *sola gratia* [by grace alone] and the risen Lord invites believers to his meal. Yet according to the Catholic understanding, the
Eucharist, as the celebration of the Church and of her communion,
cannot be circumvented through recourse to the hospitality of the
risen, glorified Lord.[54] Here an intensive discussion with the churches
of the Reformation is needed about our understanding of Church,
Eucharist, and ministry. According to the Catholic (and Orthodox)
understanding, Church and Eucharist belong together inseparably.

---

[53] Cf. Kurt Koch, *Eucharistie: Herz des christlichen Glaubens* (Fribourg: Paulusverlag, 2005),
109.

[54] Cf. *Lehrverurteilungen—kirchentrennend? Rechtfertigung, Sakramente und Amt im Zeitalter der
Reformation und heute*, Dialog der Kirchen 4, ed. K. Lehmann and W. Pannenberg (Freiburg:
Herder; Göttingen: Vandenhoeck & Ruprecht, 1986), 29–33; *Dokumente wachsender Überein-
stimmung* III: 1990–2001, ed. H. Meyer et al. (Paderborn: Bonifatius, 2003; hereafter cited as
DwÜ III).

Since the connection between Church unity and communion in the Lord's Supper is indissoluble, intercommunion can stand only at the end of the ecumenical dialogue, not at the beginning.[55] The common bond of Baptism does not suffice as the foundation for a common celebration of the Lord's Supper.[56] For Baptism is ordered to the common profession of the faith and to the one Eucharist. Eucharistic communion forms the foundation of the Church and at the same time is the expression of ecclesial communion, which according to the Catholic understanding includes the ministry and communion of the bishops. Without agreement on our understanding of Church and ministry, as well as our understanding of ecclesial communion and Eucharistic communion, there can be no common celebration of the Lord's Supper. For the Eucharist is not only a "bond of love" (vinculum caritatis), but also a "sign of unity" (unitatis signum) and symbol of harmony (symbolum concordiae).[57]

The council of the "Evangelical Church in Germany" (the association of Lutheran, Reformed, and United member churches) argues in A Vote in Favor of the Ordered Coexistence of Churches with Different Professions of Faith (2001) for an entirely different model of ecclesial communion.[58] The Vote is a response to the Vatican declaration Dominus Iesus (2000). Based on the Leuenberg Concord (1973), the Vote regards the goal of Christian ecumenism as a fellowship of churches with different beliefs, not as visible unity of the Church. The Leuenberg Concord, which adopts from the Wittenberg Concord its profession of faith about the presence of Christ in the Eucharist, led to "altar and pulpit fellowship" between the Lutheran and Reformed churches. Of course not all Lutheran or Presbyterian churches entered into the Leuenberg Concord; for example, the Lutheran Church in Sweden did not. The Concord is an association of churches with different professions of faith on the basis of the

---

[55] Cf. Karl Lehmann, "Einheit der Kirche und Gemeinschaft im Herrenmahl: Zur neueren ökumenischen Diskussion um Eucharistie- und Kirchengemeinschaft", in Eucharistie: Positionen katholischer Theologie, ed. T. Söding (Regensburg: Pustet, 2002), 171f.

[56] For a different view, see Johannes Brosseder and Hans-Georg Link, eds., Eucharistische Gastfreundschaft (Neukirchen-Vluyn: Neukirchener Verlag-Haus, 2003).

[57] Cf. DH 1649.

[58] Cf. Evangelische Kirche in Deutschland, Kirchengemeinschaft nach evangelischem Verständnis ein Votum zum geordneten Miteinander bekenntnisverschiedener Kirchen (Hannover: Hannover Kirchenamt der EKD Hannover Kirchenamt der EKD, 2001).

Evangelical message of justification. In the Concord, the traditional unity of ecclesial communion and communion in faith is abandoned. The *Vote* by the Council of the Evangelical Church in Germany is an intra-Protestant model of Church unity. The *Vote* correctly says about this model that it is obviously incompatible with the Roman Catholic idea of the visible, full unity of the Church.[59]

The controversy about the declaration *Dominus Iesus* and the *Vote* of the Evangelical Church in Germany about ecclesial communion according to the evangelical understanding shows that to this day there is no agreement about the goal of ecumenism. Ultimately the Catholic understanding of Church and her unity cannot be reconciled with the Evangelical one. The goal of the Catholic Church is the visible unity of the Church. The *Vote* of the Evangelical Church in Germany objects to such a unity. Although the *Vote* may be understandable as a reaction to *Dominus Iesus*, it has nevertheless made it clear that there are considerable differences between the Catholic Church and the Reformed churches in their understanding of Church, so that in the foreseeable future it will not be possible to arrive at Eucharistic communion.[60]

B. Ecumenism with the Churches of the Reformation

The central controversial points in understanding the Eucharist in the dialogue with the churches of the Reformation are the Eucharist as sacrifice, the presence of Christ with his Body and Blood in the gifts of bread and wine, and also the question of priestly ministry. In the Decree on Ecumenism, the Fathers of the Second Vatican Council declare concerning the churches of the Reformation:

> Though the ecclesial Communities which are separated from us lack the fullness of unity with us flowing from Baptism, and though we believe they have not retained the proper reality of the eucharistic

---

[59] Cf. ibid., no. 23.

[60] Cf. Koch, *Eucharistie*, 106. On the status of the dialogue with the Anglicans, cf. *DwÜ* III, 213–33; on the status of the dialogue with the Old Catholics, cf. *Kirche und Kirchengemeinschaft: Bericht der Internationalen Römisch-Katholischen/Altkatholischen Dialogkommission* (2009), ed. I. Mildenberger (Paderborn and Frankfurt am Main, 2010), 13–44.

mystery in its fullness, especially because of the absence of the sacrament of Orders [*defectus ordinis*], nevertheless when they commemorate His death and resurrection in the Lord's Supper, they profess that it signifies life in communion with Christ and look forward to His coming in glory. Therefore the teaching concerning the Lord's Supper, the other sacraments, worship, the ministry of the Church, must be the subject of the dialogue.[61]

This declaration defines to this day the relation of the Catholic Church to the churches of the Reformation. There continue to be deep-seated differences in the question about ministry, since the churches of the Reformation do not recognize a sacramental priestly ministry distinct from the common priesthood of all the faithful.[62] In the question about the Real Presence of Christ in the Eucharist, but also about the Eucharist as a sacrifice, significant rapprochement has been achieved without removing all differences.

Eucharistic Real Presence: The document *Das Herrenmahl* [The Lord's Supper] (1978) by the Joint Roman-Catholic and Evangelical-Lutheran Commission of the Council for Promoting Christian Unity in Rome and of the Lutheran World Federation states about the Eucharistic presence of Christ: "In the sacrament of the Lord's Supper, Jesus Christ, true God and true man, is present fully and entirely with his Body and Blood under the signs of bread and wine."[63] Lutherans and Catholics both object "to a purely memorial or figurative understanding of the sacrament".[64] The Real Presence of Christ with his Body and Blood in and under the signs of bread and wine, however, is not a "spatial or natural sort of presence".[65] Catholic and Lutheran Christians together profess today the true and Real Presence of the Lord in the Eucharist. Differences exist with regard to the conceptual definition of the Real Presence and with regard to its duration.[66]

---

[61] *UR* 22.

[62] Cf. Roman Catholic/Lutheran Joint Commission, *The Ministry in the Church* (Geneva: Lutheran World Federation, 1982).

[63] Joint Roman-Catholic/Evangelical Commission *Das Herrenmahl* (Paderborn: Verlag Bonifatius-Druckerei; Frankfurt am Main: Lembeck 1978; hereafter cited as *Herrenmahl*), no. 16.

[64] Ibid.

[65] Ibid.

[66] Cf. ibid., no. 48.

The ecumenical discussion has shown that our way of thinking about the somatic Real Presence is no longer necessarily a divisive difference. "The Lutheran tradition affirms with the Catholic tradition that the consecrated elements do not simply remain bread and wine but by virtue of the creative word are given as the Body and Blood of Christ. In this sense, Lutheran tradition could also occasionally speak with the Greek tradition about a 'transformation',"[67] as is the case in the Apologia of the *Confessio Augustana*.[68] There continues to be no consensus between Catholics and Lutherans about the question of the somatic Real Presence of Christ in the Eucharistic bread beyond the celebration of the Eucharist or about the practice of Eucharistic adoration, although in liturgical practice there has been some rapprochement, for instance through the fact that the consecrated gifts of bread and wine are consumed during the celebration of the Eucharist.

The "Faith and Order" Commission of the World Council of Churches says in the *Lima Document* (1982) about the Real Presence of Christ in the sacrament of the Eucharist:

> The Eucharistic meal is the sacrament of the Body and Blood of Christ, the sacrament of his Real Presence. Christ fulfills in a variety of ways his promise to be always with his own even to the end of the world. But Christ's mode of presence in the Eucharist is unique. Jesus said over the bread and wine of the Eucharist: "This is my body ... this is my blood...." What Christ declared is true, and this truth is fulfilled every time the Eucharist is celebrated. The Church confesses Christ's real, living, and active presence in the Eucharist.[69]

The explanatory guide by the Council of Evangelical Churches in Germany *Das Abendmahl* (2003)[70] offers an insight into the Evangelical understanding of the Lord's Supper today. As far as their understanding of Christ's Real Presence with his Body and Blood in the bread and wine in the celebration of the Eucharist is concerned, there

---

[67] Ibid., no. 51.

[68] *Apologia Confessionis* X (*BSLK* 247f.).

[69] *Dokumente wachsender Übereinstimmung, 1931–1982*, ed. H. Meyer et al. (Paderborn, Leipzig, and Frankfurt am Main: Otto Lembeck, 1983), 560.

[70] Cf. *Das Abendmahl: Eine Orientierungshilfe zu Verständnis und Praxis des Abendmahls in der evangelischen Kirche*, proposed by the Council of the Evangelical Church in Germany (Gütersloh: Gütersloher Verlagshaus, 2003; hereafter cited as *Abendmahl*).

is no longer a divisive difference between Lutherans and Catholics, even though the conceptual models for understanding this presence are different (transubstantiation, consubstantiation). Insofar as it is acknowledged that Christ with his Body and Blood is present in, with, and under the gifts of bread and wine, there is no disagreement with regard to Christ's presence with his Body and Blood in the celebration of the Eucharist, although of course there still is disagreement with regard to the presence of Christ in the consecrated Host after the celebration. According to the Lutheran understanding, the special union between the living Jesus Christ, his Body and Blood, and the elements of bread and wine exists only "during the use of them in the worship service (*in usu*)".[71]

An important step in ecumenism between Catholics and Lutherans was the rediscovery of the Eucharistic Prayer by the *Evangelische Gottesdienstbuch* (Evangelical Book of Worship) (1999) of the United Evangelical-Lutheran Church of Germany and the United Evangelical Church of the Union.[72] The development of the *verba testamenti* in a Eucharistic Prayer with anamnesis, epiclesis, praise of God, and eschatological perspective took priority in a book of worship over the tradition to restrict the text to the words of institution: the importance of this fact can scarcely be overestimated, even though this development was and is vigorously debated internally. Critics regard it as a "Eucharistizing" of the central action of the Lord's Supper that endangers the confessional identity of Lutheran theology.[73] Granted, some "Catholicizing" texts were revised or deleted. Yet this overture of the Evangelical liturgy of the Lord's Supper to the "Eucharistic Prayer" was not retracted.

---

[71] Ibid., 51.

[72] Cf. *Agende*.

[73] Cf. Dorothea Wendebourg, "Den falschen Weg Roms zu Ende gegangen? Zur gegenwärtigen Diskussion über Martin Luthers Gottesdienstreform und ihr Verhältnis zu den Traditionen der Kirche", *Zeitschrift für Theologie und Kirche* 94 (1997): 437–67; Wendebourg, "Noch einmal 'Den falschen Weg Roms zu Ende gegangen?' Auseinandersetzung mit meinen Kritikern", *Zeitschrift für Theologie und Kirche* 99 (2002): 400–440; Roland Ziegler, *Das Eucharistiegebet in Theologie und Liturgie der lutherischen Kirchen seit der Reformation: Die Deutung des Herrenmahles zwischen Promissio und Eucharistie* (Göttingen: Edition Ruprecht, 2013). For a critique of Wendebourg's essays, see Frieder Schulz, "Eingrenzung oder Ausstrahlung? Liturgiewissenschaftliche Bemerkungen zu Dorothea Wendebourg", in *Liturgiewissenschaft und Kirche: Ökumenische Perspektiven*, ed. M. Meyer-Blanck (Rheinbach: CMZ-Verlag, 2003), 91–107.

Lutherans and Reformed Christians who accepted the 1973 Leuenberg Concord agreed that Christ is present in the Lord's Supper in the word of proclamation *with* the signs of bread and wine. Since the theological differences between Lutherans and Reformed Christians with respect to Christ's presence in and under the signs of bread and wine were not removed, the "altar fellowship" brought about by the Leuenberg Concord is above all pragmatic in nature.[74] The explanatory guide *Das Abendmahl* by the Evangelical Church in Germany confirms that the theological differences between Lutherans and Reformed Christians in their understanding of Christ's Real Presence in bread and wine were not settled. The document reads:

> The 1973 Leuenberg Concord describes a common Evangelical understanding of the Lord's Supper that is the theological basis for the altar fellowship between Lutherans, Reformed, and United Christians. Since positions that continue to differentiate the Evangelical confessions (for example, those about the manner of Jesus Christ's presence in the Supper) were bracketed off in the formulation of the common basic understanding, the confessions can receive the Concord in agreement with their own traditional professions of faith.[75]

The compromise formula that was found reads: "In the Lord's Supper the risen Jesus Christ imparts himself in his body and blood, given up for all, through his word of promise with bread and wine."[76] Consequently, the contested question about the somatic Real Presence of Christ—whether Jesus Christ with his Body and Blood is present in, with, and under the gifts of bread and wine (thus the Lutheran tradition) or whether bread and wine are signs illustrating the presence of Christ in the word of proclamation (thus the Reformed tradition)—is regarded as theologically irrelevant for the pulpit and altar fellowship between Lutherans and Reformed Christians.

The Eucharist as sacrifice: The celebration of the Eucharist is an anamnesis of God's entire reconciliatory action in Jesus Christ.[77] With the help of the full biblical concept of memorial, it was possible to arrive

---

[74] Cf. *Abendmahl* 40.
[75] Ibid., 24f.
[76] Leuenberg Concord, art. 1, par. 1.
[77] Cf. *Herrenmahl* 17.

at a clear understanding of the relation between Christ's sacrifice and the Eucharist. In the document *Das Herrenmahl* we read:

> In the *memorial celebration of the people of God*, more happens than just picturing bygone events with the faculty of memory and the imagination. The decisive thing is not that one calls to mind something past and thus is confronted with Christ's saving deed. In God's creative action, the salvific event from the past becomes an offer of salvation for the present and a promise of salvation for the future. All who celebrate the Eucharist in his memory are included in Christ's life, Passion and death and Resurrection. They receive the fruits of Christ's sacrifice of his life and consequently of God's entire reconciliatory salvific action.... By receiving [the Eucharist] in faith, they [the faithful] are taken up as his body into the propitiating sacrifice, which equips them to sacrifice themselves (Rom 12:1) and enables them to offer spiritual sacrifices (1 Pet 2:5) through Jesus Christ in service to the world. Thus in the Lord's Supper the faithful can practice what is to be carried out in the whole life of Christ. With a humble heart we offer ourselves as a living and holy sacrifice, a sacrifice that must find some expression in our whole everyday life.[78]

Another passage in the document *Das Herrenmahl* reads:

> The Lord present in our midst wants to draw us into the movement of his life. The one who in his love handed himself over to death lives in us (Gal 2:20). By his grace, we have passed over with him from death to life (Jn 5:24). In our participation in the Eucharistic sacrament, we walk with him through this world into the world to come (*pascha, transitus*). As people who have been gifted and have become alive through his Spirit, we have the privilege of passing his love along and thus glorifying the Father. Although we cannot offer a real sacrifice to God by our own power, we should all the more be drawn by Christ's power into his sacrifice. If we come before God in the Lord's Supper with our sacrifice, then we do this only through Christ, that is, in reference to his sacrifice.... To sacrifice ourselves ultimately means to be open so as to receive him. Thus we are united with our Lord, who offers himself to the Father and in communion with the universal Church in heaven and on earth, renewed in the covenant sealed with

---

[78] Ibid., 36.

Christ's Blood, and offer ourselves in a living, holy sacrifice that must find expression in our entire everyday life.[79]

Christ himself is present in this "anamnesis" [of the Eucharist] with everything that he accomplished for us and for all creation (in his Incarnation, humiliation, service, instruction, Passion, sacrifice, Resurrection and Ascension into heaven, and in sending the Spirit), and he grants us fellowship with himself. The Eucharist is also the foretaste of his parousia and of the perfected kingdom of God.... In gratefully calling to mind God's great deeds of redemption, the Church asks him to give the fruits of these deeds to every person. In thanksgiving and petition, the Church is united with the Son, her great High Priest and Intercessor (Rom 8:34; Heb 7:25). The Eucharist is the sacrament of the unique sacrifice of Jesus Christ, who lives eternally to make intercession for us.[80]

The Catholic side reaffirms that the one-time sacrifice of Jesus on the Cross can be "neither continued nor repeated, nor replaced, nor supplemented".[81] When the *Roman Catechism* (1566/1567) says that the sacrifice of the Cross is renewed (*instauretur*) in the Mass,[82] that is a formula that requires clarification. Differences continue to exist in the question about the sacrifice that the Church offers. According to the Catholic understanding, not only do the faithful offer themselves in the sacrifice of the Eucharist, but the priest offers the Body and Blood of Christ together with the faithful. Vatican Council II essentially reaffirmed the doctrine of the Council of Trent about the Sacrifice of the Mass[83] when it declared in the Constitution on the Liturgy that the faithful should "give thanks to God; by offering the Immaculate Victim, not only through the hands of the priest, but also with him, they should learn also to offer themselves."[84] The new Eucharistic Prayers of the Missal of Paul VI, therefore, contain, like the *Canon Romanus*, prayers for the post-consecratory offering of the oblations.

With regard to Jesus' death on the Cross, the explanatory guide *Das Abendmahl* acknowledges that we can speak in a correctly understood

---

[79] Ibid., 18 (emphasis added by author).
[80] Ibid.
[81] Ibid., 56.
[82] Cf. *Catechismus Romanus*, pt. 2, chap. 4, q. 61.
[83] Cf. DH 1740–43, 1751.
[84] *SC* 48.

sense about Jesus' sacrifice on the Cross: Jesus is not only the *victim* (*Opfer*) of violence; for in his obedience to the will of the Father he remained faithful to his mission in his death.[85] His death on the Cross is an *Opfer* in the sense of sacrifice, which, however, is different from all other previous cultic sacrifices. For man does not placate God by a sacrifice, but rather Christ, God's Son, sacrifices himself on the Cross for the sins of mankind. Finally, it recognizes that in the New Testament Jesus' death on the Cross is understood as an "expiation" (Rom 3:25; 1 Jn 2:2; 4:10), since Jesus, in union with the will of God, vicariously takes the sin, suffering, and death of mankind upon himself so as to forgive them. Expiation, however, according to the biblical understanding of it—and this is true above all of Jesus' expiatory death—is not the work of man, but a *gift of God*.[86] Granted to us in bread and wine is the bodily presence of Jesus Christ, who died for us.[87]

Clerical ministry: On the question of ordained ministry, there continue to be weighty differences between the Catholic Church and the Lutherans that rule out any Eucharistic and ecclesial communion for the foreseeable future.[88] Thus the study aid *Das Abendmahl* reaffirmed the rejection of a priesthood of ordained ministry. "According to the Evangelical understanding, ordination to parish ministry is not a consecration that communicates a particular competence in view of the Lord's Supper and its elements. Any Christian person could lead the celebration and speak the words of institution, because through Baptism he receives a share in the entire saving work of Christ."[89] As instituted by God, clerical ministry is exclusively a public preaching ministry of proclaiming the Gospel and administering the sacraments,[90] which in its rules (*Ordnung*) can change fundamentally, even in its distinction from and coordination with the various other

---

[85] Cf. *Abendmahl* 40.

[86] Cf. ibid., 41.

[87] Cf. ibid., 42f.

[88] On the ecumenical dialogue, see *Das kirchliche Amt in apostolischer Nachfolge 3*, Dialog der Kirchen 14, ed. D. Sattler and G. Wenz (Freiburg and Göttingen, 2008); Silvia Hell and Lothar Lies, eds., *Amt und Eucharistiegemeinschaft: Ökumenische Perspektiven und Probleme* (Innsbruck: Tyrolia Verlag, 2004).

[89] *Abendmahl* 51.

[90] Cf. *CA* 5 and 14 (*BSLK* 58f., 61).

ecclesial ministries.[91] The churches of the Reformation therefore have no ministry comparable to the priestly ministry of the Catholic Church. For this reason, it is also fair to speak about the "lack" of the sacrament of Holy Orders. Consequently, a central prerequisite for a common understanding of Church that would make Eucharistic communion possible is missing. Moreover, the episcopal structure of the Church is in many cases lacking.

If we take the study aid *Das Abendmahl* on the Evangelical understanding of ministry at its word,

> the Catholic Church cannot, on the one hand, be convinced that the Eucharistic meal and apostolic succession in the episcopal office and in the priestly ministry are essential parts of the Church of Jesus Christ and, on the other hand, say at the same time that the ministry in Churches and ecclesial communities that do not reckon these same realities as an essential part of the Church, at least not in the same sense, can be recognized in the same way.[92]

Or to put it differently: one cannot be convinced that only an ordained priest can preside validly at the Eucharist but disregard that fact in the case of the churches of the Reformation, especially since they question now as before the connection between priestly ministry and Eucharist. Thus Evangelical pastors are commissioned to proclaim the word and to administer the sacraments, but presiding at the Lord's Supper is not connected with ordination. The practice of delegating non-ordained persons to preside at the Lord's Supper is of course disputed within the Evangelical Church in Germany.[93]

Thus there is quite a controversy in Evangelical theology over how to understand the instruction of the *Augsburg Confession* that no one may "preach (*CA* 5) or administer the sacraments without a proper vocation (*rite vocatus*)".[94] Does the expression *rite vocatus* refer to ordination, which is usually connected with investiture with a parish, or

---

[91] Cf. *Kirchengemeinschaft nach evangelischem Verständnis: Ein Votum zum geordneten Miteinander bekenntnisverschiedener Kirchen*, an essay by the Council of the Evangelical Church in Germany (Hannover: Kirchenamt der EKD, 2001), no. 7.

[92] Koch, *Eucharistie*, 109f.

[93] Cf. *Abendmahl* 53f.

[94] *CA* 14 (*BSLK* 69).

is the requirement of *rite vocatus* fulfilled also when a non-ordained person is delegated by one who is ordained? Wolfhart Pannenberg argues for the first interpretation. Therefore, he demands not only the ordination requirement for celebrating the Lord's Supper but also some succession in ordination as the fundamental prerequisite for an agreement about clerical ministry.[95] An Evangelical doctrine about ministry that makes a claim to continuity with tradition must be backed up by a corresponding ministerial praxis.[96] Martin Luther himself adhered to the principle of apostolic-episcopal ministerial succession and for departures from this principle cited a situation of necessity, in that no bishop was available for the ordination of Evangelical pastors.[97]

Eucharistic communion: A pragmatic agreement on the question about altar fellowship of the sort that was aimed at in the Leuenberg Concord between Lutherans and Reformed Christians cannot, from a Catholic perspective, be a model for Eucharistic communion between the churches. Since the Church and her understanding of herself is always at stake in the celebration of the Eucharist, including the question about clerical ministry, Eucharistic communion presupposes sufficient consensus in this regard. A more nuanced judgment is required on the question of Eucharistic hospitality, for instance in the case of interdenominational marriages. Catholics are not allowed to participate in the Evangelical Lord's Supper, since its validity and that of the clerical ministry are not acknowledged by the Catholic Church. Canonically it follows that Catholics may receive sacraments such as the sacrament of Holy Eucharist only from ministers "in whose churches these sacraments are valid".[98] Here there is asymmetry in the relation of the Catholic Church to the churches of the

---

[95] Cf. Wolfhart Pannenberg, *Systematische Theologie*, vol. 3 (Göttingen: Vandenhoeck & Ruprecht, 1993), 440.

[96] Cf. Gunther Wenz, "Das kirchliche Amt aus evangelischer Perspektive", *Stimmen der Zeit* 128 (2003): 378.

[97] Cf. Luther, *Dass eine christliche Versammlung und Gemeinde Recht und Macht habe, alle Lehre zu beurteilen und Lehrer to berufen, ein- und abzusetzen, Ursache und Grund aus der Schrift*, in *WA* 11:413.22—414.10.

[98] *The Code of Canon Law* in English translation by the Canon Law Society Trust (London: Collins Liturgical Publications/William B. Eerdmans Publishing Company, 1983; hereafter cited as *CIC*), can. 844, §2. Cf. *Direktorium zur Ausführung der Prinzipien und Normen über den Ökumenismus* (Bonn: Sekretariat der Deutschen Bischofskonferenz, 193), no. 132.

Reformation. For they allow Catholics to receive communion at the Evangelical Lord's Supper. The Catholic Church, in contrast, admits the admission of Evangelical Christians to the Eucharist only by way of exception, in cases of "serious necessity" (*gravis necessitas*).[99]

Since communion in the Lord's Supper must correspond to ecclesial communion, there can be no communion in the Lord's Supper without the restoration of Church unity. Communion in the Lord's Supper would create the appearance of a unity that does not exist. Hence, *intercommunion* and *concelebration* or *intercelebration* of the Eucharist by clerical ministers of different confessions are theologically untenable.[100] Church law forbids Catholic priests "to concelebrate the Eucharist with priests or ministers of churches or ecclesial communities which are not in full communion with the Catholic Church".[101] Full Eucharistic communion, according to the Catholic and Orthodox understanding, is possible only in the case of full ecclesial communion. For the Eucharist is the *sacramentum ecclesiae et unitatis* (sacrament of the Church and of unity). As long as the close relation between the mystery of the Church and the *mysterium* of the Eucharist is not obscured, in individual cases Evangelical Christians can be admitted to Holy Communion, not only in danger of death, but for example at the wedding of a Catholic with an Evangelical Christian.[102] If this is possible for a wedding, however, then in individual cases it is probably possible, too, when an Evangelical Christian participates in a Sunday celebration of the Eucharist. For Eucharistic communion/fellowship, in contrast, there needs to be a consensus between the churches of the Reformation and the Catholic Church on their understanding of Church, the Lord's Supper, and ministry. On October 31, 1999, Reformation Day, Edward Idris Cassidy, the President of the Pontifical Council for Promoting Christian Unity, and Dr. Christian Krause, President of the Lutheran World Federation, signed in Saint Anna Lutheran Church in Augsburg a

---

[99] *CIC*, can. 844, §4. Cf. *Direktorium*, no. 131.

[100] Terminologically, the following distinction is presupposed here: limited admission in an individual case is to be distinguished from general admission for all the faithful of another church (*intercommunion*). *Concelebration* in the ecumenical context is the occasional common celebration of the Lord's Supper by priests of ministers of various confessions. In the case of *intercelebration*, two or more churches allow each other's ministers to preside at the celebration of the Eucharist or of the Lord's Supper.

[101] *CIC*, can. 908.

[102] Cf. *Direktorium*, no. 159.

Joint Declaration on Justification by Faith.[103] Through this agreement on the doctrine of justification between the Catholic Church and the Lutheran World Federation, discussion on the topic of "Church Unity and Fellowship in the Lord's Supper" has had a fresh start.[104] A central feature of it is the ecclesiological question, which remains open. After the agreement on the doctrine of justification, it is time for the Catholic Church and the Lutheran World Federation to turn to the topic of their understanding of Church.[105]

C. Ecumenism with the Orthodox Churches

The Roman Catholic Church and the Orthodox Churches share the belief that the Eucharist is the heart of the Church.[106] Since the Orthodox Churches "possess true sacraments, above all by apostolic succession, the priesthood and the Eucharist, whereby they are linked with us in closest intimacy..., some worship in common (*communicatio in sacris*), given suitable circumstances and the approval of Church authority, is not only possible but to be encouraged."[107] Opinions in the Orthodox Churches and in the Roman Catholic Church differ as to what the extent of this *communicatio in sacris* can be in an individual case. In the 1980s, the dialogue between the Catholic and the Orthodox Church on the national and international level led to significant declarations of consensus about the Eucharist and ecclesial ministry.[108] In the 1990s, the dialogue was interrupted, above all

---

[103] For a critique from the Evangelical side on the Declaration about Justification, see Eberhard Jüngel, *Justification: The Heart of the Christian Faith: A Theological Study with an Ecumenical Purpose*, trans. Jeffrey F. Cayzer (London: Bloomsbury, 2014).

[104] Cf. Lehmann, *Einheit der Kirche*, 149.

[105] Cf. Kasper, "Ein Herr, ein Glaube, eine Taufe", *Stimmen der Zeit*, February 2002.

[106] Zizioulas, in *L'Osservatore Romano*, October 13, 2005: 7.

[107] *UR* 15: "Cum autem illae Ecclesiae, quamvis seiunctae, vera sacramenta habeant, praecipue vero, vi succesionis apostolicae, Sacerdotium et Eucharistiam, quibus arctissima necessitudine adhuc nobiscum coniunguntur, quaedam communicatio in sacris, datis opportunis circumstantiis et approbante auctoritate ecclesiastica, non solum possibilis est sed etiam suadetur."

[108] Cf. Gemeinsame Kommission der Griechisch-Orthodoxen Metropolie und der römisch-katholischen Kirche in Deutschland, *Die Eucharistie der einen Kirche: Liturgische Überlieferung und kirchliche Gemeinschaft*, in Die Deutschen Bischöfe, *Ökumene-Kommission 8: Die Eucharistie der einen Kirche: Dokumente des katholisch-orthodoxen Dialogs auf deutscher und internationale Ebene* (Bonn: Sekretariat der Dt. Bischofskonferenz, 1989; hereafter cited as *EeK*), 7–24.

for reasons of Church politics.[109] During the pontificate of Benedict XVI, the attempt was made to recommence the dialogue and to continue it.

The documents of the Joint International Commission for Theological Dialogue deal with the Eucharist and Church unity, faith, the sacraments, ecclesial communion, and the sacrament of Holy Orders. The documents display a broad agreement on the central questions about the faith and the sacraments. On account of their common faith, sacraments, and common possession of ecclesial ministry (bishop, priest, deacon), the Catholic Church recognizes the Orthodox Churches as "sister Churches", that is, as true local Churches of the one Church of Jesus Christ.[110] From the perspective of a sacramental understanding of the Church of Christ, the mystery of the Eucharist is to be regarded in the light of the mystery of the Holy Trinity.[111] At the Last Supper, Christ, the incarnate Son of God, instituted the sacrament of the Eucharist. The sacrament of the Christ-event has passed into the sacrament of the Eucharist. In it, Christ gives himself to us with his Body and Blood, with his life for the many, which is God's gift for the world. In reality, Christ continues to lay down his life in the Holy Spirit.[112] In the Spirit, the faithful are baptized; through him, they are also anointed at Confirmation so as to become incorporated thereby into Christ, the glorified Lord, in whom they form one body (1 Cor 12:13).

The Eucharist proclaims the mystery of the Church, the mystery of the Trinitarian *koinonia*, "the dwelling of God with us men" (cf. Rev

---

[109] The problems have to do with the so-called "Uniatism" and the "proselytism" of which the Orthodox Churches accuse the Eastern Catholic Church. Cf. the Document of the Sixth Plenary Assembly of the Joint International Commission for the Theological Dialogue between the Roman Catholic Church and the Orthodox Church (1990): DwÜ III, 555–60; *Uniatism, method of union of the past, and the present search for full communion.* http://www.vatican.va/roman_curia/pontifical_councils/chrstuni/ch_orthodox_docs/rc _pc_chrstuni_doc_19930624_lebanon_en.html.

[110] On their common understanding of the ordained ministry and also on their differences with regard to the functions of the deacon, cf. Gemeinsame Kommission, *Eucharistie* (1989), 47–58; Gemeinsame Kommission der Griechisch-Orthodoxen Metropolie von Deutschland und der Deutschen Bischofskonferenz, "Das Sakrament der Weihe (Bischof, Priester, Diakon): Eine theologisch-pastorale Handreichung" (2006), *Orthodoxes Forum* 20 (2006): 85–91.

[111] Cf. "The Mystery of the Church and of the Eucharist in the Light of the Mystery of the Holy Trinity" (1982), Introduction: http://www.vatican.va/roman_curia/pontifical_councils /chrstuni/ch_orthodox_docs/rc_pc_chrstuni_doc_19820706_munich_en.html.

[112] Cf. ibid., 1.3.

21:4). And thus the Eucharist is "the center of sacramental life".[113]
When the Church celebrates the Eucharist, therefore, she actualizes
"what she is", the Body of Christ (1 Cor 10:16). The Church celebrates the Eucharist as the "expression here and now of the heavenly
liturgy".[114] The Eucharist, however, is at the same time the sacramental celebration through which the Church is formed into the
Body of Christ. For this reason, the Eucharist, like no other celebration, is the sacrament of the Church. Without the Spirit, who in the
celebration of the Eucharist is called down upon the gifts of bread and
wine, they are not transformed into the Body and Blood of Christ.
The entire celebration of the Eucharist "is an *epiclesis* which becomes
more explicit at certain moments".[115] The epiclesis is not only a petition for transformation but also a prayer for "the communion of all in
the mystery revealed by the Son".[116]

"The eucharistic mystery is accomplished in the prayer which
joins together the words by which the word made flesh instituted
the sacrament and the *epiclesis* in which the church, moved by faith,
entreats the Father, through the Son, to send the Spirit so that in
the unique offering of the incarnate Son, everything may be consummated in unity."[117] In this agreement, the debate between the
Roman Catholic Church and the Orthodox Churches since the fourteenth century over the different importance that they assign to the
verba testamenti and the epiclesis can be surmounted. It is the common
faith of the Orthodox and of the Roman Catholic Church that the
verba testamenti and the epiclesis are both focal points of the anaphora
(Eucharistic Prayer), although in the Antiochene-Byzantine and the
Alexandrian-Roman tradition they are combined with each other in
different ways. This is not the basis for a divisive obstacle, since the
respective traditions were always regarded as "legitimate traditions of
the ancient Church".[118]

The reform of the Roman Rite of the Mass after Vatican Council
II introduced, besides the "Roman Canon", three additional Eucharistic Prayers; in them not only was the thanksgiving character of

---

[113] Ibid., 1.5.d.
[114] Ibid., 1.4.c.
[115] Ibid., 1.5.c.
[116] Ibid., 1.6.
[117] Ibid.
[118] *EeK* 18f.

the anaphora underscored but the essential importance of the epiclesis was also strengthened. Benedict XVI described the prayer-act [*Gebetshandlung*, a special kind of speech act] of the *Prex Eucharistica*, marked by the two focal points of the epiclesis and the *verba testamenti*, as the central Eucharistic action.[119] In the Roman Rite, it is underscored by the fact that the faithful kneel, which is prescribed from the epiclesis until the *Mysterium fidei*.[120] Without the invocation of the Holy Spirit in the epiclesis, the *verba testamenti* that the priest speaks *in persona Christi*, identifying the bread and wine as the Body and Blood of Christ, would not be effective. The Spirit is also the one who unifies the faithful in "one body" and makes them a spiritual sacrifice with which the Father is well pleased. The statements of Pope Benedict XVI in his letter *Sacramentum Caritatis* are of great importance for the dialogue between the Catholic Church and the Orthodox Churches, which are connected with each other by the strong bond of the Eucharist and by their complete preservation of its mystery.[121]

Besides the consensus on the question about the inseparable unity of the *verba testamenti* and the epiclesis, there is also consensus on the fact that during the celebration of the Eucharist a transformation of the gifts of bread and wine occurs. The Council of Trent understands the term *transsubstantiatio*, which is never used in the liturgy, as a more precise definition of the traditional term *conversio* (change).[122] It corresponds to the Greek term μεταβολή. Its verbal form (μεταβάλλειν) occurs, for example, in the epiclesis of Chrysostom's anaphora. The epiclesis: "make this Bread the precious Body of Your Christ ... and that which is in this chalice—the precious Blood of Your Christ" ends with the words: "changing them by Your Holy Spirit (μεταβαλών τῷ πνεύματί σου τῷ ἁγίῳ)".[123] The patristic-liturgical term "change" (*conversio*, μεταβολή) expresses "the common faith tradition" of the Roman Catholic Church and

---

[119] Cf. *SacCar* 13, 48.

[120] Cf. *GIRM* 43.

[121] Cf. *SacCar* 15.

[122] Cf. DH 1642: "Quae conversio convenienter et proprie a sancta catholica Ecclesia transsubstantiatio est appellata".

[123] *Die göttliche Liturgie des heiligen Johannes Chrysostomos* [German-Greek edition of The Divine Liturgy of St. John Chrysostom] (Münster: Theophano-Verlag, 2004), 120–23.

of the Orthodox Churches that is "asserted in the celebration of the Eucharist".[124]

The use of unleavened bread (*azyme*) for the Eucharist, a practice that prevailed in the Catholic Church after the turn of the second millennium, made it possible to emphasize the salvation-history dimension of the Eucharist as the new and true Paschal meal. It is uncertain, however, whether the Last Supper of Jesus with his disciples was a ritual Passover meal or a meal without unleavened bread. Moreover, the Passion symbolism is likewise expressed in the Divine Liturgy by the *proskomedia* [offertory].[125] As for the question of the frequency of receiving Holy Communion, there is agreement that "both the present-day Orthodox practice of restraint with regard to the reception of Communion on Sundays and also the frequent reception of Communion among the Catholic faithful that has come about since Pius X and the liturgical movement ... need to be reexamined in light of apostolic and early Christian standards."[126] The reception of the Body and Blood of Christ is the purpose of participating in the celebration of the Eucharist; it does assume, however, that the recipient is properly disposed. In the case of mortal sin, the Catholic discipline, too, demands that the sacrament of Penance be received first.

The full sign character of Holy Communion is expressed through the reception of the Body and Blood of Christ. Traditionally, the Roman Catholic Church and the Orthodox Church "agree that the testament of the 'body which is given' *and* of the 'blood which is poured out' is realized in the proclamation of the Lord's words and in the epiclesis over both species and in the reception of both species—at least by the celebrating priest."[127] Vatican Council II and postconciliar liturgical law have made more room for Communion under both species.[128] Of course, practical difficulties are often connected with the possibility of Communion in the hand and drinking from the chalice, and these stand in the way of a regular praxis of

---

[124] *EeK* 20.
[125] Cf. ibid., 17f.
[126] Ibid., 15.
[127] Ibid., 17.
[128] Cf. *SC* 55. A list of the possibilities for Communion under both species is contained in AEM, no. 242, and *GORM*, nos. 281–87.

Communion under both species. Communion in the hand compli-
cates Communion under both species, which is self-evident in the
Orthodox Churches in the form of Communion received in the
mouth from a spoon.

In venerating the consecrated gifts outside of the celebration of
the Eucharist, it should be remembered that the liturgical traditions
of the Roman Catholic Church and of the Orthodox Churches have
always shown reverence for the sanctified gifts, for those reserved
for the Communion of the sick, too, as well as for the presanctified
gifts. The consecrated gifts in the Orthodox *missa presanctificatorum*
and the reverence shown when they are transferred can "lead among
Orthodox Christians to an understanding of the procession with the
Blessed Sacrament that arose in the Roman Catholic Church during
the Middle Ages".[129] "The closer connection between reverence
for the Eucharistic gifts and the celebration of the Eucharist that has
become clear in the Roman Catholic Church in recent decades signifies a welcome approach to the practice of the ancient Church."[130]

The Catholic Church and the Orthodox Churches share the
common faith, the sacraments, and a common understanding of the
ordained ministry. What still separates them is above all an agreement about full communion with the bishop of Rome. According
to the Catholic understanding, Eucharistic ecclesiology cannot be
developed from the principle of the local Church alone; part of it is
the Petrine ministry at the level of the Universal Church. Nevertheless, the Roman Catholic Church in individual cases allows Orthodox Christians to receive Communion in a Catholic celebration of
the Eucharist and Catholic Christians to receive Communion in the
Orthodox Divine Liturgy. Since the Roman Catholic Church and
the Orthodox Churches possess in common the sacraments, the
priesthood, and the apostolic succession, in individual cases the sacraments of Penance, Holy Eucharist, and the Anointing of the Sick
can be administered to Orthodox Christians who are not in full communion with the Catholic Church, when they spontaneously ask for
them and are properly disposed.[131] Insofar as necessity demands it or

---

[129] *EeK* 16.
[130] Ibid.
[131] Cf. *CIC*, can. 844, §3.

some spiritual benefit makes it advisable, it is also possible for Catholic faithful to receive the sacraments of Penance, Holy Eucharist, and the Anointing of the Sick in the Orthodox Churches, if no Catholic minister is available.[132]

Since the Orthodox Churches associate the reciprocal admission to Holy Communion with the full Eucharistic communion (*koinonia*) of the Church, they reject as a matter of principle the reciprocal admission to Holy Communion of Churches that are still separated from each other. The reception of the Eucharist "presupposes the fullness of the entire ecclesial life which has not yet been attained".[133] The reason why a common Eucharist is not yet possible at this time does not lie in our understanding of the Eucharist and of priestly ministry. Different ideas about the development of the Petrine ministry are still the primary obstacles to full ecclesial communion. Perhaps now, however, at a not-too-distant time, Catholics and Orthodox will be able to celebrate the Eucharist together.

---

[132] Cf. ibid., §2.
[133] Eucharistie (1989), 16.

Chapter XII

CONVIVIUM PASCHALE

The Eucharist as Sacrament of the Gift

Memores et offerimus. Giving thanks, we offer—so we might translate the formula in the first post-consecratory prayer after the *verba testamenti*.[1] Offering in thanksgiving is the theological meaning of the Eucharist, which should be distinguished from the form of its liturgical celebration but cannot be separated from it. While the liturgical texts, chants, gestures, signs, and so on belong to the celebratory form of the Eucharist, the meaning has to do with the fundamental accomplishment and content of the Eucharist. At the end of our tour of its history and theology stands a systematic reflection. By way of a concluding synthesis, we inquire about the Eucharist as an offering-in-thanksgiving, the bodily presence of Christ under the appearance of bread and wine, and the transformation of the faithful. Starting from a phenomenology of the gift, the Eucharist is displayed as *gift of life* (sacrifice), *gift of presence* (Real Presence), and *gift of transformation*. Corresponding to this threefold gift in terms of the theology of time is the distinction made by Thomas Aquinas between the sacrament as *signum rememorativum* (memorial sign), *signum demonstrativum* (indicative sign), and *signum prognosticum* (foretelling sign).[2]

---

[1] Cf. the prayers *Unde et memores* (Eucharistic Prayer I: *MR* 2002³, 576); *Memores, igitur* (Eucharistic Prayer II: *MR* 2002³, 582); *Memores igitur* (Eucharistic Prayer III: *MR* 2002³, 587); *Unde et nos* (Eucharistic Prayer IV: *MR* 2002³, 595).

[2] Cf. Thomas Aquinas, *Summa theologiae* III, q. 60, art. 3.

A. Gift of Life and of Offering

In the Eucharist, we celebrate the memorial of Christ's sacrifice on the Cross and of his Resurrection by offering in thanksgiving bread and wine, which through the power of the Holy Spirit and the *verba testamenti* become Christ's Body and Blood. Christ's sacrifice on the Cross consists of his laying down his life for us. In the Eucharist, the crucified and risen Lord becomes present for us in this gift of his life. The Eucharist is therefore more than a common meal in the name of Jesus Christ. In *The Spirit of the Liturgy* (1918), Romano Guardini writes, "the essential part[s] of Holy Mass" are "the action of Sacrifice and the divine Banquet".[3] The fundamental form of the Eucharist is not the meal apart from the sacrifice. Offering and meal belong together inseparably. Joseph Pascher (1893–1979) saw the basic form of the Eucharist as the meal form, in which, however, the form of sacrifice is inscribed, since the separate Consecration of the gifts of bread and wine symbolically points to Christ's death on the Cross. Therefore, there can be no opposition between meal and sacrifice.[4]

Pascher's attempt to settle the matter was too superficial to be theologically convincing. The meaning of the Eucharist, one could say, is the *offering-in-thanksgiving* that is accomplished in the Eucharistic Prayer and has its goal in the Eucharistic banquet.[5] The Eucharist sacramentally makes present and offers the one sacrifice of Christ through the Church.[6] "As often as the sacrifice of the cross in which Christ our Passover was sacrificed (1 Cor 5:7) is celebrated on the altar, the work of our redemption is carried on."[7] The memorial of Christ's sacrifice on the Cross is more than a merely human remembering of an event

---

[3] Romano Guardini, *The Spirit of the Liturgy*, trans. Ada Lane, in Joseph Cardinal Ratzinger and Romano Guardini, *The Spirit of the Liturgy*, Commemorative Edition (San Francisco: Ignatius Press, 2018), 325.

[4] Cf. Joseph Pascher, *Eucharistia: Gestalt und Vollzug* (Münster: Aschendorff, 1947), 27.

[5] Cf. Joseph Cardinal Ratzinger, "Form and Content of the Eucharistic Celebration", in *JRCW* 11:299–318; Ratzinger, "The Eucharist—Heart of the Church", in *JRCW* 11:249–98; Lothar Lies, "Eulogia—Überlegungen zur formalen Sinngestalt der Eucharistie", in *Zeitschrift für Theologie und Kirche* 100 (1978): 67–97; Lies, *Eucharistie in ökumenischer Verantwortung* (Graz: Styria, 1996); Kasper, "Die Eucharistie", in *WKGS* 10 (2010); Kurt Koch, *Eucharistie: Herz des christlichen Glaubens* (Fribourg: Paulusverlag, 2005), 39–54.

[6] Cf. *CCC* 1362.

[7] *LG* 3.

from the past. The Eucharist re-presents Christ's sacrifice on the Cross and makes it present. Indeed, it is the glorified Lord himself who makes himself present in the Eucharist in his gift of his life for us.

When the celebration of the Eucharist as memorial, thanksgiving, and meal no longer plumbs the depths of death, it runs the risk of becoming superficial.[8] "One could describe the Eucharist, in terms of the liturgical phenomenon, as an 'assembly', or, in terms of Jesus' act of institution at the Last Supper, as a 'meal'. But this seizes on individual elements while failing to grasp the great historical and theological connections."[9] It would also be a misunderstanding to think that the Eucharist simply continues Jesus' meals with sinners. The Eucharist, Joseph Ratzinger says, is not "the sinners' banquet, where Jesus sits at the table", nor is it "the public gesture by which he invites everyone without exception",[10] an open table to which all are invited without preconditions. The Eucharist is "the sacrament of those who have let themselves be reconciled by God".[11]

The celebration of the Eucharist signifies participation in Christ's prayer of thanksgiving over the gifts of bread and wine, in which he gives himself with his Body and Blood.[12] In the gifts of bread and wine, Christ intends to be with his Church forever. As when he laid down his life on the Cross, Christ in the Eucharist is God's gift to us, which we receive and to which we respond with offering-in-thanksgiving.[13] *Sacrosanctum concilium* 48 says about the celebration of the Eucharist that the faithful "should give thanks to God; by offering the Immaculate Victim (*immaculatam hostiam offerre*), not only through the hands of the priest, but also with him, they should learn also to offer themselves."[14] Therefore the Eucharist is also called the Holy Sacrifice, which perfects all other sacrifices.[15] The sacrifice of the Eucharist is by its very nature a "spiritual sacrifice" (λογικὴ

---

[8] Cf. Ratzinger, "Eucharist—Heart of the Church", 262.

[9] Ratzinger, *The Spirit of the Liturgy*, in *JRCW* 11:30 [50]. See also *EE* 10: "At times one encounters an extremely reductive understanding of the Eucharistic mystery. Stripped of its sacrificial meaning, it is celebrated as if it were simply a fraternal banquet."

[10] Ratzinger, "Eucharist—Heart of the Church", 273.

[11] Ibid., 274.

[12] Cf. Ratzinger, "Form and Content of the Eucharistic Celebration", 310.

[13] Cf. Ratzinger, "Eucharist—Heart of the Church", 262–63.

[14] *SC* 48.

[15] Cf. *CCC* 1330.

θυσία: cf. Rom 12:1), which, however, is accomplished in a visible oblation. The heart of this oblation is the *oratio oblationis* over bread and wine in the Eucharistic Prayer—prepared by the *Offertorium*. In this offering-in-thanksgiving—an arc that extends from the prayers accompanying the offering of the gifts at the Offertory to the post-consecratory offering of the Body and Blood of Christ—the spiritual and ritual accomplishment are to be distinguished but not separated.

Christ's sacrifice is offered by the priest together with the faithful "in the name of the whole Church" in the Eucharist and in an "unbloody manner".[16] Christ's sacrifice and the Sacrifice of the Eucharist are one sacrifice, as the Council of Trent emphasizes: "For, the victim is one and the same: the same now offers himself through the ministry of priests who then offered himself on the Cross; only the manner of offering is different."[17] Offering Christ's sacrifice is part of the central ministry of the priest. In the prayer at the anointing of the hands during priestly ordination, the bishop says: "[May] the Lord Jesus Christ, whom the Father anointed with the Holy Spirit and power, guard and preserve you, that you may sanctify the Christian people and offer sacrifice to God."[18] In the 1962 "Schott" pew missal, we read as an introduction to the Preface, which begins the Eucharistic Prayer: "The high point of the holy sacrificial celebration draws near when Christ transforms our earthly oblations into his own Body and Blood and thus personally becomes our infinitely valuable offering to the heavenly Father."[19] How are we to understand these statements about the sacrifice that the priest offers together with the faithful?

The central religious concept of sacrifice (*Opfer*), as became clear in the introduction to this book, is liable to numerous misunderstandings. Quite a few theologians reject the concept of sacrifice entirely. There is a widespread notion that sacrifice has to do primarily with the destruction of the sacrificial matter. It is true that the destruction of the sacrificial gift plays a not-insignificant role in

---

[16] Vatican Council II, Decree *Presbyterorum ordinis* on the Ministry and Life of Priests (December 7, 1965), 2.

[17] DH 1743.

[18] Ordination of Priests (second typical edition), no. 133.

[19] Schott 459.

the history of religion. Yet the essence of sacrifice is not violence but, rather, the gift with and in which a person hands himself over to God, gives back to him what he has received from him. The German language cannot distinguish between *victima* and *sacrificium*. Both the victim and the sacrifice that people offer are designated *Opfer*, while other languages, for instance, English, differentiate (victim/sacrifice). The offering of the Eucharist is an *Opfer* in the sense of a *sacrificium*. In the Eucharist, Jesus' death on the Cross is not repeated; nevertheless, in it the crucified and glorified Lord becomes present for us with the gift of his life.

Vatican Council II calls the memorial of Christ's Paschal Mystery the center of the liturgy.[20] In the liturgy, the work of our redemption is accomplished in a sacramental manner.[21] This is true especially of the celebration of the Eucharist, the "fount and apex of the Christian life".[22] In it, Christ gives himself to us with his Body and Blood: "At the Last Supper, on the night when He was betrayed, our Savior instituted the eucharistic sacrifice of His Body and Blood. He did this in order to perpetuate the sacrifice of the Cross throughout the centuries until He should come again, and so to entrust to His beloved spouse, the Church, a memorial of His death and resurrection."[23]

In order to avoid understanding the offering of the Eucharist incorrectly, that is, in the sense of the cultic sacrifices that were made obsolete by the Cross of Christ, it is essential to explain more exactly the Christian concept of sacrifice. This will be done in the following pages in the context of a phenomenology of the gift.[24] "Gift" is a primordial word of theology.[25] In Romans 6:23, Paul speaks about the "gift of God" which is "eternal life" in Jesus Christ. Similarly, John 3:16 declares that God's love was made manifest when he "gave his only-begotten Son" so that we might have "eternal life". We owe

---

[20] Cf. *SC* 5–7.
[21] Cf. *SC* 2.
[22] *LG* 11.
[23] *SC* 47.
[24] Introductory material on this subject in Holger Zaborowski, "Enthüllung und Verbergung: Phänomenologische Zugänge zur Eucharistie", *Herder Korrespondenz* 57 (2003): 580–84.
[25] Cf. Veronika Hoffmann, ed., *Die Gabe: Ein Urwort der Theologie?* (Frankfurt am Main: Otto Lembeck, 2009).

the Eucharist to the gift of Jesus' body, a gift that was "given" to the disciples at the Last Supper (Lk 22:19).

The French ethnologist Marcel Mauss (1872–1950) deserves credit for having pointed out the social function of the gift. With his "Essai sur le don" (1925),[26] in which he examines the exchange of gifts in archaic societies, Mauss inaugurated a discourse about gifts that continues to this day, with disciplinary ramifications that are now almost too numerous to survey.[27] Deserving special attention are the beginnings of a *phenomenology of the gift*. Phenomenology, founded by Edmund Husserl (1859–1938), has as its object that which appears, that which is given. Since Martin Heidegger (1889–1976), phenomenology has undergone numerous further developments. Important

---

[26] Cf. Marcel Mauss, *The Gift: The Form and Reason for Exchange in Archaic Societies*, trans. W. D. Halls (London: Routledge, 1990).

[27] Cf. Kurt Wolf, *Philosophie der Gabe: Meditationen über die Liebe in der französischen Gegenwartsphilosophie* (Stuttgart: Kohlhammer, 2006); Michael Rosenberger, ed., *Geschenkt—umsonst gegeben? Gabe und Tausch in Ethik, Gesellschaft und Religion*, Linzer Philosophisch-Theologische Beiträge 14 (Frankfurt am Main and New York: Lang, 2006); Alain Caillé, *Anthropologie du don: Le tiers paradigm* (Paris: Desclée de Brouwer, 2000); Marcel Hénaff, *Der Preis der Wahrheit: Gabe, Geld und Philosophie* (Frankfurt am Main: Suhrkamp, 2009); Pierre Bourdieu, "Marginalia: Some Additional Notes on the Gift", in *The Logic of the Gift: Towards an Ethic of Generosity*, ed. A. D. Schrift (New York: Routledge, 1997), 231–44; Maurice Godelier, *Das Rätsel der Gabe: Geld, Geschenke, heilige Objekte* (Munich: Beck, 1999); Oswald Bayer, "Gabe", in *Die Religion in Geschichte und Gegenwart*, 4th ed. (Tübingen: Mohr, 2002), 3:445–46; Oswald Bayer, "Ethik der Gabe", in *Die Gabe: Ein "Unwort" der Theologie*, ed. V. Hoffmann (Frankfurt am Main: Otto Lembeck, 2009), 99–123; John Milbank, "Can a Gift be Given? Prolegomena to a Future Trinitarian Metaphysic", *Modern Theology* 11 (1995): 119–61; Josef Wohlmuth, "'... mein Leib, der für euch gegebene' (Lk 29,19): Eucharistie—Gabe des Todes Jesu jenseits der Ökonomie", in *Die Gabe: Ein "Unwort" der Theologie*, ed. V. Hoffmann (Frankfurt am Main: Otto Lembeck, 2009), 55–72; Christine Büchner, *Wie kann Gott in der Welt wirken? Überlegungen zu einer theologischen Hermeneutik des Sich-Gebens* (Freiburg: Herder, 2010); Ingolf U. Dalferth, "Alles umsonst: Zur Kunst des Schenkens und den Grenzen der Gabe", in *Von der Ursprünglichkeit der Gabe: Jean-Luc Marions Phänomenologie in der Diskussion*, ed. M. Gabel and H. Joas (Freiburg: Karl Alber, 2007), 159–91; Dalferth, *Umsonst: Eine Erinnerung an die kreative Passivität des Menschen* (Tübingen: Mohr Siebeck, 2011); Veronika Hoffmann, *Skizzen zu einer Theologie der Gabe: Rechtfertigung—Opfer—Eucharistie—Gottes- und Nächstenliebe* (Freiburg: Herder, 2013); Helmut Hoping, "Mehr als Brot und Wein: Zur Phänomenologie der Gabe", in *Glaube und Kultur: Begegnung zweier Welten?*, ed. T. Böhm (Freiburg: Herder, 2009), 187–202; Hoping, "Christus praesens: Die Gabe der Eucharistie und ihre Zeitlichkeit", in *Phänomenologie der Gabe: Neue Zugänge zum Mysterium der Eucharistie*, ed. F. Bruckmann, Quaestiones disputatae 270 (Freiburg: Herder, 2015), 197–218; Hoping, "Die Ökonomie des Opfers und die Gabe der Eucharistie", in *Die Bindung Isaaks: Stimme, Schrift, Bild*, ed. H. Hoping, J. Knop, and T. Böhm (Paderborn: Schöningh, 2009), 203–10.

initial ideas for the phenomenology of the gift came from Jacques Derrida (1930–2004) and Jean-Luc Marion.[28]

Derrida speaks about the *aporia of the gift*, which consists of the fact that the gift, for instance a present or an invitation, after an interval of time elicits a gift in return, so that we must ask whether beyond this "economy of the gift" a pure, non-economic gift can exist at all. For Derrida, the pure, non-economic gift is proclaimed in the economy of the gift as an impossible possibility, that is, as a paradox.[29] Derrida is not intent on disputing the pure gift; he wants to salvage it.[30] "I never concluded that there is no gift."[31] Derrida's idea of the pure gift takes its orientation from the disinterested praise of God and, besides that, from almsgiving in which "the left hand does not know what the right hand is doing" (cf. Mt 6:3) or from love of neighbor, which gives love without any expectation of love in return, even though it can elicit that, but also from forgiveness without the offender asking for it. Finally, the pure gift consists of giving one's life, or, as Derrida says, "giving one's death" (*donner la mort*).[32] Derrida wants to think about the possibility of the impossible, such as forgiveness, for which there is "no limitation", "no moderation, no *so far and no farther*."[33] Derrida calls this forgiveness unconditional forgiveness without sovereignty, as opposed to the governmental act of clemency. "It seems to me that one must begin with the fact that there are, indeed, unforgivable things. Is that not really the only thing that there is to forgive? The only thing that *calls* for forgiveness? If one were only willing to forgive what is forgivable, what the Church

---

[28] Cf. Jean-Luc Marion, "Esquisse d'un concept phénoménologique du don", in *Filosofia della rivelazione*, ed. M. Olivetti (Padua: CEDAM, 1994), 75–94; Marion, *Being Given: Toward a Phenomenology of Givenness*, trans. Jeffrey L. Kosky (Stanford, Calif., 2002); Marion, *Dieu sans l'être*, 3rd, rev. and expanded ed. (1982; Paris: Presses Universitaires de France, 2002).

[29] Cf. Jacques Derrida, *Donner le temps*, vol. 1, *La fausse monnaie* (Paris: Galilée, 1991).

[30] For a different view, see Dalferth, "Alles umsonst", 159f.; in his opinion, Derrida annihilates the phenomenon of the gift.

[31] Jacques Derrida, "On the Gift: A Discussion between Jacques Derrida and Jean-Luc Marion: Moderated by R. Kearney", in *God, the Gift, and Postmodernism*, ed. J. D. Caputo and M. J. Scanlon (Bloomington, Ind.: Indiana University Press, 1999), 59f.

[32] Cf. Jacques Derrida, "Den Tod geben" (1992), in *Gewalt und Gerechtigkeit: Derrida— Benjamin*, ed. A. Haverkamp (Frankfurt am Main: Suhrkamp, 1994), 331–445.

[33] Jacques Derrida, "Jahrhundert der Vergebung: Verzeihen ohne Macht—unbedingt und jenseits der Souveränität", *Lettre International*, Spring 2000: 17.

calls 'venial sin', then the idea of forgiveness would evaporate."[34] For Derrida, forgiveness worthy of the name would have to be able to forgive "the unforgivable ... unconditionally".[35]

Marion's *phenomenology of giving* aims at a pure "givenness" (*donation*) beyond intentional presence.[36] For Marion, pure givenness is experienced in phenomena that he calls saturated phenomena. Examples are, for instance, the effect of a painting, the body's pure affection for itself, or the experience of the other in the encounter with his countenance.[37] Pure givenness *par excellence* ("id quo nihil manifestius donari potest")[38] is for Marion the possible occurrence of a divine revelation.[39] Marion, too, points to dimensions of reality that go beyond the order of visible phenomena: there is more than what appears visibly. In the theological phenomenology that he produced in 1982, *Dieu sans l'être* (God without being), Marion made an attempt to think about God in radical otherness as gift of love (*agape*). *Dieu sans l'être* is the attempt to grasp our relation to God, not in terms of being, but in some other way.[40] In his later phenomenology of giving, too, in *Étant donné* (1997), Marion talks about the gift being given without presence (*présent sans présence*).[41] Here it should be noted that, according to Martin Heidegger, the history of metaphysics is a history of *présence* and, according to Jacques Derrida, the history of *présence* extends to Husserl's phenomenology of consciousness.

---

[34] Ibid., 11.

[35] Ibid., 12.

[36] Cf. Marion, *Being Given*, 79–81. The concept *donation* [in French] is not easy to translate. Thomas Alferi, "'... Die Unfasslichkeit der uns übersteigend-zuvorkommenden Liebe Gottes ...': Von Balthasar als Orientierung für Marion", in *Jean-Luc Marion: Studien zum Werk*, ed. Hanna Gerl-Falkowitz (Dresden: Verlag Text & Dialog, 2013), 103–25, prefers the German translation *Gebung* [giving], so as to avoid misunderstandings that might be connected with the word *Gegebenheit* [givenness] (in the sense of actuality or datum).

[37] Concerning the saturated phenomenon, see Jean-Luc Marion, *De surcroît: Études sur les phénomènes saturés* (Paris: Presses universitaires de France, 2001); Marion, *Le phénomène érotique* (Paris: Bernard Grasset, 2003). Dalferth, "Alles umsonst", 161f., and Dalferth, *Umsonst*, 95, accuses Jean-Luc Marion of understanding everything as gift. In doing so, he overlooks not only Marion's distinction between gift and giving but also his theory of the saturated phenomenon, which starts from the fact that the intensity of giving varies.

[38] "Something than which nothing can be given more manifestly." Cf. Marion, *Being Given*, 244.

[39] Cf. ibid., 242f., 246; Marion, *De surcroît*, 190–95.

[40] Cf. Marion, *Dieu sans l'être*.

[41] Cf. Marion, *Being Given*, 80.

Theology cannot adopt the philosophical discourse about the gift without a critical adaptation. Philosophical discourse about the gift can help us, however, to think about God, creation, and redemption as gift. Of course this is not possible without the acceptance of the presentness of the divine origin. The fundamental divine gift is the *creatio ex nihilo*, creation from nothing, from which the *creatio continua*, ongoing creation, is inseparable in a world of becoming. The gift of creation is the most original gift, the gift of existence. As gift, everything that exists is related to God. However, when the gift of creation reveals the Giver, it evokes a response, in the form of thanks or denial.[42]

When the Giver of all gifts makes himself a gift, the definitive revelation of God occurs. We believe that Jesus Christ is this definitive revelation and Gift of God. He is the "image", the "icon" of the invisible God (Col 1:15), the visibility of the Invisible One. Due to sin, which came between God and mankind, gift and forgiveness are correlated very closely in the revelation of God. The God of Jesus is the God of *unconditional* for-give-ness. If Jesus has associated God's forgiveness with *tᵉšûbāh* (conversion, repentance), like John the Baptist, he would scarcely have caused any offense by that. Yet Jesus claims to forgive sinners unreservedly by his own authority, although he exhorts them to stop sinning. Jesus' forgiveness of sins is consolidated in his dying for our sins.

Jesus laid down his life on the Cross; this is not a material gift but, rather, the hyperbolic, all-surpassing gift of unconditional forgiveness. The gift that is given to us in Jesus' death consists, not of the fact that Jesus is made an *Opfer* (*victima*/victim) by men, but rather of the utmost gift that God gives to us in his Son, in the *Opfer* (*sacrificium*/sacrifice) of his life beyond the violence.[43] Beyond this utmost gift, nothing greater can be given. In it God gave to the men who turned away from him all the love that he could give. The gift given by God, whether in creation, in Jesus' laying down his life, or in the justification of the sinner, breaks out of the exchange economy of *do ut des*

---

[42] Cf. Milbank, "Can a Gift be Given?", 135f.

[43] Cf. Josef Wohlmuth, "Opfer—Verdrängung und Wiederkehr eines schwierigen Begriffs", in *Das Opfer*, ed. A. Gerhards and K. Richter, Quaestiones disputatae 186 (Freiburg: Herder, 2000), 125.

[I give so that you might give]. God gives himself, and we receive without any merit.[44]

The gift motif defines the Eucharistic liturgy from the very beginning. In the new prayers accompanying the offering of bread and wine at the *Offertorium*, bread and wine are offered first as gifts of nature, as fruit of the earth, but also as fruit of human work. We must let God give us again and again what the priest offers at the Offertory, because bread and wine, like a good harvest, cannot be taken for granted. The invitation to prayer, *Orate fratres*, and the prayer over the oblations (*oratio super oblata*) make it clear that bread and wine are gifts that are offered to God. In the celebration of the Eucharist, they become, at a moment that escapes us, the Body and Blood of Christ. The *Offertorium* is the preparation and offering of the oblations, and not just the setting of the gifts on the altar. Yet our offering becomes God's gift to us.[45]

The Eucharistic Prayer that follows the Offertory makes this clear. The institutional narrative in the Eucharistic Prayer is not an ordinary narrative by which a past event is called to mind. The *verba testamenti* emphasized in the institutional narrative are more than a quotation. For they refer not only back to the situation of the Last Supper; in the pragmatic course of the Eucharistic Prayer, they identify the gifts of bread and wine placed upon the altar as the Body and Blood of Christ: "Hoc est enim Corpus meum, quod pro vobis tradetur." "Hic est enim calix Sanguinis mei ... qui pro vobis et pro multis effundetur." Through Christ's words and the Holy Spirit, bread and wine are transformed into the Body and Blood of Christ—for us as a gift.[46]

The *Offertorium* and the central Eucharistic action from the epiclesis over the gifts to the *Mysterium fidei* are defined by the gift motif, and this is the case, too, with the post-consecratory prayer of offering. It should be noted in this regard that Christ himself is the one who in the Eucharist celebrates the liturgy of the New Covenant in the

---

[44] Cf. on this subject, from the perspective of fundamental theology and ecumenism, Helmut Hoping, "Gottes Ebenbild: Theologische Anthropologie und säkulare Vernunft", *Theologische Quartalschrift* 15 (2005): 127–49.

[45] Cf. Thomas Ruster, *Wandlung: Ein Traktat über Eucharistie und Ökonomie* (Ostfildern: Matthias-Grünewald, 2006), 147.

[46] Cf. *CCC* 1333.

presence of the Father in the Holy Spirit and brings us into it with our offering-in-thanksgiving.[47] In the first place, the Eucharist is the liturgy of the Son among us men (cf. Heb 5:1). Christ himself is the one who leads us to the Father in our thanksgiving to God.[48] Christ offers us to him as a sacrifice as we offer ourselves to God in him. This occurs through a not merely passive but, rather, active participation in the offering of the priest, who acts in the person of Christ and who places before God's eyes the bread of life and the chalice of salvation in the name of the Church. To God is given what he gave us and what was "Eucharistized" by the Spirit's power and Christ's creative word.

> Christ is therefore not primarily a gift that we men should and could offer in the Eucharist to God, and certainly not to a wrathful God. The fact that God gave us his Son is instead already the work of his love. We give him back to God the Father in the Eucharist. God gives so that we can give. From the most ancient times this understanding of the sacrifice has been expressed in the Roman Canon, too, when it says: "De tuis donis ac datis"—"From the gifts you have given us."[49]

The Sacrifice of the Eucharist is not a sacrifice that competes with the unique sacrifice of Christ on the Cross. The offering of Christ's Body and Blood occurs in praise and thanks.[50] The Eucharist is an *oblatio* (offering, sacrifice) in the form of thanksgiving and memorial.

Therefore, the Church does not sacrifice Christ to the Father; rather, our *oblatio* presupposes God's gift to us. In our offering, God recognizes Christ, who reconciled us with him. The statement in the *Memores igitur* of Eucharistic Prayer III should be understood in this sense, too: "Respice, quaesumus, in oblationem Ecclesiae tuae et, agnoscens Hostiam, cuius voluisti immolatione placari, concede, ut qui Corpore et Sanguine Filii tui reficimur, Spiritu eius Sancto repleti,

---

[47] On the Trinitarian dimension of the Sacrifice of the Eucharist, cf. Robert J. Daly, *Sacrifice Unveiled: The True Meaning of Christian Sacrifice* (London and New York: T&T Clark, 2009), 228f. and passim.

[48] Cf. Stefan Oster, *Person und Transsubstantiation: Mensch-Sein, Kirche-Sein und Eucharistie— eine ontologische Zusammenschau* (Freiburg: Herder, 2010), 552–59.

[49] Koch, *Eucharistie*, 52.

[50] Cf. Lothar Lies, *Mysterium fidei: Annäherungen an das Geheimnis der Eucharistie* (Würzburg: Echter Verlag, 2005), 154.

unum corpus et unus spiritus inveniamur in Christo." The new English translation is quite faithful: "Look, we pray, upon the oblation of your Church and, recognizing the sacrificial Victim by whose death you willed to reconcile us to yourself, grant that we, who are nourished by the Body and Blood of your Son and filled with his Holy Spirit, may become one body, one spirit in Christ."[51]

"From below", the Eucharist is offered by the priest together with the faithful; viewed "from above", Christ is the one who makes himself food for us by transforming the gifts of bread and wine into his Body and Blood through the power of the Spirit.[52] The purpose of the Son's liturgy among us is to make our own bodily existence a living sacrifice (Rom 12:1), united with the Son's sacrifice in laying down his life. Thus, in the Eucharist, earthly time meshes with Christ's time and his all-encompassing presence.[53] Like no other celebration, the Eucharist is the liturgy of the open heaven, in which we participate by having a foretaste of the heavenly liturgy.[54] The ritual form of the Eucharist as it has developed historically must correspond to its theological content as *offering-in-thanksgiving*. The Eucharist must not be reduced to its meal character, especially since the Eucharistic meal is different from a usual common meal. The Eucharistic meal is a *sacred meal*, in which bread and wine are offered and consecrated and we receive the Body and Blood of Christ. This is expressed strikingly in the expression "Paschal meal" (*convivium paschale*).[55] The oft-repeated antiphon "O sacrum convivium" poetically consolidates the three temporal aspects of the sacrament of the Eucharist: "O holy banquet, in which Christ is received: the memory of his Passion is renewed, the mind is filled with grace and a pledge of future glory is given to us! Alleluia."[56]

---

[51] The first part is translated ambiguously in the German Missal. Cf. *MB* 496: "Schau gütig auf die Gabe deiner Kirche. Denn sie [die Kirche?] stellt dir das Lamm vor Augen, das geopfert wurde und uns nach deinem Willen mit dir versöhnt hat" (Look graciously on the gift of your Church. For it [the Church?] places before your eyes the Lamb that was sacrificed and reconciled us with you according to your will).

[52] Cf. Ruster, *Wandlung*, 147–50.

[53] Cf. Ratzinger, *The Spirit of the Liturgy*, in *JRCW* 11:33 [57].

[54] Cf. *SC* 22.

[55] Cf. *SC* 47.

[56] "O sacrum convivium, in quo Christus sumitur: recolitur memoria passionis eius, mens impletur gratia et futurae gloriae nobis pignus datur. Alleluia."

B. Gift of Presence and Communion

To what category of phenomenality does the sacrament of the Eucharist belong?[57] Neither metaphysics nor phenomenology can make the *Mysterium* of the Eucharist completely comprehensible. The phenomenology of the gift, however, allows us to grasp the Eucharist better as the sacrament of presence. The Sunday Eucharist is celebrated in the assembly of the faithful. Its prerequisite is the presence of the glorified Lord, who gave his life for us. Like any liturgical celebration, the Eucharist, too, is marked by the tension between *presence* and *absence*:

> The Eucharist is a particular form of Christ's presence in the mind, a presence that permanently carries within it as its basis his farewell before his death and testifies to it and, consequently, to his "going away". Thus the Eucharistic presence of Jesus is permanently situated in the tension between Jesus' presence and absence, and thus its place can only be the history of the Church on her pilgrim way until the definitive revelation of God's dominion.[58]

Christ's presence among us can be understood only from the perspective of his bodily Resurrection. This is true *a fortiori* of the presence of Christ with his Body and Blood in the gifts of bread and wine. The intrinsic connection between Easter and Eucharist is manifested in the New Testament in the accounts of the meal of the risen Lord with his disciples (Lk 24:13–35; Jn 21). The bodily Resurrection of Jesus and his Ascension signify for his disciples a new form of presence. Jesus is no longer "in the flesh", that is, in his earthly-bodily presence, close to the disciples. His new form of presence is a "believed bodily presence with visible absence".[59] It is the presence of a "pure gift" that is not visible but nevertheless is no less real than physical presence. Thus the disciples who are on their

---

[57] This question is posed explicitly by Jean-Luc Marion, "Die Phänomenalität des Sakraments: Wesen und Gegebenheit", in *Von der Ursprünglichkeit der Gabe*, ed. M. Gabel and H. Joas (Munich: Karl Alber, 2007), 78–95.

[58] Alexander Gerken, *Theologie der Eucharistie* (Munich: Kösel-Verlag, 1973), 30.

[59] Jean-Luc Marion, "Verklärte Gegenwart", in *Credo: Ein theologisches Lesebuch*, ed. J. Ratzinger and P. Henrici (Cologne: Communio, 1992), 182.

way to Emmaus first recognize Jesus in the stranger when he breaks bread with them and at the same moment withdraws from their sight (Lk 24:30f.). The transitory, temporally limited presence of Jesus among his disciples has consolidated with his Resurrection and Ascension into a gift of "definitive presence"[60] that is given to us in bread and wine.[61]

Pope Leo the Great writes about the present absence of the glorified Lord that the Son of Man was revealed as God's Son "when he withdrew into the glory of his Father's majesty and in an ineffable way began to be more present in his divinity, while in his humanity he became more distant.... 'When I ascend to my Father, you will touch me more perfectly and more truly.' "[62] With Christ's Ascension, the new form of his being-present has become definitive. Without Christ's going-away, which is connected with his Resurrection and Ascension, there would be neither the presence of the Holy Spirit among us nor the Eucharist *with and in* the presence of the glorified Lord. The distance between the glorified Lord and his Church leads to a new form of presence: "I go away (ὑπάγο), and I will come to you (ἔρχομαι πρὸς ὑμᾶς)", Jesus says to his disciples when he promises them the Holy Spirit (Jn 14:28). "By dint of the Ascension, Christ is not the one absent from the world but, rather, the one present in it in a new way."[63] With his Ascension, Christ does not cease to be present; his presence is perfected in the glory of God. From there Christ's presence becomes for all who are united with him a pure and universal gift in the sacrament of the Eucharist.

[60] Ibid., 181, 189.

[61] Cf. also Marion, *Dieu sans l'être*, 197–220. For a more detailed discussion of Marion's Eucharistic hermeneutics, see Hoping, "Christus praesens". It is surprising that Veronika Hoffmann, in her dissertation entitled "Sketches for a Theology of the Gift" (2013), reconstructs Jean-Luc Marion's phenomenology of giving (French: *donation*) while completely overlooking his Eucharistic hermeneutics (cf. Hoffmann, *Skizzen zu einer Theologie der Gabe*, 91–104), especially since Hoffmann's purpose is to produce sketches for a theology of the gift and the Eucharist assumes a central place therein as gift.

[62] Leo the Great, *Sermo LXXIV*, 4 (*PL* 54:398C–399A): "cum in paternae maiestatis gloriam se recepit et ineffabili modo coepit esse Divinitate praesentior, qui factus est humanitate longinquior.... Cum ad Patrem ascendero, tunc me perfectius veriusque palpabis."

[63] Ratzinger, "Himmelfahrt Christi", in *JRGS* 6/2 (2013), 856. This is an article by Ratzinger on Christ's Ascension in the *Lexikon für Theologie und Kirche*, 2nd ed. (1960), to which Marion refers in *Verklärte Gegenwart*, 186.

"Christ is neither present in his visible flesh, nor is he someone absent whose presence is commemorated in spirit and remembrance, since his Eucharistic Body is offered to us daily."[64] Christ's sacramental presence is founded on his going away. If Jesus were still physically present, he could not be present to all men of all times and places in the sacrament of the Eucharist.[65]

Christ's presence under the appearances of bread and wine is designated in theology as "somatic Real Presence". In this expression, "somatic" does not refer to a physical presence but, rather, to the sacramental presence of Christ with his glorified Body under the appearance of bread and wine. Whereas earlier the somatic Real Presence was thought of in substantial, ontological terms, today it is understood more as his personal presence.[66] Empirical research in the natural sciences has led to a change of the concept of substance, which was understood less and less as an ontological concept and, instead, as a term for the material reality of what is elementary. Physically and chemically, however, nothing happens to the gifts of bread and wine through their transubstantiation.[67] Yet even if no change perceptible to the senses occurs at the Consecration of the gifts of bread and wine, that does not mean that nothing at all happens; unless one subscribes to the reductionist assumption that all reality is nature in the sense of material conditions. Such naturalism, however, no longer leaves "room" for the reality of God, his revelation, and his presence among us.

In the 1950s, various new interpretations of the doctrine of Christ's somatic Real Presence in the Eucharist were proposed in view of the changed concept of substance. Central to these attempts were the terms *transignification* and *transfinalization*. In order to obviate the misunderstandings that the term *transubstantiation* often causes,

---

[64] Marion, *Verklärte Gegenwart*, 188.

[65] Cf. Gerken, *Theologie der Eucharistie*, 178f.

[66] Cf. Louis-Marie Chauvet, *Symbol und Sakrament: Eine sakramentale Relecture der christlichen Existenz*, German trans. Thomas Fries, Theologie der Liturgie 8 (Regensburg: Pustet, 2015), who seeks to conceptualize a personal presence "post-metaphysically", that is, while overcoming onto-theology, starting from the concept of the symbol, especially of the body.

[67] Cf. Josef Wohlmuth, "Eucharistie als liturgische Feier der Gegenwart Christi: Realpräsenz und Transsubstantiation im Verständnis katholischer Theologie", in *Eucharistie: Positionen katholischer Theologie*, ed. T. Söding (Regensburg: Pustet, 2002), 103.

Piet Schoonenberg (1911–1999)[68] and Edward Schillebeeckx (1914–2009)[69] suggested talking about the Eucharistic transformation as a transignification (change of designation or of dedication) or as transfinalization (change of purpose).[70] In the celebration of the Eucharist, the species of bread and wine are consecrated by the Eucharistic Prayer and thus gain a new meaning (*significatio*) or a new end (*finis*). Bread and wine are no longer mere food, but signs of Christ's Body and Blood. Schoonenberg developed his new interpretation in the context of a phenomenology of the sign. He distinguished between a merely informative sign (for example, a road sign) and an actualizing sign in which a person expresses himself. Thus a present can symbolize the love of one person for another. The present is a sign that not only points to the love but also expresses that love in itself. In Schoonenberg's view, sacraments are among the actualizing signs but are actualizing signs *sui generis*.

One objection to the theory of transignification and transfinalization was that the Eucharistic presence of Christ in bread and wine is not only a human *revaluation* of a thing into a symbol. Then, too, the concept of meaning and the concept of being are not simply identical. Rather, meaning presupposes being. The limitation of talk about transignification or transfinalization is that Christ's presence in the gifts of bread and wine, according to Church teaching, does not occur through human intentionality. The concept of transubstantiation implies an *ontological* assertion: bread and wine are transformed according to their being. Concepts like transignification or transfinalization, in contrast, remain on the level of intentionality.[71] This was the reason why Pope Paul VI in his encyclical *Mysterium*

---

[68] Cf. Piet Schoonenberg, "De tegenwoordigheid van Christus", *Verbum* 26 (1959): 148–57, Schoonenberg, "Tegenwoordigheid", *Verbum* 31 (1964): 395–415; Schoonenberg, "Inwieweit ist die Lehre von der Transsubstantiation historisch bestimmt?" *Con(D)* 3 (1967): 305–11.

[69] Cf. Edward Schillebeeckx, *Die eucharistische Gegenwart: Zur Diskussion über die Realpräsenz* (Düsseldorf: Patmos, 1967), 71f.

[70] See *A New Catechism: Catholic Faith for Adults*, the English edition of the Dutch Catechism, trans. Kevin Smyth (New York: Herder and Herder, 1970), 343, 345.

[71] Cf. Hans Jorissen, "Die Diskussion um die eucharistische Realpräsenz und die Transsubstantiation in der neueren Theologie", in *Beiträge zur Diskussion um das Eucharistieverständnis: Referate und Vorträge im Rahmen des Arbeitskreises "Eucharistie" im Collegium Albertinum* (Bonn: Collegium Albertinum, 1970), 46f.

fidei (September 3, 1965)[72] magisterially took up a position on the
debate about Christ's presence in the Eucharist. Although the terms
transignification and *transfinalization* were not rejected, it was determined that they alone do not suffice to explain the Eucharistic
transformation adequately and must be supplemented by the term
transubstantiation, whereby the concept of substance presupposed is
ontological and not from the natural sciences.

Recent theological essays about Christ's presence in the Eucharist
strive to attain a more intensely dynamic-personal understanding of
the Eucharistic presence of Christ and thus to free the concept of *transubstantiation* from the increasingly constricted perspective imposed
on it by the rise of empirical research into the natural sciences. Thus
Alexander Gerken[73] and the Lutheran theologian Notger Slenczka[74]
have argued for a *personal*, which means a *relational, ontology* in the
hermeneutical analysis of Christ's bodily presence in the Eucharist.
Bernhard Welte (1908–1983) had already suggested understanding
Christ's presence in the gifts of bread and wine on the basis of a
relational ontology. Yet Welte's analysis ultimately remains on the
level of meaning.[75] Bread and wine, however, do not only *signify*,
but truly *are* Christ's Body and Blood. Viewed phenomenologically,
a relational ontology of the Eucharist presupposes that all that exists

---

[72] Cf. DH 4410–13.

[73] Cf. Alexander Gerken, "Dogmengeschichtliche Reflexionen über die heutige Wende
in der Eucharistielehre", *Zeitschrift für katholische Theologie* 94 (1972): 199–226; Gerken, *Theologie der Eucharistie*, 199–228; Gerken, "Kann sich die Eucharistielehre ändern?" *Zeitschrift für
katholische Theologie* 97 (1975): 415–29.

[74] Cf. Notger Slenczka, *Realpräsenz und Ontologie: Untersuchung der ontologischen Grundlagen
der Transsignifikationslehre*, Forschungen zur systematischen und ökumenischen Theologie 66
(Göttingen: Vandenhoeck & Ruprecht, 1993), 542–82.

[75] Cf. Bernhard Welte, "Diskussionsbeiträge", in *Aktuelle Fragen der Eucharistie*, ed. M.
Schmaus (Munich: Max Hueber Verlag, 1960), 184–90. Here we find also a limitation of the
analysis by Georg Hintzen, who understands the idea of Eucharistic Real Presence entirely
in terms of the concept of meaning. Cf. Georg Hintzen, "Transsignifikation und Transfinalisation: Überlegungen zur Eignung dieser Begriffe für das ökumenische Gespräch", *Catholica*
39 (1985): 193–216; Hintzen, "Gedanken zu einem personalen Verständnis der eucharistischen Realpräsenz", *Catholica* 39 (1985): 279–310. Cf. the critique by Slenczka, *Realpräsenz
und Ontologie*, 205–27, as well as the response by Georg Hintzen, "Personale und sakramentale Gegenwart des Herrn in der Eucharistie: Zu Notker Slenczkas Buch 'Realpräsenz und
Ontologie'", *Catholica* 47 (1993): 210–37, and the further response by Notger Slenczka, "Zur
ökumenischen Bedeutung der Transsignifikationslehre: Eine Antwort an Georg Hintzen",
Catholica 48 (1994): 62–76.

is "given". The decisive thing is that in the case of Christ's presence in the signs of bread and wine, we are talking about a real and, in this sense, substantial presence. "As a result of transubstantiation, the species of bread and wine undoubtedly take on a new signification and a new finality, for they are no longer ordinary bread and wine but instead a sign of something sacred and a sign of spiritual food; but they take on this new signification, this new finality, precisely because they contain a new 'reality' that we can rightly call *ontological*."[76] When the priest pronounces the *verba testamenti*, a transignification does in fact occur. In the "human transignification", however, a "divinely caused transubstantiation" takes place.[77] This is not merely a "change of the function" (*Umfunktionierung*) of bread and wine but, rather, a "change of their substance" (*Umsubstanzierung*).[78]

Joseph Ratzinger explains the doctrine of transubstantiation on the basis of the concept of created substantiality. He distinguishes between general created substantiality and the substantiality of a personal created being. The general created substantiality of being consists of "the fact that, while it is 'being from elsewhere', it is nevertheless 'being in its own right'; as something created, it is not God but, rather, is posited in the autonomy of an independent, non-divine being that exists for itself."[79] The substantiality of a person is the spiritual self of a human being expressing itself corporeally. Bread and wine, in their being and essence as food, are transformed and thus become signs of Christ's Body and Blood. With the Eucharistic transformation, they lose, so to speak, their creaturely independence, they cease to exist simply in themselves and "become *pure* signs of his presence".[80] The sacramental word causes the created gifts "to be changed from autonomously existing things into mere signs that have lost their creaturely peculiarity and exist no longer for themselves but only for him, through him, in him. Thus they are now in their *essence*, in their being, *signs*, as they were previously in their essence *things*."[81] "The

---

[76] DH 4413.

[77] Lies, *Mysterium fidei*, 129.

[78] Koch, *Eucharistie*, 56.

[79] Ratzinger, "The Problem of Transubstantiation and the Question about the Meaning of the Eucharist", in *JRCW* 11:236.

[80] Ibid., 237.

[81] Ibid.

potential that in principle lies hidden in all creatures—the fact that they can and should be signs of His Presence—becomes here through the sacramental word a reality in the highest degree."[82] What is present is Christ's "love, which has endured the Cross, the love in which he grants to us his very self (the 'substance' of his self): his Thou, bearing the marks of his death and Resurrection, given to us as a salvific reality."[83]

Christ, therefore, is present in bread and wine with or in his glorified corporeality according to his essential selfhood.[84] Here there is an analogy to the Incarnation event. Johannes Betz (1914–1984) writes on this subject:

> In his Incarnation, the Logos seizes a human nature and makes it so intimately his own that it does not exist in its natural personal autonomy but, rather, has the ground of its subsistence in the Logos, is held by it in a hypostatic relation and unity, and becomes its sacrament, its way of appearing. Now the Eucharist presents a salvation-history remembrance and analogy. In it, the Logos seizes, in remembrance of his humanity, the oblations offered and made over to God and accepts them, too, as his own so intimately that they cease to be autonomous created things and become his sacrament, the anamnetic way in which his Body and Blood appear; indeed, they even become substantially his Body and Blood.... For the fact that the Logos accepts the gifts and makes them his own, translated into ontological terms, means that they lose their autonomy, have their ground in him, indeed, substantially become his Body and Blood.[85]

The transformation of bread and wine can be understood better in terms of *being-as-gift*, of which relation is an inseparable part. In terms of creation theology, the being of an existing thing is to be defined as *gift*. Bread and wine, fruits of human work, are God's gifts to us, and they become the Body and Blood of his Son, gifts of Christ's presence for us. Christ's presence should consequently be thought of

---

[82] Ibid.

[83] Ibid., 238.

[84] Cf. Koch, *Eucharistie*, 58.

[85] Johannes Betz, "Eucharistie als zentrales Mysterium", in *Mysterium Salutis: Grundriß heilsgeschichtlicher Dogmatic*, ed. J. Feiner and M. Löhrer, 4/2 (Einsiedeln: Benziger, 1973), 308f.

as personal, not as a thing. The grace that is given to us in the sacrament of the Eucharist is Christ as he laid down his life for us. Christ is not present in the Eucharistic gifts as a natural thing but, rather, "in a personal way and in relation to persons".[86] Yet how can Christ be present in the sacrament of the Eucharist without being reduced to the sensible presence of the Eucharistic elements? How can we receive Christ as gift?[87] Can we receive Christ, as Jean-Luc Marion thinks, "beyond being"[88] as a gift of love? This is not possible without some form of presence. Marion's concept of revelation, whereby in revelation "an authority that transcends experience is nevertheless manifested in a way that can be experienced",[89] demands a *temporal* presence. Unless the risen crucified Lord becomes Lord within the horizon of time, we could not receive him, since we exist temporally.[90] The sacramental memorial that is accomplished in the celebration of the Eucharist is to be understood phenomenologically in a more radical sense as "intentional" thinking. It is not only *retentional*— in the sense of a Christ remembered again by us. The sacramental memorial includes the self-presence of Christ, the presence of his gift.[91] And the gift of the Eucharist cannot be given unless it is present to the one who receives it. In other words: the reception of Christ's Body presupposes our corporeality.

Through Christ's donational presence, the celebration of the Lord's Supper leads to a eucharistically filled time in which past, present, and future are combined into one. The Eucharist is *signum rememorativum* (past), *signum demonstrativum* (present), and *signum*

---

[86] Koch, *Eucharistie*, 57. Cf. the more detailed discussion by Oster, *Person und Transsubstantiation*, 575–647.

[87] Cf. Milbank, "Can a Gift be Given?"; Milbank, *The Word Made Strange: Theology, Language, Culture* (Cambridge, Mass.: Blackwell, 1997), 36–52; Milbank, *Being Reconciled: Ontology and Pardon* (London: Routledge, 2003).

[88] Marion, *Dieu sans l'être*, 223ff.

[89] Jean-Luc Marion, "Aspekte der Religionsphänomenologie: Grund, Horizont und Offenbarung", in *Von der Ursprünglichkeit der Gabe*, ed. M. Gabel and H. Joas (Munich: Karl Alber, 2007), 16.

[90] Cf. the critique by Rolf Kühn, *Gabe als Leib in Christentum und Phänomenologie* (Würzburg: Echter Verlag, 2004), 88, of Jean-Luc Marion, who does correctly reject a spatial fixation of Christ's Eucharistic Real Presence but understands transubstantiation in the sense of a persistent "distance" [*écart*] of Christ's Body [cf. *Dieu sans l'être*] but in this way does not do justice to the donational presence of Christ in the Eucharistic gifts.

[91] Kühn, *Gabe als Leib*, 82f.

prognosticum (future). An exclusively dia-chronic understanding of time that is oriented toward inter-ruption and ec-stasy does not do justice to the donational presence of the Eucharist. To the "aesthetic of absence", as it is sometimes invoked in "postmodern" philosophy, George Steiner contrasted an "aesthetic of presence". In his book *Real Presences* (1989), Steiner opposes the postmodern break "between word and world",[92] the sign that stands for absence,[93] and contrasts it with the experience of "real presence" that human beings have in aesthetic creations like literature, the plastic and graphic arts, and music. Steiner speaks in this connection about "substantiation", whereby the semantics of the word, as it exists with the doctrine of the Eucharistic transformation, should be noted. In Steiner's view, form bearing the stamp of creativity ultimately cannot be understood without the acceptance of some presence of God. The experience of form that bears the stamp of creativity is the "commerce of [two] freedoms",[94] and right there in the extraordinary form of the true work of art it brings about an experience of transcendence. In "The Rebellion against the Secondary World: Remarks toward an Aesthetic of Presence", his afterword to the German edition of Steiner's book, *Von realer Gegenwart*, Botho Strauss designated "transubstantiation" as a model of an "aesthetic of presence" and referred to important figures among the creative persons, thinkers, writers, and artists of our day who profess and practice faith in the Real Presence and have protested against the secondary world. For Strauss, what is at stake is no less than the recuperation of what is primary: the experience of real presence.[95]

Of course, the presence of the Eucharistic gift is different from the presence of the things and elements surrounding us; it has the character of an event and at the same time of a gift. This donational presence cannot be explained semiotically by another use of bread and wine, and thus transignificantly or transfinally by the change of the meanings of their properties. For the donational presence of Christ

---

[92] George Steiner, *Real Presences* (Chicago: University of Chicago Press, 1989), 93.

[93] Cf. ibid., 121–22.

[94] Ibid., 186. "the ontological encounter between freedoms".

[95] Cf. Botho Strauss, "Der Aufstand gegen die sekundäre Welt: Bemerkungen zu einer Ästhetik der Anwesenheit", in Georg Steiner, *Von realer Gegenwart: Hat unsere Sprechen Inhalt?* (Munich and Vienna: Hanser, 1990), 307f.

would then be bound to the consciousness of the faithful.[96] Christ's Real Presence in the signs (*species*) of bread and wine, however, does not depend on our idea. Hence, a "substantiated" presence is indispensable.[97] The dialectic of nearness and distance, of presence and absence, which is decisive for our communion with the risen Lord, is not abolished by his Real Presence in bread and wine. At the Consecration of the gifts of bread and wine, there comes a moment in which something happens that we cannot bring about by ourselves, namely, the "reduction of what is empirically given to the miracle of the One who gives himself in all freedom"[98]—so says Josef Wohlmuth in a beautiful and at the same time precise formulation about the gift of the Eucharist. The Eucharist is the pure gift of God, which gives the Eucharistic definition "Me for you"[99] to the Tetragrammaton, the Name of God revealed to Moses. Or, in the words of the "*Doctor eucharistiae*": "It is not a man who makes the sacrificial gifts become the Body and Blood of Christ, but He that was crucified for us, Christ Himself. The priest stands there carrying out the action, but the power and the grace is of God. 'This is My Body,' he says. This statement transforms the gifts."[100]

The *verba testamenti* are a twofold speech act: an identifying speech act (This *is* my body ...)[101] and a performative speech act, namely, the giving of the gift (*given* for you ...) unto death (*donner la mort*). In the Eucharist, we receive the *body of Christ that was given over to death*

---

[96] Cf. Kühn, *Gabe als Leib*, 84.

[97] Wohlmuth, "Eucharistie als liturgische Feier der Gegenwart Christi", 108–11, speaks for this reason in favor of adhering to the concept of "transubstantiation"; on the other hand, Thomas Pröpper, "Zur vielfältigen Rede von der Gegenwart Gottes und Jesu Christi", in *Evangelium und freie Vernunft* (Freiburg: Herder, 2001), 245–65, would like to do away with the conceptual model of transubstantiation.

[98] Josef Wohlmuth, "Vom Tausch zur Gabe: Die theologische Bedeutung des neueren Gabendiskurses", in *An der Schwelle zum Heiligtum: Christliche Theologie im Gespräch mit jüdischem Denken* (Paderborn: Schöningh, 2007), 221.

[99] Ibid.

[100] John Chrysostom, *De proditione Iudae homiliae* 1.6 (PG 49:380), in *The Faith of the Early Fathers*, trans. W. A. Jurgens, vol. 2 (Collegeville, Minn.: Liturgical Press, 1979), 105: "Non enim homo est, qui facit ut proposita efficiantur corpus et sanguis Christi, sed ipse Christus qui pro nobis crucifixus est. Figuram implens stat sacerdos verba illa proferens: virtus autem et gratia Dei est. *Hoc est corpus meum*, inquit. Hoc verbum transformat ea, quae proposita sunt."

[101] Alexander Saberschinsky, *Einführung in die Feier der Eucharistie: historisch—systematisch—praktisch* (Freiburg: Herder, 2009), 151, questions whether the *verba testamenti* have an indicative function.

for us (Lk 22:19), in which we participate most profoundly when we ourselves become a gift in our death.[102] The words of the *verba testamenti* pronounced by the priest *in persona Christi* are at the same time *indicative words* and *donational words*.[103] For the ordained priest, but also for the community of the faithful, the indicative and donational words of the *verba testamenti* make an immense demand. The priest, who performs the central speech act from the epiclesis over the gifts to the *verba testamenti*, does not simply represent the absent Lord, nor is he an *alter Christus*, but, rather, as an "icon" of Christ, correctly understood, he shows that the divine gift of the Eucharist radically surpasses all human gifts and authority.[104] By himself the priest could not perform the sacred action for which he is ordained. Therefore, he invokes the Holy Spirit on the gifts of bread and wine.[105] In the bread of life and in the chalice of salvation, Christ gives himself to us as food, "transcending the very fullness of generosity, exceeding every form of love.... O singular and wondrous liberality, where the giver becomes the gift and what is given is entirely the same as the giver!" So writes Pope Urban IV in his hymn to the Eucharist.[106] Of all the sacraments, the sacrament of the Eucharist is *the* sacrament of love (*maxime sacramentum caritatis*).[107] The Eucharist, however, is a sacrament not only of life, but also of death, for it cost a death. The reality of the Eucharist would be missed if one tried to conceive of it solely as a "ritual exchange of gifts"[108] in the sense of a circulation of life in which all share.

The offering of the Eucharist is aimed at intimate union with Christ. The purpose of Christ's presence in the gifts of bread and wine

---

[102] Cf. Josef Wohlmuth, "Impulse für eine künftige Theologie der Gabe bei Jean-Luc Marion", in *Von der Ursprünglichkeit der Gabe*, ed. M. Gabel and H. Joas (Freiburg: Karl Alber, 2007), 270.

[103] Cf. Wohlmuth, "Vom Tausch zur Gabe", 222.

[104] Cf. Winfried Haunerland, "Das eine Herrenmahl und die vielen Eucharistiegebete: Traditionen und Texte als theologische und spirituelle Impulse", in *Mehr als Brot und Wein: Theologische Kontexte der Eucharistie*, ed. W. Haunerland (Würzburg: Echter Verlag, 2005), 129.

[105] This is not an argument against interpreting the *verba testamenti* as a performative speech act. Daly, *Sacrifice unveiled*, 16f., disagrees.

[106] Urban IV, bull *Transiturus de hoc mundo* (August 1, 1264): DH 847.

[107] Cf. Thomas Aquinas, *Summa theologiae* III, q. 80, art. 3 (objection 2).

[108] Thus Andrea Bieler and Luise Schottroff, *Das Abendmahl: Essen, um zu leben* (Gütersloh: Gütersloher Verlagshaus, 2007), 134–39.

is the reception of the Eucharist.[109] Yet the celebration of the Eucharist breaks out of the economy of the gift. Someone who receives Christ's Body and Blood receives without the possibility of making any gift in return.[110] The gift of the Eucharist (1 Cor 11:24) abolishes all *do ut des*. Like the justification of the godless (Rom 4:5), the gift of the Eucharist, too, can be received only in passive acceptance.[111] The gift of the Eucharist, insofar as it thwarts the economy of the gift, stands in a critical relation to the acquisition of social energy through sacrifice and transaction.[112] The Eucharist aims at the transformation of the person who receives the gift of the Eucharist in faith. The only possible response on the part of the recipient is gratitude, the Amen of agreement, and the practice of self-giving corresponding to the gift received. The Eucharist, therefore, can be celebrated appropriately only in the pragmatic framework of the Eucharist itself, that of offering-in-thanksgiving.

The reception of Holy Communion is possible only in prayer and adoration. Prayer by its very nature is attention to God. This can consist in waiting for God or in meditation on the Word of God, in quiet prayer, in silent adoration, or in vocal prayer, whether a set prayer or an entirely personal one.[113] In the work of the political mystic Simone Weil (1909–1943), attention (*attente*) plays a major role.[114] "Attention consists of suspending our thought, leaving it detached, empty, and ready to be penetrated by the object",[115] which means that "our thought should be empty, waiting, not seeking anything, but ready to receive in its naked truth the object that is to penetrate

---

[109] Cf. Betz, "Eucharistie als zentrales Mysterium", 311.

[110] Cf. Wohlmuth, "Vom Tausch zur Gabe", 221f.

[111] Bayer, "Gabe", 446, pointed out this connection. Dalferth, *Umsonst*, 231, speaks about "creative passivity".

[112] Cf. Alex Stock, "Gabenbereitung: Zur Logik des Opfers", *Liturgisches Jahrbuch* 53 (2003): 51.

[113] On a phenomenology of prayer, see Bernhard Casper, *Das Ereignis des Betens: Grundlinien einer Hermeneutik des religiösen Geschehens*, Phänomenologie 1, Texte 3 (Freiburg: Alber, 1998). In this book, esp. pages 20–34, the author pointed out the importance of "attention" in a phenomenology of prayer.

[114] On Weil's significance for theology, see Imelda Abbt and Wolfgang W. Müller, eds., *Simone Weil: Ein Leben gibt zu denken* (St. Ottilien: EOS-Verlag Erzabtei, 1999); Wolfgang W. Müller, *Simone Weil: Theologische Splitter* (Zurich: Theologischer Verlag Zürich, 2009).

[115] Simone Weil, *Waiting for God*, trans. Emma Craufurd (New York: G. P. Putnam's Sons, 1951; Perennial Library, 1971), 111.

it."[116] The Eucharist aims at attention in receptivity: "Whoever for an instant bears up against the void, either he receives the supernatural bread, or else he falls."[117] Without this readiness to receive, the corporeal love of Christ that is given to us in the sacrament of the Eucharist cannot enter into us. To receive the consecrated Host thoughtlessly or routinely would not do justice to the extraordinary significance of the gift of the Eucharist. What we need today is a new Eucharistic culture of receiving.

The sacrament of the Eucharist, however, is not only the sacrament of the *gift* (*Gabe*). From the extraordinary gift that we receive, Simone Weil says, springs the *assignment* (*Aufgabe*) to see in every human being—however disfigured and humiliated he may be, like the Man (*Ecce homo*) who gave his life for us—the humanity that constitutes his dignity.[118] We should love our neighbor for his own sake, as God has loved us—kenotically and, as it were, selflessly. Thus, "there are times when thinking of God separates us from him."[119] Weil illustrates this in the eschatological scene of the Last Judgment in Matthew 25: "In a sense, the fact that a certain beggar is hungry is far more important than if Christ himself were hungry—Christ, that is to say, considered as man. But the Word which became incarnate is hungry that this beggar should be fed, if it is possible to conceive a divine equivalent to desire."[120]

C. Gift of Transformation and Eternal Life

It is no accident that a meal became Eucharist, thanksgiving. This is connected with the natural symbolism of a meal. Nowhere does it become so clear and obvious that men are recipients than at a common meal. Eating has a natural sign character as meal fellowship, which goes beyond the mere process of assimilating food. Even with ordinary food, we assimilate God's love, insofar as we receive it as a

---

[116] Ibid., 112.

[117] Simone Weil, *The Notebooks of Simone Weil*, trans. Arthur Wills, 2 vols. (1956; London and Henley: Routledge & Kegan Paul, 1976), 1:156.

[118] Weil, *Waiting for God*, 148–49.

[119] Ibid., 151.

[120] Weil, *Notebooks*, 1:323.

gift. In this sense, we can say with Simone Weil: "If the gift is rightly given and rightly received, the passing of a morsel of bread from one man to another is something like a real communion."[121] In the Eucharist, we receive God's love, which gave itself to the utmost, even to death on the Cross, and which gives itself as a love that can be touched only in the supernatural love of the theological virtue of charity. "That which is natural is simply that which in fact has been placed within our reach; but all the different parts of human life are as densely packed with mystery, absurdity, inconceivability as is, for example, the Eucharist, and are equally impossible to contact in the real sense otherwise than through the faculty of supernatural love."[122] "It is not surprising that a man who has bread should give a piece to someone who is starving. What is surprising is that he should be capable of doing so with so different a gesture from that with which we buy an object. Almsgiving when it is not supernatural is like a sort of purchase. It buys the sufferer."[123]

Ordinary foods and drinks nourish when we consume them. Yet however much we eat, our life unceasingly is wasting away. The Eucharistic food is given so that we may be transformed and no longer be hungry.[124] Augustine describes this with the famous words of his *Confessions*: "And you shall not change Me [Christ] into yourself as bodily food, but into Me you shall be changed."[125] The idea is found also in the *Liber de sacramento eucharistiae* by Albert the Great:

> Bodily food receives from our body its power to nourish and also from the alimentary [*cibativa*] and nutritive soul, which changes the food and converts it into a likeness of the nourished body. And because

[121] Weil, *Waiting for God*, 139.

[122] Weil, *Notebooks*, 1:300.

[123] Weil, *Waiting for God*, 147.

[124] Cf. Benedict XVI, Address to the Plenary Assembly of the Congregation for the Doctrine of the Faith (March 13, 2009): in the Eucharist we experience the "fundamental transformation of violence into love, of death into life, [which] brings other changes in its wake. Bread and wine become his Body and Blood. But it must not stop there; on the contrary, the process of transformation must now gather momentum. The Body and Blood of Christ are given to us so that we ourselves will be transformed in our turn."

[125] Augustine, *Confessiones* 7.10 (CCSL 27:104): "Nec tu me in te mutabis sicut cibum carnis tuae, sed tu mutaberis in me." Translated by F.J. Sheed, 2d ed. (Indianapolis and Cambridge: Hackett, 2006), 129. Cf. also Ambrose, *Expositio Evangelii secundum Lucam* VI, 71–75 (CCSL 14:199–201); also Leo the Great, *Sermo* 63.7 (PL 54:357B-C).

the nourished body is both corruptible and destructible, the food is corrupted and destroyed in the body, and both food and body are reduced to rot. Moreover, if this divine Body were converted into us, it would do us no good but would perish with us. But because its power overcomes our weakness and changes us into itself, it is necessary for our weakness to pass over into its divine power. Thus we are strengthened and cannot perish, having been established by it in being [*in esse*] for all eternity.[126]

In the bull *Transiturus de hoc mundo* on the introduction of the Solemnity of Corpus Christi, Pope Urban IV says about the Eucharistic bread: "This bread is taken but, truly, not consumed; it is eaten but not changed; for it is not transformed into the eater; rather, if worthily received, the recipient is conformed to it."[127] He is not talking here about the *species* of the bread, about its sensible form and its material properties, but rather about Christ in his presence in the sign of bread. His presence is an "effective" presence, indeed, a presence that works in us.

Christ's presence in the Eucharistic gifts is unique and elevates the Eucharist above all the other sacraments. "The Eucharist is, as it were, the consummation of the spiritual life and the end of all the sacraments."[128] Yet without a transformation, without a resurrection and new life, the Eucharist would be no more than a memorial for a dead man. The Eucharist, however, is a "feast of life",[129] for in it we have the privilege of "assimilating the vital nourishment that supports us unto eternal life".[130] We assimilate Christ, who is the Way, the Truth, and the Life (Jn 14:6). Thus, the Eucharist is the most intensive sign of union with Christ: "As nourishment is incorporated and completely *assimilated* in the person eating, so intimate and close does the union of the believer with Christ become."[131] Man's hunger and thirst themselves have a corporeally sacramental character, in the life

---

[126] Albertus Magnus, *Liber de sacramento eucharistiae*, dist. III, tract. I, c. 5, 5 (ed. Borgnet 38, 256) [translated from Latin]. See also Thomas Aquinas, *Summa theologiae* III, q. 73, art. 3 ad 2.

[127] Pope Urban IV, bull *Transiturus de hoc mundo* (August 11, 1264): DH 847.

[128] Thomas Aquinas, *Summa theologiae*, III, q. 73, art. 3 corpus.

[129] Ratzinger, "Eucharist—Heart of the Church", 262.

[130] Gottfried Bachl, *Eucharistie: Macht und Lust des Verzehrens*, Spuren: Essays zu Kultur und Glaube (St. Ottilien: EOS, 2008), 59, 100.

[131] Ibid., 116.

and death of Jesus Christ, also (cf. Jn 19:28: "I thirst").[132] In the sacrament of the Eucharist, we receive a share of that extraordinary life that Jesus, God's Son made man, laid down on the Cross and that was perfected by God through his Resurrection from the dead. In the Eucharist, the *Triduum paschale* is in a way gathered up and concentrated forever.[133] The Eucharist is the "embodiment" of God's love. In it, man receives something on which he can live: "O sacrament of love", Augustine writes in his Commentary on John: "He who wants to live has a place to live and something on which to live. Let him approach, believe, and be embodied so that he might be made to live."[134] The Eucharist does not give fleeting life, but, rather, it gives a share in the eternal life of Jesus Christ, who has passed over (*transitus*) forever into the life that no longer knows death.

Yet one cannot truly receive Communion unless one has previously adored: "Because he himself walked here in this same flesh and gave us this flesh to eat for our salvation; however, no one eats this flesh without first adoring it."[135] Kneeling is the eloquent "bodily expression of adoration",[136] because in this posture "we remain upright, ready, available, but at the same time bow before the greatness of the living God and of his Name."[137] Kneeling is "the bodily expression of our positive response to the Real Presence of Jesus Christ, who as God and man, with body and soul, flesh and blood is present among us."[138] "Bending the knee before the presence of the living God"[139] is indispensable. To recover this posture of adoration and reverence before the Blessed Sacrament is one of the tasks of an *ars celebrandi* of the Eucharistic liturgy. This adoration leads not only to the meal; it can

---

[132] Cf. Kühn, *Gabe als Leib*, 92f.

[133] Cf. *EE* 5.

[134] Augustine, *In Iohannis evangelium tractatus* 26.13 (CCSL 36:266): "O sacramentum pietatis!... Qui vult vivere habet ubi vivat, habet unde vivat. Accedat, credat, incorporetur ut vivificetur."

[135] Augustine, *Enarrationes in Psalmos* 98.9 (CCSL 39:1385): "Et quia in ipsa carne hic ambulavit, et ipsam carnem nobis manducandam ad salutem dedit; nemo autem illam carnem manducat, nisi prius adoraverit."

[136] Joseph Ratzinger, "Eucharist—Heart of the Church", 297.

[137] Ibid. On the liturgical gesture of kneeling, see also Ratzinger, *Spirit of the Liturgy*, in *JRCW* 11 (2014), 115–22 [184–94].

[138] Joseph Ratzinger, "Eucharist—Heart of the Church", 298.

[139] Ratzinger, *Spirit of the Liturgy*, in *JRCW* 11:119 [191].

also be continued in Eucharistic adoration outside of the celebration of Mass. In the consecrated Host, the Eucharist lives on, as though "crystallized", even when the celebration of it is concluded.[140] Sacramental Communion is not the only component of a person's transformation through the Eucharist. Eucharistic adoration can transform, too. Adoration outside of Mass prolongs and, as it were, intensifies the adoration that begins already in the celebration of the Eucharist.[141] Thus the faithful are obliged to kneel during the Consecration, that is, the central Eucharistic action from the epiclesis of transformation to the *Mysterium fidei*.[142] The priest celebrant is obliged to genuflect both times after the *verba testamenti* as a sign of adoration and also before he receives Communion. The adoration during the celebration of the Eucharist is adoration that is supposed to become union.[143]

In receiving the Body and Blood of Christ, we obtain a pledge of eternal life (Jn 6:51–18). Hence very early on the Eucharist was called the "medicine of immortality" (*pharmacum immortalitatis*).[144] "I am your breadwinner, since I give myself as bread and offer myself daily as the drink of immortality."[145] Eucharistic adoration, too, points beyond earthly life to eternal life, in which God will be worshipped "neither on this mountain nor in Jerusalem" but, rather, for all eternity "in spirit and truth" (Jn 4:22–23). Adoration here is not only the incursion of eternity into time, but a lasting presence. An essential part of eternal life is "staying in grateful adoration of the absolute mystery of God".[146] The Eucharist is the sacramental memorial not only of Christ's Passion and death but also of his *transitus* [passage] from death to life, so that "through this participation at the altar ... [we] may be filled with every grace and heavenly blessing."[147]

[140] Cf. Koch, *Eucharistie*, 59.

[141] Cf. *SacCar* 66.

[142] Cf. *GIRM* 43.

[143] The demand by Pope Benedict XVI for reception of Holy Communion on the tongue while kneeling should also be seen in this context. For when Communion is received in the hand while standing, it is easy to forget that we do not receive the Body of Christ like a piece of bread that is given out. If all the faithful were to communicate while kneeling at an altar rail, the difference between Communion on the tongue and Communion in the hand would be almost insignificant.

[144] Ignatius of Antioch, *Ad Ephesios* 20 (PG 5:755A).

[145] Clement of Alexandria, *Quis dives salvus erit* 23.4 (GCS 3.175.4–5).

[146] Koch, *Eucharistie*, 60.

[147] *RM* 2010, 625 (*Supra quae*).

The Eucharist is an anticipation of heavenly glory that seeks a suitable expression in the liturgical form of the Eucharist. The eschatological dimension was established as an intrinsic part of the Eucharist by the Last Supper. When Jesus was with the Twelve, broke the bread, and handed them the chalice of salvation, he looked ahead to the fulfillment of the Kingdom of God: "I tell you I shall not drink again of this fruit of the vine until that day when I drink it new with you in my Father's kingdom" (Mt 26:29). We have the promise that the glorified Lord comes to us anew again and again in his Eucharist, so as to be present in our midst and in the gifts of bread and wine. His presence is veiled—he is present as an Absent One. The Eucharist is the visible promise of the definitive future with God in his Kingdom. There we will see God as he is and sing his praises to him eternally.[148] And so "we await the blessed hope and the coming of our Savior, Jesus Christ."[149]

The Eucharist is at the same time a promise for the earth and for the people living on it. For what else could the metaphorical talk about eating and drinking in the Kingdom of God represent but "the reconciliation of what is personal with nature"?[150] Since this life is wasting away and its destruction and fulfillment are still in the future, the Eucharist is more than a celebration of agreement with the world. The sacred banquet is an expression of joy and gratitude, but it is also a remembrance of the dead and a place in which to ask about God's ways with his creation. Part of this, too, is the scandal of the hunger that so many people suffer. The Eucharistic bread alone does not satiate. Therefore, from the celebration of the Eucharist springs the duty to give people not only the bread of eternal life, but also the bread of everyday survival, and thus to give those who hunger and thirst for justice and peace a chance to live in dignity.

The Eucharistic transformation possesses, finally, a cosmic dimension, also, for it joins heaven and earth. In it the gifts of bread and wine become the Body and Blood of Christ. Perhaps no one has grasped the cosmic dimension of the Eucharist as profoundly as Pierre

---

[148] Cf. *RM* 2010, 655: "... when you will wipe away every tear from our eyes. For seeing you, our God, as you are, we shall be like you for all the ages and praise you without end" (Eucharistic Prayer III: Mass for the Deceased).

[149] Ibid., 513 (Embolism after the *Our Father*).

[150] Bachl, *Eucharistie*, 158.

Teilhard de Chardin (1881–1955).[151] His experience of the Eucharist is expressed in the vision of a cosmic *eucharistisation*.[152] In the Eucharistic "transformation" of the natural elements of bread and wine, Teilhard de Chardin perceives the anticipation of the universal transformation of the whole cosmos into the Body of Christ.[153] Teilhard de Chardin's vision must be seen together with the bodily resurrection of the dead, just as the celebration of the Eucharist must be seen together with the appearance of the risen Lord to the disciples in Emmaus. In the Eucharist, the crucified and risen Lord gives himself to us again and again in his glorified corporeality, which is promised to us, too, in the resurrection of the dead. The biblical hope-filled image of a new heaven and a new earth (Rev 21:1) embraces the cosmic dimension of the Eucharistic transformation.

With Kurt Koch, we can speak, in conclusion, about the "Eucharistic mystery of transformation".[154] The fundamental thing is the transformation of death into love. Jesus Christ transformed death from within by an extraordinary act of divine and human love. In the celebration of the Eucharist, this love is given to us anew again and again. The Eucharist is a memorial not only of Christ's death for us, but also of his *transitus* from death to life. This *transitus* of Christ is the prerequisite for his presence in the Eucharist and the inconceivable transformation of the gifts of bread and wine into his Body and Blood. The transformation of the gifts, however, aims at the transformation of the faithful into the Body of Christ (1 Cor 10:16–17). In the Eucharist, we receive the sacramental Body of Christ and are thus transformed into his Body. Finally, again and again in the Eucharist *parousia* occurs, the coming of Christ that anticipates his *parousia* at the end of time. Therefore, the Eucharist strengthens hope in the ultimate transformation of creation in which God will be all in all. With the *Ite missa est*, the celebration of the Eucharist, which leads us into God's presence, dismisses us at the end again and again into the time of our everyday routine. The Eucharist aims at the

---

[151] Cf. Pierre Teilhard de Chardin, *Hymn of the Universe*, trans. William Collins (New York: Harper & Row, 1965).

[152] Cf. ibid., 34–37.

[153] Cf. Ernst Benz, *Schöpfungsglaube und Endzeiterwartung: Antwort auf Teilhard de Chardins Theologie der Evolution* (Munich: Nymphenburger Verlagshandlung, 1965), 243f.

[154] Koch, *Eucharistie*, 60–66.

transformation of those who receive it and also of their lives. So the apostle Paul can call Christian life a λογικὴ λατρεία, a kind of spiritual worship, and admonish Christians to offer themselves as "a holy and living sacrifice", a "spiritual offering" that is pleasing to God. "This is for you the true and appropriate worship" (Rom 12:1 in a common German translation). Life itself wants to be *eucharistia*, offering-in-thanksgiving, and that means: *gift*.

ABBREVIATIONS

AAS	*Acta Apostolicae Sedis* (Vatican City, 1909ff.).
Abendmahl	*Das Abendmahl: Eine Orientierungshilfe zu Verständnis und Praxis des Abendmahls in der evangelischen Kirche,* proposed by the Council of the Evangelical Church in Germany (Gütersloh: Gütersloher Verlagshaus, 2003).
AEM	"Allgemeine Einführung in das Messbuch" (General Introduction to the Missal), in *Die Feier der Heiligen Messe* = MB 2nd ed. 1988, 25*–75*.
Agende	*Evangelisches Gottesdienstbuch: Agende für die Evangelische Kirche der Union und für die Vereinigte Evangelisch-Lutherische Kirche Deutschlands,* 3rd ed. (1999; Berlin: Evangelische Haupt-Bibelges, 2003).
ANF	Ante-Nicene Fathers: The Writings of the Fathers down to A.D. 325, edited by Alexander Roberts and James Donaldson (1885; reprinted: Peabody, Mass.: Hendrickson, 1995).
Bomm	*Lateinisch-deutsches Volksmessbuch: Das vollständige römische Messbuch für alle Tage des Jahres: Mit Erklärungen und einem Choralanhang,* 13th ed. (Einsiedeln and Cologne: Benziger, 1961).
BSLK	*Bekenntnisschriften der evangelisch-lutherischen Kirche,* herausgegeben im Gedenkjahr der Augsburgischen Konfession 1930, 12th ed. (Gottingen: Vandenhoeck, 1998).
CA	*Confessio Augustana [Augsburg Confession]*
CCC	*Catechism of the Catholic Church,* English translation 1994, revised in accordance with the official Latin text (Vatican City: LEV; Washington, D.C.: United States Catholic Conference, 2000).
CCSL	Corpus Christianorum Series Latina (Turnhout-Paris, 1953ff.)
COD	*Conciliorum Oecumenicorum Decreta: Dekrete der Ökumenischen Konzilien,* Latin-German, 3 vols., German translation commissioned by the Görres-Gesellschaft, edited by J. Wohlmuth with the collaboration of G. Sunnus and J. Uphus (Paderborn, Munich, Vienna, and Zurich: Schöningh, 1998–2002).

CSEL   Corpus Scriptorum Ecclesiasticorum Latinorum, edited by the Austrian Academy of Sciences (Vienna, 1866ff.).

CT   *Concilium Tridentinum: Diariorum, Actorum, Epistularum, Tractatuum Nova Collectio*, edidit Societas Goerresiana promovendis inter Germanos catholicos Litterarum Studiis (Freiburg: Herder, 1901–2001).

DEL   *Dokumente zur Erneuerung der Liturgie: Dokumente des Apostolischen Stuhls 1963–1973 und des Zweiten Vatikanischen Konzils*, vols. 1–4 edited by H. Rennings with M. Klöckener (Kevelaer and Fribourg, 1983–2008).

DH   Heinrich Denzinger, *Enchiridion symbolorum definitionum et declarationum de rebus fidei et morum*, Latin-English, edited by Peter Hünermann, 43rd ed., edited by Robert Fastiggi and Anne Englund Nash for the English edition (San Francisco: Ignatius Press, 2012).

DV   Vatican Council II, Dogmatic Constitution on Divine Revelation *Dei Verbum* (November 18, 1965).

DwÜ III   *Dokumente wachsender Übereinstimmung III: 1990-2001*, edited by H. Meyer et al. (Paderborn-Leipzig-Frankfurt am Main, 2003).

EE   John Paul II, Encyclical Letter *Ecclesia de Eucharistia* on the Eucharist in Its Relationship to the Church (April 17, 2003).

EeK   Gemeinsame Kommission der Griechisch-Orthodoxen Metropolie und der römisch-katholischen Kirche in Deutschland, *Die Eucharistie der einen Kirche: Liturgische Überlieferung und kirchliche Gemeinschaft*, in Die Deutschen Bischöfe: Ökumene-Kommission 8: Die Eucharistie der einen Kirche: Dokumente des katholisch-orthodoxen Dialogs auf deutscher und internationale Ebene (Bonn, 1989), 7–24.

FC   Fontes Christiani [new bi-lingual edition of Christian source texts from antiquity and the Middle Ages] (Freiburg: Herder, 1990ff.).

FEF   *The Faith of the Early Fathers: A Source-Book of Theological and Historical Passages from the Christian Writings of the Pre-Nicene and Nicene Eras*, selected and trans. W. A. Jurgens (Collegeville, Minn.: Liturgical Press, 1970).

FOC   The Fathers of the Church. 127 vols. (Washington, D.C.: Catholic University of America Press, 1947–2013).

GCS	Die griechischen christlichen Schriftsteller der ersten drei Jahrhunderte (Berlin-Brandenburgische Akademie der Wissenschaften) (Leipzig: Hinrichs; Berlin: Akademie-Verlag, 1897ff.).
GIRM	*Institutio generalis Missalis Romani* = *General Instruction of the Roman Missal*, 3rd. ed. (1970; Washington, D.C.: United States Conference of Catholic Bishops, 2002).
GORM	*Missale Romanum, Editio typica tertia* 2002: "Grundordnung des Römischen Messbuchs", Vorabpublikation zum Deutschen Messbuch, 3rd ed. (Bonn: Sekretariat der Dt. Bischofskonferenz, 2007).
Herrenmahl	Joint Roman-Catholic/Evangelical Commission, *Das Herrenmahl* (The Lord's Supper) (Paderborn: Verlag Bonifatius-Drukerci; Frankfurt am Main: Lembeck, 1978).
IO	Sacred Congregation of Rites, Instruction *Inter Oecumenici* on Implementing the Constitution on the Sacred Liturgy (September 26, 1964).
JRCW 11	*Joseph Ratzinger Collected Works*, vol. 11: *Theology of the Liturgy* (San Francisco: Ignatius Press, 2014).
JRGS	*Joseph Ratzinger, Gesammelte Schriften*, gen. ed. Gerhard Cardinal Müller (Freiburg, Basel, and Vienna: Herder, 2008ff.).
LG	Vatican Council II, Dogmatic Constitution on the Church *Lumen gentium* (November 21, 1964).
Mansi	*Sacrorum conciliorum nova et amplissima collectio*, edited by G.D. Mansi (Florence and Venice, 1759–1827; Paris: Hubert Welter, 1899–1927).
MB	*Die Feier der Heiligen Messe: Messbuch für die Bistümer des deutschen Sprachgebiets: Autentische Ausgabe für den liturgischen Gebrauch. Kleinausgabe: Das Messbuch für alle Tage des Jahres,* herausgegeben im Auftrag der Bischofskonferenzen Deutschlands, Österreichs und der Schweiz sowie der Bischöfe von Luxemburg, Bozen-Brixen und Lüttich, 2nd ed. (Einsiedeln, Cologne, Freiburg, Basel, et al., 1988).
MR 1962	*Missale Romanum ex decreto SS. Concilii Tridentini restitutum Summorum Pontificum cura recognitum*, editio typica 1962, edited by M. Sodi and A. Toniolo (Vatican City: Libreria editrice vaticana, 2007).

MR 2002³   *Missale Romanum ex decreto Sacrosancti Oecumenici Concilii Vat-*
            icani II instauratum auctoritate Pauli PP. VI promulgatum, Ioannis
            Pauli PP. II cura recognitum, editio typica tertia (Vatican City:
            Libreria editrice vaticana, 2002).

NPNF-1   Nicene and Post-Nicene Fathers, First Series, edited by Philip
            Schaff (1886; reprinted: Peabody, Mass.: Hendrickson, 1995).

NPNF-2   Nicene and Post-Nicene Fathers, Second Series, edited by
            Philip Schaff and Henry Wace (1890; reprinted: Peabody,
            Mass.: Hendrickson, 1995).

PG   *Patrologia cursus completus: Series Graeca*, edited by J.-P. Migne
            (Paris: Garnier, 1857–1866).

PL   *Patrologia cursus completus: Series Latina*, edited by J.-P. Migne
            (Paris: Garnier, 1841–1864).

RM 2010   *The Roman Missal: Renewed by the Decree of the Most Holy Sec-*
            ond Ecumenical Council of the Vatican, Promulgated by authority
            of Pope Paul VI, and revised at the direction of Pope John Paul II:
            English translation according to the third typical edition: For Use
            in the Dioceses of the United States of America: Approved by the
            United States Conference of Catholic Bishops and confirmed by
            the Apostolic See (2010; Washington, D.C.: United States
            Conference of Catholic Bishops, 2011).

SacCar   Benedict XVI, Post-Synodal Apostolic Exhortation *Sacramen-*
            tum Caritatis on the Eucharist as the Source and Summit of
            the Church's Mission (February 22, 2007).

SC   Vatican Council II, Constitution on the Sacred Liturgy *Sacro-*
            sanctum concilium (December 4, 1963).

Schott   *Das vollständige Römische Messbuch: Lateinisch-Deutsch: Mit*
            allgemeinen und besonderen Einführungen im Anschluss an das
            Messbuch, edited by the Benedictine monks of Beuron Arch-
            abbey (Freiburg: Herder, 1958/1962).

SP   Benedict XVI, Apostolic Letter Given Motu Proprio *Summo-*
            rum Pontificum on the Use of the Roman Liturgy Prior to the
            Reform of 1970 (July 7, 2007).

TAA   Sacred Congregation of Rites, Second Instruction on the
            Orderly Carrying out of the Constitution on the Liturgy *Tres*
            abhinc annos (May 4, 1967).

UR   Vatican Council II, Decree on Ecumenism *Unitatis redintegra-*
            tio (November 21, 1964).

WA   *D. Luthers Werke: Kritische Gesamtausgabe* (Weimar: Hermann
           Böhlau, 1883–2009).

WKGS   *Walter Kasper: Gesammelte Schriften*, edited by G. Augustin
           and Kl. Krämer with the Kardinal Walter Kasper Institut
           (Freiburg, Basel, and Vienna: Herder, 2007ff.).

WSA   *The Works of Saint Augustine: A Translation for the 21st Century*, edited by John E. Rotelle, Boniface Ramsey, Augustine
           Heritage Institute et al. (Brooklyn, N.Y.: New City Press,
           1990–2005).

APPENDICES

1. Last Supper Accounts

Matthew 26:26–29

26 Ἐσθιόντων δὲ αὐτῶν λαβὼν ὁ Ἰησοῦς ἄρτον καὶ εὐλογήσας
   Now as they were eating, Jesus took bread, and blessed,
   ἔκλασεν και δοὺς τοῖς μαθηταῖς εἶπεν·
   and broke it, and gave it to the disciples and said,
   λάβετε φάγετε, τοῦτό ἐστιν τὸ σῶμά μου.
   "Take, eat; this is my body."
27 καὶ λαβὼν ποτήριον καὶ εὐχαριστήσας
   And he took a chalice, and when he had given thanks
   ἔδωκευ αὐτοῖς λέγων·
   he gave it to them, saying,
   Πίετε ἐξ αὐτοῦ πάντες
   "Drink of it, all of you;
28 τοῦτο γάρ ἐστιν τὸ αἷμά μου τῆς διαθήκης
   for this is my blood of the covenant,
   τὸ περὶ πολλῶν ἐκχυννόμενον εἰς ἄφεσιν ἁμαρτιῶν
   which is poured out for many for the forgiveness of sins.
29 λέγω δὲ ὑμῖν,
   I tell you
   οὐ μὴ πίω ἀπ' ἄρτι ἐκ τούτο τοῦ γενήματος τῆς ἀμπέλου ἕως τῆς ἡμέρας
   I shall not drink again of this fruit of the vine until that day
   ἐκείνης ὅταν αὐτὸ πίνω μεθ' ὑμῶν καινὸν ἐν τῇ βασιλείᾳ τοῦ πατρὸς μου.
   when I drink it new with you in my Father's kingdom."

Mark 14:22–25

22 Καὶ ἐσθιόντων αὐτῶν λαβὼν ἄρτον εὐλογήσας
   And as they were eating, he took bread, and blessed,
   ἔκλασεν καὶ ἔδωκεν αὐτοῖς καὶ εἶπεν· λάβετε, τοῦτό ἐστιν τὸ σῶμά μου.
   and broke it, and gave it to them, and said, "Take; this is my body."

23   αἱ λαβὼν ποτήριον εὐχαριστήσας
      And he took a chalice, and when he had given thanks
      ἔδωκεν αὐτοῖς, καὶ ἔπιον ἐξ αὐτοῦ πάντες.
      he gave it to them, and they all drank of it.

24   καὶ εἶπεν αὐτοῖς· τοῦτό ἐστιν τὸ αἷμά μου τῆς διαθήκης
      And he said to them, "This is my blood of the covenant,
      τὸ ἐκχυννόμενον ὑπὲρ πολλῶν.
      which is poured out for many.

25   ἀμὴν λέγω ὑμῖν
      Truly, I say to you,
      ὅτι οὐκέτι οὐ μὴ πίω ἐκ τοῦ γενήματος τῆς ἀμπέλου ἕως τῆς ἡμέρας
      I shall not drink again of the fruit of the vine until that day
      ἐκείνης ὅταν αὐτὸ πίνω καινὸν ἐν τῇ βασιλείᾳ τοῦ θεοῦ.
      when I drink it new in the kingdom of God."

Luke 22:14–20

14   Καὶ ὅτε ἐγένετο ἡ ὥρα, ἀνέπεσεν καὶ οἱ ἀπόστολοι σὺν αὐτῷ·
      And when the hour came, he sat at table, and the apostles with
      him.

15   καὶ εἶπεν πρὸς αὐτούς· ἐπιθυμίᾳ ἐπεθύμησα
      And he said to them, "I have earnestly desired
      τοῦτο τὸ πάσχα φαγεῖν μεθ᾽ ὑμῶν πρὸ τοῦ με παθεῖν·
      to eat this Passover with you before I suffer;

16   λέγω γὰρ ὑμῖν ὅτι οὐ μὴ φάγω αὐτὸ
      for I tell you I shall not eat it
      ἕως ὅτου πληρωθῇ ἐν τῇ βασιλείᾳ τοῦ θεοῦ.
      until it is fulfilled in the kingdom of God."

17   καὶ δεξάμενος ποτήριον εὐχαριστήσας εἶπεν·
      And he took a chalice, and when he had given thanks he said,
      λάβετε τοῦτο καὶ διαμερίσατε εἰς ἑαυτούς·
      "Take this, and divide it among yourselves;

18   λέγω γὰρ ὑμῖν·
      for I tell you
      [ὅτι] οὐ μὴ πίω ἀπὸ τοῦ νῦν ἀπὸ τοῦ γενήματος τῆς ἀμπέλου
      that from now on I shall not drink of the fruit of the vine
      ἕως οὗ ἡ βασιλεία τοῦ θεοῦ ἔλθῃ.
      until the kingdom of God comes."

19   καὶ λαβὼν ἄρτον εὐχαριστήσας ἔκλασεν
      And he took bread, and when he had given thanks he broke it
      καὶ ἔδωκεν αὐτοῖς λέγων·
      and gave it to them, saying,

τοῦτό ἐστιν τὸ σῶμά μου τὸ ὑπὲρ ὑμῶν διδόμενον·
"This is my body which is given for you.
τοῦτο ποιεῖτε εἰς τὴν ἐμὴν ἀνάμνησιν.
Do this in remembrance of me."

20 καὶ τὸ ποτήριον ὡσαύτως μετὰ τὸ δειπνῆσαι, λέγων·
And likewise the chalice after supper, saying,
τοῦτο τὸ ποτήριον ἡ καινὴ διαθήκη ἐν τῷ αἵματί μου τὸ ὑπὲρ ὑμῶν
ἐκχυννόμενον.
"This chalice which is poured out for you is the new covenant in
my blood."

1 Corinthians 11:23–26

23 Ἐγὼ γὰρ παρέλαβον ἀπὸ τοῦ κυρίου, ὃ καὶ παρέδωκα ὑμῖν
For I received from the Lord what I also delivered to you,
ὅτι ὁ κύριος Ἰησοῦς ἐν τῇ νυκτὶ ᾗ παρεδίδετο ἔλαβεν ἄρτον
that the Lord Jesus on the night when he was betrayed took bread,

24 καὶ εὐχαριστήσας ἔκλασεν καὶ εἶπεν·
and when he had given thanks, he broke it, and said,
τοῦτό μού ἐστιν τὸ σῶμα τὸ ὑπὲρ ὑμῶν· τοῦτο ποιεῖτε εἰς τὴν ἐμὴν
ἀνάμνησιν.
"This is my body which is for you. Do this in remembrance of
me."

25 ὡσαύτως καὶ πὸ ποτήριον μετὰ τὸ δειπνῆσαι λέγων·
In the same way also the chalice, after supper, saying,
τοῦτο τὸ ποτήριον ἡ καινὴ διαθήκη ἐστὶν ἐν τῷ ἐμῷ αἵματι·
"This chalice is the new covenant in my blood.
τοῦτο ποιεῖτε, ὁσάκις ἐὰν πίνητε, εἰς τὴν ἐμὴν ἀνάμνησιν.
Do this, as often as you drink it, in remembrance of me."

26 ὁσάκις γὰρ ἐὰν ἐσθίητε τὸν ἄρτον τοῦτον καὶ τὸ ποτήριον πίνητε,
For as often as you eat this bread and drink the chalice,
τὸν θάνατον τοῦ κυρίου καταγγέλλετε ἄρχι οὗ ἔλθῃ.
you proclaim the Lord's death until he comes.

2. Ordo Romanus I (circa 700)

LITURGY OF THE WORD

Action	Traditional Title	Action performed by
Entrance and chant	Introitus	Celebrant, choir
Litany (abbreviated)	Kyrie eleison	Choir, all
Praise of God	Gloria	Celebrant, choir, all
Summary prayer	Collecta	Celebrant
Reading (Prophets, Apostles)	Epistle	Subdeacon
Responsorial chant	Graduale	Choir, all
Solemn greeting of Christ	Alleluia	Choir, all
Gospel reading	Evangelium	Deacon
Explanation of Scripture	Homily	Celebrant

LITURGY OF THE EUCHARIST

Action	Traditional Title	Action performed by
Offering of the oblations	Offertorium	Celebrant
Prayer over the oblations	Oratio super oblata	Celebrant

Eucharistic Prayer	Canon Romanus	Action performed by
Thanksgiving	Preface	Celebrant
Hymn	Sanctus	Choir, all
Prayer for blessing	Te igitur	Celebrant
Commemoration of the living	Memento	Celebrant
Commemoration of the saints	Communicantes	Celebrant
Prayer for acceptance	Hanc igitur	Celebrant
Prayer for transformation	Quam oblationem	Celebrant
Words of institution	Qui pridie	Celebrant
Remembrance	Unde et memores	Celebrant
Prayer for acceptance	Supra quae	Celebrant
Communio	Supplices te rogamus	Celebrant
Commemoration of the dead	Memento	Celebrant
Communion of saints	Nobis quoque	Celebrant
Praise (Doxology)	Per ipsum	Celebrant

COMMUNION

Action	Traditional Title	Action performed by
The Lord's Prayer	Pater noster	Celebrant, all (at conclusion)
Sign of peace	Pax Domini	Celebrant
Breaking of bread (fraction)	Agnus Dei	Choir, all
Communion	Communio	Celebrant, all
Prayer after Communion	Postcommunio	Celebrant
Dismissal	Ite missa est	Celebrant
Blessing	Benediction	Celebrant

3. Ambrose: Eucharistic Prayer (Epiclesis, Words of Institution)

Fac nobis hanc oblationem scriptam, rationabilem, acceptabilem, quod est figura corporis et sanguinis Domini nostri Iesu Christi.

Make for us this oblation approved, ratified, reasonable, acceptable, seeing that it is the figure of the body and blood of our Lord Jesus Christ,

Qui pridie quam pateretur, in sanctis manibus suis accepit panem, respexit ad caelum, ad te, sancte Pater omnipotens aeterne Deus, gratias agens benedixit, fregit, fractumque apostolis et discipulis suis tradidit dicens:

Who the day before he suffered took bread in his holy hands, and looked up to heaven to thee, holy Father, almighty, everlasting God, and giving thanks, he blessed, broke, and having broken, delivered it to his apostles and to his disciples, saying,

Accipite et edite ex hoc omnes; hoc est enim corpus meum, quod pro multis confringetur.

Take, and eat ye all of this; for this is my body, which shall be broken for many.

Similiter etiam calicem, postquam cenatum est, pridie quam pateretur, accepit, respexit ad caelum, ad te, sancte Pater omnipotens aeterne Deus, gratias agens benedixit, apostolis et discipulis suis tradidit dicens:

Likewise also after supper, the day before he suffered, he took the cup, looked up to heaven to thee, holy Father, almighty, everlasting God, and giving thanks, blessed it and delivered it to his apostles and to his disciples, saying,

Accipite et bibite ex hoc omnes; hic est enim sanguis meus.

Take, and drink ye all of this; for this is my blood.

FC 3:148f.; English text from "On the Mysteries" and the Treatise "On the Sacraments" by an Unknown Author, trans. T. Thompson (London: Society for Promoting Christian Knowledge; New York: Macmillan Company, 1919), 113–14.

4. Canon Romanus/Eucharistic Prayer I

Missale Romanum[1]

Te igitur, clementissime Pater, per
Iesum Christum, Filium tuum,
Dominum nostrum, supplices
rogamus ac petimus, uti accepta
habeas et benedicas haec dona,
haec munera, haec sancta sacrificia
illibata, in primis, quae tibi offerimus pro Ecclesia tua sancta catholica: quam pacificare, custodire,
adunare et regere digneris toto orbe
terrarum: una cum famulo tuo Papa
nostro N. et Antistite nostro N. et
omnibus orthodoxis atque catholicae et apostolicae fidei cultoribus.

Memento, Domine, famulorum
famularumque tuarum N. et N. et
omnium circumstantium, quorum
tibi fides cognita est et nota devotio, pro quibus tibi offerimus: vel
qui tibi offerunt hoc sacrificium
laudis, pro se suisque omnibus: pro
redemptione animarum suarum,
pro spe salutis et incolumitatis suae:
tibique reddunt vota sua aeterno
Deo, vivo et vero.

Communicantes, et memoriam
venerantes, in primis gloriosae
semper Virginis Mariae, Genetricis
eiusdem Dei et Domini nostri Iesu
Christi: sed et beati Ioseph, eiusdem Virginis Sponsi, et beatorum
Apostolorum ac Martyrum tuorum,

Roman Missal[2]

To you, therefore, most merciful
Father, we make humble prayer
and petition through Jesus Christ,
your Son, our Lord: that you accept
and bless these gifts, these offerings, these holy and unblemished
sacrifices, which we offer you firstly
for your holy catholic Church. Be
pleased to grant her peace, to guard,
unite and govern her throughout
the whole world, together with
your servant N. our Pope and N.
our Bishop, and all those who,
holding to the truth, hand on the
catholic and apostolic faith.

Remember, Lord, your servants
N. and N. and all gathered here,
whose faith and devotion are
known to you. For them we offer
you this sacrifice of praise or they
offer it for themselves and all who
are dear to them, for the redemption of their souls, in hope of health
and well-being, and paying their
homage to you, the eternal God,
living and true.

In communion with those whose
memory we venerate, especially the
glorious ever-Virgin Mary, Mother
of our God and Lord, Jesus Christ,
and blessed Joseph, her Spouse,
your blessed Apostles and Martyrs,
Peter and Paul, Andrew, (James,

[1] MR 2002³, 571–79.
[2] RM 2010, 635–43.

Petri et Pauli, Andreae, (Iacobi,
Ioannis, Thomae, Iacobi, Philippi,
Bartholomaei, Matthaei, Simonis et
Thaddaei: Lini, Cleti, Clementis,
Xysti, Cornelii, Cypriani, Lauren-
tii, Chrysogoni, Ioannis et Pauli,
Cosmae et Damiani) et omnium
Sanctorum tuorum; quorum meritis
precibusque concedas, ut in omni-
bus protectionis tuae muniamur
auxilio. (Per Christum Dominum
nostrum. Amen.)

Hanc igitur oblationem servitutis
nostrae, sed et cunctae familiae
tuae, quaesumus, Domine, ut
placatus accipias: diesque nostros in
tua pace disponas, atque ab aeterna
damnatione nos eripi et in electo-
rum tuorum iubeas grege numerari.
(Per Christum Dominum nostrum.
Amen.)

Quam oblationem tu, Deus, in
omnibus, quaesumus, benedictam,
adscriptam, ratam, rationabilem,
acceptabilemque facere digneris: ut
nobis Corpus et Sanguis fiat dilectissimi Filii tui, Domini nostri Iesu
Christi.

Qui, pridie quam pateretur, accepit
panem in sanctas ac venerabiles
manus suas, et elevatis oculis in
caelum ad te Deum Patrem suum
omnipotentem, tibi gratias agens
benedixit, fregit, deditque discipulis
suis, dicens:
ACCIPITE ET MANDUCATE EX HOC
OMNES: HOC EST ENIM CORPUS
MEUM, QUOD PRO VOBIS TRADETUR.

John, Thomas, James, Philip,
Bartholomew, Matthew, Simon
and Jude: Linus, Cletus, Clement,
Sixtus, Cornelius, Cyprian, Law-
rence, Chrysogonus, John and Paul,
Cosmas and Damian) and all your
Saints: we ask that through their
merits and prayers, in all things we
may be defended by your pro-
tecting help. (Through Christ our
Lord. Amen.)

Therefore, Lord, we pray: graciously accept this oblation of our
service, that of your whole family; order our days in your peace,
and command that we be delivered from eternal damnation and
counted among the flock of those
you have chosen. (Through Christ
our Lord. Amen.)

Be pleased, O God, we pray, to
bless, acknowledge, and approve
this offering in every respect; make
it spiritual and acceptable, so that it
may become for us the Body and
Blood of your most beloved Son,
our Lord Jesus Christ.

On the day before he was to suffer,
he took bread in his holy and venerable hands, and with eyes raised to
heaven to you, O God, his almighty
Father, giving you thanks he said the
blessing, broke the bread and gave it
to his disciples, saying:
TAKE THIS, ALL OF YOU, AND EAT
OF IT, FOR THIS IS MY BODY, WHICH
WILL BE GIVEN UP FOR YOU.

Simili modo, postquam cenatum est, accipiens et hunc praeclarum calicem in sanctas ac venerabiles manus suas, item tibi gratias agens benedixit, deditque discipulis suis, dicens:
ACCIPITE ET BIBITE EX EO OMNES: HIC EST ENIM CALIX SANGUINIS MEI NOVI ET AETERNI TESTAMENTI, QUI PRO VOBIS ET PRO MULTIS EFFUNDETUR IN REMISSIONEM PECCATORUM. HOC FACITE IN MEAM COMMEMORATIONEM.

In a similar way, when supper was ended, he took this precious chalice in his holy and venerable hands, and once more giving you thanks, he said the blessing and gave the chalice to his disciples, saying:
TAKE THIS, ALL OF YOU, AND DRINK FROM IT, FOR THIS IS THE CHALICE OF MY BLOOD, THE BLOOD OF THE NEW AND ETERNAL COVENANT, WHICH WILL BE POURED OUT FOR YOU AND FOR MANY FOR THE FORGIVENESS OF SINS. DO THIS IN MEMORY OF ME.

Mysterium fidei.
Mortem tuam annuntiamus, Domine, et tuam resurrectionem confitemur, donec venias.

The mystery of faith.
We proclaim your Death, O Lord, and profess your Resurrection until you come again.

Unde et memores, Domine, nos servi tui, sed et plebs tua sancta, eiusdem Christi, Filii tui, Domini nostri, tam beatae passionis, necnon et ab inferis resurrectionis, sed et in caelos gloriosae ascensionis, offerimus praeclarae maiestati tuae de tuis donis ac datis hostiam puram, hostiam sanctam, hostiam immaculatam, Panem sanctum vitae aeternae et Calicem salutis perpetuae.

Therefore, O Lord, as we celebrate the memorial of the blessed Passion, the Resurrection from the dead, and the glorious Ascension into heaven of Christ, your Son, our Lord, we, your servants and your holy people, offer to your glorious majesty from the gifts that you have given us, this pure victim, this holy victim, this spotless victim, the holy Bread of eternal life and the Chalice of everlasting salvation.

Supra quae propitio ac sereno vultu respicere digneris; et accepta habere, sicuti accepta habere dignatus es munera pueri tui iusti Abel, et sacrificium Patriarchae nostri Abrahae, et quod tibi obtulit summus sacerdos tuus Melchisedech, sanctum sacrificium, immaculatam hostiam.

Be pleased to look upon these offerings with a serene and kindly countenance, and to accept them, as once you were pleased to accept the gifts of your servant Abel the just, the sacrifice of Abraham, our father in faith, and the offering of your high priest Melchizedek, a holy sacrifice, a spotless victim.

Supplices te rogamus, omnipotens Deus: iube haec perferri per manus sancti Angeli tui in sublime altare tuum, in conspectu divinae maiestatis tuae; ut, quotquot ex hac altaris participatione sacrosanctum Filii tui Corpus et Sanguinem sumpserimus, omni benedictione caelesti et gratia repleamur. (Per Christum Dominum nostrum. Amen.)

Memento etiam, Domine, famulorum famularumque tuarum N. et N., qui nos praecesserunt cum signo fidei, et dormiunt in somno pacis. Ipsis, Domine, et omnibus in Christo quiescentibus, locum refrigerii, lucis et pacis, ut indulgeas, deprecamur. (Per Christum Dominum nostrum. Amen.)

Nobis quoque peccatoribus famulis tuis, de multitudine miserationum tuarum sperantibus, partem aliquam et societatem donare digneris cum tuis sanctis Apostolis et Martyribus: cum Ioanne, Stephano, Matthia, Barnaba, (Ignatio, Alexandro, Marcellino, Petro, Felicitate, Perpetua, Agatha, Lucia, Agneta, Caecilia, Anastasia) et omnibus Sanctis tuis: intro quorum nos consortium, non aestimator meriti, sed veniae, quaesumus, largitor admitte. Per Christum Dominum nostrum.

Per quem haec omnia, Domine, semper bona creas, sanctificas, vivificas, benedicis, et praestas nobis.

In humble prayer we ask you, almighty God: command that these gifts be borne by the hands of your holy Angel to your altar on high in the sight of your divine majesty, so that all of us, who through this participation at the altar receive the most holy Body and Blood of your Son, may be filled with every grace and heavenly blessing. (Through Christ our Lord. Amen.)

Remember also, Lord, your servants N. and N., who have gone before us with the sign of faith and rest in the sleep of peace. Grant them, O Lord, we pray, and all who sleep in Christ, a place of refreshment, light and peace. (Through Christ our Lord. Amen.)

To us, also, your servants, who, though sinners, hope in your abundant mercies, graciously grant some share and fellowship with your holy Apostles and Martyrs: with John the Baptist, Stephen, Matthias, Barnabas, (Ignatius, Alexander, Marcellinus, Peter, Felicity, Perpetua, Agatha, Lucy, Agnes, Cecilia, Anastasia) and all your Saints; admit us, we beseech you, into their company, not weighing our merits, but granting us your pardon, through Christ our Lord.

Through whom you continue to create all these good things, O Lord; you sanctify them, fill them with life, bless them, and bestow them upon us.

Per ipsum, et cum ipso, et in ipso, est tibi Deo Patri omnipotenti, in unitate Spiritus Sancti, omnis honor et gloria per omnia saecula saeculorum. Amen.

Through him, and with him, and in him, O God, almighty Father, in the unity of the Holy Spirit, all honor and glory is yours, for ever and ever. Amen.

5. Martin Luther: Mass Formularies

Formula Missae 1523	*Deutsche Messe [German Mass] 1526*
Introitus	German hymn or German psalm
Kyrie	Kyrie
Gloria (may be omitted)	—
Collects	Collects
Epistle	Epistle
Gradual	German hymn
Sequence (only on Christmas and Pentecost)	—
Gospel	Gospel
Creed (Nicene)	German hymn of faith
Sermon (possible before the Introitus also)	Sermon
Preparation of bread and wine (see below)	—
	Our Father paraphrase with Lord's Supper admonition
Preface dialogue	—
Preface (introductory part only)	—
Words of institution (syntactically connected with the Preface)	Words of institution and distribution
Sanctus and *Benedictus* with elevation	• Words over the bread with elevation, distribution while a German *Sanctus* or a Lord's Supper hymn is sung
	• Words over the chalice with elevation, distribution while a German *Agnus Dei* or a Lord's Supper hymn is sung
Our Father	(see above)
Sign of peace	—
Prayer, "Domine, Jesu Christe, fili Dei vivi"	—

Based on: Hans Bernhard Meyer, *Eucharistie*, Gottesdienst der Kirche: Handbuch der Liturgiewissenschaft 4 (Regensburg, 1989), 408.

Distribution with formula of administration while *Agnus Dei* is sung and possibly a communion hymn	(see above)
Prayer "Quod ore sumpsimus" or "Corpus tuum Domine"	Prayer of thanksgiving
Benedicamus	—
Blessing (Num 6)	Blessing (Num 6)

6. Eucharistic Prayer of the Traditio Apostolica

Dominus vobiscum.
Et cum spiritu tuo.
Sursum corda.
Habemus ad dominum.
Gratias agamus domino.
Dignum et iustum est.

The Lord be with you.
And with your spirit.
Hearts on high.
We have them to the Lord.
Let us give thanks.
It is fitting and right.

Gratias tibi referimus deus, per dilectum puerum tuum Iesum Christum, quem in ultimis temporis misisti nobis salvatorem et redemptorem et angelum voluntatis tuae, qui est verbum tuum inseparabilem, per quem omnia fecisti et beneplacitum tibi fuit, misisti de caelo in matricem virginis, quique in utero habitus incarnatus est et filius tibi ostensus est, ex spiritu sancto et virgine natus.

We give thanks to you, God, through your beloved child Jesus Christ, whom, in the last times, you sent to us as savior and redeemer and angel of your will, who is your inseparable Word through whom you made all things and who was well pleasing to you. You sent him from heaven into the womb of a virgin, and he was conceived and made flesh in the womb and shown to be your Son, born of the Holy Spirit and the virgin.

Qui voluntatem tuam conplens et populum sanctum tibi adquirens extendit manus cum pateretur, ut a passione liberaret eos qui in te crediderunt.

He fulfilled your will and won for you a holy people, opening wide his hands when he suffered that he might set free from suffering those who believed in you.

Qui cumque traderetur voluntariae passioni, ut mortem solvat et vincula diaboli dirumpat, et infernum calcet et iustos illuminet, et terminum figat et resurrectionem manifestet, accipiens panem gratias tibi agens dixit:

When he was handed over to voluntary suffering, in order to dissolve death and break the chains of the devil and harrow hell and illuminate the just and fix a boundary and manifest the resurrection, he took bread, and, giving thanks to you, he said:

FC 1:223–27; English from *On the Apostolic Tradition*, 2nd ed. (Yonkers, N.Y., 2015), emended.

Accipite, manducate, hoc est corpus meum quod pro vobis confringetur.

Take, eat, this is my body, which will be broken for you.

Similiter et calicem dicens:

Likewise with the cup, saying:

Hic est sanguis meus qui pro vobis effunditur. Quando hoc facitis, meam commemorationem facitis.

This is my blood which is poured out for you. Whenever you do this, you perform my commemoration.

Memores igitur mortis et resurrectionis eius, offerimus tibi panem et calicem, gratias tibi agentes quia nos dignos habuisti adstare coram te et tibi ministrare.

Remembering therefore his death and resurrection, we offer you bread and cup, giving thanks to you because you have held us worthy to stand before you and minister to you as priest.

Et petimus ut mittas spiritum tuum sanctum in oblationem sanctae ecclesiae: in unum congregans des omnibus qui percipiunt sanctis in repletionem spiritus sancti ad confirmationem fidei in veritate, ut te laudemus et glorificemus per puerum tuum Iesum Christum, per quem tibi gloria et honor patri et filio cum sancto spiritu in sancta ecclesia tua et nunc et in saecula saeculorum. Amen.

And we ask that you should send your Holy Spirit on the offering of the Holy Church, gathering [her] into one, may you grant to all the saints who receive for the fullness of the Holy Spirit, for the confirmation of their faith in truth, that we may praise and glorify you through your child Jesus Christ, through whom be glory and honor to you, with the Holy Spirit in your holy Church, both now and to the ages of the ages. Amen.

7. Eucharistic Prayer II

Missale Romanum[1]	*Roman Missal*[2]
Dominus vobiscum.	The Lord be with you.
Et cum spiritu tuo.	And with your spirit.
Sursum corda.	Lift up your hearts.
Habemus ad Dominum.	We lift them up to the Lord.
Gratias agamus Domino Deo nostro.	Let us give thanks to the Lord our God.
Dignum et iustum est.	It is right and just.

Vere dignum et iustum est, aequum et salutare, nos tibi, sancte Pater, semper et ubique gratias agere per Filium dilectionis tuae Iesum Christum, Verbum tuum per quod cuncta fecisti: quem misisti nobis Salvatorem et Redemptorem, incarnatum de Spiritu Sancto et ex Virgine natum. Qui voluntatem tuam adimplens et populum tibi sanctum acquirens extendit manus cum pateretur, ut mortem solveret et resurrectionem manifestaret. Et ideo cum Angelis et omnibus Sanctis gloriam tuam praedicamus, una voce dicentes:

Sanctus, Sanctus, Sanctus, Dominus Deus Sabaoth. Pleni sunt caeli et terra gloria tua. Hosanna in excelsis. Benedictus qui venit in nomine Domini. Hosanna in excelsis.

Vere Sanctus es, Domine, fons omnis sanctitatis. Haec ergo dona,

It is truly right and just, our duty and our salvation, always and everywhere to give you thanks, Father most holy, through your beloved Son, Jesus Christ, your Word through whom you made all things, whom you sent as our Savior and Redeemer, incarnate by the Holy Spirit and born of the Virgin. Fulfilling your will and gaining for you a holy people, he stretched out his hands as he endured his Passion, so as to break the bonds of death and manifest the resurrection. And so, with the Angels and all the Saints we proclaim your glory, as with one voice we acclaim:

Holy, Holy, Holy Lord God of hosts. Heaven and earth are full of your glory. Hosanna in the highest. Blessed is he who comes in the name of the Lord. Hosanna in the highest.

You are indeed Holy, O Lord, the fount of all holiness. Make holy,

---

[1] *MR* 2002³, 580–84.
[2] *RM* 2010, 629–33.

quaesumus, Spiritus tui rore sanctifica, ut nobis Corpus et Sanguis fiant Domini nostri Iesu Christi.

Qui cum Passioni voluntarie traderetur, accepit panem et gratias agens fregit, deditque discipulis suis, dicens:

ACCIPITE ET MANDUCATE EX HOC OMNES: HOC EST ENIM CORPUS MEUM, QUOD PRO VOBIS TRADETUR. Simili modo, postquam cenatum est, accipiens et calicem, iterum gratias agens deditque discipulis suis, dicens:
ACCIPITE ET BIBITE EX EO OMNES: HIC EST ENIM CALIX SANGUINIS MEI NOVI ET AETERNI TESTAMENTI, QUI PRO VOBIS ET PRO MULTIS EFFUNDETUR IN REMISSIONEM PECCATORUM. HOC FACITE IN MEAM COMMEMORATIONEM.

Mysterium fidei:
Mortem tuam annuntiamus, Domine, et tuam resurrectionem confitemur, donec venias.

Memores igitur mortis et resurrectionis eius, tibi, Domine, panem vitae et calicem salutis offerimus, gratias agentes quia nos dignos habuisti astare coram te et tibi ministrare.

Et supplices te deprecamur ut Corporis et Sanguinis Christi participes

therefore, these gifts, we pray, by sending down your Spirit upon them like the dewfall, so that they may become for us the Body and Blood of our Lord, Jesus Christ.

At the time he was betrayed and entered willingly into his Passion, he took bread and, giving thanks, broke it, and gave it to his disciples, saying:
TAKE THIS, ALL OF YOU, AND EAT OF IT, FOR THIS IS MY BODY, WHICH WILL BE GIVEN UP FOR YOU.
In a similar way, when supper was ended, he took the chalice and, once more giving thanks, he gave it to his disciples, saying:
TAKE THIS, ALL OF YOU, AND DRINK FROM IT, FOR THIS IS THE CHALICE OF MY BLOOD, THE BLOOD OF THE NEW AND ETERNAL COVENANT, WHICH WILL BE POURED OUT FOR YOU AND FOR MANY FOR THE FORGIVENESS OF SINS. DO THIS IN MEMORY OF ME.
The mystery of faith:
We proclaim your Death, O Lord, and profess your Resurrection until you come again.

Therefore, as we celebrate the memorial of his Death and Resurrection, we offer you, Lord, the Bread of life and the Chalice of salvation, giving thanks that you have held us worthy to be in your presence and minister to you.

Humbly we pray that, partaking of the Body and Blood of Christ, we

a Spiritu Sancto congregemur in unum.

may be gathered into one by the Holy Spirit.

Recordare, Domine, Ecclesiae tuae toto orbe diffusae, ut eam in caritate perficias una cum Papa nostro N. et Episcopo nostro N. et universo clero.

Remember, Lord, your Church, spread throughout the world, and bring her to the fullness of charity, together with N. our Pope and N. our Bishop and all the clergy.

Memento etiam fratrum nostrorum, qui in spe resurrectionis dormierunt, omniumque in tua miseratione defunctorum, et eos in lumen vultus tui admitte.

Remember also our brothers and sisters who have fallen asleep in the hope of the resurrection, and all who have died in your mercy: welcome them into the light of your face.

Omnium nostrum, quaesumus, miserere, ut cum beata Dei Genetrice Virgine Maria, *beato Joseph, eius Sponso*,* beatis Apostolis et omnibus Sanctis, qui tibi a saeculo placuerunt, aeternae vitae mereamur esse consortes, et te laudemus et glorificemus per Filium tuum Iesum Christum.

Have mercy on us all, we pray, that with the Blessed Virgin Mary, Mother of God, *blessed Joseph, her Spouse*,* with the blessed Apostles, and all the Saints who have pleased you throughout the ages, we may merit to be coheirs to eternal life, and may praise and glorify you through your Son, Jesus Christ.

Per ipsum, et cum ipso, et in ipso, est tibi Deo Patri omnipotenti, in unitate Spiritus Sancti, omnis honor et gloria per omnia saecula saeculorum.
Amen.

Through him, and with him, and in him, O God, almighty Father, in the unity of the Holy Spirit, all glory and honor is yours, for ever and ever.
Amen.

---

*Supplement according to the Decree of the Congregation for Divine Worship and the Discipline of the Sacraments dated May 1, 2013, on the insertion of the name of Blessed Joseph into Eucharistic Prayers II–IV.

BIBLIOGRAPHY

Abbt, Imelda, and Wolfgang W. Müller, eds. *Simone Weil: Ein Leben gibt zu denken*. St. Ottilien: EOS-Verlag Erzabtei, 1999.

Afanassieff, Nicolas. *The Church of the Holy Spirit*. Translated by Vitaly Permiakov and edited with an introduction by Michael Plekon. Foreword by Rowan Williams. Notre Dame, Ind.: University of Notre Dame Press, 2012.

——. *La primauté de Pierre dans l'Église orthodoxe*. Neuchâtel: Delachaux & Niestlé, 1960.

Agamben, Giorgio. *Opus Dei: An Archaeology of Duty*. Translated by Adam Kotsko. Stanford, Calif.: Stanford University Press, 2013.

Ahlers, Reinhild. *Communio eucharistica: Eine kirchenrechtliche Untersuchung zur Eucharistie im Codex iuris canonici*. Eichstätter Studien, new series 29. Regensburg: Pustet, 1990.

Aldenhoven, Herwig. "Darbringung und Epiklese im Eucharistiegebet: Eine Studie über die Struktur des Eucharistiegebetes in den altkatholischen Liturgien im Lichte der Liturgiegeschichte". *Internationale Kirchliche Zeitschrift* 61 (1971): 79–117, 150–89.

Alferi, Thomas. "'... Die Unfasslichkeit der uns übersteigend-zuvorkommenden Liebe Gottes ...': Von Balthasar als Orientierung für Marion". In *Jean-Luc Marion: Studien zum Werk*, edited by Hanna Gerl-Falkowitz, 103–25. Dresden: Verlag Text & Dialog, 2013.

Andrieu, Michel. *Les Ordines Romani du haut moyen âge* II. Louvain: Spicilegium Sacrum Lovaniense, 1960.

Angenendt, Arnold. *Geschichte der Religiosität im Mittelalter*. 2nd ed. Darmstadt: Primus Verlag, 2000.

——. *Liturgik und Historik: Gab es eine organische Liturgie-Entwicklung?* Freiburg: Herder 2001.

——. "Missa specialis: Zugleich ein Beitrag zur Entstehung der Privatmesse". *Frühmittelalterliche Studien* 17 (1983): 153–221.

——. *Offertorium: Das mittelalterliche Messopfer*. 3rd rev. ed. Liturgiewissenschaftliche Quellen und Forschungen 101. Münster: Aschendorff, 2014.

——. *Die Revolution des geistigen Opfers: Blut—Sündenbock—Eucharistie*. Freiburg: Herder, 2011.

Ansorge, Dirk. "Jenseits von Begriff und Vorstellung: Das Wunder der Eucharistie im Mittelalter". In *Phänomenologie der Gabe: Neue Zugänge zum Mysterium der Eucharistie*, edited by F. Bruckmann, 67–103. Quaestiones disputatae 270. Freiburg: Herder, 2015.

Appleby, David. " 'Beautiful on the Cross, Beautiful in His Torments': The Place of the Body in the Thoughts of Paschasius Radbertus". *Traditio* 60 (2005): 1–46.

Aris, Marc-Aeilko. "Figura". *Das Mittelalter: Perspektiven mediävistischer Forschung* 15, no. 2 (Berlin, 2010): 63–79.

Auf der Maur, Hansjörg. *Die Osterfeier in der alten Kirche*. Posthumously edited by R. Messner. Münster: Lit, 2003.

Ausdall, Kristen van. "Art and Eucharist in the Late Middle Ages". In *A Companion to the Eucharist in the Middle Ages*, edited by I. C. Levy et al., 541–617. Brill's Companions to the Christian Tradition 26. Leiden: Brill, 2012.

Aymans, Winfried. "Communio IV. Kirchenrechtlich". In *Die Religion in Geschichte und Gegenwart: Handwörterbuch für Theologie und Religionswissenschaft*, 2:439–40. 4th ed. Tübingen: Mohr, 1999.

Bachl, Gottfried. *Eucharistie: Essen als Symbol?* Theologische Meditationen 10. Cologne: Benziger, 1983.

———. *Eucharistie: Macht und Lust des Verzehrens*. Spuren: Essays zu Kultur und Glaube. St. Ottilien: EOS, 2008.

Backhaus, Knut. "Hat Jesus vom Gottesbund gesprochen?" *Theologie und Glaube* 86 (1996): 343–56.

———. *Der Hebräerbrief*. Regensburg: Pustet, 2009.

———. "Kult und Kreuz: Zur frühchristlichen Dynamik ihrer theologischen Beziehung". *Theologie und Glaube* 86 (1996): 512–43.

———. " 'Lösepreis für viele' (Mk 10,45): Zur Heilsbedeutung des Todes Jesu bei Markus". In *Der Evangelist als Theologe: Studien zum Markusevangelium*, edited by T. Söding, 91–118. Stuttgarter Biblische Studien 163. Stuttgart: Verlag Katholisches Bibelwerk, 1995.

Bakker, Paul J. J. M. *La raison et le miracle: Les doctrines eucharistiques (c. 1250–c. 1400)*. 2 vols. Dissertation, Catholic University of Nijmegen, 1999.

Baldovin, John F. "Eucharistic Prayer II: History of the Latin Text and Rite". In *A Commentary on the Order of Mass of the Roman Missal*, foreword by Cardinal Roger Mahony, edited by E. Foley, 311–16. Collegeville, Minn.: Liturgical Press, 2001.

———. "Hippolytus and the *Apostolic Tradition*: Recent Research and Commentary". *Theological Studies* 64 (2003): 520–42.

———. "Idols and Icons: Überlegungen zum derzeitigen Stand der Liturgiereform". *Liturgisches Jahrbuch* 61 (2011): 154–70.

———. *Reforming the Liturgy: A Response to the Critics*. Collegeville, Minn.: Liturgical Press, 2008.

———. *The Urban Character of Christian Worship: The Origins, Development, and Meaning of Stational Liturgy*. Orientalia Christiana Analecta 288. Rome: Pont. Institutum Studiorum Orientalium, 1987.

Balthasar, Hans Urs von. *Dare We Hope: "That All Men Be Saved"?* with *A Short Discourse on Hell*. Translated by David Kipp and Lothar Krauth. San Francisco: Ignatius Press, 1988.

———. *The Glory of the Lord*. Vol. 1, *Seeing the Form*. 2nd ed. Translated by Erasmo Leiva-Merikakis. San Francisco: Ignatius Press, 2009.

Barba, Maurizio. *La riforma conciliare dell'Ordo Missae: Il percorso storica-redazionale dei riti d'ingresso, di offertorio, e di communion*. Rome: CLV, 2008.

Barth, Heinz-Lothar. *Ist die traditionelle lateinische Messe antisemitisch? Antwort auf ein Papier des Zentralkomitees der Katholiken*. Brennpunkte Theologie 7. Altötting: Sarto-Verlag, 2007.

———. *Die Mär vom antiken Kanon des Hippolytos: Untersuchungen zur Liturgiereform*. Stuttgart: Sarto-Verlag, 2008.

Barth, Markus. *Das Mahl des Herrn: Gemeinschaft mit Israel, mit Christus und unter den Gästen*. Neukirchen-Vluyn: Neukirchener Verlag, 1987.

Bauckham, Richard. "Sabbath and Sunday in the Post-Apostolic Church". In *From Sabbath to Lord's Day*, edited by D. A. Carson, 251–98. Grand Rapids, Mich.: Zondervan, 1982.

Baudler, Georg. *Die Befreiung von einem Gott der Gewalt*. Düsseldorf: Patmos, 1999.

Bäumer, Remigius, ed. *Concilium Tridentinum*. Darmstadt: Wissenschaftliche Buchgesellschaft, 1979.

Baumert, Norbert, and Maria-Irma Seewann. "Eucharistie 'für alle' oder 'für viele'?" *Gregorianum* 89 (2008): 501–32.

Baumstark, Anton. *Liturgie comparée: Principes et méthodes pour l'étude historique des liturgies chrétiennes*. 3rd ed. Collection Irénikon. Chevetogne, Belgium: Éditions de Chevetogne, 1954.

———. "Das 'Problem' des römischen Messkanons: Eine Retractatio auf geistesgeschichtlichem Hintergrund". *Ephemerides liturgicae* 53 (1939): 204–43.

———. "Trishagion und Quedusha". *Jahrbücher für Liturgiewissenschaft* 3 (1923): 18–32.

———. *Vom geschichtlichen Werden der Liturgie*. Ecclesia Orans 10. Freiburg: Herder, 1923.

Bayer, Axel. *Spaltung der Christenheit: Das sogenannte Morganländische Schisma von 1054*. Cologne: Böhlau Verlag, 2004.

Bayer, Oswald. "Ethik der Gabe". In *Die Gabe: Ein "Urwort" der Theologie*, edited by V. Hoffmann, 99–123. Frankfurt am Main: Otto Lembeck, 2009.

———. "Gabe". In *Die Religion in Geschichte und Gegenwart*, 3:445–46. 4th ed. Tübingen: Mohr, 2002.

Beauduin, Lambert. "La vraie prière de l'Église (1909)". In A. Haquin, *Dom Lambert Beauduin et le renouveau liturgique*, 238–341. Gembloux: Duculot, 1970.

Becker, Jürgen. *Jesus of Nazareth*. Translated by James E. Crouch. New York: Walter de Gruyter, 1998.

Becker, Karl J. "Subsistit in". *L'Osservatore Romano*, December 5–6, 2005: 6–7.

Belting, Hans. *Das echte Bild: Bildfragen als Glaubensfragen*. Munich: Beck, 2005.

Benz, Ernst. *Schöpfungsglaube und Endzeiterwartung: Antwort auf Teilhard de Chardins Theologie der Evolution*. Munich: Nymphenburger Verlagshandlung, 1965.

Berger, Klaus. *Im Anfang war Johannes: Datierung und Theologie des vierten Evangeliums*. Stuttgart: Quell, 1997.

———. *Manna, Mehl und Sauerteig: Korn und Brot im Alltag der frühen Christen*. Stuttgart: Quell, 1993.

———, and Christiane Nord. *Das Neue Testament und frühchristliche Schriften, übersetzt und kommentiert*. Frankfurt am Main: Insel Verlag, 1999.

Berger, Rupert. *Die Feier der Heiligen Messe: Eine Einführung*. Freiburg: Herder, 2009.

———. *Die Wendung "offerre pro" in der römischen Liturgie*. Münster: Aschendorff, 1965.

Betz, Johannes. "Eucharistie als zentrales Mysterium". In *Mysterium Salutis: Grundriß heilsgeschichtlicher Dogmatic*, edited by J. Feiner and M. Löhrer, 4/2, pp. 185–313. Einsiedeln: Benziger, 1973.

———. "Die Eucharistie in der Didache". *Archiv für Liturgiewissenschaft* 11 (1969): 10–39.

———. *Eucharistie in der Schrift und Patristik*. Handbuch der Dogmengeschichte 4/4a. Freiburg: Herder, 1979.

———. *Die Eucharistie in der Zeit der griechischen Väter*. Vol. 1/1, *Die Aktualpräsenz der Person und des Heilswerkes Jesu im Abendmahl nach der vorephesinischen griechischen Patristik*. Freiburg: Herder, 1955.

———. *Die Eucharistie in der Zeit der griechischen Väter*. Vol. 2/1, *Die Realpräsenz des Leibes und Blutes Jesu im Abendmahl nach dem Neuen Testament*. Freiburg: Herder, 1961.

Bieler, Andrea, and Luise Schottroff. *Das Abendmahl: Essen, um zu leben*. Gütersloh: Gütersloher Verlagshaus, 2007.

Bieringer, Andreas. *A Halfway House to Aggiornamento? Die ersten mutter-sprachlichen Messbücher in den USA (1964–1966).* Studien zur Pastoral-liturgie 38. Regensburg: Pustet, 2014.

Bieritz, Karl-Heinz. *Liturgik.* Berlin and New York: Walter de Gruyter, 2004.

Bishop, Edmund. "The Genius of the Roman Rite". In *Liturgica Historica*, 1–19. Oxford: Clarendon Press, 1918.

Blank, Josef. "Weisst du, was Versöhnung heisst? Der Kreuzestod Jesu als Sühne und Versöhnung". In *Sühne und Versöhnung*, edited by J. Blank and J. Werbick, 21–91. Theologie zur Zeit 1. Düsseldorf: Patmos, 1987.

Böhler, Dieter. "Anmerkungen eines Exegeten zur Instructio Quinta 'Liturgiam Authenticam'". *Liturgisches Jahrbuch* 54 (2004): 205–22.

Böhm, Thomas. "Die Bindung Isaaks in ausgewählten Texten der Kir-chenväter". In *Die Bindung Isaaks: Stimme, Schrift, Bild*, edited by H. Hoping, J. Knop, and T. Böhm, 128–42. Studien zu Judentum und Christentum. Paderborn: Schöningh, 2009.

Bornkamm, Günther. "Die eucharistische Rede im Johannes-Evangelium". *Zeitschrift für die Neutestamentliche Wissenschaft* 47 (1956): 161–69.

Botte, Bernard. "L'anaphora chaldéenne des Apôtres". *Orientalia Christiana Periodica* 15 (1949): 259–76.

———. *Le canon de la messe romaine: Édition critique, introduction et notes.* Textes et études liturgiques 2. Louvain: Abbaye du Mont César, 1935.

———. "In unitate Spiritus Sancti". In *L'Ordinaire de la Messe.* Études litur-giques 2, edited by B. Botte and C. Mohrmann, 133–39. Paris: Éditions du Cerf; Louvain: Abbaye du Mont César, 1953.

———. *La Tradition apostolique de Saint Hippolyte: Essai de reconstitution.* Edited by Bernard Botte and Albert Gerhards. 5th rev. ed., Liturgiewissen-schaftliche Quellen und Forschungen 39. Münster: Aschendorff, 1989.

———. "Die Wendung 'astare coram te et tibi ministrare' im Eucharistischen Hochgebet II". *Bibel und Liturgie* 49 (1976): 101–4.

Bouhot, Jean-Paul. *Ratramne de Corbie: Histoire littéraire et controverses doctri-nales.* Paris: Études augustiniennes, 1976.

Bouley, Allan. *From Freedom to Formula: The Evolution of the Eucharistic Prayer from Oral Improvisation to Written Texts.* Studies in Christian Antiquity 21. Washington, D.C.: Catholic University of America Press, 1981.

Bourdieu, Pierre. "Marginalia: Some Additional Notes on the Gift". In *The Logic of the Gift: Towards an Ethic of Generosity*, edited by A. D. Schrift, 231–44. New York: Routledge, 1997.

Bouyer, Louis. *The Decomposition of Catholicism.* Translated by Charles Underhill Quinn. Chicago: Franciscan Herald Press, 1969.

————. "The Different Forms of the Eucharistic Prayer and Their Genealogy". In *Studia Patristica* 8 (Papers presented to the Fourth International Conference on patristic studies held at Christ Church, Oxford, 1963; part 2: Patres apostolici, historica, liturgica, ascetica et monastica), edited by F. Cross, 156–70. Berlin: Akademie-Verlag, 1966.

————. *Eucharist*. Translated by Charles Underhill Quinn. Notre Dame, Ind.: University of Notre Dame Press, 1968.

Bradshaw, Paul F. "Did the Early Eucharist Ever Have a Sevenfold Shape?" *Heythrop Journal* 43 (2002): 73–76.

————. *The Eucharistic Liturgies: Their Evolution and Interpretation*. Collegeville, Minn.: Liturgical Press, 2012.

————. *Eucharistic Origins*. Alcuin Club Collections 80. London: Oxford University Press, 2004.

————. *Reconstructing Early Christian Worship* (Collegeville, Minn.: Liturgical Press, 2010).

————. " 'Zebah Todah' and the Origins of the Eucharist". *Ecclesia Orans* 8 (1991): 245–60.

————, and Maxwell E. Johnson. *The Eucharistic Liturgies: Their Evolution and Interpretation*. Collegeville, Minn.: Liturgical Press, 2012.

————. *The Origins of Feasts, Fasts, and Seasons in Early Christianity*. London: SPCK; Collegeville, Minn.: Liturgical Press, 2011.

————, and L. Edward Phillips. *The Apostolic Tradition: A Commentary*. Hermeia Series, edited by H. W. Altridge. Minneapolis: Fortress Press, 2002.

Brakmann, Heinzgerd. "Der christlichen Bibel erster Teil in den gottesdienstlichen Traditionen des Ostens und Westens: Liturgiehistorische Anmerkungen zum sog. Stellenwert des Alten/Ersten Testaments im Christentum". In *Streit am Tisch des Wortes? Zur Deutung und Bedeutung des Alten Testaments und seiner Verwendung in der Liturgie*, edited by A. Franz, 565–604. St. Ottilien: EOS Verlag, 1997.

Brandt, Sigrid. *Opfer als Gedächtnis: Auf dem Weg zu einer befreienden theologischen Rede vom Opfer*. Münster: Lit., 2001.

Brinktrine, Johannes. *Die heilige Messe*. 4th ed. Paderborn: Ferdinand Schöningh, 1950; edited with an introduction by Peter Hofmann. 5th ed. Augsburg: Bay Dominus Verlag, 2015.

————. *Der Messopferbegriff in den ersten zwei Jahrhunderten: Eine biblisch-patristische Untersuchung*. Freiburg: Herder, 1918.

Brosseder, Johannes, and Hans-Georg Link, eds. *Eucharistische Gastfreundschaft*. Neukirchen-Vluyn: Neukirchener Verlag-Haus, 2003.

Browe, Peter. *Eucharistie im Mittelalter: Liturgiehistorische Forschungen in kulturwissenschaftlicher Absicht*. Edited by H. Lutterbach and T. Flammer. Münster: Lit., 2003.

——. *Die eucharistischen Wunder des Mittelalters.* Bresaluer Studien zur historischen Theologie 4. Breslau: Verlag Müller & Seiffert, 1938.

——. *Die Verehrung der Eucharistie im Mittelalter.* Rome: Herder, 1967.

Brown, Raymond E. *The Gospel according to John (I-XII): Introduction, Translation, and Notes.* Garden City, N.Y.: Doubleday, 1966.

Bruns, Peter. *Den Menschen mit dem Himmel verbinden: Eine Studie zu den katechetischen Homilien des Theodor von Mopsuestia.* Corpus Scriptorum Christianorum Orientalium, Subsidia 89. Leuven: Peeters, 1995.

Büchner, Christine. *Wie kann Gott in der Welt wirken? Überlegungen zu einer theologischen Hermeneutik des Sich-Gebens.* Freiburg: Herder, 2010.

Budde, Achim. *Die ägyptische Basilios-Anaphora: Text—Kommentar—Geschichte.* Jerusalemer theologisches Forum 7. Münster: Aschendorff, 2004.

Buescher, Gabriel. *The Eucharistic Teaching of William Ockham.* St. Bonaventure, N.Y.: Franciscan Institute, 1950; 2nd ed., 1974.

Bugnini, Annibale. *The Reform of the Liturgy 1948–1975.* Translated by Matthew J. O'Connell. Collegeville, Minn.: Liturgical Press, 1990.

Bultmann, Rudolf. *Theology of the New Testament.* Translated by Kendrick Grobel. New York: Scribner, 1951, 1955.

——. *Das Verhältnis der urchristlichen Christusbotschaft zum historischen Jesus.* Sitzungsberichte der Heidelberger Akademie der Wissenschaften, Philosophisch-Historische Klasse. Heidelberg: Winter, 1960.

Burkert, Walter. *Homo necans: Interpretationen altgriechischer Opferriten und Mythen.* 2nd ed. Berlin and New York: Walter de Gruyter, 1997.

Burnham, Douglas, and Enrico Giaccherini. *The Poetics of Transubstantiation: From Theology to Metaphor.* Aldershot, England, and Burlington, Vt.: Ashgate, 2005.

Burr, David. "Scotus and Transubstantiation". *Mediaeval Studies* 43 (1972): 336–60.

Caillé, Alain. *Anthropologie du don: Le tiers paradigm.* Paris: Desclée de Brouwer, 2000.

Campi, Emidio, and Ruedi Reich, eds. *Consensus Tigurinus (1549): Die Einigung zwischen Heinrich Bullinger und Johannes Calvin über das Abendmahl.* Werden-Wertung-Bedeutung. Zurich: TVZ, 2009.

Capelle, Bernard. "Et omnibus orthodoxis atque apostolicae fidei cultoribus". In *Travaux Liturgiques* 2:258–68. Louvain: Centre Liturgique, 1962.

Cappuyns, Maieul. "L'origine des Capitula pseudo-célestiniens contre le semipéligianisme". *Revue Bénédictine* 41 (1929): 156–70.

Caputo, John D., and Michael J. Scanlon, eds. *God, the Gift and Postmodernism.* Bloomington, Ind.: Indiana University Press, 1999.

Casel, Odo. *Das christliche Festmysterium.* Paderborn: Bonifacius-Druckerei, 1941.

——. *Das christliche Opfermysterium: Zur Morphologie und Theologie des eucharistischen Hochgebetes.* Edited posthumously by V. Warnach, O.S.B. Graz, Vienna, and Cologne: Verlag Styria, 1968.

——. "Das Mysteriengedächtnis der Messliturgie im Lichte der Tradition". *Jahrbuch für Liturgiewissenschaft* 6 (1926): 113–204.

——. *The Mystery of Christian Worship.* Edited by B. Neunheuser. In English trans. Westminster, Md.: Newman Press, 1962.

——. "Oblatio rationabilis". *Theologische Quartalschrift* 99 (1917/1918): 429–39.

——. "Ein orientalisches Kultwort in abendländischer Umschmelzung". *Jahrbuch für Liturgiewissenschaft* 11 (1931): 1–19.

——. "Quam oblationem". *Jahrbuch für Liturgiewissenschaft* 2 (1922): 98–101.

Casper, Bernhard. *Das Ereignis des Betens: Grundlinien einer Hermeneutik des religiösen Geschehens.* Phänomenologie 1, Texte 3. Freiburg: Alber, 1998.

Chauvet, Louis-Marie. *Symbol und Sakrament: Eine sakramentale Relecture der christlichen Existenz.* German translation by Thomas Fries. Theologie der Liturgie 8. Regensburg: Pustet, 2015.

Chavasse, Antoine. "L'epistolier romain du Codex Wurtzbourg: Son organisation". *Revue Bénédictine* 91 (1981): 280–331.

——. *Les lectionnaires romains de la messe I-II.* Spicilegii Friburgensis subsidia 22. Fribourg Éditions Universitaires, 1993.

Chazelle, Celia. *The Crucified God in the Carolingian Era: Theology and Art of Christ's Passion.* Cambridge: Cambridge University Press, 2001.

——. "The Eucharist in Early Mediaeval Europe". In *A Companion to the Eucharist in the Middle Ages,* edited by J. C. Levy and K. van Ausdall, 205–49. Brill's Companions to Christian Tradition 26. Leiden and Boston: Brill, 2012.

——. "Figure, Character, and the Glorified Body in the Carolingian Eucharistic Controversy". *Traditio* 47 (1992): 2–36.

Chilton, Bruce. *A Feast of Meaning: Eucharistic Theologies from Jesus through Johannine Circles.* Leiden and New York: Brill, 1994.

——. *The Temple of Jesus: His Sacrificial Program within a Cultural History of Sacrifice.* University Park, Pa.: Pennsylvania State University Press, 1992.

Clark, Francis. *Eucharistic Sacrifice and the Reformation.* 2nd ed. Oxford: Blackwell, 1967.

Clerck, Ewald de. *La "prière universelle" dans les liturgies latines anciennes: Témoignages patristiques et textes liturgiques.* Liturgiewissenschaftliche Quellen und Forschungen 62. Münster Wetsfalen: Aschendorff, 1977.

Conrad, Sven, F.S.S.P. "Renewal of the Liturgy in the Spirit of Tradition: Perspectives with a View towards the Liturgical Development of the West". *Antiphon* 14/1 (2010): 95–136.

Crossan, John Dominic. *The Historical Jesus: The Life of a Mediterranean Jewish Peasant.* San Francisco: Harper San Francisco, 1991.

Cuming, Geoffrey J. "ΔΙ' ΕΥΧΗΣ ΛΟΓΟΥ (Justin, *Apology*, i.66.2)". *Journal of Theological Studies* 31 (1980): 80–82.

———. "The Early Eucharistic Liturgies in Recent Research". In *The Sacrifice of Praise: Studies on the Themes of Thanksgiving and Redemption in the Central Prayer of the Eucharist and Baptismal Liturgies in Honour of Arthur Hubert Couratin.* Bibliotheca "Ephemerides liturgicae", Subsidia 19, edited by B. D. Spinks, 65–69. Rome: C.L.V.–Edizioni Liturgiche, 1981.

———. *The Liturgy of St. Mark: Edited from the Manuscripts with a Commentary.* Orientalia christiana analecta 234. Rome: Pontificium institutum orientalium, 1990.

Dalferth, Ingolf U. "Alles umsonst: Zur Kunst des Schenkens und den Grenzen der Gabe". In *Von der Ursprünglichkeit der Gabe: Jean-Luc Marions Phänomenologie in der Diskussion*, edited by M. Gabel and H. Joas, 159–91. Freiburg: Karl Alber, 2007.

Daly, Robert J. *Christian Sacrifice: The Judaeo-Christian Background before Origen.* Studies in Christian Antiquity 18. Washington, D.C.: Catholic University of America Press, 1978.

———. *Sacrifice Unveiled: The True Meaning of Christian Sacrifice.* London and New York: T&T Clark, 2009.

Damerau, Rudolf. *Die Abendmahlslehre des Nominalismus insbesondere die des Gabriel Biel.* Studien zu den Grundlagen der Reformation 1. Giessen: Schmitz, 1963.

Dassmann, Ernst. *Ambrosius von Mailand: Leben und Werk.* Stuttgart: Kohlhammer, 2004.

———. "'Bindung' und 'Opferung' in jüdischer und patristischer Auslegung". In *Hairesis*, edited by M. Hutter, 1–18. Münster: Aschendorff, 2002.

Delling, Gerhard. "Zum gottesdienstlichen Stil der Johannes-Apokalypse". In Delling, *Studien zum Neuen Testament und zum hellenistischen Judentum: Gesammelte Aufsätze 1950–1968*, edited by F. Hahn et al., 425–50. Göttingen: Vandenhoeck & Ruprecht, 1970.

Derrida, Jacques. "Den Tod geben" (1992). In *Gewalt und Gerechtigkeit: Derrida—Benjamin*, edited by A. Haverkamp, 331–445. Frankfurt am Main: Suhrkamp, 1994.

———. *Donner le temps.* Vol. 1, *La fausse monnaie.* Paris: Galilée, 1991.

———. "Jahrhundert der Vergebung: Verzeihen ohne Macht—unbedingt und jenseits der Souveränität". *Lettre International*, Spring 2000: 10–18.

———. "On the Gift: A Discussion between Jacques Derrida and Jean-Luc Marion: Moderated by R. Kearney". In *God, the Gift, and Postmodernism*, edited by J. D. Caputo and M. J. Scanlon, 54–78. Bloomington, Ind.: Indiana University Press, 1999.

Deshusses, Jean. *Le Sacramentaire Grégorien: Ses principales formes d'après les plus anciens manuscrits.* Vol. 1, *Le sacramentaire, le supplément d'Aniane.* 2nd ed. Spicilegium Friburgense 16. Fribourg, Éditions Universitaires, 1979.

———. "Les sacramentaires: État actuel de la recherche". *Archiv für Liturgiewissenschaft* 24 (1982): 19–46.

———. "Le 'Supplément' au sacramentaire grégorien: Alcuin ou Bénoît d'Aniane". *Archiv für Liturgiewissenschaft* 9 (1965): 48–71.

Dijk, Stephen J. P. van. *Sources of the Modern Roman Liturgy: The Ordinals from Haymo of Faversham and Related Documents (1243–1307).* 2 vols. Studia et Documenta Franciscana. Leiden: Brill, 1963.

Dix, Gregory. *The Shape of the Liturgy.* 1945; London and New York: Continuum, 2005.

Dölger, Franz-Josef. *Die Eucharistie nach Inschriften frühchristlicher Zeit.* Münster: Aschendorffsche Verlagsbuchhandlung, 1922.

———. "Zu den Zeremonien der Messliturgie III. 'Ite missa est' in kultur- und sprachgeschichtlicher Bedeutung". *Antike und Christentum* 6 (1950): 81–132.

Draper, Jonathan A. "The Didache in Modern Research: An Overview". In *The Didache in Modern Research,* 1–42. Arbeiten zur Geschichte des antiken Judentums und des Urchristentums 37. Leiden and New York: Brill, 1996.

Drecoll, Volker Henning. "Liturgie bei Augustinus". In *Augustin Handbuch,* edited by V. H. Drecoll, 224–32. Tübingen: Mohr Siebeck, 2007.

Driscoll, Jeremy. *Theology at the Eucharistic Table: Master Themes in the Theological Tradition.* Leominster: Gracewing, 2005.

Drumm, Joachim, and Winfried Aymans. "Communio". In *LThK,* 3rd ed., 2:1280–84. Freiburg: Herder, 1994.

Dünzel, Franz. "Herrenmahl ohne Herrenworte? Eucharistische Texte aus der Frühzeit des Christentums". In *Mehr als Brot und Wein: Theologische Kontexte der Eucharistie,* edited by W. Haunerland, 50–72. Würzburg: Echter Verlag, 2005.

Ebner, Martin. *Jesus von Nazaret: Was wir von ihm wissen können.* Stuttgart: Stuttgart Katholisches Bibelwerk, 2007.

Eizenhöfer, Leo. "Das Opfer der Gläubigen in den Sermones Leos des Grossen". In *Die Messe in der Glaubensverkündigung,* 2nd ed., edited by F. X. Arnold and B. Fischer, 79–107. Freiburg: Herder, 1953.

Emminghaus, Johannes H. *Die Messe: Wesen, Gestalt, Vollzug.* 5th ed. Klosterneuburg: Österr. Kathol. Bibelwerk, 1992.

Faggioli, Massimo. *True Reform: Liturgy and Ecclesiology in Sacrosanctum Concilium.* Collegeville, Minn.: Liturgical Press, 2012.

Fahey, John F. *The Eucharistic Teaching of Ratramn of Corbie.* Dissertationes ad lauream 22. Mundelein, Ill.: Saint Mary of the Lake Seminary, 1951.

Federer, Karl. *Liturgie und Glaube: "Legem credendi lex statuat supplicandi": Eine theologigeschichtliche Untersuchung.* Paradosis IV. Fribourg: Paulusverlag, 1950.

Feiner, Johannes. "Kommentar zu 'Unitatis Redintegratio'". In *LThK*, 2nd ed., 40–123. Freiburg: Herder, 1967.

Feneberg, Rupert. *Christliche Passafeier und Abendmahl: Eine biblischhermeneutische Untersuchung der neutestamentlichen Einsetzungsberichte.* Studien zum Alten und Neuen Testament 27. Munich: Kösel-Verlag, 1971.

Feulner, Hans-Jürgen. "Der *Ordo Missae* von 1965 und das *Missale Romanum* von 1962". In *Römische Messe und Liturgie in der Moderne,* edited by St. Wahle, H. Hoping, and W. Haunerland, 103–42. Freiburg: Herder, 2013.

Fiedler, Peter. *Jesus und die Sünder.* Beiträge zur biblischen Exegese und Theologie 3. Frankfurt am Main: P. Lang; Bern: H. Lang, 1976.

———. "Probleme der Abendmahlsforschung" (1982). In Fiedler, *Studien zur biblischen Grundlegung des christlich-jüdischen Verhältnisses,* 22–69. Stuttgarter biblische Aufsatzbände 35: Neues Testament. Stuttgart: Katholisches Bibelwerk, 2005.

Fiedrowicz, Michael. *Die überlieferte Messe: Geschichte, Gestalt, Theologie.* Mühlheim an der Mosel: Carthusianus Verlag, 2011.

Fischer, Balthasar. "Vom Beten zu Christus". In *Gott feiern: Theologische Anregung und geistliche Vertiefung zur Feier der Messe und des Stundengebets,* Festschrift T. Schnitzler, edited by J. G. Plöger, 94–99. Freiburg: Herder, 1980.

Flanagan, Kieran. *Sociology and Liturgy: Re-presentations of the Holy.* London: Macmillan; New York: St. Martin's Press, 1991.

Flusser, David. "Sanktus und Gloria". In Flusser, *Entdeckungen im Neuen Testament.* Vol. 1, *Jesusworte und ihre Überlieferung,* 2nd ed., edited by M. Maier, 226–44. Neukirchen-Vluyn: Neukirchener Verlag, 1992.

Foley, Edward. *From Age to Age: How Christians Have Celebrated the Eucharist.* 2nd ed. Collegeville, Minn.: Liturgical Press, 2008.

Fortescue, Adrian. *The Ceremonies of the Roman Rite Described.* 15th ed. Tunbridge Wells: Burns & Oates, 2009.

Frank, Karl Suso. "Maleachi 1,10ff. in der frühen Väterdeutung: Ein Beitrag zu Opferterminologie und Opferverständnis in der alten Kirche". *Theologie und Philosophie* 53 (1978): 70–79.

Franz, Adolph. *Die Messe im deutschen Mittelalter: Beiträge zur Geschichte der Liturgie und des religiösen Volkslebens.* Darmstadt: Wissenschaftliche Buchgesellschaft, 1963.

Freudenberger, Theobald. "Die Messliturgie in der Volkssprache im Urteil des Trienter Konzils". In *Reformatio ecclesiae: Beiträge zu kirchlichen Reformbemühungen von der Alten Kirche bis zur Neuzeit*, Festschrift E. Iserloh, edited by R. Bäumer, 679–98. Paderborn et al.: Schöningh, 1980.

Fries, Heinrich, and Otto Hermann Pesch. *Streiten für die eine Kirche*. Munich: Kösel-Verlag, 1987.

———, and Karl Rahner. *Unity of the Churches: An Actual Possibility*. Translated by Ruth C. L. Gritsch and Eric W. Gritsch. Philadelphia: Fortress Press; New York: Paulist Press, 1985.

Fuller, Reginald H. "The Double Origin of the Eucharist". *Biblical Research* 8 (1963): 60–72.

Fürst, Alfons. *Die Liturgie der Alten Kirche: Geschichte und Theologie*. Münster: Aschendorff, 2008.

Gamber, Klaus. *Alter und neuer Messritus*. Regensburg: Pustet, 1983.

———. *Liturgie übermorgen: Gedanken zur Geschichte und Zukunft des Gottesdienstes*. Freiburg: Herder, 1966.

———. *Missa Romensis: Beiträge zur frühen römischen Liturgie und zu den Anfängen des Missale Romanum*. Regensburg: Pustet, 1970.

———. *Zum Herrn hin! Fragen um Kirchenbau und Gebet nach Osten*. Regensburg: Pustet, 1987.

Ganz, David. *Corbie in the Carolingian Renaissance*. Sigmaringen: Thorbecke, 1990.

———. "Theology and the Organisation of Thought". In *The New Cambridge Mediaeval History*, vol. 2 (c. 700–c. 900), 758–85. Cambridge: Cambridge University Press, 1995.

Geerlings, Wilhelm. "Einleitung zur Traditio Apostolica". In [Didache] *Zwölf-Apostel-Lehre: Apostolische Überlieferung*, 143–208. Fontes Christiani (hereafter abbreviated FC) 1. Freiburg: Herder, 1991.

Geiselmann, Josef Rupert. *Die Abendmahlslehre an der Wende der christlichen Spätantike zum Frühmittelalter*. Munich: Hueber, 1933.

———. *Die Eucharistielehre der Vorscholastik*. Forschungen zur christlichen Literatur- und Dogmengeschichte 15. Paderborn: Schöningh, 1926.

Gelineau, Joseph. *Die Liturgie von morgen*. Regensburg: Pustet, 1979.

Gelston, Anthony. "ΔΙ' ΕΥΧΗΣ ΛΟΓΟΥ (Justin, *Apology*, i.66.2)". *Journal of Theological Studies* 33 (1982): 172–75.

———. *Eucharistic Prayer of Addai and Mari*. Oxford: Clarendon Press; New York: Oxford University Press, 1992.

Gerber, Simon. *Theodor von Mopsuestia und das Nicänum: Studien zu den katechetischen Homilien*. Leiden and Boston: Brill, 2000.

Gerhards, Albert. "Crossing Borders: The Kedusha and the Sanctus: A Case Study of the Convergence of Jewish and Christian Liturgy". In *Jewish* and *Christian Liturgy and Worship: New Insights into Its History and Interaction*, edited by A. Gerhards and C. Leonhard, 27–40. Jewish and Christian Perspectives 15. Leiden and Boston: Brill, 2007.

———. "Entstehung und Entwicklung des Eucharistischen Hochgebets im Spiegel der neueren Forschung: Der Beitrag der Liturgiewissenschaft zur Liturgischen Erneuerung". In *Gratias Agamus: Studien zum Eucharistischen Hochgebet*, Festschrift B. Fischer, edited by A. Heinz and H. Rennings, 75–96. Freiburg: Herder, 1992.

———. "Gipfelpunkt und Quelle: Intention und Rezeption der Liturgiekonstitution *Sacrosanctum Concilium*". In *Erinnerung an die Zukunft: Das Zweite Vatikanische Konzil*, edited by Jan-Heiner Tück, 127–46. 2nd ed. Freiburg: Herder, 2012.

———. "Die literarische Struktur des eucharistischen Hochgebets". *Liturgisches Jahrbuch* 33 (1983): 90–104.

———. "Liturgie". In *Neues Handbuch theologischer Grundbegriffe*, vol. 3, edited by Peter Eicher, 7–22. Munich: Kösel-Verlag, 2005.

———. "Die Synode von Pistoia 1786 und ihre Reform des Gottesdienstes". In vol. 1 of *Liturgiereformen*, edited by M. Klöckener and B. Kranemann, 496–510. Münster: Aschendorff, 2002.

———. "Wie viele sind viele? Zur Diskussion um das 'pro multis'". *Herder Korrespondenz* 61 (2007): 79–83.

———, and Benedikt Kranemann. *Einführung in die Liturgiewissenschaft*. 2nd ed. Darmstadt: Wissenschaftliche Buchgesellschaft, 2008.

Gerken, Alexander. "Dogmengeschichtliche Reflexionen über die heutige Wende in der Eucharistielehre". *Zeitschrift für katholische Theologie* 94 (1972): 199–226.

———. "Kann sich die Eucharistielehre ändern?" *Zeitschrift für katholische Theologie* 97 (1975): 415–29.

———. *Theologie der Eucharistie*. Munich: Kösel-Verlag, 1973.

Gese, Hartmut. "Die Herkunft des Abendmahles". In *Zur biblischen Theologie: Alttestamentliche Vorträge*, 107–27. Munich: Kaiser, 1977.

Gestrich, Christof. "Opfer in systematisch-theologischer Perspektive: Gesichtspunkte einer evangelischen Lehre vom Opfer". In *Opfer: Theologische und kulturelle Kontexte*, edited by B. Janowski and M. Welker, 282–303. Frankfurt am Main: Suhrkamp, 2000.

Geuenich, Dieter. "Kritische Anmerkungen zur sogenannten 'anianischen Reform'". In *Mönchtum—Kirche—Herrschaft 750–1000*, Festschrift J. Semmler, edited by D. R. Bauer et al., 99–112. Sigmaringen: Thorbecke Verlag, 1998.

Giampetro, Nicola. *The Development of the Liturgical Reform: As Seen by Cardinal Ferdinando Antonelli from 1948 to 1970*. Fort Collins, Col.: Roman Catholic Books, 2010.

Gibson, Margaret T. *Lanfranc of Bec*. Oxford: Clarendon Press, 1978.

Girard, René. *Das Ende der Gewalt*. Freiburg: Herder, 2009.

———. *Das Heilige und die Gewalt*. Frankfurt am Main: Fischer-Taschenbuch-Verlag, 1992.

———. *Ich sah den Satan vom Himmel fallen wie einen Blitz*. Munich: Hanser, 2002.

Giraudo, Cesare. *Eucaristia par la chiesa: Prospettive teologiche sull'eucaristia a partire dalla "lex orandi"*. Aloisiana 22. Rome: Pontificia Univ. Gregoriana, 1989.

———. "Le récit de l'institution dans la prière eucharistique a-t-il de précédents?" *Nouvelle Revue Théologique* 106 (1984): 513–35.

———. *La struttura letteraria della preghiera eucaristica: Saggio sulla genesi letteraria di una forma; toda Veterotestamentaria, B^eraka Giudaica, Anafori Cristiana*. Analecta biblica 92. Rome: Biblical Institute Press, 1981.

Gnilka, Joachim. *Das Evangelium nach Markus (Mk 8,27–16,20)*. Evangelisch-Katholischer Kommentar 2/2. Zurich and Einsiedeln: Benziger; Neukirchen-Vluyn: Neukirchener Verlag, 1979.

———. *Jesus of Nazareth: Message and History*. Translated by Siegfried S. Schatzmann. Peabody, Mass.: Hendrickson, 1997.

———. *Johannesevangelium*. 2nd ed. Neue Echter Bibel: Neues Testament. Würzburg: Echter Verlag, 1985.

Godelier, Maurice. *Das Rätsel der Gabe: Geld, Geschenke, heilige Objekte*. Munich: Beck, 1999.

Gormans, Andreas, and Thomas Lentes. *Das Bild der Erscheinung: Die Gregorsmesse im Mittelalter*. Kult-Bild 3. Berlin: Reimer, 2007.

Greshake, Gisbert. "Communio—Schlüsselbegriff der Dogmatik". In *Gemeinsam Kirche sein: Theorie und Praxis der Communio*, Festschrift O. Saier, 90–121. Freiburg: Herder, 1992.

Grillo, Andrea. *Beyond Pius V: Conflicting Interpretations of the Liturgical Reform*. Translated by B. Hudock. Collegeville, Minn.: Liturgical Press, 2013.

———. " 'Intellectus fidei' and 'intellectus ritus': Die überraschende Konvergenz von Liturgietheologie, Sakramententheologie und Fundamentaltheologie". *Liturgisches Jahrbuch* 50 (2000): 143–65.

Guardini, Romano. *The Church and the Catholic. In The Church and the Catholic and The Spirit of the Liturgy*. Translated by Ada Lane. London: Sheed & Ward, 1935.

———. *Meditations before Mass*. Translated by Elinor Castendyk Briefs. 1956; Notre Dame, Ind.: Ave Maria Press, 2014.

———. *The Spirit of the Liturgy*. Translated by Ada Lane. New York: Sheed & Ward, 1937; New York: Crossroad, 1998. And in Joseph Cardinal Ratzinger and Romano Guardini, *The Spirit of the Liturgy*, Commemorative Edition. San Francisco: Ignatius Press, 2018.

——. "Über die systematische Methode in der Liturgiewissenschaft?" *Jahrbuch für Liturgiewissenschaft* 1 (1921): 97–108.

Guéranger, Prosper. *Institutions liturgiques*. 2 vols. 2nd ed. Paris: Société générale de librairie catholique, 1878.

Gy, Pierre-Marie. *La liturgie dans l'histoire*, 223–45. Paris: Éditions Saint-Paul, Éditions du Cerf, 1990.

——. "L'office du Corpus Christi et Thomas d'Aquin: État d'une recherche". *Revue des sciences philosophiques et théologiques* 64 (1980): 491–504.

——. "L'office du Corpus Christi et la théologie des accidents eucharistiques". *Revue des sciences philosophiques et théologiques* 66 (1982): 81–86.

Häfner, Gerd. "Nach dem Tod Jesu fragen: Brennpunkte der Diskussion aus neutestamentlicher Sicht". In *Wie heute vom Tod Jesu sprechen? Neutestamentliche, systematisch-theologische und Liturgiewissenschaftliche Perspektiven*, edited by G. Häfner and H. Schmidt, 139–90. Freiburg: Katholische Akademie der Erzdiözese Freiburg, 2002.

Hamm, Fritz. *Die Liturgischen Einsetzungsberichte im Sinne vergleichender Liturgiewissenschaft untersucht*. Liturgiegeschichtliche Quellen und Forschungen 23. Münster: Aschendorffschen Verlagsbuchhandlung, 1928.

Hammond Bammel, Caroline P. *Der Römerbrieftext des Rufin und seine Origenes-Übersetzung*. Freiburg: Herder, 1985.

Hanson, Richard P. C. *Eucharistic Offering in the Early Church*. Bramcote: Grove Books, 1979.

Hardt, Tom G. A. *Venerabilis et adorabilis eucharistia: Eine Studie über die lutherische Abendmahlslehre im 16. Jahrhundert*. Forschungen zur Kirchen- und Dogmengeschichte 42. Göttingen: Vandenhoeck & Ruprecht, 1988.

Harnoncourt, Philipp. "Betsingmesse". In *LThK*, 3rd ed., vol. 2 (1994), 340.

——. "Gemeinschaftsmesse". In *LThK*, 3rd ed., vol. 4 (1995), 437–38.

——. *Gesamtkirchliche und teilkirchliche Liturgie: Studien zum Liturgischen Heiligenkalender und zum Gesang im Gottesdienst unter besonderer Berücksichtigung des deutschen Sprachgebiets*. Freiburg: Herder, 1974.

Hauke, Manfred. *"Für viele vergossen": Studie zur sinngetreuen Wiedergabe des pro multis in den Wandlungsworten*. 2nd ed. Augsburg: Dominus Verlag, 2012.

——. "Das *Offertorium* als Herausforderung Liturgischer Reformen in der Geschichte". In *Operationen am lebenden Objekt: Roms Liturgiereformen von Trient bis zum Vaticanum II*, edited by Stefan Heid, 317–49. Berlin-Brandenburg: Wissenschaft Verlag, 2014.

Haunerland, Winfried. "Der bleibende Anspruch Liturgischer Erneuerung: Herausforderungen und Perspektiven heute". In *Liturgiereform—eine bleibende Aufgabe: 40 Jahre Konzilskonstitution über die heilige Liturgie*, edited by K. Richter and T. Sternberg, 52–80. Münster: Aschendorff, 2004.

———. "Das eine Herrenmahl und die vielen Eucharistiegebete: Traditionen und Texte als theologische und spirituelle Impulse". In *Mehr als Brot und Wein: Theologische Kontexte der Eucharistie*, edited by W. Haunerland, 119–44. Würzburg: Echter Verlag, 2005.

———. "Einheitlichkeit als Weg der Erneuerung: Das Konzil von Trient und die nachtridentinische Reform der Liturgie". In *Liturgiereformen: Historische Studien zu einem bleibenden Grundzug des christlichen Gottesdienstes* 1, edited by M. Klöckener and B. Kranemann, 436–65. Münster: Aschendorff, 2002.

———. *Die Eucharistie und ihre Wirkungen im Spiegel der Euchologie des Missale Romanum*. Liturgiewissenschaftliche Quellen und Forschungen 71. Münster: Aschendorff, 1989.

———. "Die Leitlinien der Revision: Texttreue und Verständlichkeit". *Gottesdienst* 39 (2005): 153–56.

———. "Lingua Vernacula: Zur Sprache der Liturgie nach dem II. Vatikanum". *Liturgisches Jahrbuch* 42 (1992): 219–38.

———. "Mysterium paschale: Schlüsselbegriff liturgietheologischer Erneuerung". In *Liturgie als Mitte des christlichen Lebens*, edited by George Augustin, 189–209. Theologie im Dialog 7. Freiburg: Herder, 2012.

———. "Participatio actuosa: Programmwort liturgischer Erneuerung". *Internationale katholische Zeitschrift Communio* 38 (2009): 585–95.

———. "Vom 'Gottesdienst' zur 'Gemeindefeier'? Herausforderungen nachkonziliarer Liturgiereform". *Theologisch-praktische Quartalschrift* 153 (2005): 67–81.

Häussling, Angelus A. *Christliche Identität aus der Liturgie: Theologische und historische Studien zum Gottesdienst der Kirche*. Liturgiewissenschaftliche Quellen und Forschungen 79. Münster: Aschendorff, 1997.

———. "Literaturbericht zu Fronleichnam". *Jahrbuch für Volkskunde und Kulturgeschichte* (1986): 228–40.

———. "Liturgie I-II: Begriff; systematisch-theologisch". In *LThK*, 3rd ed. vol. 6 (1997), 969–70.

———. *Mönchskonvent und Eucharistiefeier: Eine Studie über die Messe in der abendländischen Klosterliturgie des frühen Mittelalters und zur Geschichte der Messhäufigkeit*. Liturgiewissenschaftliche Quellen und Forschungen 58. Münster: Aschendorff, 1973.

Heid, Stefan. "The Early Christian Altar—Lessons for Today". In *Sacred Liturgy: The Source and Summit of the Life and Mission of the Church: The Proceedings of the International Conference on the Sacred Liturgy Sacra Liturgia 2013*, edited by Alcuin Reed, 87–114. San Francisco: Ignatius Press, 2013.

Heinemann, Joseph. *Prayer in the Talmud: Forms and Patterns*. Berlin and New York: Walter de Gruyter, 1977.

Heininger, Bernd. "Das letzte Mahl Jesu: Rekonstruktion und Deutung". In *Mehr als Brot und Wein: Theologische Kontexte der Eucharistie*, edited by W. Haunerland, 10–49. Würzburg: Echter Verlag, 2005.

Heintz, Michael. "Justin, 'Apology' I, 66, 2: Cuming and Gelston Revisited". *Studia Liturgica* 33 (2003): 33–36.

Heinz, Andreas. *Lebendiges Erbe: Beiträge zur abendländischen Liturgie- und Frömmigkeitsgeschichte*. Tübingen and Basel: Francke, 2010.

——. "Papst Gregor der Grosse und die römische Liturgie: Zum Gregorius-Gedenkjahr 1400 Jahre nach seinem Tod (†604)". *Liturgisches Jahrbuch* 54 (2004): 69–84.

——. "25 Jahre Liturgiekonstitution". *Liturgisches Jahrbuch* 38 (1988): 197–98.

——. "Zeige- und Darbringungsgestus: Zur Bedeutung der Elevations nach den Einsetzungsworten". In *Gemeinschaft im Danken: Grundfragen der Eucharistiefeier im ökumenischen Gespräch*, edited by Stefan Böntert, 126–46. Studien zur Pastoralliturgie 40. Regensburg: Pustet, 2015.

Hell, Silvia, and Lothar Lies, eds. *Amt und Eucharistiegemeinschaft: Ökumenische Perspektiven und Probleme*. Innsbruck: Tyrolia Verlag, 2004.

Hénaff, Marcel. *Der Preis der Wahrheit: Gabe, Geld und Philosophie*. Frankfurt am Main: Suhrkamp, 2009.

Hengel, Martin. "Proseuche und Synagoge: Jüdische Gemeinde, Gotteshaus und Gottesdienst in der Diaspora und Palästina". In *Tradition und Glaube, das frühe Christentum in seiner Umwelt*, Festgabe für Karl Georg Kuhn zum 65. Geburtstag, edited by G. Jeremias et al., 157–84. Göttingen: Vandenhoeck & Ruprecht, 1971.

——. "Der stellvertretende Sühnetod Jesu". *Internationale katholische Zeitschrift Communio* 9 (1980): 1–25, 135–47.

——. "Zur Wirkungsgeschichte von Jes 53 in vorchristlicher Zeit". In *Der leidende Gottesknecht Jes 53 und seine Wirkungsgeschichte*, edited by B. Janowski, 49–91. Forschungen zum Alten Testament 14. Tübingen: Mohr, 1996.

——, and Anna Maria Schwemer. *Jesus und das Judentum*. Geschichte des frühen Christentums 1. Tübingen: Mohr Siebeck, 2007.

Heringer, Dominik. *Die Anaphora der Apostel Addai und Mari: Ausdrucksformen einer eucharistischen Ekklesiologie*. Göttingen: V & R Unipress, 2013.

Herms, Eilert. *Einheit der Christen in der Gemeinschaft der Kirchen: Die ökumenische Bewegung der römischen Kirche im Lichte der reformatorischen Theologie; Antwort auf den Rahner-Plan*. Kirche und Konfession 24. Göttingen: Vandenhoeck & Ruprecht, 1984.

Herwegen, Ildefons. "Nachwort zu Casel, Oblatio rationabilis". *Theologische Quartalschrift* 99 (1917–1918): 429–39.

Hesse, Michael. *Die Eucharistie als Opfer der Kirche: Antwortversuche bei Odo Casel—Karl Rahner—Hans Urs von Balthasar.* Bonner Dogmatische Studien 56. Würzburg: Echter Verlag, 2015.

Hilberath, Bernd Jochen. "Eucharistie". In *LThK*, 2nd ed., vol. 3 (1995), 946–51.

———. "Eucharistie und Kirchengemeinschaft". In *Die Kirche—erfahrbar und sichtbar in Amt und Eucharistie: Zur Problematik der Stellungn von Amt und Abendmahl im ökumenischen Gespräch*, edited by J. G. Piepke, 25–52. Veröffentlichungen des Missionspriesterseminars St. Augustin bei Bonn. Nettetal: Steyler, 2006.

———. "Kirche als Communio". *Theologische Quartalschrift* 174 (1994): 45–65.

———. "Theologischer Kommentar zum Dekret über den Ökumenismus 'Unitatis redintegratio'". In *Herders Theologischer Kommentar zum 2. Vatikanischen Konzil*, vol. 3, edited by P. Hünermann and B. J. Hilberath, 69–223. Freiburg: Herder, 2005.

Hintzen, Georg. "Gedanken zu einem personalen Verständnis der eucharistischen Realpräsenz". *Catholica* 39 (1985): 279–310.

———. "Personale und sakramentale Gegenwart des Herrn in der Eucharistie: Zu Notker Slenczkas Buch 'Realpräsenz und Ontologie'". *Catholica* 47 (1993): 210–37.

———. "Transsignifikation und Transfinalisation: Überlegungen zur Eignung dieser Begriffe für das ökumenische Gespräch". *Catholica* 39 (1985): 193–216.

———, and Wolfgang Thönissen. *Kirchengemeinschaft möglich? Einheitsverständnis und Einheitskonzepte in der Diskussion.* Thema Ökumene 1. Paderborn: Bonifatius, 2001.

Hippolytus. *On the Apostolic Tradition.* Translated by Alistair C. Stewart. 2nd ed. Popular Patristic Series 54. Yonkers, N.Y.: St. Vladimir's Seminary Press, 2015.

Hoffmann, Veronika, ed. *Die Gabe: Ein Urwort der Theologie?* Frankfurt am Main: Otto Lembeck, 2009.

———. *Skizzen zu einer Theologie der Gabe: Rechtfertigung—Opfer—Eucharistie—Gottes- und Nächstenliebe.* Freiburg: Herder, 2013.

Hofius, Otfried. "Herrenmahl und Herrenmahlsparadosis: Erwägungen zu 1 Kor 11,23b–25". In *Paulusstudien*, 203–40. Wissenschaftliche Untersuchungen zum Neuen Testament 51. Tübingen: Mohr, 1989.

Hofmann, Peter. "Kirche als universale concretum: Der 'Streit der Kardinäle' und seine fundamentaltheologischen Voraussetzungen". In *Primato pontificio ed episcopato: Dal primo millenio al Concilio Ecumenico Vaticano II: Studi in onore dell'Archivescovo Agostino Marchetto*, edited by J. Ehret, 391–426. Vatican City: Libreria Editrice Vaticana, 2013.

Hoger Katechetisch Instituut, Nijmegen. *A New Catechism: Catholic Faith for Adults* [the "Dutch Catechism"]. Translated by Kevin Smyth. New York: Herder and Herder, 1970.

Hompel, Max ten. *Das Opfer als Selbsthingabe und seine ideale Verwirklichung im Opfer Christi: Mit besonderer Berücksichtigung neuerer Kontroversen.* Freiburg: Herder, 1920.

Hoping, Helmut. "Das Beten Christi und seiner Kirche: Aspekte einer trinitarischen Theologie der Liturgie". In *Liturgie und Trinität*, edited by B. Groen and B. Kranemann, 88–107. Quaestiones disputatae 229. Freiburg: Herder, 2008.

———. "Bewahren und Erneuern: Eine Relecture der Liturgiereform". *Internationale katholische Zeitschrift Communio* 38 (2009): 570–84.

———. "Die Bindung Isaaks: Zur christlichen Rezeption des Opfers Abrahams". In *Gehorsam: Geschichten von Abraham, Isaak und Ismael*, edited by Stiftung Jüdisches Museum, Berlin; P. Greenway, M. Kampmeyer, and C. Kugelmann, 46–51. Bielefeld: Christof Kerber Verlag, 2015.

———. "Christus praesens: Die Gabe der Eucharistie und ihre Zeitlichkeit". In *Phänomenologie der Gabe: Neue Zugänge zum Mysterium der Eucharistie*, edited by F. Bruckmann, 197–218. Quaestiones disputatae 270. Freiburg: Herder, 2015.

———. "The Constitution *Sacrosanctum Concilium* and the Liturgical Reform". *Annuarium Historiae Conciliorum* 42 (2010): 297–316.

———. *Einführung in die Christologie.* 3rd ed. Darmstadt: Wissenschaftliche Buchgesellschaft, 2014.

———. "Freiheit, Gabe, Verwandlung: Zur Hermeneutik des christlichen Opfergedankens". In *Freiheit Gottes und der Menschen*, Festschrift Thomas Pröpper, edited by Michael Böhnke et al., 417–31. Regensburg: Pustet, 2006.

———. "'Für die vielen': Der Sinn des Kelchwortes der römischen Messe". In *Gestorben für wen? Zur Diskussion um das "pro multis"*, edited by M. Striet, 65–79. Theologie kontrovers. Freiburg: Herder, 2007.

———. "Gottes äusserste Gabe: Die theologische Unverzichtbarkeit der Opfersprache". *Herder Korrespondenz* 56 (2002): 247–51.

———. "Gottes Ebenbild: Theologische Anthropologie und säkulare Vernunft". *Theologische Quartalschrift* 15 (2005): 127–49.

———. "Der *Introitus* und das Stufengebet als Schwellentexte der römischen Messe". In *Operation am lebenden Objekt: Roms Liturgiereformen von Trient bis zum Vaticanum II*, edited by Stefan Heid, 305–15. Berlin and Brandenburg: be.bra Wissenschaft Verlag, 2014.

———. "Kult und Reflexion: Joseph Ratzinger als Liturgietheologe". In *Der Logos-gemässe Gottesdienst: Theologie der Liturgie bei Joseph Ratzinger*, edited by R. Voderholzer, 12–25. Benedikt-Studien 1. Regensburg: Pustet, 2009.

———. "Mehr als Brot und Wein: Zur Phänomenologie der Gabe". In *Glaube und Kultur: Begegnung zweier Welten?*, edited by T. Böhm, 187–202. Freiburg: Herder, 2009.

———. *Mein Leib für euch gegeben: Geschichte und Theologie der Eucharistie*. Freiburg: Herder, 2011.

———. "Die Mysterientheologie Odo Casels und die Liturgiereform". In *Erinnerung an die Zukunft: Das Zweite Vatikanische Konzil*, expanded, updated edition, edited by J. H. Tück, 163–84. Freiburg: Herder, 2013.

———. "Offerimus tibi, Domine: Die alten und neuen Offertoriumsgebete des römischen Messritus". In *Römische Messe und Liturgie der Moderne*, edited by S. Wahle, H. Hoping, and W. Haunerland, 378–95. Freiburg: Herder, 2013.

———. "Die Ökonomie des Opfers und die Gabe der Eucharistie". In *Die Bindung Isaaks: Stimme, Schrift, Bild*, edited by H. Hoping, J. Knop, and T. Böhm, 203–10. Paderborn: Schöningh, 2009.

———. "The *Ordo Missae* of 1965: The Latin-German Altar Missal and Liturgical Renewal". In *Benedict XVI and the Roman Missal*, edited by J. E. Rutherford and J. O'Brien, 292–309. Fota Liturgy Series 4. Dublin and New York: Four Courts Press, 2013.

———. "'Die sichtbarste Frucht des Konzils': Anspruch und Wirklichkeit der erneuerten Liturgie". In *Zweites Vatikanum—vergessene Anstösse, gegenwärtige Fortschreibungen*, edited by G. Wassilowsky, 90–115. Quaestiones disputatae 207. Freiburg: Herder, 2004.

Iserloh, Erwin. "Abendmahl III/3: Römisch-katholische Kirche". In *Theologische Realenzyklopädie*, 1:122–131. Berlin and New York: Walter de Gruyter, 1999.

———. *Die Eucharistie in der Darstellung des Johannes Eck: Ein Beitrag zur vortridentinischen Kontroverstheologie über das Messopfer*. Reformationsgeschichtliche Studien und Texte 73/74. Münster: Aschendorff, 1950.

———. *Der Kampf um die Messe in den ersten Jahren der Auseinandersetzung mit Luther*. Münster: Aschendorff, 1952.

———. "Messe als Repraesentatio Passionis in der Diskussion des Konzils von Trient während der Sitzungsperiode in Bologna 1547". In *Liturgie: Gestalt und Vollzug*, Festschrift J. Pascher, edited by W. Dürig, 138–46. Munich: Hueber, 1963.

———. "Das tridentinische Messopferdekret in seinen Beziehungen zur Kontroverstheologie der Zeit". In *Il Concilio di Trento e la Riforma Tridentina: Atti del convegno storico internazionale: Trento—2–6 Settembre 1963*, 2:401–39. Rome: Herder, 1965.

————. "Der Wert der Messe in der Diskussion der Theologen vom Mittelalter bis zum 16. Jahrhundert". In *Kirche—Ereignis und Institution: Aufsätze und Vorträge*, 2:375–413. Reformationsgeschichtliche Studien und Texte, Supplementum 3. Münster: Aschendorff, 1985.

Ivánka, Endre von. *Plato Christianus: Übernahme und Umgestaltung des Platonismus bei den Vätern*. Einsiedeln: Johannes Verlag, 1964.

Jammers, Ewald. *Das Alleluja in der gregorianischen Messe: Eine Studie über seine Entstehung und Entwicklung*. Liturgiewissenschaftliche Quellen und Forschungen 55. Münster: Aschendorff, 1973.

Janowski, Bernd. "Auslösung des verwirkten Lebens". *Zeitschrift für Theologie und Kirche* 79 (1983): 25–59.

Jaubert, Annie. *La date de la Cène: Calendrier biblique et liturgie chrétienne*. Études bibliques. Paris: Gabalda, 1957.

Jeanes, Gordon P. "Early Latin Parallels to the Roman Canon? Possible References to a Eucharistic Prayer in Zenon of Verona". *Journal of Theological Studies* 37 (1986): 427–31.

————. *The Origins of the Roman Rite*. Edited and translated by G. P. Jeanes. Alcuin Club, and The Group for the Renewal of Worship 20/Grove Liturgical Study 67. Bramcote, Nottingham: Grove Books, 1991.

Jedin, Hubert. *A History of the Council of Trent*. Translated by Ernest Graf, O.S.B. 2 vols. St. Louis: B. Herder Book Company, 1957–1961.

Jeffery, Peter. "The Introduction of Psalmody into the Roman Mass by Pope Celestine I (422–33): Reinterpreting a Passage in the *Liber Pontificalis*". *Archiv für Liturgiewissenschaft* 26 (1984): 147–65.

————. *Translating Traditions: A Chant Historian Reads* Liturgiam authenticam. Collegeville, Minn.: Liturgical Press, 2005.

Jeremias, Joachim. *Die Abendmahlsworte Jesu*. 3rd ed. Göttingen: Vandenhoeck & Ruprecht, 1960.

————. "polloi (= viele)". In *Theologische Wörterbuch zum Neuen Testament*, edited by Gerhard Kittel, 6:536–45. Stuttgart: Kohlhammer, 1959.

Johnson, Maxwell E. "The Origins of the Anaphoral Use of the Sanctus and the Epiclesis Revisited: The Contribution of Gabriele Winkler and Its Implications". In *The Crossroad of Cultures: Studies in Liturgy and Patristics in Honor of Gabriele Winkler*, edited by H.-J. Feulner et al., 405–42. Orientalia Christiana Analecta 260. Rome: Pontificio istituto orientale, 2000.

————. *The Prayers of Serapion of Thmuis: A Literary, Liturgical and Theological Analysis*. Orientalia Christiana Analecta 249. Rome: Pontificio istituto orientale, 1995.

Jones, Simon. "Introduction". In Gregory Dix, *The Shape of the Liturgy*, x–xxviii. New ed. London: Bloomsbury, 2005.

Joppich, Godehard. "Christologie im Gregorianischen Choral". In *Christologie der Liturgie: Der Gottesdienst der Kirche—Christusbekenntnis und Sinaibund*, edited by K. Richter, 270–91. Quaestiones disputatae 159. Freiburg: Herder, 1995.

Jorissen, Hans. "Abendmahlsstreit". In *LThk*, 3rd ed., 1:36–39. Freiburg: Herder, 1993.

———. *Der Beitrag Alberts des Grossen zur theologischen Rezeption des Aristoteles am Beispiel der Transsubstantiationslehre*. Lectio Albertina 5. Münster: Aschendorff, 2002.

———. "Die Diskussion um die eucharistische Realpräsenz und die Transsubstantiation in der neueren Theologie". In *Beiträge zur Diskussion um das Eucharistieverständnis: Referate und Vorträge im Rahmen des Arbeitskreises "Eucharistie" im Collegium Albertinum*, 33–57. Bonn: Collegium Albertinum, 1970.

———. *Die Entfaltung der Transsubstantiationslehre bis zum Beginn der Hochscholastik*. Münsterische Beiträge zur Theologie, 28/1. Münster: Aschendorffsche Verlagsbuchhandlung, 1965.

———. "Wandlungen des philosophischen Kontextes als Hintergrund der frühmittelalterlichen Eucharistiestreitigkeiten". In *Streit um das Bild: Das Zweite Konzil von Nizäa (787) in ökumenischer Perspektive*, Studium Universale 9, edited by J. Wohlmuth, 97–111. Bonn: Bouvier, 1989.

Jounel, Pierre. "La composition des nouvelles prières eucharistiques". *La Maison-Dieu* 94 (1968): 38–76.

———. "L'évolution du Missel Romain de Pie IX à Jean XXIII (1846–1962)". *Notitiae* 14 (1978): 246–58.

Jüngel, Eberhard. *Justification: The Heart of the Christian Faith: A Theological Study with an Ecumenical Purpose*. Translated by Jeffrey F. Cayzer. London: Bloomsbury, 2014.

Jungmann, Josef Andreas. "'Abendmahl' als Name der Eucharistie". *Zeitschrift für katholische Theologie* 93 (1971): 91–94.

———. "Konstitution über die heilige Liturgie: Einleitung und Kommentar". In *Das Zweite Vatikanische Konzil. LThk*, supplemental vol. 1: 10–109. Freiburg: Herder, 1966.

———. *La Liturgie des premiers siècles: jusqu'à l'époque de Grégoire le Grand*. Lex orandi 33. Paris, L'Éditions du Cerf, 1962.

———. *Missarum Sollemnia. Eine genetische Erklärung der römischen Messe*. Vol. 1: *Messe im Wandel der Jahrhunderte*. Vol. 2: *Opfermesse sowie im Anhang: Messe im Gottesvolk: Ein nachkonziliarer Durchblick durch Missarum Sollemnia*. Messe und kirchliche Gemeinschaft. Vormesse. Reprint of the 5th revised edition. Freiburg: Herder, 1962. With a foreword for the new edition by Hans-Jürgen Feulner. Bonn: Nova et Vetera, 2003.

Translated into English by Francis A. Brunner, C.Ss.R., as *The Mass of the Roman Rite*. 2 vols. New York: Benziger Brothers, 1950, 1955.
———. *Public Worship*. Translated by Clifford Howell, S.J. Collegeville, Minn.: Liturgical Press, 1958.
———. *Symbolik der katholischen Kirche*. Stuttgart: Hiersemann, 1960.
———. "Von der 'Eucharistia' zur 'Messe' ". *Zeitschrift für katholische Theologie* 89 (1967): 29–40.
Kaczynski, Reiner. "Angriff auf die Liturgiekonstitution? Anmerkungen zu einer neuen Übersetzer-Instruktion". *Stimmen der Zeit* 219 (2011): 651–68.
———. "Die Interzessionen im Hochgebet". In *Gemeinde im Herrenmahl: Zur Praxis der Messfeier*, edited by T. Maas-Ewerd and K. Richter, 303–13. Einsiedeln: Benziger, 1976.
———. "Theologischer Kommentar zur Konstitution über die heilige Liturgie *Sacrosanctum Concilium*". In *Herders Theologischer Kommentar zum Zweiten Vatikanischen Konzil*, vol. 2, edited by P. Hünermann and B.J. Hilberath, 1–227. Freiburg: Herder, 2004.
Kalb, Friedrich. "Liturgie". *Theologische Realenzyklopädie* 21 (1991), 358–77.
Kantorowicz, Ernst H. *Laudes Regiae: A Study in Liturgical Acclamations and Mediaeval Ruler Worship*. Berkeley and Los Angeles: University of California Press, 1946.
Karrer, Martin. *Jesus Christus im Neuen Testament*. Grundrisse zum Neuen Testament 11. Göttingen: Vandenhoeck & Ruprecht, 1998.
Kasper, Walter. "Communio: Die Leitidee der katholischen ökumenischen Theologie". In *WKGS* 14 (2012), 137–67.
———. "Ein Herr, ein Glaube, eine Taufe: Ökumenische Perspektiven der Zukunft". In *Von der "Gemeinsamen Erklärung" zum "Gemeinsamen Herrenmahl"? Perspektiven der Ökumene im 21. Jahrhundert*, edited by E. Pulsfort and R. Hanusch, 217–28. Regensburg: Pustet, 2002.
———. "Die Eucharistie: Zeichen und Symbol des Lebens". In *WKGS* 10 (2010), 206–21.
———. "Gottesdienst nach katholischem Verständnis". In *WKGS* 10 (2010), 30–143.
———. *Katholische Kirche: Wesen—Wirklichkeit—Sendung*. Freiburg: Herder, 2011.
———. "Die Kirche als Communio". In *WKGS* 11 (2008), 405–25.
———. *Die Kirche Jesu Christi*. In *WKGS* 11 (2008), 15–120.
———. "Die liturgische Erneuerung—Die erste und sichtbarste Frucht des Konzils". *Internationale katholische Zeitschrift Communio* 42 (2013): 621–32.
———. "Neue Evangelisierung als theologische, pastorale und geistliche Herausforderung". In *WKGS* 5 (2009), 243–317. Freiburg: Herder, 2009.

——. "Situation und Zukunft der Ökumene". In *WKGS* 14 (2012), 343–64.

——. "Der 'Streit der Kardinäle'—neu aufgelegt: Eine Zumutung, die man sich nicht bieten lassen kann". *Stimmen der Zeit* 231 (2013): 119–23.

——. "Das Verhältnis von Universalkirche und Ortskirche: Freundschaftliche Auseinandersetzung mit der Kritik von Joseph Kardinal Ratzinger". In *WKGS* 11 (2008), 509–22.

——. "Zur Theologie und Praxis des bischöflichen Amtes". In *WKGS* 12 (2009), 482–96.

Kaufmann, Thomas. "Abendmahl 3. Reformation". In *Die Religion in Geschichte und Gegenwart: Handwörterbuch für Theologie und Religionswissenschaft* 1:24–28. Study edition, 4th ed. Tübingen: Mohr, 2008.

——. *Geschichte der Reformation*. Frankfurt am Main and Leipzig: Verlag der Weltreligionen, 2009.

Kehl, Medard. "Die eine Kirche und die vielen Kirchen". *Stimmen der Zeit* 219 (2001): 3–16.

——. *Die Kirche: Eine katholische Ekklesiologie*. Würzburg: Echter Verlag, 1992.

——. "Zum jüngsten Disput um das Verhältnis von Universalkirche und Ortskirchen". In *Kirche in ökumenischer Perspektive*, Festschrift W. Kasper, edited by P. Walter et al., 81–101. Freiburg: Herder, 2003.

Kilmartin, Edward J. *The Eucharist in the West: History and Theology*. Edited by R. J. Daly. Collegeville, Minn.: Liturgical Press, 1998.

Klauck, Hans-Josef. *Herrenmahl und hellenistischer Kult: Eine religionsgeschichtliche Untersuchung zum ersten Korintherbrief*. Neutestamentliche Abhandlungen, Neue Folge 15. Münster: Aschendorff, 1982.

——. "Präsenz im Herrenmahl: 1 Kor 11,23–26 im Kontext hellenistischer Religionsgeschichte". In *Amt—Sakrament: Neutestamentliche Perspektiven*, 313–30. Würzburg: Echter Verlag, 1989.

Klauser, Theodor. *Kleine abendländische Liturgiegeschichte: Bericht und Besinnung*. Bonn: Hanstein, 1965.

Klawans, Jonathan. "Interpreting the Last Supper: Sacrifice, Spiritualization, and Anti-Sacrifice". *Neutestamentliche Abhandlungen* 48 (2002): 1–17.

Kleinheyer, Bruno. *Erneuerung des Hochgebetes*. Regensburg: Pustet, 1969.

Klinghardt, Matthias. *Gemeinschaftsmahl und Mahlgemeinschaft: Soziologie und Liturgie frühchristlicher Mahlfeiern*. Texte und Arbeiten zum neutestamentlichen Zeitalter 13. Tübingen and Basel: Francke, 1996.

Klöckener, Martin. "Die Bedeutung der neu entdeckten Augustinus-Predigten (*Sermones Dolbeau*) für die liturgiegeschichtliche Forschung". In *Augustin prédicateur (395–411): Actes du Colloque International de Chantilly (5–7 Septembre 1996)*, edited by G. Madec, 129–70. Collection des Études Augustiniennes, Série Antiquité 159. Paris: Institut d'études augustiennes, 1998.

———. "Die Bulle 'Quo primum' Papst Pius V. vom 14. Juli 1570: Zur Promulgation des nachtridentinischen Missale Romanum: Liturgische Quellentexte lateinisch-deutsch". *Archiv für Liturgiewissenschaft* 48 (2008): 41–51.

———. "Das eucharistische Hochgebet bei Augustinus: Zu Stand und Aufgaben der Forschung". In *Signum pietatis*, Festschrift C. P. Mayer, edited by A. Zumkeller, O.S.A., 461–95. Cassiciacum 40. Würzburg: Augustinus-Verlag, 1989.

———. "Das eucharistische Hochgebet in der nordafrikanischen Liturgie der christlichen Spätantike". In *Prex Eucharistica*, vol. 3, pt. 1, edited by A. Gerhards, H. Brakmann, and M. Klöckener, 43–128. Fribourg: Academic Press Fribourg and Paulusverlag, 2005.

———. "Liturgical Renewal through History". *Studia Liturgica* 44 (2014): 13–33.

———. "Die liturgischen Vorstehergebete im Widerstreit: Theologische Begründungen, Anfragen, Konflikte, Perspektiven". In *Gemeinschaft im Danken: Grundfragen der Eucharistiefeier im ökumenischen Gespräch*, edited by Stefan Böntert, 147–77. Studien zur Pastoralliturgie 40. Regensburg: Pustet, 2015.

Knop, Julia. *Ecclesia Orans: Liturgie als Herausforderung für die Dogmatik.* Freiburg: Herder, 2012.

Koch, Kurt. *Eucharistie: Herz des christlichen Glaubens.* Fribourg: Paulusverlag, 2005.

———. "Die Konstitution über die Heilige Liturgie und die nachkonziliare Liturgiereform". In Papst Benedikt XVI. und sein Schülerkreis, Kurt Kardinal Koch, *Das Zweite Vatikanische Konzil: Die Hermeneutik der Reform*, edited by S. Ott and S. Wiedenhofer, 69–98. Augsburg: Sankt Ulrich, 2012.

Kollmann, Bernd. *Ursprung und Gestalten der frühchristlichen Mahlfeier.* Göttinger theologische Arbeiten 43. Göttingen: Vandenhoeck & Ruprecht, 1990.

Korsch, Dietrich, ed. *Die Gegenwart Jesu Christi im Abendmahl.* Leipzig: Evangelische Verlagsanstalt, 2005.

Kottje, Raymund. "Oratio periculosa: Eine frühmittelalterliche Bezeichnung des Kanons?" *Archiv für Liturgiewissenschaft* 10 (1967): 165–68.

Krahe, Maria Judith. *Der Herr ist der Geist: Studien zur Theologie Odo Casels.* 2 vols. St. Ottilien: EOS Verlag, 1986.

Kranemann, Benedikt. "Liturgie im Widerspruch: Anfragen und Beobachtungen zum Motu proprio 'Summorum Pontificum'". In *Ein Ritus—zwei Formen: Die Richtlinie Benedikts XVI. zur Liturgie*, 50–62. Theologie kontrovers. Freiburg: Herder, 2008.

———. "Die Theologie des Pascha-Mysteriums im Widerspruch: Bemerkungen zur traditionalistischen Kritik katholischer Liturgietheologie". In *Exkommunikation oder Kommunikation? Der Weg der Kirche nach dem II. Vatikanum und die Pius-Brüder*, edited by Peter Hünermann, 123–51. Quaestiones disputatae 236. Freiburg: Herder, 2009.

Kremer, Jacob. " 'Herrenspeise'—nicht 'Herrenmahl': Zur Bedeutung von κυριακον δειπνον φαγειν (1 Kor 11, 20)". In *Schrift und Tradition*, Festschrift J. Ernst, edited by K. Backhaus, 227–42. Paderborn et al.: Schöningh, 1996.

Kretschmar, Georg. "Die frühe Geschichte der Jerusalemer Liturgie". *Jahrbuch für Liturgie und Hymnologie* 2 (1956/1957): 22–46.

Kühn, Rolf. *Gabe als Leib in Christentum und Phänomenologie*. Würzburg: Echter Verlag, 2004.

Küng, Hans. "Das Eucharistiegebet—Konzil und Erneuerung der römischen Liturgie". *Wort und Wahrheit* 18 (1963): 102–7.

Kunzler, Michael. *Sein ist die Zeit: Eine Einführung in Liturgie und Frömmigkeit des Kirchenjahres*. Paderborn: Bonifatius, 2012.

Laarmann, Matthias. "Transsubstantiation: Begriffsgeschichtliche Materialien und bibliographische Notizen". *Archiv für Liturgiewissenschaft* 41 (1999): 119–50.

Lahey, Stephen E. "Late Medieval Eucharistic Theology". In *A Companion to the Eucharist in the Middle Ages*, edited by J. C. Levy and K. van Ausdall, 499–539. Brill's Companions to Christian Tradition 26. Leiden and Boston: Brill, 2012.

Lang, Bernhard. *Heiliges Spiel: Eine Geschichte des christlichen Gottesdienstes*, 241–54. Munich: Beck, 1998.

Lang, Uwe Michael, ed. *Die Anaphora von Addai und Mari: Studien zu Eucharistie und Einsetzungsworten*, 31–65. Bonn: Nova & Vetera, 2007.

———. "The Direction of Liturgical Prayer". In *Ever Directed toward the Lord: The Love of God*, edited by U. M. Lang, 90–107. New York: T&T Clark, 2007.

———. "Rhetoric of Salvation: The Origins of Latin as the Language of the Roman Liturgy". In *The Genius of the Roman Rite: Historical, Theological and Pastoral Perspectives on Catholic Liturgy*, edited by U. M. Lang, 22–44. Chicago: Hillenbrand, 2010.

———. *Turning towards the Lord*. San Francisco: Ignatius Press, 2004.

———. *The Voice of the Church at Prayer: Reflections on Liturgy and Language*. San Francisco: Ignatius Press, 2012.

Laporte, Jean. *La doctrine eucharistique chez Philon d'Alexandrie*. Théologie historique 16. Paris: Beauchesne, 1972.

——. *Théologie liturgique de Philon d'Alexandrie et d'Origène*. Liturgie 6. Paris: Cerf, 1995.

Leeuw, Gerardus van der. *Phänomenologie der Religion*. 3rd ed. Tübingen: Mohr Siebeck, 1970.

Lehmann, Karl. "Einheit der Kirche und Gemeinschaft im Herrenmahl: Zur neueren ökumenischen Diskussion um Eucharistie- und Kirchengemeinschaft". In *Eucharistie: Positionen katholischer Theologie*, edited by T. Söding, 141–77. Regensburg: Pustet, 2002.

Lengeling, Emil J. *Die Konstitution des Zweiten Vatikanischen Konzils über die heilige Liturgie: Lateinisch-deutscher Text mit einem Kommentar von E.J. Lengeling*. Lebendiger Gottesdienst 5/6. Münster: Verlag Regensburg, 1964.

——. *Die neue Ordnung der Eucharistiefeier: Allgemeine Einführung in das römische Messbuch: Endgültiger lateinischer und deutscher Text: Einleitung und Kommentar*. 2nd ed. Lebendiger Gottesdienst 17/18. Münster: Verlag Regensburg, 1971.

Léon-Dufour, Xavier. *Abendmahl und Abschiedsrede im Neuen Testament*. Stuttgart: Katholisches Bibelwerk, 1983.

Leonhard, Clemens. *The Jewish Pesach and the Origins of the Christian Easter. Open Questions in Current Research*. Berlin and New York: Walter de Gruyter, 2006.

Leonhardt, Jutta. *Jewish Worship in Philo of Alexandria*. Tübingen: Mohr Siebeck, 2001.

Lepin, Marius. *L'idée du sacrifice de la messe d'après les théologiens depuis l'origine jusqu'à nos jours*. 2nd ed. Paris: Gabriel Beauchesne, 1926.

Levy, Kenneth. *Gregorian Chant and the Carolingians*. Princeton, N.J.: Princeton University Press, 1998.

Lies, Lothar. *Eucharistie in ökumenischer Verantwortung*. Graz: Styria, 1996.

——. "Eulogia—Überlegungen zur formalen Sinngestalt der Eucharistie". In *Zeitschrift für Theologie und Kirche* 100 (1978): 67–97.

——. *Mysterium fidei: Annäherungen an das Geheimnis der Eucharistie*. Würzburg: Echter Verlag, 2005.

Lietzmann, Hans. *Messe und Herrenmahl: Eine Studie zur Geschichte der Liturgie*. 3rd ed. Arbeiten zur Kirchengeschichte 8. Berlin: Walter de Gruyter, 1955.

Ligier, Louis. "The Origins of the Eucharistic Prayer: From the Last Supper to the Eucharist". *Studia Liturgica* 9 (1973): 161–85.

Lindsey, David. "'Todah' and the Eucharist: The Celebration of the Lord's Supper as a 'Thanks Offering' in the Early Church". *Restoration Quarterly* 39 (1997): 83–100.

Lohfink, Gerhard. *Gegen die Verharmlosung Jesu.* Freiburg: Herder, 2013.

Lohfink, Norbert. "Das 'Pange Lingua' im 'Gotteslob'". *Bibel und Liturgie* 76 (2003): 276–85.

Löhr, Hermut. "Entstehung und Bedeutung des Abendmahls im frühen Christentum". In *Abendmahl*, edited by Hermut Löhr, 51–94. Themen der Theologie 3. Tübingen: Mohr Siebeck, 2012.

——. *Studien zum frühchristlichen und frühjüdischen Gebet: Untersuchungen zu 1 Clem 59 bis 61 in seinem literarischen, historischen und theologischen Kontext.* Wissenschaftliche Untersuchungen zum Neuen Testament 160. Tübingen: Mohr Siebeck, 2003.

Lohse, Bernhard. *Das Passafest der Quartodezimaner*, 74–89. Beiträge zur Förderung christlicher Theologie, Reihe 2: Sammlung wissenschaftlicher Monographien 54. Gütersloh: Bertelsmann, 1953.

Lohse, Wolfram. *Die Fusswaschung (Joh 13,1–20): Eine Geschichte ihrer Deutung.* 2 vols. Dissertation, University of Erlangen-Nuremberg, 1967.

Lowe, Elias A., and André Wilmart, eds. *The Bobbio Missal: A Gallican Mass-Book (Ms. Paris. Lat. 13246).* Henry Bradshaw Society. Suffolk: Boydell Press, 1991.

Lubac, Henri de. *Corpus Mysticum: The Eucharist and the Church in the Middle Ages: Historical Survey.* Translated by Laurence Paul Hemmings and Susan Frank Parsons. 1949; Notre Dame, Ind.: University of Notre Dame Press, 2007.

Lurz, Friedrich. *Erhebet die Herzen: Das Eucharistische Hochgebet verstehen.* Kevelaer: Butzon & Bercker, 2011.

Lurz, Wilhelm. *Einführung in die neuen Rubriken des Römischen Breviers und Missale.* Munich: Seitz, 1960.

Luther, Martin. "Smalcald Articles". In *Martin Luther's Basic Theological Writings*, edited by Timothy F. Lull, 497–538. Minneapolis: Fortress Press, 1989.

Lutz, Ulrich. "Das Herrenmahl im Neuen Testament". *Bibel und Liturgie* 57 (2002): 2–8.

Luykx, Bonifas. "Der Ursprung der gleichbleibenden Teile der Heiligen Messe". In *Priestertum und Mönchtum*, edited by T. Bogler, 72–119. Liturgie und Mönchtum: Laacher Heft 29. Maria Laach: Verlag Ars Liturgica, 1961.

Maas-Ewerd, Theodor. "Auf dem Weg zur 'Gemeinschaftsmesse': Romano Guardinis 'Messandacht' aus dem Jahre 1920". *Erbe und Auftrag* 66 (1990): 450–68.

——. *Die Krise der liturgischen Bewegung in Deutschland und Österreich: Studien zu den Auseinandersetzungen um die "liturgische Frage" in den Jahren 1939 bis 1944.* Studien zur Pastoralliturgie 3. Regensburg: Pustet, 1981.

Macy, Gary. *The Theologies of the Eucharist in the Early Scholastic Period: A Study of the Salvific Function of the Sacrament according to the Theologians c. 1080–c. 1220*. Oxford: Clarendon Press; New York: Oxford University Press, 1984.

———. "Theology of the Eucharist in the High Middle Ages". In *A Companion to the Eucharist in the Middle Ages*, edited by J. C. Levy, 365–98. Brill's Companions to the Christian Tradition 26. Leiden and Boston: Brill, 2012.

———. *Treasures from the Storeroom: Medieval Religion and the Eucharist*. Collegeville, Minn.: Liturgical Press, 1999.

Maier, Esther. *Die Gregorsmesse: Funktionen eines spätmittelalterlichen Bildtypus*. Cologne: Böhlau, 2006.

Maier, Johann. *Zwischen den Testamenten: Geschichte und Religion in der Zeit des zweiten Tempels*. Würzburg: Echter Verlag, 1990.

Margoni-Kögler, Michael. *Die Perikopen im Gottesdienst bei Augustinus: Ein Beitrag zur Erforschung der liturgischen Schriftlesung in der frühen Kirche*. Veröffentlichungen der Kommission zur Herausgabe des Corpus der Lateinischen Kirchenväter 29; Sitzungsberichte/Österreichische Akademie der Wissenschafter, Philosophisch-Historische Klasse 810. Vienna: Verlag der Österreichischen Akademie der Wissenschaften, 2010.

Marini, Piero. *A Challenging Reform: Realizing the Vision of the Liturgical Renewal (1963–1975)*. Collegeville, Minn.: Liturgical Press, 2007.

Marion, Jean-Luc. "Aspekte der Religionsphänomenologie: Grund, Horizont und Offenbarung". In *Von der Ursprünglichkeit der Gabe*, edited by M. Gabel and H. Joas, 15–36. Munich: Karl Alber, 2007.

———. *Being Given: Toward a Phenomenology of Givenness*. Translated by Jeffrey L. Kosky. Stanford, Calif.: Stanford University Press, 2002.

———. *De surcroît: Études sur les phénomènes saturés*. Paris: Presses universitaires de France, 2001.

———. *Dieu sans l'être*. 1982. 3rd, revised and expanded edition: Paris: Presses Universitaires de France, 2002.

———. "Esquisse d'un concept phénoménologique du don". In *Filosofia della rivelazione*, edited by M. Olivetti, 75–94. Padua: CEDAM, 1994.

———. "Die Phänomenalität des Sakraments: Wesen und Gegebenheit". In *Von der Ursprünglichkeit der Gabe*, edited by M. Gabel and H. Joas, 78–95. Munich: Karl Alber, 2007.

———. *Le phénomène érotique*. Paris: Bernard Grasset, 2003.

———. "Verklärte Gegenwart". In *Credo: Ein theologisches Lesebuch*, edited by J. Ratzinger and P. Henrici, 181–90. Cologne: Communio, 1992.

Markschies, Christoph. "Wer schrieb das sogenannte 'Traditio apostolica': Neue Hypothesen und Beobachtungen zu einer kaum lösbaren Frage aus der altkirchlichen Literaturgeschichte". In *Tauffragen und Bekenntnis: Studien zur sogenannten "Traditio Apostolica", zu den "Interrogationes de fide" und dem "Römischen Glaubensbekenntnis"*, edited by W. Kinzig et al., 1–74. Arbeiten zur Kirchengeschichte 74. Berlin and New York: Walter de Gruyter, 1999.

Marschler, Thomas. *Für viele: Eine Studie zu Übersetzung und Interpretation des liturgischen Kelchwortes*. Bonn: Nova et Vetera, 2013.

Martimort, Aimé-Georges. *Les lectures liturgiques et leurs livres*. Typologie des sources du moyen âge occidental 64. Turnhout: Brepols, 1992.

Marxsen, Willi. *Anfangsprobleme der Christologie*. Gütersloh: Mohn, 1960.

———. "Der Ursprung des Abendmahls". *Evangelische Theologie* 12 (1952/1953): 293–303.

Mauss, Marcel. *The Gift: The Form and Reason for Exchange in Archaic Societies*. Translated by W. D. Halls. London: Routledge, 1990.

May, Gerhard, ed. *Das Marburger Religionsgespräch (1529)*. Texte zur Kirchen- und Theologiegeschichte 13. 2nd ed. Gütersloh: Mohn, 1979.

Mayer, Cornelius P. *Die Zeichen in der geistigen Entwicklung und in der Theologie des jungen Augustinus*. 2 vols. 1969; Würzburg: Augustinus Verlag, 1974.

Mazza, Enrico. "Alle origini del canone romano". *Cristianesimo nella storia* 13 (1992): 1–46.

———. *L'anafora eucaristica: Studi sulle origini*. Bibliotheca "Ephemerides liturgicae", Subsidia 62. Rome: Editione Liturgiche, 1992.

———. *The Origins of the Eucharistic Prayer*. Translated by Ronald E. Lane. Collegeville, Minn.: Liturgical Press, 1995.

McGowan, Andrew B. *Ascetic Eucharists: Food and Drink in Early Christian Ritual Meals*. Oxford Early Christian Studies. Oxford: Clarendon Press; New York: Oxford Univesity Pess, 1999.

———. "'Is There a Liturgical Text in This Gospel?': The Institution Narratives and Their Early Interpretive Communities". *Journal of Biblical Literature* 118 (1999): 73–97.

———. "Naming the Feast: 'Agape' and the Diversity of Early Christian Meals". *Studia Patristica* 30 (1997): 314–18.

McGuckian, Michael. *The Holy Sacrifice of the Mass: A Search for an Acceptable Notion of Sacrifice*. Chicago: Hillenbrand Books; Herefordshire: Gracewing, 2005.

McKinnon, James W. *The Advent Project: The Later-Seventh-Century Creation of the Roman Mass Proper*. Berkeley: University of California Press, 2000.

McKitterick, Rosamond. *The Frankish Church and the Carolingian Reforms 789–895*. London: Royal Historical Society, 1977.

McManus, Dennis. "Übersetzungstheorie in Liturgiam authenticam". In *Papst Benedikt XVI. und die Liturgie*, 131–49. Regensburg: Pustet, 2014.

McManus, Frederick R. *The Congregation of Rites*. Canon Law Studies 352. Washington, D.C.: Catholic University of America Press, 1954.

McPartlan, Paul. *The Eucharist Makes the Church: Henri de Lubac and Jean Zizioulas in Dialogue*. Edinburgh: T&T Clark, 1993.

Meier, John P. "The Eucharist at the Last Supper: Did It Happen?" *Theology Digest* 42 (1995): 335–51.

———. *A Marginal Jew: Rethinking the Historical Jesus*. Vol. 1, *The Roots of the Problem and the Person*. New York: Doubleday, 1991.

Merklein, Helmut. "Erwägungen zur Überlieferungsgeschichte der neu-testamentlichen Abendmahlstradition". In *Studien zu Jesus und Paulus* 1:157–80. Wissenschaftliche Untersuchungen zum Neuen Testament 43. Tübingen: Mohr, 1987.

———. *Die Gottesherrschaft als Handlungsprinzip: Untersuchung zur Ethik Jesu*. 2nd ed., 139–44. Forschung zur Bibel 34. Würzburg: Echter Verlag, 1981.

———. *Jesu Botschaft von der Gottesherrschaft*. 3rd ed. Stuttgart: Verlag Katholisches Bibelwerk, 1989.

———. "Wie hat Jesus seinen Tod verstanden?" In *Studien zu Jesus und Paulus* 2:174–89. Wissenschaftliche Untersuchungen zum Neuen Testament 105. Tübingen: Mohr, 1998.

Messner, Reinhard. *Einführung in die Liturgiewissenschaft*. 2nd ed. Paderborn: Schöningh, 2009.

———. "Gebetsrichtung, Altar und die exzentrische Mitte der Gemeinde". In *Communio-Räume: Auf der Suche nach der angemessenen Raumgestalt katholischer Liturgie*, edited by A. Gerhards, 27–36. Regensburg: Schnell and Steiner, 2003.

———. "Grundlinien der Entwicklung des eucharistischen Gebets in der frühen Kirche". In *Prex Eucharistica*, vol. 3, pt. 1, edited by A. Gerhards, H. Brakmann, and M. Klöckener, 3–41. Spicilegium Friburgense: Texte zur Geschichte des kirchlichen Lebens 42. Fribourg: Academic Press Fribourg and Paulusverlag, 2005.

———. *Die Messreform Martin Luthers und die Eucharistie der Alten Kirche: Ein Beitrag zu einer systematischen Liturgiewissenschaft*. Innsbruck: Tyrolia, 1989.

———. "Reformen des Gottesdienstes in der Wittenberger Reformation". In *Liturgiereformen*, vol. 1, pt. 1, *Biblische Modelle und Liturgiereformen von der Frühzeit bis zur Aufklärung*, edited by M. Klöckener and B. Kranemann, 81–416. Münster: Aschendorff, 2002.

———. "Was ist systematische Liturgiewissenschaft?" *Archiv für Liturgiewissenschaft* 40 (1998): 257–74.

Metzger, Marcel. *Geschichte der Liturgie.* Authorized German translation by A. Knoop. Paderborn et al.: Schöningh, 1998.

———. "La place des liturges à l'autel". *Revue des sciences religieuses* 5 (1971): 113–45.

———. *Les sacramentaires.* Typologie des sources du moyen âge occidental 70. Turnhout: Brepols, 1994.

Meyer, Hans Bernhard. "Abendmahlsfeier II (Mittelalter)". In *Theologische Realenzyklopödie* 1 (1977), 278–87.

———. "Benedikt von Aniane (ca. 750–821): Reform der monastischen Tagzeiten und Ausgestaltung der römisch-fränkischen Messfeier". In *Liturgiereformen: Historische Studien zu einem bleibenden Grundzug des christlichen Gottesdienstes*, Festschrift A.A. Häussling, vol. 1, *Biblische Modelle und Liturgiereform von der Frühzeit bis zur Aufklärung*, edited by M. Klöckener and B. Kranemann, 229–61. Liturgiewissenschaftliche Quellen und Forschungen 88. Münster: Aschendorff, 2002.

———. *Eucharistie, Geschichte, Theologie, Pastoral.* Handbuch der Liturgiewissenschaft 4. Regensburg: Pustet, 1989.

———. *Luther und die Messe: Eine Liturgiewissenschaftliche Untersuchung über das Verhältnis Luthers zum Messwesen des späten Mittelalters.* Paderborn: Verlag Bonifacius-Druckerei, 1965.

———. "Odo Casels Idee der Mysteriengegenwart in neuer Sicht". *Archiv für Liturgiewissenschaft* 28 (1986): 388–95.

Meyer, Harding. *That All May Be One: Perceptions and Models of Ecumenicity.* Translated by William G. Rusch. Grand Rapids, Mich.: Eerdmans, 1999.

Milbank, John. *Being Reconciled: Ontology and Pardon.* London: Routledge, 2003.

———. "Can a Gift Be Given? Prolegomena to a Future Trinitarian Metaphysic". *Modern Theology* 11 (1995): 119–61.

———. *Theology and Social Theory: Beyond Secular Reason.* Oxford: Blackwell, 1990.

———. *The Word Made Strange: Theology, Language, Culture.* Cambridge, Mass.: Blackwell, 1997.

Mitchell, Nathan. *Cult and Controversy: The Worship of the Eucharist Outside the Mass.* Studies in the Reformed Rites of the Catholic Church 4. Collegeville, Minn.: Liturgical Press, 1990.

Montclos, Jean de. *Lanfranc et Bérengar: La controverse eucharistique du XIᵉ siècle.* Spicilegium sacrum Lovaniense, Études et documents 37. Louvain: Spicilegium sacrum Lovaniense, 1971.

Moreton, Michael J. "Rethinking the Origin of the Roman Canon". *Studia Patristica* 26 (1993): 63–66.

Mosebach, Martin. *The Heresy of Formlessness.* San Francisco: Ignatius Press, 2006.

Müller, Wolfgang W. *Simone Weil: Theologische Splitter.* Zurich: Theologischer Verlag Zürich, 2009.

Naegle, August. *Die Eucharistielehre des heiligen Johannes Chrysostomus, des Doctor Eucharistiae.* Strassburger theologische Studien 3, 4/5. Freiburg: Herder, 1900.

Nebel, Johannes. *Die Entwicklung des römischen Messritus im ersten Jahrtausend anhand der Ordines Romani: Eine synoptische Darstellung.* Pontificium Athenaeum S. Anselmi de Urbe, Pontificium Liturgicum Thesis ad Lauream 264. Rome: Pontificium Athenaeum S. Anselmi de Urbe, Pontificium Institutum Liturgicum, 2000.

——. "Die 'ordentliche' und die 'ausserordentliche' Form des römischen Messritus: Versuch einer Orientierungshilfe zum tieferen Verständnis beider Formen". *Forum Katholische Theologie* 25 (2009): 173–213.

Negel, Joachim. *Ambivalentes Opfer: Studien zur Symbolik, Dialektik und Aporetik eines theologischen Fundamentalbegriffs.* Paderborn et al.: Schöningh, 2005.

Neuenzeit, Paul. *Das Herrenmahl: Studien zur paulinischen Eucharistieauffassung.* Munich: Kösel-Verlag, 1960.

Neunheuser, Burkhard. *Eucharistie in Mittelalter und Neuzeit.* Handbuch der Dogmengeschichte 4/4c. Freiburg: Herder, 1963.

Nichols, Aidan. *Looking at the Liturgy: The Critical View of Its Contemporary Form.* San Francisco: Ignatius Press, 1996.

Niederwimmer, Kurt. *Die Didache.* 2nd ed. Kommentar zu den Apostolischen Vätern 1. Göttingen: Vandenhoeck & Ruprecht, 1993.

Niemand, Christoph. *Die Fusswaschungserzählung des Johannesevangeliums: Untersuchung zu ihrer Entstehung und Überlieferung im Urchristentum.* Studia Anselmiana 114. Rome: Pontificio Ateneo S. Anselmo, 1993.

——. "Jesu Abschiedsmahl: Versuche zur historischen Rekonstruktion und seiner theologischen Deutung". In *Forschungen zum Neuen Testament und seiner Umwelt,* Festschrift A. Fuchs, edited by Christoph Niemand, 81–122. Frankfurt am Main and New York: Lang, 2002.

Nussbaum, Otto. *Kloster, Priestermönch und Privatmesse: Ihr Verhältnis im Westen von den Anfängen bis zum hohen Mittelalter.* Theophaneia 14. Bonn: Hanstein, 1961.

——. "Die Zelebration versus populum und der Opfercharakter der Messe" (1971). In *Geschichte und Reform des Gottesdienstes: Liturgiewissenschaftliche Untersuchungen,* edited by A. Gerhards and H. Brakmann, 50–70. Paderborn: Schöningh, 1996.

Nüssel, Friederike, and Dorothea Sattler. *Einführung in die ökumenische Theologie.* Darmstadt: Wissenschaftliche Buchgesellschaft, 2008.

Oberman, Heiko A. *The Harvest of Medieval Theology: Gabriel Biel and Late Medieval Nominalism.* The Robert Troup Prize-Treatise for the Year 1962. Cambridge: Harvard University Press, 1963.

Odenthal, Andreas. " 'Ante conspectum divinae maiestatis tuae reus assisto': Liturgie- und frömmigkeitsgeschichtliche Untersuchungen zum 'Rheinischen Messordo' und dessen Beziehungen zur Fuldaer Sacramentartradition". *Archiv für Liturgiewissenschaft* 49 (2007): 1–35.

———. "Ein Formular des 'Rheinischen Messordo' aus St. Aposteln in Köln". *Archiv für Liturgiewissenschaft* 34 (1992): 333–44.

O'Malley, John W. *Trent: What Happened at the Council.* Cambridge, Mass.: Belknap Press of Harvard University Press, 2013.

———. *What Happened at Vatican II.* Cambridge, Mass.: Belknap Press of Harvard University Press, 2008.

Osten-Sacken, Peter von der. "Von den jüdischen Wurzeln des christlichen Gottesdienstes". In *Liturgie als Theologie*, edited by W. Homolka, 130–53. Berlin: Frank & Timme, 2005.

Oster, Stefan. *Person und Transsubstantiation: Mensch-Sein, Kirche-Sein und Eucharistie—eine ontologische Zusammenschau.* Freiburg: Herder, 2010.

Ottaviani, Alfredo Cardinal. *The Ottaviani Intervention: Short Critical Study of the New Order of Mass.* West Chester, Ohio: Philothea Press, 2010.

Otten, Willemien. "Between Augustinian Sign and Carolingian Reality: The Presence of Ambrose and Augustine in the Eucharistic Debate between Paschasius Radbertus and Ratramnus of Corbie". *Dutch Review of Church History* 80 (2000): 137–56.

Paget, James Carleton. *The Epistle of Barnabas: Outlook and Background.* Tübingen: Mohr, 1994.

Pahl, Irmgard, ed. *Coena Domini.* Vol. 1, *Die Abendmahlsliturgie der Reformationskirchen im 16./17. Jahrhundert.* Fribourg: Universitätsverlag, 1983.

Pannenberg, Wolfhart. *Kirche und Ökumene: Beiträge zur systematischen Theologie.* 3:11–22. Göttingen: Vandenhoeck & Ruprecht, 2000.

———. *Systematische Theologie.* Vol. 3. Göttingen: Vandenhoeck & Ruprecht, 1993.

Pascher, Joseph. *Eucharistia: Gestalt und Vollzug.* Münster: Aschendorff, 1947.

Patsch, Hermann. *Abendmahl und historischer Jesus.* Calwer theologische Monographien: Reihe A. Bibelwissenschaft 1. Stuttgart: Calwer Verlag, 1972.

Patzold, Steffen. "Visibilis creatura—invisibilis salus: Zur Deutung der Wahrnehmung in der Karolingerzeit". In *Zwischen Wort und Bild: Wahrnehmungen und Deutungen im Mittelalter*, edited by H. Bleumer et al., 79–108. Cologne: Böhlau, 2010.

Pecklers, Keith F. *Dynamic Equivalence: The Living Language of Christian Worship*. Collegeville, Minn.: Liturgical Press, 2003.

Pelikan, Jaroslav. *The Christian Tradition: A History of the Development of Doctrine*. Vol. 3, *The Growth of Medieval Theology (600–1300)*. Chicago: University of Chicago Press, 1978.

Pesch, Rudolf. *Das Abendmahl und Jesu Todesverständnis*. Quaestiones disputatae 80. Freiburg: Herder, 1978.

———. *Das Markusevangelium*. Vol. 2, *Kommentar zu Kap. 8,27–16,20*. Herders Theologischer Kommentar zum Neuen Testament 2. Freiburg: Herder, 1977.

———. *Wie Jesus sein Abendmahl hielt: Der Grund der Eucharistie*. 2nd ed. Freiburg: Herder, 1978.

Peterson, Erik. *Das Buch von den Engeln: Stellung und Bedeutung der heiligen Engel im Kultus*. 2nd ed. Munich: Kösel-Verlag, 1955.

———. *Der erste Brief an die Korinther und Paulus Studien*. Edited posthumously by H.-U. Weidemann. Würzburg: Echter Verlag, 2006.

———. "Über einige Probleme der Didache-Überlieferung". In *Frühkirche, Judentum und Gnosis: Studien und Untersuchungen*, 146–82. Rome and Freiburg: Herder, 1969.

Pickstock, Catherine. *After Writing: On the Liturgical Consummation of Philosophy*. 2nd ed. Oxford: Blackwell, 2000.

Pinelli, Jordi. "La grande conclusion du Canon romain". *La Maison-Dieu* 88 (1966): 96–115.

Plank, Peter. *Die Eucharistieversammlung als Kirche: Zur Entstehung und Entwicklung der eucharistischen Ekklesiologie Nikolaj Afanasjevs (1893–1966)*. Das östliche Christentum, Neue Folge 31. Würzburg: Augustinus, 1980.

Pratzner, Ferdinand. *Messe und Kreuzesopfer: Die Krise der sakramentalen Idee bei Luther und in der mittelalterlichen Scholastik*. Vienna: Herder, 1970.

Probst, Manfred. *Gottesdienst in Geist und Wahrheit: Die liturgischen Ansichten und Bestrebungen Johann Michael Sailers (1751–1832)*. Studien zur Pastoralliturgie 2. Regensburg: Pustet, 1976.

Pröpper, Thomas. "Zur vielfältigen Rede von der Gegenwart Gottes und Jesu Christi". In *Evangelium und freie Vernunft*, 245–65. Freiburg: Herder, 2001.

Prosinger, Franz. *Das Blut des Bundes—vergossen für viele? Zur Übersetzung und Interpretation des hyper pollôn in Mk 14,24*. Siegburg: Franz Schmitt, 2007.

Raffaele, Simone. "Die Semiotik Augustins". In *Zeichen: Semiotik in Theologie und Gottesdienst*, edited by R. Volp, 79–113. Munich: Kaiser; Mainz: Grünewald, 1982.

Rahner, Karl. "Opfer V. Dogmatisch". In *LThK*, 2nd ed., 7:1174–75. Freiburg: Herder, 1962.

——. "The Presence of Christ in the Sacrament of the Lord's Supper". In *Theological Investigations*, vol. 4, translated by Kevin Smyth, 287–311. Baltimore: Helicon Press, 1966.

Ratcliff, Edward C. "The Eucharistic Institution Narrative of Justin Martyr's 'First Apology'" (1971). In *Liturgical Studies [of] E. C. Ratcliff*, edited by A. H. Couratin and D. H. Tripp, 41–48. London: S.P.C.K., 1976.

——. *Expositio antiquae liturgiae Gallicanae*. Edited by E. C. Ratcliff; Henry Bradshaw Society 98. London: Henry Bradshaw Society, 1971.

——. "The Institution Narrative of the Roman Canon Missae: Its Beginning and Early Background". *Studia patristica* 2 (1957): 64–83.

——. "The Sanctus and the Pattern of the Early Anaphora". *Journal of Ecclesiastical History* 1 (1950): 29–36, 125–34.

Ratzinger, Joseph. "Assessment and Future Prospects". In *JRCW*, 11:558–68.

——. "Catholicism after the Council". *The Furrow* 18/1 (January 1967): 3–23.

——. "Communion—Community—Mission". In *Behold the Pierced One*, translated by Graham Harrison, 71–100. San Francisco: Ignatius Press, 1986.

——. "The Ecclesiology of the Constitution *Lumen gentium*". In *Pilgrim Fellowship of Faith*, translated by Henry Taylor, 123–52. San Francisco: Ignatius Press, 2005.

——. "The Ecclesiology of Vatican II". Conference at the Opening of the Pastoral Congress of the Diocese of Aversa (Italy), September 15, 2001. *L'Osservatore Romano*, January 23, 2002.

——. "Eucharist—Communio—Solidarity". In *JRCW*, 11:355–70.

——. "The Eucharist—Heart of the Church". In *JRCW* 11:249–98.

——. "Form and Content of the Eucharistic Celebration". In *JRCW* 11:299–318.

——. "Fortieth Anniversary of the Constitution on the Sacred Liturgy: A Look Back and a Look Forward". In *JRCW* 11:574–88.

——. "Himmelfahrt Christi". In *JRGS* 6/2 (2013), 856–58.

——. "Is the Eucharist a Sacrifice". In *JRCW* 11:207–17.

——. *Jesus of Nazareth: From the Baptism in the Jordan to the Transfiguration*. Translated by Adrian J. Walker. New York: Doubleday, 2007.

——. *Jesus of Nazareth: Holy Week, From the Entrance into Jerusalem to the Resurrection*. Translated by Philip J. Whitmore. San Francisco: Ignatius Press, 2011.

——. *Jesus of Nazareth: The Infancy Narratives*. Translated by Philip J. Whitmore. New York: Image, 2012.

———. "Der Katholizismus nach dem Konzil". In *JRGS* 7/2 (2012), 1003–25.

———. "Das Konzil auf dem Weg: Rückblick auf die zweite Sitzungsperiode des Zweiten Vatikanischen Konzils". In *JRGS* 7/1 (2012), 359–410.

———. *Milestones: Memoirs: 1927–1977*. Translated by Erasmo Leiva-Merikakis. San Francisco: Ignatius Press, 1998.

———. "On the Meaning of Sunday for Christian Prayer and Christian Life". In *JRCW* 11:187–206.

———. "Ortskirche und Universalkirche: Antwort auf Walter Kasper". In *JRGS* 8/1 (2010), 597–604.

———. "The Problem of Transubstantiation and the Question about the Meaning of the Eucharist". In *JRCW* 11:218–42.

———. "Questions about the Structure and Duties of the Synod of Bishops". In *Church, Ecumenism, and Politics*. Translated by Michael J. Miller, 51–66. San Francisco: Ignatius Press, 2008.

———. "The Resurrection as the Foundation of Christian Liturgy—On the Meaning of Sunday for Christian Prayer and Christian Life". In *JRCW* 11:187–206.

———. *The Spirit of the Liturgy*. Translated by John Saward. San Francisco: Ignatius Press, 2000. Bracketed page references are to this book, which was reprinted in *JRCW*, 11:3–150.

———. *Theological Highlights of Vatican II*. 1966; New York and Mahwah, N.J.: Paulist Press, 2009. In particular, the sections "The First Session" and "Theological Questions at Vatican Council II".

———. "The Theology of the Liturgy". In *JRCW* 11:541–54. San Francisco: Ignatius Press, 2014.

———. "The Universal Church and the Particular Church". In *Called to Communion*, translated by Adrian Walker, 75–103. San Francisco: Ignatius Press, 1996.

Rauch, Albert, ed. *Die Eucharistie der Einen Kirche: Eucharistische Ekklesiologie: Perspektiven und Grenzen*. Regensburger Ökumenisches Symposium 1981. Munich: Verlagsgesellschaft Gerrhard Kaffke, 1983.

Ray, Walter D. "Rome and Alexandria: Two Cities, One Anaphoral Tradition". In *Issues in Eucharistic Praying in East and West: Essays in Liturgical and Theological Analysis*, edited by M.E. Johnson, 99–127. Collegeville, Minn.: Liturgical Press, 2010.

Reid, Alcuin. *The Organic Development of the Liturgy: The Principles of Liturgical Reform and Their Relation to the Twentieth-Century Liturgical Movement Prior to the Second Vatican Council*. 2nd ed. San Francisco: Ignatius Press, 2005.

———. "Eine Präzisierung von 'The Organic Development of the Liturgy'—Das grundlegende Prinzip zur Beurteilung der Reform". In *Römische*

Messe und Liturgie in der Moderne, edited by St. Wahle, H. Hoping, and W. Haunerland, 73–102. Freiburg: Herder, 2013.

———. "Sacrosanctum Concilium and the Organic Development of the Liturgy". In *The Genius of the Roman Rite: Historical, Theological, and Pastoral Perspectives on Catholic Liturgy,* edited by U.M. Lang, 198–215. Chicago: Hillenbrand, 2010.

Reiser, Marius. "Eucharistische Wissenschaft: Eine exegetische Betrachtung zu Joh 6, 26–59". In *Vorgeschmack: Ökumenische Bemühungen um die Eucharistie,* Festschrift T. Schneider, edited by B.J. Hilberath and D. Sattler, 164–77. Mainz: Matthias-Grünewald-Verlag, 1995.

Riché, Pierre. *Die Welt der Karolinger.* 3rd ed. Stuttgart: Reclam, 2009. A German translation of *La vie quotidienne dans l'empire Carolingien.* Paris: Hachette, 1973.

Richter, Georg. *Die Fusswaschung im Johannesevangelium: Geschichte ihrer Deutung.* Biblische Untersuchungen 1. Regensburg: Pustet, 1967.

Richter, Klemens. "Eucharistisches Hochgebet ohne Einsetzungsworte: Überwindung eines zentralen Aspekts scholastischer Sakramententheologie durch die römische Kongregation für die Glaubenslehre". In *Gemeinschaftlich im Danken: Grundfragen der Eucharistiefeier im ökumenischen Gespräch,* edited by S. Böntert, 69–83. Studien zur Pastoralliturgie 40. Regensburg: Pustet, 2015.

———. "Ein halbes Jahrhundert Sacrosanctum Concilium: Anmerkungen eines Liturgiewissenschaftlers". In *Sacrosanctum Concilium: Eine Relecture der Liturgiekonstitution des 2. Vatikanischen Konzils,* edited by M. Stuflesser, 97–115. Theologie der Liturgie 1. Regensburg: Pustet, 2011.

———. "Die Liturgiekonstitution 'Sacrosanctum Concilium' des Zweiten Vatikanischen Konzils". In *Liturgiereform: Eine bleibende Aufgabe: 40 Jahre Konzilskonstitution über die heilige Liturgie,* edited by K. Richter and T. Sternberg, 23–51. Münster: Aschendorff, 2004.

———. "Vom Sinn der Liturgiereform". In *Ein Ritus—zwei Formen: Die Richtlinie Benedikts XVI. zur Liturgie,* edited by A. Gerhards, 62–74. Theologie kontrovers. Freiburg: Herder, 2008.

———. "Zum Verhältnis von Kirchenbild und Liturgie: Die erneuerte Liturgie und der alte Ritus im Widerspruch". In *Objektive Feier und subjektiver Glaube? Beiträge zum Verhältnis von Liturgie und Spiritualität,* 147–69. Studien zur Pastoralliturgie 32. Regensburg: Pustet, 2011.

Roloff, Jürgen. *Jesus.* Munich: Beck, 2000.

———. *Die Kirche im Neuen Testament.* Grundrisse zum Neuen Testament 10. Göttingen: Vandenhoeck & Ruprecht, 1993.

Rordorf, Willy. "La Didaché". In *L'eucharistie des premiers chrétiens,* 7–28. Le point théologique 17. Paris: Beauchesne, 1976.

――――. "Die Mahlgebete der Didache Kap. 9–10: Ein neuer 'status quaestionis' ". *Vigiliae Christianae* 51 (1997): 229–46.

――――. *Sabbat und Sonntag in der Alten Kirche*. Traditio Christiana 2. Zurich: Theologische Verlag, 1972.

――――. *Der Sonntag: Geschichte des Ruhe- und Gottesdiensttages im ältesten Christentum*. Abhandlungen zur Theologie des Alten und Neuen Testaments, 43. Zurich: Zwingli Verlag, 1962.

Rosenberger, Michael, ed. *Geschenkt—umsonst gegeben? Gabe und Tausch in Ethik, Gesellschaft und Religion*. Linzer Philosophisch-Theologische Beiträge 14. Frankfurt am Main and New York: Lang, 2006.

Rouwhorst, Gerard. "Christlicher Gottesdienst und der Gottesdienst Israels: Forschungsgeschichte, historische Interaktion, Theology". In *Theologie des Gottesdienstes: Gottesdienst im Leben der Christen; Christliche und jüdische Liturgie*, 491–572. Gottesdienst der Kirche 2/2. Regensburg: Pustet, 2008.

――――. "Didache 9–10: A Litmus Test for the Research on Early Christian Eucharist". In *Matthew and the Didache: Two Documents from the Same Jewish Christian Milieu?*, edited by H. van de Sandt, 143–56. Assen: Royal Van Gorcum; Minneapolis: Fortress Press, 2005.

――――. "The Reading of Scripture in Early Christian Liturgy". In *What Athens Has to Do with Jerusalem: Essays in Classical, Jewish and Early Christian Art and Archeology*, Festschrift G. Forester, edited by L. V. Rutgers, 305–31. Interdisciplinary Studies in Ancient Culture and Religion 1. Leuven: Peeters, 2002.

――――. "The Reception of the Jewish Sabbath in Early Christianity". In *Christian Feast and Festival: The Dynamics of Western Liturgy and Culture*, edited by P. Post et al., 223–66. Liturgia condenda 12. Leuven: Peeters, 2001.

Roy, Neil J. "The Roman Canon: Deësis in Euchological Form". In *Benedict XVI and the Sacred Liturgy: Proceedings of the First Fota International Liturgy Conference 2008*, edited by N. J. Roy and J. E. Rutherford, 181–99. Dublin: Four Courts Press, 2010.

Rubin, Miri. *Corpus Christi: The Eucharist in Late Medieval Culture*. Cambridge and New York: Cambridge Univesity Press, 1991.

Russo, Nicholas V. "The Validity of the Anaphora of Addai and Mari: Critique of the Critiques". In *Issues in Eucharistic Praying in East and West: Essays in Liturgical and Theological Analysis*, edited by M. E. Johnson, 21–62. Collegeville, Minn.: Liturgical Press, 2010.

Ruster, Thomas. *Wandlung: Ein Traktat über Eucharistie und Ökonomie*. Ostfildern: Matthias-Grünewald, 2006.

Saberschinsky, Alexander. *Einführung in die Feier der Eucharistie: historisch—systematisch—praktisch*. Freiburg: Herder, 2009.

Sage, Athanase. "L'Eucharistie dans la pensée de saint Augustin". *Revue des études augustiniennes* 15 (1969): 209–40.

Sailer, Johann Michael. *Neue Beyträge zur Bildung des Geistlichen*, vol. 2. Munich: Lentner, 1811.

——. "Rede zum Andenken an Vitus Anton Winter, Professor und Stadtpfarrer bei St. Jodok in Landshut" (1814). In *Sämtliche Werke unter Anleitung des Verfassers*, edited by J. Widmer, 38:123–56. Sulzbach: Seidel, 1830–1841.

——. *Vollständiges Gebet- und Lesebuch für katholische Christen, aus dem grösseren Werk von ihm selbst herausgezogen*. Munich: Lentner, 1785.

Sammaciccia, Bruno. *Das Eucharistie-Wunder von Lanciano*. 2nd ed. Hauteville: Parvis, 1992.

Santogrossi, Ansgar. "Historical and Theological Argumentation in Favour of Anaphoras without Institution Narrative". In *Die Anaphora von Addai und Mari: Studien zu Eucharistie und Einsetzungsworten*, edited by U. M. Lang, 175–210. Bonn: Nova & Vetera, 2007.

Sasse, Hermann. *Corpus Christi: Ein Beitrag zum Problem der Abendmahlskonkordie*. Erlangen: Verlag der Ev.-Luth Mission, 1979.

Schäfer, Rolf. "Communio 1. Dogmatisch". In *Die Religion in Geschichte und Gegenwart: Handwörterbuch für Theologie und Religionswissenschaft* 2:435–437. 4th ed. Tübingen: Mohr, 1999.

Schille, Gottfried. "Das Leiden des Herrn: Die evangelische Passionstradition und ihr 'Sitz im Leben'". *Zeitschrift für Theologie und Kirche* 52 (1955): 161–205.

Schillebeeckx, Edward. *Die eucharistische Gegenwart: Zur Diskussion über die Realpräsenz*. Düsseldorf: Patmos, 1967.

Schilling, Heinz. *Martin Luther: Rebell in einer Zeit des Umbruchs: Eine Biographie*. Munich: Beck, 2012.

Schilson, Arno. "Die Gegenwart des Ursprungs: Überlegungen zur bleibenden Bedeutung der Mysterientheologie Odo Casels". *Liturgisches Jahrbuch* 43 (1993): 6–29.

——. *Theologie als Sakramententheologie: Die Mysterientheologie Odo Casels*. 2nd ed. Tübinger theologische Studien, 18. Mainz: Matthias-Grünewald-Verlag, 1987.

Schmemann, Alexander. *Eucharistie: Sakrament des Gottesreiches*. With an introduction by J.-H. Tück. 2nd ed. Freiburg: Johannes-Verlag Einsiedeln, 2012.

Schmitz, Joseph. "Canon Romanus", in: *Prex Eucharistica*, vol. 3/1, edited by A. Gerhards, H. Brakmann, and M. Klöckener, 281–310. Fribourg: Academic Press Fribourg and Paulusverlag, 2005.

———. "Einleitung". In Ambrosius, *De Saramentis, De Mysteriis—Über die Sakramente, Über die Mysterien*, 7–68. Fontes Christiani 3. Freiburg: Herder, 1990.

———. *Gottesdienst im altchristlichen Mailand: Eine Liturgiewissenschaftliche Untersuchung über Initiation und Messfeier während des Jahres zur Zeit des Bischofs Ambrosius (†397)*. Theophaneia 25. Cologne: Hanstein, 1975.

Schnackenburg, Rudolf. *Das Johannesevangelium*. Vol. 4, pt. 2 of *Herders Theologischer Kommentar zum Neuen Testament*. Freiburg: Herder, 1971.

Schnitzler, Theodor. *Die drei neuen Hochgebete und die neuen Präfationen*. Freiburg: Herder, 1969.

———. *Der Römische Messkanon: In Betrachtung, Verkündigung und Gebet*. Freiburg: Herder, 1968.

Scholtissek, Klaus. *Mit ihm sein und bleiben: Die Sprache der Immanenz in den johanneischen Schriften*. Herders biblische Studien 21. Freiburg: Herder, 2000.

Schoonenberg, Piet. "Inwieweit ist die Lehre von der Transsubstantiation historisch bestimmt?" *Con(D)* 3 (1967): 305–11.

———. "Tegenwoordigheid". *Verbum* 31 (1964): 395–415.

———. "De tegenwoordigheid van Christus". *Verbum* 26 (1959): 148–57.

Schröter, Jens. *Das Abendmahl: Frühchristliche Deutungen und Impulse für die Gegenwart*. Stuttgart: Katholisches Bibelwerk, 2006.

———. *Nehmt—esst und trinkt: Das Abendmahl verstehen und feiern*. Stuttgart: Katholisches Bibelwerk, 2010.

Schrott, Simon A. *Pascha-Mysterium: Zum liturgietheologischen Leitbegriff des Zweiten Vatikanischen Konzils*. Theologie der Liturgie 6. Regensburg: Pustet, 2014.

Schuegraf, Oliver. *Der einen Kirche Gestalt geben: Ekklesiologie in den Dokumenten der Konsensökumene*. Jerusalemer Theologisches Forum. Münster: Aschendorff, 2001.

Schulz, Frieder. "Eingrenzung oder Ausstrahlung? Liturgiewissenschaftliche Bemerkungen zu Dorothea Wendebourg". In *Liturgiewissenschaft und Kirche: Ökumenische Perspektiven*, edited by M. Meyer-Blanck, 91–107. Rheinbach: CMZ-Verlag, 2003.

———. "Der Gottesdienst bei Luther". In *Leben und Werk Martin Luthers von 1526–1546*, Festschrift zu seinem 500. Geburtstag, edited by H. Junghans, 1:297–302. Göttingen: Vandenhoeck & Ruprecht, 1983.

———. "Luthers liturgische Reformen: Kontinuität und Innovation". In *Synaxis: Beiträge zur Liturgik*, Zum 80. Geburtstag des Autors im Auftrag der Evangelischen Landeskirche Baden, edited by G. Schwinge, 37–69. Göttingen: Vandenhoeck & Ruprecht, 1997.

Schulz, Hans-Joachim. "Christusverkündigung und kirchlicher Opfervollzug nach den Anamnesetexten der eucharistischen Hochgebete". In *Christuszeugnis der Kirche*, edited by P.-W. Scheele and G. Schneider, 91–128. Essen: Fredebeul und Koenen, 1970.

———. "Ökumenische Aspekte der Darbringungsaussagen in der erneuerten römischen und in der byzantinischen Liturgie". *Archiv für Liturgiewissenschaft* 19 (1977): 7–28.

———. *Ökumenische Glaubenseinheit aus eucharistischer Überlieferung.* Konfessionskundliche und kontroverstheologische Studien 39. Paderborn: Verlag Bonifacius-Druckerei, 1976.

Schürmann, Heinz. "Die Gestalt der urchristlichen Eucharistiefeier". In *Ursprung und Gestalt: Erörterungen und Besinnungen zum Neuen Testament*, 77–99. Kommentare und Beiträge zum Alten und Neuen Testament. Düsseldorf: Patmos, 1970.

———. "Joh 6,51c—ein Schlüssel zur grossen johanneischen Brotrede". *Biblische Zeitschrift* 2 (1958): 244–62.

———. *Eine quellenkritische Untersuchung de lukanischen Abendmahlsberichtes Lk 22,7–38.* 3 vols. Münster: Aschendorff, 1953–1957.

Schwarz, Rudolf. *Kirchenbau: Vom Bau der Kirche.* 2nd ed. Heidelberg: Verlag Lambert Schneider, 1947.

———. *Welt vor der Schwelle.* Heidelberg: Kerle, 1960.

Seifert, Oliver, and Ambrosius Backhaus, eds. *Panis Angelorum: Das Brot der Engel: Kulturgeschichte der Hostie.* Ostfildern: Thorbecke, 2004.

Seraphim, Hans-Christian. *Von der Darbringung des Leibes Christi in der Messe: Studien zur Auslegungsgeschichte des römischen Messkanons.* University dissertation, Munich, 1970.

Simon, Wolfgang. *Die Messopfertheologie Martin Luthers: Voraussetzungen, Genese, Gestalt und Rezeption.* Spätmittelalter und Reformation, Neue Reihe 22. Tübingen: Mohr Siebeck, 2003.

Slenczka, Notger. "Neubestimmte Wirklichkeit: Zum systematischen Zentrum der Lehre Luthers von der Gegenwart Christi unter Brot und Wein". In *Die Gegenwart Jesu Christi im Abendmahl*, edited by D. Korsch, 79–98. Leipzig: Evangelische Verlagsanstalt, 2005.

———. *Realpräsenz und Ontologie: Untersuchung der ontologischen Grundlagen der Transsignifikationslehre.* Forschungen zur systematischen und ökumenischen Theologie 66. Göttingen: Vandenhoeck & Ruprecht, 1993.

———. "Zur ökumenischen Bedeutung der Transsignifikationslehre: Eine Antwort an Georg Hintzen". *Catholica* 48 (1994): 62–76.

Slenczka, Wenrich. *Heilsgeschichte und Liturgie: Studien zum Verhältnis von Heilsgeschichte und Heilsteilhabe anhand liturgischer und katechetischer*

Quellen des dritten und vierten Jahrhunderts. Berlin and New York: Walter de Gruyter, 2000.

Smyth, Matthieu. "The Anaphora of the So-Called 'Apostolic Tradition' and the Roman Eucharistic Prayer". In *Issues in Eucharistic Praying in East and West: Essays in Liturgical and Theological Analysis*, edited by M.E. Johnson, 71–97. Collegeville, Minn.: Liturgical Press, 2010.

Söding, Thomas. "Für euch—für viele—für alle: Für wen feiert die Kirche Eucharistie?" In *Gestorben für wen? Zur Diskussion um das "pro multis"*, edited by M. Striet, 17–27. Theologie kontrovers. Freiburg: Herder, 2007.

———. "Gott und das Lamm: Theozentrik und Christologie in der Johannesapokalypse". In *Theologie als Vision: Studien zur Johannes-Offenbarung*, edited by K. Backhaus, 77–120. Stuttgarter Bibelstudien 191. Stuttgart: Verlag Katholisches Bibelwerk, 2001.

———. "Das Mahl des Herrn: Zur Gestalt und Theologie der ältesten nachösterlichen Tradition". In *Vorgeschmack: Ökumenische Bemühungen um die Eucharistie*, Festschrift T. Schneider, edited by B.J. Hilberath and D. Sattler, 134–63. Mainz: Matthias-Grünewald-Verlag, 1995.

Söhngen, Gottlieb. "Christi Gegenwart in uns durch den Glauben (Eph 3,17): Ein vergessener Gegenstand unserer Verkündigung von der Messe". In *Die Messe in der Glaubensverkündigung*, edited by Franz Xaver Arnold, 14–28. 2nd ed. Freiburg: Herder, 1953.

———. *Das sakramentale Wesen des Messopfers*. Essen: Wibbelt, 1946.

———. *Der Wesensaufbau des Mysteriums*. Grenzfragen zwischen Theologie und Philosophie 6. Bonn: Hanstein, 1938.

Soosten, Joachim von. "Präsenz und Repräsentation: Die Marburger Unterscheidung". In *Die Gegenwart Jesu Christi im Abendmahl*, edited by D. Korsch, 99–122. Leipzig: Evangelische Verlagsanstalt, 2005.

Spaemann, Robert. "Gedanken eines Laien zur Reform der Reform". *Internationale katholische Zeitschrift Communio* 38 (2009): 82–89.

———. "Die Präsenz des klassischen römischen Ritus in der katholischen Kirche". In *Der Widerstand gegen die alte Messe*, edited by E. Muschalek, 13–54. Denkendorf: Van Seth, 2007.

Spinks, Brian D. *Addai and Mari—The Anaphora of the Apostles: A Text for Students*. Grove Liturgical Study 24. Bramcote: Grove, 1980.

———. "The Jewish Sources for the Sanctus". *Heythrop Journal* 21 (1980): 168–79.

———. "Mis-Shapen: Gregory Dix and the Four-Action Shape of the Liturgy". *Lutheran Quarterly* 4 (1990): 161.

———. "The Original Form of the Anaphora of the Apostles: Suggestion in Light of Maronite Sharar". *Ephemerides liturgicae* 91 (1977): 146–61.

————. "The Roman Canon Missae". In *Prex Eucharistica*, vol. 3/1, edited by A. Gerhards, H. Brakmann, and M. Klöckener, 129–43. Fribourg: Academic Press Fribourg and Paulusverlag, 2005.

————. *The Sanctus in the Eucharistic Prayer*. Cambridge and New York: Cambridge University Press, 1991.

Staedtke, Joachim. "Abendmahl III/3. Reformationszeit". *Theologische Realenzyklopödie* 1 (1977), 106–22.

Steck, Wolfgang. *Der Liturgiker Amalarius: Eine quellenkritische Untersuchung zu Leben und Werk eines Theologen der Karolingerzeit*. Münchener theologische Studien 1, Historische Abteilung 35. St. Ottilien: EOS-Verlag, 2000.

Stein, Hans Joachim. *Frühchristliche Mahlfeiern: ihre Gestalt und Bedeutung nach der neutestamentlichen Briefliteratur und der Johannesoffenbarung*. Tübingen: Mohr Siebeck, 2008.

Steiner, George. *Real Presences*. Chicago: University of Chicago Press, 1989.

Steiner, Josef. *Liturgiereform in der Aufklärungszeit: Eine Darstellung am Beispiel Vitus Anton Winters*. Freiburger theologische Studien 100. Freiburg: Herder, 1976.

Stemberger, Günter. "Pesachhaggada und Abendmahlsbericht des Neuen Testaments". In *Studien zum rabbinischen Judentum*, Stuttgarter biblische Aufsatzbände 10: Altes Testament, 357–74. Stuttgart: Katholisches Bibelwerk, 1990.

Stock, Alex. "Gabenbereitung: Zur Logik des Opfers". *Liturgisches Jahrbuch* 53 (2003): 33–51.

————. *Liturgie und Poesie: Zur Sprache des Gottesdienstes*. Kevelaer: Butzon & Bercker, 2010.

————. *Orationen: Die Tagesgebete im Festkreis neu übersetzt und erklärt*. Regensburg: Pustet, 2014.

————. *Orationen: Die Tagesgebete im Jahreskreis neu übersetzt und erklärt*. Regensburg: Pustet, 2011.

————. *Poetische Dogmatik: Christologie*. Vol. 3, *Leib und Leben*. Paderborn, Munich, Vienna, and Zurich: Schöningh, 1998.

Strauss, Botho. "Der Aufstand gegen die sekundäre Welt: Bemerkungen zu einer Ästhetik der Anwesenheit". In Georg Steiner, *Von realer Gegenwart: Hat unsere Sprechen Inhalt?*, 303–20. Munich and Vienna: Hanser, 1990.

Striet, Magnus. "Nur für viele oder doch für alle? Das Problem der Allerlösung und die Hoffnung der betenden Kirche". In *Gestorben für wen? Zur Diskussion um das "pro multis"*, edited by M. Striet, 81–92. Theologie kontrovers. Freiburg: Herder, 2007.

Stubenrauch, Bertram. Book Review of Helmut Hoping, *Mein Leib für euch gegeben: Geschichte und Theologie der Eucharistie* (2011). *Theologische Revue* 109 (2013): 326–27.

Stuflesser, Martin. "Actuosa participatio: Zwischen hektischem Aktionismus und neuer Innerlichkeit: Überlegungen zur 'tätigen Teilnahme' am Gottesdienst der Kirche als Recht und Pflicht der Getauften". *Liturgisches Jahrbuch* 59 (2009): 147–86.

———. *Eucharistie: Liturgische Feier und theologische Erschliessung*. Regensburg: Pustet, 2013.

———. *Memoria passionis: Das Verständnis von lex orandi und lex credendi am Beispiel des Opferbegriffs in den eucharistischen Hochgebeten nach dem II. Vatikanischen Konzil*. Münsteraner theologische Abhandlungen 51. Altenberge: Oros, 1998.

———, and Stephan Winter. *Geladen zum Tisch des Herrn: Die Feier der Eucharistie*. Grundkurs Liturgie 3. Regensburg: Pustet, 2004.

Stuhlmacher, Peter. *Biblische Theologie des Neuen Testaments*. Vol. 1, *Grundlegung: Von Jesus zu Paulus*. Göttingen: Vandenhoeck & Ruprecht, 1992.

———. "Existenzstellvertretung für die vielen: Mk 10,45 (Mt 20,28)". In *Werden und Wirken des Alten Testaments*, Festschrift C. Westermann, edited by R. Albertz et al., 412–27. Göttingen: Vandenhoeck und Ruprecht; Neukirchen-Vluyn: Neukirchener Verlag, 1980.

Stuiber, Alfred. "Die Diptychon-Formel für die *nomina offerentium* im römischen Messkanon". *Ephemerides liturgicae* 68 (1954): 127–46.

Sullivan, Francis A. "Further Thoughts on the Meaning of subsistit in". *Theological Studies* 71 (2010): 133–47.

———. "Quaestio Disputata: A Response to Karl Becker on the Meaning of 'subsistit in'". *Theological Studies* 67 (2006): 395–409.

Taft, Robert F. *Beyond East and West: Problems in Liturgical Understanding*. 2nd ed. Rome: Edizioni Orientalia Christiana, 2001.

———. "The Frequency of the Celebration of the Eucharist throughout History". In *Between Memory and Hope: Readings on the Liturgical Year*, edited by M.E. Johnson, 77–96. Collegeville, Minn.: Liturgical Press, 2000.

———. "The Interpolation of the Sanctus into the Anaphora: When and Where? A Review of the Dossier". *Orientalia Christiana Periodica* 57 (1991): 281–308; 58 (1992): 83–121.

———. "Mass without the Consecration? The Historic Agreement on the Eucharist between the Catholic Church and the Assyrian Church of the East Promulgated 26 October 2001". *Worship* 77 (2003): 482–509.

Talley, Thomas J. "The Literary Structure of the Eucharistic Prayer". *Worship* 58 (1984): 404–19.

————. "Von der Berakha zur Eucharistia: Das eucharistische Hochgebet der alten Kirche in neurer Forschung: Ergebnisse und Fragen". *Liturgisches Jahrbuch* 26 (1976): 93–115.

Teilhard de Chardin, Pierre. *Hymn of the Universe*. Translated by William Collins. New York: Harper & Row, 1965.

Teuffenbach, Alexandra von. *Die Bedeutung des subsistit in (LG 8): Zum Selbstverständnis der katholischen Kirche*. Munich: Herbert Utz, 2002.

Theissen, Gerd. "Sakralmahl und sakramentales Geschehen: Abstufungen in der Ritualdynamik des Abendmahls". In *Herrenmahl und Gruppenidentität*, 166–86. Quaestiones disputatae 221. Freiburg: Herder, 2007.

————, and Annette Merz. *Der historische Jesus: Ein Lehrbuch*. 2nd ed. Göttingen: Vandenhoeck & Ruprecht, 1997.

Theobald, Michael. "Das Herrenmahl im Neuen Testament". *Theologische Quartalschrift* 138 (2003): 257–80.

————. "Leib und Blut Christi: Erwägungen zu Herkunft, Funktion und Bedeutung des sogenannten 'Einsetzungsberichts' ". In *Herrenmahl und Gruppenidentität*, edited by M. Ebner, 151–65. Quaestiones disputatae 221. Freiburg: Herder, 2007.

————. " 'Pro multis'—Ist Jesus nicht 'für alle' gestorben? Anmerkungen zu einem römischen Entscheid". In *Gestorben für wen? Zur Diskussion um das "pro multis"*, edited by M. Striet, 29–54. Theologie kontrovers. Freiburg: Herder, 2007.

Thomas, John Christopher. *Footwashing in John 13 and the Johannine Community*. Journal for the Study of the New Testament, Supplement series 61. Sheffield: JSOT Press, 1991.

Thönissen, Wolfgang. "Einheitsverständnis und Einheitsmodell nach katholischer Lehre". In *Kirchengemeinschaft möglich? Einheitsverständnis und Einheitskonzepte in der Diskussion*, edited by G. Hitzen and W. Thönissen, 73–125. Thema Ökumene 1. Paderborn: Bonifatius, 2001.

————. *Gemeinschaft durch Teilhabe an Jesus Christus: Ein katholisches Modell für die Einheit der Kirchen*. Freiburg: Herder, 1996.

————. *"Unitatis redintegratio": 40 Jahre Ökumenismusdekret—Erbe und Auftrag*. Konfessionskundliche Schriften 23. Paderborn: Bonifatius; Frankfurt am Main: Lemback, 2005.

Thraede, Klaus. "Noch einmal: Plinius d.J. und die Christen". *Zeitschrift für die Neutestamentliche Wissenschaft* 95 (2004): 102–28.

Torevell, David. *Losing the Sacred: Ritual, Modernity and Liturgical Reform*. Edinburgh: T&T Clark, 2000.

Torrell, Jean-Pierre. *Saint Thomas Aquinas*. Translated by Robert Royal. Washington, D.C.: Catholic University of America Press, 2005.

Töth, Franz. *Der himmlische Kult: Untersuchungen zur kultischen Wirklichkeit der Johannesoffenbarung*. Arbeiten zur Bibel und ihrer Geschichte 22. Leipzig: Evangelische Verlagsanstalt, 2006.

Toussaint, Gia. *Kreuz und Knochen: Reliquien zur Zeit der Kreuzzüge*. Berlin: Reimer, 2011.

Trapp, Waldemar. *Vorgeschichte und Ursprung der liturgischen Bewegung vorwiegend in Hinsicht auf das deutsche Sprachgebiet*. Regensburg: Pustet, 1940; Münster: Antiquariat Stenderhoff, 1979.

Tück, Jan-Heiner. "Für viele und für alle: Marginalien zur 'pro multis'-Entscheidung des Papstes". *Internationale katholische Zeitschrift Communio* 41 (2012): 348–56.

———. *Gabe der Gegenwart: Theologie und Dichtung der Eucharistie bei Thomas von Aquin*. 3rd ed. Freiburg: Herder, 2014.

———. "Memoriale passionis: Die Selbstgabe Jesu Christi für alle als Anstoss für eine eucharistische Erinnerungssolidarität". In *Gestorben für wen? Zur Diskussion um das "pro multis"*, edited by M. Striet, 93–100. Theologie kontrovers. Freiburg: Herder, 2007.

Tymister, Markus. "Epiklese und Opfer: Anmerkungen zum Römischen Messkanon". *Gottesdienst* 47 (2007): 153–55.

Vagaggini, Cipriano. *Le canon de la messe et la réforme liturgique*. French translation by A.-M. Roguet and P. Rouillard. Lex orandi 41. Paris: Les Éditions du Cerf, 1967.

———. *Theological Dimensions of the Liturgy: A General Treatise on the Theology of the Liturgy*. Translated by Leonard J. Doyle. Collegeville, Minn.: Liturgical Press, 1976.

Verweyen, Hansjürgen. *Gottes letztes Wort: Grundriss der Fundamentaltheologie*. 4th ed. Regensburg: Pustet, 2002.

———. "Liturgie in den frühen Schriften Joseph Ratzingers". In *Ein hörendes Herz: Hinführung zur Theologie und Spiritualität von Joseph Ratzinger/ Papst Benedikt XVI.*, edited by M. C. Hastetter and H. Hoping, 74–89. Ratzinger-Studien 5. Regensburg: Pustet, 2012.

Vogel, Cyrille. *Medieval Liturgy: An Introduction to the Sources*. Washington, D.C.: Pastoral Press, 1986.

Vögtle, Anton. "Grundfragen der Diskussion um das heilsmittlerische Todesverständnis Jesu". In *Offenbarungsgeschehen und Wirkungsgeschichte: Neutestamentliche Beiträge*, 141–67. Freiburg: Herder, 1985.

Vööbus, Arthur. *Liturgical Traditions in the Didache*. Papers of the Estonian Theological Society in Exile: Scholarly Series 16. Stockholm: ETSE, 1968.

Vorgrimler, Herbert. *Sacramental Theology*. Translated by Linda M. Maloney. Collegeville, Minn.: Liturgical Press, 1992.

———. "Versteht ihr, was ihr glaubt? Neuere Versuche zum Eucharistiever-ständnis". *Stimmen der Zeit* 231 (2013): 352–55.

Wagner, Johannes. *Mein Weg zur Liturgiereform 1936–1986: Erinnerungen.* Freiburg: Herder, 1993.

Wahle, Stephan. *Gottes-Gedenken: Untersuchungen zum anamnetischen Gehalt christlicher und jüdischer Liturgie.* Innsbrucker theologische Studien 73. Innsbruck and Vienna: Tyrolia-Verlag, 2006.

Wallraff, Martin. *Christus versus Sol: Sonnenverehrung und Christentum in der Spätantike.* Münster: Aschendorff, 2001.

Walter, Peter. "Ein Blick zurück und nah vorne aus dem Abstand von fast vierzig Jahren am Beispiel des Verhältnisses von Orts- und Uni-versalkirche". In *Zweites Vatikanum—vergessene Anstösse, gegenwärtige Fortschreibungen,* edited by G. Wassilowsky, 116–36. Quaestiones dis-putatae 207. Freiburg: Herder, 2004.

Wegman, Herman A. J. "Genealogie des Eucharistiegebets". *Archiv für Litur-giewissenschaft* 33 (1991): 193–216.

———. *Liturgie in der Geschichte des Christentums.* Regensburg: Pustet, 1994.

Weil, Simone. *The Notebooks of Simone Weil.* Translated by Arthur Wills. 2 vols. London and Henley: Routledge & Kegan Paul, 1956, 1976.

———. *Waiting for God.* Translated by Emma Craufurd. New York: G. P. Putnam's Sons, 1951; Perennial Library, 1971.

Welte, Bernhard. "Diskussionsbeiträge". In *Aktuelle Fragen der Eucharistie,* edited by M. Schmaus, 184–90. Munich: Max Hueber Verlag, 1960.

Wendebourg, Dorothea. *Essen zum Gedächtnis: Der Gedächtnisbefehl in den Abendmahlstheologien der Reformation.* Beiträge zur historischen Theo-logie 148. Tübingen: Mohr Siebeck, 2009.

———. "Den falschen Weg Roms zu Ende gegangen? Zur gegenwärtigen Diskussion über Martin Luthers Gottesdienstreform und ihr Verhält-nis zu den Traditionen der Kirche". *Zeitschrift für Theologie und Kirche* 94 (1997): 437–67.

———. "Noch einmal 'Den falschen Weg Roms zu Ende gegangen?' Aus-einandersetzung mit meinen Kritikern". *Zeitschrift für Theologie und Kirche* 99 (2002): 400–440.

———. "Taufe und Abendmahl". In *Luther Handbuch,* edited by A. Beutel, 414–23. Tübingen: Mohr Siebeck, 2005.

Wengst, Klaus. *Didache (Apostellehre), Barnabasbrief, Zweiter Klemensbrief, Schrift an Diognet.* Schriften des Urchristentums 2. Darmstadt: Wiss. Buchges, 1984.

Wenz, Gunther. "Communio Ecclesiarum: Die theologische Relevanz der ökumenischen Verständigung: Bestimmung und Beleuchtung einer protestantischen Zentralperspektive". *KNA Dokumentation* 7 (July 10, 2001): 1–10.

———. "Das kirchliche Amt aus evangelischer Perspektive". *Stimmen der Zeit* 128 (2003): 376–85.

Werner, Eric. *The Sacred Bridge: The Interdependence of Liturgy and Music in the Synagogue and Church during the First Millennium*. Vol. 1: New York: De Capo Press, 1959; vol. 2: New York: KTAV, 1984.

Westfehling, Uwe. *Die Messe Gregors des Grossen: Vision, Kunst, Realität.* Cologne: Schnütgen-Museum-Köln, 1982.

Wick, Peter. *Die urchristlichen Gottesdienste: Entstehung und Entwicklung im Rahmen der frühjüdischen Tempel-, Synagogen- und Hausfrömmigkeit.* Beiträge zur Wissenschaft vom Alten und Neuen Testament 150. Stuttgart, Berlin, Cologne: Kohlhammer, 2002.

Wilckens, Ulrich. "Das Abendmahlzeugnis im vierten Evangelium". *Evangelische Theologie* 18 (1958): 354–71.

———. *Theologie des Neuen Testaments.* Vol. 1, pt. 2, *Jesu Tod und Auferstehung und die Entstehung der Kirche aus Juden und Heiden.* Neukirchen-Vluyn: Neukirchener Verlag, 2003.

Wilhite, David E. *Tertullian the African: An Anthropological Reading of Tertullian's Context and Identities.* Millennium-Studien zu Kultur und Geschichte des ersten Jahrtausends n. Chr. 14. Berlin and New York: Walter de Gruyter, 2007.

Willis, Geoffrey G. *Essays in Early Roman Liturgy.* Alcuin Club Collections 46. London: S.P.C.K. for the Alcuin Club, 1964.

———. *Further Essays in Early Roman Liturgy.* London: S.P.C.K. for the Alcuin Club, 1968.

Wilson, Stephen G. *Related Strangers: Jews and Christians 70–170 CE.* Minneapolis, Minn.: Fortress Press, 1995.

Wiltgen, Ralph M. *The Rhine Flows into the Tiber.* Rockford, Ill.: TAN Books, 1985.

Winkler, Gabriele. *Das Sanctus: Über den Ursprung und die Anfänge des Sanctus und sein Fortwirken.* Orientalia christiana analecta 267. Rome: Pontificio Istituto orientale, 2002.

Winter, Stephan. *Eucharistische Gegenwart: Liturgische Redehandlung im Spiegel mittelalterlicher und analytischer Sprachtheorie.* Ratio fidei 13. Regensburg: Pustet, 2002.

Winter, Vitus Anton. *Erstes deutsches kritisches Messbuch.* Munich: Lindauer, 1810.

———. *Liturgie, was sie sein soll, unter Hinblick auf das, was sie im Christenthum ist, oder Theorie der öffentlichen Gottesverehrung.* Munich: Lindauer, 1809.

——. *Versuche zur Verbesserung der Katholischen Liturgie: Erster Versuch: Prüfung des Wertes und Unwertes unserer liturgischen Bücher.* Munich, 1804.

Witt, Thomas. *Repraesentatio sacrificii: Das eucharistische Opfer und seine Darstellung in den Gebeten und Riten des Missale Romanum 1970: Untersuchungen zur darstellenden Funktion der Liturgie.* Paderborner theologische Studien 31. Paderborn: Schöningh, 2002.

Wohlmuth, Josef. "Eucharistie als liturgische Feier der Gegenwart Christi: Realpräsenz und Transsubstantiation im Verständnis katholischer Theologie". In *Eucharistie: Positionen katholischer Theologie*, edited by T. Söding, 87–119. Regensburg: Pustet, 2002.

——. "Impulse für eine künftige Theologie der Gabe bei Jean-Luc Marion". In *Von der Ursprünglichkeit der Gabe*, edited by M. Gabel and H. Joas, 252–72. Freiburg: Karl Alber, 2007.

——. "'... mein Leib, der für euch gegebene' (Lk 29,19): Eucharistie—Gabe des Todes Jesu jenseits der Ökonomie". In *Die Gabe: Ein "Urwort" der Theologie*, edited by V. Hoffmann, 55–72. Frankfurt am Main: Otto Lembeck, 2009.

——. "Opfer—Verdrängung und Wiederkehr eines schwierigen Begriffs". In *Das Opfer*, edited by A. Gerhards and K. Richter, 100–127. Quaestiones disputatae 186. Freiburg: Herder, 2000.

——. *Realpräsenz und Transsubstantiation auf dem Konzil von Trient: Eine historisch-kritische Analyse der Canones 1–4 der Sessio XIII.* Vol. 1. Bern: Lang, 1975.

——. "Vom Tausch zur Gabe: Die theologische Bedeutung des neueren Gabendiskurses". In *An der Schwelle zum Heiligtum: Christliche Theologie im Gespräch mit jüdischem Denken*, 194–226. Paderborn: Schöningh, 2007.

Wolf, Kurt. *Philosophie der Gabe: Meditationen über die Liebe in der französischen Gegenwartsphilosophie.* Stuttgart: Kohlhammer, 2006.

Wolff, Hans Walter. *Anthropologie des Alten Testaments.* 4th ed. Munich: Kaiser, 1984.

Yarnold, Edward. "Anaphoras without Institution Narratives?" *Studia Patristica* 30 (1997): 395–410.

Yuval, Israel. *Pessach und Ostern: Dialog und Polemik in Spätantike und Mittelalter*, 10–23. Kleine Schriften des Arye-Maimon-Instituts 1. Trier: Arye-Maimon-Inst., 1999.

——. *Zwei Völker in deinem Leib: Gegenseitige Wahrnehmung von Juden und Christen in Spätantike und Mittelalter.* German translation from Hebrew by D. Mach, 69–75, 210–56. Jüdische Religion, Geschichte und Kultur 4. Göttingen: Vandenhoeck & Ruprecht, 2007.

Zaborowski, Holger. "Enthüllung und Verbergung: Phänomenologische Zugänge zur Eucharistie". *Herder Korrespondenz* 57 (2003): 580–84.

Zahnd, Ueli. *Wirksame Zeichen? Sakramentenlehre und Semiotik in der Scholastik des ausgehenden Mittelalters*. Spätmittelalter, Humanismus, Reformation 80. Tübingen: Mohr Siebeck, 2014.

Zawilla, Ronald. *The Biblical Sources of the Historiae Corporis Christi Attributed to Thomas Aquinas: A Theological Study to Determine Their Authenticity*. Ph.D. dissertation, University of Toronto, 1985.

Zerwick, Max. "Pro vobis et pro multis effundetur". *Notitiae* 6 (1970): 138–40.

Ziegler, Roland. *Das Eucharistiegebet in Theologie und Liturgie der lutherischen Kirchen seit der Reformation: Die Deutung des Herrenmahles zwischen Promissio und Eucharistie*. Göttingen: Edition Ruprecht, 2013.

Zilling, Henrike Maria. *Tertullian: Untertan Gottes und des Kaisers*. Paderborn: Schöningh, 2004.

Zirkel, Patricia McCormick. " 'Why Should It Be Necessary that Christ Be Immolated Daily?': Paschasius Radbertus on Daily Eucharist". *American Benedictine Review* 47 (1996): 240–59.

Zizioulas, Jean. *Being as Communion: Studies in Personhood and the Church*. Crestwood, N.Y.: St. Vladimir's Seminary Press, 1985.

———. *Communion and Otherness: Further Studies in Personhood and the Church*. Edited by P. McPartlan. London and New York: T&T Clark, 2006.

———. "Die Eucharistie in der neuzeitlichen orthodoxen Theologie". In *Die Anrufung des Heiligen Geistes im Abendmahl: Viertes Theologisches Gespräch zwischen dem Ökumenischen Patriarchat und der Evangelischen Kirche in Deutschland*, 163–79. Beiheft zur Ökumenischen Rundschau 31. Frankfurt am Main: Otto Lembeck, 1977.

———. *L'eucharistie, l'évêque et l'église durant les trois premiers siècles*. Theophanie. Paris: Deslée de Brouwer, 1994.

INDEX